FINANCING BUSINESS FIRMS

# FINANCING BUSINESS FIRMS
## Sixth Edition

**JAMES E. WERT**
Professor of Finance
Arizona State University

**GLENN V. HENDERSON, JR.**
Associate Professor of Finance and
    Burton R. Risinger Faculty Chair
Louisiana Tech University

1979

**RICHARD D. IRWIN, INC.** Homewood, Illinois  60430
Irwin-Dorsey Limited   Georgetown, Ontario   L7G 4B3

© RICHARD D. IRWIN, INC., 1955, 1961, 1966, 1971, 1975, and 1979

*All rights reserved.* No part of this publication may be reproduced, stored in a retrieval system, or transmitted, in any form or by any means, electronic, mechanical, photocopying, recording, or otherwise, without the prior written permission of the publisher.

ISBN 0-256-02182-1
Library of Congress Catalog Card No. 78-70980

*Printed in the United States of America*

3 4 5 6 7 8 9 0    6 5 4 3 2

# Preface

In *Financing Business Firms*, we discuss the chief problem areas of business finance under six main subheadings: the nature of business firms, financial planning and control, short- and intermediate-term financing, sources of capital, expansion and growth, and financially distressed business firms.

We feel that a survey finance course should (1) acquaint students with the more important concepts, (2) introduce them to standard methods of analysis, and (3) provide some understanding of our economic environment and current business practices. In each case, the discussions are intended to serve these ends.

In some instances, concepts must be explained before the purpose of the analysis becomes clear. In Chapter 4, the nature of operating and financial leverage is explained before breakeven analysis and the degree of leverage measures are presented.

In other cases, the theory provides the logical structure for the analysis. This was the case in Chapter 5, on Accounts Receivable and Inventory Management. In such a case the discussions of the concepts and analysis can be combined.

The capital budgeting coverage emphasizes the analysis. In addition to explaining the rationale for use of cash flows and discounting, the implicit assumptions of the various techniques are explored. Detailed worksheets for the analysis are provided and explained. A procedure for capital budgeting under rationing is also presented. The material on uncertainty is more conceptual.

Discussion of the cost of capital emphasizes calculations. Again, detailed worksheets are provided. The calculations reflect what we assess to be the current consensus on the topic. The readers are informed of the tentative nature of this consensus.

Chapter 12 covers the long-term financing problem from two perspectives. The discussion of capital structure explains that this is a matter of policy, a long-run consideration. The coverage includes an examination of the Modigliani and Miller model and its influence on modern finance literature. Some might object to this in a beginning text; however, we felt the impact of the Modigliani and Miller paper was too important to avoid or ignore. Nevertheless, we have minimized the symbolic notation and placed much of the MM coverage in an appendix, keeping in mind our audience.

The second part of Chapter 12 is pragmatic. Long-term financing decisions, although made in the context of capital structure policy, are often dictated by short-run considerations. Some of the more important of these considerations are suggested along with methods for analyzing them.

In Chapters 13–20 the various sources of financing are described in detail. It is our view that to make informed financing decisions, detailed knowledge of the available sources is a requisite.

Most of this material is descriptive. However, where analysis is needed the techniques presented are current. For example, the chapter on leasing has been extensively revised to reflect current views as to the analysis of leases. Descriptive coverage was also updated wherever it was necessary (for example, the new accounting rules for leases are explained).

Analysis of the refunding decision was also updated. A simplified worksheet makes the analysis easier to understand and reflects current thinking as to appropriate discount rates.

Chapter 20 was extensively revised. In addition to the typical descriptive material on dividends, the reader is introduced to the academic literature on the topic. The traditional thinking with respect to dividends, the Miller and Modigliani contribution, and the ensuing (and continuing) debate are covered at an introductory level. The chapter's coverage of the academic literature is brief. An appendix provides additional depth.

The balance of the book, Chapters 21–26, deals with special situations in finance such as types of combinations, recapitalizations, reorganizations, and finally liquidations. This section of the book provides information on subjects that are frequently a background to the understanding of other business courses.

These revisions, coupled with the changes made in earlier editions, have substantially altered the emphasis of the book. The analytical material has been updated throughout. Although we have tried to simplify the presentation of this material, there was a concerted effort to make the analysis theoretically current. Much institutional material still remains, however, because we feel that an understanding of the institutional arrangements is necessary for effective decision making. The consolidation of financial decision-making concepts and institutional material has resulted in a volume of considerable length. We decided that rather than shorten the book, it was better to present the material, thereby permitting the reader to select the subject areas that require emphasis. The book is intended for use in basic finance courses where a survey of current financial theory and practices is the primary goal.

We want to express our deep appreciation to the original author of this text, Charles L. Prather. Through this book and his money and banking text, and through his teaching at the University of Texas at Austin, Professor Prather helped innumerable students to understand better our economic system and the functioning of individual business firms within it. We are pleased to carry on what he started.

We are also indebted to many individuals who have read and criticized the earlier editions of this book. Recognition and appreciation for their assistance in preparing the manuscript for this edition are due former graduate students Bradley C. Johns at the University of Arizona, Mark Bogart at Arizona State University, and Mike Levin at Louisiana Tech University. In addition, three current graduate students, Timothy P. Cronan, Roland Sheehan and Bill Bradley at Louisiana Tech University should be recognized along with Kae Faith at the University of Arizona.

Ted L. Fisher of Louisiana Tech University and Ray M. Sommerfeld of Arthur Young & Company reviewed the tax chapter and made numerous suggestions which improved the coverage and exposition.

Clark A. Hawkins of the University of Arizona, reviewed sections of the manuscript and made suggestions for which we are indebted.

Dwight C. Anderson of Arizona State University and Stephen Butcher of Emporia Kansas State College reviewed the previous edition and made a number of suggestions, many of which have been incorporated into the present work. Their comments are appreciated.

Joel J. Dauten of Arizona State University and Stephen Butcher of Emporia Kansas State College provided thorough, detailed reviews of the current edition. Their suggestions undoubtedly improved the text. Joe M. Pullis of Louisiana Tech University was of immeasurable help in editing the second author's work.

Finally, recognition is due our secretaries and wives who have converted our scrawls into readable copy. Thanks to Joyce Rinehart at the University of Arizona, Rita Nenaber at Arizona State University, Brenda Sanderson and Elaine Rinaudo, both at Louisiana Tech University, and the wife of the second author, Kay Henderson.

In spite of all the assistance we have received, deficiencies and errors probably still remain, for which we take full responsibility.

*January 1979*

JAMES E. WERT
GLENN V. HENDERSON, JR.

# Contents

## part I
## NATURE OF BUSINESS FIRMS — 1

    1. **Business Finance** — 3

        *Profit Planning. Capital Allocation. Capital Procurement. Objective of Long-Run Value Maximization. National Income. Emphasis on Service.*

    2. **Tax Considerations** — 9

        Tax Factors in Choosing a Form of Organization: *Income Tax Structure. Subchapter S Corporations.* Tax Factors and Business Decisions: *Tax Treatment of Gains and Losses. Ordinary Gains and Losses. Capital Gains and Losses. Investment Tax Credit. Dividend Income Deduction. Accelerated Depreciation. Net Operating Loss Carry-Backs and Carry-Forwards. Accumulated Earnings Tax.*

## part II
## FINANCIAL PLANNING AND CONTROL — 33

    3. **Financial Statements and Financial Analysis** — 35

        *Balance Sheet—Assets. Balance Sheet—Liabilities. Balance Sheet—Owners' Equity. Income Statements. Definitions and Statements—Finance Variations.* Financial Analysis: *Financial Analysis—Liquidity Ratios. Financial Analysis—Activity Ratios. Financial Analysis—Leverage Ratios. Financial Analysis—Profitability Ratios. Financial Analysis—Sources of Comparative Data. Financial Analysis—Common-Size Statements.*

## Contents

**4. Operating and Financial Leverage** — 68
*Operating Leverage. Operating Breakeven Analysis. Limitation of Breakeven Analysis. Financial Leverage. Financial Breakeven Analysis. Leverage Measurement.*

**5. Accounts Receivable and Inventory Management** — 90
*Working Capital. Accounts Receivable Management. Inventory Management.*

**6. Financial Forecasting Statements** — 111
*Flow-of-Funds Statements. Cash Budgeting. Cash Budgets. Forecasting Statements.*

**7. Management of Cash and Marketable Securities** — 127
*Cash Balances. Cash Management.*

**8. Time Value of Money** — 138
*Compound Value. Present Value. Compound Value of Annuity. Present Value of Annuity. Nonannual Compounding.* APPENDIX: *Comprehensive Example.*

**9. Capital Budgeting** — 149
*Basic Concepts Relative to Fixed-Capital Assets. Capital Budgeting Analysis. Methods of Analysis. Ranking Projects. Capital Rationing.*

**10. Capital Budgeting under Uncertainty** — 179
*Certainty, Risk, and Uncertainty. Risk-Adjusted Discount Rate. Certainty-Equivalent Approach. Statistical Probability.*

**11. Cost of Capital** — 195
*The General Concept. Component Costs. Component Weights. Weighted Average Cost of Capital.*

**12. Capital Structure and Long-Term Financing Decisions** — 213
*The Capital Structure Problem. Long-Term Financing. Decision Criteria for Long-Term Financing Decisions.* APPENDIX: *Modigliani and Miller on Taxes, Capital Budgeting, and the Cost of Capital.*

## part III
## SHORT- AND INTERMEDIATE-TERM FINANCING — 237

**13. Short- and Intermediate-Term Borrowing** — 239
*Trade Credit. Commercial Paper. Commercial Banks. Secured Financing. Factoring. Receivables Financing. Inventory Financing. Characteristics of Term Loans.*

Contents     xi

### 14. Leasing     275

*General Aspects of Leasing. Operational or Nonfinancial Leasing. Financial Leasing. Analysis of Leases. Accounting for Leases. Legal Considerations.* APPENDIX: *Lessee Reporting under FASB Statement No. 13.*

## part IV
## SOURCES OF CAPITAL     299

### 15. Corporate Financing through Investment Bankers     301

*Function of Investment Banking. Origination of the Issue. Distribution of the Issue. Role of the Syndicate Manager. Private Placement. Regulation of New Security Issues. Regulation of Outstanding Security Issues.*

### 16. Common Stock     323

*Evidence of Ownership. Rights of Common Stockholders. Control of the Corporation. Repurchase of Common Stock. The Preemptive Right. Privileged Subscriptions.*

### 17. Preferred Stock     350

*Characteristics of Preferred Stock. Redemption or Retirement of Preferred Stock. Liquidation and Dissolution Status. Income Claim. Voting Right of Preferred Stockholders. Convertible Preferred Stock. Merger Financing with Convertible Preferred Stock. Preferred Stock with Warrants. Future Role of Preferred Stock.*

### 18. Corporate Bonds     370

*Nature of a Corporate Bond. Legal Aspects of Business Debts. Formal Procedures for Retirement of Bonds. Asset Claim. Income Claim. Participation in Voting. Special Features to Improve Marketability. Debt Extinction before Maturity. Refunding before Maturity. Debt Management at Maturity.*

### 19. Convertibles, Warrants, and Stock Options     405

*Convertible Bonds. Warrants to Purchase Stock. Special Sources of Equity Capital.*

### 20. Retained Earnings and Dividend Policy     423

*Importance of Internally Generated Funds. Dividend Policy. Dividend Policy in Academic Literature. Dividend Policy of U.S. Corporations. Bases for Dividend Policies. Payment of Cash Dividends. Stock Dividends and Stock Splits.* APPENDIX: *Dividend Policy in Academic Literature.*

## part V
## EXPANSION AND GROWTH ............................................. 457

**21. Growth of Business Enterprises** ............................. 459

*Growth Factors. Determination of the Optimum Size. Types of Expansion. Three Major Combination Movements. Alternatives to Mergers and Consolidations. Public Policies Relative to Business Acquisitions.*

**22. Business Combinations** ..................................... 481

*Promotion. Forms of Combination. Influence of Payment Procedure. Dissenting Stockholders and Creditors.*

**23. Control of Corporations by Other Corporations** ............. 495

*Corporate Investments in Securities. Types of Holding Companies. Consolidated Financial Statements. Advantages and Disadvantages of Holding Companies. Regulation of Public-Utility Companies.*

## part VI
## FINANCIALLY DISTRESSED BUSINESS FIRMS ............................ 515

**24. Recapitalization of a Business Firm** ...................... 517

*Changes in Capital Structure. Recapitalization of Common Stock. Distribution of Capital. Reclassification of Stock. Recapitalization of Preferred Stock. Redemption of Stock. Recapitalization of Debt.*

**25. Reorganization of Business Firms** ......................... 536

*Financial Structure. Inadequacy of Working Capital. Excessive Indebtedness. Out-of-Court Adjustments. Reorganization under the Federal Bankruptcy Act.*

**26. Liquidation of Business Firms** ............................ 563

*Liquidation of Solvent Business Enterprises. Liquidation of Insolvent Business Firms outside Federal Courts. Dissolution of Corporations. Liquidation under the Federal Bankruptcy Act. Greater Protection for Creditors.*

Appendix A: Present Value of $1 ..................................... 582
Appendix B: Present Value of an Annuity of $1 ....................... 588
Appendix C: Compound Value of $1 .................................... 594
Appendix D: Compound Value of an Annuity of $1 ...................... 600
Author Index ........................................................ 607
Subject Index ....................................................... 611

# part I
# NATURE OF BUSINESS FIRMS

The primary activities in the financial functions of a business enterprise include: (1) financial planning, or estimating and evaluating future cash receipts and disbursements; (2) acquisition of funds, or raising funds required for the scale of projected operations; and (3) financial controlling, or ensuring that the cash flows are consistent with the plans and that variances are noted sufficiently early so that management may review and possibly revise the original plans. Financial management is concerned with all three functions and not with just any one of them.

The methods and procedures used by firms to acquire funds needed in their operations vary with the type and size of the organization. Financial administration is influenced by the structure wherein decisions are made and carried out; therefore, before commencing operations, a legal form of organization should be selected that will least interfere with the economical management of capital. The tax consequences of adopting a certain legal form of organization cannot be disregarded in making this decision.

# 1

# Business Finance

In the 20th century, the corporate financial discipline has broadened until today each decision of the firm in some way reflects its financial policies. The maximization of the firm's long-run value should be the objective of any financial manager. To accomplish this objective, the financial manager's concerns should lie in such areas as profit planning, capital allocation, and capital procurement.

In carrying out the goal of maximization of the firm's long-run value the manager must constantly balance risk caused by the possible lack of liquidity due to variations in future cash flows with long-run profitability.

## Profit Planning

Profit planning encompasses the relationship of revenues, costs, and profits on a short- and long-term basis. The manager must develop an understanding of the effects of volume changes on different costs within the firm. A portion of expenses may not vary with a change in output, whereas many may vary proportionately with volume. This text will consider the analysis of costs in relation to output in a discussion of break-even-point analysis. In conjunction with the development of a cost structure, the financial manager must relate his decisions to revenues to attain overall profit objectives of the firm. Regardless of whether the firm's objectives call for maximizing residual income or attaining a target return on investment, the financial manager must have a strong influence on price setting. It is his responsibility to provide for other functions within the firm with an accurate representation of the changes in cost and profit based on the probabilities of output under conceivable circumstances. Therefore, it is mandatory that he have a voice in regulating the variables associated with cost and profit.

## Capital Allocation

A second major function of the corporate financial manager is the allocation of capital or selection of projects that would prove profitable to the firm. In other words, he must analyze the effect of a set of projects on the wealth of the stockholders and choose those that enhance that wealth. Caution is required in differentiating projects because of the interdependence among many of them.

A number of methods of selection are in use today. Perhaps one of the simplest and most often used is the *Payback Period* method. Here, a project must generate cash inflows that cover cash outflows within a prescribed period of time to be deemed acceptable. Other methods analyzed in this text include the *Internal Rate of Return* and the *Net Present Value* approaches.

The selection of investments, in effect, determines the amount of assets held by the firm. It is then a matter of internal financial control to ensure that these assets are held in the proper form to efficiently conduct the business operations. The financial manager must plan for cash needs by analyzing receipts and disbursements by means of a cash budget. He must also understand the relationship of production costs to inventory holding costs to meet customer demands most economically in conjunction with the overall policy of the organization.

## Capital Procurement

A third function, capital procurement, considers the sources of capital and the mix of these sources within the firm's capital structure. Basically, the firm can finance its investments through debt or equity or some combination thereof. Debt includes a multitude of short- and long-term instruments that often require periodic payments independent of the current earnings of the company. Equity includes many forms of preferred and common stock plus retained earnings. The cost of debt and equity instruments vary according to the risk and expected return faced by the investor.

The financial manager faces the task of determining what percentage of each item should be included in the capital structure. Adopting the traditional approach described in this text, he can then determine a weighted average cost of capital to the firm. The use of low-cost debt proves beneficial when earnings per investment dollar exceed the cost of debt per investment dollar. The excess accumulates in the hands of the stockholders. However, when earnings are low, the fixed costs of debt detract from the earnings available to the stockholders. Thus, the financial manager must be judicious in the use of each instrument.

The financial officers of a firm are also responsible for maintaining records of assets and income and reporting external information to stockholders, the government, and the general public. The financial executive of today must understand general price trends, the origin of national income, interest rates, and monetary management. In addition, he must be aware of the growing social responsibility of business and establish the financial norms of the firm accordingly.

## Objective of Long-Run Value Maximization

In dealing with day-to-day concerns, the financial manager is guided by the objective of maximizing the firm's long-run value. The value of a firm is not determined by the historical cost of the firm's assets nor by the earnings figures. The true value of the firm is the amount which investors are willing to pay for it. This valuation is objectively evidenced by the stock market value of the firm's outstanding common stock.

Two factors, risk and expected return, are evaluated in the marketplace in arriving at the value of the firm. Risk and return are so related that the greater the risk associated with the firm, the greater the return that will be expected by investors. Both factors are compounded in the cost of capital to the firm. While it will be developed in more detail in later chapters, for the present the cost of capital can be defined as the required rate of return on investment projects that will leave the market price of the firm's stock unchanged.

Hence, the cost of capital specifies the minimum return that must be earned to maintain the value of the firm, that is, the market value of the firm's stock. Any return earned above this minimum criteria will theoretically result in a greater valuation being placed on the firm's outstanding common stock. Likewise, a return which fails to equal the firm's assigned cost of capital will lessen the firm's value, while a return which equals the cost of capital will have no effect.

Although the objective is to maximize the firm's long-run value, the principal means of accomplishing this goal is through a policy of minimizing the cost of capital and maximizing the net cash benefits. Maximizing the value of the firm can be shown by using the capitalization form of the well-known interest formula: $P = I/N$. The fomula shows that $P$ (the value of the firm) can be increased either by increasing $I$ (the net cash benefits) or by reducing $N$ (the cost of capital).

Since the financial manager is important in planning, allocating, and securing funds for the business firm in order to maximize long-run profits, it would follow that he plays an important role in allocating resources throughout the entire economy. In general, the factors of production, that is, land, labor, and capital, are allocated by the price mechanism. Scarce supplies of each of the factors are rationed to users by means of changes in prices. The more efficiently business units allocate their resources, the more efficient will be the performance of the overall economy. Conversely, the less efficiently the factors are allocated, the slower the overall economic growth of any country. Hence, efficient use of resources at the microlevel

## Part I  Nature of Business Firms

is a requisite for optimal overall economic growth. By effectively allocating a firm's resources, the financial manager can make a contribution to greater economic growth at the national level.

## National Income

Perhaps, at this point, it would prove helpful to the reader to examine briefly the yardstick against which economic changes in our society are measured—the national income. Currently, college presidents are noting the lag in expenditures for higher education as compared to the increase in national income, and those who analyze the national-debt burden are noting how it is declining in terms of national income. The statistics of national income by industrial origin given in Table 1–1 direct attention to (1) the predominance of private enterprise as a source of national income and (2) the current importance of manufacturing and trade industries as

**TABLE 1–1**
**National Income without Capital Consumption Adjustment by Industry ($ billions)**

|  | 1973 | 1974 | 1975 | 1976 |
|---|---|---|---|---|
| National income without capital consumption adjustment | 1,072.8 | 1,152.1 | 1,246.7 | 1,399.3 |
| Domestic income | 1,063.8 | 1,139.0 | 1,236.2 | 1,384.9 |
| Agriculture, forestry, and fisheries | 47.0 | 42.2 | 42.7 | 40.8 |
| Mining and construction | 69.9 | 77.8 | 79.7 | 87.1 |
| Manufacturing | 283.5 | 297.8 | 311.5 | 365.0 |
| Nondurable goods | 107.2 | 119.3 | 127.1 | 146.9 |
| Durable goods | 176.4 | 178.5 | 184.4 | 218.1 |
| Transportation | 41.1 | 44.2 | 44.5 | 50.6 |
| Communication | 22.6 | 24.5 | 27.1 | 30.9 |
| Electric, gas, and sanitary services | 18.8 | 18.4 | 24.4 | 25.9 |
| Wholesale and retail trade | 161.6 | 175.0 | 195.4 | 220.7 |
| Wholesale trade | 65.7 | 76.6 | 82.4 | 91.1 |
| Retail trade | 95.8 | 98.3 | 113.0 | 129.6 |
| Finance, insurance, and real estate | 116.7 | 128.4 | 143.1 | 160.8 |
| Services | 136.8 | 150.2 | 168.2 | 188.2 |
| Government and government enterprises | 165.8 | 180.4 | 199.5 | 214.9 |
| Rest of the world | 9.1 | 13.1 | 10.5 | 14.4 |

Source: U.S. Department of Commerce, Office of Business Economics, *Survey of Current Business*, July 1977. p. 45.

compared to farming, mining, transportation, and other industries. As a source of national income, manufacturing leads all other industries, accounting for over 26 percent; agriculture, forestry, and fisheries account for less than 3 percent.

## Emphasis on Services

The gainfully employed may be divided into two groups—those producing goods and those providing services. Although there is some overlapping, the service industries (wholesale and retail trade; finance, insurance, and real estate; services; and government and government enterprises) have produced a greater share of national income than the goods-creating industries (manufacturing, agriculture, forestry, and fisheries). The modern emphasis on services is found even in the goods-producing industries, which sell services as well as goods when they offer guarantees, protection plans, credit, and other benefits to accompany the products they sell.

Occupational changes that have taken place during the last century reflect increasing reliance on the use of machinery and other laborsaving devices in agriculture, manufacturing, mining, transportation, and other industries that have freed labor for employment in other areas, many of which were not in existence at the beginning of the present century. An even more important change has been the wider distribution of income among the masses and the general increase in well-being. One of the best illustrations of the effect of changes in the amount and distribution of income and technical changes in productive methods is the increasing percentage of total personal expenditures for transportation and communication. Modern automobiles, airplanes, and highways reflect technological changes that make traveling more pleasurable and in greater demand by consumers.

With the increase in automation, fewer workers will be needed in most industries, but future production will require an increase in savings as well as in personnel from the professional groups (engineers, scientists, accountants, and other specialists). An outcome of the increase in the use of capital and more highly paid personnel is increased fixed costs and a greater need to increase output in order to take advantage of the resulting operating leverage.

## Summary

A business firm is a financially responsible organization owned by one or more persons for the primary purpose of returning a profit to the owners while meeting the needs of consumers. The expansion of the scope of business during this century has been paralleled by an increase of responsibilities within the finance department.

The primary objective of the financial manager is to maximize the long-run value of the firm. This can be accomplished by minimizing the cost of capital. By so doing the excess return on capital investments will eventually accrue to the stockholders. Investors will react by paying more for the stock, thereby increasing the market price of the firm's stock.

Currently, the financial manager maintains authority in such areas as profit planning, capital procurement, and capital allocation. Through profit planning, the firm is able to observe the relationship of revenues, costs, and profits over a range of outputs. To obtain the funds for conducting the business, the financial manager must decide which instruments represent the best interests of the firm. This function, capital procurement, calls for deciding the breakdown of equity and debt in the capital structure. The finance department also determines the allocation of the capital to various projects to satisfy the goals of the organization.

With the current emphasis on capital investment, the allocations for capital goods have taken on vastly increasing importance. Decisions made today will affect costs and profits for many years. For this reason, the understanding of business finance is essential to the study and operation of the business firm.

## QUESTIONS

1. Give reasons for the increase of public interest in the problems of business finance. Discuss each.
2. What conclusions may be drawn from the facts that retail and wholesale trades have the largest number of business units and originate only about 16 percent of national income, while manufacturing firms, which are considerably fewer in number, originate about 26 percent of national income?
3. Why are large firms associated with transportation, public-utility, and manufacturing industries, and small firms with service, construction, and wholesale- and retail-trade industries?
4. Describe the functions of a finance officer.
5. Distinguish between internal and external sources of funds.
6. As firms diversify, how is the financial manager's jobs made more difficult in comparison with a firm having a single product or service?
7. Why would you expect a greater return from an investment in a manufacturing firm than from an equal investment in U.S. Treasury notes or bonds?
8. The maximization of long-run value implies a minimization of the cost of capital. Explain the relationship.

# 2

# Tax Considerations

This chapter is divided into two major subsections. In the first part of the chapter the tax considerations of selecting a legal form of organization will be discussed. This will involve a review of some factors the Internal Revenue Service and the courts consider in determining the tax status of a particular legal form of organization, what tax rates the tax entities are subject to at various income levels, and how this taxable income is determined.

The second part of the chapter deals with tax considerations and financial decision-making, *in the context of the corporation*. The tax treatment of gains and losses, the investment tax credit, and the dividend received deduction will be discussed in the context of their impact on the investment decisions of the firm. Accelerated depreciation and the impact of depreciation timing on financial decisions also will be explored. The tax provision dealing with the deduction of net operating losses will be explained. Finally, the nature of the accumulated earnings tax will be considered along with its implications for corporate dividend decisions.

A disclaimer is in order before proceeding to the topical coverage. Tax statutes are periodically changed by Congress and are constantly reinterpreted by the Internal Revenue Service and the courts. As a consequence, any tax summary is, to some degree, obsolete almost as soon as it is completed. The coverage in this chapter was current and accurate at the beginning of 1978. However, it is not intended as a substitute for a tax course. Such tax courses not only provide a more detailed explanation of the individual tax issues, many also teach the necessary research methodology to determine what current tax law is, as defined by the most recent court and IRS interpretations. An aspiring finance student might consider additional study in this area.

TABLE 2-1
1977 Federal Tax Schedule for Married Taxpayers Filing Joint Return

| Taxable Income Is over | But Not over | Income Tax | of Amount over |
|---|---|---|---|
| Not over $3,200 | | 0 | |
| $ 3,200 | $ 4,200 | 14% | $ 3,200 |
| 4,200 | 5,200 | 140 + 15 | 4,200 |
| 5,200 | 6,200 | 290 + 16 | 5,200 |
| 6,200 | 7,200 | 450 + 17 | 6,200 |
| 7,200 | 11,200 | 620 + 19 | 7,200 |
| 11,200 | 15,200 | 1,380 + 22 | 11,200 |
| 15,200 | 19,200 | 2,260 + 25 | 15,200 |
| 19,200 | 23,200 | 3,260 + 28 | 19,200 |
| 23,200 | 27,200 | 4,380 + 32 | 23,200 |
| 27,200 | 31,200 | 5,660 + 36 | 27,200 |
| 31,200 | 35,200 | 7,100 + 39 | 31,200 |
| 35,200 | 39,200 | 8,660 + 42 | 35,200 |
| 39,200 | 43,200 | 10,340 + 45 | 39,200 |
| 43,200 | 47,200 | 12,140 + 48 | 43,200 |
| 47,200 | 55,200 | 14,060 + 50 | 47,200 |
| 55,200 | 67,200 | 18,060 + 53 | 55,200 |
| 67,200 | 79,200 | 24,420 + 55 | 67,200 |
| 79,200 | 91,200 | 31,020 + 58 | 79,200 |
| 91,200 | 103,200 | 37,980 + 60 | 91,200 |
| 103,200 | 123,200 | 45,180 + 62 | 103,200 |
| 123,200 | 143,200 | 57,580 + 64 | 123,200 |
| 143,200 | 163,200 | 70,380 + 66 | 143,200 |
| 163,200 | 183,200 | 83,580 + 68 | 163,200 |
| 183,200 | 203,200 | 97,180 + 69 | 183,200 |
| 203,200 | — | 110,980 + 70 | 203,200 |

## TAX FACTORS IN CHOOSING A FORM OF ORGANIZATION

While a thorough examination of the legal forms of organization is beyond the scope of this text, for financial planning, tax considerations are important to review. Some of the most often encountered forms include the sole proprietorship, the partnership, the limited partnership, the limited partnership association, the business trust, the joint venture, and the corporation. While these organizations fall into numerous legal classifications, for tax purposes they can be classified as one of two tax entities, the individual or the corporation. Tax law lists those characteristics that indicate the existence of a corporate tax entity: (1) associates, (2) an objective to carry on a business for profit, (3) continuity of life, (4) centralization of management, (5) limited liability, and (6) free transferability of interests. Organizations not having these characteristics are generally taxed as individuals.

## 2 Tax Considerations

The distinction is important because different tax rates apply to individuals and corporations. Individuals are subject to a progressive tax rate that begins at zero and reaches a maximum of 70 percent of taxable income at higher income levels. An example of such a schedule for a married couple filing a joint return is shown in Table 2–1.[1]

On the other hand, the corporation is subject to a normal tax of 20 percent on the first 25,000 of taxable income. All taxable income above $25,000 is subject to a normal tax rate of 22 percent. Taxable income over $50,000 is subject to a 26 percent surtax. Therefore, the effective corporate tax rates are as follows: 20 percent on the first $25,000, 22 percent on the second $25,000, and 48 percent (22 percent + 26 percent) on all taxable income over $50,000. Any after-tax income may be retained or paid out to stockholders in dividends. Since the corporation is the tax entity to which the income belongs, there is no additional tax if the income is used in the business; however, if the corporation disburses all or part of its income to stockholders as dividends, the earnings so distributed are ordinary taxable income of the stockholders. Because the stockholders and the corporation are separate taxpayers, the corporate income, when distributed, is subject to two federal income taxes, probably state and local taxes, and "foreign" taxes if the corporation does business in states other than the state of incorporation (hence, there is not only "double" but also "multiple" taxation of corporate income.)

### Income Tax Structure

To better understand the calculation of tax liabilities for individuals and corporations, the income tax structure is depicted in Figure 2–1.

*Inflow of assets* represents all money or property rights received by a taxpayer. These inflows may result from either (1) exchanges, such as cash or accounts receivable resulting from a sale, or (2) nonreciprocal transfers, such as gifts or prizes. Increases in wealth resulting from nontransfers, such as increases in the market value of a stock investment held, are not recognized by the taxing authorities. Some of the more familiar inflows of assets for business in addition to sales receipts include dividend income, proceeds from the sale of capital assets, and lawsuit damages received.

*Return of capital* refers to the cost of the consideration given in the case of an exchange in which assets are received, increased by any capital improvements made since its acquisition prior to its disposal, and decreased by any depreciation, amortization, or depletion taken. This "new cost" is often referred to as the asset's *adjusted basis*. The cost of goods

---

[1] There are four classes of individual taxpayers. In order of preferential treatment, these are (1) married couples filing joint returns, (2) heads of households, (3) single individuals other than heads of households, and (4) married couples filing separate returns.

sold by a manufacturing firm has as its adjusted basis—cost—since inventory is a nondepreciable item. The same is true for marketable securities. However, an asset like a building may have had a new addition that would have adjusted its basis upward and depreciation deductions that would have reduced the basis, thus resulting in an adjusted basis different than cost.

The difference between inflow of assets and return of capital may be termed *net inflow of assets*. What this represents may be shown by considering the sale of land that was purchased at a cost of $1,000 and sold for $4,000—$4,000 represents the inflow of wealth, $1,000 is the adjusted basis (land is a nondepreciable asset), and the difference, $3,000, represents the net inflow of assets. Also, the difference between *Sales* (representing an inflow of wealth) and *Cost of Goods Sold* (representing a

**FIGURE 2-1**
**Income Tax Structure**

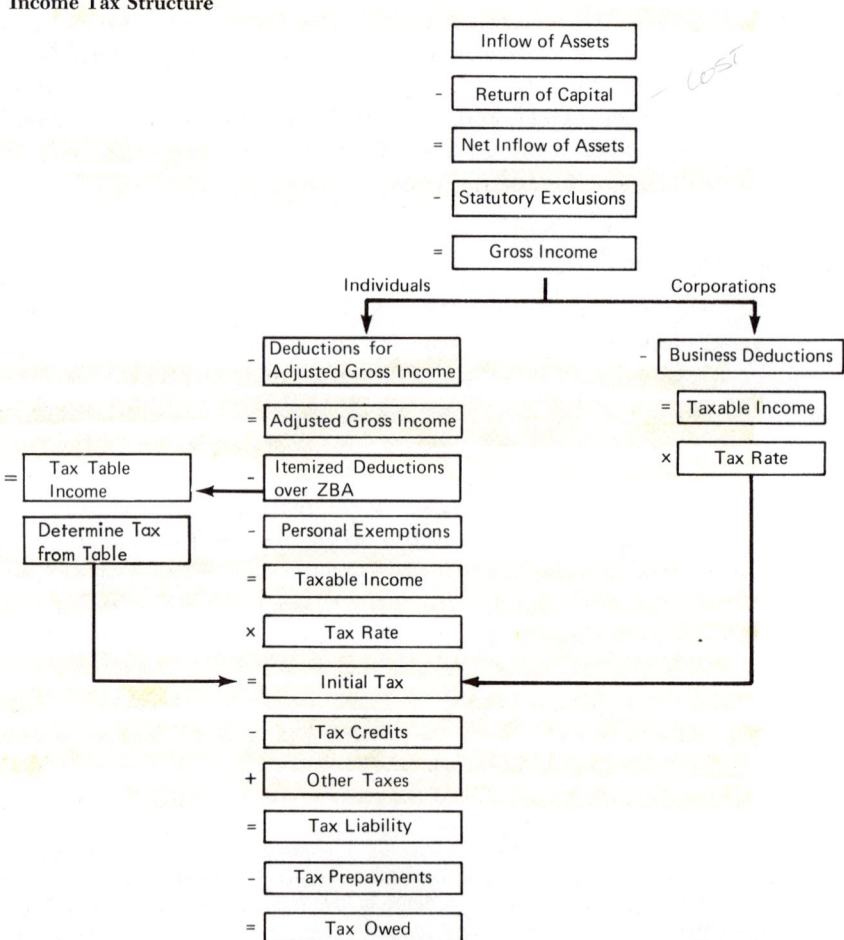

## 2  Tax Considerations

return of capital) is the net inflow of assets. In accounting terminology, this difference is referred to as *gross profit* or *gross margin*.

Certain types of inflows are excluded. Exclusions are items that are not included in the definition of gross income. They are of three types. (1) Those exclusions that cannot be taxed because of the U.S. Constitution; e.g., the interest on bonds issued by the cities and the states. (2) Those inflows that do not fit the definition of income; e.g., the return of capital as discussed above. (As a specific example, repayment of loan principal is not taxable to lenders. The lenders are merely receiving their own money back—it is not income.) (3) *Statutory exclusions,* which are items that Congress has allowed to escape taxation, even though classified as net inflows. Exclusions of types (1) and (2) are wholly excluded. Type (3), statutory exclusions, may be either wholly or partly exempt from taxation. Veterans' benefits under the GI Bill are wholly exempt, as are fellowships. Lump-sum life insurance proceeds received because of the death of the insured are generally excluded in total. However, if a beneficiary elects to receive the benefits in annuity form (periodic payments), the payments will be only partially excluded. Another common exclusion is one that allows the first $100 of dividend income of the individual to go untaxed.[2] Other net inflows of assets excluded from taxation include gifts and inheritances, many prizes and awards, and workers' compensation payments.

After this point, the method of calculating the taxable income and the taxes depends on the nature of the taxpayer—individual or corporate. Corporations generally receive the same business deductions as individuals; however, they do not receive the personal deductions allowed individuals. Corporations may deduct business expenses, which would generally include all of the normal costs of operating a business such as wages, rent, maintenance and repair, interest, taxes, advertising, and the write-off of fixed assets (depreciation, amortization, and depletion). Subtracting the total business deductions from gross income determines taxable income which is subject to the rates discussed earlier.

The tax structure for corporations is simpler than the tax structure for individuals. There are some special rules for capital assets, depreciable assets, dividend income, operating earnings, and undistributed profits. Each of these issues is discussed separately in the section on "Tax Factors and Business Decisions."

Individuals can take two types of deductions. There are "deductions *for* adjusted gross income," and there are "deductions *from* adjusted gross income." The latter are often referred to as personal deductions.

Deductions for adjusted gross income (AGI) include expenses related to running a business or profession, business-related travel expenses, de-

---

[2] If the stock is held jointly, $200 may be excluded by married individuals filing a joint return.

ductions related to rental property, losses on exchanges, moving expenses, alimony, and a deduction equal to one half of net long-term capital gains.

A review of the deductions *for* AGI will reveal that many of these deductions are analogous to the business deductions of a corporation. If the individual taxpayer engages in a business (or a profession), this is shown on a separate schedule in the tax return. The revenue and expenses are detailed on the schedule, with only the net amount being included in AGI.

Gains and losses from sales of investments are treated similarly. The gains are added to AGI and are taxable (subject to a special set of rules). The losses, subject to certain limits, are deductions *for* AGI.

Moving expenses can also be viewed as business expenses. To be allowable, such expenses must be incurred in connection with a move to a job in a new location.

Alimony refers to payments one marital partner must make to the other in the event of a divorce. Alimony payments are deductible from the AGI for the one paying and are added to the AGI of the recipient.

The long-term capital gain deduction is the most complicated of the deductions for AGI. Both individual taxpayers and corporations get a tax break on long-term gains arising from the sale of capital assets (discussion of corporate treatment is in the "Business Decisions" section).

A capital asset is defined by exclusion. It is an asset other than inventory or other property held for sale during the normal course of business, accounts or notes receivable, depreciable property and real property used in a trade or business, copyrights and other creations in the hands of the creator, and *certain* U.S. government bonds[3] and publications. The principal capital assets for individuals are investments (stocks and bonds) and personal property (jewelry and homes).

It is important to determine whether a capital transaction is short-term or long-term. If more than a year passes between the date of acquisition and the date of sale, the transaction is long-term and receives beneficial treatment.

Although it is not immediately clear when preparing the return, the effect of current capital-gains treatment is as follows:

1. All short-term transactions are totaled.
2. All long-term transactions are totaled.
3. The two totals are netted against each other.
4. If the net long-term capital gain is greater than the net short-term capital loss, the taxpayer is allowed a deduction for AGI equal to one half of the excess of the net long-term gain over the net short-term capital loss.[4] The balance is carried to AGI. (Step 4 sounds con-

---

[3] Most U.S. government bonds *are* capital assets for most taxpayers.

[4] A taxpayer may elect instead to have long-term gains taxed separately at a rate of 25 percent, subject to a $50,000 long-term gain maximum.

fusing and is easier to explain by example. If the taxpayer had only long-term capital gains, the deduction for AGI would be for 50 percent of those gains. If there were only short-term gains, there would be no deduction. If the taxpayer had net gains on both short-term and long-term transactions, the deduction is 50 percent of the net long-term amount. If the long-term transactions result in a net gain and short-term transactions result in net losses, the deduction is limited to 50 percent of the *excess* long-term gains.)
5. If the total is negative, the taxpayer can use the negative balance to offset other income to a maximum of $3,000. (Short-term capital losses offset other income dollar for dollar. Long-term losses offset 50 cents of other income for each dollar of loss. If the taxpayer has losses of both types, short-term losses are utilized first.)
6. Any unused losses are carried forward as the first entries in calculating next year's capital gains and losses.
7. The losses can be carried forward until exhausted, retaining their short- and long-term character, and offsetting ordinary income, subject to the prevailing limits, in each year.

After AGI is determined, the taxpayer can subtract certain personal deductions in excess of the zero bracket amount (ZBA). As can be seen from Table 2–1, the tax rate schedule for married people filing jointly shows the first $3,200 of taxable income as being exempt from taxation. The tax rate in this bracket is zero. Both the tax rate schedules and the tax tables have, in effect, built in a minimum deduction called the "zero bracket amount" equal to $3,200 for married taxpayers filing jointly, $2,200 for single taxpayers and heads of households, and $1,600 for marrieds filing separately. If the taxpayer itemizes deductions, allowable personal deductions include interest expense, taxes (some of which can be estimated from supplied tables; e.g., sales, gasoline), contributions (subject to maximum limits), medical expenses (subject to some complex and costly limits), and a number of other deductions such as certain employee business expenses and casualty losses.

The left-hand branch of Figure 2–1 depicts a major result of the Tax Reduction and Simplification Act of 1977. Most taxpayers, regardless of whether they itemize, will use the tax tables rather than the tax rate schedules (Table 2–1). "Tax table income" is defined as adjusted gross income less excess itemized deductions (deductions in excess of the zero bracket amount). If the tax table income is $40,000 or less, the initial tax liability can be determined directly from the tables by married couples filing jointly. (The tables go to $20,000 for singles, marrieds filing separately, and heads of households.) These tables take into consideration the number of exemptions, the zero bracket amount, and the general tax credit (discussed below).

Taxpayers with income above the table limits cannot calculate their taxes in this simplified manner. The same thing is true for some with income below the limits because of peculiarities in their returns. These taxpayers must calculate their tax liability using a tax rate schedule such as the one illustrated in Table 2–1. The tax rate schedules do not take into consideration exemptions and the general tax credit. Therefore to correctly calculate the initial tax these taxpayers should reduce taxable income for personal exemptions. Individuals are allowed a *personal exemption* of $750 from adjusted gross income for themselves, their spouses (if they file a joint return), and any dependents.[5]

*Tax credits* include certain direct offsets to the tax liability provided for in the Internal Revenue Code. The most familiar and controversial credit is probably the investment tax credit, which is discussed later in the chapter. Among other credits are those for certain political contributions, retirement income, foreign taxes paid, child care expenses, and the earned income credit.

At the present time the tax code also provides for a "general tax credit." It is the greater of (1) 2 percent of taxable income less the ZBA not to exceed $180, or (2) $35 per exemption, including those allowed for old age and blindness. This credit is available to all individual resident taxpayers. (For those taxpayers using the tax tables, the general tax credit is built in, as indicated above.)

"Other taxes" is a catchall term which refers to a number of specific taxes that might be assessed because of a taxpayer's circumstances. Self-employed taxpayers are taxed in order to be provided with the same benefits that regular employees receive through the payment of social security taxes on their wages.

Employees who receive tip income are required to calculate and pay the social security taxes on that income. There are also taxes that apply to individual retirement arrangements. One of the more recent "other taxes" is the minimum tax.

The *minimum tax on tax preferences* refers to a tax on certain items that, because of the tax law, receive preferred treatment. Its purpose is to provide some form of equity in the tax law by preventing certain taxpayers from avoiding taxes altogether. While the calculation of the tax is beyond the scope of this text, it is basically a 15 percent tax on "preference items" above a certain amount. Among the preference items are "excess" depreciation and depletion caused by the use of accelerated depreciation and percentage depletion allowances, capital gains, and certain other items.

There is also a maximum tax provision. For high income taxpayers, the maximum marginal tax rate on "personal service income" is 50 percent. Personal service income includes salaries, all or a part of self-employ-

---

[5] Additional exemptions are allowed for individuals who are 65 or older and for those who are blind.

ment income, pensions, annuities, and deferred compensation. If capital is an important contributing factor in producing self-employment income, the portion of that income that is from personal service must be determined. The personal service income, which is covered by the maximum tax provision, can be a "reasonable amount" but it cannot exceed 30 percent of the self-employment income.

The formula below is used to determine what portion of taxable income is attributable to personal service income:

$$\frac{\text{Net personal service income}}{\text{Adjusted gross income}} \times \text{Taxable income} - \text{Tax preferences} = \text{Personal service taxable income}$$

Since the enactment of the 15 percent minimum tax and the 50 percent maximum tax on personal service income, the incentive to convert what would otherwise be ordinary income into capital gains has been substantially decreased.

Finally, *tax prepayments* include amounts that have been previously applied toward satisfying any tax liability a taxpayer might have. The most common prepayments are withholding taxes, declarations of estimated tax payments, and overpayments of social security.

## Subchapter S Corporations

The Subchapter S corporation is a product of the tax law. It was created by the Technical Amendments Act of 1958 as an addition to Subchapter S of the Internal Revenue Code. Congress' original intent in establishing the provisions for the Subchapter S corporation was to try to relieve the burden of double taxation of small businesses, which, although legally established as corporations, operated like partnerships or sole proprietorships. This was accomplished by allowing those corporations meeting certain requirements to elect to have corporate income passed through directly to the stockholders to be taxed at the appropriate individual income tax rates. Subchapter S was originally intended to help smaller firms. It has evolved into a very flexible instrument for tax planning and is now probably even more advantageous for certain large corporations than for small ones.

In order for an organization to qualify as a Subchapter S corporation, the following conditions must be met:

1. The corporation must not have more than ten shareholders.[6]
2. Each shareholder must be an individual or an estate.
3. No shareholder may be a nonresident alien.
4. The corporation may not have more than one class of stock.

---

[6] For tax years after 1976, there may be up to 15 shareholders under certain conditions.

5. The corporation must not derive more than 80 percent of its gross receipts from sources outside the United States.
6. Not more than 20 percent of gross receipts may result from passive investment income, such as rents, royalties, dividends, interest, annuities, and gains from the sale of stock or securities
7. The corporation must not own 80 percent or more of the stock of any subsidiary company.
8. All shareholders must agree to the Subchapter S election.

A revocation or a failure to meet any of the above requirements terminates the election. Once revoked, another election cannot be made for five years unless the IRS consents to an earlier election.

For those corporations that meet the above requirements, the tax advantages of making a Subchapter S corporation election can be significant. The dollar benefits of the election can be seen in the following example:

Mr. A, who is married and files a joint return, owns all of the shares of stock in the X Corporation, which meets all of the requirements for a Subchapter S election. For 1977 his taxable income was $200,000. Because Mr. A lived the "good life," he wanted to have all after-tax earnings distributed to himself. If he had elected the Subchapter S status, his total tax liability would have been $108,772. Under standard corporation tax rules his total tax liability would have been $136,422—due to double taxation. The calculations are shown below.

*Tax Liability under Normal Corporate Rules*

$25,000 × 20% = $5,000
$25,000 × 22% = 5,500
$150,000 × 48% = 72,000

Corporate income tax $82,500

Amount left for distribution $117,500.
Amount taxable $117,300 ($200 dividend exclusion).

Tax on $103,200  = $45,180
14,100 × 62%  = 8,742
(Using Table 2–1)  $53,922 Personal Taxes

After-tax distribution $63,578.

*Subchapter S Corporation Tax Liability*

Tax on $200,000 = $108,772
(Using Table 2–1)

After-tax distribution $91,228.

A second important tax advantage of the Subchapter S election is that in some cases it allows the corporation to control the year in which some earnings are taxed. This is so because distributions of earnings are taxed when received, while undistributed earnings are considered received on the last day of the corporation's tax year. Thus, if the shareholders of a corporation qualifying under the provisions of Subchapter S had tax years that ended shortly before the end of the tax year for the corporation, they could either distribute earnings before the end of their tax years or retain earnings until the close of the corporate tax year, depending on whether taxable income from other sources for the shareholders was greater for the tax year just ended or whether tax liability in the coming year was expected to be greater.

Shareholders may prefer Subchapter S for one additional reason. Subchapter S allows shareholders to take advantage of investment credits and operating losses of a corporation where they otherwise could not.

## TAX FACTORS AND BUSINESS DECISIONS

Tax treatment affects many business decisions. This section discusses some of the more important of the commonly encountered decisions where taxes are especially relevant. This section limits the discussion to taxes *as they apply to corporations.*

As noted earlier, a proprietor operating a business reports the income on a separate schedule of the individual return. The nature of individual capital gain and loss calculations was discussed. The depreciation calculation was postponed, as was discussion of the investment tax credit. Although the following discussion is for corporations, the calculations are much the same for individuals.

The individual's dividend exclusion was noted. Corporations get a bigger tax break on dividend income. This will be discussed.

The material on accelerated depreciation applies to individuals as well as corporations. The net operating loss provisions and accumulated earnings tax apply only to corporations.

### Tax Treatment of Gains and Losses

Understanding income taxation of gains and losses plays an integral part in the financial management of a corporation because financial decision-making is often significantly influenced by the tax ramifications of a particular action. Since various types of activities within the firm have different tax implications, the effects of taxation can be mitigated by sound planning and management.

Gains and losses may result from either (1) sales or exchanges, or (2) other dispositions of property. The distinction is important for tax purposes because certain sales or exchanges qualify for special tax treatment if they meet the other requirements of either a capital asset or a 1231 asset.

Three types of gains are recognized by the tax law and are accorded different treatment. These include (1) ordinary gains and losses, (2) capital gains and losses, and (3) 1231 gains and losses. While the tax treatment of these gains differs, the *amount* of gain or loss to be realized exclusive of tax considerations is the same for all three. This is found by taking the difference between the fair-market value of property received and the adjusted basis of that property given up. *Adjusted basis* usually refers to the cost of the asset, plus any capital additions to the asset since acquisition, reduced by any depreciation, amortization, or depletion. For some items, such as inventories and depreciable assets, which do not qualify for a depreciation allowance under the tax law, adjusted basis typically equals cost. However, probably a greater number of business assets could apply the broader definition of adjusted basis.

As an example of how gains and losses are determined, consider the following:

> The X Corporation purchased an asset three years ago for $1,000 with an estimated useful life of five years. It has been depreciated using straight-line depreciation since its acquisition. What would be the gain or loss given the following sales prices: (1) $500, (2) $350, (3) $100 plus a machine with a fair-market value of $350.
>
> There would be a gain or loss computed as follows:

|  | (1) | (2) | (3) |
|---|---|---|---|
| FMV of property received | $500 | $350 | $450 |
| Adjusted basis of property given up | 400 | 400 | 400 |
| Gain (loss) | $100 | $(50) | $ 50 |

## Ordinary Gains and Losses

Ordinary gains and losses can best be described as those gains and losses that are neither capital gains and losses nor 1231 gains or losses. The most notable assets that would fall into this category include inventory items and real and depreciable property used in a trade or business held for a year or less. Gains classified as ordinary gains are taxed at the appropriate tax rate for corporations while ordinary losses are deducted as business expenses.

## Capital Gains and Losses

The Internal Revenue Code of 1954 defines capital assets explicitly as indicated earlier. The definition includes all assets except inventory; accounts and notes receivable; depreciable and real property used in a trade or business; short-term U.S. securities sold at a discount; and certain copyrights, literary, musical, or artistic compositions, letters, and memoranda. The most common types include investment property and nonbusiness property. While a building used as a factory by a manufacturing firm would not be a capital asset since it is depreciable property used in a trade or business, that same factory, if purchased as an investment and held for resale, might be considered a capital asset. It is clear, then, that the *intent* for utilization of a particular asset is a major determinant of whether it has the status of a capital asset.

The distinction between capital and other assets is important because capital assets receive special tax treatment. Gains or losses from the sale or exchange of capital assets are defined as capital gains or losses. The sale of a capital asset held for a year or less may result in either a short-term capital gain or a short-term capital loss. If the asset is held for more than a year before disposal, a long-term capital gain or loss results. To determine the tax treatment of the capital gains and losses, short-term capital gains and losses are added together to get the net short-term gain or loss. The same is done with long-term gains and losses.

*Net* short-term capital gains are included in the corporation's ordinary income and taxed at the applicable rates. Corporate long-term capital gains are taxed at regular tax rates, or at a 30-percent rate, whichever produces the lower tax liability. Under the present tax-rate structure for corporations, if total taxable income is $50,000 or less, the regular tax calculation will yield a lower tax liability. If income is more than $50,000, the 30-percent alternative tax may produce lower taxes.

Net capital losses, whether short-term or long-term, cannot be deducted for tax purposes but must be used to offset any capital gains of the period. The excess of capital loss over capital gain may be carried back three years and forward five years, offsetting those carry-over losses against capital gains from the earliest possible year. All losses carried over to other years are considered short-term capital losses for purposes of computing capital gains and losses for that year.

To clarify the above rules, consider the following example:

> The XYZ Corporation has made a number of sales of stock from its portfolio during 1978 and, in trying to determine its tax liability with regard to these sales, has gathered the following information:

| Security held | Purchase Date | Purchase Price | Sales Date | Sales Price |
|---|---|---|---|---|
| ABC Corp. | 12/22/77 | $10,600 | 5/4/78 | $ 8,000 |
| Scramble Corp. | 9/5/72 | 12,100 | 2/1/78 | 8,000 |
| Williams Paint Store | 3/21/48 | 9,300 | 4/15/78 | 15,100 |
| Snyder Corp. | 12/3/77 | 4,300 | 5/3/78 | 6,100 |

> The short-term capital loss from the sale of the ABC Corporation stock should be netted out against the short-term capital gain from the Snyder Corporation stock sale. The result is a net short-term capital loss of $800.
>
> Likewise, the long-term capital loss from Scramble Corporation's sale should be offset by the long-term capital gain resulting from the sale of Williams Paint Store stock. The result is a $1,700 net long-term capital gain.
>
> Since capital losses can be deducted only to the extent they offset capital gains, the net short-term capital loss should be netted out to give a

long-term capital gain of $900 for the year. This would be taxed at a rate of 30 percent, provided ordinary income is more than $50,000.

If, in this example, short-term capital loss had exceeded long-term capital gain, the difference would have been carried back to 1975 and netted out against capital gains of that period.

*1231 Gains and Losses.* Section 1231 of the Internal Revenue Code also provides special treatment for certain gains and losses resulting from sale or exchange of realty or depreciable property used in a trade or business and held for more than a year. Such assets, often called "1231 assets," consist mainly of real property and property such as machines, vehicles, and equipment. Only certain portions of gains or losses from the sale or exchange of these assets are accorded special treatment under this section. This is determined by netting out gains and losses from 1231-asset sales or exchanges to arrive at a net gain or net loss. All net losses may be deducted as ordinary losses in determining tax liability. The treatment of a net gain, however, is somewhat more complicated. To the extent that depreciation has been taken on the asset sold, the gain realized must be treated as ordinary income. This process is known as *recapture of depreciation*. Any gain realized in excess of this recapture element is treated as long-term capital gain and taxed accordingly.

To clarify these rules, consider the following example:

The BPA Corporation purchased a machine for use in its business on January 1, 1973, for $10,000. The asset had a useful life of ten years and was depreciated using the straight-line method. On December 31, 1977, the machine was sold. What would be the tax implications of the sale given the following prices: (1) $3,000; (2) $7,000; (3) $12,000?

1. A loss of $2,000 would be realized and would be deducted as an ordinary loss.

2. A gain of $2,000 would be realized on this sale. Because of the recapture of up to $5,000 of depreciation, this $2,000 would be taxed as ordinary income.

3. A gain of $7,000 would be realized on the sale. Because of the recapture of $5,000 of depreciation, this amount would be taxed as ordinary income. The remaining, $2,000 would be treated as a long-term capital gain.

### Investment Tax Credit

A part of the Revenue Act of 1962 established one of the most volatile tax incentives offered in recent tax history—the *investment tax credit*. Its dual purposes were to stimulate the domestic economy and to make U.S. businesses more competitive internationally. This was accomplished through tax provisions that encouraged the modernization of plant and equipment. Since its enactment into law, the investment tax credit has been amended, suspended, reenacted, repealed, and reenacted regularly.

The suspensions and repeals were the result of fears of inflation. The reenactments were to counter economic slowdowns. In spite of its volatility, the investment tax credit is an important tax factor in business planning. Much of its popularity can be traced to the fact that, unlike most other tax incentives for businesses, this allowance is a direct offset to the tax liability rather than a business deduction from gross income. The following example, which compares two companies whose only difference is that Company X has a business deduction of $1,000 and Company Y has an investment tax credit of $1,000, illustrates the point:

| Company X | | Company Y | |
|---|---|---|---|
| Gross income | $20,000 | Gross income | $20,000 |
| Business deductions | 1,000 | Business deductions | —0— |
| Taxable income | $19,000 | Taxable income | $20,000 |
| | | | |
| Tax (20% × $19,000) | $ 3,800 | Tax (20% × $20,000) | $ 4,000 |
| Tax credit | —0— | Tax credit | 1,000 |
| Tax liability | $ 3,800 | Tax liability | $ 3,000 |

Basically, the investment tax credit is a direct tax credit to the tax liability equal to 10 percent of any "qualified investment." This credit must be taken in the year the investment is made unless there is no tax liability. In that case, the tax credit may be carried back three years and forward seven years[7] to be applied to the tax liability, starting with the earliest year possible. The limit for each taxable year as to the amount of tax credit that may be used is $25,000 plus 50 percent of any tax liability above that amount.

To be a "qualified investment," the investment must be tangible personal property or certain real property and must have application to business activities or operations entered into for profit. Also, qualified investments must have a useful life of at least seven years.[8] If the investment is sold before the seven-year minimum but after the credit has been taken, the credit is subject to recapture much like recapture of depreciation.

## Dividend Income Deduction

Corporations are allowed a business deduction of 85 percent of all dividend income earned from domestic corporations. Thus, only 15 percent of the dividend constitutes taxable income. Assuming the present tax rate of 48 percent, the tax would amount to only 7.2 percent of the total dividend. This explains why many corporations hold investment

---

[7] In certain instances, the seven-year carry-forward may be extended to ten years.
[8] If the useful life of the investment is at least five years and less than seven years, two thirds of the cost of the investment constitutes the "qualified investment." If its useful life is at least three years and less than five years, one third of its cost represents the "qualified investment."

grade preferred stocks rather than bonds, on which the entire interest received is taxable. The rationale for this dividend credit is that to subject intercorporate dividends to the full corporate tax would lead to multiple taxation, because dividends paid by a corporation are not deductible for income tax purposes whereas bond interest is deductible.

## Accelerated Depreciation

Depreciation is the systematic allocation of the cost of an asset to the periods in which benefits are to be derived from its existence. Accelerated depreciation has long been recognized as one way of allocating these costs to benefits on the grounds that its use would help compensate for (1) sudden changes in demand or in technology that would make fixed assets obsolete prematurely and (2) premature wearing out of fixed assets due to abnormal activity or use.

The current law regarding depreciation allows a taxpayer wide latitude as to depreciation methods as long as the asset to be depreciated is used in a trade or business or for the production of income. The Internal Revenue Code specifically allows for the use of (1) the straight-line method, (2) any declining-balance method that does not exceed 200 percent of the straight-line method, (3) sum-of-the-years-digits method, or (4) any other rational and systematic method that, in the first two thirds of the useful life of the asset involved, does not exceed the allowance granted under the double-declining-balance method, without economic justification. There are exceptions to these latter rules, most notable that for the depreciation of buildings. Also, the use of the double-declining-balance method is restricted to new tangible property with a useful life of at least three years, and the sum-of-the-years-digits method can be used only to depreciate new property held at least three years. No matter what method of depreciation is selected, however, no more than the depreciated value of a fixed asset may be deducted as an expense over the life of the fixed asset.

Because there is a limit on the aggregate depreciation deduction that may be taken over the life of the asset, the selection of an appropriate method is a matter of timing. The data in Table 2–2 illustrates how different methods of depreciation realize depreciation tax savings over time.

Note that, while the double-declining-balance method yields the greatest tax savings in earlier years and therefore allows the firm to retain more cash to reinvest, over 7 percent of the cost of the asset remains unrecovered at the end of its useful life. To compensate for the unrecovered cost characteristic, tax law allows the taxpayer to change from a declining-balance method to the straight-line method at any time during the useful life of the asset.

In addition to the regular depreciation, all taxpayers can take an extra write-off in the first year. The *additional first year depreciation* allowance

**TABLE 2-2**
Assume: $500 Asset; Five-Year Useful Life; 48 Percent Tax Rate

| | Straight-line | | | Sum-of-the-years-digits | | | Double-declining Balance | | |
|---|---|---|---|---|---|---|---|---|---|
| | Depreciation Deduction | Total Cost Recovered | Depreciation Tax Savings | Depreciation Deduction | Total Cost Recovered | Depreciation Tax Savings | Depreciation Deduction | Total Cost Recovered | Depreciation Tax Savings |
| Year 1 | $100 | $100 | $48 | $167 | $167 | $80 | $200 | $200 | $96 |
| Year 2 | 100 | 200 | 48 | 133 | 300 | 64 | 120 | 320 | 58 |
| Year 3 | 100 | 300 | 48 | 100 | 400 | 48 | 72 | 392 | 35 |
| Year 4 | 100 | 400 | 48 | 67 | 467 | 32 | 43 | 435 | 21 |
| Year 5 | 100 | 500 | 48 | 33 | 500 | 16 | 26 | 461 | 12 |

is 20 percent. The taxpayer takes depreciation equal to 20 percent of the cost of new or used equipment. The tax basis of the property is reduced by that amount and then the regular depreciation is calculated. There are some limits. The asset must have a remaining life of at least six years. The provision is limited to a maximum of $10,000 in assets in any given year.[9]

## Net Operating Loss Carry-Backs and Carry-Forwards

Another important provision of the Internal Revenue Code that provides tax relief to corporations is the one that deals with net operating loss carry-backs and carry-forwards. Under this section of the law, the net operating loss of a corporation may be carried back three years and carried forward seven years, applying the loss as an offset to taxable income in the earliest year over that period in which taxable income was realized. An amended tax return must be filed for the year to which the carry-back applies, and the tax rates applicable to that year must be used. The purpose of this feature of the Internal Revenue Code is to avoid unduly penalizing firms that experience widely fluctuating income and also to aid young firms in their development period.

To better understand the basic concept of the carry-back, carry-forward provisions, study the following example, in which it is assumed there are no operating losses in previous years that would affect the tax years under question.

| Year | Taxable Income (loss) | Amount of Carry-back Applied | Taxable Income, Adjusted |
|---|---|---|---|
| 1971 | $20,000 | | $20,000 |
| 1972 | 45,000 | (30,000) | $15,000 |
| 1973 | 20,000 | | 20,000 |
| 1974 | 15,000 | (15,000) | –0– |
| 1975 | (30,000) | | –0– |
| 1976 | –0– | | –0– |
| 1977 | (40,000) | | –0– |
| 1978 | 35,000 | (25,000) | 10,000 |

The right to carry losses backward and forward can make certain corporations attractive to prospective buyers. Newspapers occasionally carry advertisements stating that a corporation experiencing losses is available for sale. Acquisitions of this type are not so prevalent today as they were before 1954. In that year certain restrictions were placed on this privilege, thereby reducing the number of mergers for the apparent purpose of using losses of the acquired company to offset profits of the

---

[9] The $10,000 provision applies to individuals and corporations. For marrieds filing jointly, the limit is $20,000 of property per year.

acquiring firm. The 1954 law specifically provided that the loss carry-over could not be used in the following instances: (1) if more than 50 percent of the stock changes hands within two years after the acquisition; and (2) if the old business is for all intent abandoned. The purpose of these restrictions is to prevent mergers solely for the purpose of taking advantage of the tax law. For tax years starting after June 30, 1978, the net operating loss carry-over is either reduced or disallowed, depending on the percentage change in ownership.

## Accumulated Earnings Tax

The presence of the accumulated earnings tax is a factor that must be considered in financial decision making. Section 531 of the Internal Revenue Code provides for a special tax (sometimes referred to as a surplus tax) on the accumulated earnings of a corporation, if the intent of the accumulation is to avoid personal income taxes on dividends and if the earnings are reinvested in excess of the reasonable needs of the business firm. (The rate is 27.5 percent on the first $100,000 of excess accumulation plus 38.5 percent on additional amounts.) Corporations whose stock is publicly traded rarely have to contend with the accumulated earnings tax. Nonpublic or family corporations that have an expanding business will generally not have a material surplus of funds that has not been designated for some business purpose. A telltale sign of earnings retained beyond the reasonable needs of the business is long-term investments in stocks, securities, and land that have no connection with the corporation's business. Such investments would attract the attention of the IRS. Funds can be retained for the purpose of buying out a minority stockholder, the purchase of a building, and the payoff of indebtedness.

A corporation may accumulate retained earnings up to $150,000 over a period of years without penalty; and, if there is an accumulation in excess of this amount, the burden of proving that the purpose is tax evasion rests with the Commissioner of Internal Revenue. Assuming that a corporation cannot support its position that an amount of $200,000 is needed but can show that $190,000 is needed, the special tax would be levied on the difference. The undistributed earnings tax has had an effect on dividend policies of small, family-owned corporations wherein the incentive to avoid high personal income tax is strong. In addition, the avoidance of the undistributed earnings tax has led to managerial policies such as unnecessary or untimely expenditures for new products, equipment, and plants.

The tax is levied on "accumulated taxable income," and not on retained earnings. This amount is specifically defined as *adjusted* taxable income minus any dividends paid and minus the accumulated earnings credit.

The adjustments to taxable income require the taxpayer to add back any net operating loss deductions, any capital loss carry-backs or carry-forwards, the dividends received deduction, and charitable contribution deductions which arise from contributions in other tax years. Federal taxes, any disallowed capital losses, and any actual contributions in excess of statutory limits are then subtracted. This, in effect, defines a "true income figure." This figure is reduced by net long-term gains after taxes (long-term gains minus short-term losses minus the related taxes).

Dividends paid is self-explanatory. The accumulated earnings credit is the *greater* of: (a) the reasonable needs of the business less net long-term gains after taxes, or (b) $150,000 less past accumulations.

Although the last two paragraphs sound complicated, the intent of the tax provision is not. If the corporation attempts to save its shareholders taxes by not declaring dividends, the corporation can be assessed a penalty. The first $150,000 accumulated does not have to be justified. For amounts over $150,000, there must be a reasonable business purpose. The tax is applied annually on that year's earnings, not on retained earnings.

**Summary**

Business firms can be classified in various ways, some of the more common being according to legal form of organization, type of industry, chief product, geographical location, method of operation, and nature of ownership. Legal forms of organization include (1) sole or individual proprietorships; (2) partnerships of various types, including general, limited, and mining partnerships, and joint ventures or syndicates; (3) corporations, which may be subdivided or classified in a number of ways; and (4) miscellaneous types of organizations. There are advantages and disadvantages inherent in each form of legal organization, and these must be considered carefully by the organizers of a business firm when selecting the form under which to operate.

There are many factors to be considered when selecting the legal form of organization. These include ease of organization, simplicity of management, ease of financing, and liability of owners for the debts of the business firm. A business firm must also give serious consideration to the possibility of lowering its federal income tax liability. Proprietors account for business profits through their individual returns by attaching a separate schedule detailing the business operation. A corporation files its own return. These two types of tax entities are subject to appreciably different tax rates and provisions.

A business firm with an option of being taxed either as a corporation or a partnership should determine which is more economical; and this depends on the policies of management as to dividends and retained earnings, and owners' tax rates. The owner-organizers of business firms may decide initially on one form of legal organization and later make changes. Basically, when tax savings is the primary objective, the general rules to follow in selecting the legal form of organization are (1) incorporate if management plans to finance future needs by retaining earnings; do not incorporate if the major portion of earnings are to be distributed to

## 2 Tax Considerations

*[handwritten annotation: Partnerships might be wise to form a corporation simply for the protection]*

owners; and (2) incorporate if large profits are anticipated during the early years of the business venture; do not incorporate if losses are anticipated during the early years of the venture. (This procedure would allow the entrepreneur to offset such losses against personal income rather than carrying the losses in the corporation.) However, general rules can be grossly misleading. The rules as stated might be referred to as "traditional wisdom." Recent changes in the tax code have severely undermined such generalities. The existence of the Subchapter S alternative and the maximum tax provisions make the corporation a more attractive choice for many small businesses. General rules are useful academic devices. The prudent entrepreneur would be better advised to enlist competent tax counsel at this crucial stage of a business.

While the organizers of a small business firm may have considerable choice as to the legal form under which to organize, a large firm usually finds it necessary to incorporate because of financial, managerial, and tax problems. The corporate form of organization is best suited to raise large sums needed to finance large business firms because new capital may be raised by the sale of capital stock or bonds in the capital market. In addition, corporations usually have perpetual charters and are legal entities separate from the individuals who own them; hence, the stockholders are not responsible for the debts of their corporations, and they may withdraw from ownership merely by selling their shares.

For these reasons, most large firms in the United States are organized as corporations. Because of this, the tax environment for corporate decision-making was examined in greater detail. As was indicated, the tax code often treats the proprietor's tax issues in a similar manner when these issues relate to business operations.[10]

## QUESTIONS

1. Could the corporate tax rate structure be described as graduated?
2. Should the marginal or average tax rates of the prospective owners be given the most consideration when determining the legal form of organization for a small business?
3. What are the three types of exclusions and how do they affect a taxpayer's tax liability?
4. What is the purpose of giving special tax treatment to capital gains?
5. What managerial policy is suggested by the following: "Under the Technical Amendments Act of 1958, small corporations may choose to be taxed as partnerships. As a result, there was a record number of new business incorporations during 1959. . . ." (*Fourteenth Semiannual Report of the Small Business Administration for the Six Months Ending June 30, 1960* Washington, D. C.: U.S. Government Printing Office, 1960, p. 7.)

---

[10] Substantial revision of the tax code was enacted after this text entered production. A capsule summary of the major changes is provided in the *Wall Street Journal*, October 16, 1978, pp. 3, 6, 10.

6. Discuss: "Changes in state and federal tax laws have increased the need for planning the form of business organization."
7. Under what conditions may a corporation choose not to be taxed as a corporation? Explain when this might be advisable.
8. Compare individual and corporate capital gain treatment.
9. How much better is an investment tax credit than a deduction in a tax bracket of (a) 20 percent? (b) 32 percent? (c) 48 percent?
10. Compare the straight-line method and the double-declining-balance method of computing depreciation. What are the advantages and disadvantages of each?
11. What is the purpose of the provisions for net operating loss carry-backs and carry-forwards?
12. Why does the Internal Revenue Code have a section treating improper accumulation of corporate retained earnings?

## PROBLEMS

1. J. R. Robinson is married and has two children. His "income" for 1977 is $26,500. Most of this is salary ($26,000) but $500 of it is corporate dividends received on stock his wife owns. Mr. Robinson files a joint return. He does not itemize deductions, taking only the zero bracket amount. Calculate the tax liability.
2. Mr. Brine owns and runs a car dealership as a sole proprietorship. He pays himself $15,000 salary. The proprietorship has been making $40,000 per year after all expenses (but before income tax). Since it is a proprietorship, this amount includes the $15,000 salary Mr. Brine pays himself. He is considering incorporating the dealership; if so, he would own all of the stock. Part of the reason for considering incorporation is that Mr. Brine is thinking of acquiring another dealership. If this occurs, he will double his income. Assume Mr. Brine is *married with no children,* and he takes the zero base amount for deductions.
    a. At an earnings level of $40,000 what would be Mr. Brine's total tax liability if the firm operated as:
        (1) a proprietorship,
        (2) a corporation that distributes all after-tax earnings, and
        (3) a corporation that distributed no earnings?
    b. Repeat the calculations for earnings of $80,000.
    c. What considerations, other than taxes, might be important?
3. Listed below is a summary of the capital gains transactions of six different taxpayers, classified as to long- and short-term:

| Taxpayer | Short-Term | | Long-Term | |
|---|---|---|---|---|
| | Gains | Losses | Gains | Losses |
| 1 | $2,000 | $3,000 | $10,000 | $ 5,000 |
| 2 | 5,000 | 2,000 | –0– | 1,000 |
| 3 | 5,000 | 2,000 | 10,000 | 5,000 |
| 4 | 1,000 | 6,000 | 1,000 | –0– |
| 5 | 1,000 | –0– | 2,000 | 10,000 |
| 6 | –0– | 1,000 | 2,000 | 10,000 |

Explain the tax treatment that would result in each case for:
  a. an individual taxpayer with other income of $50,000 or less, and
  b. a corporate taxpayer with ordinary income of $50,000 or more.

4. The ABC Corporation purchased a new widget-making machine one year ago for $5,000. What would be the tax liability on the sale of the machine today for $6,000 under the following circumstances, assuming other taxable income of $60,000?
   a. The machine was held as a part of the firm's inventory for sale to customers.
   b. The machine was used to produce widgets that were sold by the ABC Corporation. The machine had a useful life of five years depreciated on a straight-line basis.

5. John Smith, the treasurer of the MAC Corporation, is trying to decide whether to invest $100,000 in high-grade corporate bonds or stock of other corporations. He has weighed all factors except after-tax yield and has found favorable effects of each to cancel the other out. The bond investment he is considering pays 8 percent interest per year, while $4,500 in dividends would be paid from the stock investment. Which selection should Smith make based on after-tax investment income, assuming taxable income from other sources of $50,000?

6. The MBA Corporation purchased a new machine for use in its business at the beginning of its tax year for $100,000. At that time the machine was estimated to have a useful life of ten years. What is the minimum tax liability for the firm for this year assuming it exercises the investment tax credit and maximum depreciation allowances available, and that its taxable income exclusive of these calculations is $106,000?

7. Spaced-Out-Tronics, Inc., has a volatile earnings record. As a result, full advantage has been taken of the tax loss carry-back, carry-forward clause. The company's taxable income (loss) for ten years is given below. In this problem assume the current corporate tax rate for all years, even though the rates have varied. What has been the firm's yearly tax liability, and what total taxes would the firm have paid over the ten years?

| | | | | |
|---|---|---|---|---|
| 1969 | $ 35,000 | 1974 | $(30,000) |
| 1970 | 15,000 | 1975 | —0— |
| 1971 | 20,000 | 1976 | 5,000 |
| 1972 | (20,000) | 1977 | 10,000 |
| 1973 | (35,000) | 1978 | 50,000 |

## ADDITIONAL READINGS

Butters, J. K., J. Linter, and W. L. Cary. *Effects of Taxation: Corporate Mergers.* Cambridge, Mass.: Harvard University Graduate School of Business Administration, 1951.

Davies, R. M., and M. H. Lawrence. *Choosing a Form of Business Organization.* Durham, N.C.: Duke University Law School, 1963.

*Federal Tax Course.* Englewood Cliffs, N.J.: Prentice-Hall, Inc., 1977.

Holzman, R. S. *Tax Basis for Managerial Decisions.* New York: Holt, Rinehart and Winston, Inc., 1965.

Smith, D. T. *Effects of Taxation on Corporation Financial Policy.* Cambridge, Mass.: Harvard Graduate School of Business Administration, 1952.

———. *Tax Factors in Business Decisions.* Englewood Cliffs, N.J.: Prentice-Hall, Inc., 1968.

Sommerfeld, R. M. *Federal Taxes and Management Decisions.* Homewood, Ill.: Richard D. Irwin, Inc., 1978.

# part II
# FINANCIAL PLANNING AND CONTROL

Planning and control are necessary for the successful operation of a firm. Plans are guidelines for the operation of a business. Financial plans can be distinguished by their language; they are normally expressed in dollars. Control is to insure plans are properly implemented. Control is the process which monitors actions to encourage following the plan.

Planning requires information. The primary sources of financial information are the firm's financial statements; the most widely used are the balance sheet, the income statement, and the flow of funds statement. Financial analysis is a method of processing the information.

Most financial decisions involve a risk-return trade-off. Leverage is a concept which describes the nature of that choice as it applies to the firm as a whole—the nature of its operations and the way in which it is financed. Asset acquisitions and the methods of financing them must take into consideration the effect on the total firm and its riskiness; i.e., leverage.

Asset management decisions are of two general types—working capital management and capital investment (long-term capital assets). The analysis of working capital assets—cash, accounts receivable, and inventory—are all vaguely similar, involving a comparison of the costs and benefits of carrying more or less of these assets.

Capital budgeting decisions are slightly different. The assets are not as "divisible," and the analysis must stretch over a number of periods. The latter element introduces a complication. The analysis should consider the time value of the capital invested. After developing a way of handling the "time value of money," techniques of analysis can be developed which consider this aspect of the problem. Because such investments normally involve long-term, large dollar commitments, their riskiness must also be considered.

Considering money's time value requires determination of what the

33

firm pays for its funds—the cost of capital. This cost is affected by the composition of those funds—capital structure.

In this section each of these issues will be considered. In addition to a conceptual overview of each topic, methods for structuring analysis of the decisions are suggested. In the asset management areas there will also be some descriptive material about business practices. Most of the descriptive material about financing business firms is deferred until later sections, which consider the topics in detail.

# 3

# Financial Statements and Financial Analysis

All organizations must have information systems. The functions of such systems are to receive information about events that are relevant to the operation of the organization, translate this information into a form suitable for transmission, and relay it to the appropriate individual, or group, where it serves as the basis for an organizational response. The larger and more complex the organization, the greater the need for carefully devising such a system. The more removed the decision-makers are from the information sources, the greater their reliance on the information system's ability to accurately receive, translate, and transmit all necessary information on a timely basis.

Businesses have developed a wide variety of such systems depending on their needs and the nature of the information being handled. One of the financial manager's primary sources of information is the firm's accounting statements. Such statements can apprise the financial manager of the current status of the company through the balance sheet. The income statement, on the other hand, summarizes the effect of business operations between two balance sheet dates.

A company's financial statements are the primary method of communicating information about the company to interested outsiders—creditors, investors, and regulatory agencies. The public accounting profession endeavors to report fairly the nature of a firm's operations by processing its financial information in a conservative and consistent manner.

The financial manager is often using the same information to evaluate current and past operations and to plan for the future. The appropriate form of information for decision-making may well be different from what is best for financial reporting. To keep from drawing incorrect inferences from the data, the financial manager needs to know what assumptions and procedures were used in developing the statements.

Because of this dependence on accounting information, the aspiring finance student would be well advised to become thoroughly familiar with the accounting process. The purpose of this chapter will be to review briefly some accounting definitions and the form of the balance sheet and income statements.

Finance uses some terms differently than accounting and has some terms which describe different concepts. These differences are reviewed. Given the accounting and finance definitions, the topic of ratio analysis is discussed. The purpose of ratio analysis is to get more information from the accounting statements by highlighting interrelationships in the data. The more information that can be derived from the statements the better prepared the manager is to plan for future operations.

## Balance Sheet—Assets

*The Accounting Equation.* A balance sheet reports the assets, liabilities, and owners' equity of a business firm as of a given date. The term net worth is often used instead of owners' equity, but its connotation of present value is misleading. The balance sheet demonstrates the truism that the investment in assets must be equal to the sum of the creditors' and owners' claims on those assets: ASSETS = LIABILITIES + OWNERS' EQUITY. Obviously, this formula may be rearranged to emphasize residual equity (ASSETS − LIABILITIES = OWNERS' EQUITY), but the more common arrangement of the balance sheet is for assets to be placed on the left side and liabilities and owners' claims on the right. In the rare event that assets are insufficient to cover liabilities, owners' equity would be a net minus, with a deficit greater than contributed capital.

*Limitations.* While the balance sheet of a business firm has many uses, it also has many limitations. The reader of financial statements must understand their limitations and make adjustments to suit the current purpose. Accounting theory and practice have given financial reports of corporations considerable uniformity, especially when statements are accompanied by the opinion of an independent accountant. In order for the successive financial statements of a particular firm to be comparable, the basic accounting policy of consistency of treatment must be followed. If the individual analyzing financial statements does not understand the different methods, sound judgments about performance will be impossible.

The basic limitation in accounting for assets has to do with the value to be accounted for. Cost, the cash equivalent paid for the asset, provides the most objective measurement and is the most reliable base for future accounting. An asset is therefore reported at what it cost or at a lower valuation. Appreciation in market value owing to an increase in demand or higher prices due to inflation is not recorded, although it may be indicated by footnotes. Accountants have been concerned with this problem for some time, but recent inflation rates have heightened the concern. The

Financial Accounting Standards Board has issued a proposed standard for such price-level-adjusted reporting. The SEC now requires many large corporations to include supplemental information in the firms' annual reports as to replacement costs of plant, equipment, and inventories. Further, the firms are required to report how using expenses based on the price-level-adjusted costs would have changed the companies' reported earnings. It is reasonable to expect that this reporting practice will spread to firms other than those doing so to comply with the SEC regulation. On the other hand, loss in value may be recorded. Hence, balance-sheet valuation of assets tends to be rather conservative. Table 3–1 is an illustration of a simple balance sheet.

*Definition of Assets.* In a broad sense, an asset of a business firm is any item of value owned that may be measurable in terms of money. The assets of a business firm are its total resources, both tangible and intangible, plus incurred costs that are expected to benefit the firm in the future. Obviously, cash, receivables, stocks of goods or inventories, equipment, buildings, land, patents, and goodwill—as well as other resources or items that have economic value—are classified as assets; however, the justification for classifying a cost factor as an asset is less obvious. Sound accounting principles require that costs that benefit the income of a particular period be charged to that period. Consequently, an item such as prepaid expense is carried as a current asset until charged off, and

TABLE 3–1

COMPANY X
Balance Sheet
December 31, 1977

| Assets | | Liabilities and Owners' Equity | |
|---|---|---|---|
| *Current Assets:* | | *Current Liabilities:* | |
| Cash | $ 15,000 | Notes payable | $ 20,000 |
| Marketable securities | 10,000 | Accounts payable | 30,000 |
| Accounts receivable | 40,000 | Taxes payable | 2,000 |
| Inventories | 70,000 | Other accrued liabilities | 8,000 |
| Total Current Assets | $135,000 | Total Current Liabilities | $ 60,000 |
| *Fixed Assets:* | | *Long-Term Liabilities:* | |
| Land | $ 30,000 | Mortgage note payable | $ 10,000 |
| Buildings, net | 40,000 | Bonds payable | 30,000 |
| Equipment, net | 20,000 | | |
| Total Fixed Assets | $ 90,000 | Total Long-Term Debt | $ 40,000 |
| *Other Noncurrent Assets:* | | *Owners' Equity:* | |
| Investments | $ 10,000 | Capital stock | $ 33,300 |
| | | Retained earnings | 101,700 |
| | | Total Owners' Equity | $135,000 |
| Total Assets | $235,000 | Total Liabilities and Equity | $235,000 |

costs that will affect income over a long period are classified as deferred charges until amortized or written off over a period of years. If all costs were written off in the period in which payments were made, the income for that period would be understated.

**Current Assets.** Current assets are those assets that move in and out of a business regularly or are being converted from one form to another continually within a period of time. Current assets include cash and other assets that are expected to be converted into cash within a year in the ordinary course of business. Such assets include: cash; inventories or stocks of goods on hand; and receivables, which may be in the form of promissory notes, acceptances, and charge accounts. When a business firm's operating cycle is longer than one year, current assets may include items that do not meet the time qualification of this definition. However, most business firms use one year as the basis for classifying assets regardless of the length of the operating cycle.

**Cash.** The item cash includes demand deposits (checking accounts) in banks in the United States and in foreign countries (not restricted as to availability or purpose), cash receipts not deposited in banks, and currency kept on hand to meet current needs. During the normal course of business, a firm sells assets and services and receives currency and checks in payment. Although most banks give immediate credit for checks deposited, some out-of-town checks may take several days for collection, and banks usually expect their customers to keep balances large enough to cover them. Some of the checks deposited may be improperly drawn, written in amounts in excess of balances, and returned as "bad checks"; therefore, a business firm must make allowances for such items when estimating its desirable cash balance. The actual amount of deposits in commercial banks is considerably inflated, as indicated by the item "cash items in process of collection" on the combined statement of assets of insured commercial banks.

Business firms must spend money in order to make a profit on operations; therefore, there will be an outflow of funds in payment for goods, labor, utilities, and other necessary items. This outflow will rarely be matched by an inflow; consequently, a business firm is likely to have a deficiency of cash from trading operations at some times and a surplus at others. In anticipation of a period of cash deficiency, a firm may build up its cash balance or it may borrow; during other periods, the same firm may have a surplus of cash that can be invested temporarily in a marketable security to earn an investment income.

A business firm keeps part of its assets in the form of cash not only to care for normal trade needs but also to meet periodic interest payments, installments on debt obligations, dividends, taxes, and other payments. In addition, a firm ought to be prepared for unexpected declines in revenues caused by factors such as a slump in sales, difficulty in collecting receivables, strikes, and other emergencies. While it would be uneconomical to hold cash in sufficient amounts to care for every possible emergency, it is desirable to have funds in reserve to finance unusual situations. Most business firms also keep cash balances with their banks to avoid or minimize service charges on checking accounts, to meet compensatory balance requirements, to improve their credit standings, and retain good relationships with their banks.

*Temporary Investments.* It is expensive for a business firm to keep assets in the form of cash because of the resulting loss of earnings; therefore, a good finance officer will seek temporary investments for funds not needed immediately in the current operations of the business firm. There are many "near money" forms of investments (savings accounts, commercial bills or bankers' acceptances, open-market commercial paper, and short-term U.S. Treasury obligations) that make it possible to earn an income from short-term investments pending income tax payments, dividend disbursements, interest and installment payments on debts, and anticipated seasonal needs for cash.

Corporate management usually sets the same standards for its temporary investment of funds as do commercial banks. This means that temporary investments are usually in short-term securities of the highest quality so they may be sold for cash without loss or delay. Temporary investments of business firms are usually shown on their balance sheets at cost; however, some firms carry such investments either at market or redemption value or show these values by a notation on the balance sheet.

*Special Funds.* The chief financial officer of a corporation may hold cash or other assets as required by the board of directors or by contracts with creditors or others. The fact that a board of directors has appropriated part of the corporation's retained earnings for some special purpose, such as air-conditioning a building, does not mean that cash will be available when needed (as when the air-conditioning equipment is to be purchased and installed). Therefore, the board of directors may pass a resolution directing the chief financial officer to "fund" the reserve by segregating cash in a special deposit in a bank or to buy marketable government securities so that cash will be on hand or readily available when the need arises (as when a purchase is to be made).

Special funds may also be created when debt contracts call for periodically setting aside a specified amount for the retirement of the debt on or before maturity. A board of directors may also direct the chief financial officer to create a fund for payment of federal income taxes and other liabilities, such as employee-benefit and pension payments. Some of these special funds are an outgrowth of managerial decisions; others are due to collective bargaining; and still others are traced to some responsibility placed on management by governmental agencies.

*Receivables.* The amount of credit extended by a business firm to its customers at any one time is indicated by the volume of trade accounts, bills, and notes receivable. The most common types of receivables are those that result from sales of goods or services, but there may be others, such as claims against insurance companies for losses sustained; the government, for tax refunds; common carriers, for goods damaged; and stockholders, for unpaid stock subscriptions or assessments. Trade practices usually govern terms of sales when credit is given. While terms offered may be standardized, buyers do not react uniformly; as a result, business firms must have efficient policies in order to avoid losses and the tying up of large amounts of cash in receivables. Accounts receivable customarily appear on the balance sheet in a form that indicates the total claims outstanding less allowances for doubtful accounts. Most credit sales are made on an "open account" basis, with the seller keeping a bookkeeping record of claims and the buyer keeping a similar record of accounts payable.

*Inventories.* An inventory is an itemized list of goods or stock of goods on hand, with their estimated value. Inventory is usually the largest item among the current assets of a business firm; however, it is apt to be small for service companies. For a manufacturing company, inventories will consist of supplies, raw materials, work in process, and finished goods; these are valued according to some accepted rule such as "cost or market, whichever is lower."

Unless a firm chooses to speculate, its objective in inventory management should be to provide adequate stocks of goods of proper quality needed for production and sale. The actual amount will depend on the nature of business operations and on purchasing policies, but the minimum amount must be enough to keep production of sales up to schedule. The inventory management problem becomes more difficult as the number of steps and parts used in production increases and the production process lengthens. For an individual business firm, inventory control may consist of setting minimum and maximum amounts of inventories that should be kept on hand in terms of production or sales. Purchasing policies as to inventories reflect anticipated seasonal, cyclical, and trend demands for goods; therefore, changes in the volume of inventories in the hands of business firms are an important index of anticipated business conditions.

Other current assets include prepaid expenses such as outlays for interest, taxes, rent, insurance, supplies, traveling expenses, and other short-lived expenses.

*Fixed Assets.* Fixed assets are those of a somewhat fixed and permanent nature (a life expectancy of more than one year) that are used by the business firm in its normal operations. They consist of assets that cannot be sold without disrupting business operations. Fixed assets may be classified as tangible or intangible. The former includes items such as land, plants, and equipment used in operations. They have the common characteristics of long life and, as in the case of equipment, are used for the purpose for which their creative utility was manufactured. (Trucks, machines, and other equipment in possession of dealers in such items are classified as inventory pending their sale to ultimate users.) With the exception of land, valuation of tangible assets on balance sheets is usually followed by an allowance for depreciation, which, when deducted from the valuation figure of the asset, gives a net value. New plants, equipment, and other fixed assets are first valued at cost. (Although finance texts generally refer to fixed assets, the current trend in accounting is to classify such tangibles as "plant and equipment" or "plant assets.")

Intangible fixed assets increase the profit potential of a business firm; but, as the word "intangible" suggests, they are not of a physical or material nature as are the tangible assets listed above. This classification includes such items as goodwill, patents, trademarks, licenses, franchises, and other items that may be presumed to endow the firm that owns them with extra rights, privileges, or advantages. Intangibles are recorded only when they have been acquired at cost, and they may be amortized in the same way as tangible fixed assets.

*Other Noncurrent Assets.* Some assets are classified as neither current assets nor fixed assets. For illustration, an investment in common stock of a subsidiary company would not be classified as either a current asset or a fixed asset. Although common stock could be sold within a year, it does not follow that it would be sold in the normal course of business. Among the other forms of long-term investments owned by a business firm that are classified as noncurrent assets are preferred stock, bonds, mortgage notes, other securities, and real estate not being used in business operations. Investments should appear on the balance sheet at cost. Other noncurrent assets owned may include cash surrender value of life insurance policies wherein the business enterprise is the beneficiary, advances to subsidiary companies, and other items not classified as current or fixed assets.

Deferred charges, which are classified as noncurrent assets, are similar to prepaid expenses, but their nature justifies their being amortized over a period of years. Deferred charges include costs that are expected to affect income for a number of years, advertising expenditures that will benefit the firm for a period of time, costs of factory layouts or removal to new locations, discounts, and expenses associated with long-term capital financing. (The present trend is to minimize or eliminate this classification.)

## Balance Sheet—Liabilities

The claims of creditors and owners against a business firm, sometimes referred to as creditors' and owners' equity, have been identified as the sources of a business firm's assets. Originally, assets are provided by owners or owners and creditors; but, later, if the business is successful, more assets are obtained by retaining earnings. The word "liabilities" is sometimes used to include the claims of both creditors and owners; more properly, it includes only those debts owed creditors, and these may include provisions for obligations that are not yet precisely measurable. Capital stock, deferred credits to income, and retained earnings are balance-sheet liabilities only insofar as they represent balances to be accounted for rather than commitments to make future disbursements. Generally, liabilities are considered current when they will become due within one year (or within the longer operating cycle of the firm) and noncurrent or long-term when maturities are more than a year in the future.

*Current Liabilities.* The short-term liabilities of a business firm include amounts owed to banks on short-term business loans, accounts payable to trade creditors, sums due customers because of their cash advances or prepayments for goods or services ordered, amounts due governments for accrued income and payroll taxes, installment payments on long-term loans, and any other debts incurred that fall due within the current period (usually one year).

Business firms commonly borrow from their banks, and those loans that call for repayment of the principal within the year are classified as short-term liabilities. Small companies are relatively more dependent on their banks for loan capital than large companies. The policies of business firms concerning bank borrowing are considered in a later chapter. Notes payable may also have been executed to trade creditors or, occasionally, to company officers; these should be reported separately and are current liabilities only if the terms of the contract call for payment within the year.

Accounts payable result chiefly from purchases of goods or supplies. Other pending obligations are generally carried as accrued expenses: for wages earned but not yet paid, or for payroll taxes and income taxes not yet remitted. Cash dividends declared but unpaid are also reported as current liabilities.

In some industries customers may make cash advances for products or services to be delivered in the future. Such items would appear as current liabilities even though not requiring future cash disbursements.

Installment payments on term loans, serial bonds, mortgage notes, and other long-term obligations that are due within a year are current liabilities if they will be paid from current assets. Reclassification of such amounts is necessary if the net working-capital position of the business firm is to be determined or if the current ratio is to be calculated correctly.

Deferred income represents assets received in the amount that will be reported as revenue or gain when the appropriate time for realization arrives. For example, receipt of payment for a three-year subscription to a magazine would call for deferring that part of the subscription applying to months beyond the year in which the payment was received. Failure to make this allocation would result in an overstatement of current period income and the omission of a liability for future performance.

**Long-Term Debt.** Long-term debt includes term bank notes, mortgage loans, bonds, notes, purchase obligations, and other debts that have a maturity more than one year from the statement date. Such debts, or portions of them, become short-term or current in the fiscal period when they mature unless provisions are made for refinancing them with other long-term debt. The policies entailed in financing with long-term bank loans, bond issues, and other long-term credit instruments are discussed in later chapters.

**Contingent Liabilities.** A contingent liability is an obligation growing out of an existing set of conditions but dependent on some future event to determine its certainty and its amount. When the outcome is reasonably certain and the amount of liability can be measured with reasonable accuracy (such as the cost of guaranteeing the product sold), the expense and liability are recorded and reported in the liability section of the balance sheet. Among the circumstances giving rise to contingent liabilities are discounting notes or accounts receivable with recourse (which means that, if the obligor does not pay, the company is liable); contracting for future delivery; having lawsuits or damage claims pending; guaranteeing the debt instrument of another party; having disputed state or federal income tax claims unsettled. Even when the uncertainty of outcome or inability to make a reasonable estimate of the amount prevents the recording of a contingent liability, facts of the case should be disclosed in footnotes if it is a material item. Exclusion of contingencies could make the financial statement of a business firm misleading, and lenders must therefore assure themselves that all likely losses and debts are disclosed.

**Reserves.** One principle of accounting is that the accountant must subtract from revenue all anticipated costs and losses that can be assigned to the period for which the statement is being prepared. For illustration, an anticipated cost may be one associated with a guarantee or warranty and an anticipated liability may be due to bad debts, fire, and so on.

In accounting terminology, a reserve is not a fund of assets set aside for some future use (it appears as a liability). Under present consensus, the term "reserve" should be used in only one instance on the balance sheet—to signify the transfer of some part of retained earnings to another account for the purpose of disclosing limitations placed on management to declare cash dividends. Such a reserve should be reported in the same section as retained earnings, which it still represents, and should not be used to absorb charges properly made to profit and loss. Since the only effect of the "surplus" reserve is disclosure, its use is questionable because disclosure can be made in other ways, with better communication. This is not to imply that the use of such a method of reporting is common. Currently, any use of the term "reserve" is discouraged.

As noted above, the term reserve still appears on some balance sheets for two types of items: (1) cumulative deductions from an asset to reflect realizable value or (2) to report cost charged to operations, such as the "reserve for bad debts" or the "reserve for depreciation," and estimated liabilities, such as "reserve for income tax" or "reserve for contingencies." Up-to-date terminology uses the accounting titles "allowance for doubtful accounts" and "accumulated depreciation" for the asset valuation items. For liabilities, such titles as "estimated federal income tax" are preferred.

## Balance Sheet—Owners' Equity

Customarily, owners' equity is the sum of three elements: the par or stated value of outstanding shares of capital stock; contributed capital in excess of par or stated value (called paid-in capital in legal terminology); and earnings retained in the business. Of course, common and preferred issues are reported separately, as are any other classes of stock outstanding. The number of authorized shares of each class is disclosed parenthetically.

Capital in excess of par or stated value may result from (1) issuance of shares at an amount in excess of par or stated value, in which case the premium is carried in this account; (2) gifts or donations of assets or shares of the company's own stock to the corporation; (3) reduction of par or stated value; and (4) reacquisition of fully paid shares from stockholders. When transactions involving this account are numerous or especially significant, a separate supplementary statement may be prepared, such as shown in Table 3–2.

**TABLE 3–2**

XYZ COMPANY
Stockholder's Equity

|  | 1976 | 1977 |
|---|---|---|
| Capital stock: | | |
| Preferred stock, 6% cumulative, $25 par value (entitled to $100 per share on redemption, dissolution or liquidation)– authorized, 25,000 shares, outstanding, 10,227 shares | $ 255,675 | $ 255,675 |
| Common stock, $0.50 par value—authorized, 2,000,000 shares; outstanding, 1977, 1,767,213 shares; 1976, 1,761,478 shares | 880,739 | 883,607 |
| Paid-In Capital | 2,475,321 | 2,461,912 |
| Retained earnings | 2,701,541 | 2,873,827 |
| Total | $6,313,276 | $6,475,021 |

*Retained Earnings.* Retained earnings are comprised of net income previously reported on the company's income statements (including the current year) that have not been distributed to shareholders in the form of dividends, paid in cash or other assets, and not capitalized by issuance of stock dividends.

If the corporation's accounting policy is to report extraordinary and nonrecurring items of gain or loss on the income statement, direct charges or credits to retained earnings are restricted to the transfer of net income for the period and distributions or appropriations. An alternative treatment is generally accepted that permits extraordinary and nonrecurring gains or losses that would distort the comparison of income from operations of one year and the next to be entered in the Retained Earnings account without passing through the income statement. For this reason, a separate statement of changes in retained earnings is an important part of the financial reports.

Distributions of cash or other assets to stockholders (dividends) are presumed to be distributions of retained earnings rather than a return of a portion of their investment in the corporation. In some states, dividends may legally be charged in part to contributed capital in excess of par, in which case an accounting principle requires that the dividend be described as a liquidating dividend in part.

Since the retained earnings balance technically measures the book value of unspecified assets available for dividends without impairing contributed capital, management of the corporation may elect to appropriate a part of this item (or be obliged to by reason of contracts with bondholders or others) for a time, or management may choose to capitalize a part of retained earnings permanently. Neither action alters the total owners' equity. In the first instance, the appropriation is reported separately to show the intent of management in withholding dividends, but, ultimately, the reserve must be returned to the Retained Earnings account. The following illustration demonstrates the point:

| Assets | | Liabilities and Capital | |
|---|---|---|---|
| Cash | $ 1,000,000 | Preferred stock | $ 1,000,000 |
| | | Common stock | 15,000,000 |
| Other assets | 25,000,000 | Other capital paid in | 5,000,000 |
| | | Reserve for retirement, pfd. | 1,000,000 |
| | | Retained earnings | 4,000,000 |
| Total | $26,000,000 | Total | $26,000,000 |

After cash is used to retire the preference shares and the reservation is no longer applicable, the following items would be reported:

| Assets | | Liabilities and Capital | |
|---|---|---|---|
| Other Assets | $25,000,000 | Common stock | $15,000,000 |
| | | Other capital paid in | 5,000,000 |
| | | Retained earnings | 5,000,000 |
| Total | $25,000,000 | Total | $25,000,000 |

Capitalization of retained earnings is a permanent reclassification of a part of retained earnings as contributed capital. In theory, it is equivalent to distributing assets to stockholders and their immediate reinvestment of the assets in the corporation. Suppose the directors of the company whose statement is illustrated above decided to capitalize $1 million of the retained earnings, representing about a 6 percent increase in shares. The vehicle for capitalization would be declaration and payment of stock dividend, and, in the subsequent balance sheet, the contributed capital items would be increased by $1 million and retained earnings would be decreased by $1 million.

## Income Statements

An income statement summarizes the operating transactions of a company that take place during a fiscal period and shows the revenue and expenses incurred in earning that revenue. Expenses are deducted from revenue in order to arrive at net income or net loss for the accounting period—net income when revenue is larger than expenses and net loss when expenses are larger than revenue. The income statement explains the change in retained earnings from one balance sheet to the next caused by operations. The income statement usually encompasses a 12-month period of operations, although interim statements may be issued for shorter periods, such as a quarter. Management, of course, requires monthly income statements.

The income statement contains a summary of revenue transactions from which expenses of the period are deducted (REVENUE − EXPENSES = NET INCOME). The primary source of revenue is completed sales of products or services. Gross sales should be reported, with the adjustment for returns, allowances, and discounts deducted to give net sales. In the merchandising or manufacturing concern, gross profit on sales is usually shown by deducting the cost of the product sold from the net revenue. Cost is determined by taking inventory, assigning a value to it, and deducting this amount from beginning inventory and new costs to be accounted for (purchases for the trade or business, manufacturing costs for the factory), or by recording sales at cost price as well as at selling price for each transaction. Gross profit is traditionally accorded importance as a comparison of pricing policies in relation to cost incurred in buying or making the products sold. Within a given industry, the profit margin will tend to be approximately the same percentage of sales.

Typical treatment of expenses is by function, with selling expenses grouped, general administrative expenses next, and income tax expense separately stated and deducted last. Table 3–3 depicts a typical income statement.

Many variations in amount of detail and arrangement may be found

TABLE 3–3

COMPANY X
Income Statement
For the Year Ended December 31, 1977

| | | |
|---|---:|---:|
| Gross sales | | $412,000 |
| Less: Returns, allowances, and discounts | | 12,000 |
| Net sales | | $400,000 |
| Cost of goods sold | | 300,000 |
| Gross profit on sales | | $100,000 |
| Selling expenses | $24,000 | |
| General administrative expenses | 36,000 | 60,000 |
| Income before taxes | | $ 40,000 |
| Income taxes | | 8,300 |
| Net income | | $ 31,700 |

in the published reports of corporations. Selling and administrative expenses are often detailed by item, such as salaries, depreciation, loss on bad debts, supplies, property taxes, and so forth.

As was stated earlier, material extraordinary gains or losses may be reported in a final section of the income statement or in the statement of retained earnings, depending on the accounting policy of the reporting company. When dividends are the only reduction of retained earnings, the income statement is often continued beyond the point illustrated above to tie in with the retained-earnings balance appearing on the accompanying balance sheet.

| | |
|---|---:|
| Net income for the period | $ 31,700 |
| Retained earnings, beginning of the year | 80,000 |
| | $111,700 |
| Less cash dividends paid or declared | 10,000 |
| Retained earnings, end of the year | $101,700 |

The general practice of corporations that publish annual financial statements is to present comparative balance sheets, income statements, and statements of retained earnings. Access to balance-sheet information as of the first and last of the fiscal period and to income statements and retained-earnings statements of the preceding period adds some depth of analysis. In addition, some useful information is presented on a ten-year basis in many annual reports (prior years' data being made comparable with latest year's data to reflect acquisitions on a "pooling of interests" basis and other changes in capitalization). This financial history may not be covered by the auditor's opinion, but any footnotes to the financial statements themselves are subject to audit and to the criterion of full disclosure. The reader of statements should refer to footnotes in making any analysis of the reports.

## Definitions and Statements—Finance Variations

Financial managers and analysts use accounting data for different purposes than interested outsiders, the intended audience for most accounting statements. In addition, there are certain responsibilities that normally rest with the firm's finance function. As a result, finance people have developed different definitions for some terms, and in some cases they modify the financial statements slightly. These differences are generally small but can be confusing when first encountered. Therefore, the most important of these definitional differences will be reviewed.

When financial managers speak of working capital, they are generally referring to total current assets—the sum of cash, marketable securities, accounts receivable, and inventory. This is different than the accounting definition. To the accountant, working capital is the *difference* between current assets and current liabilities. The financial manager refers to this difference as *net* working capital.

The situation is complicated a little further by the concept of working capital management. Working capital management refers to the ongoing administration of the investment in and the expenses related to both current assets *and* current liabilities.

Finance texts will sometimes refer to quick assets. Quick assets are those which can be readily converted into cash with minimal shrinkage. They include cash, marketable securities, and accounts receivable.

An area of continual concern for the financial manager is the capital structure of the firm. The *capital structure,* sometimes referred to as just *capital,* is the total of all long-term funds used by the firm. Quite simply, capital structure is the right-hand side of the balance sheet less current liabilities. When current liabilities are included, the total is normally referred to as *financial structure*.

One segment of the capital structure causes some additional problems. Preferred stock is, by definition, a form of equity. To the financial manager, preferred stock is a culturally deprived form of debt. As will be explained later, preferred stock has many of the characteristics of debt. Because of the hybrid nature of preferred stock, financial analysts will sometimes refer to *common equity*. Common equity is the sum of common stock, paid-in capital, and retained earnings. It is net worth less preferred stock (and any associated discounts or premiums). Other differences in jargon are occasionally encountered, but the preceding are the main variations.

One additional item that can cause confusion is the altering of the income statement. The change is very minor and is done primarily to make analysis of financing decisions more convenient. The change is in the treatment of financing expenses, primarily interest.

Because financial managers are responsible for the expenses related to financing, they do not view them as "operating expenses." They would prefer that these expenses be treated separately and explicitly labeled as is done in Table 3-4.

The value, *earnings before interest and taxes* (EBIT), is generally referred to in finance as *operating income*. The benefit from structuring the income statement in this manner will be seen in the next chapter on leverage. For now, accept that it makes the analysis easier. When analyzing the different methods of financing, all figures down to and including EBIT can be held constant. This procedure simplifies analysis of changes in financing which alter only the figures below the EBIT.

TABLE 3-4
COMPANY X
Income Statement
For the Year Ended December 31, 1977

| | | |
|---|---:|---:|
| Gross sales | | $412,000 |
| Less: Returns, allowances, and discounts | | 12,000 |
| Net sales | | $400,000 |
| Cost of goods sold | | 300,000 |
| Gross profit on sales | | $100,000 |
| Selling expense | $24,000 | |
| General administrative expense | 31,000 | 55,000 |
| Earnings before interest and taxes | | $ 45,000 |
| Less: Interest | | 5,000 |
| Income before taxes | | $ 40,000 |
| Less: Taxes | | 8,300 |
| Net income | | $ 31,700 |

## FINANCIAL ANALYSIS

Financial analysis is a natural extension of the accounting process. The accounting system aggregates data related to numerous individual accounts and labels the total accounts receivable. The information about a wide variety of different raw materials, in-process goods, and finished products is summarized as inventory. Diverse types of equipment and real property are lumped together and called plant and equipment. The same type of information processing results in totals for the different types of liabilities and equities.

The result is a highly stylized, stop-action photograph of the firm. The balance sheet is a still picture of something in motion. Further, all of the detail has been omitted. This type of summary allows the analyst to perceive better the relationships between the major assets and liability classifications.

The income statement summarizes in one statement the result of a large number of individual transactions. It serves as a kind of time-lapse photograph of the firm. But the statement is not a true picture—it is a caricature. It is a representation of how the firm operated. This is not a criticism of the accounting process. The capacity for abstraction is one of the strengths of the system. It is because the process is stylized that one can perceive the nature of the firm's operations. It is the rare individual, if one exists, that can obtain the same perspective from seeing day-to-day operations. The efficient business firm, like a highly accomplished athlete, seems to cover more ground with less effort. It is necessary to compare the firm to some benchmarks to perceive how well it may be doing. On the other hand, the floundering firm may be a beehive of activity with very little being accomplished.

Ratio analysis further distills the information provided by the accounting system. It does not provide any new information. Its purpose is the same as that of accounting—to eliminate some detail so relationships are more readily discernible and can be more easily perceived.

All ratios involve an implied comparison between the numerator and the denominator. The question being asked is whether the *relative* values seem appropriate. The purpose is to aid the analyst in perceiving conditions and interrelationships.

Although they will be restated, some advance warnings are in order. Ratios, because they are highly distilled information, should be investigated before wide-sweeping interpretations are made. This investigation should include comparison to norms and to trends.

Ratios only indicate potential problems—they are not problems in and of themselves. Further, advice to correct a ratio is of little value. Ratios are not problems; changing a ratio is not a cure.

An analogy may help in understanding the point of the last paragraph. If a patient is running a temperature of 102°, that is not the problem, and bringing the temperature back to 98.6° is not the cure. The temperature is only a symptom.

Ratio analysis looks for symptoms. Certain patterns indicate certain financial illnesses. While ratios are efficient for localizing the problem, they are insufficient for a final diagnosis. That involves more in-depth analysis.

The appropriate ratio to use depends on the purpose of the inquiry and the perspective of the analyst. Short-term creditors are more concerned with liquidity. Long-term creditors are, of necessity, concerned about how much debt is being used and with long-run profitability. Investors are also concerned about how effectively the firm's assets are employed. Managers must concern themselves with everything. Management must insure sufficient liquidity is maintained to pay the bills. Assets must be employed actively and effectively. The aggressive firm normally employs some borrowed capital. If all aspects of the firm are well managed, the result is normally acceptable profits and returns to the stockholders.

Different analysts and different industries have resulted in a wide variety of ratios. The material that follows will review the four most basic types: liquidity, activity, leverage, and profitability.

## Financial Analysis—Liquidity Ratios

Liquidity ratios are measures of a firm's short-term bill-paying ability. They compare the assets available for meeting current obligations with the level of those obligations.

**Current Ratio.** The need to be able to meet obligations as they come due is recognized by management; hence, different ratios indicating the firm's debt-paying ability are constructed. Among the most widely used ratios that test liquidity is the current ratio, which is found by dividing current assets by current liabilities. The current ratio for Company X in Tables 3–1 would be found as follows:

$$\frac{\text{Current assets}}{\text{Current liabilities}} = \frac{\$135,000}{\$60,000} \text{ or } 2.25:1$$

The current ratio may vary with changes in either or both current assets and current liabilities, and only by studying the trends of the two can one explain what determined the relationship on the date the ratio was constructed. Many individual acts on the part of management will affect this ratio. For example, after repaying the bank loan, Company X would have a current ratio of $115,000/40,000, or 2.88:1. While repayment of the current debt does not change the net working capital of the company, it causes the company to have a more favorable current ratio.

Generally, a current ratio of 2.25:1 is satisfactory, but there is no single correct ratio. At one time a ratio of 2:1 was assumed to be satisfactory, but this is no longer the case because the conversion period for inventories or receivables may be relatively long in some fields (as in cotton-cloth mills and retailing of lumber and lumber products).

A low current ratio may be improved in several ways: repaying current debts, borrowing for terms of more than a year, collecting tax refunds, converting noncurrent assets into current assets, and increasing investments in current assets by retaining earnings. On the other hand, the current ratio may be reduced by short-term borrowing, buying goods and materials on account, accruing federal income taxes and other expenses, converting current assets into noncurrent assets, and paying cash dividends.

The chief advantage of having a high current ratio is that it protects a business firm from difficulties that might arise because of accounts receivable becoming noncollectible or inventories unsalable. When there is insufficient cash to meet maturing liabilities, a business firm is at the mercy of its creditors. Bankers are interested in making loans that will be repaid; therefore, a business firm with a weak current ratio may find it impossible to borrow additional funds when the need for them is greatest.

The chief value of the current ratio is that it provides an index of the ability of a business firm to pay its short-term debts. As is true for all ratios, the use of current ratios requires intelligent analysis and comparison to those of other companies in the same field. As indicated by analysis, the quality of current assets and current liabilities varies from time to time for a particular company and from company to company (depending on the nature of the business). For example, for different business firms the types of goods that make up inventories vary from raw materials and semimanufactured goods to merchandise held for sale. The last may range from highly marketable goods whose value may be established readily to goods having only a special market. The dollar value of goods carried as inventory may have little or no relationship to reality; also, because of different methods of valuation, any comparison of the inventory positions of different companies may be misleading.

*Quick Ratio.* Conversion of inventories into cash entails two steps—sales and then collection of receivables. Neither is assured. Inventories tend to be largest during business booms, and this gives a misleading impression of the liquidity of a business firm. Deliberate liquidation of inventories by a business firm to improve its cash position would ordinarily occur under pressing financial circumstances, irrespective of the need to maintain an adequate stock of goods for efficient operations. Thus, a current ratio of 2:1, or a higher current ratio, may not reveal a satisfactory liquidity condition during some phase of a business cycle. Because inventories are the least liquid of working-capital assets, a comparison of current assets minus inventories to current liabilities may give a more meaningful ratio than the current ratio. The so-called quick assets or acid-test ratio of Company X would be

$$\frac{\$135,000 - \$70,000}{\$60,000} \text{ or } 1.08:1$$

which is larger than the minimum rule-of-thumb ratio of 1:1.

In the final analysis, the best test of the liquid position of a business firm is its ratio of cash plus investment in money-market securities to current liabilities. Although securities are not cash, many are short term or approaching maturity. Unlike inventories and receivables, securities held by a business firm may be sold readily with practically no loss or delay to obtain cash when needed without disrupting business operations.

In further analysis of the current and quick ratios, financial management should determine the quality of current liabilities. Some current liabilities may be due within a day or two and others at the end of the year; some may be owed to open-market creditors and payable at maturity; and others may be bank loans, which are customarily renewed or extended on request at maturity. Each type of liability may have a different effect on the future working-capital position of a business firm and should therefore be considered with care.

## Financial Analysis—Activity Ratios

Activity ratios help the analyst to determine how well the company's assets are being employed. Here the comparison is between the level of activity (sales) and the investment in some type of asset.

Many of the activity ratios are referred to as turnover ratios. Reference to turnover means that the analyst has divided some measure of sales by some asset. The two most common turnover ratios are total asset turnover and inventory turnover.

*Total Asset Turnover.* The purpose of this ratio is to evaluate how well the firm is utilizing its total resources. As was stated before, turnover suggests that sales is to be divided by something. In this case, it is total assets.

For Company X, which was described in Tables 3–1 and 3–3, the ratio is

$$\frac{\text{Net sales}}{\text{Total assets}} = \frac{\$400,000}{\$235,000} = 1.70:1$$

This figure by itself is sterile. To determine if the company is performing well, the ratio must be compared to other firms, or averages, for the same industry during the same time period. Total asset turnover figures vary widely from one industry to another. The ratio is also very sensitive to prevailing economic conditions. Even considering the industry and the economy, there are problems in comparing one firm with another.

As with all ratios, any abnormality for a particular company may be traceable to either the numerator or the denominator, or a combination of the two. For example, a company with a low turnover ratio may be suffering a loss of sales or be troubled by an inflated asset base. Further, the loss in sales may be due to loss of volume or caused by erosion of product prices or, again, a combination thereof.

The denominator of the ratio may cause comparability problems. The valuation of the assets on the balance sheet involves estimation procedures. Differences in these procedures can create differences between companies. The total assets figure adds all of the differences together. The result can produce some marked effects on the turnover ratios.

To appreciate how this estimation process could produce different results, some examples might be helpful. The accounts receivable figure is adjusted for an estimate of the uncollectable accounts. The actual write-down of accounts receivable depends on when the firm determines that an account is a bad debt. The time in making such a determination varies. The value of a firm's inventory depends in part on how operating expenses are allocated. Those which are considered to be product costs are included as part of inventory. This, along with other direct costs, determines the value of the company's inventory (assuming cost is lower than market).

Part of inventory cost is direct overhead which includes depreciation.

The method of depreciation then affects inventory and the value of plant and equipment as it is carried on the balance sheet.

The age of fixed assets also determines their valuation. During times of generally rising prices, plant and equipment replacement costs will generally exceed their book values. This will tend to inflate the total asset turnover ratios of older companies when they are compared to companies which have purchased their fixed assets more recently and at higher prices.

Total asset turnover is a measure of how well a firm's resources are being used. The nature of the accounting process can create some comparability problems. However, examination of the trend for a firm compared to some appropriate norm can provide valuable insight. This can be heightened by examination of use of the individual assets.

***Inventory-Turnover Ratio.*** The avoidance of excessive investment in materials, merchandise, and supplies is an elementary rule of financial management, but, probably, no rule is more frequently violated. Usually, an inventory is not only the largest but also the least liquid of a firm's current assets. Proper analysis might use one of several ratios; one widely used is net sales divided by the inventory, which, for Company X, is as follows:

$$\frac{\text{Net sales}}{\text{Inventories}} = \frac{\$400{,}000}{\$70{,}000} = 5.71 \text{ times}$$

The inventory-turnover ratio is overstated, however, by the amount of the gross profit on sales when it is calculated on the basis of net sales, because inventories are carried at cost or market, whichever is lower, while sales reflect the gross profit markup. Based on cost of goods sold, therefore, the inventory-turnover ratio is as follows:

$$\frac{\text{Cost of goods sold}}{\text{Inventories}} = \frac{\$300{,}000}{\$70{,}000} = 4.28 \text{ times}$$

Ideally, inventory turnover should be based on cost of goods sold. However, most of the sources of comparative figures use the net sales calculation. To be comparable, the analyst must perform the calculation the same way. For this reason, inventory turnover will be calculated using sales unless specifically indicated otherwise.

The chief value of the inventory-turnover ratio is to check the freshness of the stock that makes up the inventory. Like other ratios, it is computed for comparison of one period to another or one company to a second; therefore, it is of value irrespective of the method used, provided the ratio is computed in the same way each time. However, it is not an accurate measure of physical turnover of goods because accuracy could be obtained only by counting every item in stock and comparing it to the physical sales of those same items.

Comparison of standard ratios of a business firm to those of other companies in the same line of business indicates whether a firm has too little or too much so invested. However, the dollar value of inventories is influenced not only by the stock of goods but also by the accounting method used in its evaluation, such as actual costs, which are indicated by code or number for each item in stock, or a derived cost method. Derived cost methods include: (1) average costs, found by averaging unit prices as taken from inventories or dividing total costs of goods to be accounted for by the number of units; (2) standard costs, which prices each unit at a standard or uniform cost previously determined; (3) first-in, first-out, or Fifo, which assumes goods are sold in the order acquired; and (4) last-in, first-out, or Lifo, which assumes that goods acquired last are sold first.

The method of accounting for inventories may affect not only their book value but also the net profits of the company. The use of the last-in, first-out method tends to stabilize income, and the opposite is true for the first-in, first-out method. Under the Lifo method, goods, materials, and supplies used during the period are valued near current replacement costs rather than at actual purchase costs. During periods of rising prices, this results in inventories being carried at more conservative values, serving, in effect, to increase costs of goods sold and reduce reported profits and income taxes. However, if inventories at year-end are smaller than a year earlier, some of the tax advantage is lost, because a taxable profit must be reported on that part of the inventory not replaced after being used up or sold. However, when the Lifo method is used during periods of falling prices, balance sheet inventories are overstated, serving, in effect, to decrease the cost of goods sold, increase reported profits, and expand taxable income. However, one objective of financial management would be achieved in part; namely, reports of stable earnings.

A common problem with inventory ratios is that sales occur over the entire year while the inventory figure is for one point in time; that is, at the time of the financial statement. If it is ascertained that a business is highly seasonal, it would be better to use an average inventory, computed by adding beginning and ending inventories and dividing by two.

The conclusion usually drawn from inventory ratios is that the more rapid the turnover, the smaller the amount of working capital needed in terms of net sales and the larger total profits (unless the apparent rapidity of sales is due to an excessive markdown in prices, understocking, and other factors). Holding more inventories than needed is a form of speculation that is usually criticized, but, sometimes, speculation in inventories is profitable (as for many firms that bought in excess of current needs at the outbreak of World War II and of the Korean War). The inventory-turnover record is intended to indicate the liquidity of the inventory, the degree to which management tends to overstock, and the efficiency with which inventory is being handled. A decrease in the inventory-turnover ratio as compared to previous years may raise some doubt as to the efficiency of inventory management. In the case of small business firms, banks and other lenders may give advice as to inventory policy, particularly if a reduction in inventories seems desirable, because economic indicators reveal a cautious buying policy to be in order. Relative to the total cost of a business firm's operations, the interest charges on loans to carry inventories are not large; therefore, inventory retrenchment is usually desired to prevent losses on sales due to decreases in prices and curtailment in sales volume.

*Average Collection Period (Days' Sales).* Average collection period, also referred to as days' sales, is a turnover ratio that has been given a face-lift. The early finance texts generally referred to accounts receivable turnover, which is calculated just as one would assume—sales divided by accounts receivable. To give the measure more intuitive appeal, the figures were rearranged. Sales was divided by 360 and the ratio was inverted. For Company X, average collection period is

$$\frac{\text{Receivables}}{\frac{\text{Sales}}{360}} = \frac{\$40,000}{\frac{\$400,000}{360}} = 36 \text{ days}$$

Constructed in this way, the figure seems logical. One day's sales would be $400,000/360, or $1,111 a day. There is currently 36 times that amount on the books. The discussion of the earlier calculation (which might still be encountered on occasion) is to point out the logical analogy to the other activity ratios. The question is the same. Is the investment in this particular asset, accounts receivable, reasonable, based on sales volume?

It was suggested that inventory turnover would be more correct if calculated using cost of goods sold. Average collection period would be more correct if credit sales were used rather than total sales. Sales is used here also and for the same reason. The comparative figures are calculated using total sales. However, this can result in a marked distortion if a firm makes a higher (or lower) than average percentage of its sales on credit.

Another criticism of the collection ratio is that the amount of receivables outstanding at the end of the year is not likely to be representative since receivables are usually at a seasonal low at that time while credit sales for the year have no seasonal factor affecting the total. A more accurate method would be to use daily averages of receivables, but such an average would be difficult to compute. If the accounting records do not reflect some unusual factor at the time of the balance-sheet statement, the collection ratio will indicate roughly whether collections are improving, deteriorating, or remaining the same. When compared to the collection ratios of similar firms in the same line, they will indicate the relative position of the company among its competitors. Receivables, like inventories, tend to expand when the volume of business is rising, but they are not cash until they are collected; slowing down of collections is often a factor in tightening financial conditions.

When the collection period is longer than that of the average for companies in the same line or industry and the collection ratio is increasing as compared to that of previous years, it is time for financial management to review its credit and collection policies. A business firm may not be in a position to stop credit sales to all overdue customers, but it may curtail the amount of credit extended to such customers. A credit policy that is too rigid relative to that of competitors may destroy future business, but one that is too liberal may be even less desirable. If the volume of receivables is too high, it may be necessary for some individual accounts to be written off in order to show a realistic situation. However, if the fault lies with those responsible for collecting accounts receivable, a vigorous collection policy may turn some of the past-due accounts into cash. Usually, accounts receivable become noticeably slower in payment when credit tightens.

## Financial Analysis—Leverage Ratios

There are two types of leverage ratios, but they both are asking the same question—how much borrowed money is the firm using? The answer to this question must be viewed in the context of what other firms of the same type are doing.

The two types of leverage ratios are balance sheet ratios and income statement ratios. Each type will be discussed. A common and useful example of each will be explained along with a discussion of how the example ratio might be interpreted.

*Balance Sheet Leverage Ratios.* Ratios of this type compare some measure of indebtedness to some measure of equity. The calculation is for only one point in time, the balance sheet date, but it indicates how extensively the firm is financing with loan capital.

There are a wide variety of such ratios, and the names are usually self-defining. Each involves the calculation of a ratio where the debt figure is normally the numerator and some measure of equity (or assets) is the denominator. Some examples of this type of ratio would include long-term debt to net worth, total debt to net worth, long-term debt to total assets, and long-term debt to total capital (capital here refers to capital structure, which was discussed earlier).

The particular ratios that are used generally depend on the tastes of the analyst and the availability of comparison figures. A comparison of the total debt of a firm to its total assets seems to be a straightforward approach to the issue.

The debt-to-total-assets ratio indicates that portion of total assets represented by owners' equity over and above the amount needed to repay the creditors in total. Since the creditors have legal claims superior to those of the owner, the percentage of the assets provided by creditors indicates the risk of insolvency of the business. Generally, the higher the proportion of debt to total assets, the more important consideration of the creditors becomes in influencing the actions of the company.

The purpose of this ratio is to compare the amount of the firm's obligations to its creditors against all of its assets. For Company X, the debt-to-total-assets ratio is

$$\frac{\text{Total debt}}{\text{Total assets}} = \frac{\$100{,}000}{\$235{,}000} = 43\%$$

↑ assets

The total debt includes all of the firm's current liabilities plus its long-term debt outstanding. The lower this ratio, the easier it becomes to satisfy the creditors. A low ratio provides them with assurances that their investment is protected. Thus, a firm with a low debt-to-total-assets ratio has less chance of failing when the business cycle is in a recession period, but it also has less opportunity of making high net profits when the business cycle is in an expansionary stage. Therefore, decisions to use debt extensively must balance the potential higher returns against the prospect of increased risk of failure.

***Income Statement Leverage Ratios.*** Ratios of this type generally compare a firm's ability to pay a particular type of expense to the level of that expense. This is done by dividing earnings (before the expense) by the amount of the expense to see how well the expense is "covered." Ratios calculated in this method are often referred to as *coverage ratios*.

The primary problem in dealing with creditors is fulfilling the company's legal commitments. In connection with long-term creditors, this major commitment is a payment of the interest periodically. The principal repayment may be at some distant future date; therefore, if a firm can earn in excess of the amount required for interest payments, the likelihood is good that it will make its interest payments as agreed in the contract. The times-interest-earned ratio is determined by dividing earnings (before interest and taxes) by the interest charges. For Company X, the ratio would appear as follows:

$$\frac{\text{Earnings before interest and taxes}}{\text{Interest charges}} = \frac{\$45{,}000}{\$5{,}000} = 9 \text{ times}$$

This ratio tells how far earnings can fall before the firm will run into difficulty in meeting its annual interest costs. Since payments must be made from earnings over a period of time, this ratio measures the company's ability to service its debt. Trends in this ratio are usually watched carefully by the long-term creditors. In addition, where the company has bonds outstanding, it is a partial determinant of the company's bond rating.

## Financial Analysis—Profitability Ratios

Each type of ratio discussed so far has assessed the firm's performance relative to some standard. One obviously important criterion is profit.

## 3 Financial Statements and Financial Analysis

Each ratio in this section has the same numerator—net income. Turnover requires that sales be divided by something; return indicates that net income should be divided by something. Each profitability ratio asks the same question. Are profits high enough?

*Return on Sales.* This ratio measures the percentage profit made on each dollar of sales. For Company X, the return on sales is

$$\frac{\text{Net income}}{\text{Net sales}} = \frac{\$31,700}{\$400,000} = .0793 = 7.93\%$$

As with other ratios, evaluation of trends in the ratio should be more helpful than the one ratio alone. However, the interpretations can be ambiguous. Sales profitability is the result of both pricing and cost control. Eroding returns should be evaluated to see if the problems are the result of lower volume resulting in higher per-unit fixed costs, of rising variable costs, or of lower margins resulting from price-cutting. Because of changes in tax rates, it may be desirable to use income before taxes as the numerator to avoid tax-induced distortions.

*Return on Total Assets.* This ratio measures the return on the firm's total asset base. It is calculated by dividing net income by total assets. For Company X, the ratio is:

$$\frac{\text{Net income}}{\text{Total assets}} = \frac{\$31,700}{\$235,000} = .1349 = 13.49\%$$

This investment ratio is a measure of performance widely used by stockholders and creditors as well as management.

*Return on Net Worth.* For shareholders the concern may be what return they make on their invested capital. This may be determined by comparing income to common equity. Although referred to as return on net worth, there is often an adjustment where a firm has preferred stock outstanding. For Company X, the ratio is:

$$\frac{\text{Net income}}{\text{Net worth}} = \frac{\$31,700}{\$135,000} = .2348 = 23.48\%$$

*Profitability Interrelationships.* Company X seems to be a profitable operation. However, to ascertain the source of that profitability, it is often helpful to trace through the determinants of profitability and to compare them to the industry averages. Understanding the interrelationships between some of the ratios can be helpful in this process.

The DuPont Return-on-Investment system specifies some of the more important of these relationships. The system can be stated concisely as follows:

$$\frac{\text{Sales}}{\text{Total assets}} \times \frac{\text{Net income}}{\text{Sales}} = \frac{\text{Net Income}}{\text{Total assets}}$$

$$\frac{\text{Net income}}{\text{Total assets}} \div \left[1 - \frac{\text{Debt}}{\text{Total assets}}\right] = \frac{\text{Net income}}{\text{Net worth}}$$

## Part II  Financial Planning and Control

The ROI system was originally developed as a management control device. It is used to encourage managers to think through all the implications of a particular management decision. This brief discussion of the process does not do it justice. Here, it is used merely as an organizing concept for the ratio analysis. Its use as a planning tool is more important.

Table 3–5 shows how the analysis might be organized. The industry figures in this case are entirely hypothetical to show how the interpretation might be aided through this organization.

**TABLE 3–5**

**COMPANY X**
Ratio Interrelationship

|  | Total Asset Turnover | × | Return on Sales | = | Return on Total Assets | Return on Total Assets | ÷ | 1— Debt to Total Assets | = | Return on Net Worth |
|---|---|---|---|---|---|---|---|---|---|---|
| Company X | 1.70 | × | .079 | = | .135 | .135 | ÷ | (1—.43) | = | .235 |
| Industry | .7 | × | .171 | = | .120 | .120 | ÷ | (1—.33) | = | .180 |

Viewed in this way, quite a bit about Company X's operation can be seen. Company X seems to be a low-markup, high-volume operation. This seems to be a successful strategy. Their profit on total assets is above average. They enhance profits through the aggressive use of debt capital.

## Financial Analysis—Sources of Comparative Data

The previous example makes apparent how industry averages can help interpret ratios. There are several sources for such data. They include Dun & Bradstreet, Robert Morris Associates, the Federal Trade Commission (FTC), and the Securities and Exchange Commission (SEC). Of these, probably the most widely known and used are those published by Dun and Bradstreet. They provide 14 key ratios calculated for a number of selected industries. Dun & Bradstreet gives these ratios, by quartiles, for 125 industries, based on their financial statements. The FTC and the SEC jointly publish quarterly data on manufacturing companies. The ratios are relatively current since they are published usually within six months after the data is made available by the corporations.

The main problem in the usage of industry ratios or comparisons with other specific companies is that of comparability. For example, variations in product mix, location, or even accounting methods can lead to significantly different results. Even so, these comparisons may prove useful in pointing out areas where further study might be made by management. Finally, it should be cautioned that ratio analysis does not show the existence of lines of credit and loan commitments that some companies

## 3  Financial Statements and Financial Analysis

may have with their banks and others. This ability to borrow may considerably understate the financial strength of the firm as suggested by the overall ratio analysis.

## Financial Analysis—Common-Size Statements

Ratio analysis is only one way of interpreting accounting data. Common-size statements are another. This technique involves reworking the balance sheet and/or the income statement using percentages.

In a common-size balance sheet all accounts are expressed as a percentage of total assets. This allows comparison with other companies in the industry or the industry average to see if the composition of the asset structure is in line with what would be expected.

This technique is especially effective with the income statement. All revenue and expenses are restated as a percentage of net sales. Such a statement is sometimes referred to as an *operating income* statement.

*Operating Income Statement.*  In an operating income statement, the relative importance of each major item is shown as a percentage of net sales. Table 3–6 presents such a statement for Company X using the data

**TABLE 3–6**

COMPANY X
Income Statement
For the Year Ended December 31, 1977

|  |  | Amounts | Operating Ratios (%) |
|---|---|---|---|
| Gross sales | | $412,000 | 103.00 |
| Less: Returns, allowances, and discounts | | 12,000 | 3.00 |
| Net sales | | $400,000 | 100.00 |
| Cost of goods sold | | 300,000 | 75.00 |
| Gross profit on sales | | $100,000 | 25.00 |
| Selling expense | $24,000 | | |
| General administrative expense | 36,000 | 60,000 | 15.00 |
| Income before taxes | | $ 40,000 | 10.00 |
| Income taxes | | 8,300 | 2.07 |
| Net income | | $ 31,700 | 7.93 |

from Table 3–3. When compared to similar statements for earlier periods, clues to danger spots may be uncovered. If there is a decline in cash discounts taken, the company's customers may be in financial difficulties due to a general deterioration of business—a conclusion that may be tested by checking with comparable companies in the industry. However, if management concludes that the ratio is satisfactory, it passes on to the next one and the same procedure is followed with reference to the cost of goods sold relative to sales, and so on through the list.

*Operating Ratio.* The operating ratio is found by dividing net sales into operating expenses, which include all costs *except interest,* income taxes, and other financial charges. In the income statement shown in Table 3-4, the ratio would be found by dividing $355,000 by $400,000, which would be 89 percent. The difference between this percentage and 100 is the ratio of operating income to net sales, or the operating profit (1.00 − 0.89 = 0.11). This means that the lower the operating ratio, the greater the operating profit and the more efficient the business.

Because nonoperating expenses (income taxes and financial costs) are excluded from operating expenses, the operating ratio is not a measure of the profitability of a firm's operations. A firm that is in an unfavorable financial position because of high fixed charges and income taxes may show a low net income even though the operating ratio is relatively low.

The percentage composition of items that comprise the income statement of a corporation provides the financial manager with invaluable information. If the operating ratio (the sum of the cost of goods sold plus operating expenses divided by sales) is increasing, it will give a clue to the cause of the change. As compared to the preceding year, administrative costs may have increased because of higher wages paid or higher costs of goods purchased. As a result of this analysis, management may raise prices or increase sales efforts in order to regain its former, more profitable position.

The margin of operating profit considered adequate for a business firm varies from industry to industry and even among firms in the same industry. For illustration, in the railroad industry, the operating ratio (the ratio of all operating expenses to operating revenues) is elucidated by an analysis of the "maintenance ratio," which shows the percentage of railroad operating revenues used for maintenance, including depreciation, and the "transportation ratio," which shows the percentage of railroad operating revenue used for transportation expenses. In addition, there are performance ratios—average tons per loaded freight car, train miles per train hour, car miles per car day, and so on.

Public-utility operating ratios will reflect the basic nature of each service provided (light and power, gas, water, gas and oil pipelines, or telephone), the mode of operation (hydroelectric, coal or nuclear power), and regulatory policies. Depreciation charges are an important factor in the operating expenses of both railroad and public-utility companies. The percent of annual depreciation to gross property is indicative of the rate of annual depreciation charges. Earnings reflect both economic conditions and regulatory policies. The operating ratio may be but 50 percent for a well-run hydroelectric company and as high as 75 percent for a gas company. Operating ratios for industrial companies are even more variable than those for the public-utility group, being relatively higher for a dressmaking firm than for a steel-producing company.

## Summary

The general-purpose financial statements include the balance sheet, the income statement, the statement of retained earnings, and supporting schedules and footnotes associated with them. They are the primary sources of information for the creditor, the shareowner, or the potential investor; hence, these statements must be used as the basis for decisions to lend, invest, or disinvest. Management of a business also relies on financial reports, but it may request and get as much detail as it needs.

The balance sheet, or statement of financial position, is a summary of assets owned by the firm, its known liabilities, and the residual equity of the owners. Assets are taken up in the accounts at cost at time of acquisition; and, while appreciation of value is rarely recorded, loss of utility because of use or obsolescence and loss in market value may be recorded. The balance sheet does not purport to reflect current value of assets; when price levels change substantially, the analyst must make his own judgments and adjustments. All liabilities that are reasonably certain to require future outlays of cash or other assets and can be measured in dollars with reasonable accuracy are reported on the balance sheet; significant probable liabilities not sufficiently certain or measurable to be recorded are reported by way of footnotes. Owners' equity in a corporation is reported in such a manner that the reader can distinguish contributed capital from earnings.

The income statement is a report of the results of operations carried on by an enterprise over a period of time, usually being a 12-month period. Although income statements are more and more condensed as corporate business gets bigger, they reflect the principal sources and amounts of revenue realized during the period and the expenses incurred during the same period. In the event that unusual transactions have taken place and have given rise to substantial gains or losses not identifiable with the current period, it is permissible to report these items on the retained-earnings statement instead of on the income statement.

The retained-earnings statement is an analysis of the account, detailing the items that caused the change in the balance from one balance sheet to the next. Except where extraordinary gains and losses are reported here, the statement simply shows the pickup of net income and the dividend distribution.

Supporting schedules may be prepared to give details about inventories, plant and equipment cost and depreciation, or changes in capital in excess of par or stated value, for example.

Assurance of the reliability of financial statements is provided in audited statements, for the expert review of data underlying the statements and the expression of a professional opinion by an independent certified public accountant mean that generally accepted accounting procedures have been used consistently from year to year and that evidence of transactions supporting reported figures was examined.

The beauty of accounting statements is that they include a great deal of information in an understandable structure. Ratio analysis is a way of further distilling that information so it might be better interpreted.

Liquidity ratios add insight as to a firm's short-term bill-paying ability. Activity ratios help the analyst to determine how actively the company is employing its different classes of assets. The leverage ratios are used to determine how much of the firm's capital is supplied by creditors. This may be done by comparing the relative amount of funds supplied (balance sheet leverage ratios) or by gauging how much of available income is committed to paying creditors (coverage ratios). All of the foregoing attributes contribute to the firm's profitability, which can be assessed through return ratios.

The interpretation of ratios is more revealing if the analyst understands the interrelationships between activity, profit margins, and the use of borrowed money and how these elements influence a firm's profitability. The DuPont ROI system provides a convenient conceptual framework for remembering these interactions.

To interpret ratios, they must be viewed in context. Such a background can be created by comparison to industry norms. Sources of such data were indicated.

Common-size statements provide another way of restructuring the information provided by the financial statements. The operating income statement is a particularly effective way of discovering variances in operating expenses.

Throughout the discussion the judgmental nature of the accounting process was stressed. Differing, though accepted, ways of accounting for the firm's assets, liabilities, revenues, and expenses create comparability problems that can undermine the effectiveness of ratio analysis.

To be totally competent in analysis of financial statements, the analyst must understand the methods of their construction. The accounting system is one of the chief methods of conveying financial information. Understanding of this information system is imperative for the financial decision-maker.

## QUESTIONS

1. Distinguish among operating, financial, and income-tax accounting statements. What are the most important financial statements?
2. What is the purpose of financial statements?
3. Analyze: The measurement of net income is the main feature of accounting, and so the procedure of matching revenue with costs is the main problem of accounting.
4. Discuss: In analyzing financial statements, there is a basic need to note the

industry wherein the firm is located—manufacturing, merchandising, or service.
5. Discuss briefly the purpose of: (a) liquidity ratios, (b) activity ratios, (c) leverage ratios, and (d) profitability ratios.
6. "In the U.S. economy a firm must have some characteristic, or combination of characteristics, which allows it to generate a competitive return." Discuss in the context of the DuPont ROI system.
7. Utilities often have low liquidity ratios, low activity ratios, and high leverage ratios. What characteristics of a utility allow them to carry on what would seem to be very high-risk operations?

## PROBLEMS

1. Given the financial statements provided below:

|  | (dollars in thousands) | |
|---|---|---|
|  | Baker Mfg. Co. | Able Mfg. Co. |
| Cash | $ 1,670 | $ 10,500 |
| Accounts receivable | 4,100 | 24,660 |
| Inventory | 14,250 | 37,600 |
| Net fixed assets | 53,730 | 43,550 |
| Other Assets | 26,250 | 16,090 |
| Total assets | $100,000 | $132,400 |
| Current liabilities | 7,540 | 20,300 |
| Term debt | 53,940 | 40,000 |
| Net worth | 38,520 | 72,100 |
| Total claims | $100,000 | $132,400 |
| Sales | 47,100 | 166,600 |
| Cost of goods sold | 27,000 | 115,900 |
| Operating expenses | 10,600 | 34,500 |
| Operating profit | 9,500 | 16,200 |
| Interest expenses | 2,500 | 2,000 |
| Taxes | 3,000 | 5,900 |
| Net profit | $ 4,000 | $ 8,300 |

Compute the following ratios for both companies:
a. Current ratio.
b. Average-collection-period.
c. Inventory-turnover.
d. Debt-to-total-assets.
e. Net-profit-to-sales.
f. Times-interest-earned.
g. Return-on-net-worth.
h. Operating ratio.

Compare the performance of the two firms from the information provided from the ratios.

2. Construct the balance sheet and income statement from the following information:
a. Total assets = $1,000,000.

b. Current assets as a percentage of total assets (CA/TA) = 60%.
c. Current ratio = 1.50.
d. Debt to total assets = 50%.
e. Total asset turnover = 2.
f. Gross profit rate (GP/Total sales) = 50%.
g. Return on total assets = 20%.

Set up the balance sheet and income statement as shown below:

```
Current assets      ....................
Fixed assets        ....   ................
              Total assets  ..............  $1,000,000
                                            ==========
Current liabilities ....................
Term debt           ....................
Net worth           ....................
              Total ........................
                                            ==========
Total sales         ....................
    Cost of goods sold  ...............
Gross profit        ....................
    Other expenses  ....................
              Net profit after taxes  .....
                                            ==========
```

3. Construct the balance sheet with the data given:

| | | | |
|---|---|---|---|
| Net profit/net worth ...... | 25% | | |
| Long-term debt/net worth .. | 1:2 | Sales (all credit) ........ | $10,000,000 |
| Inventory turnover | | Cost of goods sold ...... | 6,000,000 |
| (using cost of goods) ... | 4X | Gross margin ........... | $ 4,000,000 |
| Average collection period .. | 72 days | Expenses ............... | 2,000,000 |
| Current ratio ............. | 2.5 | Earnings before taxes .... | $ 2,000,000 |
| Total asset turnover ....... | 1.25 | Taxes ................... | 1,000,000 |
| Return on total assets ...... | 12.5% | Net profit .............. | $ 1,000,000 |

```
Cash .....................  _____      Current
Accounts receivable .......  _____         Liabilities ...........  _____
Inventory ................  _____
    Total current
         assets  ..........  _____
Fixed assets ..............  _____      Bonds .................... _____
    Total .................  _____      Net worth ............... _____
                                             Total ................. _____
```

4. Given the following information, analyze Wynot, Inc.:

Balance Sheet

| | | | | |
|---|---|---|---|---|
| Cash ............... | $ 9,500 | Current liabilities .... | | $ 80,000 |
| Accounts receivable ..... | 62,500 | Long-term debt ...... | | 20,000 |
| Inventory ........... | 120,000 | Common stock ....... | $60,000 | |
| Current assets ....... | $192,000 | Retained earnings .... | 40,000 | |
| Net fixed assets ....... | 8,000 | Net worth ......... | | $100,000 |
| Total assets ..... | $200,000 | Total claims .. | | $200,000 |

## Income Statement

| | | |
|---|---:|---:|
| Net sales | | $500,000 |
| Cost of goods sold | | 400,000 |
| Gross profit on sales | | $100,000 |
| Selling expense | $21,000 | |
| General and administrative expense | 25,000 | 46,000 |
| Earnings before interest and taxes | | 54,000 |
| Less: Interest | | 4,000 |
| Income before taxes | | $ 50,000 |
| Less: Taxes | | 20,000 |
| Net income | | $ 30,000 |

### Industry Average

| | | | | |
|---|---:|---|---:|---|
| Current ratio | 2.5 | Debt/total assets | .30 | |
| Quick ratio | 1.3 | Times interest earned | 15 | |
| Total asset turnover | 3 | Return on sales | 3.5% | |
| Inventory turnover | 6 | Return on total assets | 10.5% | |
| Days' sales | 30 | Return on net worth | 15.0% | |

## ADDITIONAL READINGS

Altman, E. I. "Financial Ratios, Discriminant Analysis and the Prediction of Corporate Bankruptcy," *Journal of Finance*, vol. 23 (September 1968), pp. 589–609.

Beaver, W. H. "Financial Ratios as Predictors of Failure," *Empirical Research in Accounting: Selected Studies in Journal of Accounting Research* (1966), pp. 71–111.

Benishay, H. "Economic Information on Financial Ratio Analysis," *Accounting and Business Research*, vol. 2 (Spring 1971), pp. 174–79.

Bierman, H., Jr. "Measuring Financial Liquidity," *Accounting Review*, vol. 35 (October 1960), pp. 628–32.

Donaldson, G. "New Framework for Corporate Debt Capacity," *Harvard Business Review*, vol. 40 (March–April 1962), pp. 117–31.

Helfert, E. A. *Techniques of Financial Analysis*, 4th ed. Homewood, Ill.: Richard D. Irwin, Inc., 1977.

Horrigan, J. O. "A Short History of Financial Ratio Analysis," *Accounting Review*, vol. 43 (April 1968), pp. 284–94.

———. "The Determination of Long-Term Credit Standing with Financial Ratios," *Empirical Research in Accounting: Selected Studies in Journal of Accounting Research* (1966), pp. 44–62.

Jaedicke, R. K., and R. T. Sprouse. *Accounting Flows: Income, Funds, and Cash*. Englewood Cliffs, N.J.: Prentice-Hall, Inc., 1965.

Lev, B. *Financial Statement Analysis: A New Approach*. Englewood Cliffs, N.J.: Prentice-Hall, Inc., 1974.

Murray, R. F. "The Penn Central Debacle: Lessons for Financial Analysis," *Journal of Finance*, vol. 26 (May 1971), pp. 327–32.

Sorter, G. H., and G. Benston. "Appraising the Defensive Position of a Firm: The Internal Measure," *Accounting Review*, vol. 35 (October 1960), pp. 633–40.

# 4

# Operating and Financial Leverage

It has been said that financial managers face a constant dilemma. They are forced to make a continual choice between eating well and sleeping well. Most, if not all, financial decisions involve some type of risk-return trade-off. Managers can choose to maximize the expected profits of their companies, but in so doing, they run higher risks that their plans will be undone. If they extend themselves trying to achieve maximum profits, the impact of any business reversal will be magnified. If they play it safe, profits are lower.

The purpose of this chapter is to explore one area where this dilemma is most apparent—the leverage decisions. Leverage is a concept with application in many areas of finance. In general, leveraging is a process of conscious risk assumption in order to achieve higher expected returns. This is accomplished by substituting some form of fixed cost for variable costs to lower total costs and consequently raise net profits. This text concentrates on two types of leverage—operating and financial—in the context of the business firm.

The discussion that follows provides examples that illustrate how leverage works. If decision-makers are to make choices as to the use of leverage, they must be able to analyze its impact. Techniques are provided to quantify the effect of leverage on the nature of the firm.

Breakeven analysis is one method for evaluating operations. The strengths and weaknesses of breakeven analysis are explained. A method for extending breakeven analysis to the nonlinear case is provided. A form of financial breakeven is also considered. Although breakeven analysis is a deceptively powerful tool for evaluating changes in policy, it is of limited usefulness for quantifying the effect of leverage when a firm is operating well above breakeven. Elasticity measures exist which will help

## 4 Operating and Financial Leverage

in this case. These measures are referred to as *degree of operating leverage* and *degree of financial leverage*. The purpose, calculation, and nature of these measures are explained and illustrated. Before becoming unduly concerned about measurement, it would be well to understand better the nature of leverage.

## Operating Leverage

It was stated that leverage involved substituting fixed cost for variable costs in an attempt to raise expected profits. Operating leverage involves use of fixed operating expense instead of variable expenses in an attempt to raise operating income (recall that operating income was defined as income before interest and taxes).

To illustrate the effects of this substitution, consider a hypothetical example. There exists a company with no fixed costs and with variable costs which equal 90 percent of revenue regardless of the level of those revenues. At a sales level of $1 million, a partial income statement (down to the EBIT figure) would look like Table 4–1.

**TABLE 4–1**

HYPOTHETICAL, INC.
Operating Income Statement
For the Year Ended December 31, 1978

| | | |
|---|---:|---:|
| Net sales | | $1,000,000 |
| Fixed expenses | —0— | |
| Variable expenses | $900,000 | |
| Earnings before interest and taxes | | $ 100,000 |

Hypothetical, Inc., is considering a change in its operations. The change would involve incurring a fixed cost of $250,000 a year but would lower variable costs to 60 percent of revenues. Assuming these estimates are accurate, the income statement for the same sales volume, after the changeover, would look like Table 4–2.

**TABLE 4–2**

HYPOTHETICAL, INC.
(after operations changeover)
Operating Income Statement
For $1.0 Million Sales Level

| | | |
|---|---:|---:|
| Net sales | | $1,000,000 |
| Fixed expenses | $250,000 | |
| Variable expenses | 600,000 | 850,000 |
| Earnings before interest and taxes | | $ 150,000 |

This is the essence of operating leverage—substituting fixed cost for variable costs and raising operating income. Not only does this change increase expected profits at the current level, operating leverage magnifies the benefits of any increase in volume. Consider the effect of the change if volume were to increase by 20 percent to $1.2 million. The impact is apparent in Table 4–3.

TABLE 4–3

HYPOTHETICAL, INC.
Operating Income Statement
For $1.2 Million Sales Level

|  |  | Without Leverage |  | With Operating Leverage |
|---|---|---|---|---|
| Net sales |  | $1,200,000 |  | $1,200,000 |
| Fixed expenses | –0– |  | $250,000 |  |
| Variable expenses | $1,080,000 | 1,080,000 | 720,000 | 970,000 |
| Earnings before interest and taxes |  | $ 120,000 |  | $ 230,000 |

This makes operating leverage appear extremely advantageous. This procedure raises expected operating income and magnifies the impact of any increases in sales. In this case, the leveraged EBIT increased from $150,000 to $230,000. The change amounts to a 53 percent increase in operating earnings as the result of a 20 percent rise in sales. However, it was suggested that such attempts to raise expected return involved the assumption of risk. In using operating leverage, this risk arises from the magnification effect just observed. Operating leverage not only magnifies the effect of increases in sales, it magnifies the effect of sales downturns also. Table 4–4 illustrates how a 20 percent loss in sales volume would affect the company. In this case, leveraged EBIT drops by 53 percent.

The effect of operating leverage is now apparent. *Such leverage makes good times better and bad times worse.* Whether or not this is advisable

TABLE 4–4

HYPOTHETICAL, INC.
Operating Income Statement
For $800,000 Sales Level

|  |  | Without Leverage $800,000 |  | With Operating Leverage $800,000 |
|---|---|---|---|---|
| Net sales |  | $800,000 |  | $800,000 |
| Fixed expenses | –0– |  | $250,000 |  |
| Variable expenses | $720,000 | 720,000 | 480,000 | 730,000 |
| Earnings before interest and taxes |  | $ 80,000 |  | $ 70,000 |

depends upon the circumstances within a particular company at a specific point in time. The advisability of operating leverage depends on how much variable costs can be cut by the substitution of fixed costs and how likely the firm is to experience a reduction of sales, and by how much.

To evaluate these factors, the financial managers must make some important and difficult estimates. After arriving at these estimates, they can evaluate the impact of the change using forecasted income statements as was done in the example.

Another technique that might be considered as a prelude to doing such statements is breakeven analysis. Breakeven analysis will not tell the manager what expected income will be, but it does provide a quick estimate of the minimum sales level necessary to maintain some profit. Determining the new breakeven point provides preliminary evaluation of the advisability of such a change in operations.

## Operating Breakeven Analysis

An analysis of the breakeven point for the firm provides the financial manager with a means for observing the relationship between fixed costs, variable costs, and sales revenue. The analysis considers only operating expenses. Financing expenses are considered separately in the section on financial leverage; therefore, fixed costs exclude interest charges.

Operating breakeven is the level of sales at which operating profit is zero. At higher sales levels, operating profit is positive; and at lower sales levels, operating losses are incurred. Thus, it is incumbent upon management in the interest of efficient profit planning to determine at what volume sales will cover both fixed and variable costs. However, breakeven analysis can be used only over that period of time in which both costs and selling prices are relevant. The analysis must of necessity be short run since both costs and selling prices are always subject to change. Also, the reader is cautioned at this point that breakeven analysis has several disadvantages, which will be discussed later. Thus, these deficiencies greatly restrict the use and interpretation of this profit-planning technique.

*Types of Cost.* For any firm, costs can be subdivided into fixed, semi-fixed, and variable. Regardless of the level of output, a business firm will be subject to certain costs that are fixed, to others that will change with the volume of business, and to some that have characteristics of both fixed and variable costs.

*Fixed Costs.* The fixed costs of a business firm are those that go on irrespective of the volume of goods produced or sold or the amount of business done. These costs include those for salaries of executives, insurance of buildings and equipment, depreciation due to time interest on bonds and other long-term debts, and property taxes. Since World War II, there has been a rapid increase in the relative size of fixed costs or expenses in the cost structures of business firms in the United States. The sharp increase in the proportion of fixed costs has been due not only to higher relative fixed costs in some industries but also to growth in the relative importance of the high fixed-cost industries.

In many cases, fixed costs are explainable on the basis of their contributions to production rather than on the inability of management to eliminate them. For example, the positions of many top-level employees could be eliminated, barring long-term employment contracts. A major item of overhead costs is salaries of managers, administrative personnel, technicians, engineers, chemists, market-research specialists, salespeople, accountants, and others. The activities of many of these are in the field of research and development, which may not be linked directly to the current output of the company, but their services may be required to achieve the firm's long-term objectives. Their salaries should be looked on in the same way as expenditures for improvements in plant and equipment; that is, as investments in the future of the company.

A second type of fixed cost is related to plant and equipment. These expenses, like overhead salary costs, have risen sharply since the end of World War II because of technological advances. These changes have resulted in an increase in the investment per worker, which has added to fixed costs in the form of interest and other debt-service charges, fire-insurance premiums, property taxes, depreciation charges, and utility expenses.

*Semifixed Costs.* Semifixed or semivariable expenses are those that vary with, but not in direct proportion to, changes in the volume of sales or products. Sometimes, changes in expenses are due to managerial policy rather than changes in output. For example, commissions paid to salespeople on a guaranteed minimum basis would vary, due as much to the firm's salary policy for its salespeople as to changes in production. Among the other semifixed costs are those for light and power, advertising, and fringe benefits for employees, such as incentive pay, bonuses, and various types of insurance. Even though it is extremely difficult to do, semifixed costs must be divided into fixed and variable components in order to construct a breakeven point for a firm.

*Variable Costs.* Variable costs or expenses are those that fluctuate directly with changes in the volume of sales or business. They include expenses for labor, materials, and others that vary almost in direct proportion to changes in volume of sales or output of goods and/or services.

*Breakeven Point.* The breakeven point can be derived graphically or mathematically. The algebraic solution is easier, but the chart helps to demonstrate what information is derived from the solution. A breakeven chart for Hypothetical, Inc. (the previous example), *with operating leverage,* appears in Figure 4–1. The illustration is completed by assuming that Hypothetical sells only one product at a price of $100 per unit.

The chart contains much of the same information as Tables 4–2 through

FIGURE 4-1
Breakeven Point—Hypothetical, Inc. (leveraged) ($000)

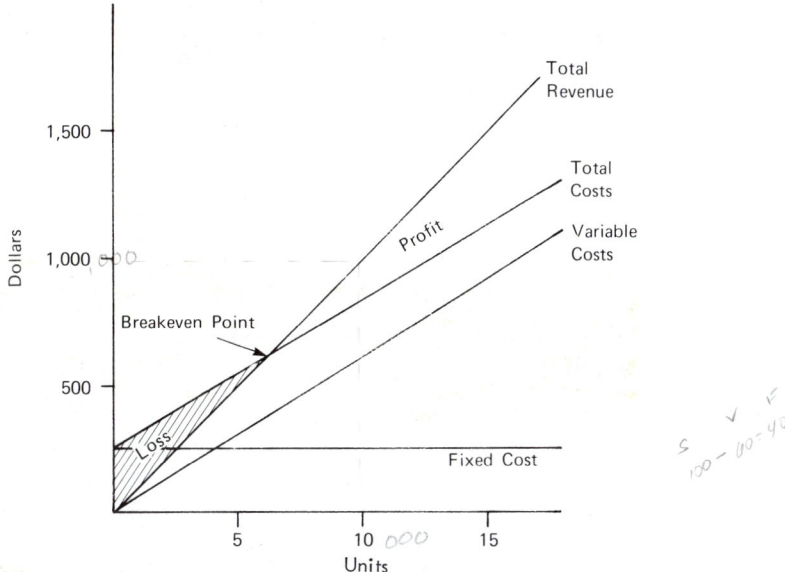

4-4. For example, company sales of $1 million (10,000 units) result in profits of $150,000. The profits for the other sales level could also be derived from the chart, making it an efficient way of developing the forecast profit figures.

In addition, the chart establishes the breakeven point. The company would continue to generate operating profits at any sales level above 6,250 units, or $625,000. This information provides some guidance for the financial manager. The manager must now assess the likelihood of sales deteriorating below that point.

Although the breakeven chart contains more than just the breakeven point, that is one of the more interesting facts to be derived from it. If only the breakeven point is wanted, it can be calculated more quickly by the following formula:

$$\text{BEP} = \frac{\text{Fixed operating expenses}}{\text{Contribution margin}}$$

where contribution margin is defined as the per-unit difference between sales price and variable cost. The contribution margin may be expressed either as a dollar amount or as a percentage. In the example, the leveraged hypothetical firm, the contribution margin was 40 percent; i.e., variable expenses were 60 percent of sales revenue. With this information, the breakeven point in dollars can be determined.

$$\text{BEP}_{\text{dollars}} = \frac{\text{Fixed operating expenses}}{\text{Percentage contribution margin}}$$

$$BEP_{dollars} = \frac{\$250,000}{.40}$$

$$BEP_{dollars} = \$625,000$$

If the analyst would prefer to have the BEP in units, the dollar figure can be divided by the unit price, which was $100 in this case. The BEP can also be solved for in units by using a dollar contribution margin.

$$BEP_{units} = \frac{\text{Fixed operating expenses}}{\text{Dollar contribution margin}}$$

In the example, each unit sold for $100. Variables costs were 60 percent of that amount, or $60. On each unit sold, the company would clear $40 over and above variable costs. Each unit sold would contribute this amount to covering fixed costs and generating a profit. At 6,250 units these contributions would be just sufficient to cover fixed operating expenses.

$$BEP_{units} = \frac{\$250,000}{\$40}$$

$$BEP_{units} = 6,250 \text{ units}$$

***Effects of Changing Variables.*** One of the strengths of this formulation for calculation of the breakeven point is the clarity with which it highlights the effect of changing variables. Anything which increases the numerator, fixed costs, will increase the breakeven point, all other things being equal. On the other hand, any increase in the contribution margin, due to either a price increase or a lowering of variable expenses, will lower the breakeven point, if there are no other changes.

Generally, a change in operations will affect both the numerator and the denominator. In those cases, the numbers can be substituted into either formula to see the effect on breakeven. As an example, if the firm has found a way to cut fixed costs to $200,000, if raw material costs have increased making variables costs $65 a unit, and if competition has forced price cuts to $90 a unit, the new contribution margin would be $25 ($90–$65 = $25). The new BEP would be

$$BEP_{units} = \frac{\$200,000}{\$25} = 8,000 \text{ units}$$

$$BEP_{dollars} = \frac{\$200,000}{.278} = \$720,000$$

## Limitation of Breakeven Analysis

The concept of breakeven analysis as presented here is useful to the extent of explaining the relationships of the three major variables confronting a firm. Its validity hinges on the management's ability to overcome several significant limitations. These deficiencies can be found in both the revenue and cost structures of the firm.

A major limitation is the assumption that selling prices are constant. Demand for a product may be elastic or inelastic; therefore, changes in the prices of a product may have a very great impact on the volume that can be produced. To take the various sales projections into account would require a whole series of breakeven points.

Second, variable costs may not be directly proportional to output. Labor costs may change as the plant approaches full capacity. Labor overtime may have to be paid. Breakdowns may occur more frequently as labor and equipment are used more intensively. Also, during periods of peak production, labor output may be lower due to the employment of more inexperienced workers who may have been hired to meet the demand for increased output.

Third, many fixed costs are not really constant over a wide range of output. More likely, these costs may rise or fall in discrete amounts. For example, an additional piece of equipment may be required or an additional clerk added to meet higher volume requirements. Large volume increases may require the addition of an entire new plant, which undoubtedly would increase the fixed overhead costs dramatically.

Fourth, another problem area is confronted when the firm produces multiple products. In this situation it would be necessary to construct separate breakeven points for each product line unless the product mix remains relatively constant over time. Even so, there would still be a major task of assigning joint costs to the various products. For multiple product lines, unless the firm can readily isolate the various joint costs, perhaps management's analysis should be confined to a calculation of the breakeven point based on total revenues and total costs.

Finally, it should be emphasized again that breakeven analysis is short-term in nature. Firms having heavy fixed costs in the form of research expenditures, such as the ethical drug companies, will not find breakeven analysis too meaningful. Research costs may not be directly related to present sales volume, but they are vital to permit the firm to remain competitive in the future. Nevertheless, breakeven analysis can provide a good beginning point in profit planning for many firms where such an analysis may be applied with validity.

*Nonlinear Breakeven Analysis.* Construction of a linear breakeven chart involves some conscious self-delusion. To construct such a chart, constant selling prices at all sales levels must be assumed. That is not normal; generally prices must be cut to sell greater volume. Rather than being linear, the revenue line should increase at a decreasing rate. The cost line would have two inflection points. First, variable costs increase at a decreasing rate as the firm achieves economies of scale. After some point these same costs start to rise at an increasing rate as production capacity is used more and more intensively, resulting in an efficiency loss. The results of these relationships would create a graph like Figure 4–2.

Although the nonlinear breakeven chart is more difficult to construct,

## FIGURE 4–2
### Nonlinear Breakeven Chart

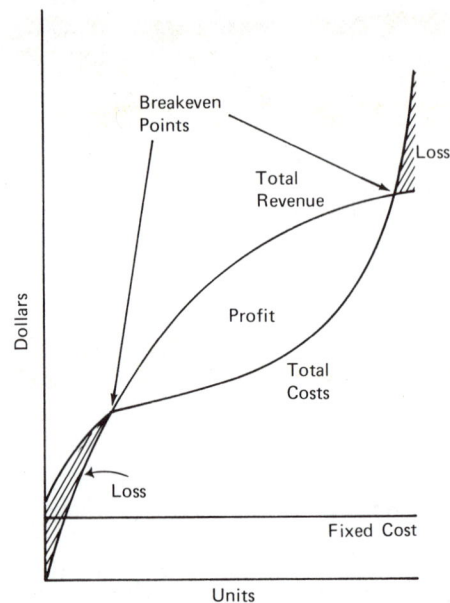

it contains some very important information that is missing from the linear version. If the axis had definitive labels, the analysis would provide the firm with guidance as to what volume level maximizes profits. The firm should operate where the vertical distance between the revenue line and the cost line is the greatest, *if it wishes to maximize profit.*

Although it takes a number of steps and involves some difficult estimates, it might be well to demonstrate how an approximation of the nonlinear breakeven chart might be constructed.

First, unit revenue lines are graphed for a number of potential prices. Each of these lines is a linear ray from the origin. The slope of each ray is the unit price (see Figure 4–3A).

Then, on each price line, a point is marked which indicates the estimated number of units that can be sold at that price. The coordinates (the X's in 4–3A) indicate the estimated unit volume and sales revenue at each price. For this product, the manager estimates that 150 units could be sold at a price of $400 for total sales revenues of $60,000. At $300 each, the sales estimate is 300 units, or $90,000. The other points are 575 units at $200 each for total revenues of $115,000; 1,210 units at $100, revenues of $121,000; and 1,550 units at $50, revenues of $77,500. By connecting these points, half (the difficult half) of the nonlinear breakeven chart is completed—the total revenue line (see Figure 4–3B).

The other half of the breakeven chart is more tedious to develop, but

## FIGURE 4–3
### Construction of Nonlinear Breakeven Chart ($000)

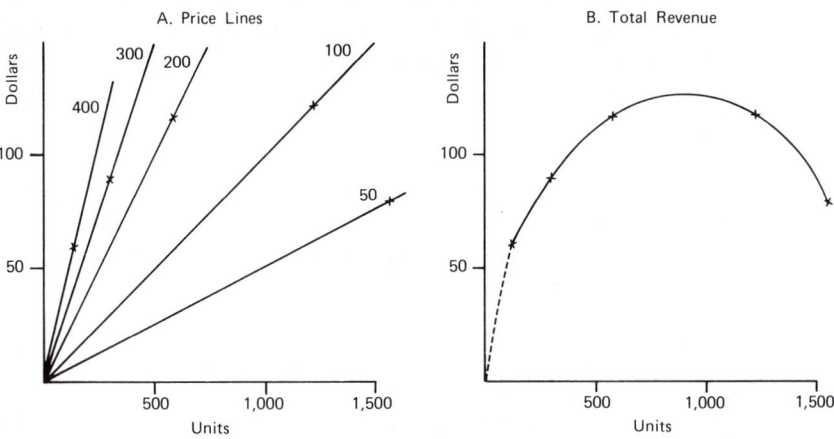

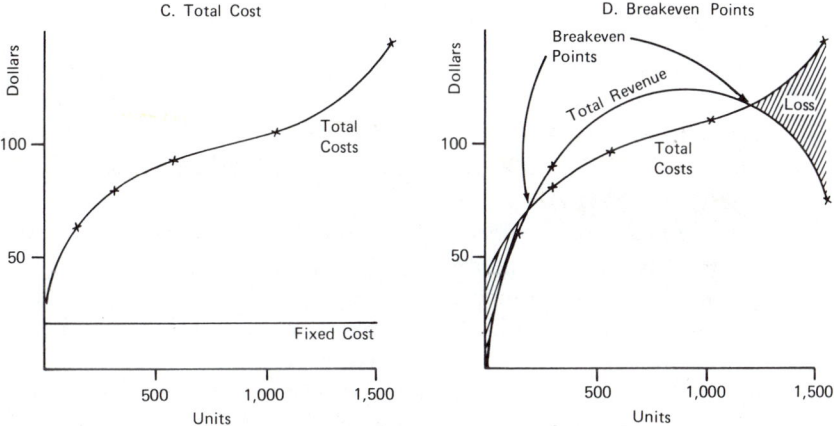

the estimation problems are somewhat easier. Generally the costs would be estimated through operating budgets for the various volume levels. To complete the example, the process is somewhat oversimplified.

If the operation were to require a minimum fixed cost of $20,000 per year, this would provide the "floor" for the cost estimates (see Figure 4–3C). Next, the variable costs would be estimated for each output level. A representative set of figures might be as follows: To produce 150 units, the variable costs would be $300 per unit; for 300 units, $200 per unit; for 575 units, $125 each; for 1,125 units, $70; and for 1,550 units, $80. (These figures represent a somewhat exaggerated example of the economies of scale phenomenon. The more units produced, the lower per-unit production costs, up to a limit.) Adding the variable costs, which would be the per-unit cost times the number of units, to the fixed costs gives the total cost estimates as illustrated in Figure 4–3C.

By combining Figures 4–3B and 4–3C, the nonlinear breakeven chart is completed. The firm has breakeven points at revenue levels of approximately $70,000 and $120,000. However, the chart contains more important information. By selling 800 units, the firm can generate a profit of approximately $20,000. Further, the chart provides guidance as to the pricing decision. The 800 units are to be sold for approximately $120,000, or $150 a unit.

One should not infer from the example that the pricing decision is simple. Derivation of the sales estimates would normally involve expensive and delicate market studies. The estimated income figures would require detailed budgeted income statements (Chapter 6). However, the preceding discussion should indicate the purpose of such studies and statements. Further, the discussion should help one better appreciate the merits of a more complex nonlinear breakeven analysis.

## Financial Leverage

Financial leverage involves the same type of cost substitution that was illustrated in the operating leverage discussion. The only difference is the costs involved. Financial leverage results when a fixed-cost form of financing, such as debt, is substituted for a variable-cost form of financing, like common stock.

Debt, such as bonds and notes, is considered to be of fixed cost because the interest payments are set by the contract. Common stock, on the other hand, has a variable cost. Issuing stock dilutes the current shareholders' claims on future earnings. How much the current shareholder forfeits depends on how high those future earnings turn out to be.

To illustrate the effects of financial leverage, recall the example used earlier. To avoid confusing operating and financial leverage, assume that the firm uses *no operating leverage* and that operating earnings (EBIT) are 10 percent of sales at all sales levels. (Note in passing that the impact of operating leverage is before the EBIT figure, and the impact of financial leverage is after that point.)

Assume, as before, that the firm is operating at a sales level of $1 million. Operating expenses are 90 percent of that figure and are all variable. Assume the firm pays taxes at a constant 40 percent rate. The firm is financed entirely with common stock—100,000 shares with market value and par value both being $10. An abbreviated income statement, including an earnings-per-share calculation, appears in Table 4–5.

Again, Hypothetical, Inc., is considering a change. In this instance the change involves altering the capital structure. The firm is considering

## TABLE 4-5
### HYPOTHETICAL, INC.
### Abbreviated Income Statement
### For $1 Million Sales Level

| | |
|---|---:|
| Net sales | $1,000,000 |
| Earnings before interest and taxes | $ 100,000 |
| Less: Interest | 0 |
| Income before taxes | $ 100,000 |
| Less: Taxes | 40,000 |
| Net income | $ 60,000 |
| Earnings per share | $.60 |

borrowing $500,000. They would have to pay 9 percent interest on the money. The funds would be used to buy up half of the outstanding stock, leaving 50,000 shares. This provides a clear-cut example of financial leverage. Though unrealistic, the example illustrates a direct substitution of one form of fixed-cost capital (debt) for a variable-cost type (stock). The effects on net income and earnings-per-share figures are illustrated in Table 4-6.

*[handwritten note: SUBSTITUTING FIXED COST CAPITAL FOR VARIABLE COST]*

## TABLE 4-6
### HYPOTHETICAL, INC.
### (after financing change)
### Abbreviated Income Statement
### For $1 Million Sales Level

| | |
|---|---:|
| Earnings before interest and taxes | $100,000 |
| Less: Interest | 45,000 |
| Income before taxes | $ 55,000 |
| Less: Taxes | 22,000 |
| Net income | $ 33,000 |
| Earnings per share | $.66 |

Like operating leverage, financial leverage, when successfully employed, benefits the shareholders by raising their expected return—earnings per share. This should, in turn, raise the value of their stock. Like operating leverage, financial leverage magnifies the benefits of any increase in volume, as illustrated in Table 4-7.

Notice that the spread between the EPS figure is even greater than at the former sales level of $1 million. Without leverage the EPS figure increased by the same amount as sales did—20 percent. Leveraged earnings increased more rapidly, from $.66 to $.90—an increase of over 36 percent. Again, leverage made good times better.

Unfortunately, financial leverage can also make bad times worse. The

TABLE 4-7

HYPOTHETICAL, INC.
Abbreviated Income Statement
For $1.2 Million Sales Level

|  | Without Leverage | With Financial Leverage |
|---|---|---|
| Earnings before interest and taxes | $120,000 | $120,000 |
| Less: Interest | –0– | 45,000 |
| Income before taxes | $120,000 | $ 75,000 |
| Less: Taxes | 48,000 | 30,000 |
| Net income | $ 72,000 | $ 45,000 |
| Earnings per share | $.72 | $.90 |

amount of interest expense does not decrease when sales volume declines. The result is a more severe erosion of EPS, as illustrated in Table 4-8.

TABLE 4-8

HYPOTHETICAL, INC.
Abbreviated Income Statement
For $800,000 Sales Level

|  | Without Leverage | With Financial Leverage |
|---|---|---|
| Earnings before interest and taxes | $80,000 | $80,000 |
| Less: Interest | –0– | 45,000 |
| Income before taxes | $80,000 | $35,000 |
| Less: Taxes | 32,000 | 14,000 |
| Net income | $48,000 | $21,000 |
| Earnings per share | $.48 | $.42 |

This illustration depicts the nature of financial leverage and its effect. Financial leverage is simply the use of fixed cost capital such as debt. If the money is successfully employed, it raises earnings per share. With debt, the impact is magnified further because interest changes are tax deductible. However, the money must be used advantageously; otherwise, the interest expense can reduce shareholders' returns.

## Financial Breakeven Analysis

Analysis of financial breakeven allows the financial manager to explore the relationship between the type of financing used and the effects on earnings per share. Although the effects of both types of leverage can be included in the analysis, it is less confusing to introduce the topic with a simplified example; namely that used in the previous section—Hypothetical, Inc., without operating leverage.

Where simple capital structures are involved, the analysis is relatively easy. First, plot earnings per share as a function of sales for each financing alternative. The illustration in Figure 4–4 uses the figures derived in Tables 4–5 through 4–8.

**FIGURE 4–4**
**Construction of Financial Breakeven Chart**

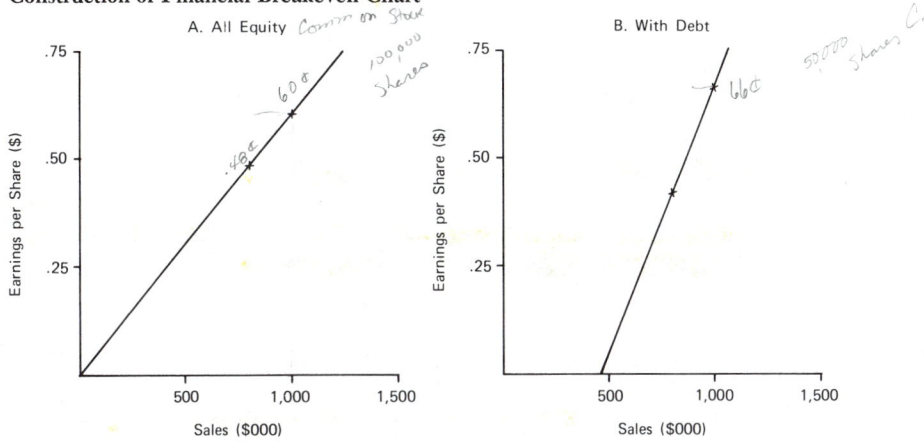

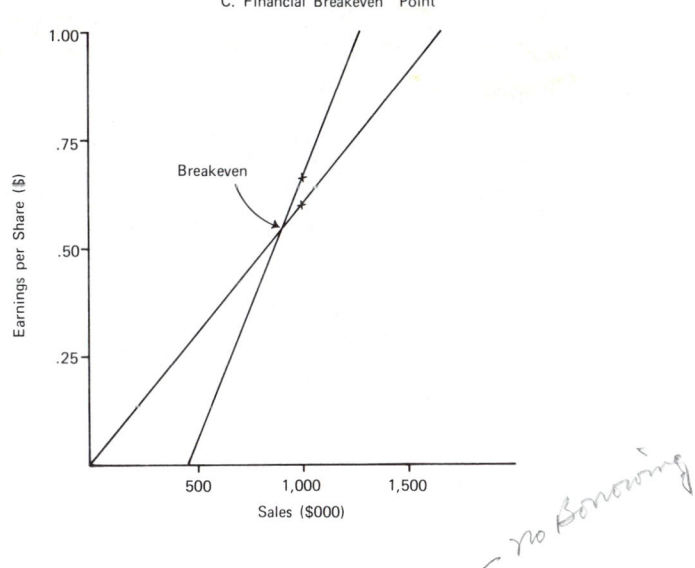

In Figure 4–4A, the EPS-sales graph for the unlevered firm is depicted. The small x's mark the earnings-per-share figures that were calculated in Tables 4–5 and 4–8. Note that only two points were necessary to determine the line. In this instance the line could have been graphed with only one point because, for a firm with *absolutely no leverage,* the line will come out of the origin. If the firm had any leverage, operating or financial, that would not be the case.

Figure 4–4B depicts the relationship if the firm had financed with debt in the manner suggested in the illustration. Again, two points determined the line. The x intercept of this line also provides some insight. Earnings per share will be zero at the sales level where operating earnings equal the interest charges. In this case, the contribution margin was 10 percent (variable costs were 90 percent). At a sales level of $450,000, operating income equals interest expense, both being $45,000.

In Figure 4–4C the two graphs are combined to determine the financial breakeven point. In this case, with no operating leverage, financial breakeven is at a sales level of $900,000. At that sales level either method of financing will produce earnings per share of $.54. What the financial manager must do next is estimate what sales will be and decide whether it is likely that sales will fall below $900,000.

If the financing alternatives are more complicated; that is, they involve use of more than one type of debt, multiple interest rates, and possibly preferred stock, and/or convertible issues, developing the EPS estimates becomes more difficult and the EPS-sales line may be nonlinear or even discontinuous. However, the technique remains valid. Simply calculate a number of EPS points, graph them for each financial plan, and combine the graphs to determine the breakeven point.

In some cases it is possible to calculate the breakeven points algebraically. To do this, derive an expression for calculating EPS for each alternative. For the example just reviewed, the expressions would be:

$$\text{EPS}_{\text{stock}} = \frac{\left[ \begin{array}{c} (\text{Contribution} \\ \text{margin} \times \text{Sales}) \end{array} - \begin{array}{c} \text{Fixed} \\ \text{cost} \end{array} \right] \times (1 - \text{tax rate})}{\text{Shares outstanding}}$$

$$= \frac{[(.1 \text{ sales}) - 0] \times (1 - .4)}{100{,}000}$$

$$= \frac{.06 \text{ sales}}{100{,}000}$$

$$\text{EPS}_{\text{levered}} = \frac{\left[ \begin{array}{c} (\text{Contribution} \\ \text{margin} \times \text{Sales}) \end{array} - \begin{array}{c} \text{Fixed} \\ \text{cost} \end{array} - \text{Interest} \right] \times (1 - \text{tax rate})}{\text{Shares outstanding}}$$

$$= \frac{[.1 \text{ sales} - 0 - 45{,}000] \times (1 - .4)}{50{,}000}$$

$$= \frac{(.1 \text{ sales} - 45{,}000) \times (.6)}{50{,}000}$$

$$= \frac{.06 \text{ sales} - 27{,}000}{50{,}000}$$

To solve for the financial breakeven, set the two expressions equal, which they will be at breakeven, and solve for the breakeven sales level.

$$\frac{.06 \text{ sales}}{100{,}000} = \frac{.06 \text{ sales} - 27{,}000}{50{,}000}$$
$$.06 \text{ sales} = 2\,(.06 \text{ sales} - 27{,}000)$$
$$.06 \text{ sales} = .12 \text{ sales} - 54{,}000$$
$$.06 \text{ sales} = 54{,}000$$
$$\text{Sales} = 900{,}000$$

Developing the algebra serves to validate the result found graphically, and to amplify the logic of the charts. However, developing the algebra for more complex financial structures can be tedious, and the charts are generally easier to follow.

## Leverage Measurement

Operating and financial breakeven allow the financial manager to appreciate the danger points in the use of leverage, but for a firm that is operating well above the breakeven points, they are of limited usefulness. As has been seen, the principal effect of leverage is to increase the volatility of a firm's earnings. Operating leverage magnifies the impact of sales volume changes on operating earnings. Financial leverage magnifies any changes in operating earnings on earnings per share. Useful measures should indicate to what degree these changes are magnified.

**Degree of Operating Leverage (DOL).** This measure of operating leverage is logically analogous to the power marking on a telescope or a pair of binoculars. A seven-power pair of binoculars magnifies the image of distant objects seven times. A firm's DOL tells about the degree of magnification within the firm.

The DOL can be defined more precisely as follows: *the degree of operating leverage is the percentage change in operating earnings (EBIT) for a 1-percent change in sales volume, at a given level of operations.* A firm's DOL is not constant. The DOL is a point measure, meaning that it is valid only at one point, the sales level for which it is calculated.

The DOL can be calculated by using the following formula:

$$\text{DOL} = \frac{\text{Sales} - \text{Variable Expenses}}{\text{EBIT}}$$

In returning to the example, for a $1 million sales level, Hypothetical's DOL would be 2.67 if it used operating leverage. Using the figures from Table 4–2, the calculation is:

$$\text{DOL} = \frac{\$400{,}000}{\$150{,}000} = 2.67$$

Thus, if sales increased by 1 percent, operating earnings should rise by 2.67 percent. That can be checked very easily. A 1-percent change in sales is $10,000. The operating income statement would then be as illustrated in Table 4–9.

### TABLE 4–9
### HYPOTHETICAL, INC.
(with operating leverage)
Operating Income Statement
For $1,010,000 Sales Level

| | | |
|---|---:|---:|
| Net sales | | $1,010,000 |
| Fixed expenses | $250,000 | |
| Variable expenses | 606,000 | 856,000 |
| | | $ 154,000 |

As can be seen, operating income would rise by $4,000, or 2.67 percent of its previous level of $150,000.

**Degree of Financial Leverage (DFL).** The DOL indicates the degree of magnification between sales and EBIT. The DFL quantifies the relative volatility of EPS with respect to EBIT. Again, a more precise definition better describes the measure: *the degree of financial leverage is the percentage change in earnings per share for a 1-percent change in operating earnings, at a given level of volume.* It can be calculated using the formula,

$$DFL = \frac{EBIT}{EBIT - \text{Interest Expense}}$$

In continuing the example used in the DOL discussion, assume Hypothetical is to use both types of leverage, operating and financial. At a $150,000 level of operating earnings, the firm's DFL would be:

$$DFL = \frac{150{,}000}{150{,}000 - 45{,}000} = 1.43$$

A 1 percent increase in EBIT, to $151,500, would raise earnings per share by 1.43 percent. Again, the result can be easily validated, as is shown in Table 4–10.

### TABLE 4–10
### HYPOTHETICAL, INC.
Abbreviated Income Statement

| | | |
|---|---:|---:|
| Earnings before interest and taxes | $150,000 | $151,500 |
| Less: Interest | 45,000 | 45,000 |
| Income before taxes | $105,000 | $106,500 |
| Less: Taxes | 42,000 | 42,600 |
| Net income | $ 63,000 | $ 63,900 |
| Earnings per share | $1.26 | $1.278 |

## 4 Operating and Financial Leverage

***Degree of Total Leverage (DTL).*** If DOL quantifies the magnification between sales and operating earnings, and DFL measures the magnification between EBIT and earnings per share, the total magnification between sales and earnings per share should be the product of the two. *The degree of total leverage is the percentage change in earnings per share for a 1-percent change in sales, at a given level of volume.*

The DTL can be calculated in either of two ways:

$$DTL = DOL \times DFL$$

$$DTL = \frac{Sales - Variable\ expenses}{EBIT - Interest\ expense}$$

As would be expected, both calculations yield the same result. For the example,

$$DTL = 2.67 \times 1.43 = 3.81$$

$$DTL = \frac{1,000,000 - 600,000}{150,000 - 45,000} = 3.81$$

Again, the result can be validated, as is shown in Table 4–11.

**TABLE 4–11**

HYPOTHETICAL, INC.
Comparative Income Statements

|  |  |  |  |  |
|---|---|---|---|---|
| Net sales |  | $1,000,000 |  | $1,010,000 |
| Fixed expenses | $250,000 |  | $250,000 |  |
| Variable expenses | 600,000 | 850,000 | 606,000 | 856,000 |
| Earnings before interest and taxes |  | $150,000 |  | $154,000 |
| Less: Interest |  | 45,000 |  | 45,000 |
| Income before taxes |  | $105,000 |  | $109,000 |
| Less: Taxes |  | 42,000 |  | 43,600 |
| Net income |  | $ 63,000 |  | $ 65,400 |
| Earnings per share |  | $1.26 |  | $1.308 |

With a 1-percent sales increase, earnings per share increased by just under a nickel, or exactly 3.81 percent.

As simple as they are, these measures allow a manager to anticipate the effect of changes in volume, both upward and downward. Further, the measures pinpoint the source of the firm's earnings volatility. That is, they tell whether the volatility is due to the nature of firm's operations or to the way in which the firm is financed.

More importantly the measures allow the managers to assess the impact of any proposed changes in either operations or financing. One other point should be made clear—the effects of leverage are multiplicative. There are obviously policy implications for the managers. Managers must be aware that the nature of the firm's operations limits the financing alternatives. If operations result in highly volatile operating income, managers must be more cautious about the method of financing and vice versa.

## Summary

This chapter has reviewed two important concepts—operating leverage and financial leverage. Operating leverage occurs when a firm has fixed costs that do not vary with changes in output. It can be analyzed by means of breakeven calculations. Since all firms have some fixed costs, every firm has a breakeven point. Until this volume of output is achieved, the firm will operate at a loss. By analyzing the relationships between fixed costs, variable costs, and prices, the firm's managers can delineate more precisely the prospective impact on profits of changes in any or all of these factors. While breakeven analysis may be helpful to management, it must be used with caution because of its inherent limitations.

A more useful form of breakeven analysis would be the often discussed, but seldom illustrated, nonlinear analysis. This format not only defines the breakeven points but can also be of help in the pricing decision.

Financial leverage occurs when the firm uses fixed cost financing such as debt. Whether this is beneficial depends on how successfully the funds are employed. Both graphical and algebraic methods of analyzing the use of financial leverage are available.

Both types of leverage increase the volatility of the firm's earnings. Measures of earnings volatility such as DOL, DFL, and DTL can help a financial decision-maker assess whether a particular plan of operations or financing is advisable, given the nature of firm. Review of these measures also illustrates the multiplicative nature of the two types of leverage.

## QUESTIONS

1. Define the general concept of leverage.
2. Within the context of a business firm, define and distinguish between operating and financial leverage.
3. Define the operating breakeven point. Using the formula, discuss the effect on the breakeven point of the firm for:
    a. an increase in wages for production personnel.
    b. a decrease in selling prices.
    c. an increase in property taxes.
    d. a decrease in raw material prices.
    e. an increase in social security taxes.
    f. an increased use of machinery to increase productivity.

4 Operating and Financial Leverage

4. Are higher fixed costs always detrimental to the profitability of the firm?
5. Define the financial breakeven point.
6. Financial breakeven considers the effect of the form of financing on earnings per share. Discuss factors that might be important considerations in financing decisions that are not considered by such breakeven analysis.
7. Define DOL, DFL, and DTL in your own words. What is the purpose of these measures?

## PROBLEMS

1. The SW Corporation produces brass lamps in which variable costs per unit equal $7 and fixed costs equal $126,000 over the entire planned production range. The selling price is $13 per lamp.
   a. What is the BEP in units? in dollars?
   b. What is the profit or loss if production and sales equal 20,000 units? 25,000 units?
   c. What volume is required to produce a $6,000 profit?

2. X Company produces and sells two products, "A" and "B," in the constant ratio of 3 A to 2 B. Costs are as follows: $VC_A = \$4$, $VC_B = \$5$, total FC = $51,000. Product "A" sells for $7 and "B" for $9.
   a. Determine the BEP for "A" and "B."
   b. What is the profit if total sales equal 60,000 units?
   c. Changing $VC_A$ to $2, $VC_B$ to $3, and FC to $135,000, recompute parts a and b and describe in general the effects of substituting fixed costs for variable costs.

3. The Jones Corporation has a choice of using either of the following relationships of fixed costs, variable costs, and revenue:

   Alternative A:  Total Revenue = $12 Q
   Total Cost = $8 Q + $14,000

   Alternative B:  Total Revenue = $12 Q
   Total Cost = $5 Q + $31,500

   Where Q = Quantity produced and sold

   a. Which alternative would you, as a manager of the Jones Corporation, choose?
   b. Would your ability to predict sales volume influence the decision? If you were confident of a 6,000-unit sales volume, which would you choose?

4. Handy-Dandy Manufacturing, Inc., maker of Handy-Dandy Indispensibles, is considering how to finance a plant expansion. After the expansion fixed costs will be $325,000 and variable costs will be 40 percent of net sales.
   The company currently has 25,000 shares of stock outstanding. The expansion can be financed by selling an additional 25,000 shares or by issuing $300,000 worth of 8-percent debt. Assume a 40 percent tax rate.
   a. Graphically determine financial breakeven.

b. What is the sales level and what are EPS?

(Using sales figures of $1 million and $600,000 is convenient though not essential).

5. Wynot, Inc., is considering a change in its financing. The current income statement appears below.

WYNOT, INC.
For the Year Ended December 31, 1977

| | | |
|---|---:|---:|
| Net sales | | $500,000 |
| Fixed expense | $125,000 | |
| Variable expense | 250,000 | 375,000 |
| Earnings before interest and taxes | | $125,000 |
| Less: Interest | | 15,000 |
| Earnings before taxes | | $110,000 |
| Less: Taxes (40% rate) | | 44,000 |
| Net income | | $ 66,000 |
| Earnings per share (30,000 shares outstanding) | | $2.20 |

The company is considering borrowing $165,000 at 9 percent. The proceeds would be used to buy half of the outstanding stock.

a. What would be the new earnings per share?
b. What are the DOL, DFL, and DTL now?
c. What would they be after the change in financing?
d. Discuss the implications of your findings.

6. Review the chapter example, Hypothetical, Inc. Assume that company has a 25 percent probability of achieving sales of $800,000, a 50 percent probability of sales of $1 million, and 25 percent probability of sales of $1.2 million.°

Construct a bar chart probability distribution (an example of a bar chart distribution appears in Figure 10–1 for those unfamiliar with the term) for earnings per share, assuming:

a. The firm uses no leverage (the necessary EPS figures are in Tables 4–5, 4–7, and 4–8).
b. The firm uses only operating leverage, (you must calculate all of the necessary EPS figures in this part).
c. The firm uses only financial leverage, (the EPS figures are in Tables 4–6, 4–7, and 4–8).
d. The firm uses both forms of leverage (you must calculate all of the necessary EPS figures in this part).
e. Discuss the concept of leverage based on your findings.

° This problem assumes students already understand something of probability. It is included for the convenience of instructors who wish to discuss leverage in terms of probability and dispersion of returns.

## ADDITIONAL READING

Baker, S. H. "Risk, Leverage, and Profitability: An Industry Analysis" *Review of Economics and Statistics,* vol. 55 (November 1973), pp. 503–507.

Crowningshield, G. R., and G. L. Battista. "Cost-Volume-Profit Analysis in Planning and Control," *N.A.A. Bulletin,* vol. 44 (July 1963), pp. 3–15.

Donaldson, G. "Strategy for Financial Emergencies," *Harvard Business Review,* vol. 47 (November–December 1969), pp. 67–79.

Ghandhi, J. K. S. "On the Measurement of Leverage," *Journal of Finance,* vol. 21 (December 1966), pp. 715–26.

Haslem, J. A. "Leverage Effects on Corporate Earnings," *Arizona Review,* vol. 19 (March 1970), pp. 7–11.

Hunt, P. "A Proposal for Precise Definitions of 'Trading on the Equity' and 'Leverage,'" *Journal of Finance,* vol. 16 (September 1961), pp. 377–86.

Percival, J. R. "Operating Leverage and Risk," *Journal of Business Research,* vol. 2 (April 1974), pp. 223–27.

Pfahl, J. K., D. T. Crary, and R. H. Howard. "The Limits of Leverage," *Financial Executive,* vol. 38 (May 1970), pp. 48–56.

Raun, D. L. "The Limitations of Profit Graphs, Breakeven Aanalysis, and Budgets," *Accounting Review,* vol. 39 (October 1964), pp. 927–45.

Shalit, S. S. "On the Mathematics of Financial Leverage," *Financial Management,* vol. 4 (Spring 1975), pp. 57–66.

# 5

# Accounts Receivable and Inventory Management

This chapter will discuss the management of the investment in and expenses related to accounts receivable and inventories. Management of these assets is part of the general topic referred to as working capital management. Discussion of the working capital concept provides a logical beginning.

From this basis, the more specific problems will be examined. Accounts receivable management can be thought of as having two levels, policy determination and decisions related to specific accounts. Policy determination will first be examined at a conceptual level as an optimization problem. This overview provides the basis for analysis of policy decisions.

Given an overall policy, implementation requires evaluation of individual accounts to ensure that they meet the requirements dictated by policy. Such evaluations are generally referred to as credit analysis.

Inventory management has many of the same characteristics as accounts receivable management, and the theory is analogous, as will be demonstrated. However, because the costs are more readily quantified, it is easier to algebraically specify the relationships. This characteristic has allowed the derivation of a valuable and widely recognized management technique, inventory models. The logic and purpose of the technique will be explored by using the economic order quantity model.

## Working Capital

Assets can be categorized as either working capital or fixed assets. Working capital includes cash and those assets that will be converted into cash within a year in the normal course of business; fixed assets include land, buildings, furniture and fixtures, machinery and equipment, and natural resources subject to depletion through operations.

The volume of working capital of a business firm depends on a number of factors; however, over a period of time, the solvency of any firm depends on its ability to generate cash. A firm that is successful will generate more cash than is required in operations; hence, cash will be available to finance the acquisition of fixed assets, retire debt, pay dividends, and increase the firm's working capital.

Current assets, because of their form, have great flexibility and can be used immediately (cash items) or after a short period (noncash items) to achieve various business objectives. Consequently, the management of working capital is one of the most vital aspects of financial management.

*Kinds of Working Capital.* Every business firm needs funds with which to finance its working-capital assets. Such funds may be obtained from proprietors, from investors (through the sale of securities), from lenders, from suppliers of goods and services, and from the firm's own operations. At the beginning of a business venture, cash is provided by owners and lenders. A part of this cash is invested in machinery, furniture, equipment, buildings, and other forms of fixed capital assets that are not to be sold throughout the year during the normal course of business. The remainder of the cash is kept available as working capital to meet the current requirements of the business enterprise, such as purchases of services, raw materials, merchandise, and other things needed to operate the business. From these expenditures, merchandise or inventories of finished goods will become available (see Figure 5–1).

FIGURE 5–1
Circular Flow of Working Capital

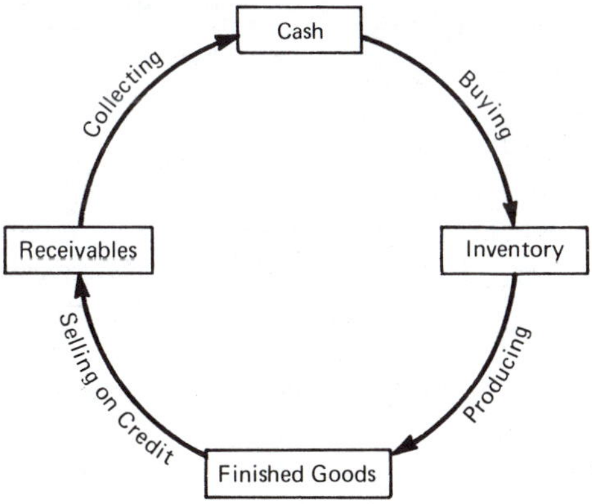

The finished merchandise of any business firm will be priced and sold to other business firms or to consumers on terms common to firms within the particular division of the industry. Credit sales will be accounted for as accounts receivable, which normally have maturities of 30 days after the billing date. Terms usually permit generous discounts for cash remittances within a specified period; therefore, many accounts receivable are paid within two weeks after the billing date. When payment is received, the circular flow of working capital is complete—that is, from cash to merchandise to accounts receivable and back to cash. If the business firm is profitable, the sum of cash obtained at the end of each cycle will be greater than the amount originally paid out. Each cycle should provide a gross profit, and the amount of net earnings for the year will depend, in part, on the number of times that working capital is turned over. The flow of working capital through the different stages of business operation does not always proceed smoothly. For example, if merchandise is difficult to sell or if receivables are impossible to collect, the normal working-capital cycle is interrupted.

Working capital may be permanent or seasonal. Permanent working capital is the minimum amount of current assets needed to conduct business even in the slowest season of the year. This amount will vary depending on the growth of the firm, the stage of the business cycle, and the general level of prices. Permanent working capital ideally should be supplied by equity capital or obtained with long-term loans.

Seasonal working capital is the additional amount of current assets required during the more active business season of the year (see Figure 5–2).

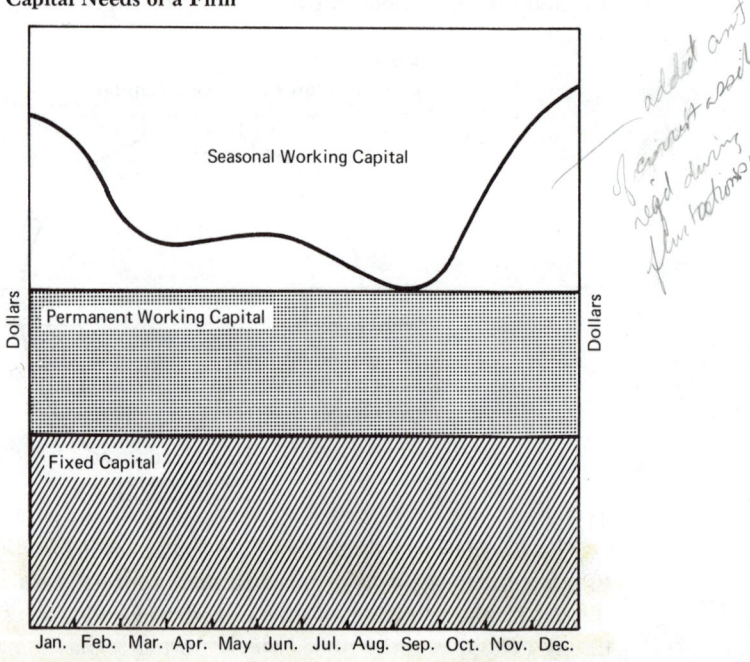

FIGURE 5–2
Capital Needs of a Firm

Normally, firms that have seasonal working-capital needs borrow short-term funds from commercial banks or other lenders to finance enlarged payrolls, accounts receivable, and inventories. A firm may provide for seasonal needs by arranging for a line of credit at the beginning of its fiscal year. A line of credit is merely an understanding with a bank that it will lend up to a certain amount if the credit standing of the firm does not deteriorate sharply. It is also possible to formalize the loan commitment by the payment of a fee. The bank would then be obligated to lend an agreed amount under specified conditions. Although a good banking connection is not reflected on the balance sheet of a firm, its presence may be as important as some assets that do appear.

The principal working-capital assets are cash and marketable securities, accounts receivable, and inventory. In this chapter the management of receivables and inventories is considered. Chapter 7 will provide the cash management coverage, which is postponed until after the discussion of forecasted financial statements. An understanding of such statements is a prerequisite for effective cash management.

## Accounts Receivable Management

Accounts receivable are the result of credit sales to the firm's customers. Management of this investment requires a comparison of the costs and benefits derived from allowing customers the convenience of credit. This will determine the firm's accounts receivable policy; that is, the general guidelines established as a target for managing the accounts receivable balance.

Policy determination can be viewed as a classical cost minimization problem, as illustrated in Figure 5–3. One of the most obvious costs of allowing credit sales is that the firm does not receive the proceeds from sales immediately. Thus, the firm must raise added capital until the customers pay. The firm's funds are tied up in accounts receivable rather than being employed in other earning assets. Firms generally define some minimally acceptable return for invested capital. This required return may well be dependent on the perceived risk of the project. If the required return on accounts receivable is constant for all levels, the capital expenses would increase linearly with the accounts receivable balance, as shown in Figure 5–3A.

Before the firm allows customers to buy on open account, it will evaluate the customers' creditworthiness. The amount of time and money spent on such investigations will depend on the industry, the dollar amount of individual sales, competitive conditions, economic conditions, and a host of other considerations. However, regardless of the nature of the individual firm, one generalization can be made. The cost of investigation will increase with an increased volume of credit sales and higher accounts receivable balances. Further, it would be expected that these expenses

94  Part II  Financial Planning and Control

**FIGURE 5-3**
Receivables Policy Determination

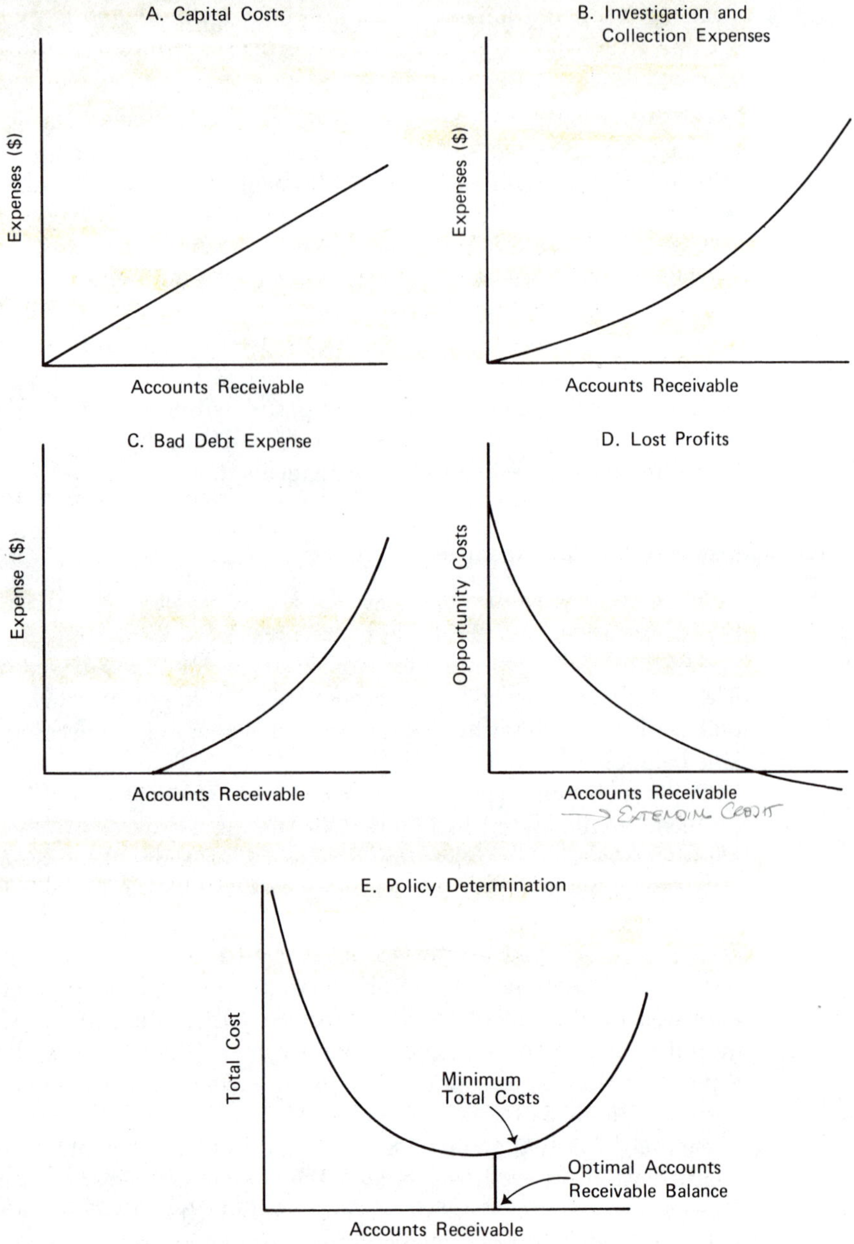

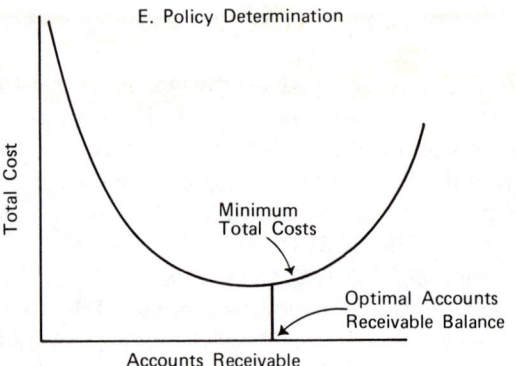

would increase at an increasing rate. This can be explained quite simply. The firm would sell on credit to the best accounts first. These would be relatively easy to evaluate. As the firm takes on more and more marginal accounts, the time, and therefore the expense, required would increase. This would result in investigation expenses consuming more and more of the sales dollar.

The same pattern would be expected for collection expenses. The best accounts, those that required little investigation due to their credit reputation, would generally require little, if any, collection effort. Such accounts can be expected to remit payment promptly after the bill is received. The more marginal accounts would be less routine. Such accounts are less prompt in paying and might require occasional reminders. The most doubtful might require even stronger collection effort and occasional legal action. Again, the expenses would increase at an increasing rate. Given the similar nature of investigation and collection expenses, they can be combined, as is done in Figure 5–3B.

Not only will marginal accounts require more investigation and collection effort, at some point the firm may encounter accounts that absolutely cannot pay or where the expenses of collection outweigh the benefit. Such accounts are written off as "bad debts." They rise from zero at some point and then increase at an increasing rate as more and more doubtful accounts are accepted, as depicted in Figure 5–3C.

The scenario thus far might well be referred to as the "credit manager's nightmare." All of the explicit costs related to accounts receivable increase as the receivables balance increases. If the analysis were to stop at this point, the optimal accounts receivable balance suggested would be zero, which minimizes all of the costs so far considered.

This process would overlook the main benefit to extending credit—additional sales which hopefully mean greater profits. Extending no credit has a very high opportunity cost. The profits that would be made by selling on credit would be lost. As credit terms are made progressively easier, such foregone profits become smaller and smaller. At some point, the lost profits are minimal—approaching zero. At that point the market is saturated, and easier credit terms would do little to affect sales. This relationship between lost profits and accounts receivable appears in Figure 5–3D.

If all of the costs are added together, the result is the familiar U-shaped total cost curve, Figure 5–3E. The optimal policy would be that which minimized total costs, explicit and opportunity. At that point the expected profit from the lost sale would barely outweigh the cost of carrying the account, the expenses of investigating and collecting it, and the chance that the customer would not pay.

Admittedly, accounts receivable management is not quite as simple as the graphs suggest. For planning purposes all of the expenses must be estimated; thus, errors of estimation occur. Further, the graphs suggest that the accounts receivable level is set to minimize cost. A firm's credit policy *influences* the level of accounts receivable, but it *does not determine that level*. The end result is to some degree determined by economic conditions which are beyond the control of the firm. The policy is established, and changes are made as conditions dictate. Any particular credit policy can be described by its components: credit standards, terms of sale, and collection policies.

**Credit Standards.** Credit standards are the criteria that determine which customers are allowed to buy now and pay later. The accounts receivable policy considers, as part of the problem, how much the firm can afford to invest in accounts receivable, how much can be spent on investigation and collection, and what percentage of bad debts the firm can afford.

Credit standards are set so that the accounts accepted fall within the overall guidelines, on the average. This is done by evaluating each individual account on the basis of its credit attributes. Although there is no clear-cut way of defining what is an acceptable credit risk, a great deal of work has been devoted to making the process less subjective. Modern quantitative methods and data processing technology hold great promise along these lines.

Regardless of whether the information is processed by man or machine, there seem to be some common elements in each credit evaluation. These are the so-called five Cs of credit: character, capacity, capital, collateral, and conditions. These attributes are important in both mercantile (business) and consumer credit.

No one implies that each of the five Cs is of equal importance. Character refers to the customer's desire or willingness to pay. It is generally the most important. A reputation for paying bills on time is built up over time. It is the "good name" of the firm, and once established, it is jealously guarded.

Wanting to pay is one thing; being able to pay is another. Capacity refers to the ability to pay. For short-term credit, such as accounts receivable, this can be measured as liquidity; for example, current and quick ratios, as discussed in Chapter 3. If the credit were to be outstanding for longer periods, profitability would also be a concern.

Capital refers to the equity base of the potential credit customer. How much of the firm is financed with borrowed money? The leverage ratios of Chapter 3 are used to gauge this characteristic.

Collateral refers to specific named security for a loan. It is generally more common to see collateral agreements in association with longer-term debt; for example, mortgages. However, if a customer is unusually shaky, or if a particular industry has a high attrition rate, sales are sometimes based on promissory notes, using the goods sold as collateral.

Conditions refers to the economic sensitivity of the borrower-customer. Some industries are extremely vulnerable to shifts in the economic climate (parts of the entertainment and amusement industry and construction are more obvious examples). In selling on credit, a firm must evaluate how well its customers are insulated from changes in the economy.

In evaluating individual accounts, strengths and weaknesses often counterbalance each other. The most honest and most seasoned business can experience hard times. Additional liquidity can offset economic sensitivity and the related vulnerability. Collateral can partially offset other weakness, but it is not a cure-all. Playing safe and turning down all marginal accounts is not the answer either, due to the lost profits. The discussion thus far has considered credit standards only as an element of policy. The problem of implementation will be examined further in the section on "credit analysis."

*Terms of Sale.* In many cases, the terms of sale are dictated by custom in the industry. If a firm's competitors are offering more lenient terms, the firm must do likewise or be prepared for a possible decline in the volume of sales. If credit terms such as "2 percent, 10 days, net 30 days" are customary, a shift by the firm to less liberal terms would be difficult to initiate without suffering a loss of goodwill and a decline in business. The offering of cash discounts speeds up payments, reduces the volume of receivables, and improves the average collection period. Although the credit position of the firm may be improved by the reduction in receivables and the increase in cash, it is an expensive method of obtaining additional funds. For instance, a firm that offers credit terms of 2/10, net 30 is actually paying an annual equivalent of 36.73 percent in order to keep down the level of accounts receivable.[1]

Unless it is deeply ingrained in the trade practices of an industry, a firm may find it expedient to abandon the cash discount system or to lower the discount. Only after a careful study of the firm's clientele has been made should such a move be considered. The trade-off in this case would be the savings of the cash discount as compared to the possible lengthening of the payment period by the firm's customers, as well as the possible loss of sales. A firm should not deviate from the industry practice on discounts unless it has made a thorough analysis of the possible repercussions on future sales.

A firm whose business is seasonal may offer liberal terms during the

---

[1] Assume a $100 balance due. If the purchaser were to pay on the 10th day, the payment would be $98. If he were to wait until the 30th day, the payment would be $100, since no discount is allowed after the 10th day. Therefore, the merchant actually pays $2 for the privilege of holding $98 for the time period between the last discount day and the final due date. Based on a 360-day year, the interest rate would be:

$$I = \frac{\text{Discount percent}}{(100 - \text{discount percent})} \times \frac{360}{(\text{final due date} - \text{discount period})}$$
$$= \frac{2\%}{98\%} \times \frac{360}{20}$$
$$= 36.73\%$$

slack season in order to encourage sales and thereby permit year-round production. A firm may encourage purchases of seasonal goods ahead of the normal buying period, arrange to make delivery, and then date the invoices according to normal delivery dates. Seasonal dating terms are important in some industries such as antifreeze, fuel oil, bicycles, and heating and cooling equipment. In seasonal industries it is hoped that the economies of evenly distributed production will more than offset the greater costs of carrying the seasonally dated receivables.

**Collection Policies.** The task of collecting accounts receivable is usually routine because most businesses pay their obligations promptly. A creditor should be punctual in mailing statements to each customer showing the amount due according to the established credit terms. If payment is not made according to the terms of the credit agreement or contract, a follow-up notice should be sent to remind the delinquent account of the obligation and to request payment.

Unless credit terms are enforced, the creditor may have to write off a large number of accounts as bad debts; therefore, there is no substitute for a systematic follow-up when granting credit. An efficient collection program will reduce the amount of receivables and prevent an undue amount of cash from being tied up in them. Even though an effective collection program is followed, it still may be necessary to use cash discounts in order to ensure the liquidity of the firm or just to speed up the turnover of the firm's receivables.

The total cost of collection efforts should be weighed against the possibility of collecting the account. If the estimated collection expenses exceed the amount of cash that can be recovered, the account should be written off immediately as being uncollectible. An account may be turned over to a collection agency, but, as the costs of using an agency are quite high, the account should not be turned over until the firm has exhausted its normal collection procedures. On occasion, a composition settlement may provide partial payment, or the firm may participate in a creditors' committee arrangement (see Chapter 25).

It is also possible for the firm to protect itself from unusual credit losses by using credit insurance. Such insurance protects against abnormal losses only and is not designed to protect against ordinary losses. Insurance companies writing such policies normally restrict the coverage to specified amounts of acceptable credit risks, as measured by the Dun & Bradstreet rating of the customer. Also, the insurer will insist upon co-insurance; that is, the firm will have to stand 10 to 20 percent of the actual loss. The use of credit insurance is not practical if the firm has adequate resources and sells to a large number of customers, none of which has unusually large accounts-receivable balances. If a loss on an account might unduly weaken the firm or even cause it to be reorganized, credit insurance should be considered. Relatively few firms use credit insurance.

One of the most difficult decisions of management is that pertaining to the continuation of credit to customers who have failed to pay in full at the due date. A study of the ledgers will reveal the past payment records. It will permit management to classify accounts as those temporarily in arrears and those calling for corrective actions, such as reductions in the maximum lines of credit. In drastic cases, the accounts might be placed on a cash basis.

*Analysis of Policy Changes.* In discussing the theory of accounts receivable management, a classical cost minimization-optimization framework was used. In reality, the problem is generally not one of determining the "best" policy; but, is instead, a question of whether a particular proposed policy shift is advisable. However, the theoretical framework is still helpful since it defines the relevant costs and benefits to consider: the capital costs, investigation and collection expenses, bad debt expense, and the additional profits.

The easiest way to demonstrate the analysis is with an example. Mid-States Suppliers, a jobber for various consumer durable products, currently sells around $2 million a year. The firm is relatively judicious in deciding to whom they will sell (all sales are credit). The total investigation and collection expenses for last year were $2,000. Bad debts were minimal, an additional $2,000. Mid-States' customers are generally prompt in paying their bills, with average collection period running 30 days. Although the firm nets considerably less, Mid-States grosses 20 percent on each dollar of sales.

Last year, the owner's oldest son graduated from college. The young man majored in business and is now working in the firm with ambitions of someday taking over operations. Based on analysis of past credit records and sales information, he suggests that sales could be doubled if credit standards were relaxed.

The credit manager has conferred with the sales manager, who believes the sales estimates are realistic. Examination of the type of new accounts that would be accepted is frightening! The credit manager is sure that the change would raise investigation and collection expenses by at least $15,000, and even at that, 5 percent ($100,000!) of the new accounts would turn out as bad debts. Further, the accounts receivable collection period would be expected to double.

The credit manager believes the change is ill-advised. The son desires additional analysis. Whether the change is advisable cannot be determined in advance. However, if the two can agree on the estimates and define a required rate of return for the added investment, the problem can be analyzed.

Assume they agree that sales can be doubled and that without the change all sales and expense figures would duplicate those of last year. The credit manager's cost estimates are used, and they feel 20 percent is a representative before-tax capital cost. The analysis appears in Table

**TABLE 5-1**
Analysis of Accounts Receivable Policy Change

*Capital Costs:*

Current $\dfrac{\$2 \text{ million sales}}{360 \text{ days}} \times 30 = \$166,667$ Accounts receivable

Proposed $\dfrac{\$4 \text{ million sales}}{360 \text{ days}} \times 60 = 666,667$ Accounts receivable

$\phantom{xxxxxxxxxxxxxxxxxxxxxxxx}$ $\$500,000$ Additional accounts receivable
$\phantom{xxxxxxxxxxxxxxxxxxxxxxxxxxx}$ .8 Variable cost

Cost of added accounts $\$400,000$
$\phantom{xxxxxxxxxxxxxxxxxxxxxxxxxxx}$ .20 Required rate of return
$\phantom{xxxxxxxxxxxxxxxxxxxxxxx}$ $\$\phantom{x}80,000$

*Collection and Investigation:*
$\$15,000$ increase per credit manager's estimates.

*Added Contribution to Profits:*

| Current | Proposed | |
|---|---|---|
| $2,000,000 | $4,000,000 | Sales |
| 2,000 | 102,000 | Bad debts (2000 + 100,000 new bad debts) |
| $1,998,000 | $3,898,000 | Net sales |

Net increase $\phantom{x}$ $1,900,000 Added sales
$\phantom{xxxxxxxxxxxx}$ 1,600,000 Cost of added sales (.8 × $2 Million)
$\phantom{xxxxxxxxxxxxx}$ 300,000 Gross contribution

*Summary:*
Gross contribution − Costs = Net benefit
$\$300,000 - 95,000 = \$205,000$

5–1. Note that it follows the theory previously discussed (see Figure 5–3).

The table is largely self-explanatory, but some attention to the details is probably warranted. Under capital costs the new accounts receivable level is calculated using an estimated collection period. There are other ways of estimating the increase. The firm might estimate how long the new accounts will take to pay on average and add the increment to the expected balance for the old accounts. The next step is important and sometimes overlooked. It does not cost $100 to create a $100 account. The account's cost is the outlay for the merchandise sold, which would have been $80 in this case. That is the additional amount to be financed and should be the basis for the capital cost calculation.

The collection and investigation costs would have to be estimated, as was suggested in this example. In some cases firms do this using percentages. The analysis is the same. It only involves an added step.

Bad debt expense could have been calculated separately. (Again the cost would be the variable cost of producing the sales.) This expense was treated as part of the sales change to emphasize the point. If bad debts are figured as an explicit and separate cost, the sales change should not be reduced for bad debts. That would be double counting. The way the example analysis is set up should minimize such problems.

In this case it appears the easing of credit standards would be profitable. Similar analysis can be tailored to most accounts receivable policy decisions. Explicit analysis is often necessary in this area. The costs of extending credit are very visible. The benefits are sometimes not. The proposed analysis considers both sides of the issue and highlights what estimates are necessary to make the decision.

*Credit Analysis.* After a policy has been established, the credit department knows the type of accounts the firm wants to accept. The credit department's function is to ensure the accepted customers are of that type. For each new credit applicant two questions must be answered: (1) Is the probability that the customer will pay as high as the policy dictates? (2) If the customer pays, will payment be as prompt as expected by policy?

Answering these questions is the purpose of credit analysis. The best source of information as to the creditworthiness of an old customer is the firm's own files. If the receivables are significant, the firm may request that an income statement and balance sheet be sent periodically to the firm by the customer. A new customer should be required to supply financial statements, including, if available, a cash-flow statement, before being granted credit. Some companies are quite agreeable to honor such a request; others may refuse. If an applicant will not supply financial statements, other sources of information may be used, or the request for credit may be rejected.

Among the most widely used sources of credit information are the reports of mercantile credit agencies—organizations that specialize in gathering and supplying information concerning the credit, reputation, and financial standing of individuals and firms engaged in business. The information is confidential and is so treated. Court decisions have held that credit reports furnished by an agency, like responses to a credit inquiry by one person to another, are "privileged communications" and this defense may be used in legal action.

The services offered to subscribers by Dun & Bradstreet, Inc., include its *Reference Book,* which is issued six times a year and contains the names of approximately 3 million commercial and industrial enterprises in the United States and Canada. Each firm is classified as to products and functions and is given a composite rating, such as "high," "good," "fair," or "limited." The *Reference Book* also contains an estimate of the financial strength of each business firm, which is usually measured by the firm's tangible net worth. Listings are classified by states and then broken down under cities, towns, and villages. Dun & Bradstreet also prepares commercial credit reports on all enterprises listed in the *Reference Book* and sends these reports to subscribers on request.

When a supplier asks a new customer for the the name of his bank, the supplier may then contact that bank for information as to the length of time the account has been there, the line of credit, payment habits, defaults, returned checks (because of insufficient funds), and its general opinion as to the customer's character, capacity, and capital. Banks usually make trade inquiries about their borrower-customers from time to time, and so they feel obliged to answer suppliers' questions about their customers. However, banks do not freely disclose detailed financial information about their customers; hence, the information received from them may be fragmentary and vague.

The discussion so far has been on the degree of credit risk the company is willing to assume and the sources of readily available information about present and prospective customers. It still must be determined if the account is to be accepted or rejected. Existing customers can be handled routinely. After a credit limit has been set, future orders may be approved as long as they are within this limit. If the customer's order exceeds the approved limit, then the customer can be treated in the same manner as a new account. In this case, ratio analysis may be used advantageously. Applicable ratios would include those pertaining to working capital, such as the current and quick ratios.

If more information is desired, the customer's Dun & Bradstreet rating can be checked. A special credit report from Dun & Bradstreet also may be requested. Finally, banks, other suppliers, and the firm's own sales force may be asked to evaluate the creditworthiness of the applicant.

Compiling any information is not costless and may take considerable time. The prospective size of the account should determine the degree of thoroughness of the credit analysis. If the potential size is quite large, perhaps all of the available sources will be required to make an evaluation.

After assembling all the necessary information, the credit manager must make a decision. It should be based on the current industry trends, the operating position of the firm, and the evaluation of the application. Statistical methods have been employed recently in credit analysis by some firms. However, these techniques (primarily, regression and discriminant analysis) give best results when there is a large number of relatively small accounts. As these techniques become more refined, it is possible they will be used more widely, but they cannot replace the subjective evaluations required in credit analysis when substantial sales and, possibly, accounts-receivable balances are at stake.

## Inventory Management

For many firms, inventories represent the most important of the working-capital assets, at least if measured in monetary terms. Since inventories are so important, it is essential they be managed efficiently. There are two key problems that confront any firm having inventories: (1) What should be the size of the order? (2) At what point should orders be placed? The answers to both of these questions will have a significant impact on the size of inventories the firm should hold. They also will determine whether or not the firm manages its inventories efficiently.

There have been changes in inventory policies since the 1950s. Perhaps the most significant force for stimulating progress has been the computer. By its use, perpetual inventories may now be maintained where formerly it was not economically feasible to do so. In addition, the computer has stimulated research into sales forecasts and inventory models. Finally, by using linear programming, warehousing costs have been trimmed by more effectively locating warehouses, thereby reducing transportation costs and often saving considerable time in filling orders.

The dollar amount of inventories varies from industry to industry and from firm to firm within the same industry, depending on the nature of the business, its size, and its managerial policies. On a manufacturer's balance sheet, inventories consist of raw materials, work in process, and finished goods; on a retailer's balance sheet, inventories consist of merchandise for resale. A service industry has no inventory for resale.

The size of a particular firm as compared with others in the same industry affects its inventory total; therefore, for comparative purposes, the amount is often expressed relative to the cost of goods sold. This relationship may be found by several other methods, but perhaps the most widely used is to divide cost of goods sold by the average inventory at cost. Management may then compare this figure with that considered appropriate for the type of business conducted. If the business is one wherein the productive process is of long duration, as in the shipbuilding and construction fields, the amount invested in raw materials and goods in process will be large; however, if the manufacturing process is of short duration, as in the paper, canning, toys, and small-value household-appliance industries, the amount invested in raw materials and goods in process will be relatively small.

The size of a firm's various inventories will be influenced by managerial policies as to buying, selling, and inventory valuation methods. The advantages of large inventories are readily apparent. It is possible that economies in production can be achieved, bargains in purchasing may be available, and customers' orders can be filled without delay. However, these advantages cannot be achieved without some cost. In keeping large inventories on hand, the firm incurs implicit as well as explicit costs. Since a portion of working capital is tied up in a noninterest-bearing form, an implicit cost of foregone investment income accompanies excessive inventories. Explicit costs of carrying inventories include, among other things, insurance, storage, and handling expenses. Like the conclusion reached regarding accounts receivable, inventories should be increased up to the point where the operating savings and total costs of carrying the inventories are equal. This requires reliable estimates of the savings as well as the costs connected with carrying the additional inventories. As with most things, these estimates are not easy to obtain; they require estimates of loss if production is interrupted or if sales are lost because of slow deliveries. On the expense side, estimates of increased deterioration, recordkeeping, and space costs will be necessary in order to assess properly the various possible inventory positions.

***Order Size.*** Management of the investment in any asset is an inventory problem of sorts. The benefits and costs must be analyzed, and a decision must be made as to the investment that achieves the best balance between the two.

Although estimating the benefits and costs related to inventory can be difficult, these factors are generally more quantifiable than in other problem areas. This has allowed the development of a mathematical decision technique referred to as inventory models.

The theory is essentially the same as that discussed under accounts receivable. There are costs that rise as the average level of inventory increases, such as capital costs, insurance, storage, deterioration, pilferage, and obsolescence. These are referred to as carrying costs (Figure 5–4A). However, there are also costs that decline as the average inventory increases. Examples of these costs would include the costs of placing and processing orders. In a production situation they would include "setup costs," the costs of arranging the equipment for a particular production run. Costs that decline as the average level of inventory increases are referred to, in aggregate, as ordering costs (Figure 5–4B). Adding these costs, a U-shaped total cost curve is derived. The best inventory would be that which minimized total costs, as illustrated in Figure 5–4C.

Inventory management has become an extremely sophisticated branch of operations management and research. Although inventory models can be intimidating because of the mathematics involved, the idea is basically simple. All of the proposed models involve an algebraic specification of Figure 5–4C, total costs. The models are then solved for the optimum inventory level.

One of the simplest of these models, the *EOQ* (economic order quantity), illustrates the process. The simplicity of this model is due to its assumptions. It assumes that the sales requirement ($R$) is known, that the firm sells the same amount every day, and that the firm receives instant delivery on orders. The model is valid for any time period as long as all elements are defined with the same period in mind, but it is simpler to think in terms of a year.

The firm wants to determine the unknown quantity, $Q$, that will minimize costs. Average inventory will be $Q/2$. If it costs $I$ dollars a year to carry one unit, total carrying costs will be the per-unit cost times the average inventory.

$$\text{Carrying costs} = I(Q/2)$$

## FIGURE 5–4
Minimizing Inventory Costs

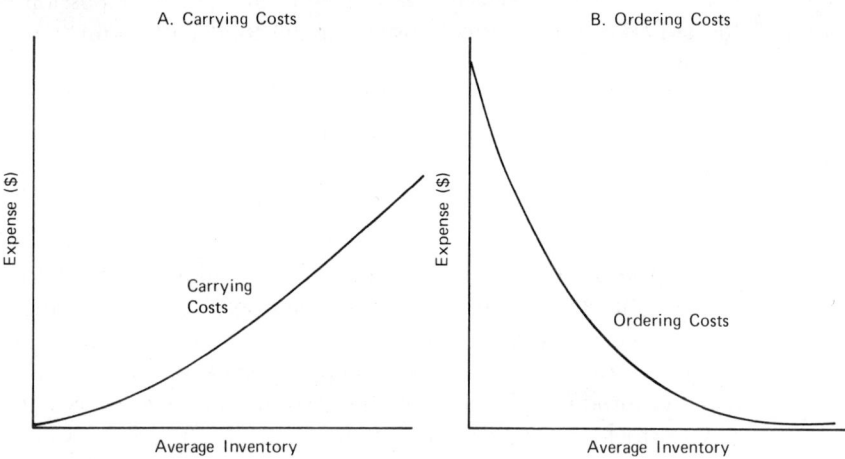

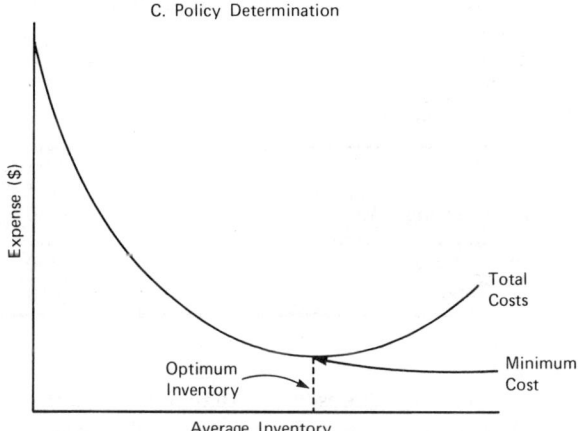

If the cost of placing one order is $O$ dollars, total ordering costs will be the per-order cost times the number of orders placed per year, $R/Q$.

$$\text{Ordering costs} = O(R/Q)$$

Total costs are the sum of the two.

$$\text{Total costs} = I(Q/2) + O(R/Q)$$

The three equations specified so far are the algebraic counterparts of Figure 5–4. The next step is to find the minimum point on the total cost curve and the best order quantity which corresponds to it.

Recall from economics that the minimum point on the total cost curve is the point where marginal cost is equal to zero. It is possible to derive the equation for marginal cost from the total cost formula by differentiation.[2]

$$\text{Marginal cost} = I/2 - OR/Q^2$$

Setting marginal cost equal to zero and solving for $Q$ gives the EOQ formula.

$$Q = \sqrt{\frac{2RO}{I}}$$

By ordering $Q$ each time, the firm will minimize the total costs associated with carrying and ordering inventories. To demonstrate the use of the formula, an example is helpful.

Assume the Davis Mattress Company needs 100,000 springs a year to make its product ($R$). Purchasing costs per order are $18 ($O$). It costs $.10 to stock one mattress spring for a year ($I$). The EOQ would be:

$$Q = \sqrt{\frac{2RO}{I}} = \sqrt{\frac{2 \times 100,000 \times 18}{.10}}$$
$$= 6{,}000 \text{ springs}$$

Table 5–2 demonstrates that ordering either more or less would raise costs.

**TABLE 5–2**
**Inventory Costs**

| | | | |
|---|---|---|---|
| Order size | 5,000 | 6,000 | 7,000 |
| Average inventory | 2,500 | 3,000 | 3,500 |
| Carrying costs | $250 | $300 | $350 |
| Number of orders | 20 | 16.7 | 14.3 |
| Order costs | $360 | $300 | $257 |
| Total costs | $610 | $600 | $607 |

Table 5–2 does more than just validate the concept of the EOQ. It demonstrates that the trough of the total cost curve is often fairly flat. This allows one to think of the EOQ as an indicator of the optimum range of order quantities rather than as a specific point where small deviations are extremely costly. The table also reasserts the theory of inventory management. Some costs rise as inventory increases (carrying costs); at the same time others decline (ordering costs). Good inventory management involves finding an appropriate balance between these two.

**Order Point.** Order quantities indicate *how much* to order; order points indicate *when*. In developing the EOQ model, there was no con-

---

[2] $T = I(Q/2) + O(R/Q)$
$\frac{\partial T}{\partial Q} = \frac{I}{2} - \frac{OR}{Q^2}$

## 5 Accounts Receivable and Inventory Management

cern about when to order. It was not necessary because of two assumptions: (1) instant delivery, and (2) uniform usage.

If deliveries are not instantaneous, then the firm must order prior to running out. The firm must have enough on hand at the time of ordering to carry on operations until the new shipment arrives. This quantity of stock on hand can be referred to as *transit stock* and would be the amount of stock the firm would expect to sell (or use) between the time the order was placed and when it was delivered.

$$\text{Transit stock} = (\text{usage}) \times (\text{transit time})$$

Assume Davis Mattress, the previous example, uses 2,000 springs a week (100,000 springs a year assuming a 50-week year). If it takes a week for delivery, the firm should order when inventory is reduced to 2,000 units.

$$\begin{aligned}\text{Transit stock} &= (2{,}000/\text{week usage}) \times (1\ \text{week}) \\ &= 2{,}000\ \text{springs}\end{aligned}$$

The development to this point assumes the firm can forecast exactly how much it will sell, in total and per week, and how long delivery will take. If the estimates are less precise, the firm will probably build in a "fudge factor." This is called a *safety stock*.

The size of the safety stock will depend on the costs and benefits associated with carrying such a stock. Another figure similar to Figure 5–4 could be drawn. The optimal safety stock is the one which balances the expected costs and benefits.

Safety stock models are slightly more complicated because they rely heavily on probability concepts. Although the math can be complex, the idea is simple. The higher the expected benefit from having stock, the lower should be the probability of running out. On the other hand, if benefits of having the extra inventory are small, and there are substantial penalties for having too much inventory, safety stocks should be minimal.

The point at which the order will be placed depends on both transit time and how much of a margin for error the firm wants to build into the system.

$$\text{Order point} = \text{Transit stock} + \text{Safety stock}$$

Davis Mattress has decided that a safety stock of 1,000 springs suits their needs. They would place an order when inventory gets down to 3,000 units.

$$\begin{aligned}\text{Order point} &= 2{,}000 + 1{,}000 \\ &= 3{,}000\ \text{units}\end{aligned}$$

The amount of the order would be 6,000 units, the economic order quantity.

## Summary

The working capital of a firm is its circulating capital, which flows from cash to inventories, to receivables, and back to cash. If the business is profitable, the amount of cash at the end of the cycle will be greater than it was at the beginning. This process will help generate the funds necessary for acquisition of capital assets, fostering the long-term growth of the business.

Throughout the cycle the firm will have funds invested in these working-capital balances. Part of the financial manager's task is to assure the firm is getting maximum mileage out of these investments.

In accounts receivable management this optimization process involves balancing the costs—interest and other capital costs, collection and investigation expenses, and bad debts—against the added profits that will be generated through the sales fostered by the availability of credit.

Although financial managers cannot directly control the accounts receivable balance, they can manipulate policy variables which indirectly affect this balance. The managers determine the credit standards customers must meet, what terms of sales are offered, and how much collection effort is exerted.

Together these components determine accounts receivable policy. Implementation requires evaluating each customer to ensure that all customers meet the policy guidelines. Credit analysis involves deciding whether a particular customer will pay and, if so, how quickly.

Inventory management involves the same type of cost-benefit analysis. Because the costs are more readily quantified, mathematical models can be derived. The *EOQ* is an example of such models which demonstrates the logic of the technique.

Deciding when to order inventory is also necessary. The analysis should make allowances for the necessary delivery time and for possible errors in the estimates. How much added inventory the firm will carry depends on the costs and benefits involved.

## QUESTIONS

1. Distinguish between permanent and seasonal working capital.
2. A policy of keeping current assets in excess of usual normal needs would free management of the need to borrow. What are the disadvantages of such a policy?
3. Should the credit policy of a firm be such that no bad debts will be encountered?
4. You hear or see a used car lot advertising instant credit, even for those new in the area, and with a recent bankruptcy or divorce. What does this imply about their:
    a. Credit standards?
    b. Collection policy?
    c. Contribution margin?
5. Using the 5 Cs of credit as a basis, consider the questions you might expect to be asked when applying for consumer credit.

5  Accounts Receivable and Inventory Management

6. Why is overinvestment in inventory sometimes called the "graveyard of business firms"?
7. Discuss the logic of the *EOQ* model and how the logic might be useful even where the model is not directly applicable.
8. Does the *EOQ* model assist management in determining:
    a. How much safety stock to carry?
    b. When to order?
    c. How much to order at a time?
9. Considering the cost and benefits involved, suggest, in general terms, a safety stock policy for:
    a. A balloon vendor at a fair.
    b. A restaurant after normal dinner hours.
    c. A Christmas tree lot.

## PROBLEMS

1. A firm with current sales of $1 million and a 45-day collection period is considering loosening credit standards.

    The change is expected to increase sales by $500,000 but the overall collection period would lengthen to 55 days. This is in spite of added collection and investigation expenses of $20,000. In addition, bad debts that are currently 1 percent of sales are expected to increase to 3 percent of sales.

    The firm's contribution margin is 10 percent and it expects to make at least a 15-percent (before tax) return on any new investment.

    Should the firm make the change?

2. Because of recent increases in their outstanding accounts, Supplier Sales, Inc., is considering tightening credit standards and increasing collection efforts.

    Sales are currently $2 million a year with accounts receivable averaging $450,000. Supplier knows such a move would hurt sales. They expect sales would drop by $300,000 but they think this would enable them to get accounts receivable down to 36 days, the industry norm.

    Investigation expense would drop but collection expenses would rise. They estimate the net effect would be a $10,000 increase in costs. This would be offset by a drop in bad debt expense. Bad debts are currently 1.5 percent a year. They believe the new policy would cut this to 1 percent.

    Supplier grosses 5 percent on each sales dollar. They would like to make 25 percent, before taxes, on invested capital.

    Analyze the policy change.

3. Analysis establishes the following relations for inventory and storage costs:
    a. Orders must be placed in multiples of 100 units.
    b. Requirements for the 50-week year are 40,000 units.
    c. Carrying cost per unit per year is $0.20.
    d. Ordering costs per order are $10.

    What is the *EOQ*? What is the optimal number of orders to be placed during the year?

4. The XYZ Corporation produces a line of electric motors, with a volume of 50,000 units per year. Currently it purchases the rotor shaft in quantities of 10,000 units per order. Inventory carrying costs amount to $0.50 per shaft per year and it costs $45 to place an order. Find the $EOQ$ and determine the yearly savings relative to the firm's current inventory system.

5. If the Quadruple-A Cleaning Supply Company uses $EOQ$ for inventory purchasing and you are given the information below, how many units of this particular item does the firm sell in a year?
   a. $EOQ$ is 5,000 units.
   b. Ordering cost per order is $12.50.
   c. Carrying cost per unit per year is $0.10.

# ADDITIONAL READINGS

Bean, V. L., and R. Griffith. "Risk and Return in Working Capital Management," *Mississippi Valley Journal of Business and Economics,* vol. 1 (Fall 1966), pp. 28–48.

Benishay, H. "Managerial Controls of Accounts Receivable: A Deterministic Approach," *Journal of Accounting Research,* vol. 3 (Spring 1965), pp. 114–32.

Beranek, W. *Working Capital Management.* Belmont, Calif.: Wadsworth Publishing Co., Inc., 1966.

Brown, R. G. *Decision Rules for Inventory Management.* New York: Holt, Rinehart and Winston, Inc., 1967.

Davis, P. M. "Marginal Analysis of Credit Sales," *Accounting Review,* vol. 41 (January 1966), pp. 121–66.

Lewellen, W. G., and R. W. Johnson. "Better Way to Monitor Accounts Receivable," *Harvard Business Review,* vol. 50 (May–June 1972), pp. 101–9.

Magee, J. F. "Guides to Inventory Policy," I, II, and III, *Harvard Business Review,* vol. 34 (January–February 1956), pp. 49–60; (March–April 1956), pp. 103–16; and (May–June 1956), pp. 57–70.

Marrah, G. L. "Managing Receivables," *Financial Executive,* vol. 38 (July 1970), pp. 40–44.

Mehta, D. *Working Capital Management.* Englewood Cliffs, N.J.: Prentice-Hall, Inc., 1974.

Oh, J. S. "Opportunity Cost in the Evaluation of Investment in Accounts Receivable," *Financial Management,* vol. 5 (Summer 1976), pp. 32–36.

Sisson, R. L., and N. L. Statland. "The Future of Computers in Credit Management," *Credit and Financial Managemennt,* vol. 67 (May 1965), pp. 13–15, 40, 44.

Smith, K. V. *Management of Working Capital: A Reader.* New York: West Publishing Co., 1974.

Snyder, A. "Principles of Inventory Management," *Financial Executive,* vol. 32 (April 1964), pp. 13–21.

Stancill, J. McN. *The Management of Working Capital.* Scranton, Pa.: Intext Educational Publisher, 1971.

# 6

# Financial Forecasting Statements

Before moving on to the topic of cash management, it will be useful at this point to first examine the tools of financial planning which the financial manager has at his or her disposal. Efficient utilization of the firm's assets requires that the financial manager be conversant with the tools of cash planning and control. The flow-of-funds statement provides information concerning how funds were acquired in the past, and how they were used. It also provides a convenient framework for future planning of sources and uses of funds. The cash budget, showing estimated cash receipts and disbursements, is essential to the proper and efficient management of cash. Finally, forecasted financial statements, called pro forma statements, can be drafted to show the ultimate effects of the firm's decisions on the operations and financial position of the firm.

The preparation of the forecasting statements should begin with an examination of the assets and liabilities held by the firm at the beginning of the forecasting period. An evaluation of the current economic environment and the possible plans of the major competitors should be made. A synthesis of the above factors must then be made in order to arrive at a sales forecast or even multiple forecasts. It is possible that a range of sales estimates under varying economic and competitive conditions can be made by using computer simulations, that is, assuming the firm is large enough to afford the costs involved in making such projections.

Once a sales forecast is completed an operating plan can be formulated. Later, pro forma statements can be made showing the consequences of the operating policies adopted to fulfill the projected sales target. Hence, the various forecasting statements show the financial consequences of the level of operations required to meet the sales estimate. If the latter forecast is considerably higher than the past level of operations, the financial impact of acquiring physical and human resources will be reflected in the cash budget. The pro forma income statement and pro forma balance sheet will reflect the acquisition of such resources.

This chapter will focus on the aforementioned financial forecasting statements. Through their analysis, the financial manager should acquire an insight into the financial needs of the firm. If the firm adheres closely to the planned levels of operations, the forecasting statements will be a reliable indicator of the financial consequences.

## Flow-of-Funds Statements

Corporate financial statements have traditionally presented the income, retained earnings, and financial position statements. However, within the last decade, a fourth statement has emerged with increased prominence—The flow-of-funds statement (or alternatively, statement of changes in financial position). This statement has particular relevance in that it conveys information about the financing and investing activities of the firm as well as changes in its financial position for the period.

The flow-of-funds statement shows the net flow of funds into a firm from all sources and the flow of funds out of the business to meet obligations. The statement is usually presented on either of two bases: (1) a working capital basis, or (2) a cash basis. Under the working capital basis, funds are defined as working capital (current assets less current liabilities). The working-capital-flow statement indicates changes in noncurrent items which require either the generation or use of working capital. The cash-flow statement shows the net flow of cash (defined as cash and marketable securities) into and out of the firm.

The latter basis, that is cash-flow, is preferred by the authors because of management's need for information about the firm's ability to generate cash, future cash requirements, and related financing. The techniques of preparation and analysis are similar for both methods, however, so that a knowledge of one will give a good understanding into the contents of the other.

The cash-flow statement depicts the sources that generate cash (examples are net income, sales of assets, sales of common stock or bonds), and the uses of cash (reduction of debt, dividends, purchase of other assets). Thus, it is a statement of (1) the beginning cash balance, (2) cash provided by operations, (3) cash provided by nonrecurring sources, (4) applications or uses of cash, and (5) the ending cash balance (see Table 6–1). The end result is to evaluate the cash flow during the period under examination.

The first step in preparing the cash-flow statement consists of converting net income computed on an accrual basis to net income on a cash basis. A convenient method involves taking the reported net income fig-

## TABLE 6-1
### X MANUFACTURING COMPANY
### Cash-Flow Statement
### For the Year Ending December 31, 1978

| | | | |
|---|---|---|---|
| Beginning cash balance (January 1, 1978) ...... | | | $52,000 |
| Cash provided by operations: | | | |
|    Net income .................. | | $110,000 | |
|    Adjustments to convert income from accrual to a cash basis: | | | |
|       Depreciation .................. | $30,000 | | |
|       Increase in prepaid insurance ...... | (1,000) | | |
|       Increase in prepaid rent .......... | (500) | | |
|       Provision for bad debts ........... | 500 | | |
|       Increase in inventories ........... | (5,000) | | |
|       Decrease in receivables ........... | 36,000 | | |
|       Decrease in payables ............. | (4,000) | | |
|       Loss on sale of fixed assets ....... | 2,000 | | |
|       Net adjustment to income ........ | | 58,000 | |
|    Cash generated by current operations ........ | | $168,000 | |
|    Nonrecurring sources of cash: | | | |
|       Sale of fixed assets .............. | $4,000 | | |
|       Sale of short-term notes .......... | 10,000 | | |
|       Total other sources .......... | | $14,000 | |
|    Total cash provided, 1978 ...... | | | 182,000 |
| Total cash ........................... | | | $234,000 |
| Cash used for: | | | |
|       Increase in sinking fund .......... | $15,000 | | |
|       Payment on short-term bank notes .. | 50,000 | | |
|       Payment on long-term notes ....... | 20,000 | | |
|       Purchase of land ................ | 75,000 | | |
|       Payment of dividends (1978) ...... | 20,000 | | |
|    Total cash used during year .... | | | $180,000 |
| Ending cash balance (December 31, 1978) .... | | | $54,000 |

ure and adding or deducting therefrom the noncash items included on the income statement. This computation is found in Table 6–1 under the section of the statement labeled "cash provided by operations."

There are no cash expenditures entailed in depreciation, provision for bad debts, and losses on the sale of fixed assets; therefore, the total for these items is added to the net income figure in the adjustment process. Changes in current asset and liability accounts are also adjustments to convert income from accrual to a cash basis. For example, an increase in inventory balances during the year would require additional cash payments even though such balances would not affect net income until sold. However, if accounts payable also increased, the amount of cash required would be less. In table 6–1 both inventories and payables went down by $5,000 and $4,000, respectively; therefore, a net cash flow of $1,000 was generated during the year by the decrease in inventories. Continuing, a decrease during the year in accounts receivable supplied a $36,000 cash-inflow because funds were not required to finance the beginning year higher balance. Finally, other items which increase the reported income figures on the income statement, but which do not result in cash-inflows (extraordinary gains, on sale of fixed assets), must be deducted from the income figure to arrive at cash provided by operations.

The next step in the statement preparation involves the identification of sources of cash originating outside of the normal operations of the firm. This category frequently includes the major sources of the firm's outside financing. The "other sources" consist of the proceeds from the sale of assets, and the issuance of debt and stock. These items, together with "cash generated by operations," are totaled to yield the cash generated by the firm during the period.

Lastly, the cash-flow statement details the uses of cash during the period. In Table 6–1, cash was used for sinking-fund payments, to pay short- and long-term notes coming due, to purchase additional land for expansion, and for payment of dividends. The net result was a $2,000 increase in the cash balance during the year.

Using the historical information given in a flow-of-funds statement, the financial manager receives a picture of internal and external operations that affect cash. For instance, he should seek to answer questions such as: What portion of cash is generated by current operations as opposed to other sources? Will total cash be sufficient to cover proposed cash outflows? Will a given level of dividends endanger the firm's cash position? What new sources of cash are available to the firm? Management must maintain a proper balance between profitability and liquidity to prevent technical insolvency (the inability to pay debts in the ordinary course of business). An inadequacy of cash to meet its obligations can cause financial embarrassment even to a firm having a large net income. Sufficiency of cash flow is therefore of paramount importance to management.

*Working-Capital-Flow Statement.* The working-capital-flow statement is a financial document that indicates changes in the sources and uses of funds affecting the amount of net working capital of a firm during an accounting period. This statement differs from the cash-flow statement in that it emphasizes the causes of changes in net working capital, not cash. The only difference between a working-capital-flow statement and a cash-flow statement is the disregarding of the changes in various current assets and current liabilities. Bankers are among the chief users of the working-capital-flow statement since they frequently require that the borrower maintain a minimum net working-capital amount, particularly on term loans. Frequently, long-term bond issues require that net working capital be maintained at a predetermined level. Otherwise, the firm might be able to pay dividends or purchase fixed assets to the detriment of the bondholders' annual interest requirements, or even payment of the issue itself. Hence, this statement would be of great concern to the bond trustee and to the investors in the firm's long-term bond issues.

# 6 Financial Forecasting Statements

## Cash Budgeting

The cash-flow statement provides pertinent data in a single statement of the past financial operations of the firm. An analysis of this statement is the proper starting point in the preparation of a cash budget. It shows from what sources the cash has been derived in the past and where it has been used. Thus, a cash-flow statement can show management where problem areas might develop, and perhaps corrective actions may be taken before the situation deteriorates significantly. A study of the past cash flows will assist the firm's managers in forecasting the cash position of the firm for specified periods in the future. The vehicle for making these future projections is the cash budget.

A cash budget is a summary of the anticipated cash receipts and disbursements for a forthcoming period of time, such as a month, a quarter, or a year. It is frequently used to forecast cash requirements to meet quarterly dividend and tax payments and requirements for bond redemption and plant expansion, but there is an equally important need for its use in planning for monthly or quarterly requirements. In order to work effectively, policies as to product mix, sales position, pricing, and financing must be appraised and modified, if necessary, in conjunction with the cash budget. Should a sizable cash deficit for any part of the forecast period be indicated, the entire plan of operation may have to be re-examined. It may be determined that sales estimates are too high, credit terms too generous, inventories too large because of too many product lines, prices too low or too high on some items, cash dividends too generous, and many other factors, such as too much cash being earmarked for capital expenditures. Many of the foregoing situations can be corrected by changing internal company policies.

The forecasts of cash receipts and expenditures and the estimates of cash balances may be short-term (from one week to a year) or long-term (for periods in excess of a year). The extent of the various forecasts is determined by the nature of the operations of the particular firm and by the purposes for which they are intended. For example, the cash-budgeting period would be short for firms with highly variable prices and sales, low cash balances, or relatively narrow margins of profit. For such firms, the cash budget may be prepared on a monthly basis.

While long-term cash budgets include those in excess of a year, they are much less detailed and more tentative in nature. Long-term cash forecasts are useful for proper planning in order to avoid excessive cash dividend disbursements. Frequently, dividend payments are more stable than corporate profits or cash flow. Therefore, an estimate of future cash receipts and expenditures would be helpful in setting the dividend rate, and possibly in the timing of sales of new securities.

It should be pointed out that a cash budget is but one step in the budgetary process, albeit an important one. Sales for future periods are first estimated; in turn they provide the foundation for other forecasts such as production, merchandise acquisition, selling and administrative, and all other operations of the firm. The cash budget functions to relate all of the these activities in terms of their effect on expected cash receipts and disbursements. It should be clear that the accuracy of the cash budget necessarily depends upon the accuracy of the estimates used in the sales and other forecasts.

## Cash Budgets

The cash budget is typically an analysis of management's estimates of future operations in order to derive expected cash receipts and disbursements during some future time period. The principle involved is that cash does not necessarily change hands at the same time that revenues are earned and expenses are incurred. Cash budgets purport to show the expected cash receipts and cash disbursements during a specified period, which may either lead or lag the specific revenues or expenses that generated the cash flow.

A cash budget deals with a discrete time period. Because it is a forecast of anticipated cash expenditures, cash receipts, and the resulting cash balance, it can be constructed for one month, and then extended month by month for three, six, nine months, or a year. The longer the period, the less reliable the forecast tends to be because of changing conditions, some of which may be favorable and others detrimental. Although the budget may be used for control purposes, operating policies must be flexible enough to make adjustments to conform to changes as they occur. Thus, periodic revisions are necessary to meet changes in conditions.

Usually, the cash budget is divided into two major sections: expected cash receipts, and expected cash disbursements (see Table 6–2). The first step in its preparation entails an evaluation of sales forecasts to determine timing of the resultant cash receipts. Knowledge of past financial records, general economic conditions, and past, present, and future credit policies of the firm will be important in order to ascertain the distribution of cash receipts over current and future periods. For example, a current period's cash receipts will normally consist of cash from the current period's sales, that is, collections on accounts receivable.

Having derived the total cash receipts for the period or periods, next it is necessary to determine what disbursements will be made. Forecasts of future operations are as necessary here as they were in determining the timing of cash receipts. Expenses are estimated, and then the periods requiring cash outlays are determined. As an example, if the firm purchases materials on which the credit terms are 1/30, n/60,[1] it may attempt

---

[1] This notation reflects a credit arrangement whereby the purchaser who pays cash within 30 days of the sale will receive a 1-percent discount; however, the entire amount is due within 60 days.

to pay the bill before the end of 30 days in order to take advantage of the discount. Therefore, items purchased in one month will normally be paid for in the next. Thus, in the cash budget, material purchased last month but paid for in the current month will be reflected as a cash disbursement in the period in which it is paid, that is, the current month.

A similar analysis should be extended to other items of expense such as manufacturing costs, labor, selling and administrative expenses, taxes, and interest. Any item for which a cash outflow will be associated in the specified period under review should be depicted as a cash disbursement in the cash budget for that period. It is important to remember that those items of expense which do not entail cash outflows should not be included in expected cash disbursements. Such items include, among others, depreciation, bad debt expense, and amortization of intangible assets.

*Monthly Cash Budget.* The procedures outlined in the preceding section are illustrated in the cash budget in Table 6–2. The closing January cash-budget figure may be estimated for a firm by making a number of assumptions along with information obtained from the ending balance sheet. Continuing, sales are assumed to equal one twelfth of the forecasted sales for the coming year. The amount of cash and inventories on hand can be obtained from last year's balance sheet. Other required data depend upon assumptions on past data and future expectations, which in this instance are: inventory costs are equal to 60 percent of net sales; cash sales are 70 percent of net sales; credit terms for buying and selling are 2/10, net 30; and the income tax provision is 10 percent of net sales. Thus, the cash budget for a hypothetical firm might be as shown in Table 6–2.

The anticipated budget for January reveals an increase in cash, no borrowing or lending, and apparently no collection problems on credit sales. The operating budget is based on past experience and anticipated sales for the month; the cash position is expected to be adequate so that

**TABLE 6–2**
**Cash Budget for the Month of January 1979**

| | | | |
|---|---|---|---|
| Cash balance, January 1, 1979 . . . . . . . . . . . . . . . . . . . . | | | $2,500 |
| Expected cash receipts (January 1979): | | | |
|   Cash sales (70% of net sales, $70,000) minus | | | |
|     2% cash discount ($980) . . . . . . . . . . . . . . . . . . . | $48,020 | | |
|   Collections, previous credit sales (30 days) . . . . . . . | 18,000 | | |
|     Total cash receipts . . . . . . . . . . . . . . . . . . . . . . . . . | | $66,020 | |
| Expected cash expenditures: | | | |
|   Payment for purchases (60% of net sales, $70,000) | | | |
|     minus discount (2% net 10 days) . . . . . . . . . . . | $41,160 | | |
|   Operating expenses . . . . . . . . . . . . . . . . . . . . . . . . | 15,000 | | |
|   Income tax (10% of sales) . . . . . . . . . . . . . . . . . . . . | 7,000 | | |
|     Total payments . . . . . . . . . . . . . . . . . . . . . . . . . . | | 63,160 | |
| Receipts less payments . . . . . . . . . . . . . . . . . . . . . . . . . | | | 2,860 |
|     Cash balance, January 31, 1979 . . . . . . . . . . . | | | $5,360 |

the firm may take its cash discounts. The increase in the ending cash balance is because of the increase in the volume of sales, 70 percent of which were for cash. However, the budget contains no provisions for cash dividends or short-term investments.

*Yearly Cash Budget.* A yearly cash budget is constructed on a month-to-month basis for the entire year. For example, in Table 6–3 the yearly budget assumes that: (1) sales are 50 percent cash, discounted at 2 percent and the remainder 30-day credit; (2) other income from investments is $40,000, paid $10,000 each quarter; (3) raw materials, payroll, and other factory expenses vary directly with sales; and (4) fixed expenses include advertising, selling, administrative, bond sinking fund, and other payments. The use of a cash budget makes it possible for management to forecast the need for bank loans in January, February, and March.

Fulfillment of plans for growth depends in part on the ability of the firm to generate cash in excess of current needs. Expenditures for new equipment, like other expenditures, should be anticipated. In many cases it is necessary to supplement cash generated by operations with funds obtained from outside sources in order to finance these acquisitions. In the case of borrowed funds, future cash budgets would be increased by interest and debt repayment obligations. The minimum penalties for improper cash budgeting are possible higher interest costs and less favorable contracts for both short- and long-term borrowings. This can happen because cash shortages require immediate funds to cover the firm's commitments. More severe cash problems may ensue if borrowing is not possible on relatively short notice.

## Forecasting Statements

Projected, or "pro forma," statements can be made to assist the financial manager in estimating the effects of current decisions upon the operations of the firm. Essentially, these pro forma statements summarize all the forecasts and assumptions made by management pertaining to specific periods and place them within the framework of the familiar financial position and income statements. Pro forma statements are tools which are commonly applied for planning and control purposes.

For planning purposes, pro forma statements are used initially to evaluate the decisions and plans adopted for the coming period. By incorporating planned policies and decisions into standard financial statements, projected figures for the period can be derived. In the event that the results appear to differ from expectations or goals, changes and modifications can be made concurrently to achieve more palatable results.

Another role of pro forma statements lies in the area of financial control. Acting as budgets, pro forma statements can be compared with actual results. Differences can be evaluated to identify unforeseen problems, or to modify existing forecasting techniques.

## TABLE 6–3
## X COMPANY—Cash Budget, 1979 (in thousands)

| | Jan. | Feb. | Mar. | April | May | June | July | Aug. | Sept. | Oct. | Nov. | Dec. |
|---|---|---|---|---|---|---|---|---|---|---|---|---|
| **Expected cash receipts:** | | | | | | | | | | | | |
| Cash sales (50%, 2% discount) | $490 | $539 | $588 | $637 | $686 | $735 | $784 | $735 | $686 | $588 | $490 | $392 |
| Collection, accounts receivable (30 days) | 400 | 500 | 550 | 600 | 650 | 700 | 750 | 800 | 750 | 700 | 600 | 500 |
| Other income (interest) | 10 | | | 10 | | | 10 | | | 10 | | |
| Total cash receipts | $900 | $1,039 | $1,138 | $1,247 | $1,336 | $1,435 | $1,544 | $1,535 | $1,436 | $1,298 | $1,090 | $892 |
| **Expected cash payments:** | | | | | | | | | | | | |
| Raw material (10% of sales) | 100 | 110 | 120 | 130 | 140 | 150 | 160 | 150 | 140 | 120 | 100 | 80 |
| Payroll (50% of sales) | 500 | 550 | 600 | 650 | 700 | 750 | 800 | 750 | 700 | 600 | 500 | 400 |
| Other factory expense (1% of sales) | 10 | 11 | 12 | 13 | 14 | 15 | 16 | 15 | 14 | 12 | 10 | 8 |
| Advertising | 1 | 1 | 1 | 1 | 1 | 1 | 1 | 1 | 1 | 1 | 1 | 1 |
| Selling expenses | 4 | 4 | 4 | 4 | 4 | 4 | 4 | 4 | 4 | 4 | 4 | 4 |
| Administration expenses | 100 | 100 | 100 | 100 | 100 | 100 | 100 | 100 | 100 | 100 | 100 | 100 |
| Bond sinking fund | 125 | 125 | 125 | 125 | 125 | 125 | 125 | 125 | 125 | 125 | 125 | 125 |
| Other payments | 75 | 75 | 75 | 75 | 75 | 75 | 75 | 75 | 75 | 75 | 75 | 75 |
| Total cash payments | $915 | $976 | $1,037 | $1,098 | $1,159 | $1,220 | $1,281 | $1,220 | $1,159 | $1,037 | $915 | $793 |
| **Expected cash balance:** | | | | | | | | | | | | |
| (Beginning) | (101) | (116) | (53) | 48 | 197 | 374 | 589 | 852 | 1,167 | 1,444 | 1,705 | 1,880 |
| Increase or decrease | (15) | 63 | 101 | 149 | 177 | 215 | 263 | 315 | 277 | 261 | 175 | 99 |
| Ending cash balance | (116) | (53) | 48 | 197 | 374 | 589 | 852 | 1,167 | 1,444 | 1,705 | 1,880 | 1,979 |

Pro forma statements are effectively employed in conjunction with cash budgets; however, whereas the cash budget is on a cash accounting basis, pro forma statements are prepared on an accrual basis. The most common projected statements of this type are the pro forma income, and pro forma financial position.

**Pro Forma Income Statement.** The pro forma income statement estimates future net income based on forecasts and assumptions about sales and costs. It incorporates much of the data contained in the cash budget, but operates on an accrual rather than a cash basis. Here again, the vital bit of information is sales for the period. A sales estimate can be developed in a number of ways, among which are forecasts from sales representatives, economic analysts or other outside consultants, marketing managers, or any subjective combination of these.

Given the sales estimate for the period, the next variable to project is the cost of goods sold. The simplest means of estimating this figure is by resorting to historical ratios adjusted for known differences from past operations. Thus if cost of goods sold has been stable in relation to sales, use of either the cost ratio or gross profit margin rate will enable cost of goods sold to be estimated. This method is used in the statement shown in Table 6–4 where the gross margin rate is 40 percent of sales, thereby resulting in a cost ratio of 60 percent (100 − 40).

**TABLE 6–4**

ABC MERCHANDISE CO.
Pro Forma Income Statement
For Period Ending December 31, 1979

| | | |
|---|---:|---:|
| Estimated sales | | $100,000 |
| Less estimated cost of goods sold (60% × $100,000) | | 60,000 |
| Estimated gross margin | | $ 40,000 |
| Less: estimated expenses: | | |
|    Selling and administrative | $10,000 | |
|    Interest | 2,500 | |
|    Other expenses | 1,500 | 14,000 |
| Estimated net income before taxes | | $26,000 |
| Less: income taxes (40%) | | 10,400 |
| Estimated net income | | $15,600 |

Unfortunately, such an approach does not always produce accurate results. Fluctuating prices and uncertain economic and business conditions are but two examples of factors which would affect the relationship between sales and cost of sales. Another means of estimating the cost of goods sold requires the forecasting of the levels of its component parts, that is, direct and indirect costs of production. Materials can be projected on the basis of prices expected to be in effect during the period. In the same manner, labor costs can be estimated by reference to current costs, and any expected wage-rate revisions. By reference to the production schedule, other costs can be approximated for the period under review.

An example of a pro forma income statement where each expense has been estimated directly is shown in Table 6–5. It has been simplified for illustration purposes by assuming a single-product firm. In a typical company where many different products are produced and sold, separate schedules and budgets are used to accumulate costs for each product line.

TABLE 6–5

X MANUFACTURING CO.
Pro Forma Income Statement
For Period Ending December 31, 1979

| | | | |
|---|---|---:|---:|
| Estimated revenues: | | | |
| Sales (200,000 units @ $4.50 ea.) | | | $900,000 |
| Less estimated cost of goods sold: | | | |
| Beginning inventory | | $ 13,500 | |
| Materials ($.50/unit) | $100,000 | | |
| Labor ($1.25/unit) | 250,000 | | |
| Depreciation (plant and equipment) | 200,000 | | |
| Other indirect costs | 82,000 | | |
| Total production costs | | 632,000 | |
| Total available | | $645,500 | |
| Less projected ending inventory | | 15,500 | |
| Estimated cost of goods sold | | | 630,000 |
| Estimated gross margin | | | $270,000 |
| Less estimated operating expenses: | | | |
| Selling and administrative | | $90,000 | |
| Financial expenses | | 18,000 | |
| Other | | 12,000 | |
| Estimated operating expenses | | | 120,000 |
| Estimated net income before taxes | | | 150,000 |
| Estimated tax liability (40%) | | | 60,000 |
| Estimated net income | | | $ 90,000 |

Other operating expenses can be estimated using past operations as the basis; but, adjustment must be made for conditions expected to prevail during the future period. The effects of current or future decisions may well negate the historical costs of the firm.

Making a pro forma income statement will force the firm's management to develop plans for controlling expense items under its control. This is especially true if the projections serve as a basis for rating performance when the pro forma income statement is compared to the actual outcome at the close of the period.

If it is warranted, management may find it useful to revise the pro forma income statement as time passes, taking into consideration significant changes of various expense or revenue categories. Of course, it may be worthwhile to prepare a range of pro forma income statements based upon a range of possible sales estimates.

*Pro Forma Balance Sheets.* The projected time interval for a pro forma balance sheet may be a budget year, a season, or a month. The length of the projection depends on management's use of the statement. For example, if the statement is made to provide information for obtaining a 90-day bank loan, a quarterly projection would be most useful. If the firm's sales are highly seasonal, it may be helpful to cover the season rather than an arbitrary time period.

Historical data is the logical starting point for the pro forma balance sheet. However, since many firms experience some growth and operate in a nonstatic economic environment, historical data must be adapted to obtain a valid estimate of future conditions. Probably the most important estimate required for projecting the balance sheet and income statements is net sales. Over a period of time many firms develop a relatively consistent relationship between sales volume and certain items, such as current assets and liabilities. Thus, it is possible to develop a pro forma balance sheet that is based primarily upon the sales estimate. The accuracy of the entire forecast rests on the reliability of the sales estimate, thereby requiring the utmost care in its development.

Let us assume that the X Corporation faces a growing demand for its product, and plans to purchase equipment for expansion with a bank loan of a year's maturity have been formulated. The current balance sheet for December 31, 1978, is shown below. A three-year historical analysis (1976–78) reveals that some balance sheet items vary consistently with sales, as shown in parentheses.

### X CORPORATION
### Balance Sheet
### December 31, 1978

| Current Assets | | Current Liabilities | |
|---|---|---|---|
| Cash (5%) | $ 100,000 | Accounts payable (12%) | $ 240,000 |
| Receivables (15%) | 300,000 | Provision for income | |
| Inventory (8%) | 160,000 | tax (6%) | 120,000 |
| Total Current Assets | $ 560,000 | Total Current Liabilities | $ 360,000 |
| *Fixed Assets* | | *Net Worth* | |
| Gross | $1,500,000 | Capital stock | $ 980,000 |
| Accrued depreciation | 440,000 | Retained earnings | 280,000 |
| Net Fixed Assets | $1,060,000 | Total Net Worth | $1,260,000 |
| Total Assets | $1,620,000 | Total Liabilities and Net Worth | $1,620,000 |

The current ratio is 1.56:1, and the quick ratio is 1.11:1. Let us assume that the quick ratio is adequate but the current ratio is only marginal for this type of firm.

# 6 Financial Forecasting Statements

At the request of the bank, the X Corporation prepares the following pro forma balance sheet showing the effect of the proposed bank loan of $200,000.

**X CORPORATION**
Pro Forma Balance Sheet
On December 31, 1978
Showing the Effect of Bank Loan

| Current Assets | | Current Liabilities | |
|---|---|---|---|
| Cash | $ 100,000 | Accounts payable | $ 240,000 |
| Receivables | 300,000 | Provision for income tax | 120,000 |
| Inventory | 160,000 | Bank loan | 200,000 |
| Total Current Assets | 560,000 | Total Current Liabilities | $ 560,000 |
| Fixed Assets | | Net Worth | |
| Gross | $1,700,000 | Capital stock | $ 980,000 |
| Accrued depreciation | 440,000 | Retained earnings | 280,000 |
| | | Total Net Worth | $1,260,000 |
| Net Fixed Assets | 1,260,000 | Total Liabilities | |
| Total Assets | $1,820,000 | and Net Worth | $1,820,000 |

The borrowing will cause the current ratio to fall to 1:1 and the quick ratio to decline to .71:1. Thus the corporation may be endangering its future borrowing capacity and its ability to pay its current liabilities.

However, if the demand for the firm's product remains strong, X Corporation might consider expanding its productive capacity by investing an additional $200,000; but, rather than endangering its ability to pay its current obligations, it should consider a term loan with a maturity long enough to repay it out of the incremental cash flows in future years.

## Summary

The cash-flow statement is an historical analysis of where the cash came from and how it was used. This statement permits management to evaluate the firm's past performance, and it may give a possible clue to where future problem areas might occur.

The need for cash is common to all business firms; hence, the management of any firm must know the firm's cash position. Because a shortage of cash may cause a firm to cease operations, management must plan for cash flows as well as income. The cash budget is an indispensable aid because it requires a forecast of income, expenditures, and a cash balance for a future period.

Cash budgeting permits better timing of disbursements to coincide with receipts, thereby possibly avoiding some short-term borrowing that otherwise might be necessary. Because the cash budget is a forecast of anticipated cash receipts, expenditures, and the resulting cash balance, it can be constructed for one month and then extended month by month. In addition to the monthly cash budget, yearly cash budgets are frequently made for management's use. Although it is prudent for management to follow a cash budget for control purposes, policies must be flexible enough to permit necessary adjustments in response to changing conditions.

Pro forma statements can be made to aid the financial manager in forecasting the effects of current decisions upon future operations. Basically the pro forma statements summarize future plans and couch them within the familiar framework of financial position and income statements. Thus, pro forma statements can be used as vehicles for financial control. Acting as budgets, pro forma statements can be compared with actual results. Differences can be identified, and if required, corrective actions may be taken.

When planning external financing, pro forma statements, such as cash budgets, balance sheets, and income statements, are useful to test the possible effects of the prospective borrowing or equity issues. A projected balance sheet can disclose weaknesses in proposed plans, such as a low current ratio, thereby signaling to management possible adverse effects of its proposed actions. The key projection in pro forma statements is the estimate of sales, since the level of sales may have a direct bearing on many of the expenditures likely to be incurred by the firm during the forecast period.

## QUESTIONS

1. Why is the sales forecast basic to the entire budgeting process?
2. In making a cash-flow statement, determine whether each of the following items is a source or use of funds. What is the effect of:
   a. An increase in the cash balance?
   b. A purchase of long-term notes payable in the open market?
   c. An increase in inventories?
   d. A sale of excess land?
   e. A decrease in current receivables?
3. Explain how a downturn in a firm's sales could have the effect of generating excess cash.
4. Explain: "Depreciation of fixed assets, amortization of patents, estimated uncollectibles, and other valuation accounts do not affect cash but do reduce profits."
5. Is it necessary to make cash budgets if the firm typically carries sufficient cash to handle all but extraordinary needs?
6. How would you correct a situation wherein the cash position is unsatisfactory due to the fact that the volume of business is too large relative to the firm's assets?
7. Why are bankers interested in cash budgets and pro forma balance sheets?
8. "Since accurate forecasts of cash are difficult, cash budgets of over a month's duration are not meaningful." Why is this attitude questionable?
9. How can pro forma statements be used as a means of financial control?

# 6 Financial Forecasting Statements

## PROBLEMS

1. The controller of the J Corporation wants to construct a cash budget for the month ending July 31, 1979. The following information is furnished to him by the various departments:
   a. Cash balance on July 1, 1979 is $3,250.
   b. July sales are forecast at 800 units.
   c. Sales price per unit is $10.
   d. 50 percent of the sales are in cash and receive a 3-percent discount.
   e. Credit sales are 3/15, net 30 days.
   f. Collections from previous sales should be $3,750 during July.
   g. Operating expenses will be $6,750.
   h. A $1,000 loan payment is due on July 23, 1979.
   i. 20 percent of net sales goes toward payment of purchases.
   What is the end-of-the-month cash balance?

2. X Manufacturing Co. Intends to replace an operating machine on April 1, 1981. Given the data below, will your firm have sufficient cash on that date to cover a cost of the machine of $10,000? (Prepare monthly cash budgets for the first quarter of 1981.)
   a. Actual and forecasted sales are:

   | | | | | |
   |---|---|---|---|---|
   | November | $28,000 | | February | $20,000 |
   | December | 35,000 | | March | 25,000 |
   | January | 15,000 | | April | 22,000 |

   b. All sales are made on credit, and accounts receivable are collected entirely in the month after sale. Purchases each month are made to satisfy next month's forecasted sales, and are paid the month after incurred.
   c. The gross margin has historically been 30 percent and is expected to remain so over the next year. Other cash expenses amount to $5,000 a month.
   d. Accrued taxes must be paid January 1 and July 1 of every year.
   e. Annual mortgage interest is due on March 1.
   f. X's balance sheet as of December 31, 1980, is:

   | Assets | | Liabilities and Owner's Equity | |
   |---|---|---|---|
   | Cash | $ 3,000 | Accounts payable | $10,500 |
   | Accounts receivable | 35,000 | Accrued taxes | 5,400 |
   | Inventory | 10,500 | Mortgage note @ 8% | 10,000 |
   | Fixed assets | 40,000 | Common stock | 15,000 |
   | | | Retained earnings | 47,600 |
   | Total | $88,500 | Total | $88,500 |

3. Management has approached the B Bank in regard to a $250,000 loan. This loan would be repaid in five annual installments of $50,000 each. The proceeds from the loan would be used as follows:
   a. $50,000 to reduce trade payables.
   b. $25,000 to increase cash balance.
   c. $50,000 to purchase inventory.
   d. $25,000 to pay off a bank note to the A Bank.
   e. $100,000 to purchase fixed assets.

Given the current balance sheet (shown below) and the uses of the loan, prepare a pro forma balance sheet.

Balance Sheet
December 31, 1978
(figures in thousands)

| | | | |
|---|---|---|---|
| Cash | $ 100 | Notes payable—A Bank | $ 300 |
| Receivables | 500 | Note payable—B Bank | 100 |
| Inventory | 600 | Trade payables | 200 |
| Current Assets | $1,200 | Accruals | 200 |
| Building and fixed assets | 800 | Current Liabilities | $ 800 |
| Other assets | 200 | Term debt | 500 |
| | | Common stock | 200 |
| | | Retained earnings | 700 |
| Total Assets | $2,200 | Total Liabilities and Net Worth | $2,200 |

4. The comparative balance sheet for the XYZ Company for December 31, 1977 and 1978 is as follows:

XYZ COMPANY
(figures in thousands)

| | 1977 | 1978 |
|---|---|---|
| Current assets | $1,200 | $1,400 |
| Fixed assets | 800 | 1,500 |
| Other assets | 200 | 100 |
| Total Assets | $2,200 | $3,000 |
| | | |
| Current liabilities | $ 800 | $1,100 |
| Term debt | 520 | 900 |
| Common stock | 200 | 200 |
| Retained earnings | 680 | 800 |
| Total Liabilities and Equity | $2,200 | $3,000 |

Construct a working-capital-flow statement for the XYZ Company for 1978. Did the increase in fixed assets contribute to a deterioration in the current position (current assets and liabilities)?

## ADDITIONAL READINGS

Chambers, J. C., S. K. Mullick, and D. D. Smith. "How To Choose the Right Forecasting Technique," *Harvard Business Review*, vol. 49 (July–August 1971), pp. 45–74.

Parker, G. C., and E. L. Segura. "How to Get a Better Forecast," *Harvard Business Review*, vol. 49 (March–April 1971), pp. 99–109.

Raun, D. L. "The Limitations of Profit Graphs, Break-Even Analysis, and Budgets," *Accounting Review*, vol. 39 (October 1964), pp. 927–45.

Weston, J. F. "Forecasting Financial Requirements," *Accounting Review*, vol. 33 (July 1958), pp. 427–40.

# 7

# Management of Cash and Marketable Securities

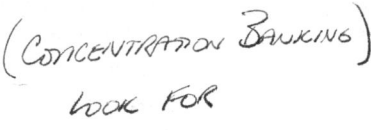
(CONCENTRATION BANKING)
LOOK FOR

The previous chapter was concerned with cash budgets and other forecasting statements. The efficient management of the firm's cash resources is the subject of this chapter. A firm's liquid assets are made up of cash and marketable securities. This chapter discusses the cash management function, particularly methods of handling cash receipts efficiently, determining the appropriate mix of cash and marketable securities, and investing excess funds temporarily.

## Cash Balances

A firm holds cash or its equivalent for three motives. They are transactions, precautionary, and speculative. A firm must hold cash resources to satisfy the first two motives; however, whether funds are held to satisfy the third is optional.

The transactions motive for holding cash is important because of the necessity of meeting day-to-day operations. Cash, and only cash, is required to carry out these normal activities.

The precautionary motive, however, generally can be satisfied by cash or near-cash assets. The greater the certainty of the cash flow, the lower the precautionary balances the firm will have to hold. In addition to the cash assets of the firm, good banking connections are a valuable resource that can be drawn upon should the need arise to satisfy the precautionary motive.

Holding cash for the speculative motive would be for the purpose of maintaining liquidity to take advantage of favorable changes in security prices. Thus, if interest rates are expected to fall significantly, the firm should invest in fixed-income securities immediately to take advantage of the rise in prices of debt-oriented securities. Conversely, if interest rates are expected to increase substantially, debt issues currently held should be sold and the proceeds held in cash until the forecasted increase is completed. Since most firms do not hold cash for the purposes of speculating on interest-rate changes, the present chapter is primarily concerned with holding cash or near-cash assets for the transactions and precautionary motives.

Taking into consideration the above motives for holding cash, the formulation of a management policy regarding the cash balance to be held by the firm poses many problems. For example, what should be the minimum cash balance the firm should hold? When cash inflows exceed cash outflows, how should the excess cash be invested? If cash is to be invested, for how long? If demands for cash exceed available cash assets, how should the excess demands be financed? The cash budget is instrumental in resolving these questions since it may indicate possible future cash imbalances during the budget period.

## Cash Management

Cash is the most liquid of assets, and as such is subject to the greatest misuse. Historically, the safeguarding of cash funds has been the main focus of cash management, and despite the expansion and sophistication of the cash management role it still receives major attention.

As cash circulates throughout the business operation, the best safeguard is an adequate system of internal control. Essential features include a plan of organization showing lines of authority, a good accounting system, and able and reliable personnel in responsible positions. These manifest themselves into policies which help to ensure that cash which should have been received was in fact received, and that cash disbursements are made only for authorized purposes.

A major rule of thumb to follow states that no single person should manage a transaction from beginning to end. This policy gives rise to the separation of authority and the division of the firm into separate departments. Thus the work of one person or department serves as a check on the accuracy and efficiency of another.

The accounting system is the key source of information for evaluating actual performance and formulating future plans. Both the cash-flow and cash budget analyses described in the preceding chapter are used to some extent by a corporation's management. The ability to predict future sources and uses of cash, and the partial resolution of the uncertainty surrounding the timing of cash flows, is essential to the efficient management of the firm's cash resources. A cash forecast should provide a reasonably good estimate of cash inflows and outflows as well as the cash position over some defined time horizon. With such information, management can ensure that there is sufficient cash to meet demands by arranging short- or long-term financing as required, or by planning to invest excess cash in marketable securities.

***Cash Sales and Collections.*** In many business operations, cash inflows are principally in the form of cash sales. Once again, the principal means of control should be the division of responsibility between receiving cash and recording it. However, this is not practical for small firms or retail stores, and additional measures must be taken. Two of the most prevalent are the cash register and the form-writing machine. In both cases a record of the day's sales is kept locked within the machine, removed by a supervisor at the end of the day, and compared with actual receipts.

Effectively managing cash collections serves a dual role in maintaining control over cash remitted by customers, and in increasing the amount of cash available to the firm by reducing the time between mailing and crediting the firm's accounts. The latter is referred to as "float," and can be reduced by implementing one of two major methods: the lock-box system or concentration banking. If either is successful, the amount of cash required to conduct the firm's operation can be reduced. The released cash funds can be used elsewhere in the business or perhaps used to reduce indebtedness.

Area concentration banking is most conducive to large national or regional firms who have many small offices scattered throughout a region or regions of the country and these offices act as payment points for customers. Illustrations of such organizations are several of the national retail department store chains and some insurance companies. The collection points will usually receive most customer remittances within one day of mailing. When payments are received by the collection center, they are immediately deposited in a local bank. The funds are then sent to a regional bank where the firm maintains its principal account used to make disbursements. These transfers are usually effected by either a bank wire or transfer check, which is a check drawn on the local bank and payable to the firm's regional bank. Further transfers may be made to the firm's major bank or disbursements may be made directly from the regional bank balances.

Probably the most common method employed to speed up collections is the lock-box. A lock-box is a post office box rented by the firm to which customers mail their payments. These boxes are usually located regionally to minimize the time it takes for the payments to reach the box location. The firm then instructs a local bank to service the box, that is, the bank collects the payments from the box, processes the checks, and forwards the details of the payments to the firm's accounts receivable department for recording. For example, a Chicago-based firm can direct its West Coast customers to send their remittances to a lock-box in San Francisco. The designated San Francisco bank periodically picks up the checks, credits the firm's account, and then notifies the firm. The bank clears the checks locally and wires available funds to the firm's Chicago bank. By doing this, the collection process is speeded up, sometimes significantly. The lock-box system eliminates the time lost in mailing the checks directly to Chicago, processing them there, depositing them in a Chicago bank, and then waiting for the funds to be collected.

The objective in both the concentration banking scheme and the lock-box system is to reduce mail delivery time, processing time, and collection time, thereby increasing the amount of cash which is available to the firm for operations. A corollary policy concerning disbursements maintains that cash disbursements should be delayed to the last possible moment. The firm should take all cash discounts by timing payments to be received on the last day of the discount period. If discounts are not available, payments should be made on the due date. Nevertheless, care should be taken at all times to maintain the firm's good standing with creditors and customers.

**The Cash Balance.** While the stewardship function of cash management is still of major significance, cash management also recognizes that there is an opportunity cost attached to the holding of cash. Thus it is desirable to minimize cash kept by the firm, yet ensure that it is sufficient to cover the firm's demand for it. As mentioned earlier, a firm may hold cash or its equivalent for three primary motives: transactions, precautionary, and speculative. The transactions motive is of major concern because every dollar on hand can be used for day-to-day operations, and each dollar on hand is subject to the same opportunity costs incurred by changing levels of interest rates and prices. Perhaps a better view sees cash as both an earning asset (used in the productive process), and as a financial asset (having an opportunity cost associated with its use). The objective of the firm should be the utilization of cash so as to maximize its utility to the firm.

**Economic Order Quantity.** Attempts have been made to construct analytical models which purport to maximize utility with respect to the firm's cash balance. Recognizing the similarity between managing cash balances and managing physical inventory, William Baumol adapted the economic order quantity model to cash asset management.[1] The model seeks to find the optimal transaction balance which the firm should maintain. In this model there are two pertinent costs to be considered. First, interest is lost by holding cash instead of interest-earning marketable securities. Second, a fixed cost (broker's fee) is involved in the buying and selling of securities. Figure 7–1 shows the *EOQ* model in diagrammatic form.

In the *EOQ* cash model, it is assumed that disbursements in the present period are paid out of receipts from a previous period. In order to use

---

[1] William J. Baumol, "The Transactions Demand for Cash: An Inventory Theoretic Approach," *Quarterly Journal of Economics* (November 1952), pp. 545–56.

## 7 Management of Cash and Marketable Securities

**FIGURE 7–1**
**EOQ Model for Cash**

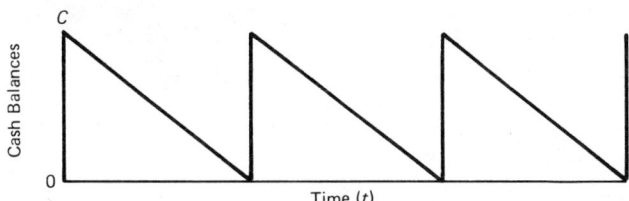

this model, transactions must be able to be forecast accurately. As a consequence, the quantity of cash to cover transactions in the present period is known with certainty. Also, the transactions are assumed to be evenly distributed during the period and are equal in amount.

Using the same assumptions and the notation of Baumol, assume that:

$T$ = Total dollar transactions to be paid out evenly over the period.
$i$ = Interest opportunity cost.
$C$ = Size of periodic cash withdrawals used to pay $T$.
$b$ = Broker's fee per transaction (assumed constant).
$T/C$ = Number of withdrawals per year.
$\dfrac{bT}{C}$ = Total brokers' fees.
$C/2$ = Average cash holdings. ($\frac{1}{2}$ of C)
$\dfrac{iC}{2}$ = Annual interest cost of holding cash.

Now, let us assume the firm starts with $C$ dollars in cash; when this amount has been disbursed it acquires $C$ more dollars by selling securities. Given the transactions amount for the year ($T$) and $C$, the firm is involved in $T/C$ withdrawals during the year. If $b$ is the broker's fee, the total fixed cost to the firm of making this number of withdrawals is $b(T/C)$. The opportunity cost of holding cash is $i(C/2)$, where $i$ is the interest rate on securities and $C/2$ is the average cash holdings for the year. The total cost to the firm is then:

$$\overline{TC} = b\left(\frac{T}{C}\right) + i\left(\frac{C}{2}\right)$$

total broker's fee / fixed cost — interest rate on securities

As $C$ increases, total broker's fees decrease, since there are fewer transactions, hence, fewer broker's fees. However, interest income foregone will increase because there is a higher level of average cash balances, $i(C/2)$, which are noninterest-bearing. The problem is to find the optimal size of cash withdrawals, $C$, which will minimize total costs, made up of transactions costs and lost interest income.

Using standard optimization techniques,[2] the cost minimizing level of cash withdrawals ($C^*$) then can be expressed as:

$$C^* = \sqrt{\frac{2bT}{i}}$$

In the model, the demand for cash ($C^*$) is proportional to the square root of the volume of transactions. This would imply that there are economies of scale, since the amount of cash demanded will not grow proportionately with the volume of transactions. If this is generally true, this finding may have some bearing on ratio analysis. Perhaps the larger firms should reasonably be expected to carry relatively smaller cash balances than smaller firms in the same industry.

The application of the *EOQ* formula for cash is similar to its use in calculating the optimal order quantity for inventory (Chapter 5). Assume a firm with estimated total cash disbursements of $10 million for the year. If the broker's fee is $100 per transaction and the interest rate is 8 percent, then the optimal transaction is $158,000. This can be calculated as follows:

$$C^* = \sqrt{\frac{2bT}{i}}$$
$$= \sqrt{\frac{2\,(100)\,(10{,}000{,}000)}{.08}}$$
$$= \$158{,}000$$

The firm will find it necessary to make about 63 transactions during the year in converting securities to cash ($10,000,000/$158,000). The average size of the firm's cash balance would be $79,000.

For many firms the model may have rather limited applicability. This is because the model has a number of operational weaknesses. Perhaps the most telling is that the model is static and allows for no changes during the time period. Thus, the model assumes a constant rate of interest, constant broker's fees, and no additional cash receipts during the period. In addition, it has been pointed out by Miller and Orr (1966) that for many firms, receipts and disbursements tend to be more random than the Baumol model implies. Therefore, the assumption that transactions demand is entirely predictable may not be valid. However, it could be

---

[2] By setting the derivative of $b(T/C) + i(C/2)$ with regard to $C$ equal to zero and solving for $C$:

$$\overline{TC} = \frac{bT}{C} + \frac{iC}{2}$$
$$\frac{dTC}{dC} = -\frac{bT}{C^2} + \frac{i}{2} = 0$$
$$C^* = \sqrt{\frac{2bT}{i}}$$

argued that this objection could be handled as in the inventory case (Chapter 5); that is, allow for a reasonable safety stock.

Many other more sophisticated models have been formulated which attack the cash balance problem, such as one presented by Miller and Orr. Their model recognizes the random nature of cash inflows and outflows, and also takes into account the cost of transferring from cash to securities, from one security to another, and then back into cash. However, their model is beyond the scope of analysis presented here.

Whether a model is useful or not for a particular firm cannot be determined here, but a model does point up the problems involved in determining the mix between cash and marketable securities. If short-term interest rates are high, there is more incentive to hold minimum cash balances. This is because the interest income on securities will more than offset the increased transactions costs caused by the limited cash balances held by the firm. Thus, if short-term interest rates climb sharply and broker's fees remain the same or increase only slightly, it would be almost inevitable that firms would accelerate their search for more efficient methods of handling cash and further economize on their cash balances.

*Investment in Short-Term Securities.* In the previous section, the concern was with the division of cash assets between cash and marketable securities. The *EOQ* model assumed that the interest rate was known precisely; hence, market fluctuations of securities were not a cause for apprehension. What securities come closest to fulfilling this ideal? The securities that best qualify would be the short-term obligations of issuers whose default risk is low or almost nonexistent. Since the issues are short-term, frequently they are known as money-market instruments. Cash is treated as a commodity that is bought by business firms and other institutions that need it temporarily to meet financial commitments and sold by others that have excess cash available. For example, if a firm has a surplus of cash on Monday that will not be needed until Thursday, the firm may put it to work during the three-day period. In the meantime, the cash may be able to earn 8 percent annually. If the available amount is $10 million, the return would be $6,575.[3] If the funds are to be converted into cash in the near future, the securities selected by the firm must be readily marketable. There are a number of money-market instruments suitable as short-term investments. The more important types of securities available for investment include U.S. Treasury bills and notes, repurchase agreements of government securities, commercial paper, and negotiable certificates of deposit.

---

[3] The return may be computed as follows:

$$\text{Income} = \text{Amount} \times \text{interest rate} \times \frac{\text{days}}{365}$$
$$= \$10{,}000{,}000 \times .08 \times \frac{3}{365}$$
$$= \$6{,}575.$$

***U.S. Treasury Bills.*** Perhaps the most popular investment with corporate investors is U.S. Treasury bills. These bills have no default risk and are available in large denominations, for example, up to $1,000,000. The Treasury issues bills weekly, and maturities run from 91 days to a year. Treasury bills have no coupon rate; they are issued on a discount basis. The market for bills is very active, and large sums can be sold on a moment's notice should the need arise. Another distinct advantage of bills is the low transactions cost involved in selling them in the secondary market.

***U.S. Treasury Notes.*** Treasury notes have initial maturities of one to ten years. Notes, as contrasted to bills, have coupons; the market for notes is also very active. They can be used by a firm seeking short-term investments because there are notes outstanding for almost any desired maturity.

***Repurchase Agreements.*** Government-security dealers offer repurchase agreements under contracts wherein the dealer agrees to reacquire the bills within a few days at an agreed-upon price. The firm receives a given yield while it holds the securities. The rates on repurchase agreements are very closely tied into the rates on Treasury bills of the same maturity but usually are slightly higher in order to make the transaction attractive to the investor.

A repurchase agreement is about the equivalent of securing a loan equal to 100 percent of the collateral tendered. Thus, the government bond dealer instead of using a bank loan arranges to temporarily sell Treasury bills with an agreement to repurchase them at the same price at some future date (possibly as short a time as one day). When the funds are no longer needed, the bond dealer reacquires the bills in accordance with the terms of the agreement.

***Commercial Paper.*** Commercial paper is the name used to describe short-term promissory notes issued by borrowers with only the highest credit ratings. Usually, commercial paper is sold on a discount basis with maturities between 30 and 270 days. Interest rates typically are slightly above the Treasury-bill rate and move in harmony with other money-market rates. The volume of commercial paper expands when money is relatively tight. At that time the commercial paper rate may be below the bank lending rate for comparably highly rated firms (bank prime rate), and borrowers may find it advantageous to use the open market rather than commercial banks. Typically, commercial paper is sold in denominations of $100,000 or more.

Commercial paper is sold to investors either directly or indirectly through dealers. The largest component of the market is paper placed directly by finance companies, such as General Motors Acceptance Corporation, C.I.T. Financial Corporation, and Ford Motor Credit Company.

Industrial firms generally sell their paper through dealers. Probably the reason for this is that they are not steady borrowers as are the finance companies; therefore, they do not find it efficient to set up their own organization to market commercial paper. The dealer purchases the paper from the issuer and resells it to the investor seeking a short-term investment. Commercial paper is expected to be paid at maturity and not renewed by the borrower.

**Negotiable Certificates of Deposit.** A firm with funds to lend may purchase a negotiable certificate of deposit (CD) from a commercial bank for a fixed period of time for a specified rate of interest. The rates offered by issuing banks are in line with other money-market rates. The yields on CD's typically are higher than on Treasury bills but about the same as on commercial paper. A secondary market has developed for the certificates of the large, well-known money-market banks.

Maximum yields on small certificates (under $100,000) are set by the Federal Reserve System under Regulation Q. However, issuers of CD's over $100,000 are permitted to pay the competitive rates in order to attract funds. The ceilings on certificates of deposits over $100,000 were suspended in two steps in 1970 and 1973.

## Summary

The previous chapter discussed cash budgets and forecasting statements. In the present chapter the chief concern is with the management of the firm's cash and near-cash resources.

A firm may hold cash or its equivalent to satisfy three motives; they are transactions, precautionary, and speculative. A firm must hold cash to satisfy the first two motives; it is optional as to whether a firm holds cash to satisfy the third.

Perhaps a more operational view is to consider the cash balances as both an earning asset and a financial asset. The objective of the firm should be the utilization of cash so as to maximize its utility to the firm. By doing so, the firm's long-run value is maximized because the net cash benefits to the firm will be increased by securing a return on the cash investment.

Cash is the most liquid of all assets and, therefore, requires an adequate system of internal control. Essential features include a plan of organization showing lines of authority, a good accounting system, and reliable personnel in responsible positions.

Effective cash management serves a dual function of maintaining control over cash remitted by customers and reducing the float in the collection process. Two methods generally are used to accomplish the latter goal, namely, the lock-box system and concentration banking. If either method is successful, the amount of cash required to operate the business can be reduced, sometimes substantially. Area concentration banking is most adaptable to large national or regional firms having many small offices spread throughout the region, or regions of the entire country.

These offices can also act as payment points for customers. The lock-box method, however, is probably the most common method employed to speed collections. A lock-box is a post office box rented by a firm to which customers mail their payments. These boxes are located to minimize the time it takes for the payments to reach the box. A local bank is then employed to service the box.

In order to prevent financial crises, a firm must have sufficient cash to meet its obligations on time; however, to prevent a loss of income, idle cash must be kept to a minimum. The economic order quantity ($EOQ$) model shows a method of analysis that can be used to determine the division between cash and near-cash assets. Funds that are not needed immediately may be invested temporarily in money-market instruments, such as U.S. Treasury bills and notes, repurchase agreements with government-bond dealers, commercial paper, and negotiable certificates of deposit. Thus, cash that would otherwise remain idle awaiting disbursement can become an income-producing asset. High interest rates on short-term investments may induce some firms to lower their cash positions to a point where they may experience difficulties meeting their obligations promptly. However, the primary goal of any firm still must be to meet its obligations on time, thereby preserving its credit standing in the business and financial communities.

## QUESTIONS

1. How does efficient cash management contribute toward management's objective of maximizing shareholder wealth?
2. What are some safeguards against misuse of the firm's liquid assets?
3. Contrast concentration banking and the lock-box system.
4. Explain how the lock-box system can free cash for other purposes.
5. How can cash be analyzed in an inventory context?
6. What cash problem can the $EOQ$ model be used to solve?
7. Explain the effects of credit and payment policies on the firm's cash flow and cash balance.
8. What role does commercial paper play in the market for short-term securities? What potential problems exist for its issuers?
9. Why do Treasury bills normally set the yield floor for money-market instruments?

## PROBLEMS

1. A small Eastern foundation currently has a weekly payroll of $100,000. Due to a drastic cut in its budget, it is seeking ways to save money. A proposal has been made to pay its employees biweekly instead of weekly. If the foundation can earn 6 percent on its invested funds, how much can

it save over the next year if the change is implemented? Recalculate savings if employees are paid monthly.

2. The Jones Company has budgeted for expenditures of $20 million in the coming year. The company's opportunity cost of holding cash is 8 percent. It will pay a brokerage fee of $100 each time it exchanges marketable securities for cash. Cash disbursements are expected to be evenly distributed and of equal amounts over the year. By using the *EOQ* model:
   a. Calculate the amount of each transaction.
   b. What is the average cash balance?
   c. What will be the total cost involved in the transaction amount calculated above?

3. A California firm sells nationally. Its East Coast sales are $9 million. The firm is planning a lock-box system in New York to reduce the time for customers' payments to be made available. Its sales are spaced evenly throughout the year, except for December's sales of $3 million. It is estimated that the float can be reduced four days by use of the lock-box system. The additional costs to the firm for the bank's services are $5,200 a year. The released funds can be invested in Treasury bills at 6 percent. Is the plan feasible? Assume a 360-day year.

## ADDITIONAL READINGS

Baumol, W. J. "The Transactions Demand for Cash—An Inventory Theoretic Approach," *Quarterly Journal of Economics,* vol. 66 (November 1952), pp. 545–46.

Miller, M. H., and D. Orr. "A Model of the Demand for Money by Firms," *Quarterly Journal of Economics,* vol. 80 (August 1966), pp. 413–35.

———. "The Demand for Money by Firms: Extension of Analytical Results," *Journal of Finance,* vol. 23 (December 1968) pp. 735–59.

Orgler, Y. E. *Cash Management, Methods and Models.* Belmont, Calif.: Wadsworth Publishing Co., Inc., 1970.

Orr. D. *Cash Management and the Demand for Money.* New York: Praeger Publishers, 1971.

Tobin, J. "The Interest-Elasticity of Transactions Demand for Cash," *The Review of Economics and Statistics,* vol. 38 (August 1956), pp. 241–47.

# 8
# Time Value of Money

The problems associated with financing and managing fixed assets are less dynamic but more troublesome than those pertaining to current assets. Although treated separately for convenience in discussion, the two are closely related. For example, if funds raised by a bond issue are invested excessively in plant improvements and equipment, then funds needed to meet interest and sinking-fund requirements might be so great as to leave an insufficient amount for working capital. Therefore, it is incumbent that management avoid exessive investment in fixed assets and keep working capital in a proper relationship to sales.

In planning and budgeting for capital expenditures, the financial manager must be aware that a poor decision on an investment in fixed assets will affect the company for many years in the future. As a consequence, specialized capital planning and budgeting procedures have evolved over the years. As time passes, the methods gradually gaining prominence rely on the concept that money has a time value. This premise is interwoven in the formal planning and budgeting techniques emphasized in the next chapter, that is, the internal-rate-of-return and net-present-value methods.

Before developing the analysis of capital budgeting decisions, it is necessary to understand the basic concepts of the time value of money. It is readily apparent to any individual who maintains a savings account in a bank that an account of $100 today will have a cash value in excess of $100 a year from today. Likewise, if you were to get a one-year, single-payment loan of $100 from a bank, you would repay an amount in excess of $100. In the first case, the bank is paying you for the use of your money. In the second case, you are paying the bank for the use of its money. The amount in excess of $100 changes as the length of time changes; thus, the value of money is a function of time.

Two basic ideas are essential to financial decision-making. They are compound value and the present value of a future sum. In the former instance, we are searching for a value of a sum at a future date when interest in succeeding periods is earned not only on the original amount, but also on the accumulated interest from prior time periods. In the latter case, present value is the current worth of a future sum discounted back to the present time at an appropriate rate of interest. In both cases the concepts for single payments and for multiple payments spread over a period of time are discussed.

## Compound Value

The explanation of the concept of compound value is most easily understood through the use of examples. Suppose you deposited $100 today in a bank account at interest rate of 5 percent compounded annually. What would be the value in one year? Clearly, the value would be equal to the sum of your original $100 plus the amount the bank would pay you for the use of your money. At an interest rate of 5 percent, the bank would pay you $(.05 \times \$100) = \$5.00$, for a total value in the account of $105. The same logic can be expressed in a mathematical formulation as shown below:

Let:  $P$ = principal
 $i$ = annual interest rate
 $n$ = number of years
 $I$ — amount of interest
 $CV$ = total value (compound value) at the end of $n$ years.

Then:
$$CV = P + I$$
$$CV = P + iP$$
$$CV = P(1 + i)$$

and, for example:
$$CV = \$100 \,(1 + .05) = \$105.$$

Now, suppose you leave the money in the bank for a period of three years. What is the compound value of the account at the end of years 2 and 3? At the beginning of year 2 (end of year 1), your account was valued at $105. Essentially, this value can be considered the principal ($P'$) for year 2. Thus, we have the following:

$$CV = P'(1 + i)$$
$$CV = \$105 \,(1 + .05)$$
$$CV = \$110.25$$

but

$$P' = P(1+i)$$
$$CV = P(1+i)(1+i)$$
$$CV = P(1+i)^2$$
$$CV = \$100(1+.05)^2$$
$$CV = \$110.25$$

Likewise, at the end of year 3:

$$CV = P(1+i)(1+i)(1+i)$$
$$CV = \$100(1+.05)^3$$
$$CV = \$115.76$$

Generally, the value of a single payment compounded over $n$ years can be expressed in Equation 1.

Eq. 1 $\qquad CV = P(1+i)^n$

Rather than calculating in each instance the value of $(1+i)^n$, tables have been constructed for various values of $i$ and $n$. Appendix C presents these values for .75 to 40 percent.

## Present Value

Rather than depositing $100 in a bank at 5 percent interest today, you deposited a sum that would give you a total of $100 at the end of the year. How much should you deposit, or, in other words, what is the present value of $100 one year from today? This concept is allied closely to that of compound value in that the amount deposited today should compound to $100 in one year, as seen below:

Let: $PV$ = Present value of a future sum
$i$ = Annual interest rate
$I$ = Amount of interest
$V$ = Value at end of a future period

Then:

$$V = PV + I$$

But:

$$I = PV(i)$$
$$V = PV(1+i)$$

and,

Eq. 2 $\qquad PV = \dfrac{V}{(1+i)}$

# 8 Time Value of Money

Continuing the example:

$$V = \$100$$
$$i = .05$$
$$\therefore PV = \frac{V}{(1+i)}$$
$$PV = \frac{\$100}{1.05}$$
$$PV = \$95.24$$

Therefore, if you deposited $95.24 today, you would have $100 in one year. Similarly, if you wish to have $100 at the end of three years:

$$PV = \frac{V}{(1+i)^3}$$
$$PV = \frac{\$100}{(1+.05)^3}$$
$$PV = \$86.36$$

## Compound Value of Annuity

In many financial transactions, a series of payments are involved rather than a single payment, as discussed above. A series of monetary payments of a specific amount over an established number of years is defined as an *annuity*.[1] Two types of annuities, an immediate annuity and an annuity due, are worthy of explanation. For both types, time begins at the present ($t_0$ in the figure below). In the case of an annuity due, the payments (indicated by an x) are made at the beginning of each period starting with $t_0$. The immediate annuity calls for payments at the end of each period, in which case the first payment is made at $t_1$.

The time between payments of an annuity is defined as the payment interval. The time from the beginning of the first payment interval to the last is called the term of the annuity. The compound value of an annuity is simply the sum of the compound values of each payment. Of course, each payment is compounded over a different period of time.

Suppose you are analyzing a three-year immediate annuity in which each payment equals $100. What would be the compound value at the

---

[1] For further discussion, see C. L. Hubbard and C. A. Hawkins, *Theory of Valuation* (Scranton, Pa.: International Textbook Company, 1969), pp. 122–23.

end of the annuity if payments are compounded at 5 percent? The illustration below explains the concept for this example.

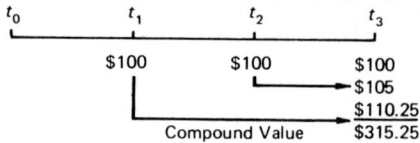

Mathematically:

Let: $CV_A$ = Compound value of an annuity
$i$ = Annual interest rate
$n$ = Number of years
$a$ = Value of each payment

Then:

$$CV_A = a(1+i)^{n-1} + a(1+i)^{n-2} + \cdots + a(1+i)^0$$
$$CV_A = a[(1+i)^{n-1} + (1+i)^{n-2} + \cdots + (1+i)^0]$$

For our example:

$$CV_A = 100[(1+.05)^{3-1} + (1+.05)^{3-2} + (1+.05)^{3-3}]$$
$$CV_A = \$315.25$$

For long annuities, the calculations become quite laborious; thus, tables have been developed for various values of $i$ and $n$. The values of immediate annuities of \$1 per year are given in Appendix D. This appendix has compound values for interest factors for .75 to 40 percent. Using these interest factors, the compound-value formula reduces to Equation 3.

Eq. 3
$$CV_A = a(S_{\overline{n}|\,i})$$

Where: $(S_{\overline{n}|\,i})$ = compound value interest factor at $i$ percent for $n$ years. Substituting into Equation 3 by using Appendix D as follows:

$$CV_A = \$100\,(3.1525)$$
$$CV_A = \$315.25$$

the identical result is obtained.

## Present Value of Annuity

Often, it is necessary to know the present value of all payments of an annuity. Subsequent discussions will introduce decision-making processes that discount all future payments to the present for comparative purposes. Here, the calculations that will permit one to compare cash flows on a present value basis are discussed.

The present value of an annuity is merely the sum of the present value

## 8  Time Value of Money

of each payment discounted over the appropriate number of years. Continuing the example of a three-year immediate annuity in which the payments are $100 per year, what is the present value of the annuity? As can be seen below, the process is just the reverse of compounding an annuity.

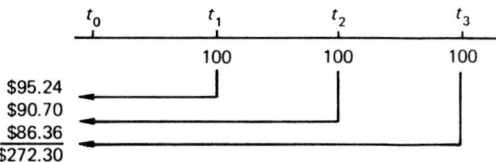

Mathematically:

Let: $PV_A$ = Present value of an annuity
$i$ = Annual interest rate
$n$ = Number of years
$a$ = Value of each payment

Then:

$$PV_A = \frac{a}{(1+i)} + \frac{a}{(1+i)^2} + \cdots + \frac{a}{(1+i)^n}$$

$$PV_A = a\left[\frac{1}{(1+i)^1} + \frac{1}{(1+i)^2} + \cdots + \frac{1}{(1+i)^n}\right]$$

For our example:

$$PV_A = \$100\left[\frac{1}{(1+.05)^1} + \frac{1}{(1+.05)^2} + \cdots + \frac{1}{(1+.05)^3}\right]$$
$$PV_A = \$100\,[.9524 + .9070 + .8636]$$
$$PV_A = \$272.30$$

Again, tables have been constructed to ease the calculations (see Appendix A). Thus, the present-value equation becomes:

Eq. 4        $PV_A = a[V_{\overline{n}|\,i}]$

Where: $[V_{\overline{n}|\,i}]$ = present value annuity interest factor at $i$ percent for $n$ years.

Appendix B is the summation of the yearly factors appearing in Appendix A.

Hence, if the present value of $100 a year for three years at 6 percent is desired, using Appendix A, it would be calculated as follows:

$$PV_A = \$100\,[.943 + .890 + .840]$$
$$PV_A = [94.3 + 89.0 + 84.0]$$
$$PV_A = \$267.30$$

Looking now at Appendix B for three years at 6 percent, the interest factor is shown as:

$$PV_A = \$100\ (2.673)$$
$$PV_A = \$267.30$$

Therefore, Appendix B can be used where an equal sum is received annually at the end of each year for a given number of years, such as in the example shown above.

**Uneven Series of Receipts (Payments).** Unfortunately for computational purposes, financial decisions do not always call for equal payments or receipts, as previously discussed. Thus, the manager must be equipped to deal with uneven cash flows. Suppose someone will pay you $100 per year for three years and $250 per year for two more years in order to pay off a debt. If the payments are discounted, what is the present value? Or, in other words, what is the value of one payment today that will make you financially indifferent to the payments over five years? Since the payments are not equal, it is not a straight annuity. However, one could assume that the payments consist of the sum of (1) a $100, five-year annuity plus (2) two payments of $150 each in years 4 and 5. The solution, assuming a 10-percent discount rate, is as follows:

$$PV_A = a[V_{\overline{n}|\ i}]$$
$$PV_A = \$100\ (V_{\overline{5}|\ 10\%}) + \$150\,[(.683) + (.621)]$$
$$PV_A = \$100\ [3.791] + \$150\,[1.304]$$
$$PV_A = \$574.70$$

The problem could have been set up another way to arrive at the same answer. For example, the same problem could have been solved by treating the first three years as one time period and the last two years as a second period. Thus:

$$PV = \$100\ (2.487) + \$250\ (3.791 - 2.487)$$
$$PV = \$248.70 + \$326.00$$
$$PV = \$574.70$$

It is necessary to subtract 2.487 from 3.791 (see Appendix B) because the $250 is not received until the fourth and fifth years.

## Nonannual Compounding

In a large number of situations, financial transactions are compounded semiannually, quarterly, or on some other nonannual basis. Examples include passbook savings accounts and revolving charge accounts. In this book, the assumption is made that payment intervals for annuities coincide with compounding intervals. To alter this assumption merely complicates the problem and detracts from the presentation of the basic ideas. If "$m$" is the number of times per year that compounding takes place, the formulas presented previously can be summarized:

### Compound Value—Single Payment

$$CV = P\left(1 + \frac{i}{m}\right)^{mn}$$

Present Value—Single Payment

$$PV = \frac{V}{\left(1+\dfrac{i}{m}\right)^{mn}}$$

Compound Value—Annuity

$$CV_A = a\left(S_{\overline{mn}|}\,\tfrac{i}{m}\right)$$

Present Value—Annuity

$$PV_A = a\left(V_{\overline{mn}|}\,\tfrac{i}{m}\right)$$

For example, what is the compound value of $100 compounded quarterly for three years at 8 percent?

$$P = \$100 \quad\quad m = 4$$
$$i = .08 \quad\quad n = 3$$
$$CV = \$100\left(1 + \frac{.08}{4}\right)^{(4)(3)}$$
$$CV = \$100\,(1 + .02)^{12}$$
$$CV = \$126.82$$

Although the tables have been discussed as "per year," in fact, they should be properly designated as "per period." That is, if compounding or discounting takes place twice a year and the annual rate is 8 percent, the per-period rate is 4 percent. As a consequence, there are twice as many periods as years. If compounding occurs four times a year, the per-period rate is 2 percent, and there are four times as many periods as years.

The concept of compound values and present values is pervasive throughout financial decision-making techniques. The chapter appendix presents a comprehensive example of the material covered thus far in the chapter. It illustrates how the tables are used for the required computations.

## Summary

The importance of time in financial decision-making cannot be overestimated. A knowledge of compound interest and present-value calculations is necessary to solve problems in capital budgeting. In this chapter, compound value, present value, compound value of an annuity, and present value of an annuity calculations are illustrated. Then, methods of handling an uneven series of payments or receipts are discussed. The chapter appendix presents a comprehensive example using the above-mentioned techniques. As a consequence, by using calculations similar to these, it is now possible to proceed into a discussion of capital budgeting. In the following two chapters the material discussed in this chapter will be employed in solving capital-budgeting problems. The concept of present value will be shown to be a valuable aid in measuring rates of return on proposed investment opportunities.

## QUESTIONS

1. Explain the difference between the following terms: (a) compound value and (b) compound value of an annuity.
2. Define the present value of an annuity.
3. What is meant by the time value of money?
4. If your savings account is earning 6 percent interest compounded annually, how long will it take for it to double in value?
5. Why do savings-deposit institutions, such as commercial banks, stress the method of compounding their accounts?
6. In legal proceedings involving compensation for loss of future earnings, the concept of the present value of an annuity frequently is employed to measure damages. How would it be used?

## PROBLEMS

1. Three years from today, Jerry Donalds plans to take a European vacation that will cost $3,000. He consults you, his banker, about methods of providing for the trip. Among your many plans, you explain to him that he can deposit a single amount today and allow it to collect interest for three years so that the account equals $3,000 in three years. Assuming that your bank pays a 6-percent interest rate compounded semiannually, how much must he deposit now? (Use Appendix A to interpolate the amount.)
2. Find the compound value of a $125, ten-year immediate annuity at 6 percent annual interest if the payment at the end of year 6 is omitted.

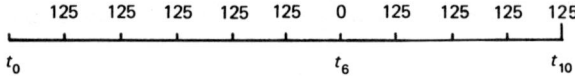

3. You have just purchased a home for $35,000, with $10,000 down. The home is financed with a 20-year mortgage at 8 percent, in which equal one-year payments must be made to discharge the mortgage. What is the value of each payment? (Assume immediate annuity.)
4. You have a rich uncle who plans to give you a gift in one of two ways. First, he proposes to give you $5,000 today and $5,000 at the end of year 5. Second, he proposes to give you $2,000 at the end of each year for five years, the initial payment being at the end of the first year. In both cases, you feel the money has a 6 percent time value. Which gift would you prefer? (Ignore taxes.)
5. A father is planning to provide a 20-year trust fund for his son. The amount deposited today will remain untouched until the end of the 20th year, but will gain interest at a rate of 8 percent compounded annually.

## 8 Time Value of Money

The money will then be transferred to another account, which pays 6 percent. The son plans to withdraw the money in six equal annual payments of $4,000 each at the end of year 20. The fund will be completely depleted after six payments. What amount should the father deposit today?

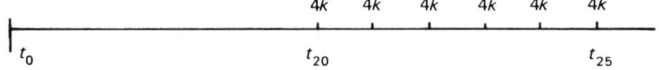

## APPENDIX: COMPREHENSIVE EXAMPLE

Richard Evans, a small businessman, is currently planning a savings fund to finance his son's college education. Assuming today as $t_0$, Evans figures he will need a lump sum of $20,000 at the end of year 18 for his son's education. Consider the additional information in each independent case below and solve as required:

1. What yearly sum must Evans place in the college fund if the payment is made at the end of each year and the fund receives interest at 6 percent compounded annually? Assume that no money is removed from the fund until year 18.

*Solution:*

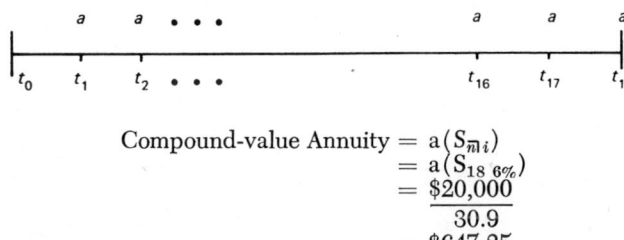

$$\begin{aligned}\text{Compound-value Annuity} &= a(S_{\overline{n}|i}) \\ &= a(S_{\overline{18}|\,6\%}) \\ &= \$20{,}000 \\ &\phantom{=}\,\overline{30.9} \\ &= \$647.25\end{aligned}$$

Evans must deposit, then, $647.25 in the fund each year.

2. Suppose additionally that Mr. Evans is considering a second savings fund to partially cover his expenses for retirement. He proposes to place $1,200 per year in a separate fund for his retirement 20 years from now. What will be the value of the retirement fund at the end of 20 years if payments earn 6 percent interest compounded annually and each payment is made at the end of the year?

*Solution:*

Using the compound-value annuity calculations:

$$\begin{aligned}CV_A &= a(S_{\overline{n}|i}) \\ &= \$1{,}200\,(36.786) \\ &= \$44{,}143\end{aligned}$$

3. When Mr. Evans' wealthy uncle learns of his retirement plans, he volunteers to give Mr. Evans the present value of his contemplated savings described in part 2 above. How much would he have to contribute?

*Solution:*

$$PV_A = a(V_{\overline{n}|i})$$
$$= \$1200 \,(11.470)$$
$$= \$13{,}764$$

As a check, find the compound value of $13,764 for 20 years:

$$CV = P\,(1+i)^n$$
$$= \$13{,}764\,(1+.06)^{20}$$
$$= \$13{,}764\,(3.207)$$
$$= \$44{,}141$$

which, except for the rounding difference, is equal to the $44,143 calculated in the preceding part of the example.

# 9

# Capital Budgeting

Financial managers must contend with working-capital problems every day. Decisions involving fixed-capital assets, such as equipment that the firm acquires for use in producing goods or services,[1] are less frequent. However, because of the nature of fixed assets, the decisions are at least as difficult and are often more important.

Acquisition of such assets generally involves larger dollar commitments, for longer periods of time, and the decisions are harder to change once a commitment has been made. Because of these characteristics, prudence is essential. Poor performance in this area can affect the long-run prospects for the firm and the near-term employment outlook for the manager.

This chapter will examine the capital investment process. A review of the importance of such investments and an overview of the planning process provide a logical introduction.

Analysis of fixed-capital investments is called capital budgeting. The different methods of analysis will be discussed in detail. Inconsistent rankings for individual projects with the different techniques can cause problems. Why this occurs and what to do about it are covered separately. The appropriate way of setting up the analysis when funds are limited is also given special attention.

## Basic Concepts Relative to Fixed-Capital Assets

Fixed assets can be defined as capitalized assets a firm acquires for use in producing goods or services. Although fixed-capital assets are not

---

[1] The tax code's definition of a capital asset excludes depreciable assets, which can be confusing. Business people and economists agree that the means of production is, by most definitions, capital.

for resale during the ordinary course of business, this does not mean they may not be disposed of if they have outlived their usefulness to the firm. As a general rule, fixed assets have specialized uses, so that, when an attempt is made to sell them, they frequently have relatively low market prices. The basic distinction between fixed- and working-capital assets is the use made of them. For illustration, a truck would be a working-capital asset (inventory) to a truck dealer but a fixed-capital asset to a trucking firm.

*Relative Importance of Fixed-Capital Assets.* The amount of fixed assets relative to total assets will vary widely among business firms because of differences in the nature of their operations. In general, firms in the service and merchandising industries have relatively small investments in fixed-capital assets and relatively large investments in working-capital assets. If a retailer leases his business building, equipment, and furnishings, most of the firm's total assets will be in cash, receivables, and inventories. If a real estate company owns a hotel together with its equipment and furnishings, the real estate company's investments in fixed-capital assets will be large, while those of the company that operates the hotel will be small.

In contrast to the relatively small investments in fixed-capital assets of most service and merchandising firms are the relatively large investments in fixed assets of public-utility, railway, and real estate companies. The latter firms need relatively small amounts of working-capital assets—cash, receivables, and inventories—because they provide services paid for with cash or receivables that are quickly convertible into cash; but their investments for fixed-capital assets—buildings, machinery, and equipment—are relatively and absolutely large. The relative importance of fixed-capital assets in other industries, including manufacturing, will be somewhere between the two extremes—service and merchandising firms, on the one hand, and public-utility, railway, and real estate companies, on the other.

*Planning Capital Expenditures.* Capital planning is based on the anticipated growth of the economy as a whole, as well as of the specific industry in which the firm is operating, and on the anticipated place of the firm within the industry. Specific proposals for capital expenditures must be considered in terms of anticipated increased revenue or cost savings. This, in turn, raises questions as to total cost of acquisitions, length of service life, operating expenses, maintenance costs, and tax-free depreciation allowances. Usually there is some discrepancy between anticipated costs and anticipated income because there are changes in the price level as well as routine miscalculations of costs and receipts. Changes in corporate income taxes, wages, and other costs over which management may have little or no control are factors that affect the profitability of fixed-assets expansion, and changes in market demand also must be anticipated by management.

Fixed-capital expenditures are usually classified as major and minor; the former would include those for plant sites, buildings, and expensive machinery, and the latter those for small additions to plants, inexpensive machinery, and other miscellaneous items that are capitalized (tools and small items may not be capitalized but rather treated as current expenses irrespective of their useful life).

Replacement investments are usually more pressing than those for expansion, but policies in this regard are complicated by the fact that some fixed-capital assets may never become completely obsolete or entirely worn out. In making decisions as to when such assets are to be replaced, the cost of replacement should be weighed against the anticipated savings and increased revenue derived from greater efficiency of new fixed assets. When such replacement investments result in an increase in output, the expenditure may contain an element of expansion. When new capital assets are designed to produce new products, estimates must be made not only of costs but also of the effect of the new products on the market for old products of the company. Expansionary investments in capital assets are those that are expected to result in an increase in output and income. Customarily, the board of directors of a corporation makes decisions pertaining to capital expenditures of this type. A vital question in this regard is whether the market will absorb the additional output in the near future in sufficient quantities to justify the outlay.

Sometimes capital investments must be made (such as replacing property that has been destroyed by fire) in order to stay in business. Other investments—such as safety or health measures to protect employees or the public—may be made to meet requirements of a governmental agency. There may be other capital expenditures by a company for the welfare of employees or the community in which it is located, such as for public meeting rooms to be used for community functions or swimming pools for employees and their families. While capital expenditures of this type may be relatively small, they may be given priority in capital budgets despite the fact that no direct profits therefrom are to be anticipated.

In planning capital expenditures, priority is usually given to projects having the greatest urgency; but the evaluation of the urgency of items may be highly subjective. There are basically two levels in the decision-making process: namely, the departmental level and general management. Planning usually starts in different departments, with department heads presenting arguments for the approval of their projects. Frequently there are several approaches forwarded to meet a recognized need. These are often conflicting because, if one is adopted, the others are immediately excluded. Since they are mutually exclusive, general or top management must make a choice. The purpose of a budgetary program of capital planning is to ensure the selection of the most profitable investments to be made with funds available that are compatible with the business activities of the firm.

The discussion of the capital investment process will emphasize the analysis because conducting the analysis is generally a functional responsibility of the financial manager. However, other critical areas in the process should be noted. First, it is essential that there be an effective mechanism for generation of proposals. The top choice indicated by the analysis can be no better than the best prospect considered. Generally, successful firms are those which are constantly trying to generate profitable new ideas. No method of analysis can compensate for a deficiency in this area.

The process can be thought of as having three stages: proposal generation, analysis, and implementation. The criticalness of the generation stage has been noted. Implementation is obviously important too. After the analysis has been done, management must act on it in a decisive and expeditious manner. This includes insuring that actions follow the plans; that is, control.

This discussion, though brief, should establish the role of capital budgeting in the investment process. Capital budgeting is the analysis of capital investment proposals submitted to management. Its purpose is to aid management in the selection of those proposals which are to be implemented. The total of "accepted" proposals constitutes the *capital budget*.

## Capital Budgeting Analysis

Analysis of any particular capital investment proposal involves three steps. First, the cost of the project must be estimated. Next, the value of the derived benefits must be quantified. Finally, the two sets of estimates must be combined in some form of reasoned analysis which is helpful to management in making a decision.

Where more than one project is being considered, the analysis should provide a way of ranking the proposals. Further, the method of analysis should provide guidance as to the total size of the capital budget. If the size of the budget is limited due to funds availability, the analysis should include this consideration.

**Cost Estimation.** *For purposes of analysis*, the cost of a capital asset is the price that would be paid for the asset *if it were bought for cash*. This would be reduced (or, in some rare cases, increased) by trade-ins. Cost would also be adjusted for any tax consequences of the trade-ins.

Although this definition of cost seems straightforward, it contains some subtle, and sometimes difficult, analytical assumptions. Regardless of *how* the asset in question is acquired, the analysis *assumes* the firm would buy it outright. The purpose of the current analysis is to determine whether an asset should be acquired. If the analysis shows that investment in the asset (or project) is justified, then the financing question can be addressed.

However, the assumption of cash purchase is more than a practical expedient; there is theoretical justification for it. As will be explained in the next section, the benefit estimates are developed in a way which assumes that an asset is bought outright.

There is also another reason for excluding the financing problem at this point. The earlier chapter on leverage suggested there might be some benefit to the use of debt capital. If a project were considered to be partially, or totally, debt financed, this would introduce bias. To avoid this, all projects are considered to be purchased outright.

Trade-ins can cause problems too. However, they can generally be dealt with by remembering that equipment should only be considered as a trade-in if it would be released from service due to the proposed acquisition. The point is that it is the logical relationship between the acquisition and the trade-in that counts, not the facts of the actual transaction.

Consider the following example. A company is analyzing the installation of a new materials-handling system. Six months later, after implementation of the new system, the firm could sell the fork lift trucks it currently is using, on the resale market. Although the seller of the new system is not taking the fork lifts in trade, they constitute a "logical trade-in" and should be considered as such in the analysis.

The opposite situation can also be envisioned. A trucking company has ten old trailers on the back lot. The trailers were not licensed this year because they are no longer compatible with the firm's other equipment. Their current market value is $800 each. The firm is considering acquiring some new tools. The tool manufacturer can use the trailers and agrees to allow $8,000 trade-in for them.

Although the trailers would be an actual trade-in, they are not a "logical trade-in" since they are not being replaced by the new tools. The trailers could be sold for $8,000 without acquiring the tools, assuming the previous estimate was correct. Analysis of the acquisition of the tools should not lower cost for the "trade-in."

When old equipment is traded, or sold, there will quite likely be tax consequences. The effect of the transaction on the current year's tax bill can be considered as part of the cost of investment.

To better visualize the proposed definition, again consider the example of the firm evaluating a new materials-handling system. The system would cost $50,000 if purchased outright. The market value of the fork lift trucks that would be released from service, and which could be sold, is estimated to be $10,000. This makes the net outlay, excluding immediate tax effects, $40,000.

To illustrate the tax calculation, assume that the book value of the fork lifts is $15,000. The tax loss on their sale would be $5,000.[2] (This is the book value of $15,000 minus market value of $10,000.) Being able to

---

[2] It is advisable to review the tax coverage in Chapter 2 where necessary.

write off this loss this year would reduce the firm's taxable income and therefore its taxes. If the firm is in the 40 percent tax bracket (this rate will be used throughout the chapter unless otherwise specified), the loss write-off will save the firm $2,000 in taxes this year. This figure is derived by multiplying the firm's tax rate of 40 percent times the tax loss[3] of $5,000.

For this project the cost would be $38,000, as shown below:

| | |
|---|---:|
| Cash price | $ 50,000 |
| Less trade-in | (10,000) |
| Less tax loss | (2,000) |
| Net cost | $ 38,000 |

***Estimating Benefits.*** Generally capital acquisitions are undertaken because they increase profits, either by increasing revenues or by decreasing expenses, or both. However, in analyzing capital proposals, the financial analyst will generally speak in terms of cash flows rather than profits.

The difference between the two concepts is relatively simple. Cash flow includes those funds flows which constitute investment or return of capital. An example might serve to clarify the distinction. Assume party B (for banker) lends party C (for client) $1,000 for one year at 10 percent interest. At the end of the year, C repays $1,100. Party B's end-of-year profit is $100. The end-of-year cash flow is $1,100, which is the profit ($100) plus the return of capital ($1,000).

In banking, the return of the original capital by the borrower is referred to as repaying the principal. The return of invested capital by a fixed-capital investment is accounted for as depreciation.

The previous example could have had party B (a business executive) investing in project C (a capital acquisition, a machine). The machine costs $1,000, only has a one-year economic life, and is depreciated accordingly. During the year, B spends $400 on materials and $500 for labor. Party B produces and sells $2,000 worth of goods for cash. The profit, ignoring taxes, would be:

| | | |
|---|---:|---:|
| Revenues | | $2,000 |
| Less: | | |
|   Direct labor | $ 500 | |
|   Direct materials | 400 | |
|   Depreciation | $1,000 | |
|     Cost of goods sold | | 1,900 |
|     Income | | $ 100 |

---

[3] Please note that the new project is not saddled with the loss. That loss is what is referred to in accounting and finance as a "sunk cost." This means that it has already occurred; there is no recapturing it, so it should not affect future decisions. The only consideration is the tax effect, which is part of the current decision.

However, at the end of the year, party B would have more than $100 in cash on hand. Recall the machine was purchased outright. The depreciation expense would involve no cash outflow. The sale of the goods would bring in $2,000. Paying for materials and labor would only require $900, leaving $1,100, the cash flow. The cash flow is the profit of $100 plus the $1,000 return of capital which is accounted for as depreciation.

This illustrates the purpose of depreciation accounting. Depreciation is the systematic allocation of the cost of capital equipment to the revenues it helps to generate. More simply, depreciation accounting is the process of writing off the cost of the means of production. This keeps the company from confusing the return of capital with income.

The distinction is important from a tax standpoint. Income is taxable. Return of capital is not; with the return of capital the investors are simply receiving their own money back. The fact that capital return is nontaxable (depreciation is deductible) preserves the definition of cash flow. With a 40 percent tax rate, party B's income would be:

```
Revenues ............................... $2,000
    Less:  Cost of goods sold
           (including $1,000 depreciation) ..........  1,900
           Earnings before taxes .................    100
    Less:  Taxes ..........................     40
                Net income ..................... $   60
```

The end-of-year cash flow would be $1,060, net income plus depreciation.

In addition to net income and depreciation, there are off-income-statement cash flows. These are flows which involve the investment or the return of capital in ways other than through depreciation. The original investment usually involves a cash outflow. Two other cash flows are frequently encountered. Working capital investment and the salvage value of capital equipment do not affect income, but they are cash flows.

The cash flow related to the investment is captured in the cost calculation. If a project involves an investment in added inventory or receivables, the cost should be added to the original investment. If equipment has value at the end of the related project's life, the estimated proceeds from its sale should be considered an added benefit and figured into the analysis. This is also true of any residual values associated with working capital investment. These flows should be considered net of any related taxes.

To recap, when speaking of the benefits from a capital investment, a financial analyst will normally refer to cash flows. This is the total flow generated by the acquisition—both parts, that which is income and that which constitutes return of capital.

Cash flow, net income plus depreciation, is the amount of cash the firm would have on hand if the asset were purchased for cash and no other accounts were changed; that is, if there were no changes in working capital and no changes in any other asset or liability accounts.

Stated in this way, the cash flow concept seems highly artificial, which it is. Cash flow is an analytical construct. Its purpose is to isolate the change due to one investment. This change is defined in such a manner as to eliminate the confusion that might result from simultaneously introducing financing considerations. Financing determines the firm's cost of capital which, in turn, determines if projects are acceptable. The cost of capital calculation is explained in Chapter 11. The relationship between the cost of capital and financing decisions is one of the topics in Chapter 12. The cash flow calculation, as defined in this text, also omits working capital considerations. If changes in working capital are required by an investment, they must be introduced separately and explicitly.

The analyst is not naive enough to believe that this is the cash flow that will actually occur when all of these other changes do take place. The problem at this point is to determine the benefits for the one project by itself. To do this, the cash flow concept is very helpful. The concept allows the analyst to concentrate on only those changes which will affect revenues, expenses, or depreciation. If working capital flows or salvage are involved, they can be "tacked on" separately.

To appreciate how the benefits might be quantified, return to the earlier example involving the materials-handling equipment. The equipment would not affect sales revenue, but it is estimated that it would reduce physical handling costs by $13,000 a year.

Assume that either the new system or the old fork lifts could perform the task for five years, and that both would be depreciated over a five-year life, straight-line, to a zero salvage value. The new system would generate depreciation of $10,000 a year ($50,000 divided by a five-year life). The fork lifts would have $3,000 a year depreciation (their book value of $15,000 divided by five years). The change in depreciation would be $7,000 a year.

Knowing the changes in revenues, expenses, and depreciation along with the firm's tax rate provides the basis for the calculation of the incremental *per-year* cash flow, as illustrated in Table 9–1:

**TABLE 9–1**
**Illustrative Cash Flow Calculation**

| | |
|---|---:|
| Increase in revenues | $ –0– |
| Decrease in expenses | 13,000 |
| Net contribution | 13,000 |
| Less: increased depreciation | 7,000 |
| Change in income | 6,000 |
| Less: taxes | 2,400 |
| Change in net income | 3,600 |
| Add: increased depreciation | 7,000 |
| Incremental cash flow | $10,600 |

# 9 Capital Budgeting

Even with the cost and benefit estimates, the problem is not solved. The figures must be combined in some way to provide useful guidance for the decision.

However, before proceeding to the methods of analysis, a warning is in order. There is no way of adequately simulating the information-gathering and estimation processes in an introductory text. Some of it is highly sophisticated and relatively precise; other parts are almost entirely subjective. A revered tenet in all decision-making states that the analysis can be no better than the input. This is abbreviated GIGO—"garbage in, garbage out." The estimation process has been covered quickly. It should be remembered that the quality of the analysis is no better than the quality of the estimates!

## Methods of Analysis

In this section five methods of analysis will be reviewed. The first two, payback and average rate of return, are covered primarily because their use persists in the business world. Their weaknesses will be indicated.

The other methods, net present value, profitability index, and internal rate of return, are preferable because they consider the time value of money. They are discounted cash flow techniques and make use of the mathematics of interest covered in Chapter 8.

There is one conscious omission in the discounted cash flow coverage. The discount rate used is taken as a value that has been supplied to the analyst. The appropriate rate would depend on the riskiness of the capital investments and how the firm is financed. These two issues will be addressed in Chapters 10 and 11. For now, the analysis will simply specify a discount rate and apply it without further explanation.

**Payback Period.** Payback has been, and still is, a widely used method of analysis. The payback period is the estimated *time* it will take the company to recover its invested capital. To determine payback, calculate a cumulative total of the cash flows. When the total reaches zero; that is, cost has been recovered, payback has been achieved. Table 9–2 illustrates the calculations for a hypothetical example. (Although it costs $38,000,

TABLE 9–2
Payback Calculation for a Project with Net Cost of $38,000

| Year | Cash Flow | Cumulative |
|---|---|---|
| 0 | ($38,000) | ($38,000) |
| 1 | 7,000 | (31,000) |
| 2 | 10,000 | (21,000) |
| 3 | 14,000 | (7,000) |
| 4 | 12,000 | 5,000 |
| 5 | 6,000 | 11,000 |

this is not the materials-handling project. These figures were made up merely to illustrate the calculation. However, a $38,000 example is used for a purpose. Comparison of this example with the $38,000 materials-handling system will be used to demonstrate one of payback's weaknesses as an analytical technique.) The project achieved payback between the third and fourth years.

It is common practice to interpolate to give the appearance of greater precision. Given a cash flow of $12,000 in year 4, the project would pay out seven twelfths of the way into the fourth year. Its payback period is 3.58 years.

If a project has the same cash inflow each year, the payback period can be calculated directly using the formula:

$$\text{Payback period} = \frac{\text{Net cost}}{\text{Annual cash inflow}}$$

In the case of the materials handling example this would be:

$$\text{Payback period} = \frac{\$38,000}{\$10,600} = 3.58 \text{ years}$$

The question arises as to whether 3.58 years is an acceptable payback period. There is neither an implicit nor explicit acceptance criterion with the payback. Management must establish some payback level as acceptable.

This lack of logical cutoff value is one of the weaknesses of the payback method. There are others. Payback does not consider the timing of the cash flows during the payback period, and it ignores cash flows after the payback period. The two examples just discussed illustrate this weakness. The materials-handling project had greater total cash flows and greater early cash flows, but its payback period was approximately the same as that illustrated in Table 9–2. However, the point is accentuated in Table 9–3. All three of the projects would have a three-year payback.

TABLE 9–3
Cash Flows for Three Projects Each with a Net Cost of $6,000

| Year | Project A | Project B | Project C |
|---|---|---|---|
| 1 | $2,000 | $3,000 | $(4,000) |
| 2 | 2,000 | 2,000 | (5,000) |
| 3 | 2,000 | 1,000 | 15,000 |
| 4 | –0– | 1,000 | 20,000 |
| 5–20 | –0– | –0– | 25,000 |

Examination of the table is enlightening. If management accepted all projects with less than a three-year payback, Project A would be acceptable even though it just returns the invested capital. It looks as good, from a payback perspective, as Project B which more than returns the capital and has better early cash flows.

Project C illustrates the type of project that is most severely penalized by payback analysis. Where a long period of product development is involved and where early research and development costs are high, payback can be slow. However, the long-run benefits of this type of project can be quite high.

The payback method survives because it is quick, it is easy to do, it is easy to understand, and because many business investments are of a nature that minimizes the problems of the technique. If the projects under analysis have relatively level cash flows and have similar economic lives, the rankings achieved by payback will be similar to those achieved by more defensible methods. However, the results can be misleading and, therefore, costly.

*Average-Rate-of-Return Method.* This method is more defensible in that it attempts to calculate a rate of return rather than concentrate on the time necessary to recapture the original investment. As such it considers both the amount invested and the *profits* generated. The average rate of return is defined as the average annual net income after taxes divided by average investment. This is an accounting income concept rather than a cash flow concept. For the example used previously, the materials-handling project, the calculation would be:

$$\text{Average rate of return} = \frac{\text{Average annual net income}}{\text{Average investment}}$$

$$.189 \text{ or } 18.9\% = \frac{\$3,600}{(\$38,000/2)}$$

The denominator, the average investment, is derived by averaging the beginning investment of $38,000 and the end-of-life value—zero. Some presentations of the technique suggest that an average of the end-of-year book values for each year of the asset's life is more accurate. Because of other problems with the technique, it seems to be of marginal benefit.

The numerator is an average of the after-tax income figures for each year of the project's life. As with payback, the time value of money and the greater importance of early flows are ignored. Because of this, the rate of return calculated by this method will often misstate the true return on invested capital, the internal rate of return.

In some cases average rate of return can approximate the true rate. If the life of a project is long (greater than twice the payback), salvage values are negligible, and annual income is fairly uniform, this method may approximate the result derived by the internal rate of return method. However, the technique's usefulness in this regard is limited. Average rate of return is more important because it is indicative of early attempts by business to make decisions based on rate-of-return projections. The fact that many business investments are of a type that allow project rankings to be close to correct may explain the continued use of average rate of return by some firms.

Since few projects would be expected to have truly uniform inflows, the approximation is bound to suffer. This is compounded by nonnegligible salvage values. Accelerated depreciation and shortened product lives add to the need for accurate methods of dealing with the time value of money. Averages simply are not sufficient; the discounted cash flow techniques are far superior.

*Net Present Value (NPV).* The material on the time value of money in the last chapter is the basis of the logic of the discounted cash flow techniques. The net present value of a project is the present value of the future benefits minus the cost. It is the difference between what is to be received, in current worth, and what will be paid for it.

Net present value quantifies the benefit from a particular investment by comparing the current dollar value of the future benefits with what is going to be expended to receive those benefits. To make the comparison, the firm must specify what rate of return it wants on its money; that is, what discount rate to use in translating future benefits to their current dollar equivalents.

Again the materials-handling project can be used as an illustration. Assume the company wants to make 10 percent on its money. A 10-percent discount rate will be used.

Recall that the project was to generate a cash flow of $10,600 a year for five years. The present value of the benefits can be calculated as the present value of an annuity of $10,600 per year discounted at 10 percent. Using the calculation from Chapter 8, this is:

$$PV_A = a[V_{\overline{n}|i}] = \$10{,}600[V_{\overline{n}|i}]$$
$$= \$10{,}600 \cdot 3.791$$
$$= \$40{,}185$$

If the company spends $38,000 to receive benefits with a current worth of $40,185, it will have been a profitable venture. Net present value simply quantifies how much of a bargain the firm is getting for its money.

$$\text{NPV} = \text{Present Value of Benefits} - \text{Cost}$$
$$\text{NPV} = \$40{,}185 - 38{,}000 = \$2{,}185$$

As the example illustrates, the actual calculation of the net present value is easy once the cost and benefits have been specified. The problem arises in making certain of counting everything once and not counting anything twice. A work sheet is helpful in this regard, even though it is simply a checklist of the potential costs and benefits that might be encountered.

The cost section of the work sheet is identical to the earlier calculation. However, the benefits section derives the cash flows in a slightly different manner for reasons that will be explained. The bottom line result is the same, but the derivation differs. The easiest way to explain the calculations is with an example. Using the materials-handling data will save time. The two approaches are illustrated in Table 9-4.

TABLE 9-4
Quantifying Benefits—Two Alternative Approaches

| Cash Flow | | Tax Shield | |
|---|---|---|---|
| Net contribution | $13,000 | Net contribution | $13,000 |
| Less: Depreciation | 7,000 | Less: Taxes | 5,200 |
| Change in income | $ 6,000 | After-tax contribution | $ 7,800 |
| Less: Taxes | 2,400 | | |
| Change in net income | $ 3,600 | Depreciation | 7,000 |
| Plus: Depreciation | 7,000 | Times: Tax rate | .40 |
| Total Benefit: | $10,600 | Tax shield | $ 2,800 |
| | | Total Benefit: | $ 7,800 |
| | | | 2,800 |
| | | | $10,600 |

Both approaches arrive at the same bottom line figure, $10,600. In the tax-shield method, the after-tax value of the contribution and depreciation are each calculated separately. If the firm saved $13,000 in expenses, *and there were no change in depreciation,* the entire amount would be taxed, resulting in an after-tax benefit of $7,800 per year. However, there is additional depreciation of $7,000. This reduces the taxes from the $5,200 which would have been paid on the $13,000 to $2,400 as shown in column one. The value of the tax saving, or shield, can also be calculated directly. Having a $7,000 depreciation deduction reduces taxable income by that same amount, $7,000. The taxes on $7,000 income at a 40 percent rate would be $2,800. Having an added $7,000 in deductible depreciation will save the firm $2,800 in taxes per year. This amount can be calculated directly as the added depreciation times the tax rate.

The main reason for advocating the tax shield method is convenience. This approach allows the effect of each change in revenues, expenses, and depreciation to be handled separately. This eliminates the need for setting up a pro forma statement like Table 9-1 for each year of a project's life. The tax-shield method is especially helpful where projects have long lives, where accelerated depreciation methods are used, where maintenance and rehabilitation costs occur in varying amounts over the life of the project, and when the analysis is replicated with varying estimates of the individual cost and benefit entries. Such complications require an analytical format which is capable of expanding with the complexity of the analysis. Table 9-5 illustrates such a work sheet. This method of analyzing capital investment is very general. It is capable of handling a wide variety of problems. (It will be used again in Chapters 14 and 18.)

The work sheet has two sections. In the first, the cost of the investment is defined; in the second, the expected benefits are detailed. Within each

TABLE 9–5
Analysis of Materials-Handling System Using the Tax Shield Work Sheet

|  | Before Tax | After Tax | Time | Discount Factor | Present Value |
|---|---|---|---|---|---|
| *Cost* | | | | | |
| Price | $50,000 | $50,000 | 0 | 1 | $50,000 |
| Trade-in | (10,000) | (10,000) | 0 | 1 | (10,000) |
| Tax loss | (5,000) | (2,000) | 0 | 1 | (2,000) |
| | | | | | $38,000 |
| *Benefits* | | | | | |
| Revenues | –0– | –0– | 1–5 | 3.791 | –0– |
| Expenses | $13,000 | $ 7,800 | 1–5 | 3.791 | $29,570 |
| Depreciation | 7,000 | 2,800 | 1–5 | 3.791 | 10,615 |
| Salvage | –0– | –0– | 5 | .621 | –0– |
| | | | | | $40,185 |

NPV = Present value of benefits — Cost
= $40,185 — 38,000 = $2,185

section the entries can vary. Analysis of the materials handling project provides a fairly typical example problem. The price of the investment is, as explained before, the cash purchase price of the asset regardless of how it is actually acquired. The price is the same before and after taxes. Capital acquisitions are not immediately deductible. They must be depreciated. The depreciation allowances are accounted for in the benefits section.

The trade-ins are "logical trade-ins." This distinction was explained earlier. Trade-ins are also the same before and after taxes. The tax consequences of trade-ins are entered separately on the next line. Losses would arise when market or trade-in value was lower than book value. Gains would occur if the asset sold for over book value. Unless otherwise specified, the firm's normal tax rate will be applied to such gains and losses.[4]

Increases in revenues and reductions of expenses constitute net contributions to fixed expenses and profits. Such increases in profits would be fully taxable. Because of this, the after-tax value is derived by multiplying the before-tax amount by *one minus the applicable tax rate*. Depreciation is beneficial because it reduces taxes. In the case of depreciation, the after-tax value would be the depreciation amount *times the tax rate*.

In every case the time column indicates when the flow occurs. For convenience it is assumed all flows occur at year end. The discount factor is determined by the "time" and the specified discount rate. If the flow is annual, the factor is an annuity factor. If the flow occurs only once, such as in the case of salvage, the factor would be the present value of a dollar. (Note that the entry for salvage is the *increase* in salvage be-

---

[4] Generally, gains would be depreciation recapture, and the losses are 1231 losses which are deducted from ordinary income. For further explanation review Chapter 2.

## 9 Capital Budgeting

tween the acquisition and the trade-in equipment.) The present value amounts are the product of the discount factor and the after-tax amount.

To calculate the project's net present value, add up the benefits, determine the cost, and take the difference. If the net present value is positive, the project generates more than the required rate of return and should be undertaken.

***Profitability Index (PI).*** The profitability index is simply a different way of presenting the results of the analysis. Every calculation *except the last one* is the same. In calculating net present value, the analyst must find the difference between the present value of the benefits and cost. To derive the profitability index, the results are presented as a ratio; that is, an index of profitability. For the materials-handling project the profitability index would be:

$$\text{Profitability index} = \frac{\text{Present value of benefits}}{\text{Cost}}$$

$$1.06 = \frac{\$40{,}185}{\$38{,}000} \quad 1.0575$$

The purpose of the profitability index is to allow a different interpretation of the results. The NPV indicated that expected benefits were worth $2,185 more than was invested. The PI says that for every dollar invested, the firm will receive future benefits with a current worth of $1.06, if it discounts future returns at a 10-percent rate.

Like net present value, the profitability index has a built-in acceptance value. If a project had a PI of exactly 1.0, the firm would be getting exactly its required return on capital. If a project's PI is greater than one, it is expected to return more than a dollar for each dollar invested, over and above the minimum return—the discount rate. Because of this, the firm would be expected to undertake all projects with PI's of one or greater.

Note that the profitability index calculated is valid only for the rate used in the discounting process. Thus, the discount rate should be specified when speaking of a project's PI. This will avoid confusing the index with a project's "rate of return." A PI of 1.06 is not a rate of return of 6 percent. The PI depends on the discount rate used; a project's rate of return is independent of the assumption of an external rate. That is why it is referred to as an *internal* rate of return.

***Internal Rate of Return (IRR).*** The calculation of a project's expected rate of return on invested capital has not yet been explained. Recalling the net present value discussion will provide a way of determining this rate of return. That discussion indicated that the NPV was how much a project was going to generate in present dollar terms *over and above* the required rate, the discount rate. Therefore, if a project had a NPV of zero, it would be generating a return exactly equal to the discount rate. This provides both a definition and a way for solving for the internal rate

TABLE 9–6
Analysis of Materials-Handling System Internal-Rate-of-Return Method

|  | Before Tax | After Tax | Time | 10 Percent | | 12 Percent | | 14 Percent | |
|---|---|---|---|---|---|---|---|---|---|
|  |  |  |  | Discount Factor | Present Value | Discount Factor | Present Value | Discount Factor | Present Value |
| *Cost* |  |  |  |  |  |  |  |  |  |
| Price . . . . . . . . | $50,000 | $50,000 | 0 | 1 | $50,000 | 1 | $50,000 | 1 | $50,000 |
| Trade-in . . . . . . | (10,000) | (10,000) | 0 | 1 | (10,000) | 1 | (10,000) | 1 | (10,000) |
| Tax loss . . . . . . | (5,000) | (2,000) | 0 | 1 | (2,000) | 1 | (2,000) | 1 | (2,000) |
|  |  |  |  |  | $38,000 |  | $38,000 |  | $38,000 |
| *Benefits* |  |  |  |  |  |  |  |  |  |
| Revenues . . . . . | –0– | –0– | 0 | 0 | –0– | 0 | –0– | 0 | –0– |
| Expenses . . . . . | 13,000 | 7,800 | 1–5 | 3.791 | 29,570 | 3.605 | 28,119 | 3.433 | 26,777 |
| Depreciation . . . | 7,000 | 2,800 | 1–5 | 3.791 | 10,615 | 3.605 | 10,094 | 3.433 | 9,612 |
|  |  | $10,600 |  |  | $40,185 |  | $38,213 |  | $36,389 |
| Salvage . . . . . . . | –0– |  |  |  |  |  |  |  |  |
| NPV . . . . . . . . . |  |  |  |  | $ 2,185 |  | $ 213 |  | ($1,611) |

## 9 Capital Budgeting

of return. The internal rate of return of a project is that discount rate which makes the project's net present value zero.

Finding the internal rate of return is, therefore, a trial-and-error process. Different discount rates should be tried until one gives a NPV of zero. Actually, the process can be somewhat more systematic than that. If the NPV for a given discount rate is positive, it indicates that the return is greater than the rate used and a higher rate is indicated. The size of the NPV can serve as a guide as to how much to increase the rate on the next trial.

The work sheet can also assist in organizing this analysis. Each trial can be calculated by simply repeating the last two columns. The materials-handling project can again be used as an example. Recall that the project had a NPV of $2,185 at a discount rate of 10 percent, which indicates that the project's rate of return exceeds 10 percent. Table 9–6 illustrates trial solutions with discount rates of 12 and 14 percent.

The analysis indicates that the project's return is approximately 12 percent. (Its NPV is very small relative to the size of the investment.) If greater accuracy is desired, the true rate of return can be approximated[5] through interpolation, as follows:

| Discount Rate | NPV | Difference |
|---|---|---|
| 12% | $ 213 | |
| 14% | ($1,611) | |
| | | $1,824 |

$$\frac{\$ 213}{\$1,824} \times 2\% = .23\%$$

$$12\% + .23\% = 12.23\%$$

The project will generate a return of 12.23 percent per year on each dollar of invested capital, if the estimates are correct. Table 9–7 illustrates this to help interpret the IRR measure.

**TABLE 9–7**
The Logic of Internal Rate of Return Using Materials-Handling Project Data

| Year | Invested Capital | Return on Investment | Repayment of Invested Capital | Cash Flow |
|---|---|---|---|---|
| 0 | $38,000 | | | |
| 1 | 32,045 | $4,645 | $5,955 | $10,600 |
| 2 | 25,362 | 3,917 | 6,683 | 10,600 |
| 3 | 17,862 | 3,100 | 7,500 | 10,600 |
| 4 | 9,446 | 2,184 | 8,416 | 10,600 |
| 5 | –0– | 1,154 | 9,446 | 10,600 |

---

[5] The interpolation is approximate because the present value of a dollar decreases at an increasing rate as the discount rate is increased. Thus, the discount factors are not linear between the two exact rates; that is, 12 and 14, which were used. However, the results obtained by interpolation are generally accurate; for example, in this case the true rate was 12.224 instead of the interpolated value of 12.234.

In the beginning of the project $38,000 is invested. During the first year the cash flow would be $10,600. A 12.23-percent return[6] on $38,000 would be $4,645; so $5,955 constitutes a repayment of invested capital, leaving $32,045 invested. The required one-year return on that investment would be $3,917, so $6,683 of the next year's flow is capital repayment. This division of each year's cash flow can be continued for the life of the project. At the end of the project's life, it will have, each year, generated a 12.23-percent return; and over the life of the project, it will have repaid all of the original invested capital.

REPETITIVE

✓ As indicated earlier, the IRR solution generally involves an iterative trial-and-error solution. However, there is a situation[7] where the solution can be derived directly. Examining this situation can improve the efficiency of the calculations for more complicated problems. Where the annual inflows are all of equal amounts, the present value of an annuity calculation from Chapter 8 can be utilized. However, in this case, the analysis is worked backward. Before, the calculation was to determine the present value. This time it is to ascertain the discount factor.

If a project is expected to generate a level benefit stream, such as our materials handling project's $10,600 a year, some present value of annuity factor exists which will make the present value of those benefits equal to the project's cost of $38,000. The factor can be found by substituting into the present value of an annuity equation.

$$PV_A = a[V_{\overline{n}|\,i}]$$
$$\$38{,}000 = \$10{,}600 \cdot V_{\overline{n}|\,i}$$
$$\frac{\$38{,}000}{\$10{,}600} = V_{\overline{n}|\,i} = 3.585$$

The implied discount rate can be ascertained by looking up this factor in the tables. Using Appendix B, go across the 5-year row until a factor of approximately 3.585 is encountered. The factor for 12 percent is 3.605, which is fairly close. The calculated factor is slightly less, so the project's return is slightly greater than 12 percent as the previous solution indicated.

Although the technique is only truly accurate for level flow projects, it can help with others, those with non-level flows, by providing a starting point. Consider a project with these flows:

| $t_0$ | $t_1$ | $t_2$ | $t_3$ |
|---|---|---|---|
| ($1,800) | $1,000 | $800 | $600 |

Recognizing that the flow averages $800 a year allows an approximation to the *IRR* by direct solution.

---

[6] To avoid rounding error, the true rate of 12.224 percent was used for construction of the table.

[7] The IRR can also be solved directly where there is only one inflow by using an analogous solution utilizing the present-value-of-a-dollar table.

$$PV_A = a[V_{\overline{m}|\,i}]$$
$$\$1{,}800 = \$800[V_{\overline{m}|\,i}]$$
$$\frac{1{,}800}{\$800} = V_{\overline{m}|\,i} = 2.25$$

Checking the table suggests that the project returns approximately 16 percent.

Using the 16-percent factors demonstrates that the approximation identified a relatively efficient first-trial discount rate:

| $t_0$ | $t_1$ | $t_2$ | $t_3$ |
|---|---|---|---|
| ($1,800) | $1,000 | $800 | $600 |
| 862 | ←——.862 | .743 | .641 |
| 594 | ← | | |
| 385 | ← | | |
| $   41 | | | |

One more iteration would provide the basis for the IRR interpolation. Many computer installations have canned IRR programs which eliminate the need for this time-saving approximation. However, where hand calculation is involved with complex problems, the technique can help reduce the drudgery.

As with the other discounted cash flow techniques, there is a logical acceptance rule that follows naturally from the analysis. If a project's internal rate of return exceeds the company's minimum required return, it is acceptable and should be undertaken.

## Ranking Projects

Each of the discounted cash flow techniques provides a ranking criterion. The higher the NPV, or PI, or IRR, the better. Therefore, if two or more projects are to be ranked, they can be placed in descending order by these measures. This ranking procedure would lead to the firm's undertaking the "best" projects first.

Generally, all three of the techniques will establish the same priority. However, because of slightly different underlying assumptions, the techniques can produce conflicting results on occasion. Two areas where the techniques differ in their assumptions are (1) the assumed reinvestment rate for interim cash flows, and (2) recognition of existence of external constraints.

The "discounting" in discounted cash flow analysis is performed to recognize the earning power that has been foregone by not having the money now. If money did not have this earning power (if it could not be invested) there would be no need for discounting. Future dollars would be just as valuable as current dollars, if there were no opportunity to invest the money in the interim.

The techniques just reviewed differ in their underlying assumptions as

168   Part II   Financial Planning and Control

to the rate of return that can be earned on the interim investment. To illustrate the difference, a simple numerical example is helpful. Assume a firm which requires a 6 percent return is reviewing an investment with cash flows as follows:

| $t_0$ | $t_3$ | $t_1$ | $t_2$ |
|---|---|---|---|
| ($2,400) | $1,000 | $1,000 | $1,000 |

The NPV can be calculated quickly because of the level flow. The NPV is $273 because the present value of the inflows is $2,673, calculated as the present value of a $1,000 three-year annuity at 6 percent. But why is the present value of $1,000 a year for three years $2,673?

The answer is made apparent by Table 9–8. If $2,673 were invested at 6 percent for three years, the balance, principal and interest at the end of three years would be $3,184. If, on the other hand, the individual $1,000 flows are invested as they are received, the ending balance is the same, $3,184. The amount of $2,673 is referred to as the present value of the annuity because it will generate the same terminal amount as the annuity if invested at 6 percent. Net present value and its alter-ego, the profitability index, both implicitly assume that the interim flows can be *reinvested* at the discount rate used in the analysis.

TABLE 9–8
Present and Future Values of a Simple Three-Year Annuity at 6 Percent

|  | | Present Value | Future Value |
|---|---|---|---|
| Flow at end of Year One | $1,000 | $ 943 | $1,124 |
| Flow at end of Year Two | 1,000 | 890 | 1,060 |
| Flow at end of Year Three | 1,000 | 840 | 1,000 |
|  |  | $2,673 | $3,184 |
| $2,673(1.06)^3 = $3,184 | | | |

Because of the way in which the analysis is done, the internal rate of return uses a different discount rate and therefore assumes a different reinvestment rate. This example problem is amenable to direct IRR solution:

$$PV_A = a[V_{\overline{n}|\,i}]$$
$$\$2,400 = \$1,000[V_{\overline{n}|\,i}]$$
$$\frac{\$2,400}{\$1,000} = V_{\overline{n}|\,i} = 2.4$$
$$IRR = 12\%$$

The return on the project is 12 percent because $2,400 invested at 12 percent will generate the same terminal amount as the interim flows if they too are invested at 12 percent (see Table 9–9). The IRR method assumes that interim flows can be reinvested at the internal rate of return arrived at in the final solution.

## TABLE 9-9
Present and Future Value of a Simple Three-Year Annuity Using the IRR Rate of 12 Percent

|  |  | Present Value | Future Value |
|---|---|---|---|
| Flow at end of Year One | $1,000 | $ 893 | $1,254 |
| Flow at end of Year Two | 1,000 | 797 | 1,120 |
| Flow at end of Year Three | 1,000 | 710 | 1,000 |
|  |  | $2,400 | $3,374 |

$2,400(1.12)^3 = $3,374

Another difference between the NPV and IRR techniques is the recognition of external constraints. Net present value, as it stands, does not consider any outside constraints; most noticeably it ignores the possibility of a capital constraint. It implicitly suggests that all projects with a positive NPV should be undertaken and that the money will be available if the firm has correctly specified its cutoff rate.

These differences in assumptions create certain biases. The NPV approach tends to favor large projects. Comparing Project A to Project B on Table 9-10 provides an exaggerated example to illustrate this point.

## TABLE 9-10
Comparison of Projects A, B, & C Using a Discount Rate of 6 Percent

| Project A: |  | $t_0$ | $t_1$ |
|---|---|---|---|
|  |  | $ (1,000) | $ 1,400 |
|  |  | 1,320 ← | .943 |
| NPV |  | $ 320 |  |
| IRR |  | 40% | PI = 1.32 |
| Project B: |  | $t_0$ | $t_1$ |
|  |  | $(100,000) | $120,000 |
|  |  | 113,160 ← | .943 |
| NPV |  | $ 13,160 |  |
| IRR |  | 20% | PI = 1.13 |
| Project C: |  | $t_0$ | $t_{10}$ |
|  |  | $ (1,000) | $ 6,192 |
|  |  | 2,390 ← | .386 |
| NPV |  | $ 1,390 |  |
| IRR |  | 20% | PI = 2.39 |

Based on the NPV method, Project B is more attractive than Project A, even though it has a lower rate of return. If the firm has unlimited capital, this conclusion is defensible. With unlimited funds a firm would be better off employing $100,000 at a 20-percent return than investing $1,000 at 40 percent. However, it is important to be aware of this bias in the NPV method. This is the principal reason for the development of the

PI—it preserves the reinvestment rate assumption of the NPV approach, but it also considers how profitably each dollar is employed.

The reinvestment rate assumption creates another bias. Because the IRR on all acceptable projects (IRR greater than the required rate) would be higher than the reinvestment rate used in calculating the NPV (and PI), the IRR tends to favor projects with earlier returns.

In Table 9–10, Projects A and C are of the same size, but they have a different time pattern of returns. Project A is expected to generate a 40 percent return at the end of a year. Project C does not generate any returns until the tenth year, but the cash flow in that year constitutes a 20-percent compound rate of return per year for the life of the project. This level of return makes the project more attractive than Project A from both a NPV and a PI perspective. However, because the IRR method implicitly assumes that Project A's cash flow can be reinvested at a rate of 40 percent, it strongly favors Project A.

All three of the discounted cash flow techniques are marked improvements over earlier attempts at analysis of capital investments. The problems arising from the differing assumptions are relatively minor. Generally, all of the techniques will give the same rankings to the firm's projects. The conflicting rankings are most perplexing where two projects are mutually exclusive; that is, accepting one project means rejecting the other. In this case, the analyst should examine the underlying assumptions of the methods and use the one which most accurately coincides with the circumstances of the firm.

If the company has relatively easy access to capital and if it can undertake most acceptable projects, then the NPV approach and its assumptions seem reasonable. For the smaller firm, where raising capital is a continuing problem, each project in effect has the next-best project as its opportunity cost. Under these circumstances, the reinvestment rate assumption of the IRR is easier to defend.

Once the problems concerning mutually exclusive projects have been resolved, the capital budget can be determined. If the firm can raise sufficient capital, it should undertake all acceptable projects; that is, those with NPV's greater than zero, PI's greater than one, or IRR's greater than the firm's required return. If the firm is limited in its ability to finance new projects, it is operating under conditions of *capital rationing*. Under such circumstances, the method of analysis should consider the existing capital constraint, or limit.

## Capital Rationing

Capital rationing may be externally or internally imposed. "Externally imposed" means that the size of the capital budget is dictated to the firm by an outside force or conditions. Examples might include limited out-

## 9 Capital Budgeting

side capital availability due to economic conditions and limitations written into previously negotiated contracts which are still in force.

In addition to such outside constraints, firms sometimes limit their capital investments voluntarily. Such "internally imposed" rationing is sometimes attributable to managers' or owners' fears of debt financing. (This reluctance to use excessive debt can be observed in a number of firms that "survived the great depression.") Reluctance to issue new equity can also constrain capital investment, which sometimes occurs when owners are concerned about loss of voting control.

Regardless of the origin of the constraint, a limit on the size of the capital budget should be explicitly considered in the analysis. There have been a number of approaches suggested. Two of them, the use of the IRR and the PI, are approximations. The other, which uses the NPV, is theoretically correct, but it is more tedious to apply.

The IRR approach ranks all projects by their IRR's and finances as many of the projects as possible. This approach attempts to select those projects which generate the maximum return per dollar. It will arrive at approximately the same result as the theoretically correct approach unless there are marked differences in either (1) the dollar size of individual projects, or (2) the time patterns of the returns of the projects. Because of the reinvestment rate assumption, the IRR approach may get maximum rate of return on the dollars invested. However, it could result in fewer dollars being invested now or, more importantly, in the future when the early return projects pay out.

The PI approach ranks all projects by their PI's and finances as many as possible. If all projects were divisible; that is, if the firm could take on part of a project, this approach would identify the same solution as the correct method. However, because projects are not divisible, the PI approach can result in less than optimal capital allocation. It is a reasonably efficient approximation where the individual projects are a small percentage of the total budget.

The best method of handling capital rationing is a constrained maximization of the NPV of the capital budget. Although that sounds imposing, the idea is not complex. Find the capital budget which gives the highest NPV without exceeding the number of dollars available. This provides the firm with the highest possible net benefit, in current dollars, that it can purchase with its constrained budget.

Development and discussion of this approach generally makes use of linear programming. However, a reasonably efficient solution can be obtained by systematic trial-and-error examination of the potential capital budgets. The program follows these steps:

1. Identify the dollar size of the capital budget; that is, the constraint.
2. Calculate the NPV of all individual projects, eliminating those that are negative.

3. List all projects in ascending order by cost and, using the constraint, determine the maximum number of projects that can be financed. This is the "upper bound."
4. List all projects in descending order by NPV. List the highest NPV project first, the next highest second, and continue in this manner down to the lowest NPV project. Use the constraint to determine how many of the projects, so ordered, could be financed. This is the "lower bound." No budget with fewer than this number of projects need be considered. Further, the budget defining the lower bound is the best budget of this number.
5. List all feasible combinations between the upper and lower bounds. Any combination which would cost more than the constraint is nonfeasible.
6. Calculate the NPV of each feasible solution.
7. Select the combination with the highest NPV which is the optimal solution, given the constraint.

Although the process sounds involved, it really is nothing more than a way of eliminating many useless possible solutions. To better envision the process, examine the hypothetical capital budget in Table 9–11.

TABLE 9–11
Determination of a Constrained Capital Budget

1. Maximum Capital budget: $250,000.
2. NPV of individual projects as follows:

| Project | Cost | NPV | |
|---|---|---|---|
| A | $ 50,000 | $22,000 | |
| B | 100,000 | 47,000 | |
| C | 80,000 | 32,000 | |
| D | 40,000 | 14,000 | |
| E | 120,000 | (30,000) | eliminated |
| F | 60,000 | 17,000 | |
| G | 25,000 | 10,000 | |

3. Establish upper bound:

| Project | Cost | |
|---|---|---|
| G | $ 25,000 | |
| D | 40,000 | |
| A | 50,000 | 4 maximum |
| F | 60,000 | |
| C | 80,000 | |
| B | 100,000 | |

4. Establish lower bound:

| Project | NPV | Cost | |
|---|---|---|---|
| B | $47,000 | $100,000 | |
| C | 32,000 | 80,000 | 3 minimum |
| A | 22,000 | 50,000 | |
| F | 17,000 | 60,000 | |
| D | 14,000 | 40,000 | |
| G | 10,000 | 25,000 | |

5. List of all feasible solutions.

## TABLE 9–11 (continued)

6. Calculate their NPV's:

| Sets of 3 | Cost | NPV |
|---|---|---|
| ABC | $230,000 | $101,000 |

All other sets of 3 will have lower NPV's.

| Sets of 4 | | |
|---|---|---|
| ABCD | 270,000* | — |
| ABCF | 290,000* | — |
| ABCG | 255,000* | — |
| ABDF | 250,000 | 100,000 |
| ABDG | 215,000 | 93,000 |
| | | |
| ABFG | 235,000 | 96,000 |
| ACDF | 230,000 | 85,000 |
| ACDG | 195,000 | 78,000 |
| ACFG | 215,000 | 81,000 |
| ADFG | 175,000 | 63,000 |
| | | |
| BCDF | 280,000* | — |
| BCDG | 245,000 | 103,000† |
| BCFG | 265,000* | — |
| BDFG | 225,000 | 88,000 |
| CDFG | 205,000 | 74,000 |

\* not feasible
† Combination BCDG has the highest NPV.

7. Select the constrained maximum.

Given the dollars involved, it seems foolish to use a shortcut which might save an hour or two, at best. The difference could be thousands of dollars. The possible benefits justify the added effort.

## Summary

Capital budgeting is the analysis of long term investment proposals being considered by the firm. The investment process involves three stages: proposal generation, analysis, and implementation. The chapter coverage concentrated on the analysis phase of capital budgeting because analysis is generally considered to be a responsibility of the financial manager. Careful analysis is important in this area because capital investments are generally expensive, long-lived, and relatively irreversible.

Capital budgeting analysis involves determining the cost of a project, estimating the expected benefits, and combining the two into some form of reasoned analysis. Because the benefits will be extended over a number of years, the method of analysis should consider the time value of money. Three approaches explicitly consider money's time value. They are net present value, profitability index, and internal rate of return.

Net present value analysis tells the analyst how much better off the firm can expect to be, in current dollars, by undertaking an investment.

The profitability index allows a slightly different interpretation. It is the number of current dollar equivalents, expected, *per dollar of investment*. The internal rate of return is the expected per-period return on the invested balance.

Although the interpretations are different, the three methods generally produce consistent results. However, in ranking two projects, the techniques can give different results if the projects are markedly different in size or in the time pattern of expected benefits. This is because of the assumptions of the techniques. When the inconsistent rankings concern mutually exclusive projects, a common sense comparison of the analytical assumptions and the real world situation can help the analyst resolve the problem.

If the problems of inconsistent rankings are resolved, all of the techniques will specify the same capital budget; that is, investment total. If the size of the capital budget is constrained by either external or internal factors, the analysis should recognize it explicitly. Use of a programming algorithm and the NPV's is generally recognized as the best approach. However, shortcuts have been suggested which are reasonable approximations under certain conditions.

Before discussing the methods of analysis, the reader was warned that the output of the calculations was no better than the quality of the estimates. Sophisticated analysis will not compensate for poor informational input. This can be summarized quite cryptically: GIGO—garbage in, garbage out. The methods of analysis covered in the chapter are among the most valuable in finance, but quality estimates are a prerequisite to sound decision-making.

## QUESTIONS

1. What are the three stages of the capital investment process? Which did the text coverage emphasize? Why?
2. Define capital budgeting and the capital budget.
3. Why is cost defined in terms of the cash purchase price of an asset?
4. What is the purpose of depreciation accounting and why must depreciation flows be considered in capital-budgeting analysis?
5. Explain the advantages and disadvantages of payback as a capital-budgeting technique.
6. Distinguish between the average rate of return and the internal rate of return.
7. In your own words, express the meaning of the results found by the three discounted cash flow techniques: NPV, PI, and IRR.
8. Under what conditions might the discounted cash flow techniques give inconsistent rankings to two projects and why?
9. Explain briefly what the programming approach to capital budgeting under rationing is doing.

## 9 Capital Budgeting

10. Why is the assembling of data so important in capital budgeting?

## PROBLEMS

1. Find the present value of the following cash flows (assuming the required rate of return equals 10 percent):

    | Year | A | B | C |
    |---|---|---|---|
    | 1 | $1,000 | $1,000 | $1,000 |
    | 2 | 1,000 | 1,000 | 1,000 |
    | 3 | 1,000 | 1,000 | 1,000 |
    | 4 | 1,000 | 1,000 | 2,000 |
    | 5 | 5,000 | 5,000 | 3,000 |
    | 6 |  | 5,000 | 5,000 |
    | 7 |  | 5,000 | 5,000 |
    | 8 |  | 5,000 | –0– |
    | 9 |  |  | 5,000 |
    | 10 |  |  | 5,000 |

2. If the cash flows in Problem 1 represent the benefits from three different investments and if the cost of each investment (cash outflow occurring in beginning year) was $4,000 for A, $9,000 for B, and $13,000 for C, find the:
    a. Payback.
    b. Net present value.
    c. Profitability index.

3. Find the internal rate of return of the following investment proposals:

    |  | A | B | C |
    |---|---|---|---|
    | Outflow | $4,100 | $ 250 | $5,250 |
    | Benefits in year |  |  |  |
    | 1 | 1,000 | –0– | 1,000 |
    | 2 | 1,000 | –0– | 1,000 |
    | 3 | 1,000 | –0– | 2,000 |
    | 4 | 1,000 | –0– | 2,000 |
    | 5 | 1,000 | 1,000 | 4,000 |

4. Elco Manufacturing, Inc., is contemplating the purchase of a new computer-controlled processing machine. The machine, including installation, would cost the company $60,000, if purchased outright. If the company bought the machine, they could trade in their two old processors for $8,000. This would involve a small loss in that the book value of the old machines is currently $10,000.

    Either the old machines or the new one would be usable for ten years. Depreciation on either would be straight-line to a zero salvage. (The company figures either would be worthless after ten years.) The principal reason for the changeover would be cost. Although no increases in revenue would be attributable to the new machine, it would cut labor costs by $13,000 a year before taxes, which are at a 40-percent rate. The firm's required rate of return is 10 percent.

a. Calculate payback and average rate of return.
b. Calculate the NPV.
c. Calculate the PI.
d. Calculate the IRR. Use the direct solution and report to the nearest whole percent (do not interpolate).

5. Elco Manufacturing, Inc., could buy an updated version of a piece of equipment they are currently using. It would cost $25,000. The purchase would allow the firm to dispose of one of its old processors and some related machinery. The old equipment could be sold for $5,000 (its current book value is $6,000). The new machinery would reduce labor costs by $5,500 a year before taxes.

Either the new equipment or the old processor would last for 10 years. Depreciation is straight-line to a zero salvage, which is a realistic estimate of the future worth of either setup. The company is in a 40-percent tax bracket and requires a 10-percent rate of return.

a. Calculate the NPV.
b. Calculate the PI.
c. Calculate the IRR.

6. A new processing system has been developed which is compatible with Elco Manufacturing's operations. The manufacturer would sell the system to them for $27,800, installed, if it were purchased outright. The manufacturer agrees to take the company's old equipment in trade upon completion of the installation. This would facilitate the changeover. However, the manufacturer will only allow the firm $7,000 for the equipment even though its book value is $10,000.

The benefits of the equipment are twofold. It produces more and it is cheaper to operate. Elco is certain it can sell the increased production. The equipment is expected to have a useful life of five years. The expected revenues and cost savings it would generate per year are:

| Year | Added Revenues | Reduced Expenses |
|---|---|---|
| 1 | $5,000 | $5,500 |
| 2 | 5,000 | 4,300 |
| 3 | 5,000 | 3,100 |
| 4 | 4,000 | 1,900 |
| 5 | 4,000 | 1,800 |

For purposes of analysis, it is assumed that both the new equipment or that which is replaced would be worthless after five years.

Depreciation on either would be straight-line over a five-year life toward a zero salvage. The firm is in a 40-percent tax bracket and expects a 10 percent return on invested capital.

a. Calculate the NPV.
b. Calculate the PI.
c. Calculate the IRR. (Don't forget the shortcut.)

7. The projects in Problems 4 and 5 could be mutually exclusive alternatives. Discuss the inconsistent rankings achieved with the NPV and the IRR measures. Why did the inconsistency occur and how would you resolve it?

## 9 Capital Budgeting

8. The projects in Problems 5 and 6 could be mutually exclusive alternatives. Discuss the inconsistent ranking achieved by the different methods. Why did this occur and how would you resolve the issue?
9. The Tucson Company is considering the replacement of a piece of molding equipment in its household appliance division. Company accountants have given you the following information. If you were the president, what action would be appropriate?

|  | (A) Present Machine | (B) Proposed Machine |
|---|---|---|
| Book value | $20,000 | |
| List price | | $65,000 |
| Expected remaining life | 5 | |
| Expected life | | 5 |
| Salvage value | –0– | $ 5,000 |
| Trade-in value | $15,000 | |
| Cash operating expense | $30,000 | $30,000 |
| Revenues | $75,000 | $90,000 |

Assume that both machines are depreciated on a straight-line basis. The firm is in a 40-percent income tax bracket and has a required rate of return of 10 percent. (Calculate the NPV and PI.)

10. Given a required return of 8 percent, which of proposals A, B, and C would you select if you had a maximum of $22,000 to invest, using:
    a. The payback method?
    b. The net-present-value method?
    c. The profitability index?

|  | A | B | C |
|---|---|---|---|
| Outlay | $10,000 | $8,000 | $12,000 |
| Benefits in year | | | |
| 1 | 3,000 | 4,000 | 6,000 |
| 2 | 3,000 | 3,000 | 6,000 |
| 3 | 3,000 | 1,600 | 4,000 |
| 4 | 3,000 | 1,600 | –0– |
| 5 | 3,000 | 1,600 | –0– |

Which two proposals would you select regardless of the method of evaluation?

## ADDITIONAL READINGS

Abdelsamad, M. H., and E. H. Hunt. "Capital Expenditure Analysis: Key to Financial Management," *Administrative Management*, vol. 34 (October 1973), pp. 63–66.

Bernhard, R. H. "Mathematical Programming Models for Capital Budgeting—A Survey, Generalization, and Critique," *Journal of Financial and Quantitative Analysis*, vol. 4 (June 1969), pp. 111–58.

Bierman, H., Jr., and S. Smidt. *The Capital Budgeting Decision,* 4th ed. New York: Macmillan Company, 1975).

Dean, J. *Capital Budgeting.* New York: Columbia University Press, 1951.

Fogler, H. R. "Ranking Techniques and Capital Rationing," *Accounting Review,* vol. 47 (January 1972), pp. 134–43.

Haynes, W. W., and M. B. Solomon, Jr. "A Misplaced Emphasis in Capital Budgeting," *Quarterly Review of Economics and Business,* (February 1962), pp. 39–46.

Johnson, R. W. *Capital Budgeting.* Belmont, Calif.: Wadsworth Publishing Co., Inc., 1970.

Lorie, J. H., and L. J. Savage. "Three Problems in Rationing Capital," *Journal of Business,* vol. 28 (October 1955), pp. 229–39.

Mao, J. C. T. "Survey of Capital Budgeting: Theory and Practice," *Journal of Finance,* vol. 25 (May 1970), pp. 349–60.

Quirin, G. D. *The Capital Expenditure Decision.* Homewood, Ill.: Richard D. Irwin, Inc., 1967.

Robichek, A. A., D. G. Ogilvie, and J. D. C. Roach. "Capital Budgeting: A Pragmatic Approach," *Financial Executive,* vol. 37 (April 1969), pp. 26–38.

Schwab, B., and P. Lusztig. "A Comparative Analysis of the Net Present Value and the Benefit-Cost Ratios as Measures of the Economic Desirability of Investments," *Journal of Finance,* vol. 24 (June 1969), pp. 507–16.

Tilles, S. "Strategies for Allocating Funds," *Harvard Business Review,* vol. 44 (January–February 1966), pp. 72–80.

Vandell, R. F., and P. J. Stonich. "Capital Budgeting: Theory or Results?" *Financial Executive,* vol. 4 (August 1973), pp. 46–56.

# 10
# Capital Budgeting under Uncertainty

The preceding chapter examined several approaches to evaluating investment proposals. The preferred methods, the discounted cash flow techniques, used the firm's required rate of return as the appropriate basis for decision making. By discounting, expected future benefits were converted into current equivalents that could be compared to current costs. In the analysis, only a single value was used for each expected cash flow even though some of the cash flows were subject to a wide range of possible outcomes. Some future events can be forecast relatively accurately. Others are subject to a wider margin of error. The potential error in a forecast is generally referred to as its riskiness. To use a single discount rate for all flows, as was done in the previous chapter, the flows should be of the same level of riskiness. Although it was not emphasized, the analysis in the last chapter assumed that all projects under consideration were of average riskiness.

If an investment had no risk, the investor would still expect to receive payment for the use of the capital but should not require an additional payment for risk assumption. The rate of return required as payment for waiting only is referred to as the *riskless rate*.

The classic example of an investment with such a rate of return is a Treasury bill that matures in one day. Governmental taxing power assures that funds will be available for payment, and the short time span eliminates the risk of other contingencies. Some business investments also offer assured returns: if a firm buys a computer, it is certain to avoid the lease payments it would otherwise incur; if the firm retires a bond issue, it is assured the future interest payments are eliminated. However, most business ventures are less certain. The degree of potential error can vary widely from one project to the next. The purpose of this chapter is

180   Part II   Financial Planning and Control

to suggest ways in which this aspect of a potential investment might be incorporated into the analysis.

Risk and uncertainty is one of the most topical areas in finance. Progress is being made on the incorporation of risk into all financial decision making. The topic has its own set of definitions, which will be reviewed. The application to capital budgeting can then be discussed.

## Certainty, Risk, and Uncertainty

The definition of these terms, in a precise sense, derives from the model of a decision. The model of a decision is descriptive of all situations which involve a reasoned choice of a course of action from among competing alternatives. The decision-maker's problem is to choose the course of action which is expected to be the best, based on a prediction about the future, and based on a specific criterion. What the decision model does is provide labels for these elements.

The different courses of action that can be taken are referred to as *alternatives*. Each possible future set of circumstances that might occur is referred to as a *state of nature*. Each state of nature has a certain likelihood of occurrence, referred to as the *probability* of that state of nature. The basis of choice is called the *efficiency measure* or *decision variable*. What a decision involves then is a choice of the best alternative based on the expected value of the efficiency measure.

The difference between certainty, risk, and uncertainty is the amount of information the decision-maker has, or assumes, about the probabilities of the states of nature. If the decision-maker knows which state of nature will occur (probability of that state equals one), the situation is one of certainty. If more than one state is likely, *and the probabilities can be specified*, the situation is one of risk. If the states can be specified, *but their probabilities cannot*, the situation is one of uncertainty.

For illustrative purposes, the following example is presented. A small entrepreneur, a street vendor near an amusement center, is contemplating the decision of what product line to carry on a given day. The vendor's cart is insulated. However, it is only capable of carrying either cold goods, ice cream and other frozen delights, or hot products such as coffee and sandwiches. The sale of frozen goods is potentially more profitable due to higher margin and high sales on hot days, but their sales are poor on cool and/or rainy days. The vendor knows the probable profits for each product under each set of circumstances. The predictions for the alternatives are presented in Table 10–1.

After reviewing Table 10–1, the nature of the vendor's problem becomes more evident, and it can serve as the basis of a discussion of the different decision situations. If the vendor knew which state of nature were going to occur, the problem would be solved—simply take the alternative which offered the greater profits. This is *decision making under*

## 10  Capital Budgeting under Uncertainty

**TABLE 10–1**
Expected Profits under Varying Conditions for Two Different Product Lines

| Alternatives | States of Nature | | | |
|---|---|---|---|---|
| | Hot and Clear | Hot and Rainy | Cool and Clear | Cool and Rainy |
| Cold goods . . . . . | 40 | (10) | 0 | (15) |
| Hot goods . . . . . . | 15 | (5) | 20 | 15 |

*certainty.* A certainty situation is one where the analyst knows, or assumes, that the probability of some state of nature is one.

If the vendor did not know which state was going to occur but could assign probabilities to the various states, the process would be referred to as decision making under risk. The prescription in this case would be to make a decision based on the *expected value* of the efficiency measure. The procedure is illustrated in Table 10–2.

**TABLE 10–2**
Decision-Making under Risk

| Alternatives | States of Nature | | | | Expected Value (Standard Deviation) |
|---|---|---|---|---|---|
| | Hot and Clear | Hot and Rainy | Cold and Clear | Cold and Rainy | |
| Cold goods . . . . | 40 | (10) | 0 | (15) | 26.25 (21.26) |
| Hot goods . . . . . . | 15 | (5) | 20 | 15 | 13.75 (6.50) |
| Probability of state . . . . . . . | .70 | .10 | .15 | .05 | |

Note that the illustration includes two summary statistics: the expected value and the standard deviation. The expected value, or mean, is a measure of central tendency and is calculated as $\hat{E} = \Sigma[P(S) \cdot E]$. Standard deviation measures dispersion, or spread, and is calculated $\sigma = \Sigma[P(S) \cdot (E - \hat{E})^2])^{1/2}$. In both cases, $P(S)$ is the probability of the state and $E$ is the value of the efficiency measure given that state. The symbol $\hat{E}$ stands for expected value and $\sigma$ is the symbol for standard deviation.

In the illustration the expected value of carrying cold goods is:

$$.70(40) + .10(-10) + .15(0) + .05(-15) = 26.25$$

This is the average profit per day that would be expected over a large number of days.

The standard deviation is the square root of the sum:[1]

$$.70[(40-26.25)^2] + .10[(-10-26.25)^2] + .15[(0-26.25)^2] + .05[(-15-26.25)^2] = 452.19$$

---
[1] This sum is called the variance.

The standard deviation is 21.26. This measure indicates that the variation in profits on a day-to-day basis could be quite large.

In this instance, the expected profit is higher with the frozen desserts. Note that decision making under risk is not synonymous with decision making that considers the degree of risk. Carrying ice cream is riskier in the sense that the potential error of the forecast is larger as indicated by the standard deviation. Decision making under risk only means that probability estimates were used. If a consideration of risk is to be included, measures such as the standard deviation can assist in the analysis.

If probabilities cannot be specified, the situation is one of decision making under uncertainty. There is no clear-cut decision rule for such a problem. There have been some attempts at guidance, but each rule proposed can be shown to have logical weaknesses.

The *maximax* rule proposes that a decision-maker take the alternative that offers the highest potential reward. In this case, carrying cold goods offers the potential of a $40 profit if the weather cooperates. No more than $20 can be made by selling coffee and sandwiches. Such an approach is appropriate only for the supreme optimist. It overlooks the greater potential losses that might be incurred with the refrigerated product line.

The pessimist can also find a decision rule to fit that pattern of decision making. The *maximin* rule says to take the alternative which has the highest low payoff. Coffee and sandwiches never lose more than $5 under any state, whereas the cold products can suffer a $15 loss. The pessimist can minimize the potential losses by selecting the hot product line.

There are other proposals for dealing with an uncertainty situation: Hurwicz criterion, La Place criterion, minimax regret, and others. However, each can be shown to have logical weaknesses. As a result, the uncertainty situation must, to some degree, involve a personal evaluation by the decision-maker as to the appropriate method of evaluating proposals with such limited information. However, the lack of probabilities does not preclude the analyst from considering the *degree of uncertainty*. By studying the matrix in Table 10–2, it is possible to ascertain that the range of outcomes is wider with cold goods and that the potential losses are greater. It could be said, therefore, that the degree of uncertainty is greater with that alternative. Because incorporation of the degree of risk or the degree of uncertainty both involve recognition of the magnitude of potential estimation error, it is common to use the terms *risk* and *uncertainty* as synonyms in this context.

The distinction between decision making under uncertainty and decision making which considers the degree of uncertainty is important because uncertainty is by far the most common condition confronting the financial decision-maker. Most future cash flows of investment proposals depend on future economic activity that is itself uncertain. When uncertainty conditions exist in the business environment, the financial manager must rely on subjective measures to allow for a correct assessment of the investment proposals considered. This is commonly done by separating investment proposals into various uncertainty categories based on management judgment. Other methods that accomplish the same result on an individual project basis include applications of a risk-adjusted discount rate and use of certainty equivalents, techniques that will be discussed in greater detail later in the chapter.

Financial managers will not always need or seek a quantitative measure of risk or uncertainty to evaluate properly an investment proposal. This may be so when the nature of the decision-maker is such that *any* possibility, no matter how small, that a potential project might fail would exclude it from consideration. Likewise, if the decision-maker is looking solely at returns on investments without the associated hazards, a risk or uncertainty measure would be of little value to him. But the typical decision-maker is a risk averter and therefore must understand the types of risks characteristic of investments at appropriate levels of risk and uncertainty.

One broad category of uncertainty of which the financial manager must be aware is economic in nature. If a firm is considering adding a product line, there is always the possibility that there will not be adequate demand for the proposed investment to make it profitable. Furthermore, there is the possibility that inflation will cause an otherwise attractive investment to become much less so. For example, a firm entering into a long-term contract that pays an annual cash inflow of $300 for 20 years may find itself at a distinct disadvantage in trying to exploit its opportunities wisely if an identical investment were open to it five years later that, because of rising prices, provided for a $600-per-year cash inflow.

For certain types of investment proposals, uncertainty of future cash flows due to financial inability of debtors to make payments or changes in estimates as to such financial inability is an important consideration. For example, if one of the investments under consideration by a financial manager is the common stock of a company on the verge of bankruptcy, there is a high degree of cash-flow uncertainty involved that cannot be overlooked.

Technological uncertainty is another type of hazard of which the financial manager should be aware. If a firm decides to purchase a computer that will result in an expected constant cash inflow for 15 years, there would appear to be a great deal of uncertainty of cash flows in the later years of the investment's life due to the rapid advance being made in computer technology in recent years.

Once the financial manager understands the nature of the uncertainty inherent in the particular investment proposal under consideration, a capital budgeting technique that incorporates the risk factor in the decision process can be applied. Some of the more common types are presented below.

## Risk-Adjusted Discount Rate

Adjusting the discount factor to take into account the degree of uncertainty of the future cash flows of an investment proposal is an appropriate capital-budgeting method when conditions of uncertainty exist. In the preceding chapter it was implicitly assumed that all investment proposals had the same degree of risk; thus, each was evaluated by applying the required rate of return as the discount factor. The following general form was the result:

$$\text{Net Present Value} = \sum_{t=0}^{N} \frac{C_t}{(1+K)^t}$$

Where

$K$ = Required rate of return
$C_t$ = Cash inflow in period $t$

However, as was explained earlier in this chapter, some invesment proposals are rather riskless while others have a very high degree of uncertainty as to future cash flows. In evaluating these former investment proposals, it would not seem appropriate to apply a discount factor that implies an average degree of risk. Instead, the riskless rate would be a logical discount rate when an investment proposal is evaluated in an environment of complete certainty as to future cash flows. Likewise, when future cash flows are highly uncertain, some discount factor above the overall required rate of return, determined by management judgment or some rule of thumb (e.g., return on total assets), may be appropriate. In any case, the general formula for finding the acceptable investment projects must be altered. When the adjustment is made to the discount rate, the following expression of the problem results:

$$\text{Net Present Value} = \sum_{t=0}^{N} \frac{C_t}{(1+K^*)^t}$$

Where

$K^*$ = Risk-adjusted discount rate

To illustrate the use of the risk-adjusted rate, consider the following example:

The ABC Corporation is trying to determine whether a new product should be introduced. The initial cost will be $100,000, with net operating cash inflows estimated to be $10,000 for the first two years and $30,000 for the remaining eight years it is expected to sell. While the firm's cost of capital is 10 percent, the financial manager believes this understates the risk inherent in the project because of lack of information about demand

and risk of obsolescence. Therefore, a discount rate of 18 percent is assigned to the project.

Net present value of $3,500 may be found using the following equation:

$$\text{Net Present Value} = -\$100{,}000 + \sum_{t=1}^{2} \frac{\$10{,}000}{(1+.18)^t} + \sum_{t=3}^{10} \frac{\$30{,}000}{(1+.18)^t}$$

$$\text{NPV} = -\$100{,}000 + \$15{,}660 + \$87{,}840 = \$3{,}500$$

Certain problems may arise in using the risk-adjusted-discount-rate approach. Raising the discount rate penalizes projects whose cash flows are heaviest in the later years of the project. This characteristic seems to indicate that only where there is an unusual increase in uncertainty in future years should this method be applied.

A case in point would be the previous example where obsolescence and uncertainty as to demand are very significant factors in the success of the project. Another problem, which is not unique to this approach, is that a quantitative measure of risk does not result from the analysis that can be used for comparing proposals.

## Certainty-Equivalent Approach

While the risk-adjusted-discount-rate approach adjusts for uncertainty in the denominator, the certainty-equivalent approach makes the uncertainty adjustment to the cash flows themselves. The resulting general formula is as follows:

$$\text{Net Present Value} = \sum_{t=0}^{N} \frac{A_t C_t}{(1+i)^t}$$

$A_t$ = Certainty equivalent coefficient in period $t$
$i$ = Riskless rate

The logic used to determine the certainty-equivalent coefficient with this approach parallels that used in arriving at the risk-adjusted discount rate previously described. That is to say, in this case the analysis recognizes that not all investment proposals have the same uncertainty and should be treated separately. However, the size of the coefficient increases as uncertainty decreases, where A takes on values from 0 to 1. Thus, where the financial manager feels the future cash flows are certain, a certainty-equivalent coefficient of 1 should be assigned. If it is felt that there is a high degree of uncertainty of future cash flows, a very low coefficient would be assigned (e.g., .20). The following relationship expresses this concept:

$$A = \frac{\text{Certain cash flow}}{\text{Uncertain cash flow}}$$

It should be noted that the cash flows adjusted for the certainty equivalent are discounted using the riskless rate as the appropriate discount factor. This rate is used since all elements of uncertainty are incorporated in the certainty-equivalent coefficient. In a sense, if a higher discount rate, such as the required rate of return, were used, "double counting" would result. It is also important to recognize that a different certainty equivalent may be used for evaluating the certainty of each period's cash flows. Thus, it would appear logical that in a number of investment proposals the certainty equivalent would diminish over time.

When the internal rate of return is used for the capital-budgeting decision, the problem involves finding the discount rate that equates the present value of the cash inflows and outflows adjusted for uncertainty with the certainty-equivalent coefficient. This rate is then compared with the riskless rate. An acceptable project would be one where the internal rate of return is greater than this riskless rate.

To illustrate the concept of the certainty equivalent, consider the following example:

> The X Corporation has $10,000 to invest for two years. The investment under consideration has expected cash inflows of $7,000 in each of the years. However, the financial manager feels it would be equally desirable to receive a certain $6,300 at the end of the first year and $5,600 at the end of year 2, instead of the two uncertain cash flows. At the present time a Treasury bill yields 7 percent on the open market.

The certainty-equivalent coefficients for the two years are .90 and .80, respectively, determined as follows:

$$A_1 = \frac{\$6,300}{\$7,000} = .90 \qquad A_2 = \frac{\$5,600}{\$7,000} = .80$$

Since the Treasury bill is relatively riskless, it can be assumed that 7 percent approximates the riskless rate. This rate may be used as the proper discount rate to find the net present value of the certain cash flows of $779 as shown below:

$$\text{Net Present Value} = 1.0\,(-\$10,000) + \frac{.90(\$7,000)}{(1.07)^1} + \frac{.80(\$7,000)}{(1.07)^2}$$
$$\text{NPV} = -\$10,000 + \$5,888 + \$4,891 = \$779$$

## Statistical Probability

Under some circumstances, information may be available to the financial manager concerning the probability of various future cash flows. As was previously mentioned, when such probabilities are known, the decision-making process takes place under conditions of risk. In order to illustrate this process, consider the following example:

> The M Corporation is trying to determine whether a particular investment project should be undertaken. The initial investment outlay will be $2,000. As shown in Table 10–3, only three discrete states of nature are possible with known probabilities for each, as well as conditional cash

inflows based on the various states. The firm's required rate is 10 percent, and the period of the annuity is six years.

Two procedures must be followed to make a proper evaluation of the investment proposal.

1. The expected value of the cash flows of the project must be determined by multiplying the probability of occurrence of a particular state of nature by the expected cash flow if that state of nature occurs. This procedure is shown in Table 10–3.

TABLE 10–3
Expected Value of Cash Inflows

| State of Nature | Probability (1) | Conditional Cash Flows (2) | Expected Value (1) x (2) |
|---|---|---|---|
| Boom | .20 | $800 | $160 |
| Normal | .60 | 500 | 300 |
| Recession | .20 | 200 | 40 |
| | | | $500 |

2. The net present value of the project must be determined by discounting the cash flow back to the present time. The resulting net present value of $177.50 is calculated as shown below:

$$\text{Net Present Value} = -\$2,000 + \sum_{t=1}^{6} \frac{\$500}{(1 + .10)^t}$$

While this example is illustrative of the concept of decision-making under conditions of risk, it does not compensate for varying degrees of uncertainty in the decision-making process. Also, it assumes that the states of nature are separate and identifiable rather than part of a continuum. Any decision tools that are to be used by the financial manager should incorporate these factors since they more closely parallel the environment of the firm. The tools most commonly used to meet this objective are the mean and the standard deviation.

In the previous example, the probability distribution of the expected cash flows could be shown as in Figure 10–1A below:

FIGURE 10–1
The Development of the Normal Probability Distribution

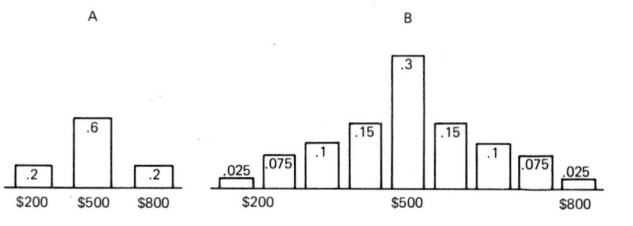
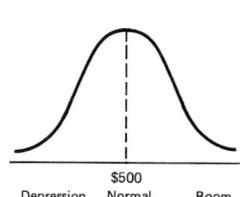

Assume that instead of only three states of nature there are nine (i.e., there are three degrees of depression, three degrees of normalcy, and three degrees of boom). In that case the probability might be as seen in Figure 10–1B. One can visualize that, if these states of nature were further subdivided, the probability distribution would approach the shape of a normal curve with an expected value, or mean, of $500 as shown in Figure 10–1C. This normal curve represents a probability distribution of expected cash flows related to states of nature shown on a continuum.

To carry this illustration one step further, assume that the probability distribution of expected cash flows is as shown in Figure 10–2A below. Since the existence of any state of nature will result in the same future cash flows, there is no element of uncertainty as to the value of these cash flows in the future.

**FIGURE 10–2**
Degrees of Risk and Expected Cash Flows

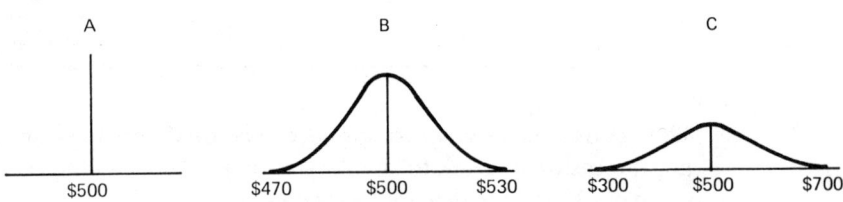

If, however, the cash flows are somewhat dispersed according to the state of nature as shown in Figure 10–2B, the financial manager is not certain the cash flows will be $500 as in the first figure. It can be said that the uncertainty is relatively small because even for the most unexpected states of nature (those states at the tails of the distribution where the probabilities are least) the resultant cash flows will only differ by $30 from what is expected. Finally, if the dispersion is similar to that depicted in Figure 10–2C, the element of uncertainty will be even greater since actual cash flows may take on values anywhere from $300 to $700. The uncertainty element, and therefore the risk to the decision-maker, can be quantitatively determined if the probability distribution is known, by using the following formula:

$$\sigma_t = \sqrt{\Sigma(X_{rt} - \bar{X}_{rt})^2 P_{rt}}$$

$\bar{X}_{rt}$ = Expected value of cash flows in period $t$
$X_{rt}$ = Cash flow for rth possibility in period $t$
$P_{rt}$ = Probability of the occurrence of the rth cash flow in period $t$

This measure of risk, known as the standard deviation, allows the decision-maker to apply the following rules in choosing among alternatives:

1. If two or more investment proposals have the same expected values, those with the lowest standard deviations should be selected.

## 10 Capital Budgeting under Uncertainty

2. If two or more investment proposals have the same standard deviations, those with the highest expected values should be selected.

This procedure is proper for decisions in which comparable expected returns or standard deviations are present. Historically, however, returns vary proportionally with the degree of uncertainty as to future cash flows; and, typically, all investment proposals under consideration are not going to have the same expected return or standard deviation. Therefore, some method must be developed for relating each proposal's measure of risk to the expected value of its cash flows. This is done by using the coefficient of variation as defined below:

$$\text{Coefficient of variation} = \frac{\text{Standard deviation}}{\text{Expected value}} = \frac{\sigma}{\bar{X}}$$

This measure is useful for assigning investment proposals to various risk classes and for selecting among alternative projects. The lower the coefficient of variation, the more attractive is an investment proposal.

This interpretation can be understood more easily if the coefficient of variation (CV) is thought of as the "percentage error." That is, a project with cash flows of $1,000 and a CV of .5 can be thought of as a project with cash flows of $1,000, give or take 50 percent of that amount. The interpretation is not exact; with normally distributed flows, the probability that the flows would be between $500 and $1,500 is 68 percent.[2] However, this interpretation of the CV may explain why a lower CV is preferable. The lower the margin of error relative to the estimate, the better off the analyst is; that is, the lower the degree of uncertainty.

To illustrate the application of the standard deviation, expected value, and coefficient of variation to the capital-budgeting problem, consider the following example:

> The KBA Corporation is trying to choose between two investment proposals. Project A has a standard deviation of $650, while Project B has a standard deviation of $800. The firm's financial manager wants to know which investment to choose, given each of the following combinations of expected values:
>
> 1. Project A and Project B both have an expected value of cash flows of $12,500.
> 2. Project A has an expected value of cash flows of $9,000, while Project B has an expected value of cash flows of $12,500.

In the first situation it is clear that Project A would be preferable, since the expected value of the projects is the same, while the standard deviation, and therefore the uncertainty of the former, is smaller. The second situation requires a comparison of their coefficients of variation. The re-

---

[2] For a normal distribution, 68 percent of the outcomes will fall within plus or minus one standard deviation from the mean.

sult is that Project B would be selected since it has a lower coefficient of variation, as calculated below:

$$\text{Project A} \qquad \text{Project B}$$
$$\frac{\sigma}{\overline{X}} = \frac{\$650}{\$9{,}000} = .072 \qquad \frac{\sigma}{\overline{X}} = \frac{\$800}{\$12{,}500} = .064$$

*Decision-Tree Analysis.* A particularly useful statistical-probability technique under conditions of risk when trying to evaluate cash flows over time is decision-tree analysis. The *decision tree* is a means of graphically illustrating the pattern of relationship among decisions involving conditional probabilities (that is, where the probability of one alternative action is tied into the outcome of another event). Figure 10–3 shows a decision-tree diagram of possible outcomes for a corporation in a two-year period, with the expectation of 0.8 of receiving $1,000 for each of two years, compared to the expectation of 0.2 of receiving no cash flow.

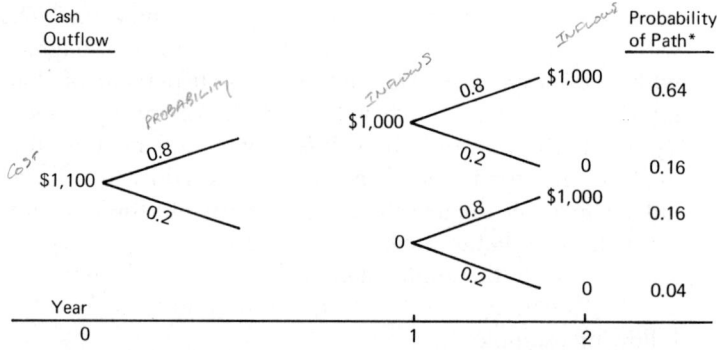

FIGURE 10–3
Decision Tree of Cash-Flow Expectations

° Probability of path equals probability of year 1 times probability of year 2.

The expected discounted cash inflows of the project costing $1,100 may be calculated, assuming a discount rate of 10 percent as the required rate of return, as shown in Tables 10–4. The expected net present value is $287 ($1,387 − $1,100). If the firm accepts the proposal, there is a 0.04 possibility of losing the entire $1,100. On the other hand, the company may gain $1,735 in discounted cash inflows, with a probability of 0.64 of achieving this result. In the other two possibilities, the outcome would result in losses, but these would not be ruinous to the firm. The value of the decision tree is that it sets out various choices and their probability of fulfillment and then proceeds to quantify the result.[3]

---

[3] See James C. T. Mao, *Quantitative Analysis of Financial Decisions* (New York: Macmillan Co., 1966), Chapter 8.

## TABLE 10-4
### Expected Present Value of Discounted Cash Flows

| Calculations (Present Value @ 10% x Conditional Cash Inflows) | Discounted Cash Flows (1) | Probability (2) | Expected Value of Discounted Cash Flows (1) x (2) |
|---|---|---|---|
| 0.909 ($1,000) <br> + .826 ($1,000) | $1,735 | 0.64 | $1,110 |
| .909 ($1,000) <br> + .826 ( 0) | 909 | 0.16 | 145 |
| .909 ( 0) <br> + .826 ($1,000) | 826 | 0.16 | 132 |
| .909 ( 0) <br> + .826 ( 0) | –0– | 0.04 | –0– |
| Expected Present Value | | | $1,387 |

## Summary

Because cash flows of investment proposals will be realized with varying degrees of certainty, capital-budgeting methods must be used that incorporate this uncertainty into the decision process. However, some investment proposals do have certain cash flows. In such cases it is appropriate to use the riskless rate to discount future cash flows.

When there is some degree of uncertainty as to the amount of future cash flows, alternative means of incorporating this uncertainty into the decision process must be found. When uncertainty exists as to future cash flows but there are known probabilities for each of these alternatives, a condition of risk exists. Risk may be evaluated by determining the standard deviation of the distribution. The standard deviation may also be related to the expected value of future cash flows with the use of the coefficient of variation to select among alternative investments. When future cash flows are dependent on present events, the probabilities of which are known, decision-tree analysis becomes a useful tool.

If only a subjective assessment of uncertainty is possible, a condition of uncertainty exists. Appropriate decision tools for such situations include the risk adjusted discount rate and the certainty-equivalent coefficient. The risk-adjusted discount rate adjusts for varying degrees of risk implicit in investment proposals by reducing or increasing the discount rate based on managerial judgment. The certainty-equivalent approach, on the other hand, makes the risk adjustment to the cash flows themselves.

## QUESTIONS

1. Explain the difference between decision making under: certainty, risk, and uncertainty.

2. Distinguish between decision making *under* risk and decision making which *considers* the degree of risk.
3. Explain why the terms degree of risk and degree of uncertainty can often be used interchangeably.
4. Risk-adjusted discount rate and certainty equivalents were suggested as methods for analysis of investment proposals under uncertainty. Can the techniques be used under conditions of risk? How?
5. How is the coefficient of variation used for selecting among alternative investment proposals?
6. Under what conditions is decision-tree analysis useful?

## PROBLEMS

1. The financial manager of a large corporation has determined his firm's required rate of return to be 10 percent. In the past, he has used 80 or 120 percent of the required rate of return as the discount rate for investments that *are not* of average uncertainty. He is currently evaluating two proposals with the following characteristics:

|  | A | B |
|---|---|---|
| Expected life | 10 years | 10 years |
| Uncertainty factor | Below average | Above average |
| Cost | $45,000 | $60,000 |
| Expected net cash flow | $ 6,500 | $12,000 |

Which project(s) would be selected applying the risk-adjusted-discount-rate approach?

2. Assuming the financial manager in problem 1 was indifferent between the cash flows given for project B and the certain cash flow given below, determine whether project B should be selected. Assume a risk-free rate of 6 percent.

| Year | Certain Cash Flows |
|---|---|
| 1–2 | $10,000 |
| 3–7 | 9,000 |
| 8–10 | 8,000 |

3. The Carpet Manufacturing Company uses a certainty-equivalent approach in its capital-budgeting decisions. The company is currently evaluating three proposals. The expected values of the net cash flows are as follows:

| Year | A | B | C |
|---|---|---|---|
| 0 | −$30,000 | −$25,000 | −$20,000 |
| 1 | 10,000 | 12,000 | 8,000 |
| 2 | 10,000 | 12,000 | 9,000 |
| 3 | 10,000 | 12,000 | 10,000 |
| 4 | 8,000 | 12,000 | 10,000 |

In analyzing the three proposals, the financial manager provided the following certainty equivalents:

## 10 Capital Budgeting under Uncertainty

| Year | A | B | C |
|---|---|---|---|
| 0 | 1.00 | 1.00 | 1.00 |
| 1 | .95 | .95 | .95 |
| 2 | .90 | .80 | .90 |
| 3 | .80 | .70 | .90 |
| 4 | .70 | .50 | .90 |

If U.S. Treasury bills are currently yielding 4 percent, which proposal(s) should be selected?

4. Begs, Inc., is faced with investing in one of the proposals listed below:

| A | | B | | C | |
|---|---|---|---|---|---|
| Probability | Net Cash Flow | Probability | Net Cash Flow | Probability | Net Cash Flow |
| .1 | $1,000 | .2 | $1,000 | .4 | $1,000 |
| .2 | 2,000 | .2 | 2,000 | .4 | 2,000 |
| .3 | 3,000 | .3 | 3,000 | .1 | 3,000 |
| .4 | 4,000 | .3 | 4,000 | .1 | 4,000 |

If the company is averse to risk, which proposal should it undertake?

5. *a.* If the company in the preceding problem was not averse to uncertainty, which proposal would it select? Why?

   *b.* If the probability distribution for proposal C was as follows, would this change your answer? Assume Begs is averse to uncertainty.

| Probability | Net Cash Flow |
|---|---|
| .1 | $1,000 |
| .2 | 2,000 |
| .5 | 3,000 |
| .2 | 4,000 |

## ADDITIONAL READINGS

Bierman, H., Jr., and J. E. Hass. "Capital Budgeting Under Uncertainty: A Reformulation," *Journal of Finance*, vol. 28 (March 1973), pp. 119–29.

Byrne, R., A. Charnes, A. Cooper, and K. Kortanek. "Some New Approaches to Risk," *Accounting Review*, vol. 63 (January 1968), pp. 18–37.

Farrar, D. E. *The Investment Decision Under Uncertainty*. Englewood Cliffs, N.J.: Prentice-Hall, Inc., 1962.

Greer, W. R., Jr. "Capital Budgeting Analysis with the Timing of Events Uncertain," *Accounting Review*, vol. 45 (January 1970), pp. 103–14.

———. "Theory Versus Practice in Risk Analysis: An Empirical Study" *Accounting Review*, vol. 49 (July 1974), pp. 496–505.

Henderson, G. V., Jr., and A. H. Barnett. "Breakeven Present Value: A Pragmatic Approach to Capital Budgeting Under Risk and Uncertainty," *Management Accounting* (January 1978), pp. 49–52.

Hertz, D. B. "Risk Analysis in Capital Investments," *Harvard Business Review*, vol. 42 (January–February 1964), pp. 95–106.

Hillier, F. S. "The Derivation of Probabilistic Information for the Evaluation of Risky Investments," *Management Science*, vol. 9 (April 1963), pp. 443–57.

Hillier, F. S., and D. V. Heebink. "Evaluation of Risky Capital Investments," *California Management Review*, vol. 8 (Winter 1965), pp. 71–80.

Lerner, E. M., and A. Rappaport. "Limit DCF in Capital Budgeting," *Harvard Business Review*, vol. 46 (September–October 1968), pp. 133–39.

Magee, J. F. "Decision Trees for Decision Making," *Harvard Business Review*, vol. 42 (July–August 1964), pp. 126–38.

Myers, S. C. "Procedures for Capital Budgeting Under Uncertainty," *Industrial Management Review*, vol. 9 (Spring 1968), pp. 1–19.

Naslund, B. "A Model of Capital Budgeting Under Risk," *Journal of Business*, vol. 39 (April 1966), pp. 257–71.

Robichek, A. A., and S. C. Myers. "Risk-Adjusted Discount Rates," *Journal of Finance*, vol. 21 (December 1966), pp. 727–30.

Van Horne, J. C. "Capital Budgeting Decisions Involving Combinations of Risky Investments," *Management Science*, vol. 13 (October 1966), pp. 84–92.

# 11

# Cost of Capital

In the capital budgeting chapters there was frequent reference to the required rate of return. It was used as the discount rate in the net present value and profitability index analyses. Proposals must generate such a rate of return to have positive NPV's or PI's greater than one and, therefore, to be acceptable. This "required rate" also defined the acceptance criterion for the IRR analysis.

The acceptance or rejection of individual projects, and, therefore, the growth of the firm, depend on the discount rate used. This makes the figure crucial in the decision process. The question naturally arises as to what rate is correct. Logic dictates that the firm at least earn as much from investment of capital as the capital costs.

The purpose of the present chapter is to determine the cost of capital. As the chapter unfolds, it will become apparent that this is an area of finance that is still in the formative stage. There is no universally accepted procedure for determining the cost of capital; and, because there are both theoretical and operational problems in estimating the cost of capital because of uncertainty, any calculation must of necessity be an approximation. Since the cost of capital is not a refined measure, given the present state of the art, any use of it should acknowledge that subjective evaluations must still be employed. As an example, forecasts of future dividends or earnings are necessary in order to arrive at an approximation of the cost of equity capital. Hence, until long-run forecasting becomes more precise (which is not imminent), the cost of capital cannot be more than an approximation. Thus, when the net present values of various capital projects approach zero or the internal rates of return approach the cost of capital, close scrutiny should be given to the projects to see if they are still acceptable.

## The General Concept

One of the primary uses of the cost of capital is capital budgeting. Therefore it seems appropriate to define the concept in terms of the firm's investment function. Professor Myron J. Gordon defines the cost of capital as follows:

> The cost of capital for a firm is the discount rate with the property that an invesment with a rate of profit above (below) this rate will raise (lower) the value of the firm.[1]

This means the cost of capital is the minimum rate of return needed when investing funds. A higher return would benefit the shareholders, and a lower return would penalize them by reducing the value of their holdings.

In the previous chapters it was shown that investments have differing degrees of profitability; therefore, they can be arranged in a descending order of internal rates of return. As seen in Figure 11–1, these investment

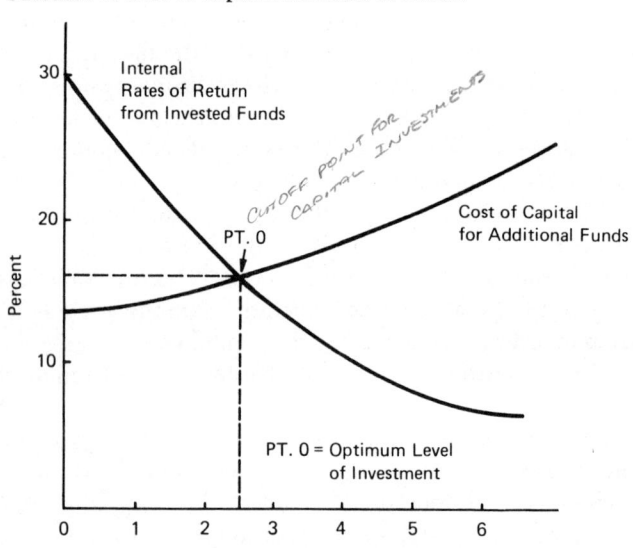

FIGURE 11–1
Schedule of Cost of Capital and Rates of Return

proposals form a negative sloping demand schedule for capital. At any given time it is possible to prepare a schedule based on investment proposals currently available to the firm. This suggests that the cost of capital cannot be determined without knowing the amount of funds to

---

[1] Myron J. Gordon, *The Investment Financing and Valuation of the Corporation* (Homewood, Ill.: Richard D. Irwin, Inc., 1962), p. 218.

## 11 Cost of Capital

be raised by the firm. However, the amount of funds to be acquired is dependent on the investment projects available to the firm.

The acquisition of capital follows the principle of increasing costs. In this connection the concern is with the various costs of securing additional funds. What the figure depicts, then, is a supply schedule of capital, with costs varying in accordance with the amounts actually raised.

Figure 11–1 depicts the diminishing marginal return on investments and the rising marginal cost of capital. Theoretically, the firm proceeds down the schedule of capital-budgeting projects to the point where the marginal cost of capital equals the rate of return offered by the marginal proposal. This is the cutoff point for capital investments. It must be emphasized that the risks of the proposed projects are assumed to be comparable and that the projects will not shift the capital market's view regarding the overall risk of the firm.

It is likely that, if the firm does not significantly alter its financing requirements from one period to the next, the supply curve will not slope upward sharply; that is, it will be raising capital in the same area of the supply curve in each period. However, if the firm does undertake a major expansion project, it is possible it may move further up the supply schedule; that is, raise its cost of capital.

It must be remembered that Figure 11–1 represents a theoretical cost of capital. A firm cannot expect to encounter a situation where the cost of acquiring funds can be so closely tied to the amounts available at that price. Although the costs and amounts of funds may not be readily identifiable without considerable effort on the part of the firm, the schedule does suggest the theoretical objective.

In Chapter 9 it was evident that a cost of capital was necessary for use of the discounted cash flow techniques in investment analysis; and, because of the nature of those techniques, the cost of capital became a cutoff rate. Viewing the concept from that perspective helped define the cost of capital. Further examination demonstrated that the use of the cost of capital as a cutoff rate was entirely in keeping with economic theory of supply and demand. However, to this point there has been no discussion of how to determine the actual figure.

Conceptually the calculation is simple. If a firm was financed half with debt and half with equity and if debt capital costs 5 percent and equity costs 15 percent, the firm's cost of capital could be calculated without hesitation. It is 10 percent! Instinctively, one would average the costs based on the percentage of each type of capital used.

The cost of capital calculation involves three steps:

1. Determination of the costs of the different types of capital.
2. Specification of the percentage of each component (the weights).
3. The calculation of a weighted average.

The preceding example should not be interpreted to mean that defining a firm's cost of capital is easy. Although there is general agreement as to the three steps, there is disagreement among finance theorists about some aspects of virtually every calculation. The method presented here is a compromise which reflects what is assessed to be the current consensus. It is certain to change. The next three sections will explain a method for accomplishing each of the steps.

## Component Costs

A corporation can obtain needed funds either externally or internally. External capital includes long-term debt as well as new preferred and common stock issues. Since the firm is concerned with financing long-term requirements for funds, short-term sources of capital may be ignored. One possible exception to this rule might occur if short-term debt is used to finance a project with the idea of funding it at its completion, or possibly when interest rates decline. Nevertheless, for present purposes, short-term sources will be disregarded.

The cost of various types of funds is typically expressed as an annualized rate. This rate is secured by determining the average annual amount that must be paid and stating it as a percentage of the amount of funds obtained. In estimating the various individual costs of capital, it is important that the costs be stated uniformly. Either before- or after-tax rates could be utilized, but, typically, the after-tax rate is the one selected. After-tax rates are used because the cost of capital is compared to rates of return that are determined by cash flows after taxes. Therefore, to preserve comparability with the rates of return calculated for a firm's proposed capital projects, after-tax costs are the most suitable.

There is one other thing to keep in mind in calculating the cost of capital. The figure is to be used to screen present investments. Such investments should generate returns high enough to offset *current capital costs*. Historical costs are inappropriate except to the extent that they help determine current costs.

**Cost of Long-Term Debt.** In discussing the cost of capital concept, it was noted that the investment of any form of capital should generate a return sufficient that the shareholders were not penalized. With debt capital the investment should return at least enough to offset the after-tax interest costs of any new debt *that was to be issued*. Although there are a number of forms of long-term debt, bonds are most prevalent. Discussion will be limited to determining the capital costs for new bonds.

There are two ways in which a firm might determine what its current interest costs would be. It could (1) contact an investment banker (a market middleman that sells new security issues), or (2) observe the prevailing yield on the firm's old bonds, if the firm had such bonds outstanding.

The second approach may require a more detailed explanation. After

## 11 Cost of Capital

a firm sells bonds, a secondary market for the securities develops where interested buyers and sellers of such securities can make exchanges, normally through middlemen such as brokers. When interest rates change in the market, the prices of all secondary market securities will also change so that they reflect current conditions. Price changes will also occur whenever individual companies become safer or riskier investments. Therefore, the current price of a company's outstanding bonds will reflect the investment community's assessment of that company and of interest rates in general.

There are bond tables available which allow an interested investor, or bond trader, to translate a bond's current market price, its coupon rate (the original interest rate of the bond), and the maturity date into a "yield to maturity" figure. The yield to maturity is the discount rate which makes the present value of the interest and principal equal to the current price. It is the bond's internal rate of return. This is the market's assessment of the appropriate interest rate for the firm.

Without bond tables the somewhat tedious IRR calculation can be avoided by use of an "approximate yield formula" as follows:

$$\text{Approximate yield} = \frac{I + (\frac{\$1000 - P}{n})}{\frac{P + \$1000}{2}}$$

where $I$ is the annual interest expressed in dollars, $n$ is the number of years to maturity, and $P$ is the current price of the bond.[2]

To demonstrate the use of the formula, assume that a firm has bonds outstanding which are currently selling for $931. The original coupon was 8 percent, or $80 per year on a $1,000 bond. The bond will mature in 10 years. The approximate yield on the bond is:

$$\text{Approximate yield} = \frac{\$80 + (\$1000 - \$931)/10}{(\$1000 + \$931) \div 2} = 9.00\%$$

This suggests that if the firm were to sell bonds in the current market the firm could expect that the bonds would have to carry an effective interest rate of approximately 9 percent.

Note that the formula also could be used for bonds selling at a premium. For example, if the bond just discussed were selling for $1,050, the approximate yield would be:

$$\text{Approximate yield} = \frac{\$80 + (\$1000 - \$1050)/10}{(\$1000 + \$1050) \div 2} = 7.32\%$$

Further, if consultations with an investment banker indicated that new

---

[2] This formulation assumes that the original price of the bond was $1,000, which is the norm. If the original price were otherwise, substitute the original price for the $1,000 in the formula.

bonds were to be sold at a discount or a premium, the formula could be used to translate an estimated current coupon into a current effective interest rate.

In the earlier discussion, it was explained that the calculation of the cost of capital would be done on an after-tax basis to preserve comparability. This requires that an adjustment be made for the cost of debt. Interest charges are deductible. Therefore, the cost of debt is less than the nominal interest rate or yield. The adjustment is simply:

$$\frac{\text{After-tax cost}}{\text{of debt}} = \frac{\text{Before-tax cost}}{\text{of debt}} (1 - \text{Tax rate})$$

Assuming the hypothetical firm had a 40-percent tax rate, the after-tax cost of debt (for the bonds selling at a discount) would be:

$$\frac{\text{After-tax cost}}{\text{of debt}} = 9(1-.4) = 5.4\%$$

**Cost of Preferred Stock.** Calculating the cost of preferred stock is the easiest of any of the components because preferred stock has no maturity date. Thus, there is no problem of amortizing premiums or discounts. The cost is the annual dividend divided by the net proceeds that would be received by the issuer. Further, because preferred dividends are not tax deductible, there is no tax adjustment calculation.

The same formula can be used for calculating the cost of preferred stock regardless of whether the calculation is based on estimates from an investment banker or by observing the prices of the firm's currently outstanding preferred. The logic of the cost of preferred is identical to that of the cost of debt. It is the rate of return being demanded by preferred stock buyers, which is determined using an IRR calculation:

$$P_p = \frac{D_p}{1 + K_p} + \frac{D_p}{(1 + K_p)^2} + \cdots \frac{D_p}{(1 + K_p)^n}$$

where $P_p$ is the price of the preferred, $D_p$ is the preferred dividend, and $K_p$ is the preferred stock buyers' required rate of return.

Given that $D_p$ is a constant, it can be factored out and multiplied by the sum of the present value factors—the present value annuity interest factor at $K_p$ for an infinite number of years, $N$.

$$P_p = D_p \cdot \sum_{t=1}^{N} \frac{1}{(1 + K_p) t}$$

The algebra of summations allows the last term to be simplified in the case of an infinite series.

$$P_p = D_p \cdot \frac{1}{K_p}$$

$$K_p = \frac{D_p}{P_p}$$

The result is:

$$\frac{\text{Cost of}}{\text{preferred stock}} = \frac{\text{Preferred stock dividend}}{\text{Preferred stock price}}$$

If the cost calculation is based on currently outstanding securities, the numerator is the existing preferred dividend, and the current market price of the preferred is the denominator. If the calculation is for new preferred, the numerator is the anticipated preferred dividend, and the denominator is the net-per-share proceeds from the sale of the new preferred.

To continue the previous example, assume the firm had preferred outstanding with a $7 dividend (7 percent preferred, par $100) and that the security was currently selling for $66.75. Any new preferred the firm was to sell would be expected to yield:

$$\frac{\text{Cost of}}{\text{preferred stock}} = \frac{\$7}{\$66.75} = 10.5\%$$

**Cost of Common Equity.** One of the most troublesome problems in determining the average cost of capital is defining the cost of equity capital. In determining the costs of debt and preferred, the problem was simplified because security holders' returns could be forecast with a high degree of accuracy. Bondholders would normally expect to receive interest payments and a return of principal. Their required return could be found by using the IRR procedure or approximated, as was done, by using a simplified calculation. Preferred stock buyers can expect to receive an infinite series of dividends of a specified amount. The IRR calculation is again appropriate; but, because there were no premiums or discounts to amortize or principal payment to recapture, the calculation could be made directly. No approximation method was necessary to make it easier.

For the common stockholders the problem is more complex—both for the investors contemplating the nature of their expected returns and for the analyst in trying to measure their required rates of return. Again, the problem is to find the discount rate being used to set the price investors are willing to pay to acquire the firm's shares. To do this, some assumption must be made about what the investors are paying for. Although there is no way of knowing exactly what stock buyers use as their basis for price determination, one reasonable assumption is that they pay for expected dividends. This is the approach used in the Gordon model, a widely recognized measure of the cost of equity.

Common stock is different from preferred stock. The dividends on common stock would normally be expected to grow over time. If it is assumed that the growth rate is constant over time, the price of the common stock can be defined as the present value of the dividend stream, as follows:

$$P = \frac{D}{1+K_e} + \frac{D(1+g)}{(1+K_e)^2} + \frac{D(1+g)^2}{(1+K_e)^3} \cdots \frac{D(1+g)^{n-1}}{(1+K_e)^n}$$

where $P$ is the price of the common stock, $D$ is next period's expected dividend, $g$ is the constant per-period growth rate, and $K_e$ is equity investors' required rate of return.

As was done in calculating the cost of preferred stock, the constant term, next period's dividend ($D$), can be factored out, leaving:

$$P = D \cdot \sum_{t=1}^{N} \frac{(1+g)^{t-1}}{(1+K_e)^t}$$

Again, the algebra of summations can be used to simplify the expression. The result is:

$$P = D \left(\frac{1}{K_e - g}\right)$$

This can be rearranged to define the cost of common equity:

$$K_e = \frac{\hat{D}}{P} + \hat{g}$$

There are two types of common equity—internal and external. Internal equity is that generated as profits and accounted for as retained earnings. There are a number of advantages to acquiring equity in this manner. There is no underwriter; therefore, there are no flotation costs. Shareholders who receive their returns in the form of price appreciation rather than dividends receive a tax break. Capital gains are taxed at a lower rate, and the tax is postponed until actual sale of the security. However, shareholders who want current income may not look at the choice from this perspective. Their need for current income may require them to restructure their portfolios to meet their needs if dividend income is insufficient. Such transactions would involve brokerage costs. The net effect of these countervailing influences has not been entirely worked out. The most common specification for the cost of retained earnings is the formula just developed:

$$\frac{\text{Cost of}}{\text{retained earnings}} = \frac{\text{Common stock dividend}}{\text{Common stock price}} + \text{Growth rate}$$

For the example firm assume current market on the firm's shares is $50, next period's expected dividend is $2.50, and the firm's dividends historically have grown at a rate of 10 percent per annum. The firm's shareholders appear to expect a return of 15 percent:

$$\frac{\text{Cost of}}{\text{retained earnings}} = \frac{\$2.50}{\$50} + .10 = 15\%$$

The sale of new common stock involves at least one expense that retention of earnings does not entail—flotation costs. Sales of original issue

## 11 Cost of Capital

securities are normally handled by investment bankers. The concessions that these underwriters receive, along with other administrative expenses associated with new issues, serve to reduce the net proceeds to the company. However, investors' expectations would be undiminished. They would expect the same dividend yield previous investors had enjoyed, and they would want the same level of growth. To accomplish this, the firm must generate a higher rate of return than the investor expects to net. The firm will have to generate the same dollar return with a reduced amount of capital. This makes new equity slightly more expensive than retained earnings:

$$\frac{\text{Cost of}}{\text{new stock}} = \frac{\text{Common stock dividend}}{\text{Net per share proceeds on sale of new stock}} + \text{Growth rate}$$

Assuming that flotation costs were 10 percent on the sale of the stock in our previous example, the cost of new equity would be:

$$\frac{\text{Cost of}}{\text{new stock}} = \frac{\$2.50}{\$45} + .10 = 15.6\%$$

$50 = STOCK
$5 = FLOTATION COSTS
$45 NET PER SHARE PROCEEDS

Before continuing, it would be well to reflect upon the meaning of this calculated cost of equity. Based on the current market price of the stock, it was determined that shareholders expect to receive a 15-percent after-tax rate of return on their investment. This figure is predicated on the assumption that these investors are buying a dividend stream and that the growth rate they used in their projections was properly defined. (If the firm sells new stock, investments will have to earn a slightly higher rate to return 15 percent to the shareholder because the underwriters would receive part of the proceeds at the time of issuance.) The whole purpose of the weighted average calculation to follow will be to determine what rate of return the firm must make to satisfy the shareholders' return requirements. What rate of return does the firm have to make so that the shareholders can receive their desired 15 percent?

## Component Weights

To calculate a weighted average cost of capital, a weight, or proportion, must be assigned to each of the different types of capital. There are at least three possible ways to define the weights. The proportions could be based on what was done in the past as indicated by the historical balance sheet figures. This is referred to as the book value method. Current theory suggests that the book value method is inappropriate because these percentages do not reflect the amount of securities outstanding at current market rates. (Recall that the bonds were selling at $931 to bring them into line with current interest yields on similar bonds.) Quite simply, it is inconsistent to use current costs and historical weights.

Another way of assigning the weights would be to use the percentages that would prevail if the firm were optimally financed. Although the use of optimal capital structure weights is theoretically appropriate, it creates a problem. If component weights from an optimal capital structure are used, the analysis should also use the component costs that would prevail under such conditions. These are not readily observable nor easy to define.

Fortunately, there is a simpler alternative. Market value (MV) weights can be used. Current theory suggests that a firm's optimal capital structure is achieved when as much debt as possible is used. The cost of capital calculation which has been suggested under these conditions results in exactly the same figure derived using market value weights if consistent component costs are used. This is illustrated in an appendix to Chapter 12.

Thus, market rates of return can be used as the basis for determining the component costs, and the relative market values can be used as the weights. This is convenient because market values for the different securities are readily observable. The formulae for the weights are:

$$\text{Weight for debt} = \frac{\text{MV of outstanding bonds}}{\text{MV of all outstanding securities}}$$

$$\text{Weight of preferred stock} = \frac{\text{MV of outstanding preferred stock}}{\text{MV of all outstanding securities}}$$

$$\text{Weight for common equity} = \frac{\text{MV of outstanding common stock}}{\text{MV of all outstanding securities}}$$

There is only one more problem to deal with before calculating the weighted average cost of capital. Common equity has two components: retained earnings and new stock. How much of the equity weight should be attributed to stock and how much to retained earnings? Although there have been various approaches suggested, none of them is beyond question. A common expedient is to apportion the weight for common equity based on book values (BV) as follows:[3]

$$\frac{\text{Weight for}}{\text{new stock}} = \frac{\text{Weight for}}{\text{common equity}} \times \frac{\text{BV of common stock}}{\text{BV of common equity}}$$

$$\frac{\text{Weight for}}{\text{retained earnings}} = \frac{\text{Weight for}}{\text{common equity}} \times \frac{\text{BV of retained earnings}}{\text{BV of common equity}}$$

## Weighted Average Cost of Capital

Given a procedure for calculating each of the costs and each of the weights, calculating the average becomes a matter of mechanics. Market value for each of the components is determined and weights are calcu-

---

[3] In cases where there is contributed, or paid-in, capital, it is considered as part of common stock.

## 11  Cost of Capital

lated. The equity weight is apportioned to new stock and retained earnings. A cost for each component is calculated. Finally, the average is calculated. The procedure is best illustrated with an example. The necessary formulae are summarized in Table 11–1.

Using the example firm discussed earlier in this chapter with the bonds selling at a discount will avoid the necessity of refiguring the cost calculations. Deriving the weights requires translation of book value figures into market values. The first column in Table 11–2 lists book values for the various components of the hypothetical firm's capital structure. Note that there is no consideration of short-term indebtedness and the procedures have not been confused with the normal definition of net worth.

The market value of the bonds was derived by taking 93.1 percent of their book value. Recall in the component cost section that the old bonds were trading at $931. The market value for the outstanding preferred stock was derived the same way. The preferred stock was currently trading at 66-¾ even though par was $100.

Market value of common stock was derived by multiplying current market price, previously specified as $50, times the number of shares outstanding—125,000 shares. For publicly traded firms, the number of shares would be readily available. In this case, the number of shares was derived from the common stock account and par value (2,500,000/20 = 125,000). After the proportions are derived, the weights for common stock and retained earnings are defined based on their book values.

The cost figures are those that were developed in the individual component cost sections. The weighted costs are the product of columns (4) and (5). Finally, the weighted costs were summed.

***Interpretation of the Results.*** The analysis indicates that if the firm undertakes projects which offer an 11.53-percent rate of return, and if the firm finances in accordance with the current capital structure, it will be able to generate a 15-percent rate of return for the common shareholders, which is what the previous analysis indicated was their required rate of return. Projects with returns higher than that are obviously better and should result in an increased demand for the firm's stock with a resultant increase in stock price.

It is possible to demonstrate the logic of the previous paragraph. Assume that the firm has the opportunity of investing in a $1,000 project. The project will last exactly one year. At that time, it will generate exactly enough funds to return the original investment plus create a before-tax profit of 19.22 percent or $192.20 (19.22 percent before-tax is equivalent to 11.53 percent after-tax; 19.22 (1−.4) = 11.53).

If the project is financed with the same proportions as exist in the current capital structure (based on market value weights), 35 percent of the money will come from 9 percent bonds, 6.27 percent will come from preferred stock yielding 10.5 percent, and 58.73 percent will come from new stock and retained earnings.

**TABLE 11-1**
Summary of Cost and Weight Formulae

| Component | Cost | Weight |
|---|---|---|
| Debt | $(1 - \text{Tax rate})\left(\dfrac{I + (1000-P)/n}{\dfrac{P+1000}{2}}\right)$ | $\dfrac{\text{MV of outstanding bonds}}{\text{MV of all outstanding securities}}$ |
| Preferred stock | $\dfrac{\text{Preferred stock dividend}}{\text{Preferred stock price}}$ | $\dfrac{\text{MV of outstanding preferred stock}}{\text{MV of all outstanding securities}}$ |
| Common equity weight (CEW) | — | $\dfrac{\text{MV of outstanding common stock}}{\text{MV of all outstanding securities}}$ |
| Common stock | $\dfrac{\text{Common stock dividend}}{\text{Net per share proceeds on sale of new stock}} + \text{Growth rate}$ | $\dfrac{\text{BV of common stock}}{\text{BV of common equity}} \times \text{CEW}$ |
| Retained earnings | $\dfrac{\text{Common stock dividend}}{\text{Common stock price}} + \text{Growth rate}$ | $\dfrac{\text{BV of retained earnings}}{\text{BV of common equity}} \times \text{CEW}$ |

**TABLE 11-2**
Illustrative Cost of Capital Calculation

| Type of Funds | (1) Book Value (in thousands) | (2) Market Value (in thousands) | (3) Proportion of Market Value | (4) Component Weight | (5) Component Cost | (6) Weighted Cost |
|---|---|---|---|---|---|---|
| Bonds | $ 4,000.00 | $ 3,724.00 | 35.00% | 35.00 | 5.4 | 1.89% |
| Preferred stock | $ 1,000.00 | $ 667.50 | 6.27% | 6.27 | 10.5 | .66% |
| Common stock ($20 par) | $ 2,500.00 | $ 6,250.00 | 58.73% | 29.37 (based on B.V.) | 15.6 | 4.58% |
| Retained earnings | $ 2,500.00 | | | 29.37 | 15.0 | 4.40% |
| | | $10,641.50 | | 100.00 | | 11.53% |

The end-of-year income would appear as follows:

| | |
|---|---|
| $192.20 | Earnings before interest and taxes |
| 31.50 | Interest ($350 @ 9%) |
| $160.70 | Earnings before taxes |
| 64.28 | Taxes (40% rate) |
| $ 96.42 | Earnings after taxes |
| 6.58 | Preferred Dividend ($62.70 @ 10.5%) |
| $ 89.84 | Available to Common |

The $89.84 available to common represents a 15.3-percent return on $587.40 (89.84/587.40 = .153). This is an average of the 15.6 percent necessary to generate a 15-percent return on the new stock and a straight 15-percent return on the retained earnings component.

***Qualifications and Extensions.*** The interpretation of the cost of capital demonstrated that the figure was based on the use of a combination of different types of capital. It is appropriate that all projects be compared to such an average cost. If some projects were considered to be debt-financed and others as being financed with equity, the standards for acceptances would be illogical and difficult to defend. The firm could be led to accept low-return "debt-financed projects" while simultaneously rejecting "equity-financed projects" with higher rates of return.

Although it is appropriate to consider projects as being financed with a combination of different forms of capital, the actual raising of funds would seldom be done in exactly the proportions used in the analysis. External sources of funds have certain minimum amounts that can be raised with reasonable flotation costs. Financing the firm's future needs must, of necessity, be done in a way that will help reduce these costs. Only the larger firms can tailor their capital requirements to include the simultaneous use of more than one source of funds, thereby partly alleviating the problem of maintaining fixed proportions. Other firms will be required to manage the various external sources in connection with the retention of earnings in order to maintain relatively fixed proportions of funds in the capital structure. Regardless of which is the case, the calculation of the cost of capital presumes that over the long run such a combination of debt and equity would exist and that it is the appropriate basis for cost measurement.

The proposed calculation of the cost of capital ignored any interrelationship between the investments being analyzed and the component costs and/or weights. It is possible that a large project, or a combination of projects, would alter the basic nature of a firm. Such a change in operations could change the risk and return prospects and, therefore, the attractiveness of the company's shares or even its bonds. Such a change in the nature of the firm could similarly affect the relative amount of debt which the firm should use; that is, the optimal capital structure, and, therefore, the weights (and incidentally, the costs, too).

All projects, to some degree, change the firm. The procedure described ignores this fact. The implication is simple. Because of measurement problems and necessary simplifying assumptions, the accuracy of the cost of capital figure is far less than indicated by the number of significant digits. However, having a ballpark estimate of the required rate of return is better than being without any guidance for the capital budgeting analysis.

## Summary

Use of the cost of capital is a practical application of microeconomic theory. The firm should undertake added investments until marginal returns are equal to the marginal cost of the capital used.

If the firm uses more than one type of capital, the appropriate cost is an average, a weighted average. This entire chapter was devoted to development of measures for calculating such an average. The formulae are summarized in Table 11-1, and the averaging procedure is illustrated in Table 11-2. The result is the minimum rate of return which can be accepted on new investment proposals which will satisfy the requirements of the shareholders *to the degree their requirements can be measured.* Measurement problems create reservations as to the exactness of the derived figure.

## QUESTIONS

1. Discuss the relationship between cost of capital and capital budgeting.
2. Why is it customary for a firm to encounter:
    a. Diminishing marginal returns on investments?
    b. Rising marginal cost of capital?
3. Why is the after-tax rather than the before-tax cost of capital used?
4. Why should market weights be used rather than book weights when developing a weighted average cost of capital?
5. Discuss the quotation: "Retained earnings are free."
6. Why are retained earnings treated differently from new common stock when determining the cost of common-stock equity?
7. The algebraic formula

$$k = \frac{D}{P} + g$$

is used to estimate $k$, the cost of common-stock equity. Explain the rationale behind the use of this equation.
8. Why would you not recommend that the cost of common-stock equity be used as a firm's cost of capital?

Part II  Financial Planning and Control

## PROBLEMS

1. Market Products, Inc., wants to know the cost of each component of their capital structure. Rather than contact an investment banker, they intend to use their current yields and prices as a basis for the calculation. That information can be summarized as follows:

   | | |
   |---|---|
   | Market price of outstanding bonds | $ 980 |
   | Coupon rate on bonds | 9% |
   | Maturity value of bonds | $1,000 |
   | Years to maturity | 7 |
   | Corporate tax rate | 40% |
   | Market price of outstanding preferred | $ 70 |
   | Par value | $ 100 |
   | Dividend (in dollars) | $ 8 |
   | Market price of outstanding common | $ 25 |
   | Common stock dividend | $ 1 |
   | Growth rate | 8% |
   | Percentage flotation cost on sale of new shares | 7% |

   a. Calculate the after-tax cost of debt.
   b. Calculate the cost of preferred.
   c. Calculate the cost of new common stock.
   d. Calculate the cost of retained earnings.

2. Using the component costs calculated for Problem 1, calculate a weighted average cost of capital, using the following weights:

   | | Weight |
   |---|---|
   | Bonds | 30 |
   | Preferred stock | 10 |
   | Common Stock | 40 |
   | Retained earnings | 20 |

3. Middleman Supply & Co. intends to calculate its cost of capital. To help do this it has contacted an investment banker who supplied estimates of what prices and yields the firm might expect to offer on new securities in order to sell them. The estimates, along with certain other data, can be summarized as follows:

   | | |
   |---|---|
   | Expected offering price net of underwriting concessions | $ 960 |
   | Anticipated coupon rate | 8.25% |
   | Maturity value | $1,000 |
   | Term (in years) | 30 |
   | Corporate tax rate | 40% |
   | Net proceeds on sale of new preferred | $ 96 |
   | Par value | $ 100 |
   | Dividend rate (percent of par) | 9% |
   | Current market price of outstanding common | $ 40 |
   | Common stock dividend | $ 0.60 |
   | Growth rate | 11% |
   | Net proceeds on sale of a new share | $ 34 |

   Calculate the cost of (a) debt; (b) preferred stock; (c) common stock; and (d) retained earnings.

## 11 Cost of Capital

4. Using the component costs from Problem 3 and the given weights, calculate a weighted average cost of capital.

|  | *Weight* |
|---|---|
| Bonds | 40 |
| Preferred stock | 5 |
| Common stock | 35 |
| Retained earnings | 20 |

5. Marketimer, Ltd., needs to determine its cost of capital for capital budgeting purposes. The company has assembled the following information.

| | |
|---|---|
| Market price of outstanding bonds | $ 940 |
| Coupon rate on those bonds | 8.25% |
| Maturity value of bonds | $1,000 |
| Years to maturity | 12 |
| Corporate tax rate | 40% |
| | |
| Market price of outstanding preferred | $ 57.25 |
| Par value | $ 100 |
| Dividend (percentage of par) | 6% |
| | |
| Market price of outstanding common | $ 72 |
| Common stock dividend | $ 5 |
| Growth rate | 6% |
| Net proceeds per share on sale of new stock | $ 65.50 |

The current capital structure, based on book value, appears as follows:

| | |
|---|---|
| Bonds | $2,500,000 |
| Preferred stock | 1,500,000 |
| Common stock (par 50) | 3,700,000 |
| Retained earnings | 2,300,000 |

Calculate the weighted average cost of capital based on market value weights (allocate common equity by book value as was done in the chapter).

## ADDITIONAL READINGS

Ang, J. S. "Weighted Average Versus True Cost of Capital," *Financial Management*, vol. 2 (Autumn 1973), pp. 56–60.

Arditti, F. D., "The Weighted Average Cost of Capital: Some Questions on Its Definition, Interpretation and Use," *Journal of Finance*, vol. 28 (September 1973), pp. 1001–7.

Arditti, F. D., and M. S. Tysseland. "Three Ways to Present the Marginal Cost of Capital," *Financial Management*, vol. 2 (Summer 1973), pp. 63–67.

Brennan, M. J. "A New Look at the Weighted Average Cost of Capital," *Journal of Business Finance*, vol. 5 No. 1 (1973), pp. 24–30.

Brigham, E. F. "Hurdle Rates for Screening Capital Expenditure Proposals," *Financial Management*, vol. 4 (Autumn 1975), pp. 17–25.

Durand, D. "Costs of Debt and Equity Funds for Business: Trends and Problems and Measurement," reprinted in E. Solomon, ed., *The Management of Corporate Capital*. New York: Free Press, 1959, pp. 91–116.

Gordon, M. J. *The Investment Financing and Valuation of the Corporation.* Homewood, Ill.: Richard D. Irwin, Inc., 1962.

Henderson, G. V., Jr. "On Capitalization Rates for Riskless Streams," *Journal of Finance*, vol. 31 (December 1976), pp. 1491–93.

Lewellen, W. G. *The Cost of Capital.* Belmont, Calif.: Wadsworth Publishing Co., Inc., 1969.

McConnell, J. J., and C. M. Sandberg. "The Weighted Average Cost of Capital: Some Questions on its Definition, Interpretation, and Use: Comment," *Journal of Finance*, vol. 30 (June 1975), pp. 883–86.

Myers, S. C. "Interactions of Corporate Financing and Investment Decisions—Implications for Capital Budgeting," *Journal of Finance*, vol. 29 (March 1974), pp. 1–25.

Nantell, T. J., and C. R. Carlson. "The Cost of Capital as a Weighted Average,' *Journal of Finance*, vol. 30 (December 1975), pp. 1343–55.

Robichek, A. A., and J. G. McDonald. "The Cost of Capital Concept: Potential Use and Misuse," *Financial Executive*, vol. 33 (June 1965), pp. 20ff.

Santow, L. "Cost of Long-Term Capital from a Corporate Point of View," *Financial Analysts Journal*, vol. 19 (May–June 1963), pp. 43–50.

Solomon, E. "Measuring a Company's Cost of Capital," *Journal of Business*, vol. 28 (October 1955), pp. 240–52.

———. *The Theory of Financial Management.* New York: Columbia University Press, 1963.

Weston, J. F. "Investment Decisions Using the Capital Asset Pricing Model," *Financial Management*, vol. 1 (Spring 1973), 25–33.

# 12

# Capital Structure and Long-Term Financing Decisions

A firm's financial manager is faced with two types of problems with regard to long-term financing. The firm needs overall guidelines as to the appropriate mix of debt and equity that it should use over time. This raises a question as to whether there is a best combination and, if so, what factors affect its composition. A long-run goal for use of debt and equity constitutes a policy. There is also the recurring problem of how to finance the firm at specific points in time. It was suggested in the cost of capital chapter that even if there is a best combination of debt and equity, it is unlikely that the firm will finance with exactly that combination on any given occasion. There are a number of reasons for this, one of the more obvious being flotation costs. Long-term financing decisions—the problem of how exactly to raise needed funds at a point in time—will generally require a cost-benefit analysis that evaluates a number of factors. Capital structure policy is only one consideration.

The optimal financing policy for a firm has been a major issue in the finance literature for the last 20 years. It has important implications for a firm's financing decisions, the cost of capital calculation, the capital budgeting process, and the valuation of the firm. Given that the generally accepted objective for all financial decisions is maximization of the value of the firm, the issue is obviously important and is indeed central to all of finance theory. The theory of capital structure serves to interrelate a number of important topics. For this reason, this chapter and its appendix delve into the theoretical issues. Capital structure theory is the basis of the analysis in a number of related areas, e.g., cost of capital and capital budgeting, as explained in the chapter appendix.

## The Capital Structure Problem

In an earlier chapter, capital structure was defined as the total of the firm's long-term financing. In balance sheet terms, this is the right-hand side of the balance sheet less current liabilities. When current liabilities are included, the total is generally referred to as financial structure. The capital structure problem then is to derive a policy which will provide guidance as to the appropriate composition of the capital structure—how much debt versus how much equity.

Attempting to determine a best capital structure implies that such an optimal policy exists. For many years financial theorists took the existence of such an optimum for granted. In the late fifties it was demonstrated that such a position was not implicit in classical economic theory. For such an optimum to exist, there must be institutional factors which create countervailing incentives for the use of the different types of capital.

A 1958 article by Franco Modigliani and Merton Miller considered the problem using the theory of equilibrium economics which they felt had been overlooked. This required reevaluation of all existing theories of valuation and the cost of capital. Their paper was quite controversial. There were heated exchanges and a great deal of rethinking on the issues. The result has been a better understanding of the factors which influence capital structure, a clearer definition of the relationship between capital structure policy and the cost of capital, and some important guidance for capital budgeting.

**The Traditional View.** To appreciate the importance of the Modigliani-Miller article, it is necessary to understand the way in which the capital structure problem was approached prior to the paper. The traditional approach, as it has since been labeled, taught that the firm could benefit from the judicious use of debt capital by lowering the average cost of capital and thereby raising the value of the firm. The relationship is depicted in Figure 12–1.

The explanation of the relationships is straightforward and intuitively appealing. The cost of debt would not be expected to rise with moderate increases in borrowing; and, therefore, the debt-cost curve would be nearly flat. If borrowing became excessive, lenders would raise their rates, and the cost of debt would rise sharply. Shareholders' required rates of return, the cost of equity, would also increase sharply if too much debt were used. For moderate increases in risk the shareholders would not be expected to become alarmed. As a result the slope of the cost of equity curve is relatively gentle until the extreme is reached.

The policy implications are obvious. For moderate amounts of debt the cost is much lower, and debt should be substituted for equity, lowering the average. The substitution should continue until the lowest possible average cost of capital is reached. This process would achieve the optimal capital structure (point X on the capital structure axis).

**FIGURE 12-1**
The Traditional View

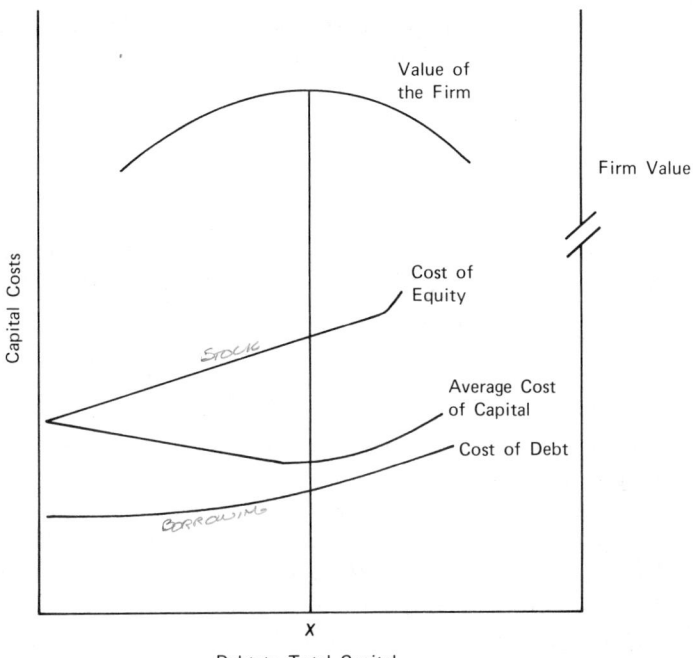

Such a policy would achieve the generally accepted goal of maximizing the value of the firm. A firm is an economic asset, therefore its value is the present value of the benefits it generates, the income stream. If the income stream is unchanged, the lowest discount rate produces the highest present value; that is, the highest valuation.

*The Modigliani-Miller Model (MM).* The MM indictment of the traditional model was complete. They showed that the model lacked rigor, was less than specific in its definition of economic earnings, and suggested little understanding of the nature of risk; most importantly, the traditional model overlooked the workings of a competitive market. They undertook to develop such a competitive market model for capital structure decisions. They recognized that there would need to be modifications to such a simplified model to make it more realistic, but unless such a pure model were developed, the more elaborate ones would continue to be on shaky footing.

Their models revealed exactly what they, as economists, would have expected. However, the results seem to startle others. In a world without institutional factors favoring one type of financing (debt or equity) there would be no optimal capital structure. All firms with the same earnings, of the same risk, would have the same value regardless of how they were financed. Market forces, through a process that MM called *arbitrage*, would guarantee it.

A numerical example of their elegant proof is the easiest way to explain the logic of the MM model. It is necessary to define the nature of the market in which the model was developed before the example can be understood.

The MM model is simply the pure competition model of economics applied to the capital market. In such a world there are no impediments to security transactions; there are no brokerage costs. No market participant has any advantage with regard to the use of debt; everyone pays the same interest rate. There are no institutional factors favoring the use of a particular type of security, such as the tax deductibility of interest payments; there are no taxes.

If the value of the firm is defined to be the market value of the firm's outstanding securities, the value of a given firm will be the same regardless of how it is financed. To appreciate why, consider two firms that are identical except for their financing.

Firm one, Auchs Manufacturing, generates operating earnings of $75,000 a year and is entirely equity-financed with the value of its outstanding stock being $300,000. A second firm, Fox Manufacturing, is in the same business and generates exactly the same operating earnings of exactly the same risk. The only difference between the two firms is that Fox uses financial leverage. Fox has $160,000 worth of 10-percent debt outstanding. The firms' income statements appear as follows (recall there are no taxes):

|  | Auchs | Fox |
|---|---|---|
| Operating income | $75,000 | $75,000 |
| Interest expense | 0 | 16,000 |
| Net income | $75,000 | $59,000 |

Assume that for some reason Fox's outstanding shares were selling for more than $140,000, making the value of Fox greater than the $300,000 which was the value of Auchs' outstanding shares. MM's position is that such a condition could not continue. Market forces would correct the situation.

If Fox's stock was selling for $160,000, the shareholders would be wise to sell it. To see why, consider the position of a major Fox shareholder who owns 10 percent of the outstanding stock. This Fox shareholder owns $16,000 worth of stock and has a claim on $5,900 worth of earnings (10 percent of $59,000). If the stock were sold and $32,000 worth of Auchs were bought, borrowing $16,000 against the securities as collateral, the shareholder would command a claim on greater earnings and would still have the same level of leverage, 50 percent borrowed money. The transactions are summarized below:

|  Transaction | New Earnings | |
|---|---|---|
| Sell: $16,000 Fox | (32/300) of Auchs earnings | $8,000 |
| Buy: $32,000 Auchs | 10% interest on borrowing | 1,600 |
| Borrow: $16,000 @ 10% | | $6,400 |

*better than $5900*

The implications are clear. If a firm were selling for a premium[1] because of its use of debt financing, the wise shareholder would unload the stock and buy a similar undervalued, unlevered stock. Prudent investors would not pay a corporation to use debt. They can do that on their own. This ability of shareholders to manufacture "homemade leverage" is the key to the MM argument. In a perfect market all participants are equally free to borrow and at the same rates. This eliminates any benefits the corporation might have in this regard. Companies will not be able to raise their value by using debt. This is equivalent to saying they cannot lower their cost of capital through management of their capital structure.

***Taxes and Optimal Capital Structure.*** After dealing with the capital structure issue in a simplified world, MM then considered the problem in a more realistic context. They doubted that transaction costs and differences in borrowers' interest costs would change their conclusions. However, taxes were another matter. In that interest payments are deductible, investors would always benefit if the firm did the borrowing. Homemade leverage just is not as good.

This led MM to conclude that the optimal capital structure, in a world with taxes, would involve maximum possible use of debt. According to their findings, a firm would best serve the interests of the shareholders if it borrowed until lenders refused to extend any further credit.

The MM tax model used the same arbitrage mechanism as their no-tax model. A numerical example is provided in the Appendix. In addition, the MM paper's implications with regard to the areas of capital budgeting and the cost of capital are explained. The MM paper has resulted in much rethinking on these topics. The teaching of these areas as well as the current understanding of capital structure owes much to the authors.

As might be anticipated, any paper which reshaped thinking on so many topics was, and is, controversial. It has been hotly debated since its appearance in the literature.

***The Debate.*** The 1958 MM article included (1) the no-tax model, (2) the tax model (which was corrected somewhat in a 1963 follow-up by MM), (3) an empirical test, and (4) a review of some of the major implications. The article has subsequently been contested and defended on virtually all counts.

The no-tax model was acknowledged to be virtually flawless in derivation, but many of the leaders in finance at that time characterized it as

---

[1] The arbitrage process works in reverse if a levered firm is undervalued. In this case, the arbitrager negates the leverage by buying a combination of stocks and bonds.

an academic exercise due to its lack of realism. It appears many of these critics chose to ignore the stated purpose of the model; that is, to provide a theoretical basis for subsequent inquiry. In addition to questioning the universality of interest rates and the lack of transactions costs, both issues which MM had anticipated, some questioned the efficiency of U.S. financial markets. Since then, a large number of studies from the capital market area have reinforced MM's assertions of financial market efficiency.

The MM theoretical development used an analytical device called "risk classes." They assumed that investors could classify firms into such risk groups. This was their more elegant counterpart to the "identical except for leverage" firm used in the text's example. The existence of such classes was questioned. The MM proof has since been redone without the use of this analytical convenience.[2]

As the fervor of the debate subsided, more time was devoted to the tax model. Numerous authors relaxed, modified, reversed, and respecified the assumptions and replicated the derivations. These studies have helped to identify factors that might be expected to affect the optimum capital structure. However, the MM model, as originally derived, still stands as a surprisingly effective theoretical construct after years of continuous evaluation. As the Appendix illustrates, much of current doctrine reflects its influence.

In addition to the theoretical models, MM's paper contained a statistical study. It involved two regressions. The first regressed the average cost of capital against capital structure. The results were interpreted to show that the cost of capital was unaffected by the degree of leverage, *except for the tax effect*. The second regression used the cost of equity as the dependent variable. The second set of results validated the first.

The two runs were criticized as being essentially identical; that is, they were not independent tests, merely two different forms of the same regression. The methodology made the second run appear important when, in fact, it merely duplicated the first results in a different form.

The sample was also criticized. A number of authors suggested that the use of regulated industries, oil companies and electric utilities, prevented the authors from finding any important differences in capital costs. The fact that the range of capital structures was limited added to this problem. Reevaluation of their findings suggested that the results were too weak to differentiate between MM's position and the traditional view which they (MM) had oversimplified.

What followed was a decade of statistical studies intent on answering the capital structure question. Regretfully, the major finding was that social science data are difficult to deal with in an exact way. One of the benefits of this search has been to increase the sophistication of finance

---

[2] Readers interested in these proofs should consult the articles by Hamada, Schall, and Stiglitz listed in the bibliography.

researchers. Suffice it to say that the issue remains unresolved from an empirical perspective.

It is impossible to summarize a debate that has continued this long and has involved so many scholars. However, it is fair to say that much of current teaching in finance reflects the Modigliani-Miller influence. They have affected the way in which capital budgeting is taught. The current method of calculating the cost of capital, using market value weights, owes homage to their model. Finally, current wisdom on capital structure owes much to the interest generated by their contribution.

**The MM View on Capital Structure.** The MM papers have had a major impact on the finance literature, but the qualitative difference with regard to capital structure policy is relatively slight. According to their tax model, the highest level of debt creates the lowest cost of capital and, therefore, the highest valuation. This made the imposition of the external borrowing constraint (L) necessary. A graphical illustration of the MM model, Figure 12-2, looks much like the traditional model.

The Modigliani-Miller View
**FIGURE 12-2**

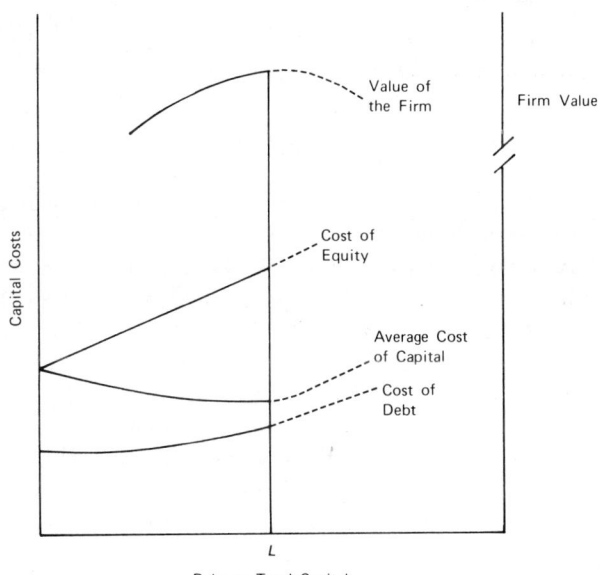

Debt to Total Capital

The explanation would differ slightly. MM felt that traditionalists had underestimated the slope of the cost of equity curve. MM felt that this cost would rise rapidly, *due to arbitrage*, and all but the tax advantage of debt would be neutralized. However, because of this tax benefit, the average cost of capital would decline until it reached a minimum at the maximum borrowing point, L, the externally imposed limit. Using the maximum reasonable amount of debt would maximize firm value.

The remaining point of contention between MM and the traditionalists is whether there is a range of capital structures, somewhere short of L, where there is room for financial decisions. The question is whether there are counterbalancing factors that offset the tax benefit. Some of the factors that have been suggested are increased bankruptcy risks, increased earnings variability, and higher covariability with market returns, which causes stock investors diversification difficulties.

Which of the two positions is correct is difficult to assess. The empirical evidence is unclear. As will be indicated in the chapter on bonds, U.S. firms do use vast amounts of debt capital which is consistent with the MM thesis. However, there are studies of debt capacity which suggest that although these firms do use a lot of debt, they still have unused debt-carrying capacity. Such a practice cannot be reconciled with the MM position. Regardless of whether they are ultimately supported or disproven, MM have made an immense contribution to our understanding of the capital structure and its importance.

## Long-Term Financing

The capital structure problem is an unresolved theoretical issue. Even when it is resolved, theory will not solve all of the front-line financial manager's long-term financing problems. Capital structure policy, even as it is now imperfectly derived, must often be ignored because of short-run considerations. The financial manager must raise funds now, and what is expedient now may not always be consistent with what would be best in the long run.

Numerous situations could be described where policy and short-run tactics would be in conflict. Two should be sufficient. It is not uncommon for small proprietors to prefer the policy of being debt-free. However, when expanding, they generally use debt capital because they prefer not to, or cannot, raise outside equity capital.

In the fairly recent past, it was possible to observe quite a few large firms wrestling with the same type of paradox. Although they desperately needed long-term capital, and their financing policy would have dictated the sale of bonds, they used other means. Because of unusually high interest rates, these firms financed with short- and intermediate-term debt or, in some cases, even sold equity issues.

These examples indicate two factors that may override policy dictates: control and timing. There are other such considerations. The desirability of the different forms of financing is a direct consequence of the legal characteristics of these securities. Subsequent chapters on the different securities will discuss these characteristics in greater detail. For now the characteristics will be discussed briefly before developing them into desirability considerations.

The discussion will be limited to pure debt and common stock. Other securities are hybrids, having some of the traits of bonds and some of those of common stock. Convertible bonds are bonds when issued but may, at some later point, be converted into stock. Preferred stock is equity by definition, but it is more like debt in that it generally receives a limited, preferential payment, a preferred dividend. Securities such as these are appropriate forms of financing when a blend of the debt and equity characteristics are desirable. This is why they were developed. For current purposes, concentrating on the simpler forms is more efficient.

*Legal Characteristics of Debt and Equity.* The security owner's rights with debt and equity differ with respect to three important features: right to recovery of original investment, claim on income, and representation. Debtholders are not investors; they are lenders. Lenders receive added safeguards with regard to recovery of their original investment and payment for its use. However, they have no rights to representation unless their preferential position with regard to principal and income appears in jeopardy.

Bondholders are contractually guaranteed they will be returned their original investment. Bonds mature; they come due just like a promissory note. At the time of maturity, the issuer is legally bound to repay the face value of the bonds or suffer the legal consequences. In the event of such difficulties, the bondholders have a preferential position with regard to participation in assets. They have prior claim over residual owners (common stockholders). The amount of their claim is limited to their original investment. This provision is seldom troublesome in that the assets are generally insufficient to satisfy court costs, attorney's fees, and creditor's claims. If there is anything remaining, that belongs to the stockholders.

Not only are bondholders contractually assured of receiving return of their invested capital, they are also assured of receiving payment for the use of that capital. Interest is the payment for the use of debt capital. Bondholders have a preferential claim on income. Interest must be paid before any distribution can be made to stockholders. Except in rare cases (income bonds will be discussed in Chapter 18), it must be paid even if there is no income. Nonpayment of interest constitutes default; and the bondholders, or their representative, can sue.

Stocks never mature. They do not come due. The buyer is in no way assured that the original investment will ever be "repaid." The investor surrenders the capital to the company and then hopes for the best.

Stockholders also receive no guarantee of payment for the use of their invested capital. Not only do they have an inferior position with respect to claim on income, they are not assured of receiving dividends even if the company does make money. However, shareholders obviously hope to receive dividends. Bondholders' claim on income is limited to the contractually agreed-upon interest payment. Common stockholders are not subject to such limitations. They have the right to unlimited participation in earnings, to the extent the corporation declares dividends. Even when common dividends are not paid, the shareholder generally benefits. The higher earnings will normally increase the value of the stock, and the investor can realize the benefit by selling part or all of the stock.

Because they have invested in the firm (surrendered their capital to it), the shareholders have a right to a voice in the management of the firm. They, through their collective vote, elect the board of directors who in turn appoint the management. It has been said that the representative process severely reduces the effectiveness of such a voice for the average shareholder. However, contests for control of firms through the elective mechanism are far from uncommon. The threat of such occurrences no doubt makes management more responsive to the perceived desires of the shareholders.

Bondholders do not vote under normal circumstances; however, it is not strictly correct to say they have no voice. The restrictive provisions (covenants) in bond contracts can restrict management. Further, most bond contracts have provisions which allow the bondholders to vote under certain conditions, such as default as to payment of either principal or interest. Because such conditions are relatively rare, it is common to speak of bondholders as not having a voice in management.

These legal characteristics (maturity, claim on income, and voice) affect the desirability of the different forms of financing in any given situation. Because the firm can choose the maturity of the debt it issues, it can choose one which is *suitable* to its needs. As mentioned, the two securities (stocks and bonds) have different rights as to representation so *control* can be an issue. Debt has a limited, enforceable, preferential claim on income as compared to equity's residual, but unlimited, claim. Because of the differences in these claims, the two securities have different effects on *earnings per share, riskiness,* and the *flexibility* of the firm with regard to future financing. Recognizing the firm will need financing again in the future raises the question as to which type of financing to use now and which to issue later. This last issue, *timing,* is often said to be the key to success in long-term financing decisions. The next section will discuss each of these decision factors.

## Decision Criteria for Long-Term Financing Decisions

Because of their legal characteristics, debt and equity capital affect the firm differently. This section will consider some of the consequences of the long-term financing decision which should be considered in making a choice.

In discussing the individual factors, analytical techniques will often be referred to which were discussed in previous chapters. Review of these earlier chapters may be necessary to recall the mechanics of the techniques.

One additional point should be made before discussing the individual decision considerations. There is no simple way of combining the analysis of the individual factors into one precise summary measure. The analysis of the individual factors cannot be added nor can it be strictly averaged. When such a financing decision is to be made, the manager must examine the total consequences of the different alternatives and choose the one which represents the best compromise solution. On some rare occasions, one type of financing will appear to be preferable in all respects. More frequently, it is a matter of selecting the best of a number of less-than-perfect choices.

*Suitability.* Suitability refers to how well the financing alternative fits the need. If the firm only needs the financing for a short period of time, long-term bonds or common stock are unsuitable. The firm would still be saddled with them after the need was past.

Debt is more flexible in this regard than equity. The firm can choose to issue debt which matures and which can be retired when the need expires. The firm can use short-term debt to finance seasonal working capital, intermediate-term debt for equipment, and long-term debt for financing plant expansion.

Equity, on the other hand, might be suitable for financing the same assets, if the need was perceived as permanent. For example, permanent increases in working capital, equipment, or plant might logically be financed with equity funds.

The idea is to use funds in such a way as to provide the company with a firm foundation, but not to burden it with unnecessary financing and its associated costs. The firm does not want insufficient or excessive financing at any time, now or in the future.

*Control.* Companies are often controlled by relatively small holdings of common stock. Although the percentage of the outstanding shares held might be small, the dollar amount of the controlling block will generally be substantial. If the firm sells new shares, the controlling shareholders must buy a proportionate amount of the new stock to maintain their percentage control. Because of the large dollar amounts involved, such purchases may be difficult.

Because they do control the company, such shareholders might prefer the sale of bonds instead of issuance of additional stock. Bondholders would have no voice in management, unless the company defaulted on interest or principal payments. In such cases the bondholders might well end up with total control. Therefore, there is even the possibility of a control issue with the sale of bonds.

*Earnings Per Share (EPS).* In Chapter 4 it was shown that debt and equity have different effects on EPS. If debt financing is used successfully,

EPS will increase. On the other hand, if volume falls, the added burden of the interest charges simply compounds the problem. This phenomenon was referred to as *financial leverage.* Equity capital does not magnify the effect of changes in volume. It does not provide leverage.

Methods for analyzing the EPS effect of the different financing alternatives were described in detail in Chapter 4. If the analyst wished to know per-share earnings at a particular sales level, pro forma income statements would provide the answer. A financial breakeven chart, such as Figure 4–4, provides that information for a wide range of volume levels. Such a chart would help the manager to evaluate the EPS consideration.

**Riskiness.** The financial breakeven chart does more than just indicate the EPS forecasts for the various financing alternatives. It highlights another aspect of the problem. Although debt capital can provide favorable leverage and raise earnings per share, it can also increase the vulnerability of those EPS to changes in volume. This is one aspect of riskiness, *earnings volatility.*

With debt financing, EPS are more volatile. This means that they are subject to wider variations with changes in the economic environment. The leverage measures (DOL, DFL, DTL) in Chapter 4 are efficient ways of describing, and are therefore helpful in assessing, this aspect of the financing alternatives.

Earnings volatility is only one feature of debt's greater riskiness. Debt also carries a risk due to the fixed interest payments involved. If the firm misses such a payment, there are severe legal repercussions, including the possibility of bankruptcy.

One way of measuring such a *default risk* is the coverage ratios of Chapter 3. However, in this case the ratios would be calculated on a pro forma basis; that is, on the basis of forecasted income statements. Because the penalties for default are so severe, firms generally are very conservative with regard to this type of risk.

**Flexibility.** Flexibility refers to the firm's ability to adapt to a changing economic environment. The firm tries to maintain flexibility with regard to future financing decisions.

If a firm issues too much debt capital, it may find itself forced to use equity financing at a time when the sale of stock is particularly unattractive. Firms are reticent to sell stock in poor markets. However, they might be forced to choose some other equally unattractive strategy. A number of such strategies could be observed in recent years. These strategies included selling callable bonds (bonds subject to accelerated retirement) at high interest rates, with hopes of rearranging the capital structure when the market environment improved; selling short-term debt, postponing the decision in hopes that the situation would improve; selling convertible bonds so the indebtedness might be extinguished through conversion when times improved; and, finally, by severely curtailing capital expenditures.

There can be a similar problem if too much equity financing is used. If a firm wanted to contract operations (i.e., become smaller by selling assets or possibly even an operating division), excessive equity can be troublesome. With debt, management can wait until the bonds mature and retire them. Management may have even reserved the right to retire the debt early through a call provision. With stock, the management is put in the delicate situation of bargaining with the stockholders in order to persuade them to sell their ownership rights.

To be flexible the firm must maintain its options. Then if the firm wishes to expand, it can do so using the most attractive financing available at the time. To be truly flexible, the firm needs to maintain its choices for either expansion or contraction, though generally the emphasis is on the former.

*Timing.* The discussion of flexibility made frequent references to time. In any financing decision financial managers must consider the current financial market environment and expected environment which might exist the next time the firm reenters that market.

It is difficult to generalize as to the correct tactics for corporate financing decisions. Any prescription for such decisions will seem over simplified if viewed against the complexities of modern capital markets and the volatile and ever-changing nature of these markets' behavior. However, some patterns do appear in the relationship between security returns and general economic conditions. These patterns suggest guides to the timing of corporate issues.

In the past, interest rates have generally been lower during recessions. This pattern would suggest that debt financing should be done during such periods. Recognize that such action will require considerable courage on the part of management. Managers will be in the position of incurring added fixed interest expenses during those periods when the outlook is the gloomiest.

Generally, interest rates reach their highest level at, or near, the peak of expansionary periods. This occurs when the government applies restraints to reduce the inflationary pressures that mount during such a boom.

These high interest rates will have a negative effect on stock prices which will have risen during the economic expansion. Stock prices would generally have risen during the early phases of the expansion due to improving profits and higher earnings-per-share expectations.

Reviewing this stylized scenario of the economy's and the market's behavior provides some insight to the timing problem. During the recessions interest rates are low. With funds being readily and cheaply available, firms are induced to make new investments, providing the base for a subsequent economic recovery. As the recovery begins, other firms are encouraged to borrow and to increase production. Increased borrowing will push interest rates upward. The pattern repeats itself and is magnified until boom conditions are reached. Because of their profits, firms' stock prices rise.

At the height of the boom, productive capacity is fully utilized, or nearly so, and increased demand results in higher prices for goods and services rather than increased production. Unusually high prices are considered to be socially undesirable, and the government reacts to keep the inflation under control. Government officials do this primarily through the management of the supply and cost of loanable funds. Monetary restraint will push interest rates even higher and cause share prices to moderate. Stock prices are restrained because the high yield on bonds makes bonds more attractive alternative investments.

The government will then attempt to keep the economy running at, or near, peak capacity. If the effects of the monetary management are too severe; that is, if interest rates climb too high, too fast, the country can be sent into a recession. The same thing can occur if the business community becomes pessimistic as to the economic future and cuts back on production. Reductions in production can snowball the same way the increases did in the expansion. Economic slumps occasionally occur out of all proportion to the economic restraint applied by the government. The economy is not a perfectly manageable system.

The prescription for the financial manager is as follows: acquire debt capital during the recession when interest rates are low and sell stock just before the peak of the expansion. To accomplish this, the manager must forecast when the recessions and booms are going to occur. Further, the decision-maker is going to be in a position of continually being exposed to ultimate financial embarrassment. Such a policy will have the firm issuing debt when profits are at their lowest, during the recession. During the expansion, when the benefits from leverage are the greatest, the financial manager will be advocating the sale of equity securities and the consequent dilution of earnings.

The previous paragraph highlights a central problem in long-term financing decisions. Accurate forecasts are the key to good timing. In addition to forecasting the firm's need for funds during the different phases of the business cycle, the manager must predict what market conditions will exist when these needs arise. This involves guessing at how and when the economy will expand and what government's response to the resulting economic conditions will be. The economy's reaction to the governmental tinkering must also be assessed. The magnitude of the forecasting problem does much to explain why financial managers stay constantly atuned to economic conditions and predictions. They read the financial press, listen to government announcements, enter economic consulting arrangements, and try anything they can to stay in touch with tomorrow's financial market environment. With the dollar amounts that are involved, an astute financial manager can save the firm millions of dollars by properly timing the issue of the firm's securities.

## Summary

This chapter considered the long-term financing decision from two perspectives. Capital structure policy prescribes guidelines as to the appropriate mix of debt and equity for a firm to use as a target over time. However, financing decisions are not made *over time;* they are made at *points in time.* The tactical decisions of this nature involve multiple considerations that must be weighed simultaneously.

The issue of capital structure policy has been hotly debated in the finance literature. The two sides of the debate, the traditional and the Modigliani and Miller views, were both presented. The increased concern with theory represented a departure for this text which has not generally devoted too much space to strictly theoretical considerations. The reason for the departure is that the impact of the MM model is too great to ignore.

The MM paper considered more than capital structure. It has reshaped the analysis of a number of important financial decisions. The cost of capital calculation and the structure of capital budgeting reflect the MM influence. The Appendix discussion examines these topics.

The desirability of debt or equity at a given point in time derives from the securities' legal characteristics: right to return of invested capital, claim on income, and voting rights. Differences with regard to these attributes result in differences with regard to the securities' suitability for the need and their impact on earnings per share and riskiness. There are limits on the amount of debt a firm can use. Maintaining flexibility requires that a firm operate below that limit. The salability of the two forms of capital varies with prevailing economic conditions. Forecasting the firm's needs and the probable economic environment at the time of the need is one of the most troublesome aspects of the financing problem. These forecasts are the key to the timing issue, which is central to the handling of the firm's recurring financing decisions.

## QUESTIONS

1. Define "capital structure."
2. Distinguish between the capital structure issue and the long-term financing problem.
3. Concisely state the conclusions of the MM "no-tax" model.
4. Concisely state the implications of the MM "tax" model.
5. Using Figures 12–1 and 12–2, state the remaining point of contention between MM and the traditionalists.
6. Review each of the "decision criteria for long-term financing decisions" discussed in the chapter. For each of these considerations, suggest a method of analysis.

228 Part II Financial Planning and Control

7. Would inflation benefit a firm with a high debt/total capitalization ratio more than a firm in the same industry with a lower ratio?
8. Considering the current economic climate, what type of financing would seem to be appropriate? Consult the financial press to see if your instincts are consistent with what is going on in the market.

## PROBLEMS

1. Two hypothetical companies, Fast Service Shoe Company and Comfort-Last (both small shoe manufacturers), generate identical operating earnings of $100,000 a year. Both companies have been offered to you as potential investments. Fast Service has $300,000 of 8 percent debt outstanding. The owners offer to sell the company for $550,000 if the liabilities are assumed. This would give almost a 14 percent rate of return. The owners of Comfort-Last offer to sell their operation, debt-free, for $800,000. Even though the return would only be 12.5 percent, the owners are certain that they are offering a better deal. Using the MM "no tax" model and the two firms' income statements as given below, evaluate the two alternatives. Assume that up to $300,000 could be borrowed at 8 percent. (Ignore taxes.)

|  | Fast | Last |
|---|---|---|
| Operating Earnings | $100,000 | $100,000 |
| Interest Expense | 24,000 | 0 |
| Net Income | $ 76,000 | $100,000 |
| Offering Price | $550,000 | $800,000 |
| Return on Investment | 13.8% | 12.5% |

2. The Equity Corporation has a capital structure comprised of all equity (200,000 shares of common stock). The firm desires to raise additional capital of $3 million. The controller is considering three alternatives.
   a. 6 percent unsecured bond issue.
   b. 5 percent preferred stock issue.
   c. 100,000 shares of additional common stock.
   Future earnings before interest and taxes have been estimated at $500,000. Determine the net effect of the proposed alternatives. Assume a 50 percent tax rate.

3. The XYZ Corporation has the following capital structure:

| | |
|---|---|
| Debt issues (6%) | $200,000 |
| Preferred stock (5%) | 100,000 |
| Common stock equity (30,000 shares) | 300,000 |
| | $600,000 |

The planning department projects earnings before interest and taxes of $60,000 for the next three years. (Assume a 50 percent tax rate.) Should the XYZ Corporation raise $100,000 of additional capital through the sale of 10,000 shares of common stock or through the use of an 8 percent bond issue?

4. The Superior Corporation has a capital structure that is all equity (100,000 shares of common stock at $3 million). The financial manager is determining which of the following three methods would be most advantageous from

## 12 Capital Structure and Long-Term Financing Decisions

the stockholders' viewpoint for raising an additional $2 million for the corporation. The three alternatives available to the firm are as follows:
- a. 8 percent debentures.
- b. 6 percent preferred stock.
- c. 50,000 shares of common stock.

The forecast of earnings before interest and taxes for the next year is $300,000. (Assume a 50 percent tax rate.)

5. The comptroller of Mythaco, Inc., recently pulled off a major coup. By waiting less than 60 days, major interest savings were accomplished. The company recently issued $400 million of 30-year bonds at an effective yield of 8 percent. Less than two months ago they withdrew the issue when rate climbed to 8-⅜ percent.
   - a. What is the annual difference in interest expense?
   - b. Assuming the firm is in a 50 percent tax bracket and discounting the interest savings at 8 percent, what is the present value of the savings?

6. Plasto Enviro Products, Inc., (PEP) is considering how to finance a major plant expansion of $200 million. The two alternatives being considered are: (1) issuing $200 million in mortgage bonds secured by the new plant, with an anticipated interest cost of 9 percent, or (2) selling 4 million additional shares of common stock at $50 each. The firm's current balance sheet and income statement are as follows:

PEP, INC.
Balance Sheet
December 31, 1978
(in millions)

| | | | | |
|---|---|---|---|---|
| Cash | $ 150 | Current liabilities | | $ 400 |
| Accounts receivable | 570 | Long-term debt | | 500 |
| Inventories | 560 | Stock (20 million shares) | $500 | |
| Total Current Assets | $1,280 | Retained earnings | 600 | |
| Net plant and equipment | 720 | Net worth | | $1,100 |
| Total Assets | $2,000 | Total Claims | | $2,000 |

PEP, INC.
Income Statement
For the Period Ending December 31, 1978
(in millions)

| | |
|---|---|
| Net sales | $5,500 |
| Fixed cost | 1,650 |
| Variable costs (65%) | 3,575 |
| Operating income | 275 |
| Less: Interest | 35 |
| Income before taxes | 240 |
| Less: Taxes (40%) | 96 |
| Net Income | $ 144 |
| Earnings per share | $ 7.20 |

By undertaking the expansion, the company can increase sales by $160 million. The variable costs will remain at 65 percent and fixed costs will rise $30 million. As indicated below, operating earnings will increase by $26 million. In addition, the company will be prepared to enter a new market area that they believe has a good potential.

PEP, INC<br>
Pro Forma Operating Income Statement<br>
For the Period Ending December 31, 1979<br>
(in millions)

| | |
|---|---:|
| Net sales | $5,660 |
| Fixed costs | 1,680 |
| Variable costs (65%) | 3,679 |
| Operating income | $ 301 |

a. Discuss the suitability of the two financing alternatives.

b. A major shareholder group currently owns 40 percent of the outstanding common stock and feels they need to maintain 33 percent ownership for control.
  (1) If these shareholders wished to maintain 40 percent ownership, how much of the new issue would they be forced to buy?
  (2) What must they spend to maintain control if 33 percent ownership is sufficient?

c. Prepare a breakeven earnings-per-share chart as illustrated in Figure 4–4. (Using the forecasted sales level as one of the points will save time.)

d. To assess riskiness, calculate:
  (1) DOL, DFL, and DTL for current operations.
  (2) The same measures for both financing alternatives, if the project is undertaken and the forecasted sales level is achieved.
  (3) Times-interest-earned figures for current operations (industry average is six times).
  (4) Times-interest-earned for both alternatives if the expansion is undertaken.

e. In this industry the average debt-to-total-assets ratio is .47. Using pro forma balance sheets and ratios, evaluate the financing alternatives with regard to their effect on the firm's flexibility.

f. PEP, Inc., manufactures environmental protection devices and is attempting to develop biodegradeable plastic containers. Currently, the economic environment is best described as "mid-cycle." Interest rates, although far from being at bargain rates, are much lower than they were in the near past. Although there have been favorable announcements by numerous government sources as to the economic indicators, the stock market and, therefore, the sale of original issues has been somewhat sluggish. PEP believes their shares might be received somewhat more enthusiastically because of the obvious future potential of environmental products and the current concern about environmental issues. Discuss the implications for the timing of the two alternatives.

## ADDITIONAL READINGS

Barges, A. *The Effect of Capital Structure on the Cost of Capital*. Englewood Cliffs, N.J.: Prentice-Hall, Inc., 1963.

Baxter, N. D. "Leverage, Risk of Ruin, and the Cost of Capital," *Journal of Finance*, vol. 22 (September 1967), pp. 395–404.

Ben-Shahar, H. "The Capital Structure and the Cost of Capital: A Suggested Exposition," *Journal of Finance*, vol. 23 (September 1968), pp. 639–53.

Beranek, W. *The Effects of Leverage on the Market Value of Common Stocks.* Madison, Wisc.: Bureau of Business Research and Service, University of Wisconsin, 1964.

Boness, A. J. "A Pedagogic Note on the Cost of Capital," *Journal of Finance*, vol. 19 (March 1964), pp. 99–106.

Haley, C. W., and L. D. Schall. *The Theory of Financial Decisions*, Chapters 10 and 11. New York: McGraw-Hill Book Co., 1973.

Hamada, R. S. "Portfolio Analysis, Market Equilibrium and Corporation Finance," *Journal of Finance*, vol. 24 (March 1969), pp. 13–31.

Melnyk, Z. L. "Cost of Capital as a Function of Financial Leverage," *Decision Sciences*, vol. 1 (July–October 1970), pp. 327–56.

Modigliani, F., and M. H. Miller. "The Cost of Capital, Corporation Finance, and the Theory of Investment," *American Economic Review*, vol. 48 (June 1958), pp. 261–97.

———. "Corporate Income Taxes and the Cost of Capital: A Correction," *American Economic Review*, vol. 53 (June 1963), pp. 433–43.

Pfahl, J. K., D. T. Crary, and R. H. Howard. "The Limits of Leverage," *Financial Executive*, vol. 38 (May 1970), pp. 48–56.

Schall, L. D. "Firm Financial Structure and Investment," *Journal of Financial and Quantitative Analysis*, vol. 6 (June 1971), pp. 925–42.

Schwartz, E. "Theory of the Capital Structure of the Firm," *Journal of Finance*, vol. 14 (March 1959), pp. 18–39.

Schwartz, E., and J. R. Aronson. "Some Surrogate Evidence in Support of the Concept of Optimal Financial Structure," *Journal of Finance*, vol. 22 (March 1967), pp. 10–18.

Solomon, E. "Leverage and the Cost of Capital," *Journal of Finance*, vol. 18 (May 1963), pp. 273–79.

Stiglitz, J. E. "A Re-Examination of the Modigliani-Miller Theorem," *American Economic Review*, vol. 59 (December 1969), pp. 784–93.

Wippern, R. F. "Financial Structure and the Value of the Firm," *Journal of Finance*, vol. 21 (December 1966), pp. 615–34.

# APPENDIX: MODIGLIANI AND MILLER ON TAXES, CAPITAL BUDGETING, AND THE COST OF CAPITAL

## The MM Tax Model

MM's pure competition model demonstrates that the lower nominal cost of debt can be misleading. There would be no incentive for the corporate use of "cheap" debt unless (1) there were institutional factors which made debt cheaper to corporations than it was to individual investors, or (2) there were market imperfections which would impede the equilibrating process.

MM pointed out that stock collateral loans are generally at rates approximately the same as those obtained by corporations. They also discounted market imperfections, suggesting that domestic capital markets were relatively efficient and that any arguments hinged on market imperfections would need rigorous development and empirical support.

The one factor that they felt clearly encouraged the use of corporate leverage was our tax system. If interest is deductible, it would always be beneficial for the corporation to use debt rather than the investor. That would maximize the tax benefit. Stockholder borrowing cannot create as high a return as corporate leverage.

This can be demonstrated by re-using the chapter example. With taxes (assume a 40-percent rate), the income statements of the two firms would appear as follows:

|  | Auchs | Fox |
|---|---|---|
| Operating earnings | $75,000 | $75,000 |
| Interest expense | 0 | 16,000 |
| Earnings before taxes | $75,000 | $59,000 |
| Less: Taxes (40%) | 30,000 | 23,600 |
| Net Income | $45,000 | $35,400 |

Now, if the large shareholder in the earlier example were to sell the Fox stock and try to create homemade leverage, the transaction would be disadvantageous, as indicated:

| Transaction | New Earnings | |
|---|---|---|
| Sell $16,000 Fox | (32/300) of Auchs earnings | $4,800 |
| Buy $32,000 Auchs | 10% interest on borrowings | 1,600 |
| Borrow $16,000 @ 10% | | $3,200 |

The shareholder is better off with 10 percent of Fox and earnings of $3,540.

With tax-deductible interest, the market value of levered firms (the market value of all the firm's outstanding securities—stock and bonds) would be higher than the market value of similar unlevered firms. Modigliani and Miller even went so far as to specify exactly how much higher. The difference between the values of the two firms would be equal to the value of the tax shields on the levered firm's outstanding debt (i.e., the product of the tax rate times the market value of the outstanding bonds).

If the shares of the unlevered firm, Auchs Manufacturing, were worth $300,000 in total, then the bonds and stock of Fox would be worth $364,000. Again, the difference is due to the tax shields, a tax rate of .4 times $160,000 worth of debt. Market forces, through arbitrage, would always preserve this difference in market values.[1]

This, then, is the MM valuation model. The value of a levered firm

---

[1] The arbitrage process is basically the same as demonstrated in the no-tax case, although it is complicated slightly by the use of risk-adjusted discount rates, a factor originally omitted by MM but subsequently corrected.

($V_L$) is equal to value of the same firm without leverage ($V_U$), plus the value of the debt-related tax shields:

$$V_L = V_U + \tau D$$

where $\tau$ is the corporate tax rate and $D$ is the *market value* of the firm's outstanding debt securities. To define the value of the unlevered firm, MM used the standard model for an economic asset: the value of the firm is the present value of its earnings stream capitalized at the appropriate rate. The value of the unlevered firm would be:

$$V_U = \frac{(1-\tau)\bar{x}}{\rho^\tau}$$

Each of the symbols used is chosen because they were used in the MM articles. The value $x$ can be thought of as operating earnings, or EBIT, although this must qualified slightly.[2] The capitalization rate, $\rho^\tau$, is the market capitalization rate for unlevered earnings streams of this riskiness.

Combining the last two equations specifies the MM tax model, which most would agree is the premier valuation model in financial theory today:

$$V_L = \frac{(1-\tau)\bar{x} + \tau D}{\rho^\tau}$$

The development of this model has had a major impact on financial management theory. The model has implications for many important financial decisions. However, its realism continues to be a center of debate.

The body of the chapter discussed only the implications for capital structure policy. The paper's impact on capital budgeting and cost of capital calculations is also important.

## Capital Budgeting—MM's Proposition III

The MM paper was organized around three central themes which they referred to as propositions. The first two concerned the average cost of capital and the cost of equity. The third was a rule for a firm's investment decisions. It specified a cutoff point for the capital budgeting process. The rule is:

> The cutoff point for investment in the firm will, in all cases, be $\rho_k$ and will be completely unaffected by the type of security used to finance the investment. Equivalently, we may say that regardless of the financing used,

---

[2] The qualification mentioned appears in Franco Modigliani and Merton H. Miller, "Corporate Income Taxes and the Cost of Capital: A Correction," *American Economic Review*, vol. 53 (June 1963), pp. 433–43.

the marginal cost of capital to a firm is equal to the average cost of capital.[3]

Proposition III was supported by mathematical arguments. These arguments were developed in the no-tax environment and might be criticized as accurate only under those conditions. The article makes it obvious that the authors recognized this limitation. However, the prominence they accorded the rule, designating it a proposition of equal importance to the cost of capital findings, suggests that the authors felt the advice was important and should be given high visibility.

Subsequent work has validated their instinct. The MM tax model suggests that firms will use maximum leverage and always operate against a maximum debt constraint. This position has been reaffirmed by numerous theorists since then. In theory a firm will always finance with maximum leverage. If all capital budgets are so financed, the average cost of capital and marginal cost of capital will be identical.

More recent work has gone even further to validate Proposition III. If markets are efficient, the value of individual projects has been shown to be a function of only the project's returns and the relationship of those returns to market returns. In this framework the value of a project is totally unrelated to the firm, its other investments, or its financing. Work on this, the capital asset pricing model approach to capital budgeting, is at the formative stage, but it is interesting to note that Proposition III appears to hold under these conditions.

Current texts and teaching in finance reflect the impact of Proposition III. The required rate of return on individual capital investments is generally defined without regard to their specific financing. Projects are considered to be financed with a combination of funds, and the projects must earn the cost of this combination, the average cost of capital. The calculation of this average cost also reflects the MM influence.

## Cost of Capital Calculation

Throughout their articles, MM spoke of capital structure in terms of market values. Most of the current texts teach the use of market values in the cost of capital calculation. It can be shown that the weighted average cost of capital calculation suggested in the last chapter is consistent with the MM formulation for the cost of capital. The MM cost of capital formulation is derived from their valuation formula:

$$V_L = \frac{(1-\tau)\bar{x} + \tau D}{\rho^\tau}$$

---

[3] Franco Modigliani and Merton H. Miller, "The Cost of Capital, Corporation Finance and the Theory of Investments," *American Economic Review*, vol. 48 (June 1958), p. 286.

## 12 Capital Structure and Long-Term Financing Decisions

By partial differentiation[4] they find the minimum acceptable return ($m$) which the firm can accept without reducing firm value. This minimum return is:

$$m = \rho^\tau \left(1 - \frac{\partial D}{\partial I}\right)$$

All of the terms in the formula have been previously defined except $\partial D/\partial I$ which is the change in debt occasioned by an investment. This is the percentage of the investment that would be debt-financed. It is a debt-to-total-capital ratio where the components are measured on a market-value basis.

MM's findings that tax deductibility would pressure firms to use maximum debt required that some type of limit be externally imposed. They suggested that lenders would impose a limit on firms. This, denoted as $L$, would be the maximum that firms could borrow, which in turn would be the optimal amount to borrow. Substituting this into the formula, and recognizing that $L$ would be the debt ratio, allows their formula to be rewritten in more conventional terms:

$$\text{Cost of capital} = \frac{\text{Cost of equity for an all-equity firm}}{} \times [1 - (\text{Tax rate}) \cdot (\text{Debt ratio})]$$

To demonstrate the equivalence of this method and the calculation of last chapter, the example from the tax model illustration can be used. Recall that the value of the levered firm would be expected to be $364,000 in equilibrium. The two cost-of-capital calculations are summarized in Table 12A–1.

The purpose of Table 12A–1 is not to introduce cost of capital calculation. Its purpose is to demonstrate that the "average cost" as is currently taught is a marginal cost under current theory—MM's Proposition III again. Current wisdom with regard to the cost of capital reflects the MM influence.

---

[4] To find the minimum such that the investment of $I$ dollars will not reduce the value of the owners' shares, find the minimum $(1-\tau) \, \partial \bar{x}/\partial I$ such that $\partial V/\partial I = 1$:

$$\frac{\partial V}{\partial I} = \frac{(1-\tau)}{\rho^\tau} \frac{\partial \bar{x}}{\partial I} + \tau \frac{\partial D}{\partial I} = 1 \qquad (1-\tau)\frac{\partial x}{\partial I} = m = \rho^\tau \left(1 - \tau \frac{\partial D}{\partial I}\right)$$

**TABLE 12A-1**
Cost of Capital Illustration

|  | Auchs | | Fox | |
|---|---|---|---|---|
|  |  | Weights |  | Weights |
| Bonds | –0– |  | $160,000 | .44 |
| Stock | $300,000 | 1.00 | 204,000 | .56 |
| Total Capital | $300,000 |  | $364,000 |  |

Costs:

Cost of equity[°] $= \dfrac{\text{Net income}}{\text{MV stock}}$   $\dfrac{\$45{,}000}{\$300{,}000} = 15$   $\dfrac{\$35{,}400}{\$204{,}000} = 17.4$

Cost of debt ............. N/A    Interest rate $(1 - \text{Tax rate})$
    $.10\,(1 - .4) = .06$

MM calculation: $m = \rho^\tau \left(1 - \tau \dfrac{\partial D}{\partial I}\right)$

$m = 15\,(1 - .4\,\{0\})$        $m = 15\,(1 - .4\,\{.44\})$
$\phantom{m}= 15$               $\phantom{m}= 12.4$

Weighted average calculation:

|  | Weight | Cost | Weighted Cost | Weight | Cost | Weighted Cost |
|---|---|---|---|---|---|---|
| Bonds | 0 | — | — | .44 | 6 | 2.64 |
| Stock | 1.00 | 15 | 15 | .56 | 17.4 | 9.74 |
|  |  |  | 15 |  |  | 12.40 |

[°] Although it appears a new cost of equity calculation is being used, that is not necessarily the case. MM stressed an earnings approach to valuation, but they demonstrated that the earnings measure for the cost of equity was consistent with the Gordon model under his assumptions. Use of the earnings measure was simply easier here.

# part III
# SHORT- AND INTERMEDIATE-TERM FINANCING

In financing their operations, business firms borrow from many sources, for a multitude of reasons. While the distinction among the various types of credit is sometimes obscure, the type of credit needed will often influence the maturity, terms, and sources employed. Beginning with Chapter 13 and continuing through Chapter 20, a detailed study is made of the various sources of funds available to the firm. In this section, short- and intermediate-term financing are discussed, before moving to long-term sources of funds.

Approximately 90 percent of wholesalers' and manufacturers' sales are made on credit; consequently, trade credit is an important, and sometimes the only, external source of funds available to some business firms. However, the average firm uses bank credit to some extent; and, in selecting a bank, it is important that the one chosen is qualified and able to handle the firm's banking needs.

Some financially stronger firms can obtain short-term funds without going to a lending institution. They sell short-term obligations directly to the investing public. The obligations are called commercial paper. This type of borrowing is discussed briefly.

While some firms can obtain unsecured short-term financing, either from a financial institution such as a bank or through the markets by selling commercial paper, many must provide collateral for such loans. The nature of such collateral arrangements is explained. Intermediate credit is often needed to finance equipment and is increasingly obtained by arranging for term loans. The growing practice of leasing instead of purchasing equipment requires an analysis of the relative costs of leasing versus borrowing.

This section covers trade credit, borrowing through commercial banks, commercial paper, secured borrowing, intermediate-term loans, and leasing.

# 13

# Short- and Intermediate-Term Borrowing

Analysis of a firm's financing requirements should answer three questions. How much financing is needed? How long is the financing needed? What type of financing should the firm use?

Short-term financing is generally required to carry seasonal working capital requirements. The amount and duration of the need are dependent on sales and the production and credit procedures used by the firm. Chapter 6 discussed cash budgets. Cash budgets develop estimates based on forecasted sales as to the amount and duration of the expected short-term financing requirements.

This chapter will address the third issue—the type of financing. It will discuss a number of ways a firm's financial needs might be met by borrowing. The chapter starts with a discussion of trade credit. This type of borrowing is almost universal. The use of trade credit is generally assumed in the construction of a cash budget. If a firm buys materials and supplies on credit, paying for the goods at some later point in time, it has, in effect, borrowed from its suppliers. Some of the more common types of trade credit will be described.

In addition to asking how much, how long, and what kind of borrowing the firm needed, it might have been asked from *whom* the firm was to borrow. This would provide a legitimate basis for organizing the discussion of short-term financing. However, because of competitive pressures in the financial marketplace, many of the traditional institutional boundaries have blurred. Many of the financial institutions which formerly specialized in particular forms of lending arrangements now seek to offer a broader range of financial services to their clients. For this reason the descriptive material is organized according to types of financing arrangements rather than types of lenders. However, one institution is covered in some detail. Because of their strategic location and because of their pivotal importance as suppliers of short- and intermediate-term financing, commercial banks are discussed separately.

In addition to using trade credit and borrowing from financial institutions, stronger firms can raise short-term funds on the open market. Because of their prominence they can sell promissory notes directly to the investing public. These publicly sold, short-term promissory notes are called commercial paper. The nature of this type of borrowing and some of the benefits derived from its use will be examined.

The remainder of the chapter concentrates on types of borrowing arrangements. Borrowing may either be secured or unsecured. Unsecured borrowing may be obtained by the stronger firms. In such an instance the firm obtains the use of funds merely by providing a contractual promise to pay. Such arrangements could be made with a bank, or the borrowing could be from other financial institutions. The mechanics would be much the same either way. The company would receive the funds in exchange for a promissory note.

Firms may provide collateral to facilitate their borrowing on better terms. In secured short-term borrowing the type of collateral used is generally consistent with the type of loan; that is, working-capital loans use working-capital collateral. Where possible, the firm will reserve capital assets to use as collateral for longer-maturity borrowing. The primary assets used as a basis for short-term borrowing are accounts receivable and inventories. The characteristics of such financial arrangements are described.

Intermediate-term borrowing is that which has a maturity of one to five years. (The five-year cutoff is somewhat arbitrary, and a one- to ten-year designation is also common.) The use of such financing has become increasingly important as the capital requirements of modern industry have surpassed firms' ability to supply such funds from retention of earnings. In addition to lending by financial institutions, many manufacturers have established finance subsidiaries to aid firms in buying their products, by making financing conveniently available. This has proven to be an effective and, in some cases, an almost essential marketing device.

In addition to the increase in the volume of term loans, the need for intermediate-term financing has created a growing new industry—leasing. The nature of leases and methods of analyzing them are the topics of Chapter 14.

## Trade Credit

***Growth of Trade Credit.*** The growth in the volume of trade credit has been due in part to the ability of large business firms to finance the credit needs of their business customers either directly, by their own credit departments, or indirectly, through wholly owned sales finance company subsidiaries. Large business corporations typically are in a liquid position and are able to finance directly in the open market and to borrow from commercial banks and other financial institutions. Most small firms find they have no access to the money and capital markets and are less able to borrow on favorable terms than large firms. The chief suppliers of trade credit are large corporations, and the chief users are small business firms. When trade receivables are compared with trade payables, only the larger firms have receivables in excess of payables, which is further evidence they are the major source of credit for small business firms.

During periods of tight money and a scarcity of credit, interest rates soar and payments of accounts receivable lag. It is during such periods that firms look for new sources of credit or depend more on other business firms for trade credit, in larger amounts and for longer terms.

It is difficult to determine the exact amount of trade credit actually used. Reliable data are hard to obtain because of the data-collection problem. Nevertheless, it is generally agreed that trade credit is a source of short-term financing used by practically all business firms.

The volume of trade credit expands spontaneously not only with an increase in business activity but also because of possible increases in prices of goods and services financed by this source of funds. Firms making the greatest use of trade credit are in the manufacturing and the wholesale and retail industries. However, even within these industries there is considerable variation in the use of trade credit.

***Basic Types.*** There are three basic types of trade credit. (1) promissory notes, (2) acceptances, and (3) open-book accounts. The latter is by far the most common form of trade credit in use in the United States today.

***Promissory Notes.*** When promissory notes are used instead of open-book accounts, the buyer is asked to sign a note that is evidence of the debt to the selling firm. In general, it is common in industries where the merchandise is of high unit value and readily recognizable or measurable. Industries using promissory notes include milling companies and fur and jewelry dealers. The promissory note narrows the differences in case there is a dispute with regard to the claim.

***Acceptances.*** Just as in the case of promissory notes, there are a few industries that make wide use of acceptances. Basically, an acceptance is a time bill of exchange drawn on a bank or business firm by another firm, usually to cover the cost of goods sold (which may be in transit or in storage). When a bill of exchange is drawn on and accepted by a bank, it is called a banker's acceptance; when drawn on and accepted by a business firm, it is called a trade acceptance. Both types of bills are used by business firms to raise cash to finance their working-capital needs.

A trade bill of exchange is drawn by the seller of goods on the buyer to cover payment. It is an order to pay as distinguished from a promise to pay (promissory note, bond, certificate of deposit, and so on). A trade bill may be either a demand or time bill. If it is a time bill, it is usually accepted by the purchaser (which makes it a trade acceptance), and the buyer of the goods becomes primarily responsible for the trade acceptance, as would be the case if he signed a promissory note for the goods purchased.

Before the Civil War, most merchandise sold on credit terms was financed with promissory notes and trade acceptances running for six to nine months. During and following the war, suppliers reduced the credit period and began to offer generous discounts for cash payments. This step was taken by suppliers in order to protect themselves from losses caused by the fluctuating value of the "greenback," and one of the aftermaths was to establish the open-book-account method of selling. Because of the lack of trade paper, commercial banks made unsecured loans to buyers to enable them to pay cash and to take the generous discounts when purchasing goods. While the trade bill has not disappeared, the volume of such paper outstanding at one time is small compared to the volume of accounts payable.

The use of a commercial or sight draft may be illustrated by the experience of a business firm in Texas that ships cotton to a firm in Massachusetts. On a delivery of the cotton to the railroad, the seller receives an order bill of lading as a receipt. The seller draws a sight draft on the buyer for the purchase price of the cotton (including freight, insurance, and all other costs prepaid by the seller), makes out the commercial invoice, and endorses the bill of lading. All of the documents are mailed to a bank in Massachusetts, as previously requested by the buyer. When the documents arrive, the buyer is notified by the bank so that complete arrangements for payment can be made and the buyer can then get the bill of lading in order to obtain the goods from the railroad. The bank will obtain the money from the buyer and remit it to the seller. The bank acts merely as a collecting agent and charges a small fee for its services. Although this is virtually a cash transaction, the seller has the advantage of retaining title to the goods until payment is made, and the buyer has the advantage of not being required to remit until the goods have been shipped.

A buyer who cannot pay for goods immediately upon receiving them may arrange for use of a trade bill with a specified maturity; that is, the bill will run for a stated period of time after presentment of the bill of exchange for acceptance. In this case, the buying and selling arrangement may be similar to that noted above, with the exception of the time interval between the receipt of the bill of lading and payment. Before the agents of the seller release the bill of lading to the buyer, they ask for and receive the buyer's signature on the face of the draft. The buyer (drawee) writes the word "accepted" across the face of the bill, followed by the date of acceptance and signature. The trade acceptance will come due at the end of a period of time that varies—it may be 30 days from the date of acceptance. In some instances, the trade terms may specify that the draft will run from the date it is drawn rather than from the date of acceptance.

The facilities of commercial banks are commonly used for presentment, with the buyer being notified of the arrival of the documents by telephone or otherwise. A local bank receiving the bill of exchange either asks the buyer to call for it at the bank or presents it at the buyer's place of business. The commercial invoice, bill of lading, and other documents accompanying the bill of exchange are checked by the buyer to see that the sales terms are met. If something is wrong, the drawee may either accept the bill of exchange with qualifications or refuse to accept it. If, after signing the draft, the buyer finds that the papers misrepresent the goods or merchandise (papers will come by mail, goods more slowly by freight), the buyer is still liable for the draft as accepted but may sue the seller for violation of the contract or misrepresentation or fraud.

If the trade acceptance is returned to the seller, the latter may discount it for cash, hold it until maturity in 30 days, or use it as security for a loan. A trade acceptance remains a secondary liability of the drawer, and the signature of the acceptor usually adds to its credit standing. If held until maturity, it is superior to an account receivable as evidence of a sale, and it is more acceptable than an account receivable as security for a bank loan.

In selling to buyers in foreign markets, the U.S. merchant may use the same sales techniques used in domestic trade, including trade acceptances, as well as other trade drafts that are payable on sight. Because of the time element, the U.S. firm may sell its claim to its bank, use it as security for a bank loan, or request the bank to honor a time draft drawn on it, with receipts from the trade draft pledged as security. In the last case, the business firm will sell the banker's acceptance to obtain cash.

*Open-book Accounts.* In lines of business not customarily using promissory notes or trade acceptances, most sales are made on open-book accounts, with the seller keeping records and copies of customers' orders, sales invoices, and shipping papers. The volume of accounts receivable of a business firm will depend on its volume of credit sales, terms of sale, paying practices of customers, collection policies, and the selection and screening of customers as to credit worthiness. Credit extended by suppliers to their business-firm customers is called mercantile credit, and credit extended by business firms to their retail customers is called retail or consumer credit.

In the mercantile-credit field, cash terms means that payment is to be made after receipt of the invoice for the goods—usually within ten days —to allow time for the buyer to examine the goods and to remit by check or draft.

When selling on an open-book basis, the custom of giving generous cash discounts is an important procedure that makes prompt payment profitable. For illustration, payment terms of "2 percent, 10 days, net 30 days" means an implicit interest rate of 36.73 percent when computed on an annual basis.[1] This is far out of line with interest charges of banks and other lenders; therefore, it is advantageous for a business firm to borrow in order to take cash discounts. From the viewpoint of the seller, cash discounts may be justified if they have the effect of stimulating sales and expediting collections.

Credit terms quoted by business firms may vary from a few days to several months from the invoice date. However, maturity terms tend to be uniform throughout a given region within an industry, and they may be influenced by state regulatory agencies (for illustration, beer may be sold only for cash delivery in some states, while in other states distributors are allowed 90 to 120 days for payment). To offset the disadvantage to some buyers caused by geographical location, the time allowed for taking discounts may date from receipt or arrival of the goods rather than from the date of the invoice.

In trade areas where buyers order several times per month, sellers may "lump" orders and allow credit terms that specify the buyer will be billed for all purchases made during a given period on a certain date (for example, beginning, middle, or end of the month, or some specified date in the following month). In such cases, the credit period and provisions for cash discounts will start from the specified date, called the billing date.

Perhaps the main advantage of open-book credit is its easy availability. As long as purchases are made steadily, accounts payable are virtu-

---

[1] Assume a $100 balance due. If the purchaser were to pay on the 10th day, the payment would be $98 ($100 − 2\%) \times ($100)$. If payment were made on the 30th day, it would be $100, since no discount is allowed after the 10th day. Therefore, the merchant actually pays $2 for the privilege of holding $98 for the time period between the last discount day and the final due date. Based on a 360-day year, the interest rate would be:

$$I = \frac{\text{Discount percent}}{(100 - \text{discount percent})} \times \frac{360}{(\text{final due date} - \text{discount period})}$$

$$= \frac{2\%}{98\%} \times \frac{360}{20}$$

$$= 36.73\%$$

A quick and easy way to compute close approximation to the annual interest is as follows:

$$I = \frac{360}{(\text{Final due date} - \text{number of days in discount period})} \times \text{discount percent}$$

For example, given terms of 2/10, net 30, the result is:

$$\frac{360}{(30-10)} \times 0.02 = 36\%$$

In effect, the firm is paying 2 percent for the use of the funds for 20 days; since there are 18 periods of 20 days in a 360-day year, the approximate annual interest rates is simply $18 \times 2$ percent, or 36 percent per year. This approximation, regardless of the cash-discount terms, would always be slightly less than the actual rate.

ally a continuous source of credit. There is no need to arrange for the financing; it is automatic.

The main disadvantage of trade credit is its cost if discounts are not taken. Even here these costs can be lowered by not liquidating the accounts payable at the maturity date. However, if payment dates are stretched too far from the due date, there is a distinct possibility of a deterioration in the credit rating of the firm. This may have the effect of raising the cost of other sources of credit, such as bank borrowings. Banks and other lenders do not ordinarily look with favor on a long history of slowness in payments of trade-credit obligations. Although this cost is difficult to measure, there is little doubt that it will color other lenders' attitudes toward granting credit to the firm. Nevertheless, it costs the firm nothing to take full advantage of the discount period. Prudent cash management dictates that all payments be made at the end of the discount period or on the maturity date if no discount is allowed by the seller.

## Commercial Paper

*Characteristics.* In order to meet their needs for working capital, large, well-known corporations with excellent credit ratings may sell their unsecured negotiable promissory notes in the open market. This is one of the least expensive methods of obtaining funds for seasonal and other temporary needs, and, by its use, a corporation may avoid exhausting its lines of credit and increasing its indebtedness at commercial banks.

The unsecured negotiable promissory notes sold directly by corporations have maturities of varying lengths; those sold to commercial paper dealers have more standard maturities of from three to six months. The minimum denomination is usually $100,000, although there are instances of $25,000 notes. The maturity is rarely more than 270 days, since longer maturities require registration with the Securities and Exchange Commission. Business firms issue commercial paper either as a substitute for or as a supplement to short-term bank loans. The cost of borrowing in the commercial-paper market varies with the credit rating of the issuer and with money-market conditions.

The prime rate is the interest rate paid on short-term loans by business corporations whose credit standings are such as to permit them to borrow in large amounts without security and to shift their fianancing between the customer-loan market and the commercial-paper market. Commercial paper rates have generally been slightly less than the existing prime rate.

The size of the market and the ability of both lenders and borrowers to shift their funds and debt issues rapidly into and out of the market demonstrate that commercial paper is a viable alternative to the use of bank financing. The market has the ability to expand and contract appreciably, depending on the rate of return prevailing in the market in contrast to the commercial-bank lending rates.

***Dealers.*** Firms that borrow in the commercial-paper market frequently use the services of commercial-paper dealers or commercial-paper houses; but some of the large sales finance companies have created their own sales organizations, which handle the sale of their companies' open-market promissory notes. When a business firm deals through a commercial-paper house, the latter takes an issue of promissory notes on a commission basis or buys the issue outright. The notes, being drawn payable to bearer, are sold without the endorsement of the commercial-paper house or other holders. If a second name appears on the notes, it is usually the endorsement of an officer or someone closely associated with the borrower. Most notes are unsecured, but, in a few cases where they are secured, the collateral is held by a trust company or the trust department of a bank. The commercial-paper house guarantees the genuineness of all notes it sells, but it does not assume the credit risk.

***Yield.*** Like other open-market paper, the short-term notes of business firms have no provisions for interest; instead, they are sold at a discount from face value with the difference being the return or yield. At maturity, the issuer pays the par or face amount, and the cost for use of the funds is the difference between the price at which notes were sold to the commercial-paper dealer and the face value. For instance, if six-month notes were sold at $98, the yield would be 4.08 percent

$$\frac{2}{98} \times 2 = 4.08$$

and a 30-day note sold at $99 would yield 12.1 percent. The market determines the cost of borrowing; therefore, the interest rate on an issue of open-market paper is very sensitive to day-to-day credit conditions.

***Borrowers.*** Corporations that borrow in the open market are the "cream of the crop" among short-term borrowers. Although there are only a few hundred business firms that borrow in the open market, there are undoubtedly thousands of others that could meet the required credit standards. The business firms that borrow in the open market include manufacturers (particularly textiles, foods and related products, metal products, leather goods, lumber, wood, paper, chemicals, drugs, and paints); wholesalers (particularly groceries and food products, hardware and paints, and textiles and leather products); retailers (particularly department and chain stores); and public-utility companies. In addition, this market includes sales finance companies, small loan companies, bank holding companies, and other finance companies whose volume of borrowing exceeds that of all business firms.

Although the standards are high, there are a large number of business firms that could finance in the open market if they so desired. Many refrain from doing so for fear of impairing their established relationships with commercial banks. Also, the terms of financing in the open market are less flexible than the terms obtainable when borrowing from commercial banks. Ordinarily, open-market promissory notes cannot be prepaid, extended, or renegotiated like bank loans.

***Sources of Funds.*** A business corporation's success in open-market financing depends on the willingness of investors to buy and hold the firm's notes. The market is an impersonal one, which means that no favors as to renewal are asked or expected at maturity of the issue. Although the open market and the customer-loan market are sometimes regarded as providing a common credit pool, this is not the case, because the open market taps sources of credit other than those provided by commercial banks. Because of the higher yield thereon, business firms have found purchasing commercial paper a profitable substitute for investing in U.S. Treasury bills and negotiable time certificates of deposit. Thus, business firms are not only suppliers but also investors in these money-market credit instruments. In effect, firms having a temporary surplus of cash are financing those having a temporary deficit.

***Advantages.*** Business firms find it advantageous to finance in the open market for a number of reasons:

1. The open market provides an additional source of funds to supplement those provided by commercial banks. In the open market, funds are provided by financial and nonfinancial institutions and corporations that have cash available for short-term investment. The transactions are in relatively large amounts and are simple and inexpensive.

2. Traditionally, it is less expensive to finance in the open market than borrowing from commercial banks, because interest rates are generally lower and a lower minimum compensatory balance will be required. Typically, the interest rate is at least one-half of 1 percent below the prime rate.

3. Borrowing in the open market advertises the firm's name and the soundness of its financial position among those who trade in this market. As a result, there may be greater interest among investors in the equity and debt issues of these firms. As a result of these developments, firms that finance in the open market are able to borrow on more favorable terms from commercial banks.

4. Larger sums may be borrowed in the open market than could be obtained directly from banks. Because of the 10-percent rule, even the largest bank may be unable to care for the needs of some open-market borrowers. (This rule is that a bank may not lend more than 10 percent of its capital and surplus to one borrower.) However, good banking relations must be maintained, for there is always the possibility that a firm will be short of cash when its open-market commercial paper matures. Hence, it is desirable to have a line of credit under which the firm may borrow when it becomes necessary to do so. Usually, a line of credit is a requisite for open-marketing borrowing, and a commercial-paper house

will check this before contracting to buy or to act as the distributing agent for the firm's paper.

5. Although money may be "tight," there is always a market for commercial paper because banks and other open-market lenders regard the money market as a source of secondary reserves that must be held at all times in order to protect the liquidity position of the holder. The prospects that commercial paper will be nonmarketable are small and the expenses of borrowing are minor. If paper is sold through a broker, the commission will be from one-eighth to one-fourth of 1 percent when computed on an annual basis. When the borrower absorbs the commission as well as the discount on the paper, the cost is still less than it would be on a bank loan. But, in case of prepayment, there may be an interest rebate on a bank loan but not on commercial paper. The other expenses, such as the cost of the paper and engraving or printing of notes, are relatively small.

## Commercial Banks

At one time, bank lending was largely limited to meeting the seasonal working capital needs of business firms. The banking industry viewed itself as having a primary responsibility for providing the liquidity and short-term credit necessary to promote commerce. This is the reason for referring to them as "commercial" banks. In recent years bankers have broadened their perspective. Banks are heavily involved in consumer lending and sales financing. In many areas they actively seek receivables and inventory financing arrangements. They make revolving credit loans. In some regions, where their deposits are relatively stable, they have become heavily involved in longer-term lending: mortgage financing for households and, in some cases, for commercial buildings. However, even with their heavy involvement in ever-increasing variety of lending arrangements, they remain primarily a short-term lender and a critically important credit source for small and medium-size firms.

***Position of Commercial Banks.*** As compared with other lenders, commercial banks are more strategically located and better equipped to make short-term loans to business firms at lower interest rates. Only a relatively small number of business firms have access to the money and capital markets; therefore, most firms depend on direct loans to finance part of their needs for working capital and other assets. Rather than risk the loss of an increasing volume of their lending business to factors, commercial finance companies, and other specialists, commercial banks are financing a large number of special types of business assets in competition with them. In addition, banks provide business firms with term loans, revolving credit, and intermediate-term loans that are not tied to any particular type of asset.

***Characteristics of Bank Lending.*** Typically, a bank loan made to a business firm is short-term, maturing in less than 90 days, is unsecured, and is used primarily to replace trade credit. However, maturities of 150 to 180 days have become prevalent, and such loans may be secured by inventories, receivables, securities, and equipment or other fixed assets. To facilitate business financing, banks offer special arrangements, under the terms of which the borrower may obtain cash up to a maximum amount, repay the loan in whole or in part, and borrow the funds again.

**Lines of Credit.** Business firms whose seasonal operations follow a fairly definite pattern customarily make advance arrangements for lines of credit with their banks. A line of credit defines the maximum limits up to which the firm may borrow. Then, when the firm needs cash, the treasurer and president sign a note for the amount, send it to the bank, and have the amount credited to the firm's checking account.

A line of credit is usually negotiated annually by the business firm, with the amount agreed upon sufficiently large enough to cover the highest seasonal needs of the firm for the fiscal year. Costs are limited to interest payments on the amount actually borrowed, and there usually are no fees or other charges for the unused portion of the line of credit; however, the firm may be expected to maintain a so-called compensatory balance, which is usually a percentage of the line of credit. A line of credit is not a contract but merely a statement as to the maximum amount a bank will lend to a firm during the fiscal year, barring adverse changes in its financial condition. However, bankers generally feel obligated to meet their line-of-credit authorizations because they consider it necessary to do so if the bank wishes to remain competitive.

When the needs for funds of a business firm are irregular, the line-of-credit arrangement may be dispensed with; instead, the firm may make formal application for loans when funds are needed. Usually, such an application will be approved when the business firm is an old customer whose financial affairs are satisfactory, as shown by financial statements, or if acceptable security can be pledged. In negotiating the amount of a loan, the interest rate, the maturity, and other terms, bankers are influenced by the average deposit balance the business firm has maintained with the bank.

**Compensatory Balances.** For a business firm to qualify for a bank loan, it may prove beneficial to be a deposit customer of the bank or become one when a loan is granted. Loan customers are frequently required to keep a compensatory deposit balance with their banks for as long as loans are outstanding or lines of credit are in effect. In fixing lines of credit, some bankers regard the compensatory balance as a minimum, some view it in terms of an average that may fluctuate above and below the fixed amount, and others do not insist on a minimum balance but consider the average size of the borrower's usual balance. The compensatory balance may vary from 10 to 20 percent of the line of credit (or a smaller or larger percentage may be required for different types of loans). The percentage required may vary with the money situation—a higher percentage may be required when money is "tight" than when it is "easy."

Some business firms regard the compensatory deposit balance as a device to force them to pay, in effect, a higher interest rate, and others regard it as a "cheap way to get the prime rate." The difference between the interest rate applicable to a loan when a compensatory balance is required and the interest rate applicable when no compensatory balance is required may be considered an imputed interest payment on the deposit balance. During periods of tight money, deposits are most profitable to banks; therefore, during such periods, they are more insistent on the maintenance of compensatory balances, particularly for large firms, whose deposits are more volatile than those of small business firms.[2]

To see how a compensatory-balance requirement raises the effective interest rate a borrower must pay, consider the following example.

A company needs $32,000 for one year; its bank requires a compensatory balance of 20 percent and charges interest at the rate of 8 percent. Since 20 percent of the money borrowed must remain on deposit, the $32,000 represents 80 percent of the total loan.

$$\text{Total loan} = \frac{\$32,000}{.80} = \$40,000$$

$$\text{Actual interest} = .08 \times \$40,000 = \$3,200$$

$$\text{Effective interest rate} = \frac{\$3,200}{\$32,000} = 10\%$$

By requiring a compensating balance, the bank is able to charge an effective rate of 10 percent on the actual funds used by the firm. However, if the firm typically maintains a deposit balance of 20 percent of the funds requested, in this instance $6,400 (20 percent of $32,000), the compensating-balance requirement would not raise the cost of borrowing. A demand-deposit balance may be kept for liquidity purposes, and it is usually a good business practice as long as the balance is not excessive in relation to the impending current liabilities.

A minimum balance requirement may also enhance the value of the bank's legal right of offset in case the firm gets into financial difficulty. This means that the bank can attach the firm's deposit in the bank in order to apply it against the firm's loan. In other words, the firm is in debt to the bank (loan payable), but it also has a claim against the bank (deposit).

Assume the following balance sheet depicts the firm's financial picture:

| | | | |
|---|---|---|---|
| Cash (bank deposit) | $ 2,000 | Bank loan | $ 5,000 |
| Others assets | 20,000 | Accounts payable | 10,000 |
| | | Net worth | 7,000 |
| Total Assets | $22,000 | Total Liabilities | $22,000 |

[2] For an interesting discussion of compensatory balances, see Thomas Mayer and Ira O. Scott, Jr., "Compensatory Balances: Suggested Interpretation," *National Banking Review*, December 1963, pp. 157–66.

Now, assume the firm is forced to liquidate because the "other assets" cannot be converted easily into cash in order to pay the bank loan and accounts payable. At liquidation the other assets bring $8,000. Without the right of offset, the bank would share proportionally with the other general creditors. There would be $10,000 ($8,000 + $2,000) available to pay claims of $15,000. Hence, the bank would receive 66.7 cents on the dollar ($10,000/$15,000 = 66.7), or $3,333, in settlement of its loan.

With the right of offset, however, the bank would use the deposit of $2,000 to reduce its claim, which would leave $3,000 outstanding. The $3,000 balance would share proportionally with the other general creditors. Remaining claims now would be $13,000. Since $8,000 was received from the sale of other assets, the ratio would be ($8,000/$13,000), or 61.5 percent. Since the bank has a claim remaining of $3,000, it would receive $1,845 as its share of the assets. With $2,000 realized from the seizure of the bank deposit, its total recovery would be $3,845, as opposed to $3,333 without the right of offset. Thus, by requiring a compensating balance, the bank can possibly minimize the risk inherent in the loan. This would occur, however, only if the firm were not forced to borrow more than it would have otherwise in order to meet the compensating balance requirement. If it borrowed more than it needed in order to meet the requirement, i.e., $5,000 instead of $4,000, the exposure to risk by the bank would be no different than if the firm maintained a deposit balance of $1,000 and borrowed only $4,000.

Even when not required to do so, most business firms maintain adequate deposit balances with their banks because they expect banks to provide services such as credit information, payroll, stock transfer, collection, etc. When a business firm plans to move or to open new branches, bankers' advice may be sought in regard to locations for outlets, local sources of labor, and housing conditions; and the firm's officers may ask bankers to introduce them to leaders of civic groups, churches, fraternal organizations, and others.

**Application for Loan.** The application for a loan form usually filled out by a borrower contains spaces for the borrower's name, date, business activity, bank balance, amount of loan, collateral or endorsers offered, amount already owed the bank, details as to the purpose of the loan, terms (demand, 60 days, etc.), renewal provisions if any, borrower's source and amount of income, and how the borrower expects to repay the loan. Loan applicants will be expected to file copies of recent financial statements, and, frequently, operating statements are requested.

Banks screen loan applications both formally and informally, and the reasons for rejecting them throw considerable light on what is expected of loan customers. In interviews conducted by the Federal Reserve System on small business financing, bankers' reasons for rejections included those involving the credit worthiness of applicants, banks' overall loan policies, and federal and state banking rules and regulations. The lack of credit worthiness was by far the most frequent reason given for rejection of loan applications.[3]

When loan applications were rejected on the basis of lack of credit worthiness, the specific reasons included insufficient owner equity in the business, questionable managerial ability, inadequate or inferior collateral, record of slow and past-due trade or loan payments, inadequate accounting system, lack of established earning record, and poor moral risk. Because banks must avoid becoming permanent investors in business firms, the lack of adequate equity capital would be a major reason for rejecting a loan applicant. While banks are interested in lending, their survival necessitates loans being repaid; therefore, a poor earning record, questionable management, insufficient collateral, a slow payment record, and other unfavorable conditions that have a bearing on the safety of a loan would be sufficient reason for rejection.

When applications for loans by small business firms were rejected because granting them would have been in conflict with bank policy, among the specific reasons for rejection were that requested maturities were too long, applicants had not established deposit relationships with the bank, the type of loan sought was not handled by the bank, and the bank's loan portfolio for the requested type of loan was already filled.

**Short-Term Loans.** A short-term business loan is one that calls for repayment of the principal in less than one year, and it is related to the working-capital position. Although the net working capital is not changed by a short-term loan, the assets acquired through such a loan are basic to the operation of the business.

In a short-term loan, the obligations of the borrower and the rights of the lender are covered in a promissory note. The interest may be taken at maturity or the note may be discounted—interest taken in advance with only the principal amount payable at maturity. When a loan is made to finance seasonal needs, the note is usually single-name paper (no cosigner) based on the financial statements of the borrower. The borrower is expected to retire the note when due, and a short-term borrower is usually out of debt to the bank for part of the year.

Most short-term bank loans are secured; but, when dollar amounts are considered, unsecured loans represent a greater volume of funds. However, this may be explained partly by the fact that large firms with good accounting systems are able to provide their banks with complete financial statements, while small firms are more likely to depend on security.

A demand or call loan made to a business firm is one that may be called by the bank or repaid by the borower at any time. Such loans are common when manufacturers or wholesalers pledge warehoused goods as security for loans. Borrowers often cannot ascertain the time that will

---

[3] Federal Reserve System, "Survey of Credit and Capital Sources," *Financing Small Business*, vol. 1, pt. 2, survey 3 (1958), pp. 37–48.

be needed to manufacture, process, package, and sell the goods. Nevertheless, they desire to time repayment of the funds to coincide with proceeds from sales of goods. On the other hand, the bank may want cash or continued protection for the loan prior to removal of the pledged goods from the warehouse; this can be arranged by substituting documents (bill of lading or trust receipt) for the warehouse receipt.

Banks also purchase accounts receivable (with or without recourse to the seller) and make loans to business firms with accounts receivable assigned as collateral. The mechanics of these secured financing arrangements are largely the same for all lending institutions. Descriptions of these procedures, as they apply to all lenders, are included in the next two sections.

Short-term business loans may be either time or demand loans. The usual maturity of time loans is 60 days. Banks permit prepayment of loans without penalty and allow rebates if the loans have been discounted (interest taken in advance). Although bank loans may be renewed freely when they mature, a more recent practice is for both borrowers and lenders to be more realistic as to the true nature of underlying business transactions and to negotiate term loans when circumstances warant loans for more than one year. Term loans are usually made for general financing purposes, such as strengthening permanent working-capital positions and purchases of equipment, machinery, or facilities. Usually, term loans are retired with funds obtained through the operation of the business—for example, depreciation allowances and earnings retained in the business.

Although bankers are important makers of term loans, they are not the only lenders. In recent years insurance companies and private pension funds have become increasingly important. A short discussion of term loans follows the material on receivables and inventory secured financing.

## Secured Financing

In the material that follows, the reader should keep in mind that the firm's legal obligation is generally the same and it is normally embodied in a contractural promise to pay—a promissory note. What varies in the different financing arrangements is the form of collateral and the legal protections afforded the lender.

Regardless of whether a firm pledges accounts receivable or inventory as security for a loan, the firm's first obligation is to meet the moral and contractual commitment it made to repay the lender the original principal plus an agreed-upon amount of interest for use of the money.

The lender is not interested in obtaining title to the borrower's accounts nor does the lender want the firm's inventories. Collateral only constitutes an added safeguard to reduce the lender's losses should the borrower encounter financial difficulty.

There is a form of short-term financing that does not involve borrowing. Factoring is the sale of assets that might otherwise be used as loan collateral.

## Factoring

In a factoring arrangement, the financial institution routinely takes title to the firm's assets. Factoring is not truly borrowing. In this arrangement a firm sells its accounts receivable. Factoring, the business of a factor, is defined as a continuing arrangement between a factor and the seller of goods or services on open account in which the factor purchases all accounts receivable, "without recourse" to the factored client should the accounts receivable be defaulted on at maturity. As a result of this basic function, the factor assumes other activities for the client, including the maintenance of ledgers and other bookkeeping duties, collection of factored accounts receivable, and assumption of losses that may follow inability to collect. In addition, factors make advances to supplement funds obtained by factoring accounts receivable and give advice on current and potential customers, market conditions, production, and other aspects of the factored firm's business. Sometimes the term "old-line factor" is used when there is a need to differentiate the firm that purchases accounts receivables outright, with no recourse to the seller, from the firm that makes loans based on accounts receivable. In the latter case, the seller of the goods or services is ultimately responsible for repayment of funds advanced.

At one time, except in the textile industry, it was considered a sign of financial weakness for a business firm to sell or assign its accounts receivable, and a firm that resorted to this practice suffered impairment of its credit standing. This attitude was doubtless created because many firms did not resort to factoring until they were faced with immediate financial collapse. Today, the typical factored company is a fast-growing concern with a large portion of its working capital tied up in accounts receivable. Although accounts receivable are being paid, they are being replaced with new accounts; as a result, the firm is continuously short of cash. Such a firm may need additional equity capital, which might be obtained by selling stock if incorporated or by inviting others to participate as partners if unincorporated. However, many proprietors are reluctant—and understandably so—to share ownership with outsiders for fear of losing control or diluting their interests in the firm.

Most small corporations are unable to utilize the securities market in financing because investors are unwilling to buy stock in little-known and untried business concerns. In most cases, small corporations find the expenses entailed in preparing and marketing securities to be prohibitive. When firms are unincorporated, equity investment may require partnership status; this creates risks and responsibilities that many individuals are unwilling to assume. Consequently, a business firm may sell its accounts receivable to avoid having to curtail operations.

**Financial Services.** When a business firm sells its accounts receivable to a factor without recourse, the factor assumes the firm's risks of nonpayment as well as its credit and collection activities. Because the factor is able to assume risks that a relatively small business firm could not afford to assume, the factor is in a position to aid in increasing sales. The factoring company has extensive resources, an accounts receivable portfolio that provides diversification of risk, detailed credit information, and personal contacts in its clients' business areas. As a result of the factor's more liberal credit policy, the client can handle a greater volume of business.

A business firm's working-capital position, as measured by the quick ratio, may be improved to a greater degree through factoring than through a loan because, when accounts receivable are factored, no matching current liability is created. Thus, cash replaces receivables, and the quality of working capital is improved without an increase in the total amount of working capital. Without factoring, it would be difficult for some business firms to continue to operate. For illustration, in the textile industry, where factoring is deeply embedded, the average company could not survive if it had to assume the financial risk due to changes in fashions. In this field, labor and material costs are high relative to total expenses; therefore, production necessitates a large amount of working capital relative to fixed capital. Thus, with the help of old-line factors and some bank credit, small firms in this field may operate successfully with a relatively small amount of capital.[4]

**Collection Services.** For the same reasons that a factor may have a more liberal credit policy than the firm using its services, it may also have a more efficient collection system. By using the services of a factor, a business firm may avoid some of the conflicts that arise from selling and collecting. The business firm's salesmen may concentrate on obtaining the maximum number of orders and maintaining friendly relations with customers as insurance for future business. The goodwill created by salesmen is not endangered when the factor rather than the firm's collection department puts pressure on customers to pay invoices when due.

When a business firm sells its accounts receivable to a factor, the latter notifies the firm's customers that they are to make payments directly to the factor. New invoices and shipping receipts are sent through the factor to the firm's customers. The factor pays the firm the full amount of the accounts receivable minus a "reserve" (usually 20 percent), which is used to cover disputes and claims for defective or returned merchandise. These claims are settled by the factor out of the 20-percent reserve, subject to

---

[4] James Talcott, Inc., New York, a subsidiary of Talcott National Corporation, and Walter E. Heller and Co., Chicago, a subsidiary of Walter E. Heller International Corporation, are two of the better-known companies doing a factoring business. Both firms engage in a wide range of other financing activities in addition to factoring.

the firm's consent, since the claims remain the firm's responsibility. (The unused portion of the reserve is turned over to the firm when accounts are collected.)

**Credit Analysis.** The factor makes two types of analyses, one of the company whose accounts receivable are being factored and a second of the company's customers. If the first is satisfactory, an agreement will be drawn up to cover the factoring arangements. Because the factor buys the company's accounts receivable, the factor's credit department will analyze the credit worthiness of the firms that buy from the factored company. In other words, the factor takes the responsibility for the credit-analysis work of all the companies with whom it has signed factoring agreements. As might be expected, most of the credit work of factors consists of analyzing the credit standings of the factored companies' customers rather than of the factored companies themselves. As a result of careful checking of accounts and effective collection practices, credit losses are usually low—a fraction of 1 percent of the total amount of accounts receivable purchased.

**Cost.** The cost of factoring varies with the risk assumed and the amount of work done by the factor. Charges are in terms of interest on the funds provided plus a commission or service fee. The interest rate on funds provided by the factor varies with money-market rates, but the amount of the commission or service fee depends on the quality of the client's accounts, terms of sale, volume of receivables, and number of invoices handled.

The quality of a client's accounts, and therefore the credit risk, will depend in part on the product (staples, seasonal items, novelties, etc.), the types of business firms to whom goods are sold, the credit standing of the client's customers, and the credit terms offered by the client. The amount of administrative work required will depend, in part, on the client's annual sales volume, the average size of the client's invoices, and extra services demanded by the client. The commission may range from less than 1 percent to 2 percent or more, and the exact rate is determined by negotiation between the factor and the client.

When large sales predominate, as in manufacturing and wholesale merchandising, rates of 1.5 percent are considered fairly high; factoring rates of 1 percent are not unusual when the average account is large, the risks are small, and the amount of bookkeeping and collection work is not excessive. The total cost of factoring is sometimes given as a percentage of total credit sales, but it is difficult to compare this cost to that of borrowing because of other services that accompany factoring. However, interest charges are usually computed monthly on daily debit balances averaged over the preceding month, and commissions are figured as a percentage of the face value of all receivables or the total amount of accounts receivable minus discount credit for merchandise returned and allowances granted by the firm to its customers. The commission is primarily a payment for assuming the credit risk plus compensation for the factor's credit, collection, and bookkeeping work.

Usually, the factored company's chief cost of financing is the commission charged. For example, if a factor charges 6 percent per year on funds advanced before the due date of receivables and a service charge of three-fourths of 1 percent on the gross volume of receivables factored, the total factoring costs, when the annual volume of receivables is $200,000 and the average amount advanced is $25,000, will be $3,000, or 12 percent of the average amount advanced. If the service charges were to increase to 1.75 percent, the total cost would be $5,000, or 20 percent of the average amount advanced. Similarly, if the service charge were increased to 3 percent, the total cost would be $7,500, or 30 percent of the average amount advanced (see Table 13–1).

TABLE 13–1
Cost of Factoring

|  | Case 1 | Case 2 | Case 3 |
|---|---|---|---|
| Advance (6%, $25,000) | $1,500 | $1,500 | $1,500 |
| Service charge (on $200,000) |  |  |  |
| Rate | (0.0075) | (0.0175) | (0.03) |
| Dollar amount | $1,500 | $3,500 | $6,000 |
| Total charges | $3,000 | $5,000 | $7,500 |
| Annual rate on $25,000 | (0.12) | (0.20) | (0.30) |

The business firm negotiating a factoring agreement must give special attention to the fees and commissions charged in factoring. The saving accruing to the firm because of avoidance of losses from bad debts and expenses involved in bookkeeping and collection work may greatly exceed the costs of factoring; however, a thorough cost study would be required to arrive at this conclusion. Another justification for factoring is that it assures the firm's ability to take cash discounts on bills payable. The factored firm usually receives a cash advance of 80 percent of the invoices when goods are shipped; and, after all charges against the accounts are paid, the balance of the 20-percent reserve is returned to the firm. As each new shipment is made, the same procedure is followed; therefore, the firm has all the advantages of operating on a cash basis.

**Effect on Sales.** A business firm that uses the services of a factor expects an increase in earnings due to an increase in sales because (1) the factor is able to assume greater risks than the client (the factor may approve sales the client would reject); (2) the factor is in a position to recommend new territories that could be developed profitably by the client due to its extensive organization and experience; and (3) the advisory services of the factor may strengthen the client's sales position. For example, the factored company may have the benefits of (a) extensive contacts of the factor's staff that aid the company in hiring sales agents and other employees; and (b) an improved competitive position because of lower per unit costs through the advice of the factor's staff of specialists on machinery replacement, work loads, and other matters. On the other hand, one of the major objections to factoring by management is the restriction placed on sales by the factor's policy of keeping risks at a minimum by prohibiting sales to customers with unsatisfactory credit ratings.

*Advances by Factors.* Since factors adjust their terms to meet the needs of their clients, they not only factor receivables (purchase them outright) but also purchase accounts receivable with recourse, discount installment notes, make loans on other forms of property, and make unsecured loans. When additional funds are made available, they may be in the form of temporary or seasonal overadvances or in the form of term loans to be repaid over a period of years in fixed installments.

Overadvances, which are made more frequently than term loans, are related to anticipated accounts receivable out of which they are repaid. They are obtained most commonly by business firms whose products are seasonal in nature (such as seasonal apparel) and those whose shipping season is limited to one period during the year. The funds obtained are used to purchase raw materials, to defray labor and manufacturing costs, and to carry the finished products until the time for shipment arrives. If security is required for overadvances, inventory is most commonly pledged. In planning for financing, the cash budget is developed jointly by the business firm and the factor. Business firms sometimes arrange for term loans from factoring companies to purchase equipment, enlarge facilities, refinance long-term debts, and acquire other assets.

*Factoring Agreements.* Factoring agreements are based on written contracts between business firms and factors. These contracts usually contain a clause permitting either party to terminate the arrangement at any time subject to 60 days' prior notice. After factoring arrangements have been established, they may continue for years if the factored firm remains satisfied with the services obtained and the factor retains confidence in the firm. Under factoring arrangements, the factor agrees to render monthly accounting to the client for the sales each month and to credit the client with the net amount of all factored receivables. Except for a reserve to care for possible returns, claims, or defenses by customers, the credit may be withdrawn by the client at any time. The net amount of receivables is the face amount of the invoices less the factor's commission and discounts and credits granted by the business firm to its customers. The factored firm may either arrange for the factor to deposit the proceeds from accounts daily or weekly with the firm's bank or draw upon these balances while they are held by the factor as funds are needed. After offsetting interest and other charges due the factor, such balances may draw interest.

***Clients of Factoring Firms.*** Factoring has little appeal for those business firms whose credit is based on letters of credit or other secured documents; those whose output is taken by a few customers of unquestioned credit responsibility or by other firms where no unusual credit risk is present; and those that have adequate lines of credit with banks. On the other hand, there are many business firms that are not desirable clients for factoring companies because present-day factoring is not a distress type of operation.

Factors are not interested in business firms whose management is basically unsound; concerns with extremely limited working capital, net worth, or sales volume; firms whose products are of such poor quality as to lead to excessive complaints and returns; and firms whose operations are static or declining in importance. Among the companies using the services of factors are rapidly-growing manufacturing concerns, which tend to be short of cash because their working capital is tied up in accounts receivable and inventories, and small and medium-sized firms that need permanent working capital but are reluctant to raise it by issues of stocks and long-term obligations. Factoring services are not available to business firms that sell to the ultimate consumer.

***Objections to Factoring.*** The criticism of factoring is based on the following: (1) it entails a loss of personal contact with customers; (2) it results in loss of sales; and (3) it is expensive. As a compromise, many factored companies retain their own collection and bookkeeping work because they feel the periodic statements sent to customers are more than "billing arrangments," in that advertising and personal note communications may be included along with statements (such as, "Our records show you have not used your account . . ." or "Thank you for your past patronage . . .").

Conflicts over selling policies may lead to arrangements whereby the factor purchases all sales credit up to a certain amount for a stated period of time; and, if more than that amount is sold on credit, the seller assumes all credit risk for the excess. The entrance of large commercial banks into the field of factoring through subsidiaries may have the effect of driving down costs of factoring, because banks' interest rates are generally lower. The First National City Bank of New York, the second largest bank in the United States, purchased the Hubshman Factors Corporation in 1965. The First National Bank of Boston had entered the field of domestic factoring earlier, in 1946.[5] The latter had previously been in the field of international factoring through coownership of the International Factors A.G., a Swiss holding company owned by the Boston bank and two British banks.

---

[5] One important effect of the entrance of commercial banks into this specialized field of finance has been to advertise this not-too-well-known type of financial endeavor.

Several U.S. factors have extended their operations to foreign countries through subsidiaries. This is the case particularly in West Germany, where business firms generally (1) are short of financial resources, (2) lack office personnel, (3) are faced with an increase in foreign trade, and (4) are concentrating on production and leaving other business functions to factors. The services offered by U.S. factoring firms to foreign business firms are practically the same as those offered U.S. firms.

Although financing through factors is expected to increase, the rate of growth is expected to slow down relative to that of commercial finance companies. The latter make loans on a recourse basis and leave the function of collecting accounts receivable to their clients, which permits them greater control over their sales policies and closer contact with their customers. At the present time, most of the old-line factoring companies have opened credit departments and are doing a commercial finance lending business as well as factoring accounts receivable. The extension of their services to include financing clients by advancing credit secured by accounts receivable is characteristic of foreign as well as domestic factoring. Abroad, as in the United States, the differences between factors and commercial finance companies are becoming less discernible.

## Receivables Financing

Loans secured by accounts receivable are made under arrangements whereby the business firm retains financial responsibility for unpaid accounts. Under a "nonnotification" arrangement, the firm's customers are not informed that their accounts payable have been pledged as security for a loan. This arrangement is preferred by a business concern because it avoids disturbing the relationship between the firm and its customers.

When receivables financing is on a notification basis, the original invoices or bills are sent to the firm's customers after being stamped to show that their accounts have been assigned and that they are to be paid directly to the lender. Under this arrangement, the essential documents include a promissory note, an agreement between the borrower and the lender that provides a schedule of assigned accounts with their actual assignment noted thereon, and a record form for reporting collections. The borrower customarily signs an agreement that (1) defines eligible accounts; (2) indicates the percentage loan value of pledged accounts; (3) permits the lender to examine the borrower's records; (4) authorizes the lender to give notice of assignment to the firm's customers, even though the lender may never plan to use the authority; and (5) indicates the procedure to be followed in accounting for cash received from assigned account customers. It also provides for handling returned merchandise, the steps to be followed in computing the lender's charges, and an agreement not to pledge or sell accounts receivable to a third party. In case of default, the lender terminates the rights of the borrower to make more loans and accelerates payments of outstanding loans. The basic agreement between the business firm and the lender sets forth the rights and liabilities of each, together with the overall conditions under which each account receivable is pledged. The borrower prepares the schedule of accounts to be assigned and executes a demand note; the lender stamps the assigned accounts in the borrower's ledger (required in many states to validate the assignment).

Successful accounts-receivable financing depends on following the procedures applicable to the loan. Care must be taken to identify accurately each account assigned and then treat it and the cash obtained therefrom as the property of the lender. For legal as well as financial reasons, lenders generally require clients to remit the actual checks received by them in payment of accounts receivable that have been assigned. The Uniform Commercial Code gives added protection to the lender, as stated in Section 9–308:

> A purchaser of chattel paper or an instrument who gives new value and takes possession of it in the ordinary course of his business has priority over a security interest in the chattel paper or instrument (a) which is perfected under Section 9–304 (permissive filing and temporary perfection) or under Section 9–306 (perfection as to proceeds) if he acts without knowledge that the specific paper or instrument is subject to a security interest; or (b) which is claimed merely as proceeds of inventory subject to a security interest (Section 9–306) even though he knows that the specific paper or instrument is subject to the security interest.[6]

Thus, a lender may perfect its security interest by filing or having possession of sales contracts, chattel mortgages, or bailment leases on automobiles or furniture being financed, although payments may have been made to an assignee under the nonnotification or indirect-collection arrangement.

The interest rates on receivable loans are usually higher than on other loans but lower than those charged by factors. In addition to the interest charges, the debtor pays a service charge based on the amount of supervision and bookkeeping required and the number of items handled. Customarily, the interest rate and other charges are indicated in the written agreement, and they will vary both as to percentage and method used in calculating and collecting interest and service charges. The loan may be discounted or interest charges may be computed on the average daily balance over a specific period of time. The interest rate charged is commonly one-thirtieth of 1 percent per day (12 percent per year) on the

---

[6] *Uniform Commercial Code, 1972 Official Text with Comments*, p. 660. Copyright 1972 by The American Law Institute and the National Conference of Commissioners on Uniform State Laws. Reprinted with permission of the Permanent Editorial Board for the Uniform Commercial Code.

outstanding loan balance, but it may be more or less, varying with the risk assumed, money-market conditions, and the cost to the lender.

Commercial finance companies, since they are specialists in accounts-receivable financing, contend they can perform these functions more economically than commercial banks. They assert they can be more liberal in lending than commercial banks because they are staffed to appraise the collateral more accurately (which necessitates periodic examination of the books of their customers). In addition, banks usually operate locally, while many finance companies and factors are regional, and three finance companies are national, in their scope of operations. As a result of their size and mode of operations, finance companies may be able to make larger loans and provide services over a geographical area as broad as the market covered by their clients. Factors and finance companies have a more diversified clientele than commercial banks and they may offer financial, advisory, and other services not offered by local banks.

A business firm that obtains funds by pledging its accounts receivable must be prepared to be examined by the lender, who is interested in verifying pledged accounts and in auditing the firm's records. The lender will want assurance of the genuineness of the pledged accounts and will ascertain if they appear properly in the books and if all payments to the borrower have been properly deposited and recorded. In addition, information will be sought as to the method of handling defective merchandise and the credit based thereon, as well as other information that would indicate uncollectible accounts.

## Inventory Financing

A business firm may improve the terms embodied in a loan contract by pledging inventories with the use of a warehouse receipt, bill of lading, trust receipt, or chattel mortgage.[7] The most acceptable type of goods that may be pledged is highly marketable, fully insured, nonperishable staples. Such goods may be in transit, in a warehouse, or in the possession of the borrower. Customarily, when goods are pledged as security, title will be evidenced by a bill of lading if in transit, by a warehouse receipt if in a public warehouse, or by a trust receipt if in the possession of the borrower.

**Bills of Lading.** A bill of lading is issued by a "common carrier" on

---

[7] See *Uniform Commercial Code, 1972 Official Text with Comments* (Philadelphia: American Law Institute; or Chicago; Commissioners on Uniform State Laws, 1972), p. 459. Article 7, Part 1 of the Uniform Commercial Code contains provisions for the consolidation and revision of the Uniform Bills of Lading Act, Warehouse Receipts Act, and provisions for the Uniform Sales Act. Article 7 is cited as *Uniform Commercial Code Documents of Title.*

receipt of goods, and it must be surrendered to the transportation company at the place designated in the shipping agreement. A bill of lading may be negotiable; that is, made out to order; or it may be negotiable or straight when made out to the buyer. It is the negotiable type that is used in borrowing.[8]

***Warehouse Receipts.*** A warehouse receipt is a document that acknowledges storage of the goods and indicates the terms and conditions on which they will be delivered. When the receipt is nonnegotiable, goods will be delivered only to the person specified in the receipt; when negotiable, delivery may be made to the bearer or a person designated by the holder of the receipt. The warehouse receipt customarily states the quantity and quality of goods stored (neither is absolutely necessary, but the best warehousing practice is to state both). When lenders grant loans, they must be sure the warehouse receipt is valid, so that, in the event of bankruptcy, they will have a legal claim to the goods pledged. The Uniform Warehouse Receipts Act and the United States Warehouse Act provide certain standards that must be met by a bona fide warehouseman, who is defined as "a person lawfully engaged in the business of storing goods for profits." Use of a warehouse receipt permits the lender to have title to goods stored while the warehouse company has possession of the goods.

In order to reduce the cost of storage and the inconvenience of not having goods on the business premises, so-called field warehousing has been developed. Therein, goods are stored on the premises of the business firm under conditions that permit them to be segregated, controlled, and supervised by the lender. When pledged as security, title is transferred to the lender. Upon payment of the loan in whole or in part, goods will be released, with a designated bank official supervising the physical release. When surrounded by proper physical safeguards and adequate insurance, field warehousing may provide adequate safeguards to the lender and may result in lower costs and greater convenience to the borrower. For example, expenditures for a fence or partition and a lock are all that is needed to field warehouse goods, such as petroleum in a storage tank or grain in an elevator.

Field warehouses are established almost exclusively for credit purposes, while "general storage" and "cold storage" warehouses are used to hold goods awaiting marketing and distribution. Over the last ten years, field warehousing has been a factor in the rapid growth of inventory debts, which rank first among secured loans of manufacturing, mining, and wholesale merchandising enterprises. Among the goods that are field warehoused, bulk commodities predominate. Usually, goods are only held for a short period of time, pending resale or use in manufacturing. If local

---

[8] Ibid., pp. 479–512.

financing is inadequate, the services of a national field-warehousing organization may be used. The latter will not only take complete responsibility for arranging loans, bonding, crediting, and supervising but also pass along its know-how on inventory and warehouse control.

Among the risks associated with lending on goods stored in warehouses and evidenced by warehouse receipts are those associated with safeguarding the goods (collateral risks), which include protection against spontaneous combustion and germination for grains, suitable refrigeration for perishable goods, protection against moisture for most goods, and fire protection for all goods. Since warehouses do not always carry complete insurance coverage, it must be maintained by the borrower.

The warehouseman should be qualified to handle the simple but necessary accounting associated with storage and release of goods, and the lender should occasionally make spot checks for quality and condition of goods. Greatest protection is provided when the warehouse is being operated under state and federal laws. Bonds are deposited by warehouse companies to protect owners against theft of goods, and, unless stored as fungible, the identical goods must be held and returned.

In addition to collateral and bailment risks, there are other risks associated with fluctuations in the value and nature of the goods stored. Adequate protection is assured when the loan is for only a percentage of the current or anticipated future value of the goods, varying from 50 to 80 percent.

Since all loans are dependent primarily on the ability of the borrower to repay them out of the normal receipts of the business, the credit risk is present when warehouse-receipt loans are made, as it is in all other credit transactions. While lenders may make spot checks on warehoused goods, it is impractical for them to inspect every item of goods pledged; thus, considerable reliance must be placed on the borrower's description of the goods and their value. The credit-analysis work is similar to that entailed in making unsecured loans.

**Trust Receipts.** A trust receipt, used when goods are in the possession of the borrower, gives the lender title to the goods that are being held in trust for him by the borrowers.[9] In practice, a business firm may have difficulty in obtaining funds by this method because unsecured or general creditors may be successful in challenging the prior claim of the holder of a trust receipt to goods and cash resulting from their sale. In effect, holders of trust receipts may be classified as general creditors unless they can prove that the specific goods covered by the trust receipts belong to them. However, if the items, such as automobiles, office machines, equipment, and watches, have serial numbers, the trust receipt may contain adequate identification and provide satisfactory protection for the lender.

---

[9] Ibid., pp. 637 ff.

## Characteristics of Term Loans

During the last 40 years, one of the most important developments in the field of finance has been the increase in the use of term loans. A term loan is defined as one made to a business firm for a period of time in excess of one year. The fact that they are made to business firms distinguishes them from other loans maturing in more than one year (such as credit extended to financial institutions, consumers, and farmers). In some cases, term loans are made to replace short-term loans that had been renewed periodically; hence, the statistics of term lending now as compared with the past may be misleading.

Term loans came into prominence for a number of reasons, one of which was the need for credit to finance producers' goods. The need for this is apparent when a comparison is made between the amount of funds needed to equip a store, shop, factory, or any other business unit today with the amount needed two generations ago. Large business firms that are able to satisfy their needs for intermediate funds by the sale of notes in the open market may choose between negotiating term loans with commercial banks and other lenders and borrowing in the open market; however, most business concerns must depend on commercial banks, commercial finance companies, and other lenders as sources of intermediate funds.

**Purposes.** When a business firm arranges for a term loan with a bank, the purpose may be to replace or supplement working capital or to finance new equipment. Manufacturers in fields such as equipment and heavy machinery are not able to liquidate their products seasonally because their production cycles run for months. Even though a business concern in this field may obtain some advance payments to meet payrolls and other short-term expenses, it will not be able to pay off its creditors until delivery of its products. The solution for such a firm's problem may be to obtain a term loan that would supply cash for operating expenses and other purposes. Thereby the firm could pay off its small creditors and consolidate existing short-term debts. Handling a large number of payments is time-consuming and any delay in making payments will reflect adversely on the credit of the debtor company. (Small creditors tend to be more critical and less considerate about delays than large firms.)

A corporation may obtain a term loan when its cash flow from operations is insufficient to meet all expenses, including those for repairs, replacement of equipment, and others due to modernization of the plant. Although depreciation allowances and retained earnings, as shown on the firm's financial statements, may indicate an amount sufficient for these purposes, no cash may be available for spending.

Business firms may obtain term loans for purposes that are unproductive in that they do not add to the cash flow or gross income. For illustration, term loans may be made to refund outstanding long-term debt. The motive in refinancing long-term obligations may be to reduce interest costs, to simplify the corporation's capital structure, or to eliminate a bond issue or loan because of restrictive clauses contained in the bond indenture or loan contract.

When a large corporation finds the market temporarily unfavorable for permanent financing through a public offering of securities or the placement of a long-term mortgage, it may arrange for a term loan. Many large corporations have a policy of using both sources of funds—arranging for term loans with banks or other lenders, such as insurance companies, and offering security issues with the assistance of investment bankers. When term loans are used for refinancing purposes, the debt may be repaid at or before maturity, either in one lump sum or in installments. In some cases, the loan agreement will provide for installment payments but with a considerable amount still unpaid at maturity. The remaining note (called a balloon note because of its large size) will have to be refinanced at a future date.

**Cash Flow.** When term loans are made to finance working-capital assets and business expansion, management should appraise the financial situation in terms of the anticipated cash flow. A cash budget showing anticipated cash receipts and disbursements in detail over the life of the loan is generally required by the lender, and it is also desirable when considered from the viewpoint of management. Project budgets, pro forma balance sheets, and income statements are more helpful in planning term borrowing than in short-term borrowing.[10] Earning power and depreciation allowances are emphasized in term loans, while working-capital strength is stressed in short-term loans.

The growth in term lending by commercial banks has caused some concern among central bankers. The fear is that U.S. banks will be borrowing short (deposit liabilities) and lending long, which will reduce their liquidity and make them unduly dependent on the Federal Reserve System. The attitude of central bankers toward term lending by commercial banks may have considerable effect on the way business firms may finance their intermediate term needs in the future. In term lending, it should be noted that commercial banks are competing with the capital market and shifting away from their traditional function of supplying short-term credit needs of business firms. This shift is also indicated by the growth in consumer and homeowner loans among commercial banks' assets. Hence, it may be that, in the future, business firms will become more dependent on insurance companies, pension funds, and other noncommercial bank lenders for their intermediate- and long-term funds.

---

[10] A project budget is separate from the general budget of a business firm, and it contains estimates for a contemplated activity, such as a new product. A pro forma ("for the sake of form") statement is used to describe financial and other statements or conclusions based on assumed or anticipated facts.

***Maturities.*** Maturities of term loans to business firms vary, but there is a tendency for maturities to be longer when interest rates are low and loanable funds are abundant and shorter when interest rates are high and loanable funds are scarce. In the 1930s, when term loans to business first became common, initial maturities were usually for three, four, or five years; but, by 1940, about half of the volume of term loans had maturities exceeding five years. Today, term loans of over five years are found regularly in the portfolios of many large city banks.

***Repayment.*** One characteristic of term lending is the flexibility of repayment terms. Although there are many exceptions, the provision for installment repayment is common. The terms may be regular, calling for annual, semiannnual, quarterly, or monthly installment payments; or they may be irregular, depending on the nature of the business, the regularity of income, and maturity dates of other obligations, such as corporate income taxes and debt obligations. Banks usually permit prepayment of term loans without penalty, but insurance companies customarily attach a penalty, which is similar to the penalty payment by issuers when they call preferred stock or bonds before maturity. Term-loan agreements contain detailed provisions for installment payments, prepayments, the allocation of funds, and other actions by borrowers that would tend to reduce the protection provided creditors.

***Interest Rates.*** Interest rates on term loans of business firms may range from 8 to 15 percent, being lower for large firms than for small ones. One possible reason for this discrepancy is that large firms have access to the capital market; hence, banks must compete for their loans. Although interest rates on term loans tend to be higher than on short-term loans, the difference is surprisingly small (from one-half of 1 percent to 2 percent per year). Some term-loan agreements contain an "escalator" clause that provides for increasing or decreasing the interest rate under certain circumstances, such as changing interest rates to correspond to changes in the prime rate or the discount rate of the Federal Reserve Bank of New York.

Banks are handling an increasing portion of their term loans, particullarly to small businesses, on an installment-contract basis. As noted in the preceding section, the repayment terms may be regular or irregular, depending on the nature of the business. The costs of installment-term loans probably are concentrated at the upper end of the range of rates charged by banks on term loans to their customers. This is likely because of the greater risk involved in small-business lending, but also because of the higher administrative costs inherent in installment-loan contracts.

***Security.*** Business firms may facilitate borrowing by pledging assets, such as land and buildings, machinery, equipment, securities, and working-capital assets. In term lending, the most important factor in determining the safety of loans is anticipated cash flow and anticipated earnings. In analyzing the credit position of a borrower, emphasis is on the market for the firm's products; the competitive position of the firm; the firm's inventory position; the influence of cyclical, seasonal, and other price changes on the firm's net profits; depreciation, depletion, and other charges; and the financial position of the officers and chief stockholders. The capital nature of such loans is illustrated by the types of business firms that account for a high percentage of funds borrowed—metal and metal-products firms; petroleum, coal, chemical, and rubber companies; and transportation and public-utility corporations—all of which have heavy fixed-capital requirements.

*Documents.* In term-loan contracts, two documents are important—the promise to pay and the term-loan agreement. The latter covers the manner in which the borrower is to conduct his financial affairs until the loan is repaid. The agreement is signed at the time the loan is negotiated and is one of the conditions under which the loan is made. The details of the agreement are drawn so as to fit the needs of the particular business firm, but the objective is always to keep the anticipated earnings of the borrower unimpaired so it will be able to meet the interest and installment payments on the term loan. To have these details in writing and agreed to before a loan is made reduces the possibility of misunderstandings and protects not only the lender but also the borrower (changes in the lender's loan policies could be embarrassing to the debtor).

*Syndication.* Since most banks are prohibited from lending more than 10 percent of their capital and surplus to one business firm, large term loans made by banks in small communities must be syndicated, and this may also be necessary for extraordinarily large loans made by city banks.

When a term loan is syndicated, it is divided among several banks or insurance companies. When loans are made in partnership with insurance companies, the banks take the shorter maturities and the insurance companies the longer ones. One lender serves as the leader for the group; the amounts lent, the repayments, and the losses, if any, are prorated among the members. The borrower deals with the syndicate leader, who is compensated for his work by being paid a service fee.

*Flexibility.* Flexibility is one of the most interesting aspects of financing with term loans: maturities, installment payments, and so forth, may be tailored to meet the needs of individual borrowers. Usually, the term loan is for at least five years and seldom for more than ten years. Terms may be arranged so the proceeds of the loan may be taken in installments as funds are needed.

The development of term loans has made it possible for bankers to meet the political pressure from various government officials who claimed that bankers were not cooperating in solving the financial problems of small business firms. Term lending has benefited business firms—small firms have access to more bank funds than formerly, but many firms still have intermediate-term financing problems.

## Summary

Trade credit is an important aspect of working-capital financing because about 90 percent of wholesalers' and manufacturers' sales are made on credit. Distributors and retailers are usually small firms and are the chief beneficiaries of trade credit. When they obtain assets on credit, funds are released to be used in other ways. Buyers may be able to convert goods into cash before the end of the credit period and thus operate on the proverbial shoestring.

When credit terms include a credit period of a given number of days from the invoice date, the buyer may be given an option of discounting the invoice price and remitting cash within a definite period of time or waiting until the end of the credit period and paying the invoice price (for example, 2 percent, 10 days, net 30 days).

The factors in credit-granting decisions include the suppliers' profit margin and the demand for the product, in addition to the more obvious one—the credit position of the buyer. Also, there are factors such as general and anticipated business conditions that will influence the terms on which credit is granted.

Companies with excellent credit standings find that issues of unsecured short-term negotiable notes sold through the open market are the cheapest way to meet seasonal or temporary needs for cash without exploiting or disturbing their normal lines of credit at banks. Borrowing by issuance of commercial paper has been used by business firms not only as a means of raising cash but also as a device for establishing their credit standing on Wall Street with an expectation of future intermediate- or long-term security issues.

Issues vary in size from a minimum of about $100,000; however, there is no established maximum. Most of the commercial paper is handled by a few large dealers, but there are smaller firms that handle paper for smaller business concerns. The large sales finance companies handle the sale of their own open-market commercial paper.

The typical business loan obtained from a commercial bank is short-term, with repayment due in less than one year and with the obligation of the borrower and the rights of the lender covered in a promissory note. Although unsecured loans represent a greater volume of funds, a greater number of short-term bank loans are secured. Among the assets most commonly pledged or assigned are inventories, accounts receivable, securities, plant, and equipment.

When the operations of a business firm follow a fairly definite pattern, the firm may arrange for a line of credit where the bank sets a maximum limit up to which the firm may borrow during a specified period of time. Before granting a line of credit, the bank makes a careful study of the record of the firm; usually, after the line is granted, a compensatory deposit balance of from 10 to 20 percent of the line is required to be maintained by the borrower. Other business firms borrow as funds are needed without the use of lines of credit.

Businesses can borrow from a number of sources. The loans offered by factors, commercial finance companies, sales finance companies, and other financial institutions such as insurance companies and pension funds offer competitive alternatives to the bank loan. The mechanics of borrowing from the different institutions is very similar. For this reason, the nature of the different borrowing arrangements were considered rather than concentrating on the operations of the different lenders.

Short-term loans may be unsecured or secured. Unsecured loans are made without the added protection of collateral for the loans. Both types of borrowing involve promissory notes. The difference is the added safeguard provided a secured loan in the event of default. If a secured loan is defaulted the lender has a preferential security interest in some named asset such as accounts receivable or inventory.

Factoring consists of outright purchase of accounts receivable; thus, the factor usually assumes other activities for the clients. These activities include analyzing credit and market conditions, keeping records, and offering advice as to production plans and sales policies. A factor subjects prospective clients to the same sort of credit analysis as does a commercial bank when making a loan. Factoring of the revolving-credit type may be advantageous in that it allows the firm to operate on the equivalent of a cash basis, but it also entails close supervision by the factor. Now, most factoring companies are functioning more like general finance companies than like old-line factors.

As an alternative to factoring, many business firms are selling their accounts receivable "with recourse" or assigning them as security for loans made by finance companies or banks. When financing in this way, the business firm borrows against receivables and retains the credit risk as well as the collection function.

Inventory-secured borrowing may use a number of different collateral arrangements. If goods are in transit, the borrower may use the shipping document, the order bill of lading, as security for a loan. If the goods are in a public warehouse, the warehouse receipt provides the lender with evidence of the collateral's existence and protection. The use of a bonded warehouse increases the protection. However, use of a public warehouse may be inconvenient and costly due to the nature of the inventory. A field warehouse may reduce the problem for the borrower while protecting the lender. For large, easily identified inventory items, the trust receipt can provide the borrower maximum access to the inventory while evidencing the lender's preferential status with regard to the named collateral.

In order to secure intermediate-term funds, a business firm may obtain a term loan from a bank or other lender. A term loan has a maturity in excess of one year, and it may or may not be repayable on the install-

### 13 Short- and Intermediate-Term Borrowing

ment plan, depending on the purpose for which funds are obtained. A business firm may arrange for a term loan in order to replace or consolidate short-term loans that have had to be renewed regularly, to supplement working capital, and to purchase equipment and other fixed assets. A term-loan contract entails the use of a promissory note and a term-loan agreement. The latter contains provisions designed to protect the lender from loss and the borrower from changes in the lender's loan policies. Flexibility is one of the most important characteristics of term loans because the provisions therein may be tailored to fit the needs of the borrower as to maturity, amount, and repayment schedule.

## QUESTIONS

1. Distinguish among the three methods in use today to extend trade credit.
2. Indicate why cash discounts are usually large when computed on an annual basis.
3. What are the advantages of financing in the open market with commercial paper?
4. The availability of bank loans is of greater importance to smaller firms than larger ones. Why?
5. Interest actually paid by corporations on loans is higher than the posted rate because banks generally require that some portion of a loan be kept on deposit, reducing funds available to the borrower. These compensating balances usually are 20 percent of the loan. If the prime rate were reduced to 8 percent from 8.5 percent, what would be the effective rate reduction for a borrowing firm? Assume no balances normally would be kept in that bank.
6. Identify: (a) line of credit, (b) revolving credit arrangement, and (c) compensatory balance.
7. When a bank discounts a note, what does this practice do to the cost of the loan?
8. What is the effect, if any, of a compensating balance on a bank loan?
9. How would the lending practices of two commercial banks differ if one bank has 60-percent time deposits and 40-percent demand deposits, while the second bank has the opposite deposit mix?
10. Distinguish between (a) short-term and long-term borrowing, and (b) secured and unsecured borrowing.
11. a. Identify: (1) factor, and (2) factoring.
    b. What are the chief characteristics of factoring?
12. Discuss: "At one time, except in the textile industry, it was considered a sign of financial weakness for a business firm to sell or assign its accounts receivable."
13. What are the advantages and disadvantages of factoring?

14. How does discounting accounts receivable differ from factoring them? Are the risks the same as when loans are made with receivables pledged as security? Why?
15. Identify: (a) warehouse receipt, (b) trust receipt, (c) order bill of lading, and (d) field warehousing.
16. Suggest an industry that might use each of the following forms of financing:
    a. Factoring.
    b. Pledging of accounts receivable.
    c. Warehouse receipts.
    d. Field warehouse receipts.
    e. Trust receipts.
    f. None of the above.
    Explain your choices.
17. Identify: (a) cash flow, (b) project budget, and (c) "balloon" note.
18. The popularity of term loans has increased greatly over the last 25 years.
    a. How do you account for the increased demand?
    b. Why have lending agencies shown an increased willingness to make such loans?
    c. Are term loans ordinarily self-liquidating in the sense that short-term loans are supposed to be self-liquidating?

## PROBLEMS

1. On credit sales of $2 million, what would a firm sacrifice in profits if its credit terms were 2/10, n/30, and 30 percent of the customers took the cash discount? What if the terms were 1/20, n/40, and 50 percent of the customers took the cash discount?
2. The sales of the Able Company now amount to $300,000 per month; credit terms are 1/10, n/30. At the present time, half of their sales are on credit and half of all credit customers take the cash discount (i.e., they pay by the tenth day).
    a. Assuming no past-due accounts, what is the average monthly level of accounts receivable carried by the Able Company?
    b. Given the data above, what would be the level of receivables if *all* credit customers took the cash discount (i.e., paid by the tenth day)?
    c. What if credit terms were changed to 3/10, n/60, and, as a result, all customers bought on credit and half of them paid by the tenth day?
3. Company X has just received the invoices for $10,000 worth of merchandise purchased on terms of 2/10, n/30. Due to a temporary shortage of cash, Company X will not take its discount on this purchase.
    a. When should they pay the bill?
    b. What is the cost of not taking the discount, stated on an annual basis?
    c. Do you think the decision to lose the discount is wise? Why?
    d. Suppose that Company X decided to borrow money from a bank for 30 days in order to take the discount. How high a rate of interest could they pay and still *not* be worse off in dollar terms? (They can borrow only in multiples of $1,000.)

4. Fast Pace, Inc., has for many years been an active borrower in the commercial-paper market. The financial manager can use any one of the three methods listed below to meet the cash requirements of the firm:
   a. 90-day paper quoted at $98.
   b. 360-day paper quoted at $90.
   c. 180-day paper quoted at $96.
   The decision will be based exclusively on yield (i.e., cost). Which method should be used? What other factors should be taken into consideration in this decision?
5. Aside from trade credit, the commercial bank is the major source of short-term credit.
   a. Why are bank lending policies more conservative than those of other lending institutions?
   b. How much will the charging of the discount and requiring a 20-percent compensatory balance add to the actual interest cost on a loan of $10,000 at 5 percent for one year? No balance is normally maintained at the bank.
   c. On the average, secured bank loans bear a higher rate of interest than unsecured loans. Explain.
6. The Tucson Hardware Company is faced with the decision of borrowing money from its local bank to take advantage of cash discounts or forgoing the discount. The inventory cost is $10,000 and the terms are 1/30, net 50. The bank is currently charging 12 percent to borrow money. Should the company take out the loan?
7. The Mountain City Bank follows the practice of discounting its loans. What is the effective rate of interest for the following loans:
   a. A $10,000 loan for six months at 10-percent interest?
   b. A one-year loan of $40,000 at 6-percent interest?
   c. A one-year loan of $75,000 at 5-percent interest?
8. The Midtown National Bank has a policy of requiring a 25-percent compensating balance of all firms that borrow over $2,000 per year. In return for this feature the bank charges interest of 8 percent and does not discount its loans.
   a. If a firm borrows $45,000, how much will the bank credit to its account?
   b. How much will the firm have to borrow to obtain the immediate use of $45,000?
   c. What is the effective rate of interest for the use of $45,000 in part b?
9. What is the effective interest rate a company must pay for the use of $8,000 if its bank is charging 8 percent to borrow funds and requires a 20-percent compensating balance?
10. The ESP Corporation is considering the use of a factor in regard to handling all of its accounts receivable. The factor will charge the firm 8 percent on all advances and 1 percent on the gross volume of receivables. ESP currently has annual credit sales of $5 million and an average accounts-receivable turnover of ten times. If there is no change in sales or receivables, what will ESP pay (annually) for the services of the factor? What is the effective rate of interest for these services?

## ADDITIONAL READING

Abraham, A. B. "Factoring: The New Frontier for Commercial Banks," *Journal of Commercial Bank Lending*, vol. 53 (April 1971), pp. 32–43.

Adler, M. "Administration of Inventory Loans Under the Uniform Commercial Code," *The Journal of Commercial Bank Lending*, vol. 52, (April 1970), pp. 55–60.

Baxter, N. D. *The Commercial Paper Market.* Princeton, N.J.: Princeton University Press, 1964.

Beckhart, B. H. *Business Loans of American Commercial Banks.* New York: Ronald Press Co., 1959.

Brosky, J. J. *The Implicit Cost of Trade Credit and Theory of Optimal Terms of Sale.* New York: Credit Research Foundation, 1969.

Daniels, F. L., S. C. Legg, and E. C. Yuille. "Accounts Receivable and Related Inventory Financing," *Journal of Commercial Bank Lending*, vol. 52 (July 1970), pp. 38–53.

Denonn, L. E. "The Security Agreement," *Journal of Commercial Bank Lending*, vol. 50 (February 1968), pp. 32–40.

Fisher, D. J. "Factoring—An Industry on the Move," *The Conference Board Record*, vol. 9 (April 1972), pp. 42–45.

Hayes, D. A. *Bank Lending Practices: Issues and Practices.* Ann Arbor: University of Michigan, 1964.

Hungate, R. P. *Interbusiness Financing: Economic Implications for Small Business.* Washington, D.C.: Small Business Administration, 1962.

Meltzer, A. H. "Mercantile Credit, Monetary Policy, and Size of Firms," *Review of Economics and Statistics*, vol. 42 (August 1960), pp. 429–37.

Popma, J. "A Behind-the-Scenes Look at Factoring," *Credit and Financial Management*, vol. 65 (May 1963) pp. 31–33.

Quarles, J. C. "The Floating Lien," *Journal of Commercial Bank Lending*, vol. 53 (November 1970), pp. 51–58.

Selden, R. T. *Trends and Cycles in the Commercial Paper Market.* New York: National Bureau of Economic Research, 1963.

Stone, B. K. "How Secure is Secured Financing Under the Code?" *Burroughs Clearing House*, vol. 50 (April 1966), pp. 46 ff.

Wellman, M. T. "Field Warehousing—Protective Measures!" *Robert Morris Associates Bulletin*, vol. 47 (March 1965), pp. 302–12.

# 14

# Leasing

Leasing is another method of financing the firm's asset needs. In the last 30 years, the volume of lease financing has grown enormously. It is reasonable to expect that this trend will continue.

This chapter will discuss the general aspects of leases, providing definitions, background, and a discussion of the sources of lease financing. The differences between operational and financial leasing will be explained.

Methods for analyzing leases are presented. This topic has generated a large volume of literature. Two general approaches to the analysis have evolved. Both are presented. The two approaches are generally compatible, but there are points of conceptual difference. These differences are discussed.

The nature and volume of lease financing have created a problem in financial reporting. Although most agree that leases are quite similar to debts, there has historically been less disclosure in financial statements which has been unsatisfactory to some users of such statements. Effective January, 1977, the rules for reporting leases have changed markedly. The nature of the new rules for lessee reporting is explained.

Finally, some legal factors are considered. The IRS has certain requirements for acceptable leases. Although leases are like debts, they receive different treatment by the courts. These issues are covered briefly.

## General Aspects of Leasing

*Definition.* Leasing is a grant by one party (lessor) to a second party (lessee) of an interest in a property that permits the second party to use it for a period of time. Thus, leasing is a means whereby a business firm may obtain the use of a fixed asset without obtaining title to it. The asset may be in the form of real property or personal property, and the time period for which the lease is granted may be from one day to 99 years.

**_Early Development._** Records indicate that leasing may have existed as early as the fifth century B.C. and that it was common during the Grecian and Roman periods. In more modern times, the products of certain types of industrial companies have been made available to users on a lease basis, as exemplified by those of some telephone companies and some shoe machinery and other plant-machinery companies. More recently, a wide range of physical assets, as well as patents and other intangibles, has been made available on a rental basis. Such assets include office equipment, electronic computers, and equipment used in the production of textiles, containers, tobacco, and machine tools.

Most of the foregoing leases are of the operational type; that is, marketing devices used to enable manufacturers or dealers to profit from renting, rather than selling, their products. By spreading the income from a product over a period of time, tax savings accrue to the manufacturer, and the lessee is able to obtain the use of equipment that it prefers not to buy.

Much of the expansion in leasing that has taken place since World War II has been due both to the increase in output of companies that have traditionally leased their products and to the use of leasing as a form of financing. Now, department stores, supermarkets, and other nationwide chain stores are obtaining their fixtures, buildings, and land on a rental basis; and some large industrial companies are leasing their entire plants, equipment, and machinery.

**_Attitude of Lessees._** Managers of business firms who are prejudiced against factoring or borrowing from commercial finance companies and other lending institutions seem to welcome leasing as a respectable means of obtaining fixed assets needed in their operations. Expensive machinery that could not be purchased may be leased and put into immediate use. Even companies enjoying a strong cash position often lease when their funds can be invested more profitably in ways other than purchasing equipment. By leasing, they not only avoid disturbing their lines of credit but also keep their other credit sources open for future financing.

In some instances the firm may have no alternative but to lease. Owners may be unwilling to sell all or any part of a piece of property. This would be the situation that frequently confronts a retailing enterprise as it endeavors to expand by establishing new branches. The owners of a shopping center may only permit entry into their facilities by the signing of a lease by the retailing firm. However, in most instances, a firm does have the option of buying or renting. Therefore, the method chosen should be the result of a comparison between the relative costs of owning the asset directly or leasing it.

***Sources of Lease Financing.*** In some fields, business firms may lease equipment from manufacturers or independent lessors, including insurance companies, banks, trusts, special leasing companies, and subsidiaries of manufacturing, commercial, transportation, and financial corporations. Some manufacturers organize subsidiary corporations to lease their equipment to users. Being interested primarily in profits from manufacturing rather than from leasing equipment, their subsidiaries may offer more favorable terms than independent lessors. Since rental fees will replace installment payments in the case of a sale, the effect may be to give the lessor more stable income over the life of the equipment.

An independent lessor purchases the equipment or machinery it leases to users directly from the manufacturer, often having it delivered directly to the lessee. An independent lessor's profits are derived from leasing fees, agency or dealer discounts, and markups on the list price of the equipment. Much of the profit results from selling the equipment to the user at the end of the lease period or selling it in the open market as used equipment.

Since banks have been permitted to engage in direct leasing,[1] the significance of their entrance into this business is far-reaching because most commercial and industrial companies have direct access to banks.[2] Unlike manufacturers and dealers who use leasing as a merchandising device, national banks and leasing companies make their profits from leasing rather than from the equipment being leased. Because lessors' profits are derived from the lease arrangement, they must take great care in dealing with both the manufacturers from whom the property is purchased and the business firms to whom the property is leased. Customarily, a lessee would negotiate the purchase of the equipment according to its own specifications and then issue a purchase order in the name of the lessor.

Ordinarily, the independent leasing company pledges the lease as security for loans obtained from a bank or other financial institution. This could result in the business firm paying the rentals and other obligations to the lessor and then losing the equipment because the lessor has defaulted on the bank note secured by the leased property. Therefore, the company using leased property should be given the right in the lease agreement to make rental payments directly to the bank or other lender rather than to the lessor. Then, even if the leasing company should cease to operate, the lessee's right to the leased property would not be jeopardized. Another protective measure taken against repossession is to insert

---

[1] The Comptroller of the Currency, U.S. Treasury, in a letter dated March 18, 1963 addressed to all national bank presidents, stated in part: "The leasing by the bank of personal property acquired upon the specific request of and for the use of its customers, and the incurring of such additional obligations as may be incident to becoming an owner of personal property and the lessor thereof, is a lawful exercise of the powers of a National Bank...."

[2] Eugene F. Brigham, "The Impact of Bank Entry on Market Conditions in the Equipment Leasing Industry," *National Banking Review* (September 1964), p. 12.

a clause in the assignment that permits the lessee to take title to the property by paying off all remaining rentals at the time of default of the lessor.[3]

**Leasing as a Merchandising Method.** The widest development of leasing has occurred in those industries that use leasing as a merchandising device. At one time, many forms of equipment could be obtained only through purchase for cash or on the installment plan. At the same time, there were a few companies, such as Pullman, Inc., and International Business Machines, whose products could be obtained only through leasing, until the federal courts took action to force them to offer their products for sale. Now, many companies, having been influenced by the financial records of those who have followed the policy of leasing for years, are offering to lease as well as sell their products. The spread of leasing was accelerated when independent leasing firms entered the field. The entry of independent lessors reduced the dependence of equipment users on manufacturers and made the leasing market more competitive.

The manufacturing company that offers direct leasing benefits both from the enlarged market for its products and the spreading of its rental income over the lease period, which may entail tax advantages. Furthermore, this mode of operation affords the lessor better control over the secondhand market for its products. (In order to maintain the market for the equipment, the manufacturer may scrap used equipment rather than sell it in the secondhand market.)

## Operational or Nonfinancial Leasing

The older type of lease, called an operational lease, is one whose basic purpose is to transfer property from one party to another who uses it in a business. There is an incidental financial commitment that is less binding than the financial lease. It entails rental payments in an amount less than the purchase price of the asset, with an option that permits a renewal of the lease or purchase of the asset at a specified price when the basic contract terminates.

Operational or nonfinancial leasing contains all the provisions that make traditional leasing attractive to business firms. The basic characteristic of a lease is that ownership remains with the lessor rather than being transferred to the user, as in a loan transaction. By leasing instead of buying, the lessee avoids large capital outlays and the danger of having funds tied up in low-yielding capital assets for long periods. By leasing, companies may conserve their limited capital funds for working capital purposes and avoid the cash down payment usually required when financing with chattel mortgages. Leasing might provide more financing

---

[3] See Samuel J. Lee, *Introduction to Leasing* (San Marcos, Calif.: Auto Book Press, 1965), p. 58.

than borrowing (the amount depends on the required down payment on the normal loan).

Being expenses, rental costs are deductible for income tax purposes; but the lessee, not being the owner, loses the deduction for depreciation for depreciable assets. The possibility of large savings on federal income taxes was one of the major factors in the increase in leasing in recent years, but the advent of accelerated depreciation applicable to assets which have been purchased has changed this situation somewhat.

The lessee, not being the owner of leased property, may depend on the owner to provide maintenance and replacement services that can normally be supplied by the manufacturer or the leasing company at a lower cost than could be obtained by the user. Thus, the lessee may avoid many expensive breakdowns that delay production and affect employee morale adversely. Because there may be a tendency for lessees to be less careful of leased property than their own, a clause may be inserted in the contract that requires minimum standards of use to be met and provides for the assessment of penalties if they are violated. Sometimes, business firms need additional fixed assets for short periods of time, such as the interim between being awarded and fulfilling the terms of a government contract. Such emergencies may be met by leasing rather than buying because buying could entail having surplus assets at the end of the contract period.

Management may object to leasing because rental payments seem to be much higher than interest payments plus other financing charges; but this difference frequently is illusory, as can be seen when one analyzes all aspects of leasing as compared to borrowing. However, in leasing, the user loses the terminal value of the leased asset at the end of the lease period. This value may be considerable because of possible improvements made in the assets by the lessee, appreciation in the case of land, and higher prices because of inflation. If management attempts to protect the firm by inserting an option to buy at a stated price in the contract, the Internal Revenue Service may rule that the lease contract is in fact a conditional sale in intent and disallow rental payments as deductions.

When a company sells mortgage bonds, the mortgage sometimes covers not only currently owned property, but property which is acquired later; that is, after the bond issue has been sold. Such an "after-acquired property" clause serves to strengthen the issue and improve its salability. However, such provisions can make obtaining future financing more difficult. By leasing, management may avoid "after-acquired property" clauses and other restrictions found in term-loan agreements and in bond indentures. In addition, leasing has little effect on a corporation's cash position or lines of credit with banks. Since no increase in the firm's bank borrowing is involved, no increase in its compensatory bank balance is needed. Leasing provides management with greater flexibility in financing because the lease contract may be drawn so as to meet the firm's needs, and payments may be adjusted so as to correspond with cash receipts.

The restrictions to which management is subject when leasing property in some cases may be more annoying than those found in debt contracts. For example, a lessee is expected to obtain approval of the lessor before making changes in leased property. As a result, delays may occur before needed improvements are made. If assets, such as buildings, are leased for long periods, they may become obsolete before the end of the lease period; and, if the contract is noncancellable, it may be difficult to obtain improvements in the property or adjustments in the rentals.

The risk of obsolescence cannot be avoided by leasing. Lease payments will reflect the estimate by both the lessor and lessee of the rate of technological change occurring in the lessee's particular industry. The faster the rate of change, the higher the lease payments, and, probably, the shorter the lease period.

## Financial Leasing

A financial lease is a contract that is noncancellable, and the lease period is usually shorter than the useful life of the asset being leased. During the life of the contract, all of the cost of the property plus financing and servicing charges should be recovered through periodic payments. The lessee assumes complete financial responsibility for the leased asset; and, if operated successfully, the lessor or owner will recover the original investment.

Commercial, industrial, and mercantile firms are able to escape the burdens of ownership by leasing because others are able and willing to assume them. When the financial manager of a corporation finds it difficult to finance all of the company's needs with funds generated by operations and from outside sources, help may be obtained from trusts, life insurance companies, other institutional investors, and banks that are willing either to buy the firm's assets and lease them back to it or to buy the new equipment needed and lease it to the company. The terms of such leases or leaseback arrangements may be tailored to fit the requirements of the particular business firm.

One of the first types of financial leasing was developed in the merchandising field when large department stores, chain groceries, and supermarkets made use of sale and leaseback techniques. As early as 1936, this type of financial leasing was used by Safeway Stores, Inc., and it has become standard procedure in financing land and equipment needed by major retailers and also in other areas.[4]

---

[4] In 1949, the Equitable Life Assurance Society of the United States announced its plan to purchase locomotives, freight cars, and other forms of equipment to lease to railroads.

***Sale and Leaseback Financing.*** The basic procedure used in sale and leaseback financing is for the business firm to purchase and develop business or store sites to meet their needs, then sell them to investors, lease them back for long periods, and insert a clause in the lease that permits the lessee to purchase the property at the end of the lease period. The repurchase price is fixed so it will meet the approval of the Internal Revenue Service.

Originally, life insurance companies were prohibited from participating in sale and leaseback financing because they could not own nonresidential property; but, after the law was changed, they became the dominant institutions in this financial area.[5] Most of the early financing of this type was done by tax-exempt institutions—trust companies that were tax exempt because their beneficiaries were educational and similar tax-exempt institutions.[6]

Sale and leaseback financing of real estate is also used to obtain a tax advantage due to the appreciation of land on which old buildings are located. Such property may have a higher value than the original cost, so the business firm that owns it may sell it at market price and lease it back, thus obtaining extra funds with which to operate. The firm's current expenses will be increased because the rental payments are based on the current value and will amount to more than the depreciation allowances taken by the company on the old building. When land that is not depreciable is the chief element of value in a sale and leaseback arrangement, there will be a small amount of depreciation allowance to deduct in computing taxable income, which makes leasing relatively more attractive than ownership. (When property is sold, the gain thereon is subject to a capital-gains tax.) The sale and leaseback method of financing real estate is well developed, generally understood, and adequately covered by state laws. The credit rating of a company in such an arrangement has minimal effect on the terms of the lease because the real estate usually provides adequate security.

Sale and leaseback financing is widely used in the retail field, where there are many large firms that have no ownership interest in the buildings and fixtures wherein their merchandise is sold.[7] All of their capital is tied up in working-capital assets—cash, inventories, and receivables—which can be turned over rapidly and profitably. In shopping centers, the

---

[5] Limited direct ownership of real estate is permitted in all states. See Albert H. Cohen, *Long Term Leases–Problems in Taxation, Finance and Accounting* (Ann Arbor: University of Michigan Press, 1954), pp. 26–30.

[6] In 1943, Gimbel's sold its store property in Philadelphia to the Fidelity-Philadelphia Trust Company, a tax-exempt institution because its beneficiaries included Cornell, Rochester, and Yale universities. Two years later, the Allied Stores Corporation made a sale and leaseback agreement for the premises occupied by stores in six cities with Union College of Schenectady, New York, the nominal investor. See ibid., pp. 23–26.

[7] Lee, *Introduction to Leasing*, p. 16.

tenants agree to pay the owner a specified rental for an agreed period and frequently an "overage" related to profits or the sales volume of the tenant. In addition to the specified rental terms, the lease arrangement frequently contains an option that permits the lessee to buy the property at the end of the lease period.

**Straight Financial Leases.** A straight financial lease is identical to a sale and leaseback arrangement *except* that the lessee firm has not previously owned the property. The user firm negotiates with the seller and specifies what it needs with respect to the equipment or building. The firm then negotiates with a financial institution to buy the property while the user simultaneously executes a lease agreement with the institution (lessor).

The straight financial lease is essentially a loan agreement with minor modifications. However, because it is a lease instead of a loan, the transaction receives different tax treatment which may benefit the firm. Analysis of the transaction will be explained in the next section.

Lease financing and debt financing are similar in that they entail contractual obligations that have maturities that are long enough for the investor to recover the investment and the business firm to meet its obligations at specified times in the future. Both instruments give a "return" to the investor and have a "cost" to the user that can be measured fairly accurately in dollar amounts. The soundness of both instruments depends on the general debt-paying ability of the business firm, whether it is a lessee or a debtor. The objectives of management to obtain new property may be achieved by borrowing in order to buy or by leasing.

Major corporations, able to finance their needs by borrowing at favorable interest rates in the money and capital markets, have relied less on financial leasing than have smaller firms in the industrial field; but this does not mean that financial leasing is due to a lack of credit facilities. The factors that have been responsible for the growth of financial leasing include flexibility of the leasing device, cost differentials, and tax effects.

One of the advantages of leasing is the flexibility of the rental terms, which may be tailored to fit the needs of the lessee. For example, payments may be set within the firm's ability to generate cash. Payments may be high during the early life of the asset, when maintenance and repairs are at a minimum, and low during the remainder of the life of the assets, when maintenance and repair costs tend to increase. In other cases, the rental payments may be linked directly to the revenue created by the equipment being leased.

Rental payments may be monthly, quarterly, semiannual, or annual, or they may be discontinued during some periods for a firm having wide seasonal or cyclical fluctuations in income. In the repayment schedule an attempt is made to avoid the need for drawing on the firm's existing working-capital assets. This is achieved by having payments made from current revenue. In leasing, rental payments are due on specified dates after the leased asset is acquired; and, if assets are to be delivered at different times, each is included in the master lease arrangement as it is put into use. It is frequently alleged that a major advantage of lease financing is that the lessee is able to obtain 100-percent financing. In a conditional-sales arrangement, a down payment of 20, 30, or 40 percent is expected. The implication here is that leasing supplies more assets to the firm than debt financing. It is also implied that leasing may not greatly affect the firm's general borrowing capacity. However, this is unlikely, since leasing does entail fixed commitments for the lessee.

In the long run, it is improbable that the total of leased assets can greatly exceed assets acquired by conventional borrowing since both methods involve fixed obligations. Nevertheless, in the short run, it may seem that leasing offers greater financing opportunities. If this situation does carry over into a longer period, then the financial markets are not adequately recognizing leasing obligations as being very similar to debt instruments. For most firms this situation would not seem likely to prevail over long periods. In a lease contract the lessee pays an "implied" interest and other financing charges and an amount equal to the cost of the leased asset.

When comparing the costs of leasing with those of intermediate borrowing, the three items that must be considered by financial management are (1) the cost of the equipment, which should be the same in both cases; (2) differences in the real and "implicit" interest rates; and (3) costs of financing and other items included in the rental payment but which the owner pays in a credit transaction. For example, "transfer costs" assumed by the lessor are expenses due to administrative, clerical, and legal work, together with commitment fees and expenses entailed in arranging financing. However, there are other expenses that may be paid by either lessees or borrowers, including federal excise taxes, local taxes, insurance premiums, and, usually, normal costs of maintenance.

If it were not for quirks in the U.S. tax code, one would expect the cost of leasing assets and the cost of owning them to be identical.[8] Loan payment schedules can be adjusted to make them just as flexible as leases. If lenders are astute, they will accurately assess the loss of debt-carrying capacity resulting from a lease commitment. Leasing institutions and lending institutions (often one and the same) must receive payments sufficient to cover principal, interest, transfer costs, and maintenance.

The main difference between a lease payment and a loan payment is the tax treatment. On a loan payment, only the interest portion is defined as an expense, which is deductible. The payment on principal is simply return of invested capital. It is not taxable to the lender, and it is *not tax*

---

[8] This has been rigorously demonstrated in the efficient markets case by Merton H. Miller and Charles W. Upton, "Leasing, Buying and the Cost of Capital Services," and Wilbur G. Lewellen, Michael S. Long, and John J. McConnell, "Asset Leasing in Competitive Capital Markets," both in *Journal of Finance* (June 1976).

*deductible for the borrower.* On a lease the entire payment is for the use of the associated asset; it is all expense and is therefore all deductible.

All of the lease payment is taxable income to the lessor. The lessor recaptures its invested capital through depreciation of the leased asset, which it owns, and by sale of the asset at the end of the lease. In effect, the lessee has transferred the tax benefits of ownership to the lessor (depreciation and tax credits) and agreed to make payments for the use of the asset. If the lessor can better utilize the tax benefits than the user, the lease payments might be set low enough to make leasing cheaper than owning. The lessee can only determine this by thorough analysis.

## Analysis of Leases[9]

In the chapter on capital budgeting the cost of any asset to be analyzed was consistently defined as its cash purchase price, regardless of the method by which it was financed. This is justifiable in a number of ways. First, the definition of the benefits (i.e., cash flow) implicitly assumes cash purchase. Second, the cost of capital calculation takes into consideration the combination of capital used; to introduce financing into the analysis again in the cost or benefits section would be double counting. Third, leverage is a characteristic of the firm, depending upon its capital structure. To consider financing flows in the analysis of individual assets or projects would suggest that leverage was specific to those assets, which is illogical. All of the above can be summarized in Modigliani and Miller's "Proposition III" as discussed in the appendix to Chapter 12. Proposition III says that the required rate of return on any asset is the same regardless of how it is financed. The asset must make a return equal to the cost of capital. The analysis should ignore the specific form of financing used.

This prescription causes a problem when analyzing leased assets. There is no convenient way to ignore the specific form of financing used. The analysis must consider (1) whether the lease form of financing is cheaper than normal borrowing, and (2) whether the asset is worth acquiring, based on the estimates of the operating benefits.

Because of the amount of lease financing and because the analysis is tricky, there has been a large volume of literature on the analysis of leases. The approaches to the problem fall into two general categories: those that analyze the financing decision (lease-or-borrow analysis), and those that analyze the investment decision (lease-or-buy analysis).[10]

---

[9] This section is limited to the analysis of financial leases; that is, fully amortized noncancellable leases. For analysis of cancellable leases see David O. Jenkins, "Purchase or Cancellable Lease," *Financial Executive*, vol. 38 (April 1970), pp. 26–31.

[10] Instructors my wish to conserve class time by limiting coverage to one of the two approaches. Either approach may be omitted without loss of continuity.

## 14  Leasing

***Lease-or-Borrow Analysis.*** Lease-or-borrow models suggest that leases are essentially debt contracts, and the issue is to see if the lease, due to its unique place in the tax structure, is cheaper than a similarly structured loan when compared on a present value of cost basis. Analysis of the financing issue is easier than most capital budgeting problems in one respect—estimation error. The flows involved are highly predictable. The lease payments, the comparable loan payments, their interest and principal components, depreciation deductions, and the applicable tax rates are all virtually certain. Because of this, most analysts agree that these flows should be discounted at a risk-free rate. Recent work suggests that the firm's current pre-tax cost of debt is the best specification of that rate.[11,12]

One part of the analysis should use a risk rate. If the firm buys an asset (with or without borrowing), it obtains claim to the salvage value. The discount rate used for salvage should be the cost of capital, just as it would be for the analysis of any other cash flow subject to normal estimation error.[13]

Given this background, the analysis of the lease-or-borrow options can be examined. To make the decision, a comparison must be made of the present value of the after-tax cost for the lease, and the acquisition assuming it were financed with a comparable loan.

To illustrate, consider the following example: An asset costing $10,000 could be leased for six years for $2,300 a year (end-of-year payments). If purchased, the asset would be depreciated, straight-line, over a six-year life toward a realistic salvage estimate of $1,000. The firm is in a 40-percent tax bracket and can borrow money at 8 percent.

The present value, after-tax cost of the lease, can be found in a number of ways. It will facilitate comparison with the "borrow" analysis if it is performed in two steps. First, the present value of the payments is found by multiplying the value of a single payment by the factor for the present value of an annuity for six years at 8 percent (the firm's pre-tax cost of debt).

Next, the tax benefits, or shields, from the lease are calculated. Lease payments are totally deductible. Each $2,300 payment reduces taxes in that year by $920 (.4 × $2,300 = $920). The cost of the lease is reduced by the present value of these tax savings. The analysis of the lease alternative appears in Table 14–1.

---

[11] For a detailed analysis of the appropriate discount rates, see Glenn V. Henderson, Jr., "A Decision Format for Lease or Buy Analysis," *Review of Business and Economic Research* (Fall 1976), pp. 63–72.

[12] For a detailed discussion of the different discount rates used by the various authors, see Richard S. Bower, "Issues in Lease Financing," *Financial Management* (Winter 1973), pp. 25–34.

[13] Richard Bower's article suggests there is consensus on this point, ibid., p. 28.

Evaluation of the borrow alternative is more complicated. First, a comparable loan must be constructed for purpose of analysis. If the firm were to borrow from its normal sources, at 8 percent, the payments on a $10,000 six-year loan with end-of-year payments would be $2,163. The payments are calculated using the present value of an annuity factor for six years at 8 percent as discussed in Chapter 8: $10,000/4.623 = $2,163.

**TABLE 14–1**
**Lease-or-Borrow: Analysis of Lease**

| Item | Before Tax | After Tax | Time | Discount Factor | Present Value |
|---|---|---|---|---|---|
| Payments | $2,300 | — | 1–6 | 4.623 | $10,632 |
| Less: Tax shields | (2,300) | (920) | 1–6 | 4.623 | (4,253) |
| | | | | | $ 6,380 |

Recalling that only the interest portion of a loan payment is deductible requires that the interest and principal components be separated. The amortization schedule illustrated in Table 14–2 provides such a breakdown.

**TABLE 14–2**
**Amortization Table for Comparable Loan**

| Time | Payment | Principal | Interest | Balance |
|---|---|---|---|---|
| 0 | –0– | –0– | –0– | $10,000 |
| 1 | $2,163 | $1,363 | $800 | 8,637 |
| 2 | 2,163 | 1,472 | 691 | 7,165 |
| 3 | 2,163 | 1,590 | 573 | 5,575 |
| 4 | 2,163 | 1,717 | 446 | 3,858 |
| 5 | 2,163 | 1,854 | 309 | 2,003 |
| 6 | 2,163 | 2,003 | 160 | –0– |

In each row of the table the payment is separated into interest, which is deductible, and principal repayment, which is not. For example, the first year's interest is $800—8 percent on the original balance of $10,000. The rest of the payment ($2,163 − 800 = $1,363) reduces the remaining balance to $8,637 ($10,000 − 1,363 = $8,637). Second-year interest is 8 percent of that amount, $691 = .08($8,637). The amortization process is continued for the entire life of the loan.

The analysis of the borrow alternative is similar to that of the lease. The first entry is the present value of all the payments, which, by definition, must equal the asset's cost of $10,000. Then the tax shields derived from the interest deductions are quantified. Ownership also affords tax

14  Leasing        287

shields from depreciation. They are accounted for next.[14] Finally the present value of expected salvage is included. As explained before, salvage should be discounted at a risk rate (this analysis assumes that the risk rate for the company is 15 percent). The analysis of the borrow option appears in Table 14–3.

TABLE 14–3
Lease-or-Borrow: Analysis of Borrow

| Item | Before Tax | After Tax | Time | Discount Factor | Present Value |
|---|---|---|---|---|---|
| Payments  6yrs × 2163 = 12,973 |  | 2163 | 1–6 | 4.623 | $10,000 |
| Less: Interest shields | $(800) | $(320) | 1 | .926 | (296) |
|  | (691) | (276) | 2 | .857 | (237) |
|  | (573) | (229) | 3 | .794 | (182)  970 |
|  | (446) | (178) | 4 | .735 | (131) |
|  | (309) | (124) | 5 | .681 | (84) |
|  | (160) | (64) | 6 | .630 | (40) |
| Less: Depreciation shields | (1,500) | (600) | 1–6 | 4.623 | (2,774) |
| Less: Salvage value | (1,000) | (1,000) | 6 | .432 (15%) | (432) |
|  |  |  |  |  | $5,824 |

BENEFIT TO BORROWING = 6380 − 5824 = 556

The analysis suggests that in the present case, lease financing is more expensive than the use of the firm's normal debt financing when salvage and depreciation benefits are taken into account.

The example was purposefully simplified. If there are added factors to be considered, they can be "tacked on" individually. For example, if the lease included maintenance, the present value (at an appropriate discount rate) of the added costs, after tax, could be added to the cost of the borrow alternative. If there was an investment tax credit to be derived from ownership, the value of the credit could be subtracted from the cost of owning via borrowing. The work sheets are very general and can, with imagination, handle all the complications one might encounter in such a financing decision.

The analysis suggests that, in this case, the lease financing is more expensive. However, this does not answer the question of whether or not the asset should be acquired. In this case that would not present a problem. The problem could be re-analyzed using the $10,000 cost figure for the analysis. If the lease had turned out to be cheaper, the acquisition analysis might be performed using cost as $10,000 minus the benefit to

---

[14] The correct discount rate for depreciation shields was debated following an article by Robert W. Johnson and Wilbur G. Lewellen, "Analysis of the Lease-or-Buy Decision," *Journal of Finance* (September 1972), pp. 815–23. For the debate see "Comments" and "Reply," *Journal of Finance* (September 1973), pp. 1015–28. Current consensus would suggest that depreciation shields, again due to the lack of forecast error, should be discounted at a risk-free rate such as the pre-tax cost of the firm's debt.

leasing; that is, cost equal to purchase price minus the difference between the cost of owning and the cost of leasing.

Note that the cost as defined in Table 14–3 should not be used; that is, the $10,000 less the value of the interest shields. This figure ($10,000 − 970 = $9,030) is too low by the amount of the interest shields. This is simply numerical proof of an assertion made earlier: to attribute the use of borrowed money to a particular project creates a bias favoring the adoption of that project because borrowed funds are less expensive.

**Lease-or-Buy Analysis.** The lease-or-buy models suggest that the analytical surgery was performed on the wrong alternative. If the analysis is to be of the acquisition, the buy option's cost was correctly defined to start with; it is the asset's cash purchase price. The problem is to specify correctly the cost of the lease alternative for the investment analysis. This section will use a numerical example to show how that can be accomplished.

Although this approach to lease analysis is conceptually different from that in the preceding section, it is similar in most respects. Many of the flows under consideration are readily forecast; for example, lease payments, loan payments, the interest and principal components of those payments, depreciation, and the firm's marginal tax rate. Because of the certainty of these flows, they are discounted at a risk-free rate, the firm's pre-tax cost of debt. Salvage and operating benefits, being risk estimates, are discounted at the firm's cost of capital.

Like the lease-or-borrow approach, lease-or-buy analysis makes use of the concept of a comparable loan, the loan the firm could use to purchase the asset if it decided not to lease. To facilitate comparison for those who study both methods, the same example will be used. The firm can either (1) purchase the asset at a cost of $10,000, or (2) lease it for six years at a cost of $2,300 a year (end-of-year payments).

Regardless of the method of financing, the asset will afford the firm operating benefits of $5,000 a year. If purchased, the asset will be depreciated straight-line over six years to an expected salvage of $1,000. The firm's tax rate is 40 percent. It can borrow money at 8 percent, and its cost of capital is 15 percent.

Using this approach, the analysis of the buy option is almost identical to that used in the capital budgeting chapter, Chapter 9. There is only one change. The depreciation tax shields are discounted at a riskless rate of 8 percent. The analysis appears in Table 14–4.

It appears that the acquisition would be beneficial based on a "risk-adjusted" net present value. Although it is a little more complicated, the lease analysis can be formulated in a similar work sheet.

Understanding the analysis is made easier by recognizing that it concentrates on incremental flows. The lease is considered to be just like any other loan except that it involves different payments and different deductions. Higher payments increase costs, and higher deductions, through greater tax shields, increase benefits. To define these elements, the payments and deductions on a normal loan must be defined.

TABLE 14–4
Lease-or-Buy: Analysis of Buy

| Item | Before Tax | After Tax | Time | Discount Factor | Present Value |
|---|---|---|---|---|---|
| Cost | $10,000 | $10,000 | 0 | 1 | $10,000 |
| Benefits |  |  |  |  |  |
| Operating benefits | $ 5,000 | $ 3,000 | 1–6 | 3.784 (5%) | $11,352 |
| Tax shields DEPRECIATION | 1,500 | 600 | 1–6 | 4.623 (8%) | 2,774 |
| Salvage | 1,000 | 1,000 | 6 | .432 (15%) | 432 |
|  |  |  |  |  | $14,558 |
| Net Present Value = $14,558 − 10,000 = $4,558 |  |  |  |  |  |

*POSITIVE BENEFITS TO FIRM*

In the lease-or-borrow section the payments for a comparable loan using the firm's normal debt were calculated. The payments were found using the calculation from Chapter 8: $PV_A = a[V_{\overline{n}|i}]$. Substituting $10,000, the cost of the asset, and 4.623, the present value of a six-year, 8-percent annuity into the formula, the payments on a comparable loan were determined to be $2,163 a year. In that section each payment was separated into principal and interest components. An amortization table for this loan appears in Table 14–2. (This is the only material used from that section. For those skipping the lease-or-borrow material, reviewing the table and the one explanatory paragraph should be all the review that is necessary.)

$\frac{10,000}{4.623}$

Having defined the normal loan and knowing the lease payments, the extra payments and the extra deductions can be calculated. To the extent that the lease payments are higher than loan payments, cost is increased. If the lease deduction (the entire lease payment) is greater than the normal interest deduction, the firm has an added benefit. These "extras" are detailed in Table 14–5.

All that remains left to be done is to substitute into the work sheet. Before doing so, it should be recognized that some items will be omitted

TABLE 14–5
Incremental Payments and Deductions

| Time | Payments |  |  | Deductions |  |  |
|---|---|---|---|---|---|---|
|  | Lease | Loan | Extra (LEASE−LOAN) | Lease | Interest | Extra (LEASE−INTEREST) |
| 1 | $2,300 | $2,163 | $137 | $2,300 | $800 | $1,500 |
| 2 | 2,300 | 2,163 | 137 | 2,300 | 691 | 1,609 |
| 3 | 2,300 | 2,163 | 137 | 2,300 | 573 | 1,727 |
| 4 | 2,300 | 2,163 | 137 | 2,300 | 446 | 1,854 |
| 5 | 2,300 | 2,163 | 137 | 2,300 | 309 | 1,991 |
| 6 | 2,300 | 2,163 | 137 | 2,300 | 160 | 2,140 |

in the case of a lease. There will be no depreciation shields because the firm does not own the asset. For the same reason there will be no salvage. The analysis of the lease-financed acquisition appears in Table 14–6. The same discount factors that were used for the buy analysis are employed. Riskless flows are discounted at the cost of debt. Risky flows are discounted at the cost of capital.

**TABLE 14–6**
Lease-or-Buy: Analysis of Lease

| Item | Before Tax | After Tax | Time | Discount Factor | Present Value |
|---|---|---|---|---|---|
| Cost | $10,000 | $10,000 | 0 | 1 | $10,000 |
| Plus extra payments | 137 | 137 | 1–6 | 4.623 (8%) | 633 |
| | | | | | $10,633 |
| *Benefits* | | | | | |
| Operating benefits | $ 5,000 | $ 3,000 | 1–6 | 3.784 (15%) | $11,352 |
| Plus extra shields | 1,500 | 600 | 1 | .926 (8%) | 556 |
| | 1,609 | 644 | 2 | .857 | 552 |
| | 1,727 | 691 | 3 | .794 | 549 |
| | 1,854 | 742 | 4 | .735 | 545 |
| | 1,991 | 796 | 5 | .681 | 542 |
| | 2,140 | 856 | 6 | .630 | 539 |
| | | | | | $14,635 |
| Net Present Value = $14,635 − 10,633 = $4,002 | | | | | |

Again, it appears that acquiring the asset is beneficial. The risk-adjusted net present value is substantially positive. However, it is not as worthwhile as an outright purchase. Although the lease generated more benefits, due to higher tax shields, the higher payments more than offset those benefits. Because of the higher payments the firm had, in effect, paid $633 more for the asset, reducing the net present value.

**Summary of Analysis.** Both of the analytical approaches arrived at exactly the same conclusion. The lease was not advantageous *in this particular case*. Further, the amount of the advantage to normal acquisition was the same using both methods. With the lease-or-borrow analysis the cost of borrowing was $556 less. Using the lease-or-buy technique, the buy alternative's risk-adjusted NPV was $556 higher. The two techniques will always give compatible results if (1) they use the same definition of a comparable loan, and (2) they use the same discount rates.

The lease-or-borrow approach is easier. It involves slightly fewer calculations. The only problem is that it understates the cost of both alternatives. It makes both options appear cheaper than they actually are. This could confuse the investment decision.

The lease-or-buy approach is more theoretically correct. It defines cost in the normal way for the buy analysis and removes the effects of "normal" financing from the definition of cost under leasing. It is logically consistent with MM's Proposition III. However, it is conceptually more difficult and computationally more tedious.

## Accounting for Leases

In discussing leases, finance texts have traditionally included a section which discussed the advantages of leases from a financial reporting perspective. Historically leases were less visible than normal debt, being reported in footnotes rather than as balance sheet accounts. Such reporting could lead the unwary to consider a lessee firm as less leveraged than an otherwise identical firm that used a comparable amount of contractual indebtedness.

This has all changed. With the publication of *FASB Statement No. 13*, the disclosure of lease obligations is essentially on a par with debt disclosure.[15] The *Statement* deals with classification of leases and their reporting for both lessees and lessors. It provides background information as to prior accounting treatments and details the basis for the prescribed changes. A brief outline of *FASB No. 13 as it applies to lessees* is included in an appendix to this chapter.

The most pronounced change in lessee reporting applies to financial leases (which the *Statement* refers to as capital leases). These commitments are no longer buried in the footnotes. The present value of the payments is carried as an asset and is balanced with a corresponding long-term liability. This high visibility should assure that such commitments are not overlooked.

## Legal Considerations

To receive tax treatment as leases, the contracts must meet the IRS requirements for leases. In addition to receiving different tax treatment, leases also are treated differently by the courts.

**IRS Requirements.** In order to be deductible, rental payments must meet conditions found in the rulings of the Internal Revenue Service. The main problem is to be sure the lease is not a conditional-sale contract. "Rental or other payments required to be made as condition to the continued use or possession, for purposes of trade or business, of property to which the taxpayer has not taken or is not taking title or in which he has no equity,"[16] are deductible for tax purposes.

Because many leases contain an option to buy at the end of the lease period and rental payments give the lessee the opportunity to build up equity, the Internal Revenue Service issued Ruling 55–540. In general,

---

[15] *Statement of Financial Accounting Standards No. 13*. Stanford, Calif.: Financial Accounting Standards Board, 1976.
[16] Internal Revenue Code, Section 162(a)(3).

the ruling states that the lease could be ruled a conditional sale if the total of the rental payments and any option price payable in addition thereto approximates the price at which the equipment could have been acquired by purchase at the time of entering into the agreement, plus interest and carrying charges.[17] Specifically, a lease could be ruled a conditional sale if the rental terms include any of the following: rental payments are made applicable to any equity to be acquired by the lessee; title passes to the lessee after a stated number of payments have been made; required payments over a short period are inordinately large compared to the total sum needed to secure a transfer of title; contracted rental payments materially exceed the current value, so the payments include more than compensation for use of the property; a purchase option provides a nominal price relative to the value of the property at the time the option may be exercised or a small amount relative to total required payments; or some portion of the periodic payments is designated or recognizable as the equivalent of interest.

**Court Treatment of Leases.** In reorganization and bankruptcy proceedings, rental payments frequently are treated more favorably than debt obligations. Because the property leased does not belong to the business firm in financial difficulties, it may not be seized by creditors. The receiver or trustee may decide to retain the leased asset and pay rentals on it; otherwise, the lease is broken when the leased property is returned to its owner, accompanied by a payment of three years' rentals in cases of reorganization or bankruptcy. Unless the property can be identified, which becomes more difficult with the passage of time, the leased equipment may be held for the benefit of all creditors.

In reorganization or bankruptcy cases, the trustee or receiver may seize property purchased with funds raised by borrowing. If the property is secured by a chattel mortgage, the lender has first claim to the pledged asset; if the receipts from the sale of the property are insufficient to satisfy the claims of the lender, the lender becomes a general creditor for the remainder of his claim.

## Summary

Leasing is the grant by one party (lessor) to a second party (lessee) of an asset that permits the second party to use it for a specified period. Leases are classified as operational and financial. The chief distinguishing characteristic of a financial lease is that the user or lessee assumes complete financial responsibility for the leased asset.

Leasing may be used as a substitute for debt financing or as a supplement thereto. The payment procedure in leasing equipment is similar to that used in conditional sales, with payments for the equipment made

---

[17] Internal Revenue Code, Ruling 55–540, Section 4.05.

on the installment plan. There is no unqualified answer to the question of whether leasing or borrowing in order to buy is preferable. Each situation merits special attention. All the costs of leasing—rental payments, fees, service and maintenance charges, insurance fees, and miscellaneous charges—must be weighed against all the costs entailed in borrowing and buying.

Two ways for setting up the analysis were examined. Both used work sheets similar to those used in the earlier capital budgeting coverage. The primary difference was the treatment of leasing's financial flows. Financial flows were added to the buy option in the lease-or-borrow approach. In the lease-or-buy method, the normal financial flows implicit in the lease were neutralized. The two forms of analysis produced compatible results.

Accounting for leases has changed a great deal recently. Current treatment provides greater visibility to lease obligations, treating them as debts. The nature of the new accounting is covered in some detail in this chapter's Appendix.

## QUESTIONS

1. Identify: (a) leasing; (b) operational leasing; and (c) financial leasing.
2. Explain: "Leasing is a merchandising tool."
3. Explain the use made of leasing in financing stores, shopping centers, and large department stores.
4. Compare and contrast the provisions of a lease contract versus the provisions on other debt instruments, such as conditional-sales contracts.
5. Can a firm hedge against the risk of inflation by leasing equipment?
6. Can a firm hedge against any technological change in its industry by leasing?
7. In general terms what is the difference between lease-or-borrow analysis and lease-or-buy analysis?
8. In terms of *FASB Statement No. 13*, what is a capital lease?
9. How are capital leases accounted for?
10. Given the difference in the treatment by the courts, would you prefer to provide equipment to a financially shaky customer on an installment sales contract (loan) or on a financial lease? Why?

## PROBLEMS

1. The Rapid Photo Best Corporation, a processor and developer of quality photographic films, has recently lost its competitive advantage because of industry acceptance of a new film-development process. This innovative processing equipment is offered as an outright purchase for $5,000, or it can be leased from the sole manufacturer for $1,300 a year, with end-of-year payments for 5 years. The equipment has a useful life of 5 years with

no salvage value. RPB's tax rate is 40 percent, its loan rate is 8 percent, and it uses straight-line depreciation.

    *a.* Should RPB lease the equipment or borrow from their normal sources? (Assume the loan, if acquired, would have end-of-year payments.)

    *b.* If the equipment would increase before tax profits by $2,000 a year, is the acquisition economically justified, that is, is its risk-adjusted NPV positive? (Assume that RPB's cost of capital is 15 percent.)

2. Fictional Corp. is considering acquisition of a $100,000 piece of capital equipment. The equipment has an economic life of 8 years. The company estimates the machinery would save $26,000 a year before taxes. Depreciation would be straight-line (8 years, zero salvage). The company requires an 18 percent return on risky flows.

    The company can borrow the money from the bank at 10 percent or lease from the manufacturer's leasing subsidiary for $18,000 a year. Using either plan there would be eight equal end-of-year payments. The tax rate is 40 percent.

    *a.* Prepare the lease-or-borrow analysis.
    *b.* Compare the present value of the operating benefits to these "costs."
    *c.* Prepare the lease-or-buy analysis.
    *d.* Discuss your findings.

3. Whymzee, Inc., is evaluating the acquisition of some new electronic data processing equipment. The equipment is estimated to have an economic life of 5 years.

    If purchased the equipment would cost $17,500. It would be depreciated using the sum-of-the-years-digits method over a five-year life to a realistically estimated salvage of $2,500. In addition to the depreciation, ownership would entitle Whymzee to an immediate $1,167 investment tax credit. (Two thirds of a 10 percent credit due to the depreciable life of 5 years.) If the firm borrows from their bank, they could secure a 10 percent loan; equipment secured financing.

    As an alternative, the manufacturer will lease the equipment for $4,500 a year, end-of-year payments. If the equipment is leased, the manufacturer will provide all necessary maintenance. If Whymzee bought the equipment the maintenance would cost $500 a year. (Assume that the manufacturer will provide a long-term maintenance contract with end-of-year payments. This type of contract is fairly common and makes these payments certain, that is, riskless.)

    The company estimates the new equipment would save them $6,000 a year before taxes. Their cost of capital is 16 percent. The tax rate is 40 percent.

    *a.* Prepare the lease-or-borrow analysis.
    *b.* Prepare the lease-or-buy analysis.

## ADDITIONAL READINGS

    Bower, R. S. "Issues in Lease Financing," *Financial Management* (Winter 1973), pp. 25–34.

    Gordon, M. J. "A General Solution to the Buy or Lease Decision: A Pedagogical Note," *Journal of Finance*, vol. 29 (March 1974), pp. 245–50.

Henderson, G. V., Jr. "A Decision Format for Lease or Buy Analysis," *Review of Business and Economic Research*, vol. 12 (Fall 1976), pp. 63–72.

———. "Understanding the Analysis of Leases," *Arizona Business*, vol. 24 (February 1977), pp. 8–11.

Jenkins, D. O. "Puchase or Cancellable lease: Which is Better?" *Financial Executive*, vol. 38 (April 1970), pp. 26–31.

*Statement of Financial Accounting Standards No. 13*, Stanford, Calif.: Financial Accounting Standards Board, 1976.

Vancil, R. F. "Lease or Borrow—New Method of Analysis," *Harvard Business Review*, vol. 39 (September–October 1961), pp. 122–36.

## APPENDIX: LESSEE REPORTING UNDER *FASB STATEMENT NO. 13*

*FASB Statement No. 13* affects most, if not all, aspects of accounting for leases. It changes the reporting of lessors as well as lessees. A short summary of the statement is virtually impossible. This appendix will discuss the statement only as it affects the lessee and primarily as it changes the reporting of financial (capital) leases.

### Classification of Leases

For lessees' reporting purposes, leases are of two types: capital and operating. Capital leases are analogous to what finance literature refers to as financial leases. However, the *Statement's* definition is necessarily more precise. For accounting purposes, a lease is, by definition, a capital lease if it meets any one of the following four requirements:[1] (1) ownership of the leased property transfers to the lessee at the end of the lease, (2) the lease contains a purchase option at such a low price that it is relatively certain that the lessee will exercise it, (3) the term of the lease equals 75 percent or more of the economic life of the asset,[2] or (4) the *present value* of the *minimum lease payments* (excluding that portion attributable to insurance, maintenance, and/or taxes) equals or exceeds 90 percent of the *fair value* of the asset (adjusted for any investment tax credit taken by the lessor).

All of these provisions are straightforward except the last. It requires explanation because it uses some uniquely defined terms.

The *minimum lease payments* include minimum rental payments over the term of the lease, any residual value guaranteed by the lessees,[3] and any payment the lessees must make (or can be required to make) if they do not renew at the end of the current term. To calculate the *present*

---

[1] FASB, *Statement No. 13*, p. 9.

[2] This provision does not apply if the lease starts in the last 25 percent of the economic life of the asset.

[3] If the lease contains a "bargain purchase option" (as described in (2) above), the bargain purchase price is included here.

*value* of these payments, a discount rate must be defined. The prescribed rate is the lower of the current loan rate the lessee would be charged to obtain funds for a similar transaction, or the implicit rate in the lease. (The "implicit rate" is the lessor's IRR—the discount rate which makes the present value of the rental portion of the payments equal the worth of the leased asset.)

The *fair value* of an asset is the price that would be arrived at in an arm's-length transaction between independent parties. The fair value is the normal selling price of the asset reduced by usual trade and/or quantity discounts.

Operating leases are defined by exclusion. Any lease which does not qualify as a capital lease is an operating lease.

## Reporting of Leases

The *Statement* affects the reporting of all leases. The change with regard to capital leases, as defined above, is quite pronounced. The balance sheet shows an asset and a corresponding liability account for the leased asset. The amount of these accounts is the smaller of (1) the *present value* of the *minimum lease payments* (excluding again, that portion which is for insurance, maintenance, and taxes) or (2) the *fair value* of the asset. The definitions of these specialized terms are the same as before.

The lessee's income statements will treat the leased asset essentially as a loan-purchased asset. The "asset" account on the balance sheet will be depreciated in a manner consistent with the firm's normal depreciation policy. If the lease contains a purchase requirement or a bargain purchase option, the depreciable life is the economic life of the asset. Otherwise, the asset will be depreciated over the term of the lease.

The lease payments are treated as if they were loan payments. The interest rate, as described above, is used to set up an amortization schedule. Each loan payment is considered to be part interest, which is reported as expense in the income statement, and part principal, which reduces the balance sheet liability.

The assets created by such accounting and their accumulated amortization; that is, depreciation, must be separately identified in the balance sheet, or its footnotes. Likewise, the corresponding created liability should be identified separately. The same consideration is required for the income statement entries.

The reporting of operating leases is largely unchanged. The rentals are changed to expense as they become payable. However, if the payments are not straight-line, an adjustment may be required. Unless the firm can justify some other pattern on a rational basis, the expense must be recognized as straight-line.

In addition to these changes in financial reporting, *Statement No. 13* requires greater disclosure as to a firm's use of lease financing. For capital leases it requires that the statements disclose:

1. The gross amount of assets under capital lease classified by nature or function.
2. The future minimum lease payments, in aggregate and for each of the next five years.
3. Sublease rentals.
4. Total contingent rentals.

For operating leases, with remaining noncancellable terms exceeding a year, the firm must disclose:

1. Future minimum rental payments required currently, in aggregate and for each of the next five years.
2. Minimum rentals due in the future from noncancellable subleases.

For all operating leases the firm must provide detailed breakdowns as to rental expense and subleases.

Finally, the firm's financial statements must include a general description of the firm's leasing arrangements. At a minimum this description must include:

1. The basis for contingent rental payments.
2. The nature of any renewal, purchase, or escalation clauses in the leases.
3. Any restrictive covenants in the lease contracts.

In addition to these general provisions covering capital and operating leases, *Statement No. 13* has specific requirements with respect to leases involving real estate and leases based on sale-and-lease-back arrangements.

## Background, Impact, and Implementation

*Statement No. 13* is the most recent effort of the accounting profession to deal with the disclosure of lease obligations. Accountants have been grappling with this issue as far back as 1949 when the AI[CP]A issued *Accounting Research Bulletin No. 38*, "Disclosure of Long-Term Leases in Financial Statements of Lessees." The current statement to a large degree reconciles the inconsistencies in the reporting requirements for lessors and lessees. It should also serve to reconcile the profession's requirements with those of the Securities and Exchange Commission.

Most of the financial community regards leases as a specialized form of debt. The new reporting requirements treat them exactly that way. The revised accounting should eliminate any confusion that might be attributed to the use of this specialized and important form of financing.

Effective January 1, 1977, all new leases must be reported as, in effect, loans. After December 31, 1980, the provisions will also be applied to any outstanding leases. At that time, prior period statements presented for comparison will be required to be reformulated on a basis consistent with *Statement No. 13*. Lease financing can no longer be described as "off-statement debt."

# part IV
# SOURCES OF CAPITAL

In considering the financing of business firms, it is difficult to treat one aspect of the problem without taking others into account. For instance, a discussion of how and why business firms finance with funds from operations while disregarding the effects of using funds from external sources would tend to lead to incorrect conclusions. Also, the relationship between financing short-, intermediate-, or long-term needs with equity capital and short- and long-term obligations cannot be ignored. In other words, all aspects of financing business firms are interrelated.

In business finance the term "capital structure" is used to include all long-term debt, preferred stock, and common-stock equity. The latter consists of paid-in capital, capital surplus, and retained earnings. The term "financial structure" is used to describe all of the above plus short-term obligations. In other words, the financial structure includes all items on the right-hand side of the balance sheet. Emphasis in this section is on the services provided by investment bankers in the sale of bonds and equities. The investment banker also gives advice on dividend policies and on business financing practices. In addition, the various attributes of common stock, retained earnings, and bonds are identified and studied.

# 15

# Corporate Financing through Investment Bankers

While small business concerns usually must depend on their commercial bankers for financial advice and services, large corporations have, in addition, the assistance of investment banking firms. A corporation that has not previously financed in the capital market may approach (or be approached by) a representative of an investment banking house with a proposal to underwrite a new security issue. Among the proposals commonly presented are those for funding the short-term debt, refunding outstanding issues of long-term bonds with other issues, raising new capital with stock or bond issues, and financing combinations or mergers of two or more corporations. Large investment houses are able to assist corporations in working out these and other plans for raising new funds and revising their financial structures.

When raising funds in the capital market, a business corporation may sell either stocks (equities) or bonds (debts). In either case, it has two options—to dispose of the issue through a public offering or by direct placement. The corporation may negotiate with an insurance company or another institutional investor for the private placement of a long-term loan or bond issue. When two or more lenders participate in a capital loan or in buying a bond issue, the promissory notes or bonds seldom reappear in the capital market; but, when stocks or bonds are sold through investment bankers in the capital market, they may change ownership many times before their retirement.[1] The roles of investment

---

[1] An offering of two or more types of securities may be placed in one package. For illustration, in April 1970 the American Telephone and Telegraph Company offered its shareholders approximately $1.57 billion principal amount of 30-year, 8¾ debentures, accompanied by warrants to purchase 31.4 million shares of A.T.&T. stock at $52 a share. For each 35 shares held on the record date, owners could subscribe for $100 of

bankers and others who aid business firms in placing long-term obligations and equities, and of dealers and brokers who make a secondary market for the securities issued by business corporations, are considered in this chapter.

## Function of Investment Banking

The primary economic function of investment bankers is providing long-term capital funds for business enterprises and governments. They do this by purchasing issues of securities from business corporations and governments and selling the securities to institutional and individual investors. They assume the risk of being unable to sell the securities at a price that will provide a net return large enough to meet expenses and yield a profit. Investment bankers are middlemen between sellers and buyers of securities; but, because of the nature of the merchandise handled, investment bankers are expected to act as financial advisers not only to the business firms whose securities they originate and distribute but also to the investors to whom they sell the securities (which raises the question of whether both can be served impartially at the same time).

When investment bankers assist in raising new capital for a business corporation, they advise the corporation as to the type and form of securities that should be offered: if a stock offering is to be made; whether preferred or common stock should be issued; and, if bonds are to be issued, whether they should be convertible or nonconvertible. Because the methods used to raise capital funds may be varied and because market conditions are subject to change, the advice of investment bankers will depend not only on the requirements of the corporation and its capital structure but also on the prevailing conditions in the capital market. In some cases, a public offering may be preferred over private placement; in others, private placement with a small number of institutional investors may be advisable. Under other circumstances, an offering may be made to old stockholders or an entire issue may be sold to the highest bidder.

While investment bankers are primarily interested in purchasing and selling entire issues of new securities, they also contract with corporations to assist in selling new issues of stock or convertible bonds, which are offered first to old stockholders through subscription rights. Under a contract called a standby agreement, investment bankers help corporations by buying the portion of the issue for which old shareholders have not subscribed. (See Chapter 16.)

**Best Effort Basis.** Investment bankers may contract with corporations

---

debentures at par value. Each $100 of debentures carried warrants to purchase two shares at the exercise price between November 15, 1970 and May 15, 1975. This $3 billion plus offering represented the largest financing ever undertaken by any private business concern. (*Wall Street Journal*, April 14, 1970, p. 3.)

to sell new issues on a "best effort" basis. Under this arrangement, an investment banker acts as an agent for the business corporation and receives a commission on sales. He does not take title to the securities, that is, he signs no underwriting or purchasing agreement. Because of the smaller risk, the commission is smaller than the underwriter's gross spread between the purchase and sale prices. Because of his established clientele, an investment banker can usually distribute securities more effectively than the issuing corporation.

The best effort basis is used by two types of corporations; namely, the very strongest financially, or the weakest. The strongest firms' securities are so well established in the financial markets there is no need to pay an underwriting commission. At the other end of the spectrum, the weakest firms either can find no investment banking organization willing to underwrite their issues, or else the cost is deemed excessive. Therefore, the investment bankers in either case are instructed to do the best that they can. In any event the risk of not being able to attract the funds is placed on the issuing firm, and not the investment banking firms. In general, such issues usually state that if a minimum amount of capital is not raised all payments by those who have subscribed for the securities will be returned to the prospective purchaser.

***Secondary Offerings.*** At times the members of a family or a few owners of a business seek the assistance of investment bankers to market their stock. Thus, the purpose of the sale of these securities is to distribute already outstanding stock to the general public. The reason the investment bankers' services are employed is to ensure the success of the offering. The relatively large number of insider shares otherwise might depress the price of the stock, if the current owners attempted to sell them in the open market. To avoid this outcome frequently the insiders combine their shares to be sold, and use the investment bankers in the same manner as the firm would use them for a new issue of stock.[2] From the corporation's standpoint, wider ownership of stock is valuable because it may facilitate raising new equity capital in the future and perhaps stimulate investors' interest in the firm's products.[3]

***Advisory Capacity.*** Investment bankers must consider the interests of both buyers (investors) and issuers (corporations) of securities. In order to safeguard the interests of the former, the investment banker must supply information as to conditions in the industry as well as the characteristics of the securities offered. Apparently, the interests of issuers have been represented more adequately than those of the thousands of widely

---

[2] See Albert J. Fredman and James E. Wert, "An Analysis of Secondary Distributions," *Financial Analysts Journal* (November–December 1968), pp. 165–68.

[3] Sometimes a company's stock may be combined with a secondary offering. For illustration, on November 9, 1973, Avery Products Corp. had a negotiated stock offering of 600,000 common shares, 100,000 of which were from selling stockholders. ("Financing Record," *Institutional Investor*, vol. 8, no. 1 [January 1974], p. 44)

scattered investors because the federal and state governments have found it necessary to make provisions for regulation of new security issues in order to protect investors. Investment banking houses, realizing that their futures as "merchants of securities" depend on having satisfied investors as clients, negotiate with corporations for provisions in bond issues as to interest rates, sinking funds, redemption and call prices, maturities, and other features that would have investor appeal. For example, when a preferred stock issue is to be offered, the negotiations pertain to the dividend rate, redemption or call price, conversion feature, and, possibly, sinking-fund provisions.[4]

## Origination of the Issue

Investment bankers are sometimes classified according to the nature of their merchandising business such as originators of issues, underwriters, and retailers. While no investment house necessarily limits itself to only one of the above phases of the business, there are a few investment houses that originate and participate in underwriting new securities, and do practically no retail selling. Such investment houses act as managers of underwriting syndicates and also as dealers in placing large blocks of securities with other dealers, retailers, and large institutional investors. A few such houses may also have sales representatives who sell some securities at retail, but this is usually not a significant phase of their overall business.

Many investment houses in the underwriting-retailing group are primarily interested in selling securities, but they also participate in underwriting activities and may act as originators of new security issues. On occasion they may head purchasing syndicates that acquire issues; but for the most part, they obtain the merchandise they sell by participating in purchasing or selling syndicates originated and managed by larger houses.

The largest group of investment bankers are primarily retailers of securities. Because their financial resources are usually limited and their staffs small, they are unable to assume the risks of originating or participating in underwriting new issues and acquire most of their merchandise (at a discount from the offering price) from other houses that are members of purchasing syndicates or selling groups.

Most managers of firms that finance with security issues have estab-

---

[4] The services that investment bankers offer investors must meet high professional standards because so many of the investors are insurance companies, pension funds, banks, educational foundations, religious and charitable associations, and other institutional investors, as well as individuals. The major investment houses offer investment advisory and portfolio management services, including continuous review of investments, conferences with portfolio managers, collection of dividends and interest, and safekeeping services. The staff of a large investment firm will include lawyers, accountants, economists, and research specialists.

lished contracts with originating houses; therefore, a proposal for a new issue may come from either the investment house or the corporation. Investment houses keep close watch on the capital needs of their customer corporations and may anticipate their requirements and help to crystallize corporate management's plans for issuing securities.

There is a tendency for investment banking firms to become specialists in originating issues in certain fields, such as transportation, public utilities, petroleum, aviation, rubber, and so on. This development is based in part on the fact that, once a house has successfully underwritten an issue of a corporation, it often becomes its permanent investment banker. After having acquired the techniques and skills essential for handling an issue in a certain industry, the banker's services may be sought by or offered to others in the same industry. Other investment houses may solicit the services of such an investment banker to originate an issue; to manage the underwriting syndicate, either alone or with a second house; or to be a member of the underwriting or selling syndicate. Once a banking house has established a reputation in a certain field, it may have established a clientele not only among business corporations in this field but also among investors interested in that type of securities (which would facilitate retail sales of new securities).

**Negotiated Issues.** The oldest and most common method whereby investment bankers obtain new issues is by direct negotiation with financial managers of firms. When an issue is negotiated, the financial officers of the corporation meet with the investment banker with whom the firm has done business previously to discuss the characteristics of the tentative issue (nature, terms, market or placement, timing, and so on). If the prospects seem to be favorable, the necessary preparations will be made, including the prospectus, trust indenture, financial statements, and other documents necessary for registration with the Securities and Exchange Commission.

If an agreement can be reached as to terms of sale, a detailed formal purchase contract will be signed. The engraving of securities will be arranged for by the investment banker. The corporation is responsible for contracting for the services of a trustee, but the trustee is usually selected at the suggestion of the investment banker. The purchase agreement sets forth the plan, time, and method of payment for the securities, along with provisions for delivery of the securities.

Several plans for financing often are considered, and conditions in the capital market will affect both the details of the plan selected and the actual timing of the issue. While market conditions may be unsatisfactory for a short-term issue, they may be favorable for a long-term issue. At any particular time, there is a best plan for financing a specific company's capital needs; however, there is no specific plan that is best for financing any company's needs at all times.

Since the passage of the Securities Act of 1933, most purchase agreements have contained a "market-out" clause that allows the purchase agreement to be terminated by the underwriter or purchasing syndicate prior to the offering of securities if certain unfavorable conditions develop. These conditions may be due to a change either in the company's affairs, such as legal proceedings against the company by stockholders, or in general market conditions, such as the outbreak of hostilities. Fortunately, the market-out clause is seldom used, but it usually appears in purchase agreements when securities are registered with the SEC because much can happen during the required 20-day minimum waiting period.

In the last stage of negotiation, the corporation and the investment banker will agree upon the offering price (the price at which the securities are to be offered to the general public) and the price paid to the corporation by investment bankers. The difference between the two prices is the "gross spread." The offering price must be selected to meet anticipated market conditions, and it will be influenced by market prices of the corporation's outstanding securities and of similar securities of other corporations in the same industry, as well as by general market conditions. The gross spread is the underwriter's compensation, but the underwriter may also receive cash or securities as compensation for expenses incurred. When the issuer is a new corporation, an allotment of common stock is often made to the underwriter.

**Competitive Bidding.** The high quality of the securities of some corporations makes it possible to sell them at public auction instead of through investment houses after negotiation. This method has been used for many years in selling state and municipal issues, railroad-equipment obligations, and—in some states—certain securities of gas and electric companies. In 1941, the Securities and Exchange Commission adopted Rule U–50, which, with certain exceptions, requires that securities of corporations subject to the Public Utility Holding Company Act of 1935 be sold by competitive bidding.[5] In 1944, the Interstate Commerce Commission took a somewhat similar position in regard to the sale of railroad debt issues.[6]

---

[5] Competitive bidding in accordance with the provisions of Rule U–50 became effective on May 7, 1941. The commission retained the right to grant exemptions by order where it appears that competitive bidding is not necessary or appropriate to carry out the provisions of the Public Utility Holding Company Act. For a summary statement of financing pursuant to Rule U–50, see Securities and Exchange Commission, *19th Annual Report for the Fiscal Year Ended June 30, 1953* (Washington, D.C.: U.S. Government Printing Office, 1954), pp. 79–80.

[6] The Interstate Commerce Commission has regulatory authority over the issuance of securities by the railroads and can withhold approval if its policies are not followed. See Interstate Commerce Commission, *Ex Parte 158*, In the Matter of Competitive Bidding in the Sale of Securities Issued Under section 20a of the Interstate Commerce Act, 257 I.C.C. 129. An exception to competitive bidding was granted the Atchison, Topeka and Santa Fe Railroad in 1970 for a $37-million issue of 8¾ percent equipment-trust certificates. "The offering, which sold out soon after reaching the market, represented the first negotiated sale of certificates by a U.S. railroad," a spokesman said. The company was granted an exemption from the competitive-bidding proce-

Competitive bidding may be used by other companies even though there are no legal or regulatory requirements. For example, on August 18, 1954, the American Telephone and Telegraph Company announced it would sell $250 million of new bonds at competitive bidding on September 21, 1954. The registration statement covering the issue was filed with the Securities and Exchange Commission on September 1. Thus, the selling date conformed to the effective date of the registration statement; that is, at the expiration of the 20-day waiting period.

When corporations sell securities by competitive bidding there is always the possibility that there will be no bids or that the bids will be so low as to make the costs of financing prohibitive. However, to date, experiences with competitive bidding have been satisfactory, and those corporations that have been able to dispose of securities in this way generally have attracted bids that have reduced their costs of financing.

When securities are to be sold by competitive bidding, management usually specifies the time of the offering in its "red herring" or preliminary prospectus distributed among investment bankers, insurance companies, pension funds, and other prospective bidders.

In the published invitation for bids, the time, place, and other conditions are indicated. Usually, investment bankers withhold bids until the deadline in order to set their bid prices in accordance with the latest prevailing market prices. At closing time, investment bankers exchange information about their bid prices and those on Wall Street may know who the successful bidder is even before the vendor can open the bids, determine the highest bidder, and make the announcement.[7] The successful bidder may even sell the issue at retail on an "if-and-when-acquired basis" before the purchase has been confirmed. Competitive bidding has been effective in reducing underwriting margins and other costs and has been a factor in corporations obtaining better prices for their securities. At the same time, competitive bidding has provided corporations that negotiate the sales of their securities with "bench marks" for comparative purposes.

From the viewpoint of investment bankers, the development of competitive bidding has tended to weaken the relationships between investment houses and corporations that had been built up over years of direct negotiation for security issues. On the other hand, competitive bidding has permitted other investment houses to participate in the underwriting of the securities of companies that formerly dealt exclusively with particular investment banking firms. However, even when an issue is to be sold through competitive bidding, the issuer customarily uses the advisory services of an investment banking firm during the preoffering

---

dure because its issue was substantially larger than most similar issues. (*Wall Street Journal*, March 26, 1970, p. 21.)

[7] In rare instances identical bids may be submitted. If that occurs, the underwriting groups usually are asked to submit new bids.

stage, and this investment house often is the successful bidder for the issue.

Regardless of the method used to raise capital funds, business corporations may utilize the services of investment bankers in preparing bond indentures, selecting corporate trustees, making charter amendments in the case of stock issues, obtaining approval of the appropriate state regulatory agencies when needed, preparing applications for listing securities on exchanges, and preparing registration statements and other documents required by the Securities and Exchange Commission and state agencies.

## Distribution of the Issue

In the preceding section, emphasis was on the relationships between issuers and investment banking firms; in this section, emphasis is on the relationship among investment houses in processing an issue.[8] This interrelationship necessitates agreements between the issuer of the securities and the members of the underwriting or purchasing group, among underwriters or purchasers, and between members of the purchasing or underwriting syndicate and other investment houses participating in the selling group.

**Underwriting the Issue.** In investment banking, underwriting refers to the guarantee by investment bankers to a business firm of a definite sum of money on a specified date in return for issues of bonds or stock. Because such issues are usually for large amounts, two or more investment banking houses form underwriting syndicates to handle most bond or stock issues. The number of participants in such a syndicate varies with the size of the issue, the resources of the investment houses, the degree of risk of the issue, and the condition of the market wherein the securities are to be sold at retail. Typically, the number of participants is large when a corporation is financing for the first time. Because many issues have to be carried several days before distribution, investment houses obtain short-term loans from commercial banks.

Let us assume that the negotiation between the corporation and an investment banker (called the originating house) has reached the stage where the corporation is ready to sign the mutually agreed upon purchase agreement. Now, the investment houses that have been invited to join in the financing will be asked to participate by signing the purchase agreement. This agreement is usually drawn so that each member of the syndicate participates separately in the purchase of the issue. If an investment house agrees to take $1 million of bonds in an issue of $10 million, its liability to the issuer is limited to that figure. In other words, it may

---

[8] In October 1953, Harold R. Medina, U.S. Circuit Court Judge for the Southern District of New York, dismissed civil charges brought by the government against 17 investment banking houses. It had been charged that "defendants entered into a combination, conspiracy and agreement to restrain and monopolize the securities business of the United States and that such business was thereby unreasonably restrained and in part monopolized." *United States* v. *Morgan*, 118 F. Supp. 621 (S.D.N.Y. 1953).

not be held by the issuer for the purchase of the remaining $9 million of bonds.

When investment bankers contract among themselves for handling an issue, their liability may be limited or unlimited. If the limited form of contract is used, an investment house meets its obligation when it sells its portion of the issue; but, if the unlimited form of contract is used, each house is expected to assume its pro rata responsibility for the unsold balance at the end of the syndicate period. The limited or divided account is most popular among investment houses that have a strong sales organization; but, if there is an excellent market for the securities, it is a matter of indifference whether the divided or undivided account form of contract is used. When serial bonds are issued, there may be a strong demand for maturities at both ends of the issue with little demand for the middle maturities. Thus, a participant could discharge his obligation to the syndicate by selling the popular securities. This difficulty may be overcome either by using the undivided account system or prorating the bonds of each maturity among the investment houses.

## Role of the Syndicate Manager

Much of the success of a security issue depends on how well the syndicate manager performs his functions. The syndicate manager advises participants as to the affairs and structure of the corporation; the size, yield, and terms of the issue; and the class of buyer to whom the issue will appeal. In addition, he has the major responsibility for selection of the time of offering the securities. When there is direct negotiation for a corporate issue, the originating house customarily acts as syndicate manager, but the manager may be a larger investment house that has had more experience in obtaining participation of other houses. After the purchasing contract has been signed, underwriters assume all of the risks arising from inability to resell the securities to investors and possible losses arising from a decline in the securities market during the underwriting period; hence, there is a need for organizing a group of proven firms to assure rapid distribution.

After the organization of the purchasing or underwriting syndicate, the duties of the syndicate manager depend on the nature of the issue; they are fairly simple when he is handling corporate issues that are to be sold by competitive bidding, and they are more difficult when he is managing negotiated issues. If the issue is to be sold by competitive bidding, the participating houses will designate one of their number as syndicate manager to work out the price to be offered. Usually, the investment house so designated is one whose previous experience justifies its selection. Many such groups may be formed for competitive bidding, and, unless the successful bidder has appraised the market accurately, severe losses may be incurred. Because investment houses want to be associated with the successful group, they are inclined to follow the leadership of those with whom they have had successful experiences in the past. A new underwriting group is formed for each security issue; therefore, an individual house may be associated with different investment houses for each new issue. Investment managers who are specialists in handling issues in certain fields tend to have an advantage over others in bidding on issues in their respective fields.

The members of the purchasing syndicate expect the syndicate manager to provide them with papers and documents pertaining to the issue; see that the issue is properly qualified under the laws of different states, registered with the Securities and Exchange Commission if necessary, or approved by the Interstate Commerce Commission if required; prepare and supply sales material that will be helpful in selling the securities, give opinions as to the eligibility of the issue as legal investments for life insurance companies, pension funds, trust funds, and savings banks, and provide statistical comparisons to other securities in the market; attend meetings and assume leadership in fixing the bid price paid the issuer and the offering price to the general public; arrange settlement with the issuer, accept delivery of the securities, and arrange for their distribution among underwriters and others; handle repurchase of securities that reappear on the market during the distribution period; and make a final accounting to members and initiate plans for the sale of securities still on hand. Customarily, the manager is reimbursed for expenses out of the syndicate earnings; in addition, he may receive a management fee.

When securities must be registered with the Securities and Exchange Commission, the underwriters must depend on the business corporation to see that certain provisions of the law and regulations of the commission are met. Therefore, the syndicate manager requires the corporation in the covenants to do certain things, such as prepare and file a registration statement and a prospectus that meet the requirements of the law and the regulations of the commission; provide properly certified copies of the corporation's most recent financial statements; assert that there has been no adverse change in the corporation's affairs since the date of the last balance sheet; use the net proceeds of the issue for the purpose stated in the registration statement; and attest that there are no pending lawsuits against the corporation except as specifically stated. The corporation also agrees to indemnify the underwriters against any liabilities (under provision of the Securities Act of 1933) because of any untrue, misleading, or incomplete statements in registration statements or in the prospectus.

Actually, the essential documents used in financing are drawn up prior to signing the underwriting contract, and the corporation will have worked closely with the syndicate manager or originating house in their preparation. In addition, the investment bankers will have been advised as to the contents of the bond indenture, the selection of a corporate trustee, the charter amendments in case of a stock issue, the listing application in case of registration on a securities exchange, and other matters.

At any particular time, a typical originating investment banking firm will have several issues in different stages of processing, and the ideal situation is one wherein a steady stream of issues is going through investment banking channels into the hands of investors. The ultimate profitability of many investment banking firms is more dependent upon the number of issues they either manage or underwrite than the number of securities actually sold to the investors.

**Selling the Security Issue.** The purchasing syndicate may offer other investment houses an opportunity to participate in selling the issue. In this way the syndicate manager, as agent for the purchasing syndicate, may mitigate the disappointment of other houses that were unsuccessful in obtaining membership in the underwriting syndicate (at competitive bidding or otherwise). Among the "outsiders" there may be houses with good distributing facilities and with customers interested in the issue.

The syndicate manager may offer selected dealers a specified amount of securities, subject to acceptance within a specified time, or he may offer them the privilege of subscribing for a part of the issue. If a dealer accepts a specific allotment, he makes a definite commitment; but, if he merely subscribes for a part of the issue, the transaction is subject to rejection or confirmation, in whole or in part, at the discretion of the manager of the underwriting syndicate or his representative.

The members of the underwriting syndicate can usually sell small corporate issues without help from other dealers; but selling groups are usually organized for large corporation issues. The selling-group agreement covers the terms of public offerings, the dealers' commission (a portion of the gross spread between the price to the issuer and the offering price), and the provisions for terminating the selling group. A corporation is vitally interested in the effectiveness of the distribution method used by the investment managers. If an investment house is successful in distributing a corporation's securities among many investors, it will facilitate public financing in the future.

## Private Placement

Private placement of security issues means the purchase and retention of the securities (they may never be sold publicly) by one, two, or a small group of investors. One reason for private placement is to avoid the expenses of the middleman, the investment banker. Also, the costs entailed in registering securities with the SEC can be avoided by forgoing a public offering. In making plans for the private placement of an issue, corporate managements may contact large institutional investors, such as life insurance companies and private pension funds, and negotiate the terms and conditions for a potential issue of securities. The terms may be tailored to meet the needs of both parties—type of issue, security provided, sinking-fund provisions, dividend payments, and others, including restrictions on the corporation.

By paying a small commitment fee, a corporation may arrange in advance for future capital needs by obtaining an advance commitment from an insurance company or other lender. The contract typically permits the corporation to cancel all or part of the issue if the need for funds does not materialize. This arrangement would permit the firm to use internally generated funds for the proposed financing, but still have the assurance of another source if the funds did not materialize as forecasted.

An investment banker usually assists in working out the details of the offering and in approaching prospective buyers.[9] When negotiations are completed successfully, the securities are delivered to the purchasers and the corporation receives cash. After placement of securities, clauses in the contract may permit the interest rate and maturity to be renegotiated to conform to changes in the needs of the issuer or the lender. Generally, a bond issue is more suitable for private placement than a stock issue.

The increase in the volume of direct placements since 1933 has been caused by the ability of insurance companies and other institutional investors to absorb entire issues. In addition, the widespread retention of earnings by corporations has made it more difficult for institutional investors to find suitable equity investments.[10] In negotiating directly with corporations, institutional investors have many advantages over investment bankers. In their negotiations, institutional investors may emphasize the facts that, in private placement, the corporation saves the initial expense effort incidental to registering the issue with the SEC; principal officers and directors of the issuing corporation avoid the personal liability for incomplete, misleading, or untrue statements assumed in filing registration statements with the SEC; the corporation avoids the minimum 20-day waiting period normally required before the registration statement becomes effective; management avoids an underwriting agreement and the market-out clause therein; and the corporation avoids the underwriting fees and other expenses associated with financing through investment bankers. Thus, the chief advantages of this method of financing are the speed with which transactions may be completed, the savings in costs compared with public offerings, and the avoidance of disclosures concerning financial affairs required when other methods are used.

Investment bankers may be able to assist business firms in obtaining capital funds under favorable terms through private placement because they are aware of the types of securities in which institutional investors

---

[9] The fee of the investment banking firm would not be so large as in the case of an underwritten public offering. The investment banking firm acts as an agent in the transaction.

[10] In the late 1960s, however, some institutional investors began to acquire debt issues having features that permitted them ultimately to receive an equity position in the borrowing concern. This may be accomplished by the use of convertible bonds, bonds with warrants, or dual offerings of both bonds and stock.

are interested. To issuers, a disadvantage of private placements is that the securities as placed are not as a rule resold, thereby not affording the firm the same investor recognition as would be the case with public offerings. This loss of recognition possibly could be a deterrent to the ready acceptance of future public offerings.

In addition, in many cases public issues sell at lower yields than comparable issues that are privately placed. Therefore, issuers must weigh the savings in financing costs through private placement against the possible higher interest rates that may be incurred.

Figure 15–1 shows that there are wider yearly swings in volume of publicly placed bonds than for privately placed obligations. This is probably accounted for by the availability of funds for lending by institutional investors (insurance companies, pension funds and others) since a large percentage of their incremental yearly cash inflows may be determined by contractual agreements. Thus when these lenders are committed fully, the prospective borrowers are compelled either to postpone the anticipated financing, or else resort to a public offering. As a consequence, the greater variation in the amount of publicly placed bonds can be explained by both demand and supply factors.

## Regulation of New Security Issues

When business corporations obtain capital funds from investors, they must abide by the regulations of securities markets by governmental agencies. All states except Nevada regulate some aspects of security offerings within their boundaries; but, since 1933, the most extensive coverage has been by the federal government. In 1934, the Securities and Exchange Commission was created to assume responsibility for administering the Securities Act of 1933 and the Securities Exchange Act of 1934.

*Disclosure Principle.* The Securities Act of 1933, as amended, is based on the premise that full, fair, and accurate disclosure of the character of securities offered publicly for sale in interstate commerce or through the mail will lessen fraud in the sale of securities. In five subsequent acts, Congress followed this same principle in legislating on various aspects of the securities market.[11] The procedure required in the Securities Act of 1933 includes filing a registration statement with the Securities and Exchange Commission and securing its approval of the prospectus that is to be made available to the public. The SEC either permits or refuses to permit the registration statement to become effective,[12] however, it does

---

[11] These acts include: Securities Exchange Act of 1934, Public Utility Holding Company Act of 1935, Trust Indenture Act of 1939, Investment Company Act of 1940, and Investment Advisers Act of 1940. All of the regulatory acts have been amended at various times.

[12] The number of registration statements declared effective in 1976 was 2,813, for $88 billion. Securities and Exchange Commission, *42nd Annual Report, for the Fiscal Year Ended June 30, 1976* (Washington, D.C.: U.S. Government Printing Office. 1977), p. 198.

**FIGURE 15-1**
Corporate Security Issues—Gross Proceeds by Type of Issue (annually)

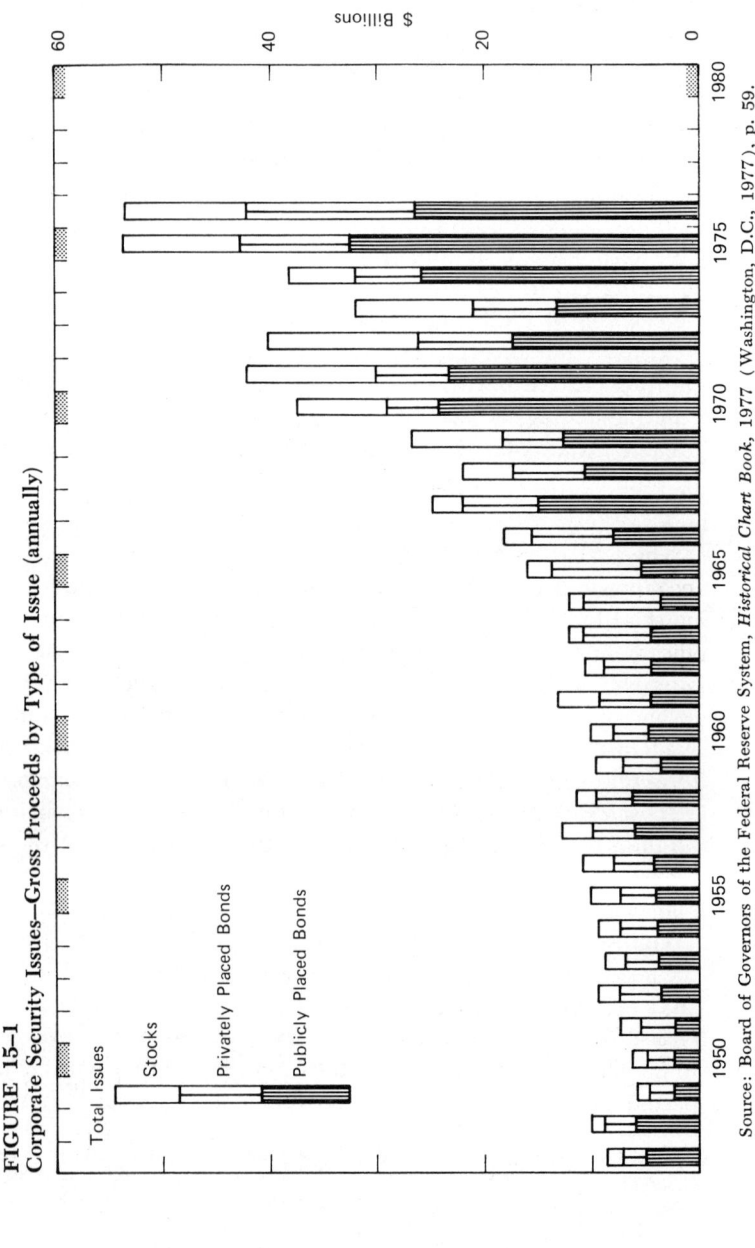

Source: Board of Governors of the Federal Reserve System, *Historical Chart Book, 1977* (Washington, D.C., 1977), p. 59.

not pass on the quality of the securities, and any representation to the contrary is a criminal offense (which is something for sellers of registered securities to remember).[13] (See Figure 15–2.)

The registrant (corporation) pays the SEC a fee of one cent for each $500 of the proposed issue. The effective date is 20 days after the filing date, unless shortened by the commission. If the statement must be amended, the waiting period starts from the date of filing the amendment. Amendments may be required to meet objections raised by the SEC in a "letter of comment." If the registration is already in effect, the commission may issue a stop order suspending the effectiveness of the registration statement. In this case the issue must be withdrawn or withheld until the registration statement and prospectus meet the standards set by the SEC.

Although the 1954 amendment gave investment bankers and business corporations more freedom in making offers to sell their securities during the 20-day waiting period, they may not be bought or sold by a "binding contract" until registration is effective. Furthermore, a complete statutory prospectus must be given each buyer. Often, a preliminary prospectus is filed with the registration statement in order to get information into the hands of investors before the actual offering date.

The Securities Act of 1933 makes the sponsors of registered securities accountable for misrepresentations, omissions, and untrue statements of material facts. Persons who may be held accountable include directors, officers, and partners of the issuer; underwriters; accountants, engineers, appraisers, and other professional persons who have been named in preparation or certification of any part of the registration statement (how much professional fees have increased as a result of this contingent liability is not known); and all others who sign the registration statement. Civil or criminal liabilities may also arise because of illegal acts such as selling a security before the registration becomes effective, engaging in any fraudulent scheme, and using the mails to defraud (a provision of the federal law before the passage of the Securities Act of 1933).[14]

The Securities Act of 1933 provides for the exemption from registra-

---

[13] Each prospectus for registered securities customarily contains in large print on the first page, "These securities have not been approved or disapproved by the Securities and Exchange Commission nor has the Commission passed upon the accuracy or adequacy of this prospectus. Any *representation* to the contrary is a criminal offense."

[14] The Securities and Exchange Commission has developed criminal cases in fiscal year 1976 as follows:

| Cases Referred to Justice Dept. | Indictments | Defendants Indicted | Convictions |
|---|---|---|---|
| 116 | 23 | 118 | 97 |

SOURCE: Securities and Exchange Commission, *38th Annual Report, for the Fiscal Year Ended June 30, 1976* (Washington, D.C.: U.S. Government Printing Office, 1977), p. 207.

FIGURE 15-2

---

**PROSPECTUS**

3,000,000 Shares

# Tucson Gas & Electric Company

### Common Stock
($2.50 Par Value)

---

THESE SECURITIES HAVE NOT BEEN APPROVED OR DISAPPROVED BY THE SECURITIES AND EXCHANGE COMMISSION NOR HAS THE COMMISSION PASSED UPON THE ACCURACY OR ADEQUACY OF THIS PROSPECTUS. ANY REPRESENTATION TO THE CONTRARY IS A CRIMINAL OFFENSE.

|  | Price to Public | Underwriting Discount(1) | Proceeds to Company(2) |
|---|---|---|---|
| Per Share | $14.625 | $.48 | $14.145 |
| Total | $43,875,000 | $1,440,000 | $42,435,000 |

(1) The Company has agreed to indemnify the several Underwriters against certain liabilities, including liabilities under the Securities Act of 1933.

(2) Before deducting expenses payable by the Company estimated at $110,000.

---

The shares of Common Stock are offered by the several Underwriters when, as and if issued by the Company and accepted by the Underwriters and subject to their right to reject orders in whole or in part. It is expected that the certificates for the shares will be ready for delivery on or about November 16, 1976.

---

### Merrill Lynch, Pierce, Fenner & Smith
Incorporated

### Blyth Eastman Dillon & Co.
Incorporated

---

The date of this Prospectus is November 9, 1976

Reproduced with permission of Tucson Gas & Electric Company.

---

tion of certain types of issues. From the viewpoint of business finance, the most important of these issues are those that are privately offered and railroad securities, which, like all securities issued by common carriers, are subject to regulation by the Interstate Commerce Commission.

Among other issues exempt from registration are (1) direct and guaranteed obligations of the U.S. government, any state or territory thereof, and political subdivisions of states and territories; (2) national and state chartered banks; (3) nonprofit organizations; (4) short-term commercial paper; (5) insurance policies and contracts; and (6) receivers' and trustees' certificates.

## Regulation of Outstanding Security Issues

Few investors are interested in holding securities indefinitely; therefore, they find attractive corporate issues having a secondary market. Secondary markets for securities include organized exchanges and over-the-counter markets.[15] A securities exchange is an unincorporated association or incorporated company wherein brokers and dealers trade in securities for others and for themselves. Since 1934, securities exchanges whose business is predominantly interstate, called national securities exchanges, have been under the general supervision of the Securities and Exchange Commission. At mid-year 1976, 11 exchanges were registered with the SEC, but the Detroit Exchange was in the process of de-registering. It ceased operations on June 30, 1976.

The largest and most important national securities exchange is the New York Stock Exchange, where stocks and bonds of national and international importance are bought and sold. The ability of business corporations to raise capital funds through the sale of bonds or stock is enhanced if the owners can resell them to others. While not equally important to all investors, the quality of marketability adds to the investment status of securities. For this reason, large investment banking firms maintain trading departments and memberships on the leading securities exchanges.

As a distributor of securities, an investment banking firm also handles sales of large blocks of securities that cannot be sold on securities exchanges in the regular way. Such shares are usually sold after the close of trading on an exchange on a nonauction basis at a price that is fixed at or near the prevailing one when the exchange closed for the day. Under the terms of the Securities Act, a "secondary offering" must be registered with the SEC if the seller has a controlling interest in the business firm. An investment banking firm's trading department also facilitates the purchase and sale of stocks and bonds not listed on securities exchanges.

---

[15] In addition to the exchange markets for listed securities and the over-the-counter markets for unlisted securities, there is an expanding "third market" where listed stocks can be bought over-the-counter. A "fourth" market also has developed, which consists of direct trading among institutional investors, such as charitable foundations, mutual funds, and trust departments of banks. The principal motive in direct trading is to avoid commissions that institutional investors would pay if they dealt through brokers.

The securities of most of the business corporations in the United States are bought and sold in the over-the-counter market, but those of major business corporations are listed on national securities exchanges. A corporation may register a security on a national exchange by filing an application for registration with the exchange and giving a copy of the application to the SEC. This application contains comprehensive information about the issuer, and, if the corporation's application for listing is approved, the corporation is required to keep this information up-to-date by filing periodic reports. The information required for listing is the same as that required for registration of a new security issue; therefore, investors in stocks and bonds who limit their purchases to those listed on a national exchange have access to more complete information than may be true for other investors.

The purpose of the Securities Exchange Act of 1934 is to ensure fairness and honesty in securities transactions on the organized exchanges and in the over-the-counter markets. The act forbids trading in a security on a national exchange unless it is registered (exclusive of federal government and other exempt securities that include corporate issues that were previously admitted to unlisted trading privileges because of a request made by a member of an exchange and not by the corporation). In 1910, the New York Stock Exchange adopted a rule that abolished unlisted trading. The Securities Exchange Act of 1934 provides for continuance of unlisted trading privileges for those issues admitted prior to March 1, 1934; an amendment of the law in May 1936 provided for unlisted trading privileges for securities already listed on other national exchanges and for further extension of unlisted trading privileges to unlisted securities (provided information substantially equivalent to that required for listing on a national exchange is available).[16]

An application for listing is usually refused if the anticipated trading in the issue is small. To be accepted for listing on the New York Stock Exchange, annual earnings of a company are expected to be at least $2.5 million before income taxes; pretax earnings averaging $2.0 million in the preceding two years; an aggregate market value of publicly held shares should be equal to $16 million; the number of common stockholders should be at least 2,000, after substantially discounting odd lots (less than 100 shares), and they should hold 1 million shares exclusive of centralized or family holdings; and there should be a broad national interest in the security so that an adequate auction market in the security can be expected. Standards for listing on other exchanges are less stringent; in

---

[16] A security admitted to trading at the request of a member of the exchange as opposed to the issuer is said to be "admitted to unlisted trading privileges." Such privileges must have the approval of the SEC. A security listed and registered on one exchange may trade unlisted on another exchange. This latter policy of the SEC may have the effect of somewhat decentralizing trading by encouraging trading on a second exchange on the strength of full listing elsewhere.

many cases, these exchanges are used as seasoning markets prior to listing on the New York Stock Exchange.

Business corporations find listing desirable because of the advertising value derived from having securities traded on national exchanges. In addition, listing tends to result in a broad distribution of stock which prevents excessive concentration of ownership. Finally, stocks that are marketable tend to trade at better prices, and the issuer would tend to save on future financing costs. The "blue-sky" laws of most states waive their state registration requirement for securities listed on a national exchange; and, for corporate managers planning future financing, this is an important reason for listing securities.

Securities may be delisted on applications originated either by the securities exchange or the corporation that issued the securities. The chief reason for withdrawing or delisting a security is a decline in trading activity owing to a decrease in the volume of securities outstanding because of retirement or redemption of bonds and preferred stock and concentration of ownership of the securities in the hands of a few. Most commonly, bonds that are being retired, either by redemption or by conversion into other securities, are removed from listing simply by certifying their delisting with the Securities and Exchange Commission.

Although listing securities on a national exchange has advantages, a firm's management may not apply for listing because of failure to meet some of the tests noted above, the existence of current satisfactory trading on an unlisted basis or in the over-the-counter market, and the expenses associated with listing. Since 1965, some corporations have applied for listing because the information they objected to providing in order to have securities listed is now required of unlisted securities.

The costs incurred in listing securities on a national exchange include a registration fee, expenses of preparing forms that must be submitted to the securities exchange and the Securities and Exchange Commission, and payment of an annual fee if the issue is stock. If the issue is listed on the New York Stock Exchange, the corporation must also bear the expense of having a transfer agent and registrar in the Borough of Manhattan.

Most of the direct regulation of the securities markets has been left to the industry, which operates under its own rules and under the general supervision of the SEC. The managers of the various stock exchanges police their organizations, and the National Association of Securities Dealers does the same for the over-the-counter-market trading.

## Summary

Investment bankers are middlemen between issuers and investors; in this capacity, they are advisers of both issuers and investors. While some investment houses are primarily underwriters, others primarily retailers, and others participants in originating, purchasing, and selling syndicates, there is a considerable overlapping in their functions. Investment bankers customarily assist in financing business firms by advising the corporation on its financing problems and assisting it in solving them. The investment banking firm may purchase an issue from the corporation through negotiation or competitive bidding, make a standby commitment that involves purchasing any part of an issue not sold by the issuer, or agree to use its best effort to sell a new issue of securities. Competitive bidding is required for certain classes of securities and may be used in other cases when the quality of securities is high enough to warrant this method of selling. In some cases, entire issues may be placed privately, thereby bypassing the investment banker and avoiding the expense and delay incurred in registering the issue with the Securities and Exchange Commission.

Underwriting and distributing corporate securities calls for cooperation among investment houses and usually entails three distinct agreements: one between the issuer and members of the underwriting or purchase group, a second among the members of the underwriting syndicate, and a third between the purchasing or underwriting syndicate and the selling group.

Most new corporate issues are subject to registration by state or federal agencies. The Securities Act of 1933, as amended, requires full, fair, and accurate disclosure of the character of securities offered publicly for sale in interstate commerce or through the mail. The Securities Act of 1933 is implemented with the requirement that a registration statement and a prospectus be filed with the Securities and Exchange Commission. The commission either permits or refuses to permit the registration to become effective but does not pass on the quality of securities. The Securities Act of 1933 provides for exemption of certain transactions, including those privately placed and certain issues including those of railroads and domestic governments.

After the primary distribution of a security issue, the securities may be traded on one of the secondary markets—securities exchanges or over-the-counter markets. Of the national securities exchanges, the New York Stock Exchange is the most important. Listing the securities of a corporation on a stock exchange necessitates registering the issue, meeting the standards set by the exchange, and fulfilling the requirements of the Securities and Exchange Commission. These standards have to do with the size of the issue, the annual earnings and assets of the corporation, the number of stockholders, and the amount of trading interest in the security.

## 15 Corporate Financing through Investment Bankers

## QUESTIONS

1. "The machinery for distribution of new securities is complex, but it is fundamentally only merchandising on a broad scale." Explain.
2. How may investment houses be classified? Explain.
3. (a) How do investment bankers serve issuing corporations in an advisory capacity? (b) Why must the investment banker consider the wishes of investors?
4. Identify: (a) security issue, (b) investment house, (c) underwriting, (d) standby underwriting, and (e) best-effort commitment.
5. (a) How does a corporation tend to benefit from the sale of its securities by competitive bidding? (b) Does the sale of securities by competitive bidding deprive the issuing corporation of the advice of investment bankers? Explain.
6. Account for the use of private placements.
7. In handling a large corporate issue of bonds, what three types of contracts or agreements are involved? Why?
8. How has public financing been affected by regulations of the Securities and Exchange Commission?
9. Distinguish between primary and secondary markets for securities.
10. What are corporate management's reasons for (a) listing securities, (b) delisting securities, and (c) not listing securities?
11. Why is the size of the issue an important determinant of the gross spread of the underwriting group?
12. Why are many high-grade industrial bonds now placed privately with institutional buyers?
13. Do you feel that nonregulated corporations should be required to sell their securities by competitive bid, as is currently required of regulated firms?
14. Investment bankers price new securities relative to outstanding securities. Why does a spread exist between the yields of new and outstanding securities?
15. Do you believe that investors are benefited by price-support practices of underwriting syndicates?
16. In May 1969, the New York Stock Exchange member firm of Donaldson, Lufkin and Jenrette, Inc., notified the exchange's board of governors of its intention to issue its equity securities to the public, and it filed a registration statement covering a proposed offering of its common stock with the SEC. At the same time, it proposed changes in the constitution and rules of the exchange that would permit the firm to retain its membership. (Securities and Exchange Commission, *35th Annual Report, for the Fiscal Year Ended June 30, 1969* [Washington, D.C.: U.S. Government Printing Office, 1970], p. 9) Comment on why this was an important filing.
17. The Monongahela Power Company raised $20 million through a dual public offering of $15 million of 30-year 9¾ bonds and 50,000 shares of $100 par value preferred stock. The bonds were underwritten by a group led by Merrill Lynch, Pierce, Fenner, and Smith; the preferred stock, by a group

led by Merrill Lynch and Salomon Brothers and Hutzler (*Wall Street Journal*, May 14, 1970.) Why were two underwriting groups used?

## PROBLEMS

1. The Allied Manufacturing Company is issuing 200,000 new shares of its common stock through an underwriter. The stock will be sold at $45 to the existing stockholders. If 180,000 shares were sold, what would be the proceeds to the company if the issue were underwritten on a standby basis? What if the stock were issued with no underwriting agreement? (Note: Ignore commissions and fees.)

2. Selected data for a pending bond issue are provided below. The bond issue is for $5 million with a ten-year maturity. The investment banker states the bonds can be sold publicly with a 9-percent coupon and a $120,000 gross spread, and the company nets $4.88 million. Alternatively, the company can place a 9.5-percent note privately, with a $20,000 investment banking advisory fee. If the firm did not repay either loan arrangement before maturity, it would make annual interest payments, and it has an after-tax cost of capital of 10 percent (assume a 40-percent tax rate). Which financing should the firm choose?

3. The Tri-State Utility Company is issuing $50 million of 7-percent, 30-year bonds. The bid of the investment firm of O'Conner and Goldberg of 98.5 was accepted.
   a. Compute the proceeds to Tri-State.
   b. Compute the approximate effective yield to Tri-State for a $1,000 bond.
   c. What is the gross profit to the investment firm if the bonds are sold to the public to yield 7 percent?

## ADDITIONAL READINGS

Block, E. "Pricing a Corporate Bond Issue: A Look Behind the Scenes," in *Essays in Money and Credit*. New York: Federal Reserve Bank of New York (1964), pp. 72–76.

Cates, D. C. "Bank Capital Management: Investment Banker Selection," *The Bankers Magazine*, vol. 157, no. 1 (Winter 1974), pp. 11–12.

Cohan, A. B. "Yields on New Underwritten Corporate Bonds," *Journal of Finance*, vol. 17 (December 1962), pp. 585–605.

———. *Private Placements and Public Offerings: Market Shares Since 1935*. Chapel Hill: School of Business Administration, University of North Carolina, 1961.

Ederington, L. H. "Negotiated Versus Competitive Underwritings of Corporate Bonds," *Journal of Finance*, vol. 31 (March 1976), pp. 17–28.

Miller, G. R. "Long-Term Business Financing from the Underwriter's Point of View," *Journal of Finance*, vol. 16 (May 1961), pp. 280–90.

Nair, R. S. "Investment Banking: Judge Medina In Retrospect," *Financial Analysts Journal*, vol. 16 (July–August 1960), pp. 35–40.

Wyndham, R. "The Underwriters Have to Offer Even More," *Fortune*, vol. 87, no. 1 (January 1973), pp. 116 ff.

# 16

# Common Stock

*[handwritten: long-term financing — good to list on exchange — most popular form of financing]*

Owner's equity or proprietary capital consists of capital contributed by shareholders and earnings retained by a business. The distinction between the two is not always clear on a corporation's balance sheet because of stock dividends that have been paid, recapitalizations, reorganizations, and mergers. The word "stock," which appears frequently in business finance, has two connotations: to a corporation, it refers to capital acquired through the sale of shares to investors; to an investor, it refers to the actual certificates of ownership interest in a corporation. Different classes of both common and preferred stock, as well as various types of debt obligations, may be used because of their effects on the control, income, and assets of a corporation. The various aspects associated with common stock are dealt with in this chapter.

## Evidence of Ownership

The proprietary rights of owners are usually evidenced by written documents, which tend to become longer and more complicated as the number of owners increases. Because of the nature of proprietorships and partnerships, the instruments indicating the rights of proprietors and partners are less formal than those of stockholders of corporations. These instruments may include documents indicating title to real and personal property; in the case of a partnership, there is usually a written agreement covering each partner's rights, obligations, and privileges. Ownership in business trusts, joint stock companies, or corporations is usually evidenced by transferable certificates; and the units into which proprietary interests are divided are called shares. Thus, a stock certificate is written or printed evidence of ownership indicating that the holder whose name appears on the face is the lawful owner of a designated number of shares of capital stock. But the issuance of a stock certificate is not necessary to make one a stockholder of a corporation. Legally, one becomes a stockholder as soon as one's subscription has been accepted and the consideration has been paid (usually in cash but sometimes in exchange for other assets). A person who buys stock in the open market is entitled to vote or receive dividends thereon only after the shares have been transferred to his name on the books of the corporation.

**Stock Certificates.** Customarily, a stock certificate contains the following: the name of the issuing company and the state wherein it is incorporated; the amount of "par value" if par value stock,[1] or a statement that it is "no par value" stock; a statement that the stock is "fully paid and nonassessable"; the name of the owner; and the name of the officers and others authorized to sign for the company (such as president, treasurer or secretary, transfer agent, and registrar). The back of the certificate will contain provisions for transfer of title with spaces for dates, name of transferee, and signature of the owner. If the company has several classes of stock, the certificates of each class may summarize the rights and privileges pertaining to it, but these provisions are usually found in the articles of incorporation or bylaws of the corporation. Each share of stock within a class carries the same rights and privileges. Among those who have claims to the assets and earnings of a corporation, common stockholders are last in point of priority. Common stock represents the final equity in a corporation; that is, common stockholders have claims to whatever capital or income remains after all prior claims are satisfied.

Since certificates may be issued for any number of shares, an owner may have his total ownership in a corporation represented by a single certificate; but, if he acquired interest in the company at different times by additional purchases or by stock dividends, he may have several stock certificates.

**Ownership of Record.** The shares of stock of major companies are bought and sold on organized stock exchanges and in the over-the-counter market. The resulting turnover in ownership creates a continuing problem for management—namely, that of determining owners who are entitled to receive dividends (when declared by the board of directors) and to vote at annual and other meetings of stockholders. The details for handling this problem are usually covered in the bylaws of the corporation rather than left to the discretion of management.

---

[1] In 1964, the New York Stock Exchange announced that listed companies would no longer be required to print the par value of shares on their stock certificates except in states where required. This ruling makes it unnecessary to retire old stock certificates when there is a change in par value for companies chartered in New York, New Jersey, Delaware, and others.

When dividends are declared by the board of directors, they are payable on dates specified in the bylaws to those whose names appear on the books as owners on predetermined dates (usually a specified number of days prior to the dividend dates). This is the explanation for items such as the following on financial pages of newspapers: "Dividends Reported June 16" and in columnar arrangement below, "Company" as Transamerica Corp.; "period" as quarterly; "amount" as 16½ cents; "payable date" as 7–29–77. and "record date" as 7–6–77. This means that the board of directors of Transamerica Corp. has declared a quarterly dividend on its common stock, payable on July 29, 1977 to those whose names appear on its stock book as owners on July 6, 1977. Therefore, those who plan to buy or sell shares must remember that a stock listed on the New York Stock Exchange on which a dividend has been declared will be purchased or sold "ex dividend" (literally, without dividend) four full days before the date of record of ownership. This rule is applied because of the time required to deliver the stock and to record it in the name of the new owner in the stock ledger. This means that, during a period beginning four days before the record date and extending to the payment date, a buyer acquires the stock without the dividend that has been declared and the seller receives the dividend after it has been sold.

***Stock Transfer Procedure.*** The Uniform Commercial Code, which replaced the Uniform Stock Transfer Act and the Uniform Negotiable Instruments Act, applies uniform rules to all formal aspects of negotiation, transfer, and registration of all recognized types of investment securities, whether registered or bearer (see Article 8). Title may be transferred by delivery of the certificate endorsed by the owner (either in blank or to a specified person) or by delivery of the certificate and a separate written assignment, drawn either in blank or to a specified person and signed by the owner. When stock certificates are sold through brokers, they are usually endorsed in blank. But the transfer of title to a stock certificate does not mean that title to the stock represented by the certificate is transferred. To complete the transaction, the books of the corporation must be changed to show the transfer of title to the stock, and the old certificate must be canceled and a new one issued in its place.

A large corporation may have its own stock transfer department or office, or it may employ a trust company to supervise transfers of its corporate stock and other securities. The transfer agent or office keeps the stock certificate book, cancels surrendered certificates and attaches them to their proper stubs in the stock book, and issues new stock certificates to the transferees. These new certificates must be signed by the designated officials and, if required, imprinted with the corporate seal. The bank or trust company employed as registrar supervises the work of cancellation and issuance of stock certificates and countersigns them. The transfer agent of the corporation will deliver the new certificate to the transferee, Corporations whose shares are listed on the New York Stock Exchange

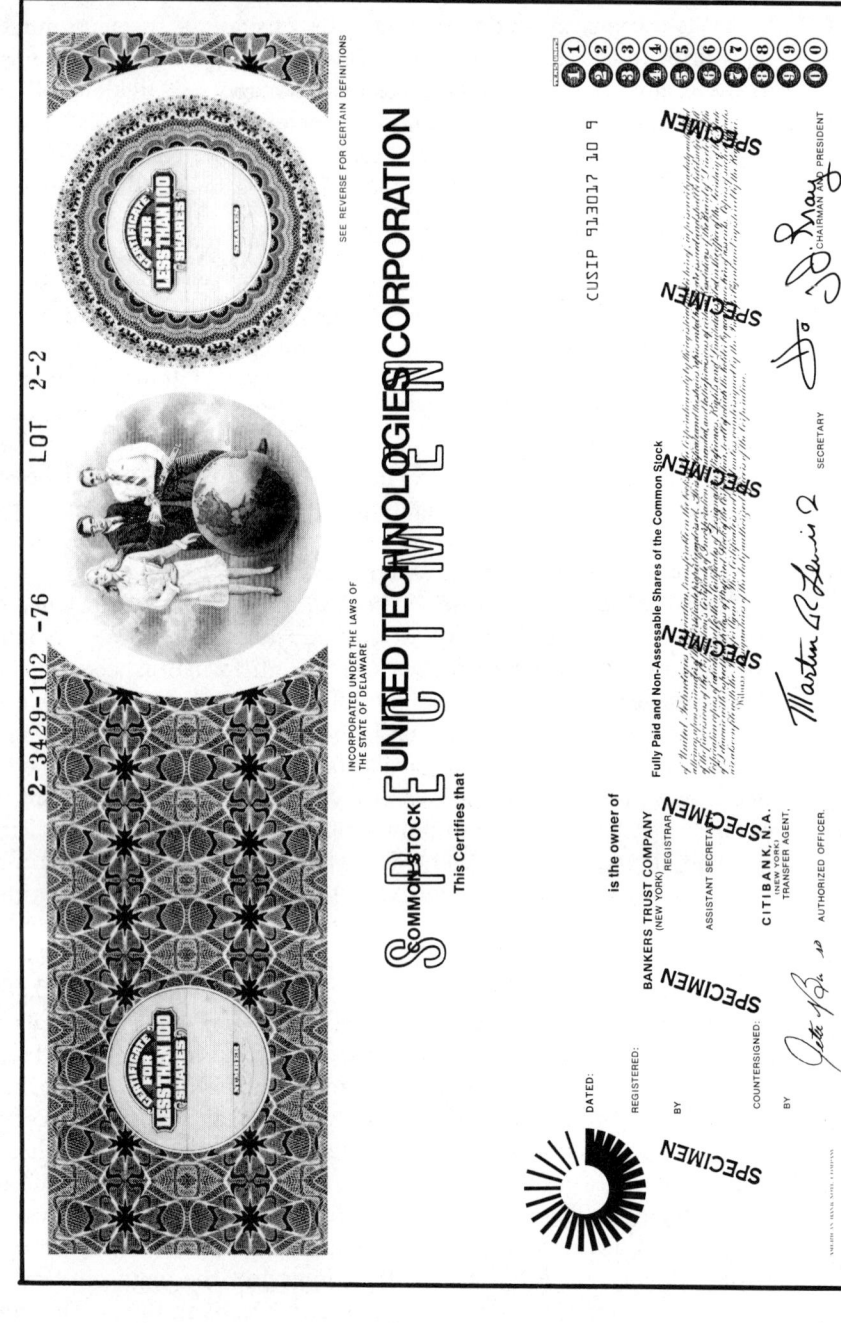

## UNITED TECHNOLOGIES CORPORATION

The following abbreviations, when used in the inscription on the face of this certificate, shall be construed as though they were written out in full according to applicable laws or regulations:

| | | | |
|---|---|---|---|
| TEN COM | — as tenants in common | UNIF GIFT MIN ACT — | ............Custodian............ |
| TEN ENT | — as tenants by the entireties | | (Cust)         (Minor) |
| JT TEN | — as joint tenants with right of survivorship and not as tenants in common | | under Uniform Gifts to Minors Act............ (State) |

Additional abbreviations may also be used though not in the above list.

The Corporation will furnish without charge to each stockholder who so requests the powers, designations, preferences and relative, participating, optional or other special rights of each class of stock or series thereof of the Corporation and the qualifications, limitations, or restrictions of such preferences and/or rights. Such request may be made to the Corporation or the Transfer Agent.

For Value received,_____ hereby sell, assign and transfer unto

PLEASE INSERT SOCIAL SECURITY OR OTHER
IDENTIFYING NUMBER OF ASSIGNEE

_____

PLEASE PRINT OR TYPEWRITE NAME AND ADDRESS OF ASSIGNEE

_____

_____ Shares

of the capital stock represented by the within Certificate, and do hereby irrevocably constitute and appoint _____ Attorney to transfer the said stock on the books of the within-named Corporation with full power of substitution in the premises.

Dated,_____

NOTICE: THE SIGNATURE TO THIS ASSIGNMENT MUST CORRESPOND WITH THE NAME AS WRITTEN UPON THE FACE OF THE CERTIFICATE IN EVERY PARTICULAR, WITHOUT ALTERATION OR ENLARGEMENT OR ANY CHANGE WHATEVER.

THIS SPACE MUST NOT BE COVERED IN ANY WAY

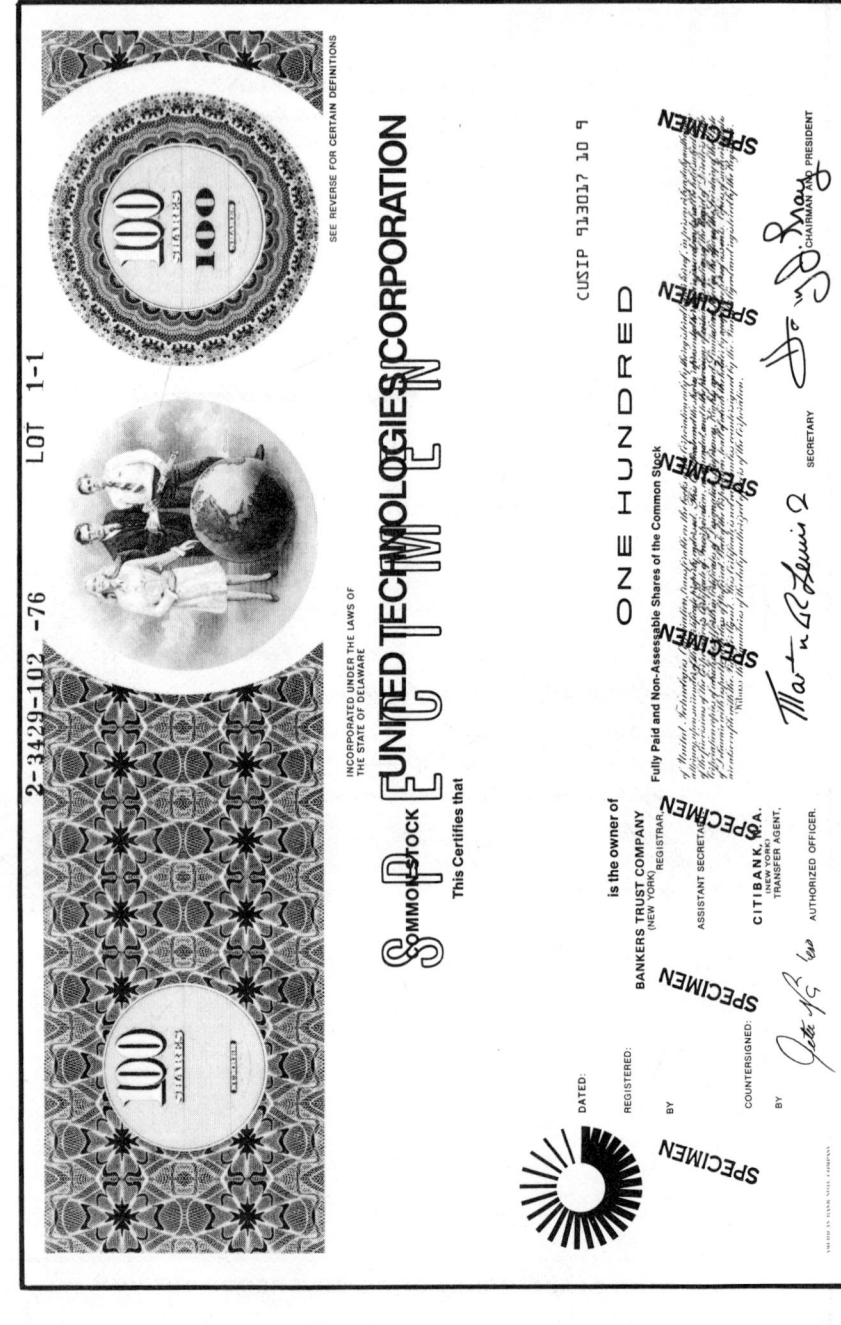

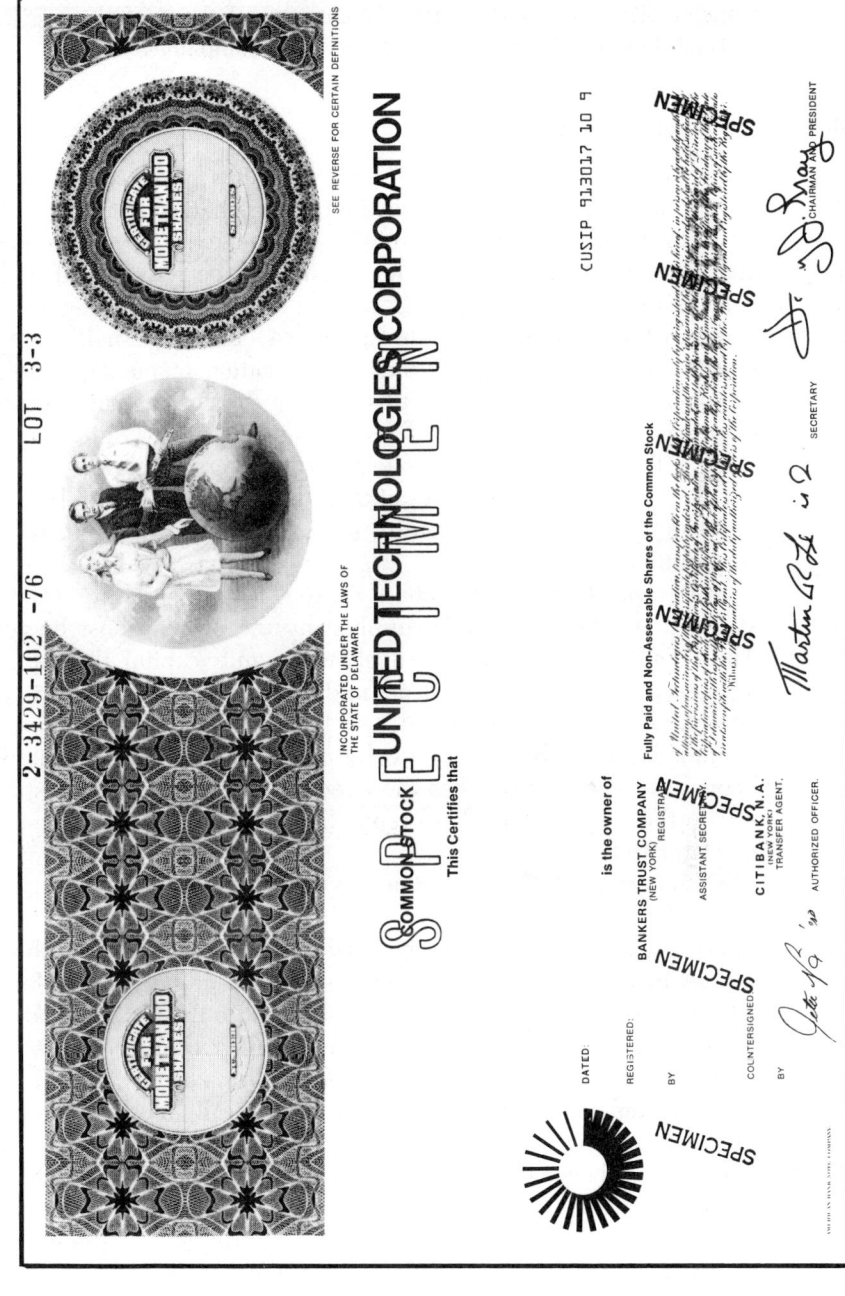

must have both a registrar and either a transfer office or transfer agent in the Borough of Manhattan. The duties of the transfer agent—or the transfer office operated by the company—and those of the registrar are distinct and must be performed by different companies.

## Rights of Common Stockholders

Equity or proprietary capital refers to funds provided by the owners of a firm. It has the following distinguishing characteristics: (1) there is no stated date on which the funds must be returned; (2) there is no contractual obligation as to how much must be returned, if a decision is made to return any funds; (3) there is no contractual obligation to pay a return for the use of the funds; and (4) there is usually reserved to those supplying the equity funds an obligation to manage and control the operations of the firm. In this section, the contractual nature of the maturity, claim on assets, claim on income, and voting rights on common stock will be examined. In the next two chapters on preferred stock and bonds, the same characteristics of these financing media will be discussed to show the contractual nature of these latter securities with the issuing corporation.

*Maturity.* If the corporation charter is in perpetuity there is no stated time when the funds supplied by the owners must be returned. Thus, if a firm is financed exclusively with equity capital, the risk of being weakened by the withdrawal of funds at a prearranged date is entirely absent. Of course, some owners may be persuaded to sell back a portion of their holdings voluntarily to the corporation. This reacquired stock, known as treasury stock, has the effect of reducing the ownership interests in the corporation. These repurchases will be treated in more detail in a later section.

*Claim on Assets.* Dissolution of a corporation can be either voluntary or involuntary. In the former case, the owners may decide to terminate the corporation by selling off the assets, or by merger with another corporation. In the latter case, dissolution may occur because of failure. In either alternative, the common stockholders are the residual claimants to the firm's assets in case of dissolution. All other claimants, whether debt or preferred stock, have prior claims to the firm's assets. When a business is terminated voluntarily the stockholders typically receive proceeds from the liquidation of the firm's assets. However, this is not the usual outcome when a firm becomes bankrupt. The equity holders assume the greater risk; the residual nature of the common stockholders means that they usually receive nothing in a bankruptcy proceeding. Presumably the equity holders make permanent investments in the firm. Shareholders may sell their ownership interest to others, or the firm may be liquidated and the proceeds divided among the owners after paying off the prior claims, but neither of these possibilities is prearranged. Thus, in regard to the claim on the firm's assets, the equity holders are the greatest risk-bearers.

***Claim on Income.*** The owners of equity capital are entitled to net earnings after taxes, interest, and all other obligations of the firm are met. They are the residual claimants to the income of a business enterprise which may be much, little, or nothing. Net earnings may be retained in the business rather than being paid to the owners; therefore, despite large earnings, common stockholders' dividends may lag for long periods of time depending upon the investment opportunities available to the firm.

A corporation's board of directors is under no contractual obligation to pay dividends on common stock; but it may feel morally obligated to do so. When earnings are retained temporarily rather than paid out as dividends, earnings may increase in the future; as a result, more earnings will be available for dividend payments at a later date. If retained earnings are capitalized by a stock dividend, the common stockholders' investments in terms of the number of shares will be increased. Generally, investors are more interested in receiving cash dividends than stock dividends.

The prospect of large returns on an investment in the common stock of a corporation may far outweight the disadvantages of stock ownership. In any business venture, the creditors and preferred stockholders, in effect, "pay" for their more secure position by accepting a limited return on their investments and surrendering control over corporate assets. In buying credit instruments, individual investors must compete with institutional investors (commercial banks, savings institutions, insurance companies, trusts, and others), and the demands of these investors for credit instruments is a factor in their yield. Among institutional investors and financial intermediaries, important buyers of equities include private pension funds, mutual investment companies, and trust departments of commercial banks. As state laws are being changed, institutional investors are competing more actively for preferred and common stock, but not to the extent that is true for bonds and other credit instruments. Since World War II, inflation has been a powerful factor in the price appreciation of common stock. However, this appreciation has not been continuous, since the stock market has suffered several rather severe reversals in the post-World War II period. Inflation tends to reallocate the value of assets of corporations among their security holders by reducing the real value of fixed-income securities and increasing the real value of variable-income securities. If a firm with assets of $1 million has creditors' claims against it for $500,000, its stockholders' share in assets is $500,000. Assuming inflation of 100 percent, the corporation's assets will have a value of $2 million, creditors' claims will be $500,000, and the stockholders' share in assets will be $1.5 million. If net earnings maintain the same ratio to net worth after inflation as before, the net earnings available for dividends will increase 300 percent even though the corporation's assets increase only 100 percent. Therefore, the disproportionate rise in net earnings on common stock equity should support further price appreciation in the common stock. The reason the increase cannot be calculated with great precision can be explained by the fact that as market conditions change, the price-earnings ratios adjust to the constantly changing environment.

**Control.** The fourth characteristic of equity capital is that those who provide it are responsible, at least in theory, for the control and management of the business enterprise. However, some equity capital is supplied under contracts that limit the control rights of those who supply it, such as limited partners in partnerships, preferred stockholders of corporations, and beneficiaries of trusts. Stockholders of corporations usually permit their elected representatives, the members of the board of directors, to select the officers and other agents to manage the affairs of their corporations. This does not invalidate the owner-control aspect of equity capital if the owners of equity capital do not surrender their rights to exercise control by waiving them.

## Control of the Corporation

The final authority to manage a corporation resides in the common stockholders. This control in large corporations is indirect, that is, the stockholders elect the members of the board of directors. The election of the directors typically takes place at the annual stockholders' meeting. Since most stockholders find it impractical to attend the annual meeting, the use of proxies by management is widespread. The election of directors is usually the most important business to be transacted at the annual meeting of the stockholders.

**Stockholders' Meetings.** Stockholders' meetings may be held at the registered or principal office of the corporation or at such places within or outside the state of origin as are permitted by the state's business corporation act and provided for in the bylaws of the corporation. There are three kinds of stockholders' meetings: annual, special, and consent. The day for the annual meeting is specified in the bylaws and may be, for example, "the fourth Tuesday in April." Annual meetings are held for the purpose of selecting new directors, hearing reports of officers, answering questions of stockholders, and voting on matters brought before the stockholders.

Special meetings may be called by the holders of no less than one-tenth (or some other specified percentage) of the shares entitled to vote at the meetings, the board of directors, the president, or such officers or persons as may be designated in the articles of incorporation or bylaws. If a special meeting is to be held, the purpose or purposes for which it is called must be indicated. Such a meeting may be called to secure approval of a new stock issue or some other proposal of the board of directors that necessitates action prior to the next annual meeting. The business corporation act prescribes that, in order to conduct business, a quorum (usually a majority) of shareholders must be present or be represented by proxy holders. Although consent meetings are not provided for in the bylaws, they are legal if all stockholders are present or if those not present have indicated in writing their waiver of the call and notice. Special meetings of the consent type are naturally limited to companies having relatively few shareholders.

**Proxies.** A shareholder may vote in person or by proxy (one who is authorized to act for another). In corporation law, it is customary to require this authorization to be in writing and properly signed by the stockholder or by his duly empowered attorney-in-fact. Management usually solicits proxies from shareholders for each meeting in order to assure enough representation to hold an official meeting, to obtain votes to support managerial policies, or to elect directors who have been nominated by them. Under the terms of the Securities Exchange Act of 1934, the Securities and Exchange Commission regulates the conditions under which proxies may be solicited by mail or other channels of interstate commerce.

Although regulations of the commission pertaining to solicitation of proxies have changed from time to time, they do include these requirements: (1) a clear statement identifying the solicitor of the proxy (usually this is the existing management); (2) names of auditors to be named at the meeting for which the proxies are being solicited; (3) a statement of matters that the minority interests are expected to raise at the proposed meeting; (4) a statement as to the action management proposes to take on items affecting officers and directors (such as profit-sharing plans; bonus, pension, or retirement plans; and rights or options to purchase securities) and a space to indicate how the proxy holder is to vote; (5) names of officers, directors, and members of the nominating committee and, when pertinent, data on the cost of soliciting proxies; and (6) information about stock holdings and about the slate of candidates for directorship.

Customarily, proxies are solicited only by management; however, a stockholder may appoint any person planning to attend a meeting to vote his shares.[2] Sometimes, one or more groups other than management may solicit proxies; however, without strong financial backing, such groups

---

[2] In 1959, in a move to strengthen stockholders' rights, the New York Stock Exchange ruled that all "actively operated" companies listed on the Exchange (including nine railroads operated under lease and two companies operated by trustees classified as nonoperating) must solicit proxies from shareholders and allow them to vote on matters to be considered at the annual meeting. Previously, 28 companies did not solicit proxies and stockholders could vote only by going to the meetings or by finding their own proxies to represent them. There is no ruling by the Securities and Exchange Commission requiring that proxies be solicited. (*Wall Street Journal*, April 3, 1959, p. 20.)

are usually unsuccessful in their attempts to obtain enough votes to elect their own candidates for directorship. Corporations pay the expenses of soliciting proxies for management—but not for minority groups. In a proxy fight, such as the successful one in 1954 to gain control of the then New York Central Railroad by Robert R. Young and associates, the expenses of soliciting proxies may run into millions of dollars.

Prior to the stockholders' meeting, a minority group will need to control or acquire a relatively large block of stock. This may necessitate purchasing shares at relatively high prices, which would add to the cost of obtaining control. If and when there is a change in management resulting from a successful proxy fight, it is more often due to having the support of a few large stockholders than to obtaining the support of small stockholders, who traditionally follow management. However, if small stockholders hold the balance of power, a strong appeal may be made to them through newspapers, pamphlets, and letters; in some cases, use is made of proxy-soliciting firms.[3]

Proxies are printed with spaces for the signatures of stockholders and for marking "for" or "against" votes on matters to be voted on at the proposed meeting. If no preference is indicated, a committee for management customarily votes as indicated in the proxy statement. In recent years, corporate management has frequently requested stockholders to vote on matters pertaining directly or indirectly to remuneration of personnel (such as bonus and stock-option plans and pension and retirement plans) and to changes in capitalization of corporations. As a consequence of proxy regulation by the SEC, many items appear on proxy statements at the request of minority groups. These have included such things as proposals to limit officers' salaries, limit pension benefits, have women directors, have meetings of stockholders elsewhere than the corporation's registered office, and permit cumulative voting.

**Provisions for Voting.** Under common law, each shareholder has one vote, irrespective of the number of shares owned, but this method of voting is not in keeping with the risks assumed in stock ownership of business corporations. Consequently, corporation laws of the various states provide that each outstanding share is entitled to one vote if it is not of a class of stock that is denied the right to vote by the articles of

---

[3] Proxy fights are usually most common during recession years, and the record number in 1958 was attributed not only to the business recession but also to the publicity given proxy fights in the 1950s. Charges of violation of proxy rules by both sides usually lead to court action and delays that are to the advantage of one or the other group. Some proxy fights are compromised and result in split boards of directors. A partially successful fight is often followed by another proxy fight the next year. (*New York Times*, January 12, 1959, p. 81.) Proxy contests are usually accompanied by low rates of return on common-stock equity. Nevertheless, in 45 proxy contests between 1956 and 1960, only about one in three successfully challenged management. (See Richard M. Duvall and Douglas V. Austin, "Predicting the Results of Proxy Contests," *Journal of Finance*, vol. 20 [September 1965], pp. 464–71.)

incorporation, as it may be for preferred stock. There are two common methods of voting in use today. They are (1) majority, and (2) cumulative voting. Under the majority voting system a stockholder may cast no more votes for any director than the number of shares that the stockholder owns or controls through proxies. Thus, if a stockholder controls 100 shares, only 100 votes may be cast for any one director. Therefore, this method of voting prevents minority representation on the board of directors because a group owning or controlling 50 percent of the voting shares plus one can elect its slate of candidates for directors.

The alternative method of voting is called cumulative voting. In some states, statutory provisions are made for cumulative voting (also by the federal government for national banks) in order to give minority stockholders representation on boards of directors if they want to use this voting privilege. In cumulative voting, a stockholder may cast votes equal to the number of shares held (assume 100) times the number of directors to be elected (assume 10), for any one candidate (thus, 1,000 votes), or he can divide them among two or more candidates. If we assume that there are 1,000 shares of voting stock outstanding, the stockholder owning 100 shares could elect a candidate to the board of directors. By taking the number of shares to be cast times the number of directors to be elected, a stockholder or group of stockholders could compute how best to prorate their votes among candidates so as to elect the largest number of directors.[4]

To ensure election of one director, a stockholder or group of stockholders must have the number of shares computed as follows:

$$\frac{\text{Number of voting shares} \times \text{number of directors desired}}{\text{Number of directors to be elected} + 1} + 1$$

---

[4] By using classified boards (terms of office for directors of more than one year), much of the impact of cumulative voting can be nullified. The formula for cumulative voting is frequently expressed by using the following notation:

$$r = \frac{S \times d}{D + 1} + 1$$

where $S$ is the number of voting shares, $d$ the number of directors desired. $D$ the number of directors to be elected, and $r$ the number of shares required to elect one director.

If a group controls a given number of shares before an election (e.g., 200 shares), it is possible to arrive at how many directors it can elect through the following formula:

$$\begin{aligned} d &= \frac{(r-1)(D+1)}{S} \\ &= \frac{(200-1)(10+1)}{1,000} \\ &= \frac{199(11)}{1,000} \\ &= \frac{2,189}{1,000} = 2.189 \text{ directors} \end{aligned}$$

If 1,000 shares are to be voted and 10 directors are to be elected, a minimum of 91 shares or 910 votes will be needed to elect one director.

$$\frac{1{,}000 \times 1}{10 + 1} + 1 = 91$$

Some managements have opposed cumulative voting because it favors special groups and does not represent the interest of all stockholders indiscriminately. Sometimes cumulative voting permits a minority group to elect a majority of the directors, which is not the intent of the cumulative-voting provision. In order to accumulate votes intelligently, a group must have an estimate of (1) the number of shares that will be voted (in person and by proxy), (2) how the independents will vote, and (3) the plan of the opposition as to accumulating votes. It is possible under cumulative voting to give one candidate so many votes that those votes in excess of the number needed for election would have elected a second candidate. Foreknowledge of the extent to which independents are supporting a candidate would permit diversion of votes to other candidates. In case no prior list of candidates is prepared and there is no knowledge that some shareholders plan to cumulate their votes, management may spread its votes over the entire slate of candidates and end up with minority representation on the board of directors.

Cumulative voting is not the usual procedure, and the wisdom of authorizing it has been questioned. While diversified representation is usually desirable, it is not necessarily assured by selecting board members by means of cumulative voting. There have been instances in which such directors seemed to take the position that they were obliged to disagree with management regardless of the merits of the issues.

**Classified Common Stock.** During the 1920s many corporations issued more than one class of common stock, usually designated as Class A and Class B. Although both shared equally in earnings and—upon liquidation—in assets of a corporation, usually one class, such as Class B, had voting preference or sole voting rights. The amount of voting stock was usually small compared with the amount of nonvoting stock; as a result, control was vested in a few. Voting stock may be issued to management, former creditors if the corporation has undergone a financial crisis, and bankers who have purchased bonds or other securities of the corporation. In practice, voting common stock may be used as a substitute for a voting trust.

The issuance of nonvoting common stock, to be sold to the general public in order to acquire assets, has been criticized as being out of step with public policy.[5] Even though the voting rights of a class of stock may

---

[5] The New York Stock Exchange, Securities and Exchange Commission, and bankruptcy courts not only frown upon but also take measures to prevent issuance of nonvoting stock when such action falls within their provinces.

be limited or denied, the owners of this stock cannot be deprived of the privilege of voting on issues that affect their interests (such as the right to vote on consolidations and mergers, on sale or mortgage of assets not in the regular course of business, and on voluntary dissolution).[6]

Common stock may be issued to care for special situations, as with Series I and Series II of Communications Satellite Corporation, which was chartered in the District of Columbia in 1963 as authorized by the Communications Satellite Act of 1962. In order to protect the extensive experimental, research, and other interests of the American Telephone and Telegraph Company, International Telephone and Telegraph Corporation, General Telephone and Electronics Corporation, RCA Corporation, and (with the approval of the Federal Communications Commission) over 150 other common carriers, they were permitted to buy one-half of the capital stock of 10,000,100 shares classified as Series II stock. In order to recognize the public interest, the charter of the corporation provided for the sale of the remaining half of the common stock to the public through the facilities of Merrill Lynch, Pierce, Fenner, and Smith and ten other investment banking houses. Although the corporation is not an agency or establishment of the U.S. government, the Federal Communications Commission has regulatory powers over the financing, accounting systems, issuance of securities other than those assigned to some common carrier, and borrowing of funds.[7]

## Repurchase of Common Stock

Common stock that has been issued and subsequently reacquired by the issuing firm is called treasury stock. Such stock is then treated as a deduction from the stockholders' equity. In recent years a number of companies have repurchased their common stock. For example, International Business Machines (IBM) offered to purchase 4 million shares of its own common stock at a price of $280 beginning on February 22, 1977, and continuing through March 7, 1977. It retained the option to purchase up to a total of 5.5 million shares. The offer to purchase was extended to March 9, 1977. At the close of the tender offer on the latter date IBM reacquired 2,546,000 shares at a cost of $713 million. Stock can be repurchased by either a tender offer to the existing stockholders, or by purchases in the open market. If a tender offer is made, all stockholders

---

[6] The limitation of voting rights occurs most commonly with preferred-stock issues.

[7] Reference is to the Series II stock sold to the American Telephone and Telegraph Company (2,895,750 shares), International Telephone and Telegraph Corporation (1,050,000 shares), General Telephone and Electronics Corporation (350,000 shares), RCA Corporation (250,000 shares). (See Communications Satellite Corporation, *Prospectus, 10,000,000 shares, common stock (without par value)*, dated June 2, 1964.

must be given an equal opportunity to tender their shares. If more shares are tendered then the firm agrees to purchase, the tendered stock is pro-rated. For example, if the firm agrees to purchase 100,000 shares and 200,000 are tendered, each tender offer would be allocated 50 percent. An alternative method would be to have the stockholders set the price at which they are willing to sell. Then the company would purchase the least expensive shares and continue to purchase them until the 100,000 shares are acquired. As a rule, a company will specify the maximum price that it will pay.

A number of reasons are advanced for the repurchase of a firm's stock. When the price of common stocks is relatively low, many corporations may reacquire outstanding shares and justify the action on the need for reducing dividend requirements, lowering the amount of capital to conform to changed business conditions, finding a profitable outlet for funds on hand, supporting the market for the stock in order to protect stockholders' interests, and acquiring stock for future corporate needs at bargain prices. In reporting the reacquisition of stock to shareholders, management usually justifies its action by pointing to the increase in earnings per share due to the smaller number of shares outstanding.

A repurchase of common stock implies that this is the best opportunity available to the firm at that time. In other words, a firm lacks investment opportunities that have returns equal to or greater than the firm's cost of capital. The surplus funds could be returned to the owners either by raising the cash dividend, or by reacquiring part of the common stock. Since cash dividends are taxed at ordinary income rates, and stock repurchases are taxed as capital gains, the tax advantage favoring repurchases appears to be a strong motivation for the action on the part of management.[8]

Management has been criticized for repurchasing the firm's stock, because using corporate assets in this way might weaken protection of creditors (bond indentures usually prohibit the use of corporate assets to reacquire stock except under special conditions that give adequate protection to creditors). In addition, repurchasing stock may permit insiders to perpetuate their control, to the possible disadvantage of other interests.

For example, if Firm X makes a tender offer to the stockholders of Firm Y, the management of Firm Y can counter with a tender offer above the price of Firm X. The probable outcome will be that many stockholders may sell to the highest bidder with the result that the possible takeover by Firm X will be thwarted. However, treasury stock is not permitted to be voted and it may not be counted to obtain the necessary number of shares required by many provisions of business-corporation acts, such as a quorum of shares for legal meetings of stockholders.

---

[8] Harold Bierman, Jr., and Richard West, "The Acquisition of Common Stock by the Corporate Issuer," *Journal of Finance*, vol. 21 (Deccember 1966), p. 690.

## The Preemptive Right

The preemptive right is the right of stockholders, under corporate charters or state laws, to subscribe to additional shares of their corporation's stock before it is offered for sale to others.

*Justification for the Preemptive-Rights Principle.* The preemptive right of common stockholders permits them to participate proportionately in any increase in the capital stock of their company. Hence, they are given the opportunity to maintain their percentage interest in their company, and, if they use their privilege to buy new stock when offered, they protect their interest in the company from being diluted.

The first argument in support of the common-law preemptive-right principle is that it permits old common stockholders to protect their voting positions. Assume that an individual owns 10 percent of the 20,000 shares of voting stock of a corporation through ownership of 2,000 shares. If a new issue of stock were sold to outsiders in an amount equal to the shares outstanding, the voting rights of the original stockholder would be reduced from 10 percent to 5 percent. If he were given the right to subscribe to an additional 2,000 shares before they were offered to others, he would have the opportunity to protect his voting position.

A second argument in support of the preemptive-right principle is that the shareholders must be permitted to retain their proportionate share in the retained earnings of their corporation. If we assume that this value is $100, and the par value is the same, each share of common stock outstanding has a book value of $200 (capital stock, $2,000,000 + retained earnings, $2,000,000 $\div$ shares outstanding, 20,000 = $200 book value per share). If we assume that 20,000 shares of a new issue are sold for the par value of $100, it would mean that the book value of each share of common stock outstanding would be reduced from $200 to $150 (capital stock, $4,000,000 + retained earnings, $2,000,000 $\div$ shares outstanding, 40,000 − $150). In effect, selling new shares at par value transferred $50 "on the books" from old stockholders to new stockholders.

The third argument in support of the common-law preemptive-right principle is that the old stockholders must be permitted to retain their proportionate interest in the earnings of their corporation. If the corporation is earning $160,000, or 4 percent, after taxes on the net worth of $4 million ($160,000 $\div$ $4,000,000 = 0.04$), it would amount to $8 per share ($160,000 $\div$ 20,000 = $8$). If 20,000 new shares are sold for $100 per share, the net worth of the corporation would be increased by $2 million, which would earn $80,000 at the rate of 4 percent after taxes and would thereby increase total earnings to $240,000. When these earnings are divided by the number of shares outstanding, the earning rate per share would be $6 ($240,000 $\div$ 40,000 = $6$). In effect the old stockholders' interest in earnings would have been reduced from $8 to $6 per share and the interest in earnings of the new shareholders would have been increased from $4 to $6 per share. In principle, usually management is not justified in undertaking new financing with outsiders unless earnings per share on the company's old stock are expected to be maintained or increased.

**Applicability of the Preemptive-Rights Principle.** If the common-law principle pertaining to the preemptive right of old stockholders to buy new common stock is justified, the preemptive-right principle is equally applicable to issues of preferred stock, bonds, and other securities that are convertible into common stock. If the right to exchange preferred stock, bonds, or other securities for common stock at the option of the owner has any value, the rights of old common stockholders as to voting, equity, and earnings of the corporation will be diluted at the time of conversion in the same way as noted above in the case of sales of new common stock to new stockholders.

Business-corporation acts provide that the preemptive right is applicable to reissued treasury stock of a corporation, unless limited or denied in the articles of incorporation. With a majority affirmative vote of the shares entitled to vote thereon, treasury as well as other stock may be offered to officers and employees without first being offered to shareholders.[9]

The preemptive-right rule does not apply when new stock is issued in exchange for property. A corporation may wish to obtain control of a second company by exchanging authorized but unissued shares for the stock of the second company, or a corporation may acquire assets from a second company by giving such stock rather than by paying cash.

Preemptive rights are based on common law, but they may be withdrawn by statutory law. To an increasing extent, business-corporation acts make provisions for the waiver of preemptive rights in the articles of incorporation of corporations. The California, Delaware, Kansas, and Vermont codes go even further and provide that no preemptive rights exist unless they are specifically included in a corporation's charter. More commonly, the statutes require incorporators to specify in the articles of incorporation "any provision limiting or denying the shareholders the preemptive right to acquire additional or treasury shares of the corporation." On the other hand, business-corporation acts also permit the articles of incorporation to be amended so as to "grant to shareholders of any class the preemptive right to acquire additional or treasury shares of the corporation whether then or thereafter authorized."

## Privileged Subscriptions

Privileged subscriptions exist when old stockholders, employees, officers, or others are given the first right to buy new securities of their corpo-

---

[9] See Sections 26 and 26A of the Model Business Corporation Act.

rations. Usually, the term "privileged subscription" suggests that only certain parties may subscribe for the securities and that special advantages are associated with offering terms that make the privilege valuable. The term is usually used when new securities are being issued, but it could be applied to sales of treasury stock. Such offerings under preemptive rights may be voluntary or they may be mandatory, as when required by common law, statutes, or charters of issuing corporations.[10]

*Market for Preemptive-Rights Offerings.* The market for securities sold under preemptive rights is assumed to be limited to old stockholders; but purchase warrants or rights are transferable and they may be sold. The size of a new issue is an important factor in the success of a rights offering in that old stockholders are in a better position to absorb all the shares offered when the ratio of new to old securities is small—assume 1:20 as compared to 1:1. In the first case, the stockholders would be asked to increase their investments by about 5 percent; in the second case, they would be asked to approximately double their investments. A careful analysis by management of the distribution of existing shares should throw light on the question of the size of the issue that could be absorbed by existing stockholders. The stock may be owned by a few large stockholders who are unable to purchase more shares or are unwilling to do so because they want to diversify their investments. On the other hand, there may be a small number of institutional investors including investment companies that are both willing and able to acquire new shares at "bargain prices." Generally speaking, the best market for privileged subscription sales of new securities exists when there are a large number of satisfied shareholders. Previous sales of new securities by privileged subscription may have demonstrated to stockholders that the degree of dilution of each share was negligible and that any possible depressing effect on the market price of the stock was only temporary.

On the assumption that everyone is interested in purchasing at "bargain prices," the key to successful financing is the spread between the subscription price and the market price. In other words, a new issue is certain to be a success if the subscription price is sufficiently below the market price. If we assume a market price of $150 and a subscription price of $125, one could expect an offering of new stock to old stockholders to be successful. Of course, the lower the subscription price, the smaller will be the return to the company for each new share sold; and a greater number of new shares will have to be sold to raise a given amount of funds. The greater the number of new shares sold, the greater

---

[10] Regardless of the provisions of state business-corporation acts pertaining to preemptive rights, stockholders have the right to sue members of the board of directors of their corporation if their interests are being affected adversely by a public sale of securities. The strength of their case will depend on the amount of dilution of their claims to earnings and net worth and the reduction in their proportionate voting power.

will be the dilution in earnings of each old share, which, in turn, may have a depressing effect on the market price of each share.

Management may set an unusually low subscription price in order to adjust the market price of the stock downward; if so, management may be guided in part by the same motives that lead a corporation to declare a stock dividend or stock split. In fact, if there is no objection to a reduction in the market price of the stock and no pressure on management to maintain the old dividend rate, there is no reason why the subscription price for a new issue may not be at a substantial discount.

**Legal and Routine Procedures.** After financing plans are drawn for a new stock issue, they must be approved by the corporation's board of directors. This approval takes the form of a resolution stating the amount of stock to be sold and the purpose of the issue. When authorized but unissued stock is available, the financing plan may be put in operation directly; otherwise, the board of directors will instruct the officers to submit a charter amendment to increase the authorized capital to shareholders for their approval (at a regular or special meeting). Following approval of the charter amendment, the resolution customarily states that new shares will be offered to stockholders and that transferable subscription warrants evidencing their rights to subscribe for new shares will be distributed.[11]

After the charter amendment has been filed as required by law and a registration statement has been filed with the Securities and Exchange Commission, an officer of the corporation will notify the shareholders of the action taken and the details of subscription rights offered to stockholders, including the record date for determining who will receive subscription warrants, the offering period (when the offering will open and when it will end), the date subscription warrants will be mailed, and how rights for less than enough to acquire one share will be handled. This letter is issued for information purposes only and is in no way a formal offering or commitment on the part of the corporation to sell securities.

As soon as practical after the record date, the corporation will transmit to stockholders of record the subscription warrants, together with a letter of transmittal containing instructions as to the use of the subscription warrants and a copy of the prospectus, which contains the basic facts about the company and the issue. Since the subscription warrants are transferable, they customarily state the terms of the issue, the number of rights to which the stockholder is entitled, the subscription price, the office that

---

[11] A subscription warrant is a certificate issued by a corporation specifying the conditions under which shareholders of record are entitled to purchase additional new stock which the corporation plans to issue imminently. It should be distinguished from a long-term stock purchase warrant giving the holder the right to purchase a certain number of shares at a specified price within a specified time. The long-term stock purchase warrant is discussed in Chapter 19.

will receive payment for the stock, the final date for using the rights, and the date of issue of the new stock. On the back of the subscription warrant there is a form for the assignment of the warrant (in case the shareholder wishes to transfer it to others) and also a subscription agreement to be signed by the one exercising the subscription rights.

Usually, two or more rights are needed to purchase one new share; therefore, most stockholders will have more or less rights than the number needed to purchase one or more shares. To prevent the stockholder from losing his extra rights, management may arrange for a trust company or bank to act as agent to sell the extra rights or to buy the additional rights at the market price according to the request of the owner when he exercises his subscription rights. Also, management may arrange to have subscription rights listed on a stock exchange, where they would be traded until the end of the offering period. Thus, those wishing to buy or sell additional rights would have to make such purchases or sales in the open market through regular brokerage channels.

Customarily, the formal offering documents will contain a copy of the prospectus, together with a description of the securities offered and the subscription. Also provided will be information pertaining to the company's planned use of the funds, its financial statements, the nature of the business, litigations involving the company, and any special information (for example, regarding license or other contracts) that may affect the company. As a matter of policy, management usually states what the anticipated dividend rate will be.

When a corporation plans to sell stock by privileged subscription, the success of the financing may be enhanced by permitting stockholders to oversubscribe for new shares. Thus, if a common stockholder has rights for ten shares, he may subscribe for ten shares and request an additional ten shares if and when available. All such requests will be added and the shares not subscribed for by those holding rights will be prorated among those requesting additional shares. It does not follow that the subscribers will receive all the additional shares requested; but they may get part of them, because, no matter how attractive the subscription privilege may be, there will be some who will not use their rights.

**Value of a Right.** The theoretical value of a right can be calculated readily. However, first it is necessary to determine whether the stock is selling "rights-on" or "ex-rights." The procedures for handling rights are somewhat analogous to those for handling dividends on stock. In an earlier discussion on dividends, it was explained that the dividends go with the stock until the ex-dividend date, which is four days before the stock of record date. Rights are generally traded in the same manner.

Thus, on January 15 the board of directors might announce that rights will be mailed out March 1 to stockholders of record as of February 15. Any investor purchasing the stock between January 15 and February 11 would receive the rights; hence, the stock would be selling rights-on.

After February 11 until the end of the subscription period, the stock would be selling ex-rights, or separately from the rights. Using $200 as the market price of the stock, $175 as the subscription price, and five rights, necessary to purchase one share, it is possible to calculate the theoretical value of the rights.

**Rights-on.** When the stock is selling rights-on, the following formula is applicable for determining the market price of each right:

$$R = \frac{M - S}{N + 1}$$

where $R$ is the value of the right, $M$ the market price of the stock, $S$ the subscription price of the stock, and $N$ the number of rights needed to buy one share. Given the assumptions noted above, the value of the right would be $4.17:

$$R = \frac{\$200 - \$175}{5 + 1} = \$4.17$$

Another way of viewing the problem would be as follows: to become entitled to an additional share at $175, a stockholder would have to own five shares worth $200 each. Exercising the right at $175 would result in six shares having a total value of $1,175 [5($200) + 175]. The average price of the six shares would be $195.83. Therefore, it is necessary to add one additional share to the denominator of the above formula $(N + 1)$ when calculating the theoretical rights-on value.

Any investor not choosing to exercise his privilege would find that his investment would depreciate if he did not make any provision to sell his rights before the expiration date. This decline would occur because the new shares can be purchased at a bargain price of $175. Therefore, an active market usually develops for the rights as soon as they are separated from the stock.

**Ex-Rights.** At the ex-rights date the purchaser of the stock does not receive the rights. At that time the market price of the stock should fall by the value of the right, or to $195.83 in our example. This decline in price can be confirmed by the use of the ex-rights formula:

$$R = \frac{M_e - S}{N}$$
$$R = \frac{\$195.83 - \$175}{5} = \$4.17$$

The $M_e$ is the market value of the stock ex-rights. Frequently, rights sell above their theoretical value during the ex-rights period. This is because of their speculative appeal. For example, if the stock price ex-rights should rise from $195.83 to $215.83, the value of a right would climb to $8.17. An investor with $195.83 to invest before the price rise could have bought one share of stock or 47 rights. The subsequent gain on the rights would have been $188 (47 × $4.00), or almost double the original investment. This outcome is possible because 47 rights would have purchased 9.4 shares of common stock at $175 a share. Thus, the subsequent gain on the rights would have been $188 vs. $20 if the stock were purchased outright.

While the purchaser of 47 rights would have had a claim on 9.4 shares thereby magnifying his potential gain if the stock price rises, it should be remembered that the opposite also may occur. If the price of the stock falls $20, from $195.83 to $175.83, the value of a right would decline to $.17, or to a total value of $8.00. In the first instance when the stock rose $20 a share, a profit of $188 would be realized; in the latter case, a loss of $188 would be incurred if the stock price falls by a like amount. This example illustrates why rights offerings can have speculative overtones if there is a substantial movement in either direction of the common stock during the rights period.

*Standby Underwriting.* Corporate management may arrange for "standby" underwriting; that is, it may negotiate a contract with an investment banking syndicate to purchase the unsold portion of an issue to be offered to its stockholders. Under such an arrangement, the corporation may pay either a flat commission on the entire issue or a smaller commission on the issue plus a higher one on each bond or share not subscribed for by existing stockholders. When planning to offer an issue under subscription rights, the corporation usually uses the services of its investment banker in preparing forms, pricing the stock, registering the issue with the Securities and Exchange Commission, preparing the prospectus, and handling other details associated with distribution of the securities.

## Summary

There are two main sources of capital funds: owners and lenders. Equity or proprietary capital refers to that provided by owners and has the following distinguishing characteristics: the firm is under no contractual obligation to pay a return thereon, there is no stated date on which the funds must be returned to the investor, and those who provide funds are responsible for the management and control of the firm. Sometimes the term "risk capital" is used; this emphasizes the fact that owners of equities assume risks to a greater degree than do lenders. Even though owners must assume risks inherent in stock ownership, this may be more than offset by prospects for high returns.

Evidence of ownership in a business will vary according to the form of organization. If the business is incorporated, ownership is evidenced by stock certificates. In most instances, stock can be sold at will by the owner; even though a stock certificate is not a credit instrument, it has some of the characteristics of negotiable instruments.

Corporation-law statutes of the various states usually provide that each outstanding share of stock is entitled to one vote if it is not of a class of stock that is denied the right to vote by the articles of incorporation. Directors may be elected either by majority or cumulative voting. In the former instance, one vote is cast for each director to be elected. In cumulative voting, a stockholder or his proxy may cast votes for any one candidate equal to the number of shares owned or controlled times the number of directors to be elected, or the stockholder may split them up among two or more candidates.

If a company repurchases or otherwise acquires some of its own stock, it is called treasury stock. It may not be voted by management.

The common-law preemptive-right principle holds that old stockholders should be given the right to protect their proportionate voting power and commensurable share in the net worth and earnings of their company. As a financing device, such an offering is most important to old stockholders when the value of subscription rights is substantial. For rights to have value, the market price must be above the subscription price.

## QUESTIONS

1. What is the chief disadvantage of financing with common stock in comparison with debt?
2. What are the most important characteristics of equity capital?
3. From the viewpoint of the investor in common stock, what justification is there for calling common stock "risk capital"?
4. What is a stock certificate? Is it negotiable? Transferable? Explain.
5. a. When is a stock "ex dividend"? b. What is meant by "holder of record"?
6. Why would a firm repurchase its own common stock?
7. "In pricing a new stock issue, an unknown company is no better or worse off than a known company." Discuss.
8. Discuss and analyze the reasons supporting the preemptive-rights principle.
9. Why is there usually a discrepancy between the calculated price of a right and the actual market price?
10. How would you respond to stockholders' complaints that the subscription price in a recent stock offering was too low, thereby unduly depressing the market price of the company's stock?
11. What are the advantages to a corporation of having a classified board of directors (one in which the terms of office are staggered and only a portion of the board is elected annually)?

## PROBLEMS

1. The common stock of KLS Incorporated is selling at $40 per share, rights-on. Find the value of the right if the stockholders are offered one new share at a subscription price of $30 for every four shares held.

2. The Southwest Company has the following balance sheet and income statement for the year 1978. The firm is contemplating a stock rights offering.

SOUTHWEST COMPANY
Balance Sheet before Rights Offering for the Year Ending December 31, 1978

| | | | | |
|---|---|---|---|---|
| Total Assets | $900,000 | Bonds (6%) | | $400,000 |
| | | Common stock (par value $1) | | 100,000 |
| | | Retained earnings | | 400,000 |
| Total Assets | $900,000 | Total Liabilities and Capital | | $900,000 |

Earning rate, 10% on total assets:
Total earnings ............................. $90,000
Interest on bonds .......................... 24,000
Earnings before income taxes ............... $66,000
Income taxes (50% rate assumed) ............ 33,000
Earnings after Taxes ....................... $33,000

Earnings per share .......... $0.33
Dividends per share ......... $0.20
Price-earnings ratio ........ 13 times
Market price per share ...... $4.29

The Southwest Company seeks to raise an additional $200,000 by a rights offering. The new funds will earn .15 percent on assets. The price-earnings ratio will probably rise to 14 times because of improved market conditions. Dividends are not expected to change. Assume that the subscription price will be set at $4 per share.

   *a.* How many additional shares of stock will be sold?
   *b.* How many rights will be needed to purchase one new share?
   *c.* What will be the new earnings per share?
   *d.* What will be the new market price per share?
   *e.* Why did the earnings per share decline slightly?
   *f.* Would this rights offering succeed?

3. Gas Lite, Inc., is preparing a new issue of common stock. They have one million shares currently outstanding and will issue 100,000 new shares of common stock.
   *a.* How many rights must they issue?
   *b.* How many shares is each right entitled to?
   *c.* If the current market price of Gas Lite is $50 and the subscription price is $44.50, what is the value of each right?
   *d.* What is the value of each right when the stock is traded ex-rights? (Assume the price of the stock remains at $50.)

4. On June 1, Corporation D announced it was offering subscription rights to its stockholders of record as of June 15 to subscribe to new shares in the ratio of one new share for each five held. The subscription price of this stock was $55 a share and the rights were to expire June 30. From May 20 until June 24 the price remained stationary at $60 a share. On June 25 it declined to $58 a share and remained there through June 27.
   *a.* What would be the probable market value of a right on June 27?
   *b.* Why is there said to be a strong element of compulsion in most rights offerings?
   *c.* Will this one probably succeed?

5.  *a.* If cumulative voting exists in the corporation, how many shares must a minority group have or obtain to assure themselves the election of 4 directors if 19 are to be elected and 100,000 shares are outstanding and entitled to vote?
    *b.* How many cumulative votes must the minority have in the problem above?
6.  If a group holds 40,000 of the 200,000 shares outstanding, how many directors can they elect if nine are going to be elected?
7.  Assuming there are 6,000 shares of stock in a corporation, the stockholders have the right of cumulative voting, and seven directors are to be elected:
    *a.* How many shares are needed to elect two directors? All the directors?
    *b.* Assuming majority voting, how many shares could unquestionably elect a single director? All the directors? (Give the minimum number.)
8.  Assuming there are 1,000 shares of stock in a corporation, the stockholders have the right of cumulative voting, and ten directors are to be elected:
    *a.* How many shares are needed to elect a single director? A majority of the directors? All the directors?
    *b.* If you had 170 shares of stock, how many directors could you be sure of electing?
    *c.* Do you think cumulative voting permits a greater degree of democracy in the control of a corporation?
9.  The management of AR, Inc., is contemplating a common-stock issue as a means of financing the firm's capital requirements. Its current financial position is as follows:

    | | |
    |---|---|
    | Net profit after taxes | $20,000,000 |
    | Number of shares outstanding | 5,000,000 |
    | Market Price | $80 |

    If the firm uses common stock as a means of raising money, management estimates they will have to issue 500,000 new shares and that the use of funds should result in a $4-million after-tax increase in profits. They will go ahead with the stock issue only if it does not reduce the market price of the stock. Assuming the price-earnings ratio remains the same after the stock issue (and the increase in profits), should AR, Inc., issue the new common stock?

## ADDITIONAL READINGS

Bacon, P. W. "The Subscription Price in Rights Offerings," *Financial Management*, vol. 1 (Summer 1972), pp. 59–64.

Ellis, C. D. "Repurchase Stock to Revitalize Equity," *Harvard Business Review*, vol. 43 (July–August 1965), pp. 119–28.

Grier, P. C., and P. S. Albin. "Nonrandom Price Changes in Association with Trading in Large Blocks," *Journal of Business*, vol. 46, no. 3 (July 1973), pp. 425–33.

Guthart, L. A. "More Companies Are Buying Back Their Stock," *Harvard Business Review*, vol. 43 (March–April 1965), pp. 40–53.

Hubbard, P. M., Jr. "The Many Aspects of Dilution," *Financial Analysts Journal*, vol. 19 (May–June 1963), pp. 33, 36–40.

Meyers, S. L. "A Re-examination of Market and Industry Factors in Stock Price Behavior," *Journal of Finance*, vol. 28, no. 3 (June 1973), pp. 695–705.

Nelson, J. R. "Price Effects in Rights Offerings," *Journal of Finance*, vol. 20 (December 1965), pp. 647–50.

O'Neal, F. H. "Minority Owners Can Avoid Squeeze-Outs," *Harvard Business Review*, vol. 41 (March–April 1963), pp. 150–52.

Sametz, A. W. "Trends in the Volume and Composition of Equity Finance," *Journal of Finance*, vol. 19 (September 1964), pp. 450–69.

VanHorne, J. C., and W. F. Glassmire, Jr. "The Impact of Unanticipated Changes in Inflation on the Value of Common Stocks," *Journal of Finance*, vol. 27, no. 5 (December 1972), pp. 1081–92.

# 17

# Preferred Stock

When the objective of the organizers of a corporation is to give management considerable latitude in financing the corporation, the articles of incorporation may contain provisions authorizing the issuance of one or more classes of preferred stock in addition to common stock. Preferred stock represents ownership and is placed with common stock in the owners' equity section of the balance sheet. Since World War II the relative amount of equity funds provided by preferred stock has declined sharply when compared to the sum provided by common stock equity for practically all United States corporations. The main disadvantage embodied in preferred stock, as compared to bonds, is that dividends thereon are not deductible as a cost in computing federal income tax obligations.

## Characteristics of Preferred Stock

Preferred stock has been given preferences over common stock by the charter of the corporation, and in exchange for these preferences has lost some of the rights inherent in common stock ownership. In general, the preferences given preferred stockholders are detrimental to the common stock owners' interests. The areas of bargaining, as outlined in the previous chapter, are concentrated on provisions for retirement, income and asset claims, and voting rights. Preferences over common stock usually are given to claims on income, and assets in case of liquidation of the corporation. However, in each instance the prior claim usually is limited. Although preferred stockholders have no contractual rights to dividends, they come first if and when dividends are declared. Until their claims are settled, common stockholders may not receive dividends.

In general, if no specific mention is made in a corporation's charter, preferred stockholders are entitled to voting privileges. However, voting rights are usually limited by the charter, and are contingent upon the occurrence of some event.

The creditors have prior claims over both preferred and common stockholders to income and assets; hence, those who want maximum protection in their investments will purchase bonds rather than preferred or common stock.

A typical preferred stock is a hybrid type of security possessing characteristics of both a stock and a bond. As a stock, it represents equity capital, and, as such, it entails no interest obligations or maturity contract. The corporation has a legal obligation to pay interest on bonds at a specified rate, but it has only a moral obligation to pay dividends on preferred stock at the rate specified in the articles of incorporation.

The preferred stockholders of a prosperous, well-managed corporation receive income just as regularly as they would if they had legal claims to income. In fact, many preferred stockholders themselves are often confused as to the nature of their investments—calling the income thereon interest rather than dividends. However, the risks assumed by a preferred stockholder are greater than those assumed by a bondholder (assuming other things are equal), because there is a difference between a "moral" and a "legal" obligation. As a consequence, at a given point in time a corporation's market dividend yield on preferred stock may be higher than the market interest yield on its bonds.

*Preferred Stock as a Financing Device.* Preferred stock is the least important of the three major classes of corporate securities issued each year (bonds, common stock, and preferred stock—in that order). Preferred stock is issued most often by corporations whose earnings are stable (i.e., public-utility companies). Although preferred stock is seldom used by manufacturing companies as a major financing device, some major industrial companies, such as General Motors Corporation and E. I. du Pont de Nemours and Co., have preferred-stock issues outstanding. Instead of using preferred stock, in many cases financial managers are shifting to financing with junior ranking debt (subordinated debentures) convertible into common stock. Subordinated-debenture holders have claims on the firm's assets only after the claims of the senior debtholders have been satisfied. (See Chapter 18.) The main motive for the use of subordinated debentures is to qualify for the tax deductibility of the interest payments.[1]

---

[1] The main disadvantage of preferred stock is that the dividends paid on it are not deductible as a tax expense by the issuer. It is this factor that makes preferred-stock financing more expensive than bond financing. For instance, assume that a corporation is in the 50-percent tax bracket and has the choice of financing with either 8-percent bonds or 10-percent preferred stock. To obtain $20 million it would cost the corporation $2 million per year in dividends to finance with preferred stock, whereas it would cost $800,000 in interest cost after taxes to finance with bonds. Since bond interest is a tax-deductible expense, it reduces income by $1.6 million per year and requires the corporation to earn only $1.6 million before taxes. However, for the corporation to pay

With the consent of both common and preferred stockholders, management may refinance and eliminate its preferred stock. For example, on June 30, 1965, the stockholders of the American Tobacco Company (now American Brands Company, Inc.), at a special meeting, approved a plan to give each of the company's preferred stockholders $150 in cash for each share held, or $50 in cash and one 4⅝-percent, 25-year subordinated debenture with $100 face value that was nonredeemable for five years. The president of the company estimated that common stockholders' earnings per share would increase about $0.06 as a result of tax savings. The cash used for retirement of the preferred stock came from working capital.

In a later section of this chapter the reasons for the frequent use of convertible preferred stock in mergers are reviewed from both the issuers' and investors' viewpoints.

## Redemption or Retirement of Preferred Stock

Management may provide for the retirement of preferred stock at the time of issuance by inserting the call feature or by making provisions for sinking funds. The investment bankers who underwrite an issue of preferred stock may insist on the sinking-fund provision in order to assure improvement in the quality of the securities over the years. They may also insist on a provision to retire a specified percentage of the shares over a series of years. The preferred-stock certificate, the contract between the corporation and the shareholder, may contain a clause permitting the corporation to repurchase the stock at a specified price at the option of the corporation or according to some prearranged plan. The purpose of including such an option is to permit the corporation to retire these securities if management finds it desirable to do so. In other cases, preferred stock is noncallable.[2]

The legal procedure for redemption of preferred stock usually requires that the owners receive 30 days' (or some other specified number of days) prior notice that the preferred stock is being called on a certain date for redemption, the place where stockholders are to receive payment on surrender of their stock certificates, and the call or redemption price. Arrangements may be made with a bank or trust company in the United States to make payment with funds deposited by the corporation for this purpose.

After the shares have been reacquired by the corporation, such shares

---

the preferred dividends, it must earn $4 million before taxes, because the preferred dividends are not a deductible expense. Assuming a 50-percent tax, the corporation needs to earn $4 million before taxes to have $2 million left after taxes to pay the preferred-stock dividend.

[2] Illustrations of noncallable preferred stock are American Can Company, 7-percent cumulative preferred, par value $25, and Celanese Corporation, 7-percent cumulative second preferred, par value $100.

are cancelled by the corporation (which should not be confused with cancelling old stock certificates and issuing new ones when ownership of stock is transferred "on the books"). Later, such shares may be restored to the status of treasury stock or "authorized but unissued shares"; sometimes, however, the provisions under which the shares are issued call for their permanent retirement. In either case, when shares are cancelled, the corporation is required to file a statement of the cancellation with the secretary of state. Since permanent retirement necessitates a change in the amount of authorized capital, the filing of the statement of cancellation amounts to an amendment to the articles of incorporation.

*Voluntary Retirement.* The call price is of interest to preferred stockholders because the call option would tend to be used when it is to the advantage of the corporation to do so. In order to refinance economically, management must keep the call price as low as possible without seriously reducing the salability of the preferred stock. The call price is above the par or stated value of the stock; the amount above par or stated value —the call premium—will be highest when financing in the capital market is most difficult and vice versa. Therefore, the same factors that necessitate a high dividend rate also necessitate a high call premium.[3]

The most important advantage to corporations in issuing callable preferred stock is the ability to replace an issue carrying a high dividend rate with one carrying a lower dividend rate. However, refinancing may be expensive and even unprofitable. At the time of refinancing, the corporation must issue enough new preferred stock not only to finance repurchase of the old shares but also to pay for the premium thereon plus underwriting and legal fees and other costs of refinancing. Since many of the preferred stocks issued during the 1920s had a call price of $120, the number of new shares issued would have had to exceed the old by at least 20 percent, assuming a par value of $100. But, if the dividend rate on the new shares is reduced enough, the refinancing will be worthwhile in spite of the fact that dividends must be paid on more shares.

In some cases, a corporation merely establishes the right to redeem or call stock without making any specific provisions as to sinking funds or other details except a call price. There may be a provision that the corporation may not pay more than par or stated value plus the accrued unpaid dividends for the preferred stock. The conditions under which a corporation may provide for the retirement of its preferred stock may be similar to those used in the case of sinking funds, except that retirement would be on a voluntary basis, with the corporation purchasing the securities in the open market or directly from stockholders. The corporation may announce to preferred stockholders that it will repurchase some

---

[3] Illustrations of call prices for preferred stock are: Generals Motors, $5.00 cumulative preferred, callable at $120; and Quaker Oats Company, $3 cumulative convertible preferred, par $50, callable at $58.

of the preferred shares at a stated price or merely that it will buy a certain number of shares, requesting that preferred stockholders notify the company as to the price at which they will sell their shares. The latter method permits the corporation to buy shares of preferred stock from those who tender their stocks at the lowest price.

*Mandatory Retirement.* At the time of issuance of preferred stock, a corporation may make provisions for its retirement. Instead of planning to refinance the preferred stock issue if and when market conditions are favorable, the terms under which the stock is issued may require the corporation to redeem a specified amount of the stock each year or to set aside a definite sum for this purpose. The pool of assets earmarked to retire preferred stock is called a sinking fund. Usually, funds required for redemption purposes must be set aside before dividends are paid on common stock. The use of sinking funds to retire preferred stock provides for orderly liquidation when the capital needs represented by such securities are only temporary. Provisions for sinking funds appear most commonly for preferred stock issues of industrial companies.

In using the assets set aside to retire preferred stock, the corporation may purchase the stock directly from stockholders or in the open market at or below the redemption price; purchase preferred shares as determined by lot (placing serial numbers in a container and retiring the numbers drawn); or retire stock on a pro rata basis, each shareholder being required to surrender stock equal to certain percentage of his holding. At the time of issuance, these terms are agreed to by those purchasing the stock; therefore, stockholders would have no choice but to surrender their shares in return for the redemption payment offered under the conditions cited above. Retiring preferred stock by lot is more commonly used than the pro rata method.

As in the case of callable preferred stock, the sinking-fund redemption price is customarily above the par or stated value of the shares. This price may be adjusted downward with the passage of time, because the preferred stockholder's cost of investing will gradually have been "amortized" out of dividends on the preferred stock. The justification for the downward adjustment in the redemption price is that the higher premium during the early life of the stock is a compensation to the investor for reinvesting; the investors who hold preferred stock for 20 years have less claim to compensation than those who hold it for only 1 year.

The primary purpose of management in providing for sinking funds when issuing preferred stock is to obtain capital under more favorable terms (higher price for the stock). Many companies whose market for preferred stock is thin expect the purchases of the preferred stock by the managers of the sinking fund to keep up the market price (or at least to maintain an orderly market for it). However, sinking-fund provisions at the time of issuance of preferred stock may not have the expected beneficial effect on the market for the stock in future years unless the total authorization is limited. Many corporations issue preferred stocks in series; while old stock is being retired, larger amounts of new stock may be issued, to the detriment of the market price for all of the company's preferred stock issues.

Provisions for compulsory sinking-fund contributions may be disadvantageous to a corporation at a time when cash is needed for other purposes. At the time a corporation's earnings are growing, it will lose the use of cash; at the time its earnings are declining, it will have to choose between withdrawing cash or defaulting on its sinking-fund contributions. If the latter is chosen, the corporation is usually subject to certain restrictions on its activities, such as borrowing, paying dividends on common stock, and reacquiring stock already issued.

## Liquidation and Dissolution Status

In case of liquidation or dissolution of a corporation, corporate charters usually give preferred stockholders priority over common stockholders as to assets as well as dividends. But, if the articles of incorporation give them preference as to dividends only (being silent in regard to priority as to assets), preferred stockholders share pro rata with common stockholders in case of liquidation or dissolution. The purpose of giving preferred stock priority as to assets is to facilitate financing by making the stock more salable, in the same way that pledges of property make bonds more salable.

The preferred stockholders' preference to assets, like the preference to dividends, is subject to limitations. In the case of involuntary liquidation or dissolution, priority to assets of preferred stock is limited to the par value, or stated value if no-par. If the corporation is reorganized, the preferred stockholders may be permitted to exchange old preferred shares for new preferred or common stock in the new corporation, while the old common stockholders' claims may have no value. If the corporation is liquidated, preferred stockholders have the first claim to any cash remaining after debts are paid. In case of liquidation, if one assumes that after paying debts the amount of equity per share of stock—both common and preferred—is $25 and that there is an equal number of shares of each kind of stock, the owners of preferred $100 par value shares will receive $50 a share and the common stockholders will receive nothing.

Sometimes the corporate charter will make a distinction between the right to assets of preferred stock in voluntary or involuntary dissolution. If so, preferred stock's right to participate in assets is usually higher when the dissolution is voluntary. The general rule seems to be that, if there is any uncertainty, preferred stock is entitled to a fair investment value, which may be more than par or stated value. But, if there is a statement to the effect that preferred stock has a preference as to assets in an amount equal to par value or in some other specified amount, a contract exists that limits the claims of preferred stockholders to that amount. The current and future value of preferred stock will depend primarily on the earning record of the corporation, because investors are interested secondarily in what preference they have to assets in case of liquidation or dissolution.

*Special Protective Features.* It is not unusual for management to issue preferred stock that has special features that provide additional protection for investors. For example, the terms under which preferred stock is issued may make it obligatory for a corporation to limit long-term borrowing, forego expenditures that would reduce working capital, and refrain from additional issues of preferred stock. There are cases wherein such restrictions are important to investors. For instance, when a large issue of preferred stock is offered in order to increase the equity base for future debt financing, investors may be interested in features that limit the future debt of the corporation.

## Income Claim

*Dividend Rate.* Customarily, the dividend rate on preferred stock is provided for in the corporate charter, being fixed by management at a rate that will assure the sale of the stock at the time of issuance. When preferred stock has par value, the dividend rate is expressed as a percentage; when it is no-par stock, the rate is expressed as a specific amount per share. The name of a no-par preferred stock includes the dividend rate: for example, General Motors Corporation, $5 cumulative preferred stock with no-par value and $3.75 cumulative preferred stock with no-par value. Since 1964, the New York Stock Exchange has permitted the companies whose securities are listed thereon to omit a statement of par value from preferred stock certificates except when the dividend is expressed as a percentage of par value.

On the typical preferred stock, the dividend rate is limited to the specified rate, but on common stock there is no limit on the amount of dividends that may be declared if earned. For instance, if a corporation has net profits after interest and taxes of $200,000, has outstanding 10,000 shares of 5-percent preferred stock and 10,000 shares of common stock, the preferred stock has prior claims to $50,000 of net profits and the remaining $150,000 will be available for dividends on the common stock.

*Cumulative Dividends.* The often-stated advantage to the issuer of financing with preferred stock—that dividends may be passed and cash retained—is a technical rather than a practical advantage. While preferred stock permits the use of leverage without legally increasing fixed charges, management usually finds it necessary to meet dividend payments on preferred stock to prevent the corporation's credit standing from being adversely affected. When preferred stock is cumulative—a common feature—the pressure to pay dividends thereon is magnified because unpaid dividends accumulate as claims against future earnings of the corporation that must be met before dividends can be paid on common stock. (When dividends have not been paid on cumulative preferred stock, dividends are referred to as being in arrears.) Corporations try to avoid dividend arrearages on preferred stock issues because they have a depressing effect on the corporation's credit and on the market price of its common stock as well as on its preferred stock. The amount of preferred stock outstanding is usually small as compared with the amount of common stock; hence, it is more important to maintain the market value of the common stock than to pass dividends on preferred stock so as to prevent the cash drain entailed.

If preferred-stock dividends are postponed for any length of time, the amount in arrears may be so great as to make it almost impossible for earnings to catch up. In this case the board of directors may propose a settlement, such as giving some cash and preferred stock for the dividends in arrears. However, unless expected earnings are sufficient to meet the dividends on the new as well as the old preferred stock, such financing is meaningless. Such a change would need the approval of at least the required percentage of the shares affected to be binding on the stockholders.

**Noncumulative Dividends.** The articles of incorporation may permit the avoidance of the risk of preferred-stock dividend arrearages by specifying that dividends on a preferred-stock issue are noncumulative. During periods of low earnings, dividends on noncumulative preferred stock may be passed as freely as on common stock without creating future claims to dividends that are prior to claims to dividends on common stock. Many of the preferred-stock issues outstanding, having the noncumulative feature, have resulted from involuntary reorganization of corporations in which bondholders had been required to exchange bonds for preferred stock of this class. When noncumulative preferred stock is sold, it customarily has a higher dividend rate than would otherwise be necessary. It would be well to point out, however, that the great majority of preferred stock outstanding today includes the cumulative feature.

Since the proprietary interest of those in managerial positions is usually represented by common stock and because the noncumulative feature works to the advantage of common stockholders, directors may be tempted to pass dividends on preferred stock even though the earnings of the company justify their payment. In general, directors have not done so except in rehabilitation cases wherein the temporary retention of large earnings is justified. In the classic case on this subject, the court ruled in part:

> When the net profits of a corporation out of which a dividend might have been declared for the preferred stock are justifiably applied by the directors to capital improvements, the claim of the stock for that year is gone,

if by the terms of the articles of incorporation and the certificates, the preferential dividends are not to be cumulative.[4]

*Participating Dividends.* As noted earlier the typical preferred stock does not participate in dividends beyond the rate specified on the stock certificate. Since there is some doubt as to rights of preferred stockholders to participate in dividends beyond the stated rate, the board of directors may remove any uncertainty by inserting a provision in the stock certificate such as "preferred as to dividends at the rate of 5 percent annually (or $5 per share) and no more." On the other hand, in order to make a preferred stock more attractive to investors, the corporation may make specific provisions for participation in dividends beyond the rate stated in the preferred stock certificate (illustrated by Southern California Edison, 5-percent cumulative participating preferred stock). Typically, the participation feature would not be provided if it were not necessary for selling the stock. Probably the most exceptions to this generalization would occur in a closely held corporation where participating preferred stock is granted to a particular stockholder because of some key relationship (past or present) with the corporation.

In the absence of specific provisions for participation, there is doubt as to the right of preferred stock to participate in dividends beyond the rate stated for preferred stock. Thus, the assumption is that the stated preferential rate is at the same time a "statement of limitation." When a participation clause exists in preferred stock contracts, the most common form is one that permits it to share equally with common stock if and when a dividend in excess of the rate provided for preferred stock is declared on common stock. If the dividend rate on preferred stock is 5 percent and a 7-percent dividend is declared on common stock, the preferred stockholders would receive 7 percent rather than 5 percent.

*Taxability of Dividends.* One important market for preferred stock is its use as an investment vehicle by other corporations. If a corporation purchases the preferred stock of another corporation, it is entitled to deduct 85 percent of the preferred dividends it receives in determining its income. Thus, if the corporation is in an unfavorable tax position (i.e., in the 50-percent tax bracket), it would be better off to purchase an 8-percent preferred stock rather than an 8-percent bond. It would receive 4 percent after taxes on the bond, whereas it would receive 7.4 percent after taxes on the preferred stock. Of course, if the investing firm is desirous of maintaining a liquid asset, the preferred-stock issue normally would not fill that need because of its limited marketability.

## Voting Right of Preferred Stockholders

Voting right refers to the privilege of voting for directors and on policies and other matters brought before annual and special meetings of

---

[4] *Wabash Ry. Co.* v. *Barclay*, 250 U.S. 197.

stockholders. Unless specifically stated to the contrary in the articles of incorporation, preferred stockholders have the same voting right as common stockholders. Since the right to vote is a fundamental one, any limitations placed on preferred stockholders regarding this right must be permitted by the state business-corporation act as well as included in the articles of incorporation and printed on the preferred stock certificate. Usually, this disfranchisement is modified by law or by agreements covering temporary circumstances. In other words, complete disfranchisement is unusual.

**Consent Voting Rights.** Among the more common circumstances whereby preferred stock is permitted to vote is one in which the assets of the corporation or the rights and privileges of the preferred stock are involved. This means that consent of the preferred stockholders must be obtained before any such proposed action is taken. Since preferred stockholders vote as a class on proposals affecting their rights and privileges, a proposal is defeated unless favored by the required percentage of the stock affected (usually two-thirds), even though a much larger number of common stockholders favor it. If management is insistent on the proposal in spite of its rejection, it may be necessary for the parties representing management to acquire the preferred shares, to obtain a court ruling to permit the corporation to proceed with its plans, or to amend the proposal to make it acceptable to preferred stockholders. The existence of preferred stock may be a serious obstacle to management in new financing if the proposed new shares have rights and preferences superior or equal to those of old preferred shareholders.

**Variation in Voting Strength of Preferred Stockholders.** If and when preferred stock is given temporary or permanent voting right as to the election of directors and on other matters, the effect of this right is determined by the relative voting strength of preferred stockholders. The number of shares of preferred stock relative to common stock may be such that the preferred stockholders are able to select all or none of the directors. If cumulative voting for directors is permitted, the minority group may obtain representation. In all cases, shareholders must vote in person or by proxy. If the voting arrangement is "one share, one vote," (majority voting) preferred stock is usually outnumbered and so special charter provisions may be made to give preferred stock representation on the board of directors. Preferred stockholders may be given two or three votes per share; but, most commonly, the principle of class voting is applied to selection of directors, with preferred stockholders being permitted to select a given number or a given percentage of directors.

As provided for in the articles of incorporation, preferred stockholders' right to vote may be temporary or permanent. Management may take the position that common stockholders are the risk takers and, as such, should have the entire responsibility for management. To the extent that preferred stock dividends are being paid regularly, as provided for in the corporate charter, the status of preferred stockholders is different from that of common stockholders. But, if preferred stock dividends are passed, preferred stockholders are in the same relative position as common stockholders and should have a share in management. Customarily, preferred stockholders are entitled to vote if dividends on preferred stock are passed a specified number of times (usually four consecutive quarters). In some cases, when dividends on preferred stock are in default in an amount equivalent to four full quarterly dividend payments, the preferred stockholders may be authorized to elect a majority of the board of directors until all the arrearages have been paid.

The Securities and Exchange Commission has been instrumental in securing protective charter provisions for preferred stockholders. In the past, the abuses associated with the issuance of preferred stock by operating and public-utility holding companies resulted in heavy losses to investors in these securities. Now, the issuance of preferred stock by such companies is prohibited except under limited circumstances subject to approval by the commission.[5] The New York Stock Exchange has been instrumental in increasing the practice of giving temporary voting rights to preferred stockholders when dividends are in default by refusing to list preferred stock that, as a class, does not have the right to elect at least minority directors when the dividends have been in arrears or default.

***Proposals Requiring Class Voting.*** Class voting is required on proposals to increase or decrease the authorized number of such shares, to permit an exchange or create a right of exchange whereby another class of stock may be converted into this preferred class, to create a new class of shares having rights or preferences prior to those of existing preferred shares, to increase the rights and preferences of any class that has inferior rights so they become equal to or prior to those of the preferred shares, to limit or deny any existing preemptive rights, and to cancel or otherwise affect dividends on shares that have accrued but have not been declared. While this list is not complete, it suggests the difficulties

---

[5] The Securities and Exchange Commission has insisted that the articles of incorporation of companies in the public-utility field must contain various features to protect the rights of preferred stockholders.

"These usually consist of the right to elect a majority of the board of directors in the event of default in the payment of four quarterly preferred stock dividends, and certain voting rights in connection with the following matters: the issuance of short-term debt in excess of prescribed amounts, mergers and consolidations, the authorization of any class of stock ranking prior to or on a parity with the outstanding preferred stock, the amendment of the charter to change the express terms of the preferred stock in any substantially prejudicial manner, the issuance of authorized but unissued preferred stock and increasing the amount of authorized but unissued preferred stock. In addition, the Commission has required that the charter limit the amount of initially authorized but unissued preferred stock and contain certain provisions with respect to the payment of common stock dividends which will reasonably safeguard the interests of the preferred stockholders." (*Tenth Annual Report of the Securities and Exchange Commission Fiscal Year Ended June 30, 1944, A Ten Year Survey 1934–1944* [Washington, D.C.: U.S. Government Printing Office, 1945], p. 103.)

a corporation may encounter in financing with a second issue of preferred stock (assuming that preferred stockholders would be reluctant to approve any change that would affect their interests adversely).

## Convertible Preferred Stock

In addition to the features of preferred stock already discussed, management may add a number of fringe provisions that are included at the time of issuance in order to enhance the attractiveness of the stock. The title of preferred stock may indicate that it is convertible into common stock at the option of the holder (for example, Atlantic-Richfield Company $3 cumulative convertible preference preferred, par $1, may be exchanged for 3.4 common shares for each preferred share, and it may be converted into common at any time). Management expects to make preferred stock more salable by giving the conversion privilege to enable holders to share in the future growth of the company. In effect, holders are given an option to acquire common stock at a fixed price in exchange for preferred stock. At the time of issuance of convertible preferred stock, shares of authorized common stock are reserved to be issued upon conversion of preferred stock.

Generally, preferred stockholders have no prior or preemptive rights to subscribe for new shares of convertible preferred or common stock. In other words, they are usually treated as "outsiders" when the corporation issues new securities convertible into common stock. Preferred stock may be par or no-par stock, and, among more recent issues, stock with par value of less than $100 seems to be predominant.

The conversion option may be expressed as a price—for example, two shares of common stock may be acquired for $50 in exchange for one share of preferred stock; or it may be expressed as a ratio—for example, one share of preferred may be exchanged for two shares of common stock. The conversion price or ratio may be variable, with the value of the conversion privilege being lowered progressively over a period of years. Usually, a date is fixed beyond which the preferred stock is no longer convertible into common stock (for example, Altec $.80 cumulative convertible preferred, class B, convertible into one common share until March 1, 1988). The ratio of conversion may be fixed so as to make immediate conversion profitable, but this is not the usual practice. So, the conversion feature usually adds only a speculative value to the preferred stock. The fact that there are many convertible preferred stocks outstanding suggests that, in many cases, owners have not yet found conversion sufficiently attractive. Nevertheless, it still may be valuable.[6]

When one share of $20 par value preferred stock may be exchanged for

---

[6] In the event conversion does become feasible the firm may force conversion by including the call feature when the preferred stock is issued.

two shares of common stock with a market value of $10 or more, conversion may take place. Investors in common stock may purchase common stock directly or may purchase convertible preferred stock to exchange it for common stock. The cheaper method of obtaining common stock will be used; therefore, the market value of the preferred stock will tend to be at the same ratio to common stock as the conversion ratio when the market price of the common stock is above the conversion price. If one assumes that one share of preferred stock is convertible into two shares of common stock, the preferred position of the preferred stock may cause it to sell for $20 while common stock may be selling for $8 or $9 per share; but, if the common stock is selling for $11, one would expect the preferred stock to be selling for about $22.

If and when conversion is profitable, shifts of buying and selling orders between common and preferred stock will tend to eliminate any differential, with the result that the price of the preferred will reflect the price of the common stock. In practice, arbitragers in securities will sell the common stock "short" and make delivery by buying the preferred and converting it into common (depressing the price of the common and increase the price of the preferred stock, thereby eliminating the price differential).

The conditions under which an owner of convertible preferred stock may convert it into common stock are determined primarily by the market prices of the two issues and how long this situation is expected to continue. Owners may decide to use the conversion privilege when dividends on common stock are so much larger than on preferred stock as to offset the added risk; when the conversion privilege is about to expire and the value of the preferred stock without the conversion right will be less than the value of the common stock into which it is convertible; when the convertible preferred stock is to be redeemed and the value of common stock is greater than the redemption price of the preferred stock; or when other advantages possessed by common stock justify conversion (voting rights, privileged subscriptions, etc.)

As noted above, the conversion privilege is inserted into charter provisions for preferred stock to make it more salable. But what is to be the long-run effect on the corporation's capital structure and the rights and privileges of old common stockholders? While issuance of convertible preferred stock may permit the corporation to finance more cheaply with temporarily beneficial effects to common stockholders, subsequent conversion may have a depressing effect on the price of common stock because of the increase in the number of shares and resulting dilution of earnings and assets represented by each share. However, a reduction in the amount of senior stock outstanding will strengthen the claim to earnings of common stockholders if the corporation's earnings decline. Furthermore, the elimination of preferred stock will simplify the corporate financial structure, will broaden the market for common stock, and, finally, will clear the way for future issues of preferred stock under market conditions that may be favorable to the corporation.

## Merger Financing with Convertible Preferred Stock

In the last 30 years preferred stock has played a rather minor role in new corporate financing. However, convertible preferred stock has become more popular in the financing of corporate mergers and acquisitions. During the 1960–67 period, less than 15 percent of all the convertible preferred stock issued was employed for uses other than financing corporate mergers.[7]

There are two important reasons for using convertible preferred stock over common stock in mergers and acquisitions. First, it enables the acquiring firm to obtain immediate earnings leverage. If the after-tax net earnings of the acquired firm are larger than the dividend requirements on the newly issued preferred stock, the surviving firm will show increased earnings available for its common stockholders. To illustrate this point, assume that Corporation A is to be merged into Corporation B using preferred stock of B as the means of payment to A's stockholders. The premerger net earnings after taxes of Corporation A and B are $20,000 and $50,000, respectively. Now, assume the following post-merger facts:

### Corporation B

| | |
|---|---:|
| Net earnings after taxes ($20,000 + $50,000) | $70,000 |
| Number of new preferred shares issued by B | 5,000 |
| Dividend rate on new preferred shares | $3.00 |
| Number of common shares of Corporation B outstanding | 10,000 |
| Net earnings per share before merger of Corporation B ($50,000 ÷ 10,000) | $5.00 |
| Net earnings per share after merger of Corporation B ($70,000 − 15,000 = 55,000 ÷ 10,000) | $5.50 |

The post-merger earnings per common share are $5.50 as compared with the pre-merger per-share earnings of $5.00. However, in order to get the stockholders of Corporation A to agree to the merger it probably would be necessary to offer them dividends on the preferred stock that are higher than they received on the common stock of Company A, or perhaps make the preferred stock convertible into Corporation B's common stock. It might even be necessary to offer them both inducements.

Second, it enables the acquiring and acquired firms to reconcile divergent cash-dividend policies. The use of preferred stock permits the acquiring firm to maintain its existing cash-dividend policy on its common stock, and still pay the acquired firm's stockholders their former divi-

---

[7] George E. Pinches, "Financing with Convertible Preferred Stock, 1960–1967," *Journal of Finance*, March 1970, p. 62.

dends.[8] If the acquiring firm pays no dividends at all on its common stock, issuing preferred stock will enable the firm to pay dividends to the stockholders of the merged firm.

In addition to the advantages cited for the merging firm, a merger using convertibles is also advantageous to the selling shareholders. If bonds are used, the recipient stockholders are subject to a capital-gains tax on the proceeds they receive over and above their original cost. This is not the case when convertible preferred stock is used. Also, the shareholders of the acquired firm may be more easily persuaded to sell out if they are provided with a fixed-income security.

The majority of the mergers and acquisitions financed with convertible preferred stock does not use any additional financing instruments (other securities or cash). In those cases where convertible preferred stock is used for other purposes (i.e., issued for cash) it is mainly in the industries that require substantial capital outlays (public utilities, chemicals, metals, heavy machinery, data processing, etc.).[9] From all indications, it seems that convertible preferred stock will continue to play an active role in corporate mergers and acquisitions.

## Preferred Stock with Warrants

Sometimes preferred stock is issued with warrants attached that permit the stockholders to purchase common stock at a price, or prices, stated in the contract. At the time of issuance, the option price is usually substantially above the market price. The stock-purchase warrant is an option similar to that of the conversion privilege, but it has an additional advantage to the corporation in that it brings in additional cash when it is exercised. The warrant usually elapses at the end of the stated time, but, during the interim, the option price of common stock as stated in the warrant may have been increased progressively ($20 until a certain date, then $22 until a second date, etc.). Warrants may be detachable or nondetachable. If detachable, the warrant may be separated from the stock certificate and sold at any time; if nondetachable, it may be separated when presented to the corporation together with cash for common stock. Corporations issue preferred stocks with warrants attached for the same reason they issue convertible preferred stocks—to enhance their attractiveness to investors.

The use of preferred stock with warrants adds a speculative appeal to the issue. Since the option price is above the market price of the underlying common stock at the time of issuance, the warrant will have only a speculative appeal until the market price of the common stock equals the option price. The warrant can have no other value until that event occurs.

---

[8] Ibid. p. 59.
[9] Ibid.

## Future Role of Preferred Stock

Corporate financing in the past 30 years has emphasized internal financing and corporate debt when external funds are sought. Preferred stock issues have been virtually ignored as a source of new corporate funds. The unpopularity of preferred stock with corporate managers probably stems from the fact that preferred stock dividends are not deductible for tax purposes from corporate income, whereas interest charges on bonds are deductible. For a company paying dividends on its common stock, the prior claim on income of preferred stock becomes an unavoidable fixed charge on income; hence, a company would be further ahead by paying interest on a bond issue that does have the deductibility advantage. Corporate boards of directors therefore have resolved that, if debt is cheaper than preferred stock and if the firms' policies imply that preferred dividends must be treated similarly to bond interest, debt should be used whenever there is a cost advantage.

Nevertheless, preferred stock is not destined to disappear completely from corporate balance sheets. As long as convertible preferred stock can be used advantageously in corporate acquisitions and mergers and public utilities require large sums of outside capital, preferred stocks will continue to be employed in these special instances. In capital-intensive industries such as public utility enterprises, the use of tax credits by the federal government to stimulate economic growth may make preferred stocks more attractive. Income tax credits will lower the effective after-tax cost of preferred stock by lowering the corporation income taxes payable by such firms. However, it will require a drastic shift in the corporate tax structure before preferred stocks will become a significant factor in the new corporate-funds market. For example, if the corporate tax laws were changed to permit the partial or full deductibility of dividend payments, preferred stock again would become an important alternative to bond financing.

## Summary

In return for giving preferred stock priority over common stock as to dividends and, usually, as to assets in case of liquidation, management customarily places limitations on the dividend rate and on the right to vote for directors. Preferred stock may be cumulative or noncumulative; that is, when dividends are passed, they may or may not accumulate as claims to future earnings that will have to be paid before dividends may be paid on common stock. Preferred stock may participate in dividends beyond the rate specified on the stock certificate, but usually does not.

Redemption or retirement of preferred stock issues may become desirable at some future time, and corporate management may anticipate this situation by making preferred stock callable. The most important advantage to corporations in issuing callable preferred stock is the ability to replace an issue carrying a high dividend rate with one carrying a lower rate. The corporate charter may also provide for issuance of various series of preferred stocks differing as to the rate of dividends, price, and terms under which shares may be redeemed, amount payable to shares in case of voluntary or involuntary liquidation, sinking-fund provisions, and terms and conditions under which shares may be converted.

Corporate management may issue convertible or nonconvertible preferred stock if provided for in the charter. The objective of management in issuing convertible preferred stock is to make the stock more salable by giving holders an opportunity to benefit from future growth of the company by use of the conversion privilege; however, the long-run effects on the corporation's capital structure are uncertain. While mass conversion of preferred stock may affect the status of common stock adversely in the short-run, the corporate financial structure will thereby be simplified, the market for common stock broadened, and the way cleared for future issues of preferred stock when market conditions are favorable. Corporations sometimes issue preferred stock with warrants attached that permit the holders to purchase common stock at a price stated in the contract.

Although preferred stock usually has limitations placed on voting rights, complete disfranchisement is rare. Preferred stockholders have the right to vote on any proposals that affect their rights and privileges, and it is not uncommon for them to have a temporary or permanent right to vote for representation on the board of directors.

The main disadvantage of preferred stock, as compared to bonds, is that dividends are not deductible as a cost in computing federal income taxes. Bond-interest expense is deductible, and this difference probably is the single most important factor accounting for the decline in usage of preferred stock by corporations in the post–World War II period.

## QUESTIONS

1. Is one justified in calling the typical preferred stock a "hybrid type of security" that possesses certain characteristics of common stock and certain characteristics of a long-term bond? Explain.
2. May the covenants for a preferred stock issue be drawn so the securities will have more of the characteristics of a bond than a common stock? Explain. May the opposite be true? Explain.
3. What justification would there be for assuming that many of the high-grade, high-dividend, noncallable preferred stocks now outstanding represent a financial mistake by the issuing corporations? Explain.
4. Assume that financing is difficult and it is necessary to offer attractive terms to investors. What features would you include in order to make preferred stock attractive and still keep the dividend rate in line with outstanding

preferred stock issues? Explain. Assume that financing is easy and it is possible to negotiate favorable terms. Would your answer differ?

5. What is meant by the statement that the conversion option may be expressed as a ratio or as a price? If the option is used, how would the position of old common stockholders be affected? Would the capital structure of the corporation be strengthened? Explain your answers. Is there justification for concluding that conversion is frequently offered by management to divert attention of investors from some corporate weakness?

6. Discuss the advantages and disadvantages of a preferred stock sinking fund from both the issuing corporation's and the stockholder's viewpoints.

7. There is *no* difference between the investor's or issuing corporation's preference as to whether a preferred stock has a low or a high call price. Discuss.

8. Should preferred stock be considered as debt or equity when measuring a firm's financial leverage? Would the method of classification be different for a creditor-versus-equity investor?

9. Briefly distinguish between the characteristics and features of convertible preferred stock and preferred stock with warrants attached.

## PROBLEMS

1. The Sun Country Utility Company currently has four preferred stock series outstanding. They are as follows:

    |  | Shares |
    |---|---|
    | Series A, 3%, $50 par value | 100,000 |
    | Series B, $6, $100 stated value | 150,000 |
    | Series C, $4.50, $100 stated value | 150,000 |
    | Series D, 9%, $100 par value | 200,000 |

    What amount of preferred dividends does Sun Country Utility pay annually?

2. What is the current dividend yield for each series if their respective market prices are as follows:

    | | |
    |---|---|
    | Series A | $ 20 |
    | Series B | 75 |
    | Series C | 50 |
    | Series D | 100 |

3. The Tucson Clothing Company has 10,000 shares of cumulative preferred stock outstanding; it pays annual dividends of $8 per share. In 1978, the company could pay only $4 per share to preferred stockholders, due to poor earnings.

    a. What will be the total payment in 1979 if the company becomes current on the dividend payments?

    b. Would it make any difference if the preferred stock were participating, but noncumulative, if only $4 is paid in 1978?

4. The board of directors of the XYZ Corporation is discussing the possibility of making one of the following investments. The investment will consist of $500,000. The alternatives are:

a. 8-percent corporate bonds.
b. $40 per share common stock, which is currently paying $1.50 per share dividends.
c. 5,000 shares of 6-percent preferred stock, par $100.

Which investment should they make? Assume a 50-percent tax bracket for the firm. Disregard possible capital gains on each investment.

5. The ABC Corporation is attempting to determine whether it should raise $10 million through a bond or a preferred stock issue. It is in the 50-percent tax bracket and feels the bond issue would have to sell at 8 percent, whereas the preferred stock could go for 6 percent if warrants were attached. How much does the corporation have to earn before taxes to pay the preferred dividends and the bond interest?

6. The College Company recently distributed a convertible preferred stock issue. The preferred stock pays annual dividends of $8 per share; each preferred stock share is convertible into four shares of common at a price of $25; the preferred shares were issued at $100 per share. Sometime later, the following events occurred:

a. The dividend yield for comparable preferred stock rose to 10 percent and the price of the College Company's common rose to $35.
b. The dividend yield for comparable preferred stock dropped to 5 percent and the price of the common dropped to $30.
c. The dividend yield remained at 5 percent while the price of common rose to $60.

What was the market price of the College Company's preferred stock for each of the three conditions above?

7. The executive committee of BC Inc. is considering three financing proposals. Assuming a marginal tax rate of 40 percent, the proposals are:

Proposal A: 9-percent corporate bonds.
Proposal B: Common stock paying a dividend of $3 annually, with a market value of $40 a share.
Proposal C: $5.50 convertible preferred, par $100.

Determine the after-tax interest or dividend cost to the firm of each proposal. Which proposal minimizes the after-tax interest or dividend cost to the firm? Assume there are *no* flotation costs.


## ADDITIONAL READINGS

Bildersee, J. S. "Some Aspects of the Performance of Non-Convertible Preferred Stocks," *Journal of Finance*, vol. 28, no. 5 (December 1973), pp. 1187–1201.

Donaldson, G. "In Defense of Preferred Stock," *Harvard Business Review*, vol. 40 (July–August 1962), pp. 123–36.

Fergusson, D. A. "Preferred Stock Valuations in Recapitalizations," *Journal of Finance*, vol. 13 (March 1958), pp. 48–69.

Fischer, D. E., and G. A. Wilt, Jr. "Non-Convertible Preferred Stock as a Financing Instrument, 1950–1965," *Journal of Finance*, vol. 23 (September 1968), pp. 611–24.

Pinches, G. E. "Financing with Convertible Preferred Stock, 1960–1967," *Journal of Finance*, vol. 25 (March 1970), pp. 53–63.

———. "Preferreds in Your Portfolio," *Financial World*, vol. 139, no. 11 (March 14, 1973), p. 9.

Santow, L. J. "Ultimate Demise of Preferred Stock as a Source of Corporate Capital," *Financial Analysts Journal*, vol. 18 (May–June 1963), pp. 47–50.

Sprecher, C. R. "A Note on Financing Mergers with Convertible Preferred Stock," *Journal of Finance*, vol. 26 (June 1971), pp. 683–85.

Stevenson, R. A. "Retirement of Non-callable Preferred Stock," *Journal of Finance*, vol. 25 (December 1970), pp. 1143–52.

# 18

## Corporate Bonds

When business corporations use external financing to raise long-term funds, they frequently use bonds and long-term notes to finance their requirements for fixed capital. Although the same in substance, bonds and long-term notes differ in form. Either may be secured or unsecured, and both are issued under provisions designed to minimize risks associated with long-term credit.

From the viewpoint of both corporate issuers and potential bond investors, areas of concern should include the maturity date, income and asset claims, and possible voting privileges. The same format of the preferred and common stock chapters will now be used to examine these topics for corporate bonds. In addition, the nature of a corporate bond, legal aspects of business debts, special features to enhance marketability, refunding before maturity, and other methods of eliminating debts are topics requiring additional specialized treatment.

### Nature of a Corporate Bond

A bond is a written promise to pay the holder a specific sum of money after a term of one year or more after issuance. Under common law a bond is more formal in its execution than a promissory note. A note is a simple promise to pay signed by the party bound, without any formality as to the seal or witnesses. A bond has been called a glorified long-term promissory note and, basically, it is the same as a note. Customarily, a bond is one of a series of similar credit instruments, all of which may or may not be of like denomination and maturity. If a corporation borrows $10 million for 25 years, the resulting debt may be represented by 10,000 bonds of the standard $1,000 denomination. The aggregate is called a bond issue, and it is supported by the general credit of the debtor and any security that may be specifically pledged. The great bulk of corporate bonds are in $1,000 denominations or multiples thereof; but $500 and $100 bonds, commonly called baby bonds, are infrequently issued. While baby bonds may appeal to small investors, they are not favored by corporations because of the costs of engraving certificates and the handling fees charged by trustees (which may be a set amount for each bond certificate transferred or registered regardless of denomination). The demand side of the corporate-bond market is dominated by institutional investors, who usually prefer large-denomination bonds.

*Maturity.* Bonds are usually thought of as long-term credit instruments with maturities of five years or more; however, to some extent, there is a connection between maturity patterns and the industry of the issuer, with railroad and public-utility-companies' bonds having the longest maturities and industrial bonds having the shortest. In a serial-bond issue, some of the bonds may come due in 1 year, some in 2 years, and so on, with the result that maturities from 1 to 15 years may be included in a 15-year serial-bond issue. Although seldom issued in the United States, bonds may be issued with no maturity dates (called perpetual bonds, on which interest is paid in perpetuity). However, bonds with maturities of more than 40 years at the time of issue have been distributed (most commonly in connection with the financial reorganization of railroad companies).

*Interest Payments.* Usually, a bond contains a promise to pay interest on stated dates: quarterly, semiannually, or annually. The discount type of bond (such as the Series E savings bond) is seldom issued by U.S. corporations. Some business corporations issue a type of bond that requires the obligor to pay interest only when it is earned during any one interest period after other expenses have been met. A corporation may make its periodic interest payments by checks that are mailed to registered holders (those in whose names bonds are registered on the corporation's books as of a certain predetermined date—for example, the last business day in June and December). A second method is to meet interest obligations by keeping deposits in certain conveniently located banks to be used to pay interest coupons as they are presented (customarily by other banks acting as collection agents for the holders of the bonds to which the coupons were previously attached).

*Bearer and Negotiable Bonds.* A corporation may issue either bearer bonds, which are payable to the bearer, or registered bonds, which are promises to pay money to those whose names are registered in the books of the corporation. Like a stock certificate, a registered bond has the name of the owner on its face. Ownership may be transferred by written assignment by the registered owner only when presented at the office of the corporation or the designated transfer agent. In order to complete the transfer of ownership, the corporation's bond register must be changed to indicate the change in ownership. A corporation's bonds may be "fully registered," that is, registered both as to principal and interest. Then, interest is paid by check to the owner of record on a predetermined date (as in the case of preferred stock dividends, except that bond interest dates are fixed in the trust indenture rather than in the corporation's by-laws), and the nuisance of handling and accounting for bond coupons is avoided. A bond certificate has a place for entering the date of registration, the name of the registered owner, and the signature of the transfer agent. When bonds are transferred, the entries are recorded on the bond certificate and in the records of the company or its transfer agent.

Some bonds are registered as to principal only and not as to interest. In this case, provisions for interest payment take the form of dated coupons attached to the bonds and are payable to the bearer. As each interest-payment date arrives, the bondholder customarily clips the proper coupon and sends it to his bank to be collected by the bank from the issuing corporation. Unlike registered bonds, which are payable only to the registered holder, bearer bonds are payable to any person having possession of them. The fact that ownership passes by mere delivery—no endorsement is needed—facilitates purchase and sale of such bonds but adds to the hazards of ownership.[1]

In deciding whether to issue fully registered bonds, bonds registered as to principal only, or bearer bonds, corporations are guided by preferences of investors as indicated by investment bankers. Because corporations try to please creditors, they customarily make provisions for changing the status of their bonds if desired at a later date. Thus, a bearer bond may be changed to a registered bond, and a registered bond of the coupon type may be converted into an unregistered bond by simply making the bond payable to bearer and so recording it in the bond register. A fully registered bond can be converted by either attaching coupons to the old bond certificate or replacing it with a new bond certificate with coupons attached.

Fully registered bonds appeal to institutional investors and others who expect to hold them for a long period of time, but the negotiable type appeals to those who trade in bonds. However, the current rule of the New York Stock Exchange states that registered bonds are "good delivery" when sold as such. In order to reduce the amount of paper to be handled, bonds may be issued or reissued in multiples of the standard $1,000 denomination ($5,000, $10,000, etc., but denominations of $1 million are more common for United States Treasury bills than for corporate bonds).

---

[1] The present tendency is toward the use of registered bonds, which save on insurance and mailing costs. Also, space requirements for storage are reduced when registered bonds are issued.

## Legal Aspects of Business Debts

*Right to Go into Debt.* Except for the common-law restriction that borrowing must be for the benefit of the company, businesses have an implied right to borrow unless specifically prohibited from doing so. Sometimes the articles of incorporation or bylaws of a corporation (or comparable documents of other types of business enterprises) place restrictions on the amount and conditions under which management may obligate the firm. Restrictions limiting borrowing and other activities of management are also found in debt contracts, such as mortgages, bond indentures, term-loan agreements, collateral-form notes, loan agreements when accounts receivable are assigned, and guarantees of various types.

When business concerns borrow, the lender inevitably assumes some risk of loss. When loans are negotiated, lenders may try to reduce these risks by requiring security, by limiting the loan period, by making certain specific provisions for repayment of the principal, by restricting the borrower's activities, and by making other specific requirements of the debtor firm. At a later date, these requirements and restrictions may seriously handicap the activities of a business concern. Probably no banker or other lender would deliberately insert a clause into a debt contract that would interfere with the normal operation of a debtor business firm, but the history of business finance is replete with cases where the normal operations of business firms were hampered by such clauses.

*Execution of Forms.* If a corporation is financing with a bond issue, its board of directors must provide proof of power to authorize such an issue (as provided for by charter, bylaws, or approval of stockholders and directors). For any type of borrowing, creditors usually request a resolution of the board of directors authorizing certain officers to sign documents, to pledge assets, and to act in other financial capacities for the corporation. There is a possibility that, after a resolution has been presented, the legality of a loan may be challenged by a stockholder or some other interested party; however, a creditor has the right to assume that the bylaws have been observed (regarding the presence of a quorum of directors, a properly conducted meeting, etc.). Certain powers possessed by officers of business concerns—to make contracts, incur liabilities, and borrow for normal business purposes—are binding on business firms. For example, notes of a corporation executed by its president and secretary are legal if the proceeds are used for business purposes.

*Regulation of Security Issues.* If a bond issue is to be offered to the general public, the legal procedures found in the Securities Act of 1933 and other federal or state laws that affect financing through public sales of securities must be followed. The legal aspects relative to issuance and retirement of securities are usually clear-cut; the major problems of finance officers are those pertaining to the cost and ease of selling securities and of servicing and retiring debts. Management usually follows procedures customary in such cases. If new precedents are established, it is usually the major companies in the industry that initiate them. Regulatory agencies (such as the Interstate Commerce Commission in the railroad field and Securities and Exchange Commission in the public-utility field) have influenced the techniques and procedures used by corporations in raising funds by borrowing. In some cases, this influence has had the effect of increasing private placement of debt to avoid registration requirements.

**Laws to Protect Creditors.** Laws have been passed that are designed to give business-concern creditors the same protection enjoyed by other creditors. Most of these are state laws; hence, there are many variations among the commercial codes of various states. About three-fourths of the states have special statutes covering "false financial statements" (which provide for punishment of those who issue false financial statements for the purpose of obtaining money or merchandise), and all states have "bad check" and "false pretense" statutes. The Federal Criminal Code (Section 215) makes anyone who uses the mail to defraud or to obtain money or property by means of false or fraudulent pretenses subject to fine or imprisonment. States have also adopted laws covering warehouse receipts, negotiable instruments, and sales. Of the federal laws designed to protect creditors, the Federal Bankruptcy Act has been the most important in its effects.

While creditors customarily assume some risks, they want to make sure these risks do not include the validity of their claims against debtors. While no lender would knowingly make a loan to an individual whose integrity he questions, nevertheless, the case books in business law are filled with litigations involving the legality of the claims of creditors. Most lenders prefer to have debt obligations repaid with cash obtained during the normal course of the debtor's business; that is, they want to be assured of repayment without resorting to foreclosure and forced sale of the borrower's assets. Because most business is done on credit, business concerns must protect themselves against nonpayment of obligations by debtors.

**Rights in a Trust Indenture.** In addition to being a promise to pay, a bond is also an instrument representing the rights of the owner to participate in the trust indenture. When a mortgage bond is issued, a mortgage trust deed is drawn up and deposited with a trustee. If intangible personal property is pledged (such as stocks and bonds) by the corporation, the trustee may take physical possession of the collateral used as security. The indenture customarily contains a preamble giving the purpose of the indenture, the proceedings taken by the corporation to make the issue legal (such as a resolution by the board of directors), and something about the nature of the bonds, bond coupons (if any), and other details. The indenture names the two parties of the contract—the debtor corporation (issuer) and the trustee—and also indicates the fees, commissions, and other payments to be received by the latter. The indenture states the conditions covering the issuance of the bonds (amount, form, certification, delivery, registration, and so on), callable features, right to convert into common stock, and other features.

A trust indenture contains a complete description of the pledged property and a statement as to whether or not property acquired in the future is to be included in the mortgage (after-acquired property clause). The debtor corporation agrees to keep mortgaged property in good repair, to insure it against loss from fire and other risks, to pay all assessments and taxes levied upon it, to defend the title and to see that the mortgage is properly recorded, and, possibly, to make provisions for a sinking fund.

The agreement entered into by the corporation usually prevents it from creating any debt having priority over the claims of creditors covered in the indenture, paying dividends until earnings exceed interest and sinking-fund requirements by a specified amount or percentage, permitting net working capital to fall below a certain figure, and selling fixed assets unless the proceeds are applied to retiring the debt. Other restrictions cover the lease of property, consolidations, and mergers. The trust indenture also specifies the action that may be taken by trustees and bondholders in the event of default on any of the conditions laid down. In case of default, the trust indenture may permit the trustee to take possession of the mortgaged property and operate it for the benefit of the creditors, to sell the property to the highest bidder, to foreclose the mortgage and dispose of the property under judicial sale, to bring suit for specific performance of any agreement, and to declare the principal due (the acceleration clause) and take action to recover the unpaid portion of the debt. The trustee may be given discretion in applying any of these remedies or he may be forced to take action by a written request of 10 percent or more of the creditors.[2] As may be surmised from this brief summary, a trust indenture may be a long document; the length of the average trust indenture is slightly over 100 pages.

**Corporate Trustee.** When a business concern borrows directly from a bank or other lender, the lender holds the promise to pay and other documents, and it is the lender's responsibility to see that the debtor meets the terms of the contract. In contrast, when a bond issue is sold, hundreds of investors may participate in lending; hence, provisions are made for their protection during the life of the bond. Business corpora-

---

[2] Sometimes a trust indenture will contain a clause that permits the company and the trustee to modify the terms of the trust agreement within limits. If the power is used, it appears as a supplement to the original trust agreement. Often, modifications of indenture provisions necessitate the approval of holders of two-thirds (or some other percentage) of the bonds or debentures.

tions employ trust companies or banks to act as agents for them and also as trustees for bondholders.³ Because the trust company or bank is compensated for its services by the debtor corporation, one might assume that the corporation would be favored in case of conflict between the interests of the corporation and the bondholders. However, there are certain basic principles a qualified and disinterested trustee cannot violate. Most bondholders are dependent on trustees to care for their interests; consequently, Congress has set standards that trust companies and banks must meet before they can serve as trustees of bond issues in which a wide public interest is present.

**Trust Indenture Act of 1939.** The Trust Indenture Act of 1939 requires business corporations to select trustees that are disinterested and competent. (In practice, the trustee selected by the corporation is the one recommended by the investment banker.) To be "disinterested" a trustee must have no financial or other interest in the issue that would be in conflict with the interests of investors. A copy of the indenture is filed with the Securities and Exchange Commission when the nature of the security issue or the method of financing brings it under the commission's supervision. Before a trust company or bank selected to hold the trust indenture is permitted to act as trustee, the approval of the Securities and Exchange Commission must be obtained. Like other provisions for registration, there are exceptions to the registration requirement. These exceptions include corporate securities when the principal amount of the issue is less than $1 million. In performing their functions, trustees must provide the bondholders with periodic and special reports on the status of the trust, condition of property held in trust, and other matters, and must notify bondholders of any default within 90 days. After default, the trustee must exercise its powers with the same degree of care and skill as a prudent man would conduct his affairs under similar circumstances (the "prudent man" rule).

### Formal Procedures for Retirement of Bonds

In making formal provisions for the retirement of bonds, corporations may either issue serial bonds or sinking-fund bonds. The terms under which cash is set aside or used to extinguish long-term-debt may be so inflexible as to handicap a corporation or may be flexible enough to prevent financial embarrassment except during extraordinary times. It is not unusual for a corporation that is able to handle all interest charges to have difficulty in meeting periodic debt-retirement obligations. The terms of debt retirement result from negotiations between investment bankers and the corporation in public financing or between the firm and the

---

[3] As an illustration, the trustee for the Union Electric Company is the St. Louis Union Trust Company for the company's mortgage and deed of trust obligations.

lender—insurance company, commercial bank, or other institutional lender—in private placement of bonds or notes.

*Significance of the Maturity Date.* Various reasons are given by management for making provisions for the extinction of bonds. They include the following: (1) to strengthen the financial position of the corporation; (2) to offset the decline in property value due to depreciation; and (3) to comply with an American tradition that insists that debts be paid. Without question there is a bias against perpetual bonds—issues that never come due; therefore, practically all bonds issued by U.S. corporations have a due date or maturity date. The significance of a maturity date is that management must face the problem of bringing about the extinction of bonds on or before maturity. In the case of bonds convertible into common stock, if bondholders use the conversion privilege, no repayment is necessary; however, management has no prior assurance that bondholders will be able to use the conversion privilege.

Retirement of a bond issue may take place at maturity, when all the bonds come due; on a call date, as set by management; periodically, as provided for in serial bond issues; piecemeal, by open-market purchases or direct negotiation with individual bondholders; or through the use of two or more of these methods. When cash is exchanged for bonds at maturity, the debtor meets his contractual obligation to repay the principal. For the convenience of bondholders, bonds are usually redeemed at designated banks in financial centers as well as at the principal office of the debtor.

*Using Sinking Funds.* Sinking funds are created to have a beneficial effect on bond issues. A sinking fund for debt retirement requires periodic appropriations of cash by the debtor to redeem the bonds or long-term notes before or at maturity. Customarily, sinking funds are provided for in the trust indenture or loan agreement, but the board of directors of a corporation may establish sinking funds by resolution at any time. Usually, a sinking fund for a bond issue is administered by the trustee who holds the trust indenture, but it may be administered by a second trust company or some other agency. Sometimes, in lieu of cash, a debtor corporation is permitted to deposit reacquired bonds of the issue being redeemed to fulfill sinking-fund requirements. This provision is advantageous to the corporation if and when bonds can be acquired at less than par or less than their call price. The trustee administers bond redemption according to the provisions set forth in the trust indenture or other contract. When they are on a contractual basis, contributions of a corporation to the sinking fund are usually compulsory. Therefore, a corporation is technically insolvent when it fails to meet its sinking-fund obligations as well as when it fails to meet interest and principal payments when due.

A corporation's sinking-fund payments may be in variable annual amounts to fit into other financial plans of the corporation. As an illustration, if the proceeds of a bond issue are spent for construction of a plant, the improvement of the company's income would tend to be gradual; and, for several years, the increase in income may be insufficient to cover average annual sinking-fund requirements. Therefore, management may arrange to postpone sinking-fund contributions for a number of years, keep constant the total of sinking-fund contributions and interest payments throughout the life of the bond issue (annuity method), or fit the "carrying charges" of the new debt into those already in existence so as to smooth out the total debt burden of the corporation (all sinking funds and interest charges).

**Annuity Method.** This method necessitates determining the sum to be set aside periodically to provide the required amount of maturity. The assumption is that no part of the debt is to be eliminated until maturity. The first year, the corporation pays the interest on its bonds and the required sinking fund payment to the sinking-fund trustee, who promptly invests it in the bonds. The second year, the corporation makes the same interest and sinking-fund payments, but now the trustee is able to invest in a larger amount of bonds because it has both the sinking-fund contribution and the interest on the bonds that were reacquired the first year. At maturity, the trustee will have accumulated the amount needed to retire the debt. In practice, the bonds may be retired as they are reacquired; but the annuity principle may be maintained if the corporation increases its sinking-fund contribution each year by the amount that its interest charges are reduced (thereby keeping the annual combined installment constant).

**Variable Payments.** Interest is a fixed charge and a firm may arrange for contributions to the sinking fund so they will not interfere with this obligation. After provisions have been made for taxes, interest, and other charges, a corporation may provide that all net profits up to a designated amount will be paid to a sinking-fund trustee. Funds above this amount would be available for dividends, other debt retirement, and retention in the business. Even when the sinking-fund contribution is a percentage of earnings, there may still be a specified minimum amount that must be contributed regardless of earnings. The policy of requiring management to make mandatory sinking-fund payments may be supplemented by an optional one. For example, management may reserve the right to make an additional optional sinking-fund payment based on a percentage of the mandatory sinking-fund contribution. This privilege would have the most value to the corporation when interest rates have declined, but not sufficiently to warrant a call for refunding purposes.

In the case of wasting-asset corporations (for example, mining and petroleum companies), provisions for sinking-fund contributions may be in terms of output: the greater the rate of depletion, the greater the amount paid into the sinking fund. Thus, the contribution would increase in direct proportion to output—a specified number of dollars for each ton of coal or copper, each barrel of oil, or each 1,000 feet of lumber produced. However, such a plan may call for a minimum annual contribution plus a variable one based on output.

*Sinking-Fund Investments.* Sinking-fund contributions are usually invested in the bonds of the issue for which the sinking fund was created, but they may be invested in other securities or assets of the issuing corporation or in securities of other corporations. If invested in the bonds for which the sinking fund was created the method whereby the sinking-fund trustee may reacquire the bonds must be determined. Because open-market purchases of bonds would be expensive when bonds are selling above par, provisions may be made at the time of issuing the bonds for calling the bonds by lot or calling a certain percentage of those held by each bondholder at specified intervals. (The latter method may be impractical because it could entail fractional parts of bonds.)

When the bonds are selling at a discount, it would be profitable to reacquire them through open-market purchases. If bonds are noncallable and the market for them is inactive, the trustee or issuing corporation may request bondholders to offer (tender) their bonds for redemption. In this case, bondholders who are willing to sell make sealed offers, and the trustee accepts those having the lowest offering prices up to an amount sufficient to exhaust the cash available for this purpose.

The ultimate purpose in creating a sinking fund is to protect the credit of the issuing corporation; to this end, the sinking-fund trustee may invest in any obligation of the debtor corporation. In some cases, the trust indenture may permit or require the annual contributions to the sinking fund to be invested in additions, improvements, or acquisitions of property by the debtor corporation. These sinking-fund investments tend to improve the corporation's debt-paying ability and to strengthen the position of its outstanding bonds.

A provision in the bond indenture permitting the corporation to deliver bonds rather than cash to the trustee to fulfill sinking-fund requirements may expedite bond redemption. (The trustee may be required to accept such bonds at par or at the call price, irrespective of the price paid to reacquire them.) Although sinking funds provide for an orderly reduction of the debt of the issuing corporation, equally orderly procedures for retirement of corporate bonds may be achieved by issuing serial bonds. Sinking funds may be used in providing for retirement of long-term notes, but, usually, debts of this type, when held by one or a few lenders, are retired on the installment basis.

*Serial Bonds.* A serial-bond or note issue is one made up of a series of bonds or notes with maturities arranged so that a specified number of bonds or notes come due each year throughout the debt period. A firm may sell the bonds of a serial-bond issue with a different coupon rate for each maturity or with the same coupon rate for all maturities. If bonds are sold so the coupon rates reflect the yield curve in the market, all the bonds sell at par. If the bonds have the same coupon rate, the market price of each maturity will reflect the yield curve in the market (see Table 18–1).

TABLE 18–1
Yield Curve, Coupon Rate, and Price of Serial Bonds

| Maturity Year | Price Constant, Varying Coupon Rates | | | Coupon Rate Constant, Varying Prices | | |
|---|---|---|---|---|---|---|
| | Yield Curve | Coupon Rate | Price | Coupon Rate | Price | Yield Curve |
| 1 | 4.00% | 4.00% | $100 | 6% | $101.94 | 4.00% |
| 2 | 4.50 | 4.50 | 100 | 6 | 102.84 | 4.50 |
| 3 | 5.00 | 5.00 | 100 | 6 | 102.75 | 5.00 |
| 4 | 5.25 | 5.25 | 100 | 6 | 102.67 | 5.25 |
| 5 | 5.50 | 5.50 | 100 | 6 | 102.16 | 5.50 |
| 6 | 5.75 | 5.75 | 100 | 6 | 101.25 | 5.75 |
| 7 | 6.00 | 6.00 | 100 | 6 | 100.00 | 6.00 |
| 8 | 6.10 | 6.10 | 100 | 6 | 99.37 | 6.10 |
| 9 | 6.20 | 6.20 | 100 | 6 | 98.64 | 6.20 |
| 10 | 6.30 | 6.30 | 100 | 6 | 97.80 | 6.30 |
| 11 | 6.40 | 6.40 | 100 | 6 | 96.88 | 6.40 |
| 12 | 6.50 | 6.50 | 100 | 6 | 95.88 | 6.50 |

Since the use of bond tables permits ready estimates of bond prices under varying yield curves, it is a matter of indifference whether varying or fixed coupon rates are used.[4] If a corporation wants a definite number of dollars, interest rates are negotiated at the time the bonds are issued; but, if the corporation sets the interest rate in advance, dollar receipts from the sale of the issue will be unknown until the actual sale of the bonds.

In determining the number of serial bonds that will mature each year, corporations are faced with the same problems as in determining the annual appropriation to a sinking fund. Maturities may be arranged to come due in equal amounts each year or they may be arranged so the total amount needed for interest and principal payments will be the same each year. Usually, the serial bonds having more distant maturities are callable; this gives flexibility to the redemption plan. When longer term bonds are callable, more rapid retirement than originally anticipated may be effected if conditions are favorable. The bond indenture may require the creation of a sinking fund for the bonds having the longest maturity;

---

[4] If the yield curve appearing in the second column of Table 18–1 were charted, it would be on an upsweeping yield curve. It would show, as of one date, that the interest rate on each maturity of the same class of credit instrument increases with its maturity, with the lowest rate on 1-year obligations and the highest on 12-year obligations. A down-sweeping curve is just the opposite, with the highest rate being for the shortest maturity and the lowest rate being for the longest maturity. Yield curves or "patterns of interest rates" are as of one time and are not a time series.

it also may require that the bonds be called in reverse order when calls are made (that is, the first call will be for bonds having the longest maturities).

Market conditions, as reflected in yield curves, may be a factor in the decision whether to issue serial bonds or sinking-fund bonds. When short-term interest rates are relatively low (an upsweeping curve), there is a preference among investors for short-term obligations. This would indicate a good market for a serial-bond issue because it includes short-term and intermediate-term bonds as well as long-term bonds; therefore, the total interest charges would be less than on an equivalent issue of long-term bonds.[5] It is sometimes said that, if long-term sinking-fund bonds are issued, the higher interest paid may be offset by savings when the bonds are reacquired; for this to be true, however, the sinking-fund trustee of the corporation would have to reacquire the bonds at a discount. When the yield curve is upsweeping and the credit position of the issuing corporation is sound, the market price of long-term bonds is usually high until they mature.[6]

While sinking-fund contributions may be more flexible than serial-bond maturities, the maturities of serial bonds may be arranged so that none mature in the years that other obligations become due. The number of bonds in each series may vary; the maturities of the earlier years may be omitted, and other maturities may be arranged so that the bond maturities may be fitted into the overall debt-retirement plan of the corporation. Serial bonds are issued by corporations in all major industries. They are used in financing railroad-equipment obligations and real estate when there is a fairly steady rate of depreciation of the property pledged and a reasonably stable cash flow.

## Asset Claim

The claim on assets frequently gives the specific bond or note issue its identification. Thus, a bond may be known as a first mortgage, second mortgage, collateral trust, or debenture bond. The name generally denotes the type of asset pledged, or lack of a pledge in the case of a debenture bond. While the claims to assets and income are intertwined, they will be discussed separately so that emphasis can be given to each. It should be emphasized that bondholders look to the corporation's earnings to secure the payment of principal and interest. The pledging of specific assets is only done in case the corporation is unable to fulfill its commitments. As

---

[5] Frank C. Jen and James E. Wert, "The Effect of Sinking Fund Provisions on Corporate Bond Yields," *Financial Analysts Journal*, March–April 1967, pp. 127–28.

[6] If the upsweeping curve prevails and there is no change in the level or shape of the curve, the market yield on an outstanding security goes down with the passage of time. So, a 15-year bond that had a 6-percent yield at the time of issuance will sell at a higher price, or lower yield, after 5 years of its term have elapsed.

noted, if no specific assets are pledged, the bond or note is known as a debenture.

***Closed-End and Open-End Mortgages.*** When long-term capital funds are needed, it is customary for business concerns to offer real property as security. Thus, the creditor will have, in addition to the debtor's ability to pay, the pledged property as assurance that the bonds or notes will be paid according to the terms of the mortgage indenture. Although several mortgages may be based on the same property, the first mortgage lien has the best rating in the market.

The use of second, third, or even higher mortgage liens on property has declined since the 1920s. The reason for the decreasing incidence of junior mortgages since that time has been the greater use of open-end mortgages in place of closed-end or partly closed-end mortgage bonds. An open-end mortgage bond is one secured by a mortgage that permits the issuance of additional bonds against the same mortgage, while a closed-end mortgage bond prohibits the issuance of additional bonds against the same mortgage. When closed-end mortgage indentures contain the after-acquired property clause, all property obtained thereafter comes under the existing mortgage. Under these conditions, the business firm in need of additional long-term funds can either issue junior mortgages or borrow on an unsecured basis. (In either case, the cost of financing may be higher.) Limited open-end mortgages and partly closed-end mortgages permit additional borrowing under the first mortgage up to a specified amount.

The typical terms in closed-end mortgage covenants cover borrowing wherein the entire amount of the authorized debt is created at one time. Under open-end mortgages, supplementary financing is anticipated and first mortgage bonds may be floated at different times under the original mortgage indenture. The interest rates on new series mortgage bonds will be determined by those prevailing in the capital market at the time of issue (assuming they are issued at or near par).

Normally, the indenture of an open-end mortgage contains detailed coverage of the conditions under which the corporation may obtain additional funds. Among the common provisions are those that limit additional financing on the basis of the relationship between interest charges and earnings, new debt and property acquired, mortgage debt and net current assets, and mortgage debt and net worth. To illustrate, the indenture may specify that earnings available for interest payments must be twice the interest charges on existing funded debt plus the debt to be created; the corporation must have earned each month for the preceding 24 months an amount equal to twice the computed interest charges; and the property acquired must have more value than the new debt (for example, the new debt may be only 50, 60, or 70 percent of the fair value or actual cost of the new property).

The Securities and Exchange Commission "with respect to first mortgage bonds requires ... that dividends or other distribution to common stockholders be limited so as to preserve an 'equity cushion' beneath the claims of the bondholders." Most of the security for bonds is in the form of depreciable plant and equipment, hence, another aspect of the commission's protection policy for secured creditors is the requirement of "periodic renewal and replacement of such property as to maintain the book value of the underlying security" or "to deposit cash or outstanding bonds with the trustee" in sufficient amounts to meet policy needs.[7]

**Value of Mortgage Liens.** A business firm may give a mortgage lien on real property in order to obtain funds at a lower cost; however, if the earnings of the debtor are inadequate to meet interest and principal payments on the debt, the value of the assets pledged as security will probably be inadequate to meet the same obligations in case of a foreclosure or liquidation sale. Nevertheless, the creditors have prospects of collecting something of value from the sale of the mortgaged assets; in addition, they also participate on the same basis as the unsecured creditors in the distribution of the remaining assets of the corporation.

The chief value of a first mortgage lien to creditors is that it gives them a prior claim to the earnings of the debtor corporation. Earnings must be available for the accumulation of funds to retire debts and to meet interest obligations. A prior lien is important because it indicates the relative treatment in reorganization or liquidation, but earning power is essential to the preservation of values. When a company is being operated under supervision of the court, the receiver may continue to meet interest payments on senior obligations while junior obligations are in default.

The holders of first mortgage notes or bonds have the same type of prior claim to earnings and assets as creditors have over stockholders or preferred stockholders have over common stockholders. It is true that a corporation may pass a preferred or common stock dividend without exposing itself to legal proceedings, as would be the case if it failed to pay interest on a junior debt; but the essential difference among the securities of a company is in the priority of claims to earnings and assets.

**Collateral Notes.** A popular form of direct borrowing from banks is by means of collateral notes secured by stocks and bonds. Usually, such loans are for only a part of the value of the securities pledged (the amount depends on the securities pledged, the purpose of the loan, and the credit standing of the borrower). A collateral note contains a pledge of securities in addition to a promise to pay. One requirement in connection with a pledge is delivery of the pledged property to the pledgee (lender). In case of default, the lender is authorized to sell the pledged

---

[7] This concerns only those bonds issued by companies regulated under the Public Utility Holding Company Act of 1935.

securities and to apply the proceeds to the loan. The borrower is entitled to any part of the net proceeds in excess of the obligations and is responsible for any deficiency. Unless there are specific provisions to the contrary, interest and dividends on the securities pledged are paid to the owner in the same manner as they would be if the securities were in his possession. Practically the same procedures are used in open-market financing with collateral trust bonds.

**Collateral Trust Bonds.** Collateral trust bonds are secured by pledges of stocks or bonds. As in other bond issues, a trust indenture held by a trustee includes the standard provisions of any indenture. Therefore, emphasis in this discussion is on the collateral aspects of this type of financing.

As provided for in a collateral trust indenture, the pledged property will be delivered by the corporation to a trustee to be held for the protection of bondholders. Customarily, the trustee will not authenticate (give authority, as by legal proof) the collateral trust bonds until the pledged securities are deposited with it. Stocks and registered bonds may remain in the name of the debtor or they may be transferred to the trustee or its nominee. In the case of a default of interest or principal payments on the collateral trust bonds, pledged securities remaining in the name of the debtor corporation are transferred to the name of a nominee or the trustee.

As long as interest and principal payments on collateral trust bonds are being met, the income from the pledged securities will be turned over to the pledgor (debtor); but, in case of default, all interest and dividend payments on securities held as collateral will be retained by the trustee. Usually, all forms of capital distribution, such as stock dividends, cash received as principal repayments, and liquidating dividends on any securities held as collateral, will be retained by the trustee as security for the collateral trust bonds.

**Securities Pledged for Collateral Trust Bonds.** Although a business corporation with large investments in stocks and bonds could avoid borrowing by selling these securities, there are many reasons why this is not done. The corporation may own stock in other corporations for control purposes, as best illustrated by a pure holding company. If such a corporation is to borrow in order to buy more stock, it may pledge the shares it already owns as security for an issue of collateral trust bonds.

Many holding companies assume responsibility for financing their subsidiaries by buying their issues of mortgage bonds and then pledging these bonds as security for an issue of collateral trust bonds that bear a lower interest rate than those of the subsidiary. By using a mortgage loan, the subsidiary can avoid the expense of originating a bond issue for public distribution and the holding company can pledge the mortgage loan to raise funds in the open market. The latter also may combine the mortgage loans of more than one subsidiary in order to save on financing costs.

Because it is a common practice for one corporation to invest in the securities of other corporations, collateral trust bonds may be secured by bonds and stocks of corporations that are entirely independent of the pledgor.

**Reasons for Use of Collateral Trust Bonds.** If and when a corporation pledges stocks or bonds as security for a bond issue, the basic reason is to obtain a more favorable interest rate than could be obtained on an unsecured loan or debenture bond issue. While the credit rating of collateral trust bonds depends primarily on the credit standing of the borrower, a pledge of securities will improve the credit rating if the pledged collateral has sufficient value. Thus, in addition to the credit standing of the borrower, the factors determining the credit rating of collateral trust bonds include the earning power behind the pledged securities, the marketability of the collateral during adverse conditions, and the protection provided by the terms of the trust indenture. In bond financing there seems to be a preference for real property as security; but, in an emergency, real property may lack the marketability possessed by stocks and bonds. In recapturing investments, marketability may be the most important quality possessed by pledged property. Because of court decisions in bankruptcy reorganizations, creditors may be entitled to damages resulting from the postponement of the sale of pledged collateral. Therefore, holders of collateral trust bonds may be in a stronger financial position when a corporation is being reorganized in bankruptcy than are mortgage bondholders.

**Debenture Bonds.** In its broadest meaning, the term debenture includes all bonds issued by a corporation; in fact, the terms debenture and bond are sometimes used interchangeably, as both are promises by corporations to pay debts. In its more restricted meaning, a debenture is a direct obligation of the issuing corporation based solely on the general credit of the issuer without the assignment, mortgage, or pledge of property. But debenture bonds are more than mere promises to pay, because they are issued under trust indentures containing provisions that restrict the issuer for the protection of the creditors.

The fact that debenture bonds are unsecured by any specific lien on property is less important than their status with reference to other securities issued by the corporation. If there are no senior obligations outstanding and no sizable amount of short-term debt, the status of a corporation's debentures is about the same as that of a first mortgage bond. In bankruptcy, unsecured creditors may sue, obtain judgments, and attach specific property to satisfy their claims; and, in practice, this amounts to the same thing as when property is assigned or pledged under a mortgage or other lien. Debenture bondholders, as creditors, have a claim to earnings and assets senior to that of preferred and common stockholders.

The credit status of debenture bonds is usually protected by provisions in the trust indenture that forbid or restrict the issuance of any debt having a prior lien. The issuance of mortgage bonds may be permitted if the outstanding debenture bonds are given prior or equal coverage to the newly issued bonds. As a consequence, the debenture bondholders in effect become first mortgage bondholders even though their bonds are still called debenture bonds.

Debentures are most common among issues of industrial companies rather than railroad and public-utility companies, because industrial companies usually have fewer fixed assets to pledge as security. In addition, because of its specialized nature, industrial property is not considered high-grade security for mortgage bonds (this has not prevented insurance companies from making loans on industrial property). When industrial corporations having high credit standings finance with bond issues, they usually issue debenture bonds. Now, companies financing with debentures represent practically every industry. To some extent, the more formal type of debenture is being replaced by ordinary promissory notes held by banks, insurance companies, and other lenders, with the term-loan agreement taking the place of the trust indenture.

**Subordinated Debenture Bonds.** A special type of debenture bond has received increasing attention in recent years. The conditions under which the debentures are issued usually include making them subordinate to other specified creditors as to claims to interest and principal. What constitutes senior debt must be clearly defined in every subordinated debenture issue. Bank loans are generally specified as senior debt; bonds outstanding frequently are included in the senior-debt category. Of course, mortgage bonds still would have a prior claim against the specific asset that has been pledged. Accounts payable are generally not defined as senior debt, and they probably would share on a par with the subordinated debenture issue as general creditors of the firm. The advantage of the subordination agreement to the senior debtholders is that any amounts to which the subordinated debtholders are entitled as general creditors are applicable to the senior creditors' claims. After the senior debt is satisfied in full, any excess amounts would then be applied to the claims of the subordinated debenture holders.

This feature in the event of insolvency may be illustrated by using the simple example shown in Table 18–2. The allocation of proceeds with and without subordination for the claims on the assets is shown. It is assumed that at the liquidation of the assets only $600 was received. If there were no subordination agreement, all the creditors would receive 60 percent and the residual owners would receive nothing. However, since there was subordinated debt, the senior debt would be paid in full, as shown by the following calculation:

$$\frac{\text{Senior debt (\$400)} + \text{subordinated debt (\$300)}}{\text{Total debt (\$1,000)}} \times \$600 = \$420$$

TABLE 18–2
Liquidating Payments (with and without a subordination agreement)

|  | Amount of Claim | Without Subordination | With Subordination |
|---|---|---|---|
| Senior debt | $ 400 | $240 | $400 |
| Subordinated debt | 300 | 180 | 20 |
| Accounts payable | 300 | 180 | 180 |
| Net worth | 1,000 | 0 | 0 |
| Total claims | $2,000 | $600 | $600 |

The claims of the trade creditors are unaffected by the subordination feature. In either case, the equity holders would receive no share of the assets. The inclusion of a subordination agreement on notes or bonds is a valuable right for the senior debt. The subordinated debt improves the borrowing power of the firm because it serves as a base upon which further senior debt may be superimposed.

The use of subordinated debentures or notes makes it possible for management to obtain cash without disturbing priorities of the corporation's existing debt structure and without issuing common or preferred stock. In effect, it is a debt instrument that ranks immediately before preferred stock; but, unlike preferred stock, the yield thereon is treated as a fixed charge and is deductible for tax purposes. Subordinated debentures provide an attractive method of raising cash while retaining the corporation's borrowing power in the form of senior secured bonds and notes for future requirements.

The indenture agreement under which subordinated debentures and notes are issued contains restrictions on management. For example, the indenture may prohibit cash dividend payments on common stock and the repurchase of outstanding common stock if the effect is to reduce net worth below a stated dollar amount. This restriction seldom applies to cash dividends on preferred stock and the repurchase of preferred stock for retirement under terms of a sinking fund previously set up for this purpose. Provisions may or may not be made for conversion of the subordinated debentures into common stock, a sinking fund, and the "call" feature.[8]

---

[8] Typically the call price is above the principal amount of the bond or note. The call premium makes debentures and bonds more attractive to investors because it reduces the likelihood of their being called at an early date; if they are called, the premium is a compensation for having to reinvest the funds. However, if interest rates fall far enough to make refinancing by corporations profitable despite paying the premium on outstanding obligations, investors will be at a disadvantage despite the premium, because the return on new investments will be lower than on those redeemed. Of course, it is assumed that the refinancing takes place in order to lower the interest cost.

## Income Claim

The main advantage of financing with debt as compared to equity is the lower cost. In addition to the income-tax saving, debt financing avoids immediate dilutions of the rights of common stockholders. When funds are borrowed, creditors receive an income claim that takes precedence over that of the owners. In a vast preponderance of cases, however, the prior claim to earnings is limited to a fixed sum. Hence, debt creates fixed interest charges and possible sinking fund obligations for repayment of the principal that create a drain on cash regardless of the economic conditions confronting the industry and the firm. In order to minimize this potential cash shortage, management may issue income bonds. Nevertheless, despite the advantages of income bonds over preferred stock, such bonds have not been used voluntarily on a wide scale by corporations. This is likely explained by the fact that historically many of the outstanding income bonds are the consequence of a corporate reorganization. The use by solvent corporations may be inhibited by this possible association.

**Income Bonds.** The indenture under which income bonds are issued specifies that interest is to be paid only when earned, thereby creating a contingent rather than a fixed charge. Income bonds are of two types: those resulting from financial reorganizations due to bankruptcies and those issued by financially sound corporations. The first of these could be called adjustment bonds because they are used to adjust the claims of creditors. The second type of income bonds could be known as preference bonds in that they are selected as a preferred financing device.

The income bonds issued by a corporation may be secured or unsecured, cumulative or noncumulative, and registered or coupon bonds. The trust indenture usually provides that interest payments must be declared by the corporation's board of directors when earned after certain specific deductions; but the decision as to whether or not interest is paid if not earned is left to the discretion of the board of directors. While income bonds bear a stated interest rate, the board of directors may vote to pay whatever funds are available, even though it may be only a fraction of the amount due bondholders. If income bonds are cumulative, interest that has been passed becomes part of the amount that must be paid when the principal comes due (the cumulative period may be limited to a period such as three years). Holders of noncumulative bonds lose all claims to interest not paid unless there is a provision that they have claims to whatever interest has been earned. Then, that part of their claims to earned interest if not paid will accumulate, as in the case of cumulative preferred stock.

Most of the income bonds now outstanding are of the adjustment type; but the preference type of income bonds may be used to advantage by new or established corporations having uncertain or widely fluctuating incomes. To date, the chief users of preference income bonds have been companies operating in the railroad industry. Established companies that have fairly steady income may find institutional investors willing to buy the preference type of income bonds when they are not permitted to buy preferred stock. The main advantage to the issuing corporation in the use of preference bonds in place of preferred stock is the tax saving; interest paid on such bonds is deductible as an expense in computing the base for federal income tax payments while dividends paid on preferred stock are not.

The legal problem for corporate management is to see that the conditions under which income bonds are issued are such that the courts will treat them as debts rather than as preferred stock. If an income bond is legal, there is no reason why corporations should not replace preferred stock with income bonds in financing, particularly when preferred stock is to be redeemed. Using income bonds is advantageous because (1) the market for them may be wider than for preferred stock (some institutional investors may be permitted to purchase the former but not the latter); and (2) interest payments provide tax savings while dividends on preferred stock do not. The difference in earnings per share of common stock when financing with preferred stock and income bonds is illustrated in Table 18–3.

**TABLE 18–3**
**Earnings per Share of Common Stock, Using Preferred Stock and Income Bonds**

| | | |
|---|---:|---:|
| Assumed level of earnings | $2,000,000 | |
| Less federal corporate income taxes (50%) * | 1,000,000 | |
| Net after federal income taxes | $1,000,000 | |
| Less dividends on preferred stock (100,000 shares at $5) | 500,000 | |
| Available to common stock (100,000 shares) | $ 500,000 | |
| Earnings per share of common stock | | $5.00 |
| Assumed level of earnings | $2,000,000 | |
| Less interest ($10,000,000 bonds at 5%) | 500,000 | |
| Earnings less interest | $1,500,000 | |
| Less federal corporate income taxes (50%) * | 750,000 | |
| Net after federal income taxes | $ 750,000 | |
| Available to common stock (100,000 shares) | 750,000 | |
| Earnings per share of common stock | | $7.50 |

* To simplify the illustration, the same rate was used for all levels of income.

***Participating in Earnings.*** On rare occasions, bondholders are permitted to share in the earnings of a corporation in an amount in excess of the fixed rate of interest, thereby receiving—in excess of a minimum stated amount—additional sums depending on the earnings of the issuer. Such bonds are called participating bonds. Participation may be cumulative or; it may be limited to a maximum rate; or the provision in the trust indenture may be so stated as to give bondholders a stated proportion of the earnings of the corporation before federal income taxes. Participation gives to bonds a speculative feature that some investors find attractive. As would be expected, this feature is limited primarily to smaller corporations, experiencing difficulties in securing adequate capital funds.

*Stabilizing Purchasing Power.* Stabilized bonds are those whose principal and interest are adjusted to changes in the price level as measured by an index number (such as the consumer price index prepared by the Bureau of Labor Statistics) to allow for changes in the purchasing power of the dollar. Proposals for this type of bond are given attention during periods of inflation, but little use has been made of such bonds in financing U.S. business firms.

Considered from the viewpoint of investors whose incomes have been affected most adversely by inflation, a stabilized bond would offer compensation for the decrease in value of their investments; however, considered from the viewpoint of the economy as a whole, there is danger of accelerating the inflationary spiral by the expansion of interest and principal payments. More important, however, is the inflationary bias that may be imparted to the investment community as a whole. The best solution to the problem would be to maintain sound governmental monetary and fiscal policies with a goal of achieving a relatively stable dollar.

## Participation in Voting

Ordinarily, bondholders have no voice in the management of the corporation; but, under certain circumstances, bondholders may be permitted to elect a given number of directors. Provisions for voting may result from concessions made to investment bankers at the time a bond issue is negotiated; but, more often, this provision results from reorganization of the corporation and the replacement of other debts with income or adjustment bonds. The indenture under which the income bonds are issued may provide for bondholders' representation on the board of directors if interest is passed for a specific number of successive interest-payment dates.

In general, bondholders have no control over management policies if the interest is paid as agreed, and as long as other trust indenture covenants are not violated. If, however, interest or principal payments are in default, the bondholders have remedies that are more direct and effective than participation in the election of directors. Therefore, with the exception of income bonds, voting privileges for bondholders are not common.

## Special Features to Improve Marketability

In order to make bonds more attractive to potential investors, corporate management may arrange for trading privileges. In addition, in special circumstances guarantees, assumptions, or joint bonds may be used to advantage.

*Trading Provisions.* Corporations may arrange to have their bonds listed on securities exchanges. The New York Stock Exchange listed some 2,600 bond issues at the end of 1975, and the American Stock Exchange, the Midwest Stock Exchange, and other exchanges listed a smaller number. Over the last 35 years, the aggregate value of listed bonds has increased, largely due to the increase in U.S. government securities and convertibles; and the volume of trading on organized exchanges has shown some increase in the 1970s, but the over-the-counter market still dominates trading in bonds. To increase bond trading on the floor of the New York Stock Exchange, it adopted the "nine bond rule." This rule requires members to buy and sell listed bonds on the exchange, unless a better price can be obtained for the customer in the over-the-counter market, when the orders are for less than $10,000 par value. Trading is on an auction basis, with the unit being one bond with a par value of $1,000; however, smaller denomination bonds may be traded if buyers can be found.

Corporations may avoid the expense of listing their bonds because most of the trading in corporate and other bonds, whether listed or not is in the over-the-counter markets (a term covering trading outside organized national securities exchanges). Usually, purchases and sales of bonds are negotiated over the telephone through dealers who quote bid and asked prices; that is, they buy at the bid price and sell at the asked price. The spread between the bid and asked price is the dealer's gross margin of profit; the more actively a bond is traded, the smaller is the spread. Quotations on bonds are in terms of percentages of face value; for example, when a $1,000 bond is quoted at 94.5, the price is $945.[9] Accrued interest is added to the purchase price computed from the last coupon or interest-payment date to date of the purchase. Bonds on which interest is in default and income and adjustment bonds are quoted "flat," that is, without the payment of accrued interest by the purchaser.

*Guaranteeing Bonds.* Sometimes owners guarantee or endorse the promissory notes of their corporations so as to obtain credit on more favorable terms from their banks. This practice of making two or more parties responsible for the debts of business firms has been extended to include bonds that may be guaranteed by a second party, assumed by a second corporation, or issued jointly by two or more corporations. The relationship between the guarantor and the corporation whose obligations are guaranteed is usually close, such as a parent company and a subsidiary. Customarily, the guarantor assumes full responsibility for fulfillment

---

[9] Customarily, U.S. government bonds are sold in terms of dollars and fractions (32nds) rather than dollars and cents. Therefore, bid and asked prices of $98.18 and $98.20 mean $98 18/32 and $98 20/32. Thus, on a $1,000 bond, a price of $98.18 means [$98 + (18/32) (10)], or $985.625.

of the debt contract, and, in case of default by the party whose obligations are guaranteed, the guarantor is responsible.

The value of a guarantee depends on the financial standing of the guarantor and the terms of the guarantee; the credit standing of a bond is enhanced when the credit of the guarantor is better than that of the issuer. A guarantee may apply to either interest or principal or both, and it may be secured by a deposit of collateral, which would give the bond some of the characteristics of a collateral trust bond. A guarantee may be covered by a lease agreement, by a special contract with the debtor corporation, or by endorsement of the bonds by the guarantor.[10] In the latter case, the guarantee is direct; in the other two, it is indirect. Most commonly, guaranteed bonds result when one corporation leases property of a second corporation and guarantees the interest and principal payments on its long-term debt. The purpose of the guarantee is to insure that the lease payments will be sufficient to pay the interest when due, and to liquidate the principal at maturity.

*Assuming Bonds.* An assumed bond is one that has been issued by one corporation and made the liability of a second corporation or individual who has voluntarily assumed responsibility for it. The party assuming the obligation customarily makes no changes in the indenture as signed by the original issuer; but, when any changes are made, they must have the approval of the bondholders or trustee. In addition, such a contingency must have been provided for in the bond indenture (covering mergers, consolidations, and sales of assets, as by a subsidiary corporation to a parent corporation).

Assumed bonds are common in U.S. business finance, where business combinations are prevalent. They are of the same dual nature as guaranteed bonds, usually being secured obligations of the original issuer but involving only the general credit of the second corporation. If the bonds have a better investment status following assumption by a second corporation, it is because the corporation that has taken over responsibility for the bond indebtedness has a greater earning power.

*Joining with Others.* Bonds that are the joint obligation of two or more corporations at the time of original issue are known as joint bonds. Sometimes the term "joint and several" is used; this means that the signers are bound jointly as well as individually for the full amount of the debt. Joint bonds may be secured or unsecured. When several railroad companies in large cities use the same terminal facilities, a subsidiary

---

[10] Over the signatures of the proper officers and seal of the grantor, this guarantee may read as follows: "For value received, the $X$ corporation hereby guarantees the punctual payment of the principal and interest of the within bond, at the time and in the manner therein specified, and covenants, in default of payment of any part thereof by the obligator to pay the said principal and interest of the within bond, as the same shall become due, upon the demand of the holder thereof."

corporation may be organized to own and manage these facilities. When bonds secured by a mortgage on this property are issued by the subsidiary, the parent corporations severally and jointly may guarantee the bonds either on the face or in an operating or lease agreement. In some cases, where the terminal property is owned by one operating company, the other roads using the facilities may guarantee the bonds secured by a mortgage on the terminal facilities.

## Debt Extinction before Maturity

In an earlier section it was suggested that corporations make formal provisions for retirement of bonds by use of either sinking fund or serial bonds. However, if market conditions are favorable (interest rates have fallen since the bonds were sold), the corporation may wish to reacquire the outstanding bonds and sell a new bond issue having a lower effective rate of interest. In order to accomplish this end, it is necessary to include a call feature when a bond issue is originated.

***The Call Privilege.*** Today, practically all issues of bonds of corporations are covered by trust indentures containing a section that permits the bond issues to be called and redeemed in whole or in part, either immediately or after a passage of time, at the option of the issuing corporation. The call privilege is inserted at the request of the corporation so as to permit adjustments in the capital structure. Corporations may use the call privilege to take advantage of a decline in interest rates, to eliminate bond issues with unfavorable indenture clauses, to reduce debt, and to replace long-term bonds with term loans or possibly short-term obligations.

Because interest rates fluctuate with the business cycle, the call option has been exercised most often during recessions to replace bonds bearing high interest rates with bonds bearing low interest rates. Over a period of years a corporation may refinance its bond indebtedness several times in order to reduce interest charges.

When corporations finance with callable bonds, management must anticipate a less favorable reaction from investors than when financing with deferred callable or noncallable bond issues. If a corporation gains from refunding at lower interest rates, investors lose. Buyers of callable bonds can anticipate having their bonds redeemed at a time when it is more difficult to obtain the same rate of return on new investments.

Consequently, a cost can be attached to the issuance of freely callable bonds as compared to deferred callable bonds. This cost can be measured at the time the bond is issued by the difference in yield between what a company would be forced to pay if the bonds had a deferred call or were noncallable and what the firm would have to pay with an immediate call feature. "Generally speaking, investors should place a value on a deferred call privilege only when their expectations of future interest rates are such that the bond would possibly be called within the period of deferment for refunding purposes."[11]

The value of the call feature will depend upon how the investors view interest-rate expectations. If interest rates are high and are expected to fall significantly, the call privilege should have a significant value to the corporation. From the investors' viewpoint, the deferred call would be most beneficial for their needs at that time. For the call feature to have a measurable value in the market, interest-rate expectations must be such that a freely callable bond might be called during the period of deferment applicable to comparable deferred callable bonds. Thus, the immediate call privilege has the greatest value, and the greatest cost to the firm, when interest rates are relatively high and are expected to fall in the foreseeable future. This is so because investors will prefer deferred callable bonds to hedge against a possible early call. The reluctance on the part of investors to purchase immediately callable bonds will cause yields to rise on immediately callable bonds vis-a-vis yields on deferred callable bonds. In order to minimize this immediate cost, corporations frequently lengthen the period of deferment from five years to ten years or more on new issues.

Trust indentures require that trustees or issuing corporations notify bondholders when bonds are to be called, and, unless bonds are surrendered promptly, bondholders incur a loss of interest. When thousands of bonds are outstanding, it is inevitable that some will not be presented on the redemption date after which all interest ceases. Holders of registered bonds will be notified by letter, but holders of nonregistered bonds must depend on notices in newspapers and financial publications. Usually, prior notice of from 30 to 60 days is given with announcement of the details of the redemption. Bond indentures usually provide that bondholders will receive a premium (more than par value) if and when bonds are called before maturity.

**The Call Price.** The call or redemption price is negotiated when bonds are issued, and it will vary according to capital-market conditions and the credit position and bargaining power of the issuing corporation. A well-known corporation having a high credit rating may offer a low call premium, such as 2 percent, but a less well-known corporation may have to offer a higher one, such as 5 or 6 percent.[12] Frequently the call privilege is deferred so that bonds may not be called until the lapse of a specified number of years, and a declining schedule of call prices is provided (for

---

[11] Frank C. Jen and James E. Wert, "The Value of the Deferred Call Privilege," *National Banking Review*, vol. 3 (March 1966), p. 370.

[12] Frequently, the call price is equal to the principal amount plus one year's nominal interest. Thus, a 6-percent bond might have an initial call price of 106.

example, 105 during the first three years, 104 during the next three years, etc.) in order to increase compensation to investors if bonds are called during the early part of the debt period.

The influence of the call price on the market price of bonds depends upon the interest rates prevailing in the market. When the market rate is below the coupon rate, corporate management will consider refunding at a lower interest rate; but, if the market rate is above the coupon rate, no savings in interest would result from refunding. In the latter case, if refunding is planned, it would be for reasons other than savings on interest charges.

If callable bonds are issued when interest rates are extremely low, there is less likelihood that bonds will be called. (If and when the interest rate changes, it should be upward.) Hence, a low call premium and an immediate call can be used because they will have little effect on the offering price of bonds. If interest rates are high and are expected to decline, the call feature will tend to depress the market price of bonds for the reason that investors would expect the debtor corporation to refinance when interest rates decline. In a new issue, the call price will have to be substantial and a deferred call period will be included to lower the effective interest rate (which in later years may be a serious deterrent to refinancing).

Before deciding to call a bond issue, the issuing corporation will compare the savings in interest over the remaining life of the bonds with the costs of refinancing, including call premium, underwriting fees, legal expenses, cost of engraving new bonds, routine expenses of retiring old bonds and issuing new ones, cost of preparation of the registration statement, and extra interest payments. (Refunding necessitates extra interest payments because a corporation will not call an old issue until the new issue has been sold and because old bondholders must be given 30 or 60 days' notice prior to the redemption date, which means that interest will be paid on both issues for the 30- or 60-day period). When making a refunding decision, the net present value of the interest savings is compared with the cash outlays required for refunding so as to determine if the refunding is advantageous to the corporation.

## Refunding before Maturity

The refunding decision is simply another capital budgeting decision. The net-present-value method of analysis can be used. This problem is made easier because the cost and benefit estimates are virtually certain. At the time of the refunding, the costs and the benefits can be calculated for the life of the "investment." Because of this a risk-free rate is used for the discounting. Recent work in this area would suggest that the before-tax rate on the new bonds is the appropriate discount rate.[13] The reasoning is similar to that explained in the analysis of leases (Chapter 14).

A detailed example will show how refunding calculations are made. Assume that a firm has a $25-million, 8-percent bond issue outstanding and the issue still has 20 years to run before maturity. Interest rates have fallen sufficiently since the bond issue was sold so that the company can now sell a $25-million issue of 20-year bonds at an effective interest rate of 6 percent. These assumptions are summarized on Table 18–4. (An income tax rate of 40 percent is assumed.)

**TABLE 18–4**
**Bond Issue Facts**

|  | Old | New |
|---|---|---|
| Principal amount outstanding | $25,000,000 | $25,000,000 |
| Coupon rate | 8% | 6% |
| Years to maturity | 20 | 20 |
| Unamortized bond discount | $ 50,000 | |
| Unamortized issue expense | $ 20,000 | |
| Call premium | 5% | |
| Issue expenses, etc. | | $ 150,000 |
| Duplicate interest (.06 × $25,000,000 × 45/360) | | $ 187,500 |

Refunding analysis, being a specialized capital budgeting problem, can be organized in a work sheet similar to that used in Chapter 9. Table 18–5 is much like Table 9–5.

For a refunding, the costs are as follows: the call premium, issue expenses, and duplicate interest. Trading in a bond issue, like trading in old equipment, can create a tax loss. Any unamortized premiums, discounts, or expenses related to the old issue become immediately deductible.

In calling the old issue, the firm must pay a premium of 5 percent. This expense of $1.25 million (.05 of $25 million) is tax deductible. The after-tax cost is then 60 percent (1 minus the 40 percent tax rate) of that amount. Issue expenses are not immediately deductible; they must be amortized. Therefore, before-tax and after-tax amounts are the same.

This example assumes that there is a 45-day overlap of interest payments on the two bond issues. This overlap occurs because most corpora-

---

[13] This rate was suggested by M. J. Gordon, "A Generalized Solution to the Buy-or-Lease Decision: A Pedagogical Note," *Journal of Finance*, vol. 29 (March 1974), p. 249, and further explained in A. R. Ofer and R. A. Taggert, Jr., "Bond Refunding: A Clarifying Analysis," *Journal of Finance*, vol. 32 (March 1977), pp. 21–31. This specification of the discount rate can be derived directly from MM's cost of capital formula as explained in the appendix to Chapter 12. Recall it was $m = \rho\tau[1 - \tau(\partial D/\partial I)]$. For riskless flows the appropriate capitalization rate for unlevered flows ($\rho\tau$) would be the interest rate ($i$). Refunding would not change the amount of debt the firm had outstanding ($\partial D/\partial I = O$). Substituting, the result is $m = i[1 - \tau(O)] = i$.

## TABLE 18-5
### Analysis of Refunding

| Cost | Before Tax | After Tax | Time | Discount Factor | Present Value | |
|---|---|---|---|---|---|---|
| Call premium | $1,250,000 | $750,000 | 0 | 1 | $750,000 | |
| Issue expense | 150,000 | 150,000 | 0 | 1 | 150,000 | |
| Duplicate interest | 18,750 | 11,250 | 0 | 1 | 112,500 | |
| Unamortized discount | (50,000) | (20,000) | 0 | 1 | (20,000) | TAX SHIELD |
| Unamortized expense | (20,000) | (8,000) | 0 | 1 | (8,000) | TAX SHR. |
| | | | | | $984,500 | |
| *Benefits* | | | | | | |
| Interest savings  2% | $500,000 | $300,000 | 1–20 | 11.470 | $3,441,000 | |
| Tax shields | 4,000 | 1,600 | 1–20 | 11.470 | 18,352 | |
| | | | | | $3,459,352 | |

NPV = Present value of benefits − Cost
NPV = $3,459,352 − $984,500 = $2,474,852

tions desire to avoid the risk of not being able to sell a new issue. Therefore, the call on the old bonds is not made until the proceeds of the new issue are assured. Because of the refunding the company will be paying interest on an extra $25 million for 45 days. The rate on this "extra" is the new issue's rate of 6 percent.[14]

As mentioned earlier, calling a bond issue accelerates the deduction of the related expenses. When the old issue is retired the discount and issue expenses, which would otherwise be written off yearly, afford the company immediate tax savings which reduces the cost of the refunding. The tax savings, or shields, would be the amount of these deductions times the tax rate.

There are two benefits the firm normally receives by refunding. The first, and most important, is interest savings. Refunding in this case saves the company 2 percent (the difference between the old 8 percent and the new 6 percent) on $25 million each year for the next 20 years. The difference is $500,000 a year before tax, or $300,000 after tax. The present value of these savings, discounted at 6 percent, is considerable!

There is also a change in the firm's financing-related tax shields. Before, the firm's *annual* expenses were:

$$\begin{array}{rl} \text{Discount:} & \$50,000/20 = \$2,500 \\ \text{Expenses:} & 20,000/20 = \underline{1,000} \\ & \$3,500 \end{array}$$

The new deductible expenses are:

Issue Expenses: $150,000/20 = $7,500.

---

[14] Some analysts use the rate on the old issue. It is the authors' feeling that the new interest is the incremental cost of changing over. The old interest would have been paid regardless of whether or not the call on the old bonds had been made.

The firm has $4,000 more in deductible expense per year which affords the firm an added tax savings of $1,600 per year.

As is apparent, this refunding operation is a very worthwhile undertaking. The example used a spread of 2 percent between the old issue and the new to make the calculations easier to understand. The results indicate refunding is often financially desirable when much smaller interest-rate differentials are involved.

Refunding is advantageous as long as the net present value is positive. If it is negative, the firm would not be justified in refunding an issue unless other considerations, such as desiring to remove restrictive bond covenants, were of paramount importance to management.

Two additional points concerning the above refunding example should be mentioned at this time. First, in the example it was assumed that the new bond issue has the same maturity as the old bond issue. Frequently, the new issue has a longer maturity than the old one; however, the analysis should only consider the cash benefits up to the maturity of the old bond issue. Second, while it may be profitable to refund the bonds now, in the near future it may be even more profitable if interest rates decline further. Therefore, timing of a refunding issue is of utmost importance in order to gain the maximum savings from the decline in interest rates subsequent to the time of the initial offering.

***Other Uses of the Call Feature.*** The call feature may be used to implement other methods of debt retirement; for example, when a corporation notifies bondholders that their convertible bonds are being called on a certain date, the holders have the option of using their conversion privilege immediately or selling their bonds to someone who will convert them. If the conversion privilege is valuable, the bonds may be sold at a premium.

Corporations are financing their long-term capital needs to an increasing extent by long-term loans from banks, insurance companies, and other institutional investors. The loan agreement may permit prepayment of the loans, in whole or in part, at the convenience of the debtor. Usually, commercial banks permit prepayment without penalty, but insurance companies and others are inclined to attach a premium to prepayment similar to the excess of a bond call price over par. Most lenders will permit prepayment of debts without penalty out of earnings, but they will assess a penalty if prepayment is accomplished by refunding at a lower rate of interest. During the years when there is the greatest uncertainty as to the future of the borrower's business, the lender is assuming the greatest risk. If the borrower's credit position improves sufficiently to enable borrowing at a lower interest rate, the lender who assumed the risk originally may feel that if the loan is repaid it means the loss of the loan when it is most attractive. (Conversely, if the borrower's credit position does not improve as anticipated, the loan may not be repaid and the

## Debt Management at Maturity

When management makes no formal provisions for the retirement of its bonds, it depends upon either the ability of the corporation to refund them at maturity with a new issue, or the willingness of the bondholders to exchange their bonds for preferred or common stock.

*Refunding at Maturity.* When a corporation refunds its bond issues at maturity, it may either issue new securities to obtain cash with which to repay those outstanding or offer new securities directly to bondholders in exchange for those they hold. In the latter case, bondholders who are unwilling to exchange their bonds are paid off in cash. Because refunding is a debt replacement rather than debt liquidation, the problems in refunding differ from those of sinking-fund and serial-bond issues.

To meet maturing bond obligations, a corporation may issue new bonds, preferred or common stock, or it may negotiate for a direct loan from insurance companies or banks. Old bondholders may accept new bonds in exchange for old ones if offered one or more special inducements, such as a cash bonus, better security, a sinking-fund, or a conversion privilege. Since most corporate bonds are held by institutional investors, the bondholders may negotiate with the debtor corporation for a direct exchange of old bonds for new. This practice doubtless would be more common were it not for the regulation requiring that new bond issues of certain regulated companies be sold to the highest bidder.

When a large bond issue matures, the credit position of the issuer and the conditions in the capital market will influence the method of refunding. It would be fortuitous if both the credit position of the corporation and the situation in the capital market happened to be favorable on the maturity date of the old debt. In the face of an unsettled capital market, a corporation would normally reappraise and postpone new financing plans; but this option of postponement is not present when obligations mature. The maturing debt in this instance may be retired by issuing short-term notes in the capital market or obtaining loans from commercial banks or insurance companies.

In the event a corporation cannot meet its maturing bond obligations, management may ask bondholders to extend the maturity of an issue. If there are only a few bondholders, some plan of extension may be agreed upon; however, if there are many bondholders, arranging for an extension becomes difficult. If an extension is arranged, the debtor corporation is usually required to make substantial concessions to bondholders. Creditors may agree to an extension in the hope of averting principal losses that would tend to result if the corporation were forced into bankruptcy.

## Summary

A bond is usually one of a series of similar credit instruments that make up a bond issue. The individual bonds are not necessarily of like denomination or maturity. For example, in a serial-bond issue, some bonds come due in successive years. The most common corporate bonds are those in $1,000 denominations or multiples thereof.

A bond usually contains a promise to pay interest on stated dates. The exception is the income bond, on which interest is paid only when earned. Bonds may be registered as to principal and interest, as to principal only, or unregistered. When bonds are fully registered, interest payments are made through the office of the corporation or through a paying agent. Nonregistered bonds are coupon bonds with the interest date printed on each coupon. The coupons may be mailed to designated payees when the interest date arrives or they may be deposited in the holder's bank to be collected for him.

The real estate mortgage loan is the most common form of long-term loan and the principles involved therein are adapted for use in financing with mortgage bonds. The two basic documents in a simple real estate mortgage loan are the note and the mortgage; in a mortgage-bond issue, the documents include a mortgage, a trust indenture, and a bond. When an indenture limits the amount of notes or bonds of equal rank that may be issued under its provisions, the mortgage is said to be closed when this amount of debt has been created. A mortgage that permits more borrowing under the mortgage is called an open-end mortgage. When a limit is fixed for new issues of notes or bonds, it is known as a limited open-end mortgage.

The issuance of bonds with maturity dates necessitates making plans for their extinction. Such plans may provide for redemption, refunding, or conversion. Redemption or retirement of a bond issue may take place when all bonds come due; on a call date, as provided in the trust indenture; periodically, over the life of the issue when serial bonds are issued; or piecemeal, by repurchase of bonds in the open market or by negotiation with individual bondholders. Sinking funds may be set up to redeem bonds, other debt obligations may be created to obtain funds with which to redeem the original issue (refunding), or extinction may be brought about by exchanging the bonds for other securities (conversion).

The call feature in bonds permits corporations to (1) reduce interest charges by replacing high-interest-bearing bonds with obligations carrying a lower interest rate, (2) eliminate bond issues having unfavorable indenture clauses, and (3) expedite conversion when bonds have the conversion feature. A sinking fund for debt retirement provides for periodic appropriations of cash for redeeming bonds on or before maturity. During the interim, sinking-fund contributions are invested by the trustee in accordance with provisions in the trust indenture. Both sinking-fund and serial-bond issues provide for an orderly reduction in debt, and market conditions determine which type will be issued. When bonds are refunded before maturity, the corporation will issue new securities, which may be sold to obtain cash to redeem those outstanding or may be offered directly to bondholders in exchange for those they hold. Refunding is contemplated when there is a decline in market interest rates large enough to provide net cash savings to the firm if the old bond issue is called and replaced with a new issue at a lower interest rate. Refunding before maturity is treated as a riskless capital-budgeting project. The conversion privilege gives bondholders the right to convert their bonds into another security, usually common stock, of the issuing corporation. The conversion rate or price as well as the conversion period are set forth in the trust indenture.

## QUESTIONS

1. Large business firms that raise funds by public financing usually depend more on bond issues than on sales of common or preferred stock. Why?
2. What provisions are usually found in a trust indenture? Compare to those found in a term-loan agreement. Which document is usually the most restrictive to the corporation? Why?
3. What are the functions of a trustee under provisions of a trust indenture? How did the Trust Indenture Act of 1939 affect the selection of trustees?
4. (a) What are the reasons given by management for making provisions for the extinction of bonds? (b) What devices may be employed to facilitate bond extinction?
5. (a) "Refunding is debt replacement rather than debt liquidation." Explain. (b) How do refunding operations differ from those used in sinking-fund and serial-bond repayment plans?
6. What are the advantages to a corporation of using open-end mortgages? Explain the clauses in mortgage indentures designed to protect bondholders.
7. Discuss the advantages of a first mortgage lien over an unsecured loan from the creditor's viewpoint.
8. Compare and contrast the uses of the two types of income bonds. What special advantages do they offer to corporate management over the use of preferred stock?
9. Compare the features of subordinated debenture bonds with those of preferred stocks. With respect to the issues of a given corporation, which could appear to be safer for an investor?
10. Identify the following: (a) redemption, (b) refunding, and (c) conversion.

11. Identify the following: (a) call privilege, (b) deferred call, and (c) immediate call.
12. "Investors should place a value on a deferred call only if they expect interest rates to fall during the deferment period." Discuss.
13. If an investor purchased a bond at $104 and it is called for sinking-fund purposes at $102, he loses $20. How can this be reconciled with the statement that bondholders are benefited by a sinking-fund provision?

# PROBLEMS

1. In 1979, the Coast-to-Coast Railroad exchanged new 8-percent income bonds due in 2019 for its outstanding 8-percent preferred stock in order to retire the latter. The new income bonds were junior in rank and matured subsequent to all other Coast-to-Coast bonds. How did this change affect:
   a. Coast-to-Coast's federal income tax liability.
   b. The position of the common stockholders.
   c. The position of Coast-to-Coast's other bonds.
   d. The position of the preferred stockholders who accepted the new bonds.
   e. The position of the preferred stockholders who did *not* accept the new bonds.

2. You bought a high-grade corporate bond bearing an 8-percent coupon rate and due in 25 years, at par, to yield 8 percent. Suppose the market yields on such obligations decline to 6 percent within a period of six months. Reverse the supposition and assume that, in a period of six months, interest rates rise and your bond now sells on a 9-percent yield basis.
   a. How much is your bond worth in each instance?
   b. What factors may have caused the above shifts in rates?
   c. Would you have the same answer in part *a* if the bonds were callable?

3. Given the facts below, analyze the indicated refunding decision. Assume the firm has a 40 percent tax rate. The present value of an annuity factor for 15 years at 7 percent is 9.108.

**Bond Issue Facts**

| | Old | New |
|---|---|---|
| Principal amount outstanding | $10,000,000 | $10,000,000 |
| Coupon rate | 8% | 7% |
| Years to maturity | 15 | 15 |
| Unamortized bond discount | $ 90,000 | |
| Unamortized issue expense | $ 150,000 | |
| Call premium | 8% | |
| Issue expenses | | $ 300,000 |
| Duplicate interest [1] (.07 × $10,000,000 × 60/360) | | $ 116,670 |

[1] Assumes 60-day overlap.

4. The RPB Corporation has pretax earnings of $4 million. Its present capitalization includes 100,000 shares of $6 preferred stock, par value $100, and 1 million shares of no-par common stock. The corporation plans to retire its preferred issue and offer $10 million of 6-percent income bonds to the pre-

ferred shareholders. Determine the effect of the proposed change on the earnings per share available to common stockholders, assuming a marginal tax rate of 50 percent.

5. During the credit crunch of 1974 and the resultant upheaval in the money and capital markets, you purchased at par a BAA corporate bond with a 10-percent coupon. Assume that presently the market rate of interest for similar quality bonds is: (a) 12 percent (b) 10 percent, (c) 8 percent, (d) 6 percent. Assume 20 years remain until maturity. Calculate how much your bond is worth under each rate of yield. (Assume annual interest payments.)

6. What is the price which investors would be willing to pay for each of the following:
    a. A 20-year $1,000 par value bond, nominal annual interest at 9%, purchased to yield 8% effective interest?
    b. A 15-year $1,000 par value bond, five years after its issuance, annual nominal interest is 6%, current yields are 9%?

7. Ajax, Inc., has issued $100,000 in mortgage bonds. The bonds have a life of 20 years. The indenture requires that a sinking fund be established which, through equal annual contributions, will be sufficient to redeem the entire bond issue on the maturity date.
    a. What is the annual sinking fund deposit if the fund earns no interest?
    b. How much must each annual contribution be if the fund can earn 5 percent compounded annually?
    c. How much must each annual contribution be if the fund can earn 8 percent compounded annually?

## ADDITIONAL READINGS

Bernstein, P. L. "What Rate of Return Can You 'Reasonably' Expect?" *Journal of Finance*, vol. 28 (May 1973), pp. 273–82.

Bowlin, O. D. "The Refunding Decision: Another Special Case in Capital Budgeting," *Journal of Finance*, vol. 21 (March 1966), pp. 55–68.

Ellis, C. D. "Bonds for Long-Term Investors," *Financial Analysts Journal*, vol. 26 (March–April 1970), pp. 81–85.

Fraine, H. G., and R. H. Mills. "Effect of Defaults and Credit Deterioration on Yields of Corporate Bonds," *Journal of Finance*, vol. 16 (September 1961), pp. 423–34.

Halford, F. A. "Income Bonds," *Financial Analysts Journal*, vol. 20 (January–February 1964), pp. 73–79.

Hopewell, M. H., and G. G. Kaufman. "Bond Price Volatility and Term to Maturity: A Generalized Respecification," *American Economic Review*, vol. 63 (September 1973), pp. 749–53.

Jen, F. C., and J. E. Wert. "The Value of the Deferred Call Privilege," *National Banking Review*, vol. 3 (March 1966), pp. 369–78.

———. "The Effects of Call Risk on Corporate Bond Yields," *Journal of Finance*, vol. 22 (December 1967), pp. 637–52.

Johnson, R. E. "Term Structure of Corporate Bond Yields as a Function of Risk of Default," *Journal of Finance*, vol. 22 (May 1967), pp. 313–45.

Mayor, T. H., and K. G. McCoin. "The Rate of Discount in Bond Refunding," *Financial Management,* vol. 3 (Autumn 1974), pp. 54–58.

Pye, G. "The Value of Call Deferment on a Bond: Some Empirical Results," *Journal of Finance,* vol. 22 (December 1967), pp. 623–36.

Wilbur, W. L. "Return and Risk Characteristics of High-Grade Bonds," *Quarterly Review of Economics and Business,* vol. 12 (August 1972), pp. 45–54.

Winn, W. J., and A. Hess, Jr. "The Value of the Call Privilege," *Journal of Finance,* vol. 14 (May 1959), pp. 182–95.

# 19

# Convertibles, Warrants, and Stock Options

In addition to the sources of long-term financing discussed in earlier chapters, there are certain specialized subjects that should be considered at this time. These areas include the use of convertible securities, warrants, and stock options. Convertible securities can be either junior bonds or preferred stock. The discussion here deals primarily with bonds, but the reasoning is equally applicable to convertible preferred stock. Warrants provide corporations with a mechanism for raising funds when other means may not be available at reasonable prices. They may make more marketable an otherwise rather unattractive issue and thereby provide certain corporations access to long-term funds.

Customers, suppliers, and employees are another source of capital, especially for small business firms. This source may not be important for large business corporations, but the latter frequently have special stock purchase arrangements for employees and executives. The primary purpose of these stock purchase plans is not to raise long-term funds but to serve as an incentive mechanism for key personnel.

The topics covered in this chapter include convertible bonds, warrants, and special sources of equity capital.

## Convertible Bonds

A convertible bond permits the holder, at his option, to exchange such a security for another of the same company under certain specified conditions. Usually, the securities that may be exchanged are bonds. Thus, the holder is relinquishing a bond having a fixed-income return and changing it into a more speculative security that lacks the fixed return but has the right to share in the residual income of the company. When this privilege is made attractive enough, the use of the option will eliminate outstanding bonds during the conversion period; however, the choice or option lies with the bondholders rather than with the issuing corporation. Whether or not they use it depends on the terms of conversion and the market price of the corporation's stock.

**Use of Convertible Bonds.** The arguments in favor of the use of convertible bonds by corporations include the following: (1) The cost of borrowing is lower, the assumption being that investors will pay more for a bond or accept a lower interest rate if they have the option of converting it into common stock in the future. If stock prices are high and there is an active market for such convertible securities, convertible bonds may have a special appeal to the more speculative-minded bond buyer. (2) If and when bonds are converted into common stock, the capital structure of the corporation will be simplified, fixed-interest charges will be reduced, and the way will be cleared for additional bond financing. (3) Conversion will tend to increase the number of common stockholders and thus broaden the market for future equity financing. By raising funds by a sale of convertible bonds, the firm will eventually issue fewer common shares than if it sold common directly. New common stock must be sold slightly below the market to make it attractive, while conversion prices of common stock are usually above the market price at the time of issuance of the convertible bond.

**The Conversion Clause.** The conversion clause in the trust indenture may be expressed as a ratio or as price; that is, it may permit either the exchange of a $1,000 bond for 20 shares of stock or the use of the bond to buy shares of stock at $50 per share, irrespective of the market price. In the latter case, a $1,000 bond could be exchanged for 20 shares of stock. The conversion ratio or price may vary from year to year; if so, it is usually most favorable to bondholders during the first years of the bond, becoming progressively less favorable with the approach of the maturity date.

Very infrequently the conversion ratio or price may be fixed so that conversion will be profitable when the bonds are issued or when the conversion period goes into effect. However, the conversion price is usually fixed above the market price of the stock into which bonds may be converted, so bondholders will be required to wait until the market price of the common stock makes conversion profitable—when the market price of the stock at least equals the conversion price. It is possible that a small number of bondholders may use their conversion privilege even when the market price is slightly below the conversion price because it is less expensive to convert a bond than to buy the same stock directly through regular brokerage channels.

The conversion period may, and usually does, run throughout the life of the bond. However, in some cases it may not become effective until several years have elapsed; while in other cases it may expire at the end of a stated number of years before the bond matures. Making such bonds callable adds an element of uncertainty to the value of the conversion privilege. The conversion clause has been compared to subscription rights, with the former running for years, while the latter is in effect only during the offering period. However, the use of rights brings cash to the corporation, while the use of the conversion privilege usually only changes the form of the capital structure—decreasing debt and increasing equity capital. More appropriately, subscription rights should be compared to stock purchase warrants that are sometimes attached to bonds. Nevertheless, both stock warrants and the conversion privilege tend to add a speculative element to bonds.

*Antidilution Clause.* The trust indenture usually includes the antidilution clause, which means that, if the corporation weakens the bondholders' claims, an adjustment is made. For example, if the corporation splits the stock two for one, or declares a stock dividend of one share of new stock for each share held, the bond becomes exchangeable for twice the number of shares originally provided for in the trust indenture. In addition to covering stock splits and stock dividends, the trust indenture usually covers subscription rights for sales of additional stock, and sales of other securities having conversion rights. The antidilution provision is included to provide an adjustment of the stated ratio or price so as to maintain the relative position of the bondholders at the time of issuance in case more shares are issued in the future. If such a provision were not included it would be possible for management to negate the value of the conversion right by splitting the stock or issuing new shares substantially below the conversion price when the market price of the stock approached the conversion price.

*Valuation of a Convertible.* The convertible bond's market value is based on two underlying factors. They are its value as a debt instrument and its potential value as converted common stock. Thus, the investor can effectively hedge when he purchases a convertible security. If the market price of a corporation's common stock rises above the conversion price of its convertible bonds, this increase will be reflected in the market price of the bonds. For example, if a $1,000 bond may be exchanged for 20 shares of stock or has a conversion price of $50 per share, when the market price of the stock is $60 per share the market price of the convertible bond will be about $1,200. When common stock is selling below the conversion price, the market price of the bond depends primarily on its investment value as a credit instrument.

The theoretical value of a convertible bond is its value without the conversion privilege. In other words, it is the price for which a comparable straight bond of the same company (or a similar company) would sell in the marketplace. This is the present value of a stream of income to be received from the bond over its remaining life. As an example, suppose that the X Company has a 6-percent convertible bond outstanding with a due date in ten years. At the present time a comparable ten-year nonconvertible bond would have to yield 8 percent in order to sell at par. A ten-year, 6-percent convertible bond would be selling at a discount, or, more specifically, at about $866. Thus, the floor of the convertible bond would be its value as a straight bond. However, it should be recognized that this floor changes as market interest rates rise or fall for the company. If the market interest rate should fall to 6 percent, the bond value floor would rise to $1,000. Market interest rates to the firm vary according to the interest-rate movements in the capital markets and any changes in the market's appraisal of the financial risk inherent in the company's bonds.

If the price of the underlying common stock rises past its conversion price, the convertible bond will sell at its conversion value. This value is the market price of the common stock into which the bond can be converted at the current conversion ratio. The bond will never sell significantly below its conversion value once the market price of the stock exceeds the conversion price. If it did, arbitrage by some investors would take place. For example, if the stock in the earlier example is still selling for $60 but the bonds falls to $1,100, investors would purchase the bond and immediately convert it into common stock. They would make $100 on the transaction if they then sold the common stock ($60 × 20 = $1,200 − $1,100). As a consequence, the market price of the bond would rise and the price of the stock would fall.

Frequently, a conversion premium is present in convertible bonds, which is the difference between the market price of the bond and the higher of either its theoretical bond value or conversion value. A conversion premium is often built into the convertible bond at the time of issuance. This is possible because the investor receives a fixed return and, in addition, receives the privilege of converting the bond into common stock on some prearranged schedule. Therefore, the company issues the bond at a lower yield than it would be forced to pay on a nonconvertible bond and, at the same time, the bond is sold above its conversion value by perhaps 10 to 20 percent. This differential represents the conversion premium, which exists because a trade-off is being made by the investor. He is willing to accept a lower yield on his bond in order to receive an opportunity to purchase stock in the future at a prearranged price even though the conversion price is above the present market price of the stock. Therefore, the investor has the security of a bond investment while he awaits the hoped-for increase in the price of the stock. The size of the premium will depend on its appeal both as a bond and a common stock. However, it is possible that some part of the premium can be explained by the fact that certain institutional investors may be restricted in the amount of common stock that may be held in their portfolios.[1]

Figure 19-1 shows the conversion premium on a 10-year 6-percent bond issued at par when the investment value of a straight bond of similar quality is 8 percent. For a bond issued at par the conversion premium would be $134 ($1000 − 866). If the common stock is selling for $40 (conversion value $50), the value of the bond based on the common stock would be $800 [$1000 − (20 shares × $40)]. Clearly, the bond would sell at its investment value, or $866.

Therefore, the market price of the bond will never be less than either its investment or conversion value. The excess of the market price over

**FIGURE 19-1**
Market Value of a 6-percent Convertible Bond with a
10-Year Maturity, Assuming 8-percent Current Yields

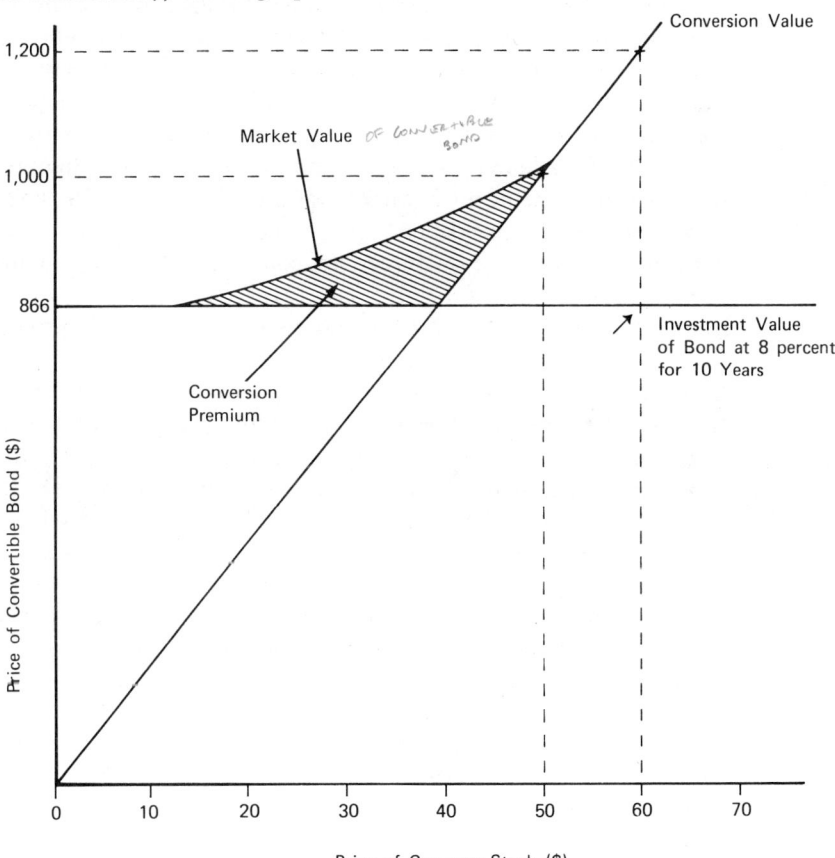

---

[1] Eugene F. Brigham, "An Analysis of Convertible Debentures: Theory and Some Empirical Evidence," *Journal of Finance* 21 (March 1966), p. 53.

the higher of these two values is the conversion premium. As Figure 19–1 shows, the conversion premium eventually disappears. This is probably explained by the existence of a call option. For example, the conversion premium would disappear when the market price of the stock reached $60 because the issuer could force conversion by calling the bond. Hence, it would be risky to pay more than the conversion value because the bond is now subject to a call by the corporation.

**Conversion Timing.** Actual conversion will occur under two distinct sets of circumstances. Conversion can either be forced by the corporation or it can be voluntary on the part of the bondholder. If the bonds are callable, which is usually the case, the corporation can force conversion. Assume that the call price is $1,050 and the bonds are selling for $1,200. If the conversion ratio is 40, the market price of the stock is $30. When the corporation issues a call for the bonds, the investor is confronted with receiving $1,050 as opposed to $1,200, the present market value of the underlying stock. He will naturally convert or sell the bond to someone who will convert. Therefore, the company can force conversion because the bondholders would sustain an appreciable capital loss by turning in the bonds for redemption. When convertible bonds are callable, the corporation customarily gives bondholders call notice of 30 days or more prior to the redemption date.

A bondholder may be forced to convert, depending on the market price of the stock, if the conversion privilege is nearing expiration or if the conversion ratio is about to decrease (for example, from 40 to 36 shares). These provisions, on occasion, are included in convertible bond indentures. While these situations appear to be voluntary, in actual fact they smack of coercion because the bondholders are forced to convert in order not to sustain a capital loss.

Assuming the market price of the stock remains at $30, if the ratio falls to 36 from 40, the bondholders will hold bonds having a market value of $1,080 instead of $1,200. Thus, the bond-indenture provisions cause an involuntary conversion. Should the existing bondholders not choose to convert, they would be forced to sell the bonds to someone who would exercise the privilege or else lose part of their investment value.

Nevertheless, this circumstance is a bit different from a conversion induced by a call. The timing of a call is uncertain, while in the former case the various conversion ratios or prices are known by the investors at the time of their purchases. The changes in conversion prices represent an attempt by the firm to anticipate part of the expected growth in its stock value.

Voluntary conversion may take place if the dividends on the common stock are increased, thereby persuading the bondholders to give up their more secure position as creditors. A corporation may encourage conversion by declaring an extra dividend on common stock and then notifying holders of convertible bonds so they may participate in the extra dividend by converting their bonds into stock before a specified date. Although holders of convertible bonds are not obligated to convert them, they may do so if the inducements offered are sufficiently attractive.

## Warrants to Purchase Stock

A warrant is an option to purchase a specific number of shares of a company within a given time period at a given price. The warrant is usually attached to a senior security at the time of sale. As a general rule, warrants permit purchases of common stock. Warrants are used typically when the company is issuing bonds. They serve as "sweeteners" to assist in the sale of an otherwise rather unattractive issue. For instance, if market interest rates are very high by historical standards, warrants may be attached to the bond issue to obtain a lower interest rate and still meet investor acceptability. Warrants are used both in public offerings and private placements of securities. In fact, warrants may have been used because the debt would otherwise have been unmarketable at any reasonable terms. When warrants are attached to bonds, usually debentures, the investor receives not only the fixed-interest-rate return on a debt instrument but also an option to purchase common stock at a prearranged price. If the company's stock price rises, this option to purchase stock will become valuable. If it does not rise in price, the investor will have to be satisfied with the interest payments on the bonds. In this respect warrants are similar to convertible securities.

The price at which warrants may be exercised is usually above the price of the common stock at the time the warrants are issued. Therefore, the common stock must advance sufficiently in price to surpass the option price within the effective time period if the warrants are to have more than a speculative appeal to investors.

***Provisions of Warrants.*** Warrants may be either detachable or nondetachable. A detachable warrant can be separated from the bond and sold independently. In the case of the nondetachable warrant, only the owner of the senior security to which it is attached can exercise the privilege. However, in most cases, the warrant is detachable. Examples of detachable warrants that trade actively can be found listed on the New York Stock Exchange and the American Stock Exchange. The holder of the senior security can detach the warrant and either exercise or sell it in the open market. Thus, a detachable warrant is assignable. If the owner does not wish to exercise it, he may sell it by means of the usual brokerage channels.

Most of the detachable warrants outstanding are exercisable for a given number of years. In other words, the warrants may be exercised anytime up to, for example, January 15, 1985. Up to the expiration date, the value of the warrant will fluctuate, depending on the value of the company's common stock.

In some instances warrants are outstanding as long as the corporation is in operation. These are classified as perpetual warrants. They remain outstanding as long as the corporation is in existence and they have not been exercised by the holder. In many instances, should the company issuing the warrants be merged and subsequently lose its identity, the warrants would expire.

The price at which warrants may be exercised can be either fixed or variable. If the price is fixed the holder may purchase common stock at a certain price (say, $25) for the life of the warrant. If the price is variable it increases periodically until the life of the warrant expires.

Since the warrant must specify a price at which the stock can be acquired, dilution is possible due to stock dividends and stock splits. As was the case with convertible bonds, an antidilution clause is usually present. This clause provides that the option price of the stock shall be reduced and the number of shares increased proportionally in the event of such actions on the part of the corporation.

Because a warrant is only an option to purchase the stock, the holder does not have the usual rights of a stockholder to vote or to receive dividends when declared by the corporation. The payment of cash dividends can be a powerful force working toward the exercise of outstanding warrants, particularly if the dividends permit a generous rate of return when compared to the option price.

**Value of Warrants.** The formula for the theoretical value of a warrant at any given time is

$$V = S(P) - S(O)$$

Factoring,

$$V = S(P - O)$$

where $V$ is the value of the warrant, $P$ the market price of the common stock, $O$ the price of the option, and $S$ the number of shares that can be purchased by each warrant. Assume the warrants of a corporation entitle the holders to purchase two shares of common stock at $20 per share and the current market price of the stock is $28. The value of the warrant would be $16 [2($28 - $20)].

The price of a warrant may go above the formula price, but it should rarely fall much below it because of arbitrage in the security markets. An arbitrager would purchase warrants, exercise them, and then sell the stock. As a result of these transactions, the market price of the warrants would rise and the price of the stock would decline, thereby eliminating the differential.

Figure 19-2 shows the relationship between the market value of the warrant and its theoretical value. The theoretical value as the formula implies, is the discount from the market value of the common stock. In Figure 19-2 the theoretical value of the warrant is zero when the market

## 19 Convertibles, Warrants, and Stock Options

**FIGURE 19-2**
Market versus Theoretical Value of a Warrant

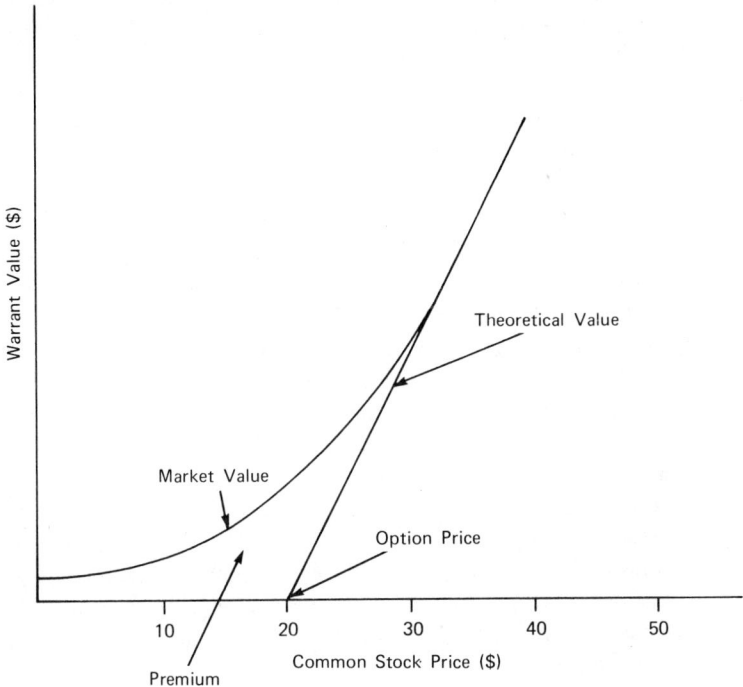

price of the common stock is below $20. When the stock price rises above $20 the theoretical value is the market price less the option price. In general, when the market value of the common stock is substantially below the option price, the market price of the warrant will be above the theoretical value. As the stock price continues its rise above the option price, the market value and the theoretical value of the warrant will gradually converge. This is because the leverage effect of the warrant decreases as the market price of the stock increases.

Over the broad range of stock prices, however, substantial premiums may exist. For example, Occidental Petroleum warrants illustrate this point. The Occidental warrants are exercisable at $16.25 per share until April 22, 1980. On August 11, 1977, the price of the common stock was $26.50, and the warrant's price on the same day was $13. The theoretical value of the warrant would be

$$V = S(P - O)$$
$$V = (\$26.50 - \$16.25)$$
$$V = \$10.25$$

The premium on that date was $2.75 ($13 − 10.25). If the market price of the stock were to rise further before the expiration date of the warrant, the market price of the warrant should approximate the theoretical value.

When the market assumes that there is little or no possibility of a warrant being exercised, the warrant price should fall to zero which is its theoretical value. No premium would then be available in the market to the present owners of the warrants. For this to occur, the market price of the stock would have to be substantially below the option price and the expiration date impending.

**The Use of Warrants.** The advantage of warrants from the corporation's viewpoint is that they are a means of obtaining additional equity funds in the corporation at a price higher than the company could obtain if the stock were issued directly instead of using a debt issue. A distinction should be made between the use of warrants and convertible bonds. When warrants are exercised, the common stock of the company is increased and the bond issue remains outstanding. In a convertible issue, the common stock would also increase but the bond issue would be extinguished. The effect of warrants is to increase the overall size of the capital structure of the corporation.

The potential increase in the number of shares due to the existence of outstanding warrants may have some adverse effect on the price of the common stock. If there is a large number of warrants outstanding, considerable dilution of earnings per share is possible. The market will recognize this and place a lower price-earnings ratio on the stock than would otherwise have been the case.

## Special Sources of Equity Capital

Although customers, suppliers, and employees are not important sources of capital for large business corporations, under certain conditions they may be important sources of capital for small business firms. Large corporations usually have special investment arrangements for employees and privileged subscriptions for executives. Even though the primary purpose of these special arrangements for customers, employees, and executives is not to raise equity capital, they fall under the area of special equity sources.

**Customers and Suppliers.** The customers of some corporations are among the special groups to whom stock may be offered. In some lines of business, such as public-utility companies, approaching customers with stock offers is not difficult. Some small public-utility companies, such as those providing water, communications, and transportation services, originate as community projects, with much of the venture capital provided by potential users of the services.

Manufacturing companies have sought to expand the sales of their products by selling stock to retail and wholesale distributors so as to give them a direct interest in the company. The same sort of customer relationship may result when the customer takes the initiative in providing new capital to the manufacturer in order to be assured a source of supply.

**Employees.** The United States Steel Corporation, E. I. duPont de Nemours & Company, Procter and Gamble Company, and Commonwealth Edison Company were among the first companies to attempt to break down the barrier between employers and employees by encouraging the latter to become coowners. Now, almost one-half of the companies whose stocks are listed on the New York Stock Exchange have investment arrangements for their employees.

The present-day employee stock-purchase plans are of two basic types: one operates under privileged subscription plans where stock is sold to employees below market prices; the other operates under arrangements where stock is purchased in the open market and sold to employees at market prices. The sponsors of both types of plans seem to assume that the company's stock has investment merits because employees stock-purchase plans are presented as savings plans.

Stability of dividends is the first test of the suitability of corporate stock for employee investment; if the earnings of a corporation are stable and large enough to permit regular payment of dividends, one requisite for a successful employee stock-purchase plan is present. The dividend rate should be high enough to make investment in the stock attractive as compared to other investments (Series E bonds, savings deposits, and savings-and-loan association accounts), or the securities should be issued by companies having excellent growth records and policies of declaring stock dividends or stock splits.

A second test of the investment quality of a security suitable for purchase under an employee stock-purchase plan is marketability—the ability to sell with little or no capital loss and with little or no delay. Because the price of common stock is subject to considerable fluctuation, some companies make loans to employees with their stock pledged as security, which may eliminate the necessity to sell stock at a possible loss when funds are needed by the employee.

The third and most important test of investment quality is safety. Most of the employee-ownership plans initiated during the 1920s were discontinued as a result of the stock market collapse beginning in the fall of 1929. Employees, like other investors, lost heavily when the market prices of their companies' shares declined. When this loss was accompanied by unemployment, employees lost not only their chief source of income (jobs) but also most of the value of their savings when they were forced to sell their securities. This danger of double loss (income and savings) is inherent in any employee stock-purchase plan.

If the market price of a company's stock is subject to wide fluctuation, it may be wise for management to refrain from inaugurating any company-sponsored employee stock-purchase plan unless the corporation is willing to risk serious losses by agreeing to repurchase all stock sold to employees at a prearranged price. Even when a company's stock has all the qualities that make it a safe investment, management should at least provide for repurchase of stock sold to participants in the company-sponsored plan during the first year after its sale.

The current trend is for corporations to arrange for purchase of securities through payroll-deduction plans at market prices rather than through fixed-price contracts, which are a feature of privileged subscriptions. The stock purchased may be delivered to the employee as soon as practicable after the end of the calendar year or it may be held by a trustee in a trust fund until the employee terminates his service with the company.

When considered from the viewpoint of management, the primary purposes of employee stock-purchase plans are to improve labor-employer relationships, to reduce labor turnover, to increase the efficiency and responsibility of labor, and to obtain new funds. While the financial advantage to a corporation of selling stock to employees is usually placed last among the advantages of stock-ownership plans, it may be among the first for small companies. That the ability to obtain funds from employees is occasionally a valuable asset is illustrated by the purchase of stock of the Endicott Johnson Corporation in January 1961 (operated since 1971 as a wholly-owned subsidiary of the McDonough Company), which was an important factor in keeping the company under the control of existing management.

**Privileged Subscription for Officers.** The various plans under which officers acquire stock usually include the right or privilege to purchase a given number of shares of the company's stock at a certain price within a certain time. This option varies from the ordinary type of "call" contract bought and sold in the securities market in that it is for a number of years rather than up to six months. Options may be granted for shares that are authorized but unissued, held as treasury stock, or reacquired at the market price on the date the option is granted.

The primary purpose of stock-option plans is to promote the interests of the company by encouraging key personnel to remain with the company and to provide them additional "incentive for unusual industry, efficiency, and loyalty by enabling them to acquire a proprietary interest in the company." Since key officers often acquire shares through regular brokerage channels, the value of a stock-purchase option depends on the difference between the option price and the market price of the stock when the option is used. In order to retain the stock purchased under officer stock-purchase plans, the participants are under contract not to leave the company except under certain specified conditions (such as ill-health and reaching retirement age).

Usually, the salaries of key personnel increase as corporations grow in size; but, because of high personal income taxes, "take-home pay" increases at a slower rate. To accumulate an estate, officers depend on capital appreciation. This has been a factor in the decision of many former executives to start their own businesses, usually in the same field as that in which they obtain their practical experience. Their departures were doubly disadvantageous to the former employers—the services of key officials were lost and new competitors were created. The stock-option purchase plan seems to be a practical solution to this problem. By linking the financial interest of key personnel to the future growth of the company, management anticipates that both the company and the officers will benefit.

Because executives sometimes lack the funds necessary to exercise their options, some corporations (General Motors, for instance) give cash and stock bonuses in addition to the options. Stock-option plans are usually effective in holding key people; and those given by smaller companies are often more valuable than those given by larger corporations because the market price of the stock of a successful, expanding, small company may rise more rapidly than that of a large, older corporation.

One of the advantages that has been claimed for the use of options is that "it costs the company little or nothing"—in fact, it brings cash into the company when the option is used. However, if a corporation purchases stock in the open market at the time of issuing an option, it is deprived of the use of assets during the option period while the stock is being held as treasury stock. Another fallacy in the assertion that stock options cost nothing is that it ignores the effect of stock purchased under options on old stockholders' rights to earnings. As the number of shares distributed under stock-option plans increases, the proportionate interest of other stockholders decreases.

When stock options are exercised, stockholders' rights to earnings, assets, and voting privileges are diluted. Therefore, it is important to balance the cost of stock options to the corporation and the dilution of old stockholders' interests against the extent to which the benefits bestowed on optionees are reflected in higher net profits. Presumably, boards of directors regard the potential dilution of stockholders' earnings and other rights to be more than offset by past, current, and anticipated contributions of optionees. While this may be true to some extent, it must be pointed out that many times external factors are more important in explaining the prosperity of a company than the internal factors for which management is responsible.

Perhaps the most conclusive evidence of the merit of stock-option plans is the fact that many corporations whose boards of directors are dominated by "outside" directors are using them. The authority to issue new shares and to distribute shares under conditions proposed in executive stock-option plans must be obtained from stockholders. When stockholders have been asked to vote thereon, they have customarily approved them by considerably more than the required number of affirmative votes. When such plans have been brought before the federal and state courts, they have been upheld.

Although the giving of stock options to executives had been criticized for years, it was not until the Securities and Exchange Commission revealed that officers of the Chrysler Corporation had gained $4.2 million on options they sold in 1963 that steps were taken by Congress to tighten up on the conditions under which such profits could be treated as capital gains. The present rules for qualified stock options are as follows: (1) The option price must be the same as the market price. (2) The unused options are automatically canceled at the end of five years. (3) In order to be taxed as capital gains, the stock must be held three years. (4) New options may not be issued to replace old ones when the market price declines. (5) Executives who own as much as 5 percent of the stock of their corporations are barred from stock options.[2] (6) Stockholders' approval of a stock-option plan is effective for only 12 months. (7) The option is nontransferable, except at death. (8) The person to whom the option is given must be an employee of the granting corporation, its parent, or subsidiary continuously from the time of the grant to three months prior to its exercise. (9) The options must be granted under a plan that may not have a total time duration of more than ten years.

## Summary

A convertible bond is one that permits the holders, at their option, to exchange such an issue for another of the same company under certain specified conditions. In most instances the securities that may be converted are bonds having a fixed or limited income. Such securities are convertible into common stock, which has the right to the residual income and benefits of the corporation. The conversion clause in the trust indenture may be expressed as ratio or a price. The conversion ratio or price may vary from year to year; if so, it is usually more favorable to bondholders during the earlier years. The conversion period may, and usually does, run throughout the life of the issue.

A convertible bond's market value is based on two factors—its value as a bond and its potential value as a converted stock. Conversion can be either forced by the corporation or it can be voluntary on the part of the holder. If the bonds are callable, which is the usual case, the corporation can force conversion when the market price of the underlying stock multiplied by the conversion ratio is above the call price. Voluntary conversion may take place if the dividend yield on the underlying common stock is greater than the interest yield on the bond (using the present conversion ratio or price).

---

[2] This applies to corporations with equity capital in excess of $2 million. Should the equity capital be less than $1 million, a person may own not more than 10 percent of the stock. For corporations with equity between these amounts, proportional changes in limits are permitted.

A warrant is an option to purchase a specific number of shares of a company within a given time at a given price. The warrant is generally attached to a bond at the time of sale. A warrant may be either detachable or nondetachable. In the case of a nondetachable warrant, only the holder of the bond to which it is attached can use the privilege. In most cases the warrant is detachable. Most of the detachable warrants are exercisable for a given number of years, although there are a few perpetual warrants outstanding at present. Warrants are frequently used as "sweeteners" because they may make it possible for companies to sell debt that otherwise could not be sold at reasonable prices. For many companies, the use of warrants will permit lower interest costs for the senior securities distributed. The warrant options provide for the future sale of common stock at a price above the present market price. The options, therefore, permit a sale of stock in the future at more favorable prices than are available at the time of issuance. As a result, fewer shares will have to be issued to raise a given amount of funds. The exercise of the warrant will add to the equity of the firm but it will leave the debt still outstanding. This is different from a convertible, which will extinguish the debt and change it into equity capital. A convertible will provide no new funds to the company.

Many corporations provide for sales of their stock to employees and officers under special stock-purchase plans, and a relatively few companies offer stock to their customers. While all such plans have the effect of raising funds, they are typically used in an effort to build better employer-employee relations. To make an ideal security for an employee stock-purchase plan, a stock should be marketable, and have a stable dividend rate. Many corporations have stock-option plans for officers, which are used as an inducement to obtain and keep key personnel. When such plans result in increased efficiency and better management, they are justified.

## QUESTIONS

1. Identify:
    a. Convertible securities.
    b. Warrant.
    c. Stock option.
2. "Debts may be eliminated by conversion into stock," but the option lies with the bondholders. Does the time when bondholders tend to use the conversion privilege coincide with the time when doing so would be most beneficial to the corporation? Explain.
3. Explain what is implied by the statement that a purchaser of a convertible bond pays more for the bond than it is really worth.
4. Explain the different effects on the balance sheet of the conversion of a bond into stock and the exercise of a warrant.

5. Why do warrants frequently sell at market prices that are above their theoretical value?
6. Why do convertible bonds frequently sell at prices higher than their theoretical values both as converted stock and straight debt?
7. What is the purpose of an antidilution clause?
8. Why will the warrant have a market value even though the market price of the stock is substantially below the exercise price of the warrant?
9. Why will a speculator prefer trading in warrants rather than purchasing the stock directly?
10. Indicate how a company's dividend policy might affect the following:
    a. The prospects of conversion taking place.
    b. The prospects of warrants being exercised.
11. Why might corporate executives prefer a stock option over a large cash bonus?
12. Why do stockholders have to approve employee and corporate executive stock options?

## PROBLEMS

1. The Great Southern Corporation decides to finance a $5-million expansion with a convertible bond issue, which it is able to sell at par. The bonds will be convertible at $40 a share, or 25 shares per bond. The market value of the corporation's stock at present is $36. The firm's balance sheet shows (in millions of dollars):

   | Assets | | Liabilities | |
   |---|---|---|---|
   | Assets | $50 | Liabilities | $15 |
   | | | Capital stock, 1 million shares | 10 |
   | | | Paid-in surplus | 5 |
   | | | Retained earnings | 20 |
   | Total | $50 | Total | $50 |

   a. If conversion is forced when the stock price has risen to $50, what is the effect on the book value of the common?
   b. By what means can the Great Southern Corporation, or any corporation, force conversion?

2. The General Corporation has an issue of $2 million in 6-percent subordinated convertible debentures outstanding. These bonds are $1,000 par value and can be converted at any time into 30 shares of $25-par value common stock. They are callable at $110 at any time.
    a. Will conversion take place if the price of the stock goes to $28 a share? $40 a share?
    b. Can the call provision in the bonds bring about their conversion in each instance in part a?
    c. At approximately what price must the debentures have been selling for in each instance in part a?
    d. If the dividend per share of common stock is increased from $1.50 to $1.75, causing the market price to increase from $28 to $34, will all the subordinated convertible debentures be converted?

e. In relation to the market price of common stock, where would you expect the conversion price of a *typical* convertible security to be placed at the time of issuance?

3. Company A has an issue of $2 million in 5-percent subordinated convertible debentures outstanding. These bonds are $1,000 par value and can be converted at any time into 20 shares of $5 par value common stock. They are callable at $105 at any time.
   a. Will conversion take place if the price of the stock goes to $25 a share? $55 a share?
   b. Can the call provision in the bonds effect their conversion in each instance in part *a*?
   c. Approximately what price must the debentures have been selling for in each instance in part *a*?
   d. Could conversion take place in some instances because of a decrease in market yields on the bonds rather than an increase in the price of the common stock?
   e. Is the conversion price of stock always higher than its market price at the time convertible securities are issued?
   f. Why do companies issue convertible bonds?

4. One of the owners of ABC Corporation's warrants is debating whether it is now advantageous for him to exercise his warrant. The warrant allows him to purchase 3.2 shares of common stock at $30 per share.
   a. Should he exercise his warrant if the market price of the common stock is $35?
   b. What is the market value of his warrant when the stock price is $35?
   c. Would you pay $18.50 for the warrant in part "b"?

5. The common stock of ECC sells at a P/E ratio of 20. The firm earns $2.50 per share after taxes and has a dividend-payout ratio of 40 percent. ECC plans to issue $5 million of 4-percent, ten-year convertible debentures with a call price of $108 and an initial conversion premium of 25 percent. ECC's capitalization presently is 1 million shares. Determine:
   a. The conversion price in dollars.
   b. The conversion ratio per $1,000-par value bond.
   c. The initial conversion value of each bond.
   d. How many new shares of equity must be issued if all the debentures are converted?

6. The Great American Corp. sold a bond issue which included detachable warrants to purchase stock of the company. If each warrant entitles the holder to buy two shares of common stock at $11 a share and the current market price is $15 a share, calculate the theoretical value of the warrant. Calculate the value if the stock market price of the stock is $10.

7. Jackie Jones is debating whether to invest $500 in warrants or in common stock of WYZ Corporation. The current market price of its stock is $22. Jones could purchase warrants which entitle the holder to purchase one share of stock per warrant at an option price of $20. These warrants have a market price of $2. Evaluate the following investments: (1) 23 shares of stock for $506; or (2) 250 warrants for $500 (ignore transaction costs). Assume that one year afterward:

*a.* The market price of the stock has risen to $28 a share.
*b.* The market price of the stock has fallen to $18 a share.
*c.* Why are the results between the stock and the warrants purchases so dissimilar?

## ADDITIONAL READINGS

Ayers, H. F. "Risk Aversion in the Warrants Market," *Industrial Management Review*, vol. 5 (Fall 1963), pp. 45–53.

Bacon, P. W., and E. L. Winn, Jr. "The Impact of Forced Conversion on Stock Prices," *Journal of Finance*, vol. 24 (December 1969), pp. 871–74.

Baker, J. C. "Stock Options at the Crossroads," *Harvard Business Review*, vol. 41 (January–February 1963), pp. 22–31.

Brigham, E. F. "An Analysis of Convertible Debentures," *Journal of Finance*, vol. 21 (March 1966), pp. 25–54.

Broman, K. L. "The Use of Convertible Subordinated Debentures by Industrial Firms, 1949–1959," *Quarterly Review of Economics and Business*, vol. 3 (Spring 1963), pp. 65–76.

Campbell, E. D. "Stock Options Should Be Valued," *Harvard Business Review*, vol. 39 (July–August 1961), pp. 52–58.

Hayes, S. L., and H. B. Reiling. "Sophisticated Financing Tool: The Warrant," *Harvard Business Review*, vol. 47 (January–February 1969), pp. 137–50.

Lewellen, W. G. "Executives Lose Out, Even with Options," *Harvard Business Review*, vol. 46 (January–February 1968), pp. 127–42.

Nelson, J. R. "Price Effects in Rights Offerings," *Journal of Finance*, vol. 20 (December 1965), pp. 747–50.

Parkinson, M. "Empirical Warrant-Stock Relationships," *Journal of Business*, vol. 45 (October 1972), pp. 536–69.

Pease, F. "The Warrant—Its Power and Its Hazards," *Financial Analysts Journal*, vol. 19 (January–February 1963), pp. 25–32.

Samuelson, P. A. "A Rational Theory of Warrant Pricing," *Industrial Management Review*, vol. 6 (Spring 1965), pp. 13–31.

Shelton, J. P. "The Relation of the Price of a Warrant to the Price of Its Associated Stock," *Financial Analysts Journal*, vol. 23 (May–June and July–August 1967), pp. 143–51 and 88–99.

Thorp, E. O,. and S. T. Kassouf. *Beat the Market*. New York: Random House, 1967.

Vinson, C. E. "Rates of Return on Convertibles," *Financial Analysts Journal*, vol. 26 (March–April 1970), pp. 81–85.

Walter, J. E., and A. V. Que. "The Valuation of Convertible Bonds," *Journal of Finance*, vol. 28 (June 1973), pp. 713–32.

Weil, R. L., Jr., J. E. Segall, and D. Green, Jr. "Premiums on Convertible Bonds, *Journal of Finance*, vol. 23 (June 1968), pp. 445–63.

# 20

# Retained Earnings and Dividend Policy

As successful firms grow and mature, they have more financing alternatives open to them. When a firm is young, it is generally unable to sell marketable securities, stocks and bonds, in large amounts through the national markets. Although there are exceptions, the majority of firms are started with equity capital supplied by an individual, or a small group of entrepreneurs. Early growth is usually dependent upon the availability of trade credit and bank, or finance company, loans. Only after some record of success has been established can firms market their securities to the investing public.

Whenever lenders or investors are evaluating a corporation, one of the concerns will be adequacy of the equity base. The corporation can build up that base in a couple of ways. The firm can retain earnings, or it can sell additional stock. In their early years most firms rely heavily on retained earnings because the market for their common stock is limited. However, the heavy dependence on retained earnings is not limited to new companies. It will be shown that U.S. corporations generally finance a large proportion of their needs with internally generated funds, of which retained earnings is a sizable component.

In mature firms, financial managers must consider whether the company's earnings should be retained or whether they might be more advantageously used in paying dividends. If stock prices are favorably influenced by a particular type of dividend policy, it is possible that paying the dividend, and selling new stock at resulting higher prices, could provide cheaper equity financing for the firm.

Whether dividend policy does, or should, affect stock prices has been a matter of controversy in the finance literature. The nature of the debate is similar to that presented in the study of capital structure. There was a traditional view regarding dividend policy, and it was challenged—again by Miller and Modigliani. The academic literature is considered briefly. An introductory review of this literature is provided in an appendix.

Although the impact of dividend policy is still unsettled, business practices seem to show a pattern. The nature of that pattern is described. Not only does there seem to be some consensus in business policy, but also the bases for such policy have been identified. These are discussed.

Finally, the mechanics of cash dividend payment will be outlined. The mechanics and rationale for stock dividends and stock splits are also considered.

## Importance of Internally Generated Funds

Internally generated funds are represented by retained earnings, depletion, and depreciation charges. They represent funds available to the firm that have been generated by the operations of the firm. To a large degree, the total amount of internally generated funds is dependent on the profitability of the firm. A change in dividend policy or the method of charging off depreciation can also affect the funds generated internally by the firm.

Retained earnings and depreciation funds are available to the firm for reinvestment purposes—they can be used as the firm sees fit, either in the working-capital sector or as a means to finance long-term capital expenditures. Of course, the more success the firm has in profitably employing these funds, the greater the beneficial impact it will have on the future profits and, therefore, the future level of internally generated funds. Over the years, retained earnings and depreciation funds have been the single most important source of corporate funds. Table 20–1 illustrates the relationship between internally generated funds and funds raised through the issuance of corporate stocks and bonds.

For the ten-year period shown in Table 20–1, internal sources accounted for about three quarters of the total funds raised. However, while depreciation accounted for about half of the total sources of funds, it does not constitute a net addition to the firm's total resources. The firm is faced with the problem of replacing existing fixed assets; depreciation, therefore, will really only permit the firm to maintain its existing size, although it may change the composition of its asset structure through the reallocation of funds derived from this source. Retained earnings, on the other hand, represent a net addition to the flow of funds to the firm. In this light, it should be clear that retained earnings are a most important source of funds for financing the future growth of the firm.

Corporate management usually has greater freedom in spending funds generated internally than funds from outside sources, such as banks and insurance companies, because the latter are usually borrowed for specific

## TABLE 20-1
Contributions of Internally Generated Funds to Total Sources of Corporate Capital Funds, 1967–1976 (in billions of dollars)

| Year | Retained Earnings | Capital Consumption Allowances* | Total Internal Sources | Stocks and Bonds† | Total Funds | Capital‡ |
|---|---|---|---|---|---|---|
| 1967 | $ 25.3 | $ 43.0 | $ 68.3 | $ 24.8 | $ 93.1 | (73.3%) |
| 1968 | 24.2 | 46.8 | 71.0 | 22.0 | 93.0 | (76.3) |
| 1969 | 20.5 | 51.9 | 72.4 | 26.7 | 99.1 | (73.0) |
| 1970 | 14.6 | 56.0 | 70.6 | 38.9 | 109.5 | (64.4) |
| 1971 | 22.5 | 60.4 | 82.9 | 45.1 | 128.0 | (64.7) |
| 1972 | 29.3 | 65.9 | 95.2 | 42.0 | 137.2 | (69.3) |
| 1973 | 42.7 | 71.3 | 114.0 | 33.4 | 147.4 | (77.3) |
| 1974 | 43.5 | 81.6 | 125.1 | 38.3 | 163.4 | (76.6) |
| 1975 | 40.9 | 89.5 | 130.4 | 53.6 | 184.0 | (70.9) |
| 1976 | 56.4 | 97.2 | 153.6 | 53.4 | 207.0 | (74.2) |
| Total | $319.9 | $663.6 | $983.5 | $378.2 | $1361.7 | (72.2%) |

\* Includes depreciation, capital outlays charged to current accounts, and accidental damages.
† Includes gross proceeds of bonds, preferred stock, and common stock newly issued by the corporate sector.
‡ Figures in parentheses represent retained earnings and capital-consumption allowances as a percentage of "Total Capital Funds."
Sources: *Federal Reserve Bulletin*, April 1974, p. A42 and p. A44, and December 1977, p. A36 and p. A38.

purposes and the terms under which they are obtained may contain provisions that limit their use and restrictions that affect the activities of the borrowing corporation. Thus, when financing with internally generated funds, the advantages to the stockholders of close scrutiny by creditors are lost. This absence of scrutiny for retained earnings has bothered some financial analysts because of the inherent possibility that the funds will not be employed advantageously by the firm. It is argued that dividend policies should direct funds from the less profitable firms to the more profitable ones. Perhaps this concern is a bit overstated because business firms that depend on the money and capital markets for part of their marginal needs for funds do not lose the advantage of outside review of financial policy.

By expanding operations, a firm may be able to increase its profits in several ways. For example, it may be able to decrease average unit cost by increasing output; it may be able to install new, efficient factors of production; or it may be able to gain more control over its markets. Overall, the objective of corporate growth is to enable the firm to maintain or improve its competitive position. The growth or expansion of a firm may be financed in several ways: retention of earnings, new outside financing, and the accumulation of assets by means of depreciation allowances. As shown in Table 20-1, the contributions of retained earnings to the growth of U.S. corporations cannot be underestimated. Clearly, the benefits of retained earnings are reflected in their effects on long-term corporate growth and profitability. Thus, by simply reinvesting funds as generated from the operations of the firm, the corporation is able to make a significant contribution to its permanency and perhaps, more important, its growth. A most important aspect of corporate growth is that the resources available to a firm be allocated in a manner that will provide the firm with maximum long-term benefits, for the decision to commit funds currently to certain sectors of the firm will be realized in the future in the form of profits and cash flow.

## Dividend Policy

Because of the great importance of retained earnings, dividend policy, which determines the division of corporate earnings between outflows and retention, should be considered one of the central decision areas for financial management. In fact, the question of retained earnings and dividend policy are really two parts of the same problem. Hence, in practice, they should be considered together, not only by evaluating the benefits of retained earnings and dividends but also by noting the interrelationship of the two areas. Attention has been devoted above primarily to retained earnings; it will now shift to dividend policy. However, the reader is cautioned to bear in mind the intimate relationship that does exist between these two areas.

A dividend is a periodic payment made to stockholders to compensate them for the use of and risk to their investment funds and most commonly is declared out of current earnings. The firm's board of directors determines the type, size, and time of dividend payments. The firm may declare one dividend each year, or several interim (usually quarterly) and a final (year-end) dividend instead. The two most common types of dividends are (1) those that reduce the assets of a corporation, such as cash dividends; and (2) those that neither decrease assets nor increase liabilities, such as stock dividends. Of the two types, those payable in cash are the most common and most important, and, when the term is used without qualification, reference is made to a cash dividend.

### Dividend Policy in Academic Literature

The literature of dividend policy can be thought of as having gone through three phases: pre-MM (Miller and Modigliani), MM, and post-MM. In the pre-MM era it was tacitly agreed that dividend policy was a factor in determining common stock prices. The literature at that time was somewhat contradictory. It was suggested by security analysts that shareholders preferred stocks with liberal dividends and would pay a premium for such stocks. However, theoretical prescriptions for dividend policy treated dividends as a "leftover," by-product of investment policy. Corporate management should retain earnings if the funds could be put to good use. Any unused remainder could be distributed to the shareholders. This prescription has since been labeled the "residual theory of dividend policy." It was suggested that such a policy would maximize shareholder wealth.

Miller and Modigliani did the same thing for the dividend policy issue that they had done for capital structure. They developed a perfect markets model and demonstrated that in such an environment dividend policy was of no consequence to share valuation. For firms' dividend policies to affect their stock prices, some market imperfection must exist.

After MM's first paper (the one on leverage discussed in Chapter 12), traditionalists raised a number of objections to the way in which the authors ignored the dividend policy problem. In a 1961 paper they "proved" dividends did not matter, and the debate concerning dividends began in earnest. Both sides offered theoretical and statistical support for their contentions. This discussion continues in current literature. It seems fair to suggest that the issue remains unsettled.

It is generally agreed that if the capital markets were perfectly "efficient" dividend policy would be of no consequence. But efficiency in this sense is a very stringent requirement. For markets to be truly efficient, there must be little or no cost to securities transactions, taxes should not play a part in investors' dividend preferences, and complete information about all firms' economic circumstances should be readily available at no cost to anyone who is interested.

Many academicians doubt that U.S. capital markets are that efficient. This makes the relevance of dividend policy an empirical issue. Do stock prices react favorably to certain types of dividend policies?

The statistical information does not provide a clear-cut answer to the relationship between stock prices and dividends. However, the evidence does seem to establish discernible patterns of corporate dividend policy. Whether corporations *should* adopt particular types of dividend policies is unclear, but it can be suggested that they *seem to* do just that. The next section examines the dividend policy of domestic corporations.

## Dividend Policy of U.S. Corporations

One early study of dividend policy has become a classic. It serves as the basis for most textbook descriptions of dividend policy. John Lintner took a very straightforward approach to the problem of determining how firms set such policies. He interviewed the managers of a number of major firms. The study provided a model of dividend behavior, *in aggregate*, and explained the more important factors used in determining dividend policy for individual firms.

**The Lintner Study.**[1] From the outset, Lintner emphasized that the

---

[1] This entire section is based on John Lintner, "Distribution of Incomes of Corporations Among Dividends, Retained Earnings and Taxes," *American Economic Review*, vol. 46 (May 1956), pp. 97–113.

study would deal with dividend decisions and policies, not retention rates. He was emphatic in this regard because he found that companies viewed the problems from a policy perspective. Managers did not consider how much to retain and distribute the remainder. Lintner found that the decision-making behavior of the firms observed was inconsistent with the residual theory of dividend policy.

Lintner's sample of firms was in no way random. He had been quite careful to get diversity. The firms represented a wide cross-section with regard to level of investment, durables versus nondurables producers, consumer versus producer goods industries, size, return on investment, price-earnings ratios, earnings stability, liquidity, and stock ownership concentration. By building diversity into the sample the generality of the results was enhanced.

What Lintner found can be summarized rather briefly. Corporate directors regarded their shareholders as having a right to earnings distribution. However, the managers were reluctant to increase dividends if there was any possibility that dividends might have to be cut back later. The directors set policy so as to pay out a reasonable percentage of earnings but dividends were adjusted only if it was felt the new and higher level of dividends could be sustained.

Lintner developed a symbolic description of such a policy, which is referred to as the "lagged adjustment model." Lintner's findings suggested that directors focused on the *change* in dividend, where the normal tendency would be to forgo an increase unless it was felt such an increase in dividends could be sustained. Lintner stressed that negative changes in dividends were avoided if at all possible due to anticipated negative market reactions.[2]

Lintner's model specified the determinants of the change in dividend in terms of earnings, payout ratio, and an adjustment factor as follows:

$$\triangle D_t = c(rP_t - D_{t-1}) \qquad c = ADJ. FACTOR$$

where $D_{t-1}$ is last period's dividend and $\triangle D_t$ is the change in dividend. This year's earnings per share are denoted $P_t$. The policy variables are $r$, the target payout ratio, and $c$, the adjustment factor. This year's dividend, $D_t$, would then be last year's dividend plus the change:

$$D_t = \triangle D_t + D_{t-1}$$

To appreciate how such a policy might work, consider a firm that intends to maintain a payout ratio of 60 percent ($r = .6$). Over the long run this firm expects to distribute, that is, pay out, 60 percent of corporate earn-

---

[2] Case studies of firms cutting dividends indicate that market reactions can be severe. See Carol J. Loomis, "A Case for Dropping Dividends," *Fortune* (June 15, 1968), pp. 181–85 *et. seq.*

ings to shareholders. However, to avoid overreacting and increasing dividends too soon, dividends are only increased by 50 percent of the indicated amount in any one year.

Assume that the firm paid a $2.00 dividend last year $(D_{t-1})$ and has earnings per share $(P_t)$ of $5.00 this year. The situation is summarized below. What is this year's dividend?

| | |
|---|---|
| Last year's dividend $(D_{t-1})$ | $2.00 |
| Current EPS $(P_t)$ | $5.00 |
| Target payout ratio $(r)$ | .60 |
| Adjustment factor $(c)$ | .50 |

If the firm were to pay out 60 percent of earnings, this year's dividend would be $3.00 (.6 × $5.00). This would be a change of $1.00. If the adjustment of dividends is "lagged," the dividend increase would only be half that amount. The indicated dividend under this type of policy would be $2.50.

When Lintner tested his model, he found that most firms had, or acted as if they had, a relatively stable target payout ratio. The majority also behaved as if there were reasonably definite rates of adjustment in mind.

Lintner found that payout ratios and adjustment factors for individual firms reflected those firms' growth prospects, cyclical movements in the firms' investments and funds requirements, tax considerations of the firms' shareholders, financial strength, access to financial markets, and policies with respect to use of outside financing. Market preference for dividend stability was also considered when setting policy. On rare occasions dividends were also affected by indenture requirements or the need to repay existing debt.

Lintner stressed that dividends were seldom, if ever, affected by current investment opportunities, counter to the suggestions of the residual theorists. However, the two positions can be reconciled to a degree. The theorists, dealing in the abstract, suggest that profitable investments reduce the payout in a given period. Lintner's work suggests that a growth firm (one with profitable opportunities over a number of years) would have a lower target payout ratio. Although profitable opportunities would be considered in setting a firm's policy, the opportunities for a given year would be unlikely to alter that year's dividend.[3] The two positions, although different, are compatible.

In addition to testing his model as it applied to individual firms, Lintner evaluated it as a description of the dividend policy of U.S. corporations in total. The results suggested that the model was reasonably accurate. U.S. corporations appear to distribute a relatively constant proportion of

---

[3] More recent evidence reinforces Lintner's position that dividend policy is affected by equity needs over time rather than a point in time. See Robert G. Higgins, "The Corporate Dividend-Savings Decision," *Journal of Financial and Quantitative Analysis*, vol. 7 (March 1972), pp. 1527–41.

their earnings. In some cases the proportion distributed may appear to change due to the lag effect. If corporate earnings increase markedly, the proportion drops. If earnings growth slows, or actually declines, the percentage of earnings paid out will increase until the system restabilizes.

Given the amount of time that has passed, the results of the study are remarkably current, and the description still seems accurate. Changes in the U.S. tax structure have introduced some distortion. Because of more liberalized rules with respect to depreciation accounting for tax purposes, it appears that a greater percentage of earnings is being paid out. It is possible this phenomenon reflects either (1) the firm's higher cash flow due to the reduced taxes,[4] or (2) an understatement of economic earnings due the higher depreciation changes. Either would create the appearance of a higher target payout. Although other models of dividend policy have been proposed, simulations suggest that Lintner's model describes dividend policy as well as any of the newer models and better than most of them.[5]

**Dividend Payouts.** With the Lintner study as background, data on the dividends and earnings of U.S. corporations can now be examined, and the dividend policy behavior can be characterized. Table 20–2 lists the dividend payout percentages of U.S. corporations since 1950. The payout percentages generally range from 40 to 60 percent, with a mean of 45 percent.

Lintner's model helps discern patterns in the figures. In general, the low payouts are in years where earnings have grown rapidly. On the other hand, low growth years have raised payouts.

In 1951 corporate earnings declined, and the proportion distributed increased. From 1952 until 1954 earnings were fairly stable, as were payouts. In 1955 earnings rose markedly. Dividends lagged, resulting in a low payout ratio. Next year's earnings (1956) were little changed, and the payout percentage edged back toward the previous average. When 1957–58 earnings were down, the proportional payout increased. In 1959 earnings jumped and payouts dropped. In 1960–61 earnings were down. When dividends rose slightly, the payout ratio was increased markedly. In 1962 and 1963 earnings were up modestly and payouts dropped slightly. From 1964 through 1967 earnings soared and payouts dropped. When earnings moderated in 1967–68, payouts crept back toward 50 percent. When earnings dropped in 1969–70, payouts went to historic highs as corporations resisted cutting dividends. In 1971–72, as earnings fell back

---

[4] Adjustment for the tax change can be made by using "cash flow" variables instead of profits. Such an adjustment improves the statistical fit of the model over recent years. See John A. Brittain, "The Tax Structure and Corporate Dividend Policy," *American Economic Review*, vol. 54 (May 1964), pp. 272–87; and John A. Brittain, *Corporate Dividend Policy*, chap. iv. Washington, D.C.: The Brookings Institute, 1966.

[5] Eugene F. Fama and Harvey Babiak, "Dividend Policy: An Empirical Analysis," *American Statistical Association Journal* (December 1968), pp. 1132–60.

**TABLE 20–2**
Corporate After-Tax Profits and Dividends, 1950–1977
(in billions of dollars)

| Year | Profits after Taxes | Dividends | (dividends ÷ profits) Payout % |
|---|---|---|---|
| 1950 | $ 24.9 | $ 8.8 | 35% |
| 1951 | 21.6 | 8.6 | 40 |
| 1952 | 19.6 | 8.6 | 44 |
| 1953 | 20.4 | 8.9 | 44 |
| 1954 | 20.6 | 9.3 | 45 |
| 1955 | 27.0 | 10.5 | 39 |
| 1956 | 27.2 | 11.3 | 42 |
| 1957 | 26.0 | 11.7 | 45 |
| 1958 | 22.3 | 11.6 | 52 |
| 1959 | 28.5 | 12.6 | 44 |
| 1960 | 26.7 | 13.4 | 50 |
| 1961 | 27.2 | 13.8 | 51 |
| 1962 | 31.2 | 15.2 | 49 |
| 1963 | 33.1 | 16.5 | 49 |
| 1964 | 38.4 | 17.8 | 46 |
| 1965 | 46.5 | 19.8 | 43 |
| 1966 | 49.9 | 20.8 | 42 |
| 1967 | 46.6 | 21.4 | 46 |
| 1968 | 47.8 | 23.6 | 49 |
| 1969 | 44.8 | 24.3 | 54 |
| 1970 | 39.3 | 24.7 | 63 |
| 1971 | 47.6 | 25.1 | 53 |
| 1972 | 55.4 | 26.0 | 47 |
| 1973 | 72.9 | 29.6 | 41 |
| 1974 | 74.5 | 31.0 | 42 |
| 1975 | 73.3 | 32.4 | 44 |
| 1976 | 92.2 | 35.8 | 39 |
| 1977 * | 104.3 | 40.3 | 39 |
| Total | $1,189.8 | $533.4 | 45% |

* Based on second-quarter data, annualized, and seasonally adjusted.

Sources: *Economic Report of the President*, 1973 (Washington, D.C.: U.S. Government Printing Office), p. 273; *Federal Reserve Bulletin*, February 1974, p. A48; November 1974, p. A43; December 1977, p. A38.

in line, payouts receded to the 50-percent level. Since 1973 when corporate profits jumped markedly, payout ratios have hovered around 40 percent. Corporations appear reluctant to raise dividends until they are assured that the new levels of profits can be sustained.[6]

While many business firms may follow a policy of using profits to provide for anticipated needs, the payment of cash dividends appears to

---

[6] There is an alternate explanation for recent low payouts. High profits in recent years are partly due to inflation; that is, higher prices with the same margins generate higher dollar profits. During this period, external financing has been relatively unattractive. Interest rates have been high and stock prices generally have been depressed. However, the need for capital assets persists, and at higher prices the problem is compounded. Greater internal financing may be a result of this squeeze play.

take precedence over retention of earnings with dividend stability and growth carrying a high premium. Cash dividends have been more stable than either corporate income after taxes or income retained in the businesses. Figure 20–1 illustrates this point. It can be seen that undistributed profits, *not* dividends, have carried the brunt of annual variations in profits.

That dividends to stockholders sometimes come first can be illustrated by the fact that, from 1931 to 1933, when most corporations were operating at a loss, dividends were being paid. Also there has been a steady, virtually uninterrupted rise in dividend payments since 1950.

## Bases for Dividend Policies

The primary basis for corporate dividends is earnings. Dividends are distributed based on current earnings and the relationship of those earnings to expected future earnings. Firms strive for stability in such policies. However, the firm must consider more than the current level of earnings in setting policy. Some of these additional considerations, all of which were suggested by the Lintner study, are discussed briefly.

*Legal Restrictions.* The first and basic fact management must take into account before declaring dividends is to be sure that realized earnings are available for distribution and their payment will not impair the paid-in capital of the firm. Payment of cash dividends when a corporation is insolvent or would be made insolvent by such payment is illegal. The concept of solvency will be discussed in some detail in Part VI, "Financially Distressed Business Firms." A firm can be insolvent in basically two ways: (1) liabilities exceed assets, or (2) there is insufficient cash to meet current obligations. Directors are responsible, jointly and severally, for such illegal dividend payments. Legal phraseology varies from state to state, and a corporation's board of directors must be sure that a proposed cash dividend payment is legal under the statutes of its state of incorporation. More specifically, management must be sure that, even under the most critical court review, negative answers would be given to these four questions regarding payment of a cash dividend: (1) Would it impair the corporation's capital? (2) Would it impair the claims of creditors? (3) Is the corporation insolvent? (4) Would the payment cause insolvency?

Some state laws provide for modification of the basic rule requiring that cash dividends be paid out of retained earnings or net profits only. For illustration, an exception is usually made for a consuming- or wasting-assets corporation exploiting natural resources; part of such a corporation's cash dividends may be a return of capital. A consuming-assets corporation may be permitted to pay cash dividends in an amount not exceeding its total depletion and amortization reserves; however, the cash dividend may be illegal if it is made when the corporation is insolvent or if its

**FIGURE 20–1**
Corporate Profits, Taxes, and Dividends (seasonally adjusted annual rates, quarterly)

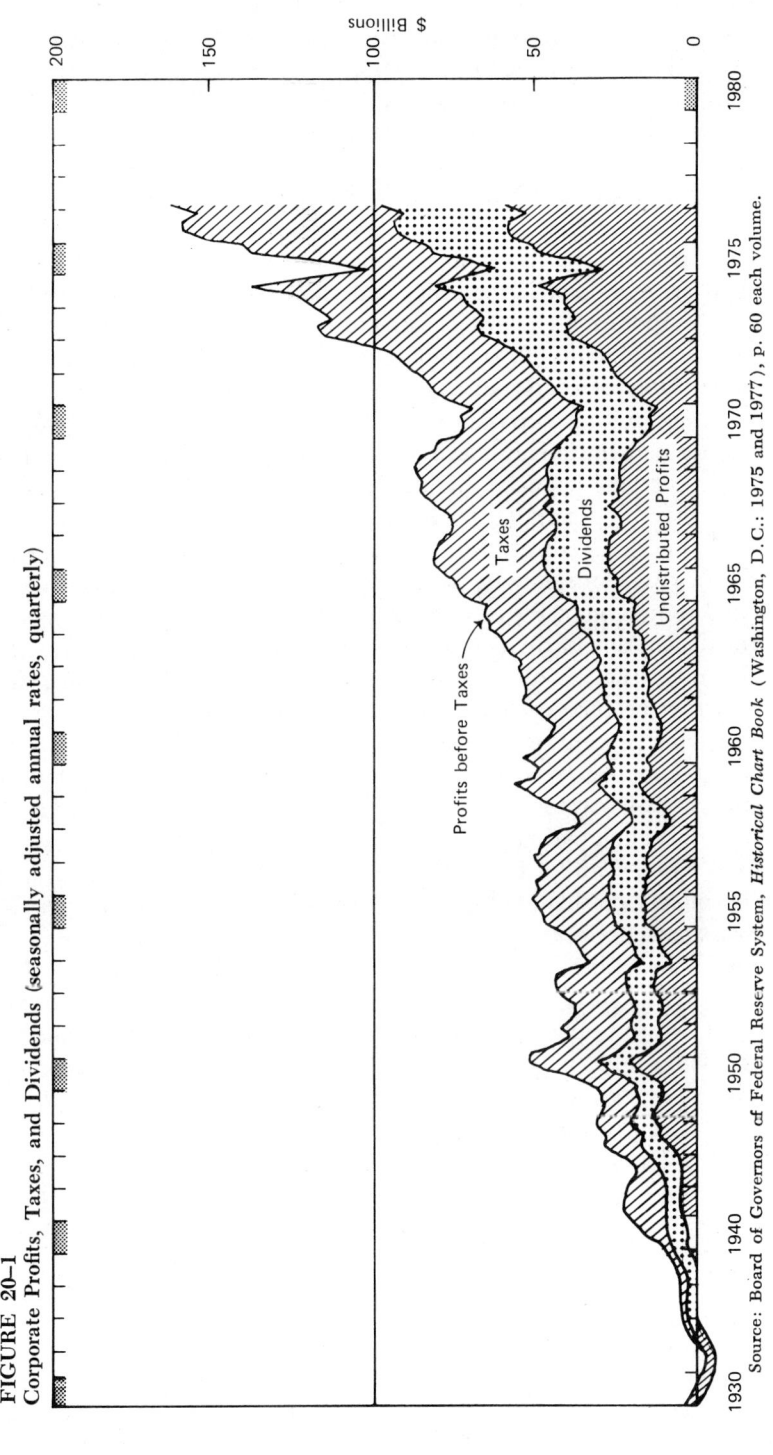

Source: Board of Governors of Federal Reserve System, *Historical Chart Book* (Washington, D.C.: 1975 and 1977), p. 60 each volume.

payment causes insolvency. However, the amount of cash available and the amount required for expansion may be more important than legal restrictions or the amounts reported as retained earnings or earned surplus.

**Contract Restrictions.** Before declaring a cash dividend, a corporation's board of directors must be careful to comply with restrictions on payment of dividends as found in debt contracts or other contracts. Most frequently, such restrictions are found in long-term debt contracts, but they may also be found in intermediate- and short-term debt contracts, such as term-loan agreements and short-term debt agreements.

A corporation's board of directors may also be denied the right to declare dividends on common stock because of contracts pertaining to prior rights of preferred stockholders over common stockholders to the earnings of the corporation. In some cases, clauses in a corporation's charter or bylaws may make it illegal to pay dividends on common stock unless certain financial standards have been met and are maintained. This may be illustrated by the requirement that net current assets must be 150 or 200 percent of the par value of the outstanding preferred stock before dividends may be paid. In other cases, compliance with a sinking-fund requirement for retirement of debt or preferred stock may prevent the declaration of dividends. The purpose of these restrictions is to ensure the maintenance of a corporation's liquidity and solvency; hence, a policy of keeping cash and increasing retained earnings is desirable. The foregoing precautions should be taken even when there are no restrictions being imposed by debt and preferred stock contracts or by statutory provisions when the business firm's earnings are subject to wide seasonal or cyclical fluctuations.

**Working-Capital Position.** Two factors are important in determining the effects of dividend payments on the working-capital position: the firm's cash position and its debt-servicing requirements (or need to repay debt). In voting a cash dividend, a board of directors creates a current liability; when these dividends are paid, there will be a loss of working-capital assets. Because other current liabilities may be coming due at the same time, need for cash and other assets must be projected. If a cash dividend would divert funds needed for operating purposes or for meeting current liabilities, it might be unwise to use working capital for dividend purposes. However, management may feel it is important to maintain a stable dividend policy and may borrow to do so. The theory is that, if retained earnings and current profits justify payment of a cash dividend, the issue should not be decided solely on the basis of a corporation's cash position. Corporations frequently borrow to discharge obligations for payrolls, goods, and income taxes. But, if a cash dividend would weaken the corporation's working-capital position unduly, it should not be paid.

**Debt Repayment.** When the capital structure of a corporation is top-heavy with debt, using all or part of net profits to build up equity is sound financial policy. Among the major corporations, some railroad companies have been most consistent in using net profits to reduce their fixed debts in recent years. The ability of a corporation to finance fixed charges depends on both the amount and stability of its income.

If outside financing is necessary, management may find it desirable to pass all cash dividends in order to improve the corporation's borrowing position with creditors; but, if a new stock is being considered, management may want to pay cash dividends at the old rate, or even at an increased rate.

*Nature of Net Earnings.* Corporations having stable incomes are in a better position to adopt settled dividend policies than those whose earnings fluctuate widely. For illustration, public-utility companies may have a more stable dividend policy than mining companies or those companies manufacturing durable producers' goods. Until a company is well established, it may have no dividend policy; after becoming established, it may distinguish between normal or regular and extra dividends.

In some states, dividends may be paid only with current earnings, and the dividend payments of corporations organized under such statutes tend to be more variable than those of corporations chartered in other states that permit earnings of prior years to be used for dividend purposes. Limiting dividend payments to current earnings (considered by some authorities to be the best index of a corporation's ability to pay dividends) would tend to have the effect of forcing stockholders to give more attention to the affairs of their corporations. Nevertheless, in most instances, a corporation's ability to pay dividends depends on its net current earnings plus earnings that have been retained from preceding years.

*Access to Capital Markets.* A factor that is important to many firms in the determination of their dividend policies is the availability of capital funds from outside sources. If a firm has access to capital markets at reasonable costs, it would follow that the firm would have less need to rely on internally generated funds as a source of capital than a company that has not established itself in the marketplace. In effect, when a firm has established alternative sources of funds, it has greater discretion in determining its dividend policy and is more able to establish a stable dividend payout. Thus, a well-established firm is more likely to have a stable rate than a new or small firm, not only because it may have fewer expansionary needs but also because it has greater access to capital markets.

*Tax Aspects.* Cash and property dividends received by stockholders are taxable as cash or at the fair-market value of the property distributed. The high tax rate on personal income has been a factor in the reluctance of some boards of directors to declare cash dividends. Federal tax rates on individual personal income contain graduated rates by brackets ranging from zero to 70 percent of taxable income. If earnings are retained, the net worth and productive capacity of a company tend to increase, and the market price of its stock may appreciate; then, if the taxpayer sells the stock, the gain will likely be subject to the capital-gains tax. When the capital stock of a corporation is owned by a few stockholders who are also directors or officers, it is reasonable to assume that the corporation's dividend policy will reflect the desires of the stockholders. Such firms may pay out most or all of the earnings or they could retain them. However, as pointed out in a preceding chapter, there are limitations on the tax-free retention of earnings.

**The Human Element.** Although dividend payments may be discussed in legal, financial, or economic terms, in practice it is not possible to keep the human element out of decisions made by directors. Corporations are regarded as continuing business enterprises, but stockholders may withdraw by selling their interest to others if they are dissatisfied with current or anticipated dividend policies. A board of directors must protect the interests of both creditors and stockholders; therefore, protection of capital assets must come ahead of dividend payments. However, if stockholders are to be induced to provide venture capital, in the long run the return on stock must be equal to a normal interest payment plus enough to compensate for the risks assumed.

The decision as to when and under what circumstances stockholders are to share in the earnings of their corporation is left to the board of directors; once a cash dividend has been declared, it becomes a liability of the corporation. A board of directors may be under pressure from common stockholders to declare dividends when retained earnings are large and current profits are satisfactory; and preferred stockholders may feel their dividends should be paid if current earnings are adequate, even if the financial position of the corporation is weak.

Stockholders have met with little success in attempting to force directors to vote dividends through court proceedings; nevertheless, stockholders have the power to force a change in management if they act collectively. One of the best known of these cases (an exception to the general rule) was the action brought by stockholders of the Ford Motor Company in a Michigan state court in 1916 which resulted in the board of directors being ordered to declare a dividend aggregating $19 million. While dividends entail a distribution to stockholders of something belonging to the corporation, it should not be forgotten that the corporation is owned by the stockholders.

## Payment of Cash Dividends

A cash-dividend declaration is effected by a resolution by a majority of the directors at a regular or special meeting. Usually, the minutes of meetings at which dividends are declared are covered in more detail than those of other meetings of the board of directors. The minutes contain a record of the information received from the chief financial officer on the net profits of the company and the amount of retained earnings. When the board of directors declares a dividend, the directors want the record to show they acted on the assumption that the payment is legal, and they want a resolution drawn to show that the dividend payment is justified. The declaration gives the name of the stock on which the dividend is to be paid, the amount per share, the date and time when the names of stockholders are to be determined for dividend purposes (such as at the close of business on December 15, 1978), and the date on which the dividend checks are to be dated and mailed to stockholders. The New York Stock Exchange requires management of companies whose stocks are listed to declare dividends at least ten days before the record date.

A corporation not only must have the legal right to declare a cash dividend but it also must have cash available to use in payment. The bylaws of a corporation may prescribe the dates for cash dividend payments—quarterly, semiannually, or annually—or merely state that "the directors may from time to time declare dividends upon the capital stock from net profits or retained earnings of the company." Only when all stockholders agree and the board of directors does not object may a valid dividend be declared without the prior approval of the directors. Although such so-called consent dividends are rare, they are sometimes made by "closed" corporations (those owned by a few stockholders). The advantage to the board of directors in permitting stockholders to declare a consent dividend is that responsibility for any adverse development caused by the payment thereof would be shifted from the board of directors to the stockholders.

**Designation of Cash Dividends.** Cash dividends may be called regular, irregular, extra or special, interim, final, or liquidating (or they may have no label attached).

Regular dividends may be made quarterly, semiannually, or annually (in rare cases, even monthly)[7] If a board of directors designates a dividend as the "regular quarterly dividend of $1 per share of common stock," it indicates that the policy of management is to maintain that rate. "Regular" dividends are most frequently related to preferred stock; however, when a corporation has a long record of paying a specified dividend on common stock at regular intervals, it is known as a regular dividend. One of the best illustrations of this is the $2.25 quarterly dividend that had been paid on the common stock of the American Telephone

---

[7] Monthly dividends are popular with stockholders who have reached retirement age. From the viewpoint of management, the greatest drawback to paying monthly dividends is the cost of sending checks. Among the corporations that distribute monthly dividends is the William Wrigley, Jr., Company. Usually, corporations enclose "stuffers" (advertising leaflets) with each check mailed, and the extra mailing costs may be more than offset by the advertising value.

and Telegraph Company from 1922 to 1959, when the stock was split three-for-one and a quarterly rate per share was fixed at 82.5 cents. In 1964 the stock was again split, this time two-for-one, and the quarterly rate (1978) was $1.15. Companies that have paid at least one dividend each year for many years include National City Bank of New York (now Citicorp), since 1813; Hartford Fire Insurance Company since 1873, American Telephone and Telegraph Company, since 1881; General Electric Company, since 1899; and a score or more other major companies, for over 50 years.

Irregular dividends are those paid in varying amounts, usually associated with companies whose earnings fluctuate widely (big earnings, big dividends and low earnings, low or no dividends). Irregular dividend policies are usually unpopular with shareholders, but those who hold stock in companies with such policies should expect fluctuations in cash-dividend payments. It may even be that the average return on stock of these companies will be larger over a period of time than dividends paid by companies having a regular dividend policy.

A corporation may share its profits with shareholders in a variety of ways, one of which is to declare an extra dividend rather than increasing the regular dividend rate. This practice does not commit the board of directors to a future increase in the dividend rate and places stockholders on notice that they are not justified in assuming that the extra dividend will be declared on the next dividend date. When an extra dividend is paid, it is usually distributed along with the regular dividend as a year-end dividend. If the extra amount were to be prorated and distributed along with each regular dividend, it might be considered as an increase in the regular dividend rate. A special dividend, whether in the form of cash or property, may be in the same category as an extra dividend, but, usually, the connotation is that some event not likely to recur has made it possible. The largest increase in distribution of cash dividends usually takes place during the last quarter of a corporation's fiscal year, when the board of directors has a clearer view of the profitability of operations likely for the entire year.

Some U.S. corporations have adopted the English terminology, calling dividends paid through the year "interim" dividends. Interim dividends may be paid as often as seems appropriate throughout the fiscal year. A final or year-end dividend is one paid at the end of the fiscal year. This terminology is used along with the concept of interim dividends.

When a cash dividend represents a return of capital, it may be termed a liquidating dividend. Liquidating cash dividends may be paid when a consuming- or wasting-assets corporation pays a cash dividend (part of the amount may represent profits and part a return of capital); a corporation is overcapitalized and returns part of the capital to owners; or a business firm is being liquidated either voluntarily or involuntarily under supervision of a federal court or otherwise.

## Stock Dividends and Stock Splits

***Stock Dividends.*** Some companies have a policy of distributing stock dividends so as to conserve cash; others distribute regular stock dividends along with cash dividends. A stock dividend is one distributed in stock of the same kind as that on which the dividend is declared. Although a corporation could distribute a different class of stock as a stock dividend, this is rarely done. The distribution of a stock dividend results in an increase in the corporation's capital account and a decrease in its retained earnings, but has no effect on its total net worth. When stockholders are given a choice of being paid a cash dividend or receiving a stock dividend and cash is chosen, the corporation sells the stock and remits cash.

***Effect on Owners' Equity.*** When stockholders receive a stock dividend, there is no change in their proportional equity. The number of shares have been increased, but the book value of the corporation's assets represented by owners' holdings has remained unchanged. If a stockholder owns 100 shares, representing 1 percent of the corporation's capital, and receives a stock dividend of 10 percent, he or she still owns 1 percent of the capital stock. While the shareholder will have more shares, each share will represent proportionately less equity; but the total proportional interest will be unchanged. This generalization is subject to minor qualification because of the provision for fractional shares. For illustration, if a stock dividend is declared on the basis of 1 new share for every 20 held, a fractional share may be issued for shares not multiples of 20. Usually, fractional shares have no voting or dividend rights, and they sometimes lose their value unless they are surrendered for full shares within a specified period of time. Therefore, in order to avoid a loss, owners of fractional shares must either sell them or buy other fractional shares to make up whole shares. Failure of a stockholder to use the fractional share would mean he or she would lose part of the equity and that other stockholders' equity would be increased by that amount. To prevent this injustice, particularly to small shareholders, corporate practice is to issue only whole shares and to pay a cash dividend in lieu of fractional shares.

***Periodic Stock Dividends.*** Since World War II, stock dividends have been distributed to supplement or replace cash dividends in order to conserve cash and at the same time appease stockholders calling for more dividends. Although stock dividends give stockholders nothing they did not already have, the extra shares may be sold; therefore, stockholders may consider the receipt of a stock dividend preferable to receiving no dividend.

The chief justification for a regular stock dividend is that it condones financing with retained earnings. Stock dividends are less expensive than omitting dividends. Frequently, business firms continue to pay the same cash-dividend rate on stock after a stock-dividend distribution, and so the cash outlay is larger because the number of shares has increased. If the intent of management is to increase the return to shareholders, this could be done by increasing the cash-dividend rate. (Stockholders must pay brokerage fees when they sell stock, and it may be an expensive way to obtain cash if their holdings are small.)

Proceeds from the sale of stock dividends are taxed at the rate for capital gains, which is below that on ordinary income for long-term gains, and this is important for those in the higher income brackets. Of course, if dividends were omitted entirely, stockholders would have the same tax advantage if they sold some of their shares for income. If stockholders retain their shares and the payment of regular cash dividends is resumed, their dividend receipts will increase. In addition, retention of earnings that might have been distributed as cash dividends should have a favorable effect on the market price of the stock in the future, permitting larger cash dividends than would otherwise have been possible.

**Stock Splits.** A stock split is not a dividend. In a split the par value of the stock is changed. Again, the stockholders have no change in their proportional equity, but in this case there is no shifting of funds from the retained earnings account into common stock as is done with stock dividends. Stock splits and stock dividends are considered together because the major exchanges view them to be analogous.[8]

The traditional wisdom justifying stock splits was to "broaden" the market for the stock. Because of the economies of buying in round lots (multiples of 100 shares), it was felt there would be greater demand for low-priced stocks than for those that are high-priced. This seems unlikely.

**Market Effects.** The academic literature with regard to stock dividends and stock splits is in general consensus. They are a waste of time. Stockholders receive nothing of value; their proportionate ownership is unchanged. Unless something else about the firm changes, the total value of the stockholders' shares will be unchanged. The stock price should adjust to make the value of the holdings of all investors the same as the values were before the split or dividend. For example, if a stockholder owned 100 shares selling at $100 and the stock split two for one, the investor would end up owning 200 shares of $50 stock. A 25-percent stock dividend would create 125 shares of $80 stock. There would be no net benefit in either case. Giving the stockholder extra pieces of paper cannot create real value.

Empirical studies support this position. Barker found that unless the total cash dividends on the after-split shares exceeded the total dividend before the split the price increases generated by the split generally dissi-

---

[8] The New York Stock Exchange defines a stock split as a distribution of stock that involves 25 percent or more of the number of shares of stock; anything less is called a stock dividend.

pated.[9] The study by Fama, Fisher, Jensen, and Roll,[10] is the best-known work on this topic. Their study suggests that stock splits per se would have no price effect. They reported that in most split stocks, unusual return activity could be detected far in advance of the split announcements. They theorized that an observed effect of a split could be from reduction in uncertainty. A split serves to formalize information already in the market, making the stock less risky, and therefore worth more. Their results on cash dividends paralleled Barker's. Where an increase in dividends was not forthcoming, the returns deteriorated, leading them to conclude that the split only contained information relative to management's expectations. Such information could be transmitted by either a dividend change or a split.

This suggests that stock dividends and splits are nothing more than advertising. They are a way of calling the market's attention to the stock. Like cash dividend increases, stock dividends and splits reflect optimism on the part of management. If that optimism is not backed by performance, any short-run price effect will quickly fade.

## Summary

Retained earnings—net profits not distributed as dividends—may be used for any business purpose. When taken in conjunction with capital-consumption allowances, they represent internally generated funds; that is, funds generated by the firm itself through the actual conduct of the business. The importance of internally generated funds is reflected in the fact that these funds account for about two-thirds of the total capital employed by corporations. Retained earnings are an important source of funds in meeting the requirements of corporate growth; they make a significant contribution to the firm's future profitability as well as its ability to maintain or improve its competitive position. While the retention of earnings is influenced by the firm's present and future financial requirements, dividend policy is also an important determinant. Retained earnings and dividend policy are really two parts of the same problem.

A firm must establish guidelines as to its distribution of corporate earnings. The periodic dividend decisions are made within the framework set by dividend policy. The purpose of such a policy should be to work for the best interests of the shareholders—to maximize their wealth. Some academicians have questioned whether a company can increase the shareholders' wealth through dividend policy. They argue that an increase in dividends results in a corresponding and exactly offsetting

---

[9] C. Austin Barker, "Effective Stock Splits," *Harvard Business Review* (January–February 1956), pp. 101–06.
[10] Eugene F. Fama, Lawrence Fisher, Michael C. Jensen, and Richard Roll, "The Adjustment of Stock Prices to New Information," *International Economic Review*, vol. 10 (February 1969), pp. 1–21.

decline in value of the shareholders' stock. This argument is less than universally accepted and has served as the center of a heated debate.

Regardless of whether or not they should worry about dividend policy, it appears corporate management is vitally concerned over the dividend decision. Their description of how policy is set provides a model which describes not only the behavior of individual firms but of the corporate sector's dividend policy in aggregate.

Decisions as to dividend payments may be influenced by a number of factors. Some of the more important considerations were identified as follows: working-capital position, the attitude of stockholders and directors, income tax rates on individual incomes, legal aspects of provisions as to retained earnings, and—the basic consideration in all such decisions —the net profits and the amount of retained earnings available.

Cash dividends may be regular, with the rate and the dividend date uniform over a period of time; extra or special, and paid with a regular dividend (usually at the end of a corporation's fiscal year); or liquidating, representing a return of capital. Presumably, management will consider the immediate and future needs of the corporation as well as the desires and objectives of its stockholders. In addition, consideration also may be given to the effect on plans for external financing, stockholder relations, and the market value of the company's stock.

## QUESTIONS

1. How important are funds accounted for as retained earnings in explaining the growth of U.S. business enterprises?
2. Retention of earnings, it has been said, represents an involuntary form of investment by stockholders. In what way do stockholders benefit from retained earnings?
3. "Earnings should be retained to the point where they contribute more to stockholders' wealth than the payment of dividends." Explain.
4. Explain why MM feel that dividend policy cannot be used to improve the wealth of the individual shareholder.
5. Briefly characterize the three phases of the academic literature related to dividend policy.
6. What does Figure 20–1 suggest as to the order in which net earnings after income taxes are applied?
7. *a.* In view of the fact that a declaration of cash dividends creates a current liability, why must a board of directors give consideration to the corporation's working-capital position?
   *b.* What factors are favorable to the adoption of a regular dividend policy?
   *c.* How does the firm's access to capital markets affect its dividend policy?
8. Discuss some of the legal implications faced by the board of directors in determining dividend policies.

## 20 Retained Earnings and Dividend Policy

9. Identify the following types of dividends: (a) cash, (b) regular, (c) interim, (d) stock, and (e) liquidating.
10. Distinguish between stock dividends and stock splits and analyze what effects, if any, they have on the market price of a company's common stock.

## PROBLEMS

1. The Waldon Corporation is determining whether to pay dividends or retain the earnings within the firm. The firm's cost of capital is 15 percent. The company has $2 million in current earnings. It has sufficient liquidity to pay any dividends it might declare. It can also, if it likes, invest in any, or all, of the following projects:
   a. $300,000—New machinery that will yield a 22 percent return;
   b. $500,000—Inventory that will improve customer service and consequently profit. The return from such an investment is estimated to be 18 percent;
   c. $400,000—Plant expansion, generating a net return of 14 percent per annum on invested capital;
   d. $800,000—Purchase of raw land for future expansion; land prices are increasing at 8 percent a year.
   If the firm were to use the residual theory of dividend policy and had 600,000 shares outstanding, what per-share dividend would it pay?

2. Consider the data on the two firms below:

   |  | Firm A | Firm B |
   | --- | --- | --- |
   | Last year's dividend | $1.00 | $2.50 |
   | Current EPS | $4.00 | $5.00 |
   | Target payout ratio | .3 | .6 |
   | Adjustment factor | .2 | .5 |

   Based on the Lintner, lagged-adjustment model calculate this year's dividend for:
   a. Firm A.
   b. Firm B.
   c. Which firm would you guess to be in the higher growth industry? Why?
   d. Which is in the more stable industry? Why?

3. Find two firms from the *Wall Street Journal* or *Standard and Poor's Corporation Stock Guide* that have the following dividend policies:
   a. Regular cash dividend.
      (1) Large cash dividends.
      (2) Small cash dividends.
   b. Regular stock dividend.
   c. No dividends.
   d. Stock splits.
   For each of these categories, discuss possible reasons for the apparent dividend policies.

4. Selected items from the balance sheet of the Ace Company are shown below (in thousands of dollars):

Part IV    Sources of Capital

| | | | |
|---|---|---|---|
| Cash | $ 3,000 | Bonds payable | $2,000 |
| Investments | 1,000 | Retained earnings | 9,000 |
| Fixed assets | 11,000 | Common stock (100,000 shares @ $50 par) | 5,000 |
| Patents | $ 2,000 | | |

The board of directors is considering four separate possibilities:
 a. A cash dividend of $5 a share.
 b. A 50-percent stock dividend.
 c. A four-for-one split.
 d. A dividend of the Ace Company's investments.
Prepare a tabulation for the board showing the effect of each possibility on the selected items from the balance sheet.

## ADDITIONAL READINGS

Brigham, E. F., and M. J. Gordon. "Leverage, Dividend Policy, and the Cost of Capital,' *Journal of Finance*, vol. 23 (March 1968), pp. 85–104.

Dobrovsky, S. P. "Economics of Corporate Internal and External Financing," *Journal of Finance*, vol. 13 (March 1958), pp. 35–47.

Elton, E. J., and M. J. Gruber. "The Cost of Retained Earnings—Implications of Share Repurchase," *Industrial Management Review*, vol. 9 (Spring 1968), pp. 87–104.

Fama, E. F. "The Empirical Relationships Between the Dividend and Investment Decisions of Firms," *American Economic Review*, vol. 64 (June 1974), pp. 304–318.

Fama, E. F., L. Fisher, M. Jensen, and R. Roll. "The Adjustment of Stock Prices to New Information," *International Economic Review*, vol. 10 (February 1969), pp. 1–21.

Friend, I., and M. Puckett. "Dividends and Stock Prices," *American Economic Review*, vol. 54 (September 1964), pp. 656–82.

Gordon, M. J. "The Savings, Investment and Valuation of a Corporation," *Review of Economics and Statistics*, vol. 44 (February 1962) pp. 37–51.

Harkavy, O. "The Relation Between Retained Earnings and Common Stock Prices for Large Listed Corporations," *Journal of Finance*, vol. 8 (September 1953), pp. 283–97.

Henderson, G. V., Jr. "Shareholder Taxes and the Required Rate of Return on Internally Generated Funds," *Financial Management*, vol. 5 (Summer 1976), pp. 25–31.

Higgins, R. C. "The Corporate Dividend-Saving Decision," *Journal of Financial and Quantitative Analysis*, vol. 7 (March 1972), pp. 1527–41.

Lintner, J. "Distribution of Incomes of Corporations among Dividends, Retained Earnings, and Taxes," *American Economic Review*, vol. 46 (May 1956), pp. 97–113.

———. "The Cost of Capital and Optimal Financing of Corporate Growth," *Journal of Finance*, vol. 18 (May 1963), pp. 292–310.

Miller, M. H., and F. Modigliani. "Dividend Policy, Growth, and the Valuation of Shares," *Journal of Business*, vol. 34 (October 1961), pp. 411–33.

———. "Some Estimates of the Cost of Capital to the Electric Utility Industry," *American Economic Review*, vol. 56 (June 1966), pp. 333–91.

Porterfield, J. T. S. "Dividends, Dilution, and Delusion," *Harvard Business Review,* vol. 37 (November–December 1959), pp. 56–61.
Van Horne, J. C., and J. G. McDonald. "Dividend Policy and Equity Financing," *Journal of Finance,* vol. 26 (May 1971), pp. 507–519.
Walter, J. E. *Dividend Policy and Enterprise Valuation.* Belmont, Calif.: Wadsworth Publishing Co., Inc., 1967.
Watts, R. "The Information Content of Dividends," *Journal of Business,* vol. 46 (April 1973), pp. 191–211.

## APPENDIX: Dividend Policy in Academic Literature

Dividend policy has been a "hot topic" in the finance literature. The chapter characterized this debate as having three phases. This appendix attempts to describe the academic work on dividends using that framework. A condensed review, such as this one, will invariably slight some important contributors. Such oversights are regrettable and unintentional.

## The Traditional View

The traditional view had evolved over time based on statistical studies followed by theoretical models. Two of the earliest empirical studies were done by Johnson, Shapiro, and O'Meara,[1] and Harkavy.[2]

The purpose of the Johnson, Shapiro, and O'Meara study was to discover any relationship that might exist between stock prices and earnings, dividends, and book values. Their method involved applying multiple regression analysis to a sample of firms selected from Moody's *Manual of Investments, Industrials.* They concluded that

> of the three factors examined (earnings, dividends, book value) book value is the least dependable, and annual dividends the most reliable, index to the price of industrial common stocks listed on the New York Stock exchange.[3]

The Johnson et al., paper was a marked improvement over earlier statistical studies. Harkavy characterized many of the early papers as "analysis where small samples of stock are chosen to illustrate a hypothesis rather than to test it."[4] In his own study Harkavy attempted to recon-

---

[1] Lyle R. Johnson, Eli Shapiro, and Joseph J. O'Meara, "Valuation of Closely Held Stock for Federal Tax Purposes: Approach to an Objective Method," *University of Pennsylvania Law Review* (November 1951), pp. 166–95.

[2] Oscar Harkavy, "The Relation Between Retained Earnings and Common Stock Prices for Large Listed Corporations," *Journal of Finance,* vol. 8 (September 1953), pp. 283–97.

[3] Lyle R. Johnson, Eli Shapiro, and Joseph J. O'Meara, "Valuation of Closely Held Stock for Federal Tax Purposes: Approach to an Objective Method," *University of Pennsylvania Law Review* (November 1951), p. 170.

[4] Oscar Harkavy, "The Relation Between Retained Earnings and Common Stock Prices for Large Listed Corporations," *Journal of Finance,* vol. 8 (September 1953), p. 286.

cile a conflict between the views of fiscal theorists, who suggested a preference existed for earnings retention due to capital gains tax treatment, and security analysts who believed that the market generally favored higher dividend stocks. His method involved the investigation of both the short-run and long-run effects of dividend policy.

Citing other studies[5] as "statistical support to the proposition that the greater the proportion of a given amount of earnings that is paid in dividends, the higher the price of the stock."[6] Harkavy investigated the tenability of such a belief. To do so, he regressed price-earnings ratios on payout ratios. His results were highly significant, in a statistical sense. However, Harkavy had reservations about the validity of the regression technique due to the form of the variables. As an added test he ran a correlation analysis of price on earnings and payout ratios. These results were much less conclusive although the correlation results were consistent with those of the regression analysis.[7]

Harkavy also investigated growth rates and payout ratios to discover what type of association might exist between earnings retention and long-term stock price appreciation. He found a significant difference in median growth between groups characterized as to payout.[8] Harkavy warned against inferring causality from the results. He pointed out there was a large overlap as to rates of appreciation between the two groups, and that only a small portion of stock price variation could be explained by earnings retention.[9]

Harkavy's conclusions summarize, to a large degree, the results of many of the earlier studies. He found:[10]

1. At any point in time stock prices tend to vary directly with payout ratios.
2. Over time, higher retention rate stocks tend to show greater appreciation. However, this appreciation is not automatic. To be beneficial, such retentions must be paired with the productive use of such funds.

Another early leader in the empirical work was David Durand. In the mid-50s he investigated the bank capital problem.[11] He wished to determine what banks could do to maintain their stock prices at, or above, book value. Only at such prices could they afford (avoid dilution) to raise equity funds and keep up with the growing need for bank capital.

Durand attempted to specify the relationship between bank share prices and other explanatory variables. Although the study encountered a number of statistical difficulties, its conclusions provided further foun-

---

[5] Ibid., n. 8.
[6] Ibid.
[7] Ibid., pp. 288–89.
[8] Ibid., p. 292.
[9] Ibid.
[10] Ibid., p. 297.
[11] David Durand, *Bank Stock Prices and the Bank Capital Problem* (New York: National Bureau of Economic Research, 1957).

dation as to the importance of dividends in stock price valuation. In concluding his second chapter, Durand wrote:

> While bank stock prices are undoubtedly influenced by many other factors both financial and institutional in nature, the analysis implies that the influence of these others is of a much smaller order of magnitude than that of book value, dividends, and earnings.[12]

All of these studies, and a number of other similar ones, imply that stock prices will generally respond to changes in dividends. The Harkavy study identified the importance of the alternative—earnings retention. If earnings could be profitably employed by the firm, greater stock price appreciation might be achieved by retention. How much to retain depends on the profitability of the firm's investments. The appropriate level of retention is an important theoretical issue.

In March of 1956 Walter presented a valuation formula which captured the essential elements of what has since been called the "residual theory of dividend policy." Walter's formulation was as follows:

$$V_c = \frac{D + \frac{Ra}{Rc}(E - D)}{Rc}$$

where $V_c$ is stock price, "$D$ is cash dividends, $E$ is earnings per share, $Ra$ is the rate of return on additional investment, and $Rc$ is the market capitalization rate."[13]

Inspection of the formula will reveal the implicit dividend policy prescription. If $Ra$ were greater than $Rc$, moving a dollar from dividends to retained earnings would increase price and should be done. Walter recognized that market imperfections would complicate the above relationship but felt the specification was generally accurate.

Later the same year, Gordon and Shapiro,[14] through a more elegant proof, developed an essentially identical model. It is different in form and has gained wide recognition. By discounting an infinite stream of certain receipts (dividends) by a constant capitalization rate, the Gordon model was derived:

$$P = \frac{D}{K_e - g}$$

This is a rearrangement of the cost of equity specification that was used in Chapter 11. The price of the stock ($P$) is the dividend ($D$) divided by the quantity ($K_e - g$). The shareholder's required rate of return is $K_e$ and $g$ is the firm's growth rate.

The dividend policy prescription is found by using calculus. By op-

---

[12] Ibid., pp. 24–25.
[13] James E. Walter, "Dividend Policy and Common Stock Prices," *Journal of Finance*, vol. 2 (March 1956), pp. 29–41.
[14] Myron J. Gordon and Eli Shapiro, "Capital Equipment Analysis," *Management Science*, vol. 3 (October 1956), pp. 102–10.

timizing $P$ with respect to the retention rate,[15] a result identical to that implicit in Walter's model is obtained; it will be price-enhancing to retain earnings as long as internal profitability exceeds the market capitalization rate.

Both of the models, Walter's and Gordon's, imply that dividends are a remainder, a "leftover." Even though stock prices are expected to move in association with changes in dividends, the shareholder will be better off if the company keeps and invests available funds at rates greater than the cost of capital. Walter's model implies retention of earnings if $Ra$ is greater than $Rc$. Gordon's model says the same thing with different symbols and more mathematics.

Some academicians at the time characterized the residual theory as oversimplified. (The Lintner study reviewed in the chapter is one example.) As Harkavy noted, security analysts felt that corporate finance theorists had underestimated the importance of paying adequate dividends. However, no one suggested that dividend policy was unimportant, much less irrelevant. That would be heresy. That was the Miller and Modigliani position on dividends.

**Miller and Modigliani on Dividends.** In their 1958 capital structure paper MM virtually ignored the dividend policy issue, asserting that the division between retained earnings and dividends in any given period was a "mere detail." This non-treatment of dividends ignored all of the statistical and theoretical work that had been done by the traditionalists as to appropriate guides for dividend policy. There were numerous objections to this aspect of their paper. In 1961 MM answered their critics with a rigorous defense of their earlier position.[16]

As in their earlier paper, MM started by developing a valuation model in an idealized market setting. The hypothesized market was perfectly competitive; no buyer or seller was large enough to affect prices, information was free and completely available, and there were no transfer costs and no taxes. All investors in the market were rational wealth-maximizers. The model assumed certainty; future profits and investments of every firm were known to all.

Next, the authors specified a valuation formula for the firm. The value of the firm was defined as the present value of next period's dividends plus the present value of the stock of the firm at the end of the period.[17] This firm valuation formula was derived from a stock valuation formula

---

[15] Myron J. Gordon, "The Savings, Investment and Valuation of a Corporation," *Review of Economics and Statistics*, vol. 44 (February 1962), pp. 37–51.

[16] Merton H. Miller and Franco Modigliani, "Dividend Policy, Growth, and the Valuation of Shares," *Journal of Business*, vol. 34 (October 1961), pp. 411–33.

[17] MM's assumptions allowed them to derive the models for a firm that was entirely financed with equity. This simplified the theoretical development. However, they alluded to similar models they had developed for levered firms which gave the same results.

## 20 Retained Earnings and Dividend Policy

identical to the Gordon model. However, by dealing with the total firm rather than individual stocks, MM could introduce a factor others had overlooked—the effect of new stock financing. Their model was as follows:[18]

Value of the firm at the beginning of a period = Present value of all the stock at the end of the period
+ Present value of all dividends paid during the period
− Present value of any new stock that must be sold during the period

MM used this specification because it is especially revealing. It highlights the three ways in which dividends affect the current value of the firm. In a certain world the dividends paid during this period could not affect the value of the firm at the end of the period. The end of period value would reflect only future prospects. Past dividends would be of no consequence.

What the authors did next was to show that if the firm's investment policy were given, current dividends and current financing needs cancel each other out. *Every dollar paid in dividends requires that an additional dollar's worth of new stock be sold.*[19] For the individual shareholder this means that an additional dollar in dividends causes the forfeiture of a dollar's worth of price appreciation.

Then, in a series of mathematical models, MM demonstrated that the four approaches to share valuation then in the literature were identical, under perfect market conditions. Further, all of the models could be reduced to the earnings valuation approach they had used in their leverage article. The value of the firm was equal to the present value of the net returns from investment (profits less the reinvestment of the necessary capital to maintain the profits).[20]

Then the authors examined what they assessed to be the flaw in the residual theory of dividend policy as derived from the Gordon model.[21] The logical error was to confuse the effects of the investment and the dividend decisions. Assuming corporate growth was entirely financed by retained earnings makes it impossible to distinguish between the effects of dividend policy and the effects of investing. MM would agree that investments that earned greater than the cost of capital should be undertaken. However, it is not necessary to retain earnings to do so. Such investments could be financed with new stock or other forms of external capital.

---

[18] Ibid., p. 413.
[19] Ibid.
[20] Ibid., p. 420.
[21] Ibid., pp. 421–26.

The study did not limit itself to consideration of dividend policy in the rarefied world of perfect markets. It also addressed the issue in a more realistic context. Although a generalized valuation model was not developed, the paper did consider the relevance of dividend policy in an uncertain world where investors *acted* rationally.[22] Again MM postulated dividend policy irrelevance. However, MM noted that dividends might appear important in an uncertain world because of their "information content." If firms adopt policies of stabilizing dividends and resist cutting them, dividends will only be raised when it is believed that earnings will continue to support a new and higher level of dividends. (The Lintner model discussed in the section on "Dividend Policy of U.S. Corporations" suggests this is a realistic description. The Lintner article predates the MM paper.) In such a business environment an increase in dividends may signal optimism on the part of management as to future earnings prospects. On the other hand, a cut in dividends would indicate hard times ahead.

This information effect would explain why traditionalists had found strong associations between dividends and stock prices. It was not dividend policy *per se* which was affecting stock prices. It was the information implicit in the dividends that was triggering the stock price changes. Such a phenomenon would make construction of statistical tests of dividend policy extremely difficult.[23]

As MM note, the next step after introducing uncertainty would be to introduce market imperfections and examine the influence of these factors. They left that task to others who they hoped would follow their lead. However, they pointed out that identification of market imperfections would not be sufficient. To be of importance to dividend policy, such imperfections must be "systematic," creating a permanent bias either for retention of earnings or payment of dividends.

Even if such impediments to market perfection did exist, market participants might undo them. For example, if some investors had a strong preference for current income, this might not make high-dividend stocks sell at a premium. If enough such high-dividend stocks were available, these investors could buy them. Others, who preferred low payouts, would buy according to their preferences. This would result in each type of dividend policy attracting its own *clientele*. However, no particular dividend policy would command a premium as long as each group could find sufficient suitable investments.[24]

If the "clientele effect" exists, it makes devising a particularly attrac-

---

[22] The distinction here is between rational investors and those who *act* rationally. MM's second set of assumptions resulted in the latter.

[23] Ibid., p. 430, n. 30.

[24] Ibid., p. 431.

tive dividend policy difficult. To capitalize on dividends, managers must devise a policy that is sufficiently different so as to attract some segment of the investing public that cannot find exactly what they want in any existing stock, or combination of stocks. Viewed from this perspective, innovation with respect to dividend policy appears unlikely.

**The Debate Concerning Dividends.** MM's articles heightened academic interest in dividend policy. The 1958 paper, which pointedly ignored divided policy, brought objections from those who had done previous work in the area. Durand[25] suggested their handling or, more correctly, nonhandling of the dividend issue overlooked some critical details. MM, in the 1958 paper, suggested that retention of earnings was logically analogous to selling a preemptive stock issue. Durand said they had overlooked one element—the price, and that their theory needed more work. He also reviewed some of the empirical results from his earlier bank stock study which supported dividend relevance.

In replying[26] to Durand, MM indicated some of what was to come in the 1961 paper. As to his empirical findings, MM chided Durand for his failure to understand the importance of the "information effect."

Gordon did a regression study[27] using more sophisticated variable definitions. The importance of dividends was again supported. He also respecified his (the Gordon) model. In the revised model he assumed that later returns, dividends, would be discounted at higher rates because of their greater riskiness. The result was a model where current dividends would be preferable to retention.[28]

Then came the 1961 MM dividend paper. Although the paper was discussed in some detail, one element was intentionally deferred until now. Although Gordon's 1962 paper, discussed above, was not published yet, MM had seen advance copies and felt it compounded an error made in the original model. The first model had confused the returns from investment with the returns from retention. The revised model confused the risk of investment with the risk of retention. There was no reason to capitalize future returns at higher rates unless the investments were riskier.[29]

The debate was rekindled. Gordon conceded MM's findings under certainty but objected to their contentions of dividend irrelevance under

---

[25] David Durand, "The Cost of Capital, Corporation Finance, and the Theory of Investment: Comment," *American Economic Review*, vol. 49 (September 1959), pp. 639-55.

[26] Merton H. Miller and Franco Modigliani, "The Cost of Capital, Corporation Finance, and the Theory of Investment: Reply," *American Economic Review*, vol. 49 (September 1959), pp. 655-69.

[27] Myron J. Gordon, "Dividends, Earnings and Stock Prices," *Review of Economics and Statistics*, vol. 41 (May 1959), pp. 98-105.

[28] Myron J. Gordon, "The Savings, Investment and Valuation of a Corporation," *Review of Economics and Statistics*, vol. 44 (February 1962), pp. 37-51.

[29] MM, op. cit., p. 425.

uncertainty. He reasserted his increasing discount rate position.[30] Walter observed[31] dividend irrelevance required that both corporate growth and shareholders' required rates of return be unaffected by the rate of retention. He felt that was unlikely.

John Lintner did a number of articles on dividend policy and leverage.[32] Although it is somewhat unfair to him to paraphrase all three articles at once, this may serve to highlight the thrust of the series.

Lintner, like MM, worked first with the assumptions of perfect markets and certainty, but he added a " 'profit possibility' function which exhibits diminishing returns *as of* any given point in time. . . ."[33] This means that all projects do not generate the same profitability. The more the firm invests, the lower the marginal return. Lintner specified a particular mathematical form for this return function. Under these assumptions, he demonstrated that there was a retention level which maximizes share prices. The firm should invest in all projects generating greater than the current earnings yield. (This is lower than the cutoff rate advocated by MM.)[34]

However, the existence of an optimal retention level would not mean that such projects must necessarily be retention financed. In perfect markets all forms of financing are perfect substitutes. The firm could use retained earnings, new stock, or debt capital. However, Lintner was not siding with MM on the leverage and dividend issues. He said that under these restrictive assumptions the earnings capitalization theory (MM) is equivalent to generally recognized economic theory which values any economic asset as the present value of its income stream; that is, the value of a share of stock is the present value of the dividends. To assert a more general application of the earnings capitalization theory would require more rigorous proof.[35]

Lintner demonstrated that under more generalized conditions of transaction costs, personal taxes, leverage, uncertainty, and corporate taxes the equivalence of the two approaches is destroyed. To achieve share value

---

[30] Myron J. Gordon, "Optimal Investment and Financing Policy," *Journal of Finance*, vol. 18 (May 1963), pp. 264–72.

[31] James E. Walter, "Dividend Policy: Its Influence on the Value of the Enterprize," *Journal of Finance*, vol. 18 (May 1963), pp. 280–91.

[32] John Lintner, "Dividends, Earnings, Leverage, Stock Prices and the Supply of Capital to Corporations," *Review of Economics and Statistics*, vol. 44 (August 1962), pp. 243–69; John Lintner, "The Cost of Capital and Optimal Financing of Corporate Growth," *Journal of Finance*, vol. 18 (May 1963), pp. 292–310; and John Lintner, "Optimal Dividends and Corporate Growth Under Uncertainty," *The Quarterly Journal of Economics*, vol. 78 (February 1964), pp. 49–95.

[33] John Lintner, "Optimal Dividends and Corporate Growth Under Uncertainty," *The Quarterly Journal of Economics*, vol. 78 (February 1964), p. 50.

[34] Ibid., p. 63.

[35] John Lintner, "Dividends, Earnings, Leverage, Stock Prices and the Supply of Capital to Corporations," *Review of Economics and Statistics*, vol. 44 (August 1962), p. 251.

maximization under such conditions required use of the dividend valuation approach.

Lintner disagreed with MM on virtually every point. Under certainty conditions, he felt their cost of capital was too high.[36] Under uncertainty, Lintner concluded the MM cost of capital was too low. Some of the factors that raised this required return were as follows: serially related returns to invested capital (year-to-year returns are interdependent), a demand for increasing returns over time, and increasing variance of returns with capital budget size. In essence, Lintner felt MM had omitted factors that increased the risk that shareholders faced when their capital was reinvested by the firm. In so doing, MM underestimated the returns such investors would require.[37]

Further, even if they were correct, Lintner felt the MM models were redundant and therefore unnecessary. In his view, MM's models lacked applicability except under fully idealized conditions when the dividend models also hold. Under more realistic assumptions dividend valuation models work where the earnings capitalization models will not. Lintner's dividend models are not the Gordon model. His valuation models, while based on dividends, are a good deal more complex than the early models.[38]

At this point it might be well to review the debate so far. MM's models demonstrate dividend policy irrelevance under certainty in perfect markets. The theoretical soundness of these models is generally acknowledged, but dividend theorists doubt that the irrelevance description is accurate in a stock market where there are so many potential market imperfections and events are everything but certain. MM would point out that imperfections per se are not enough because of the clientele effect. Dividend relevance is then, to a large degree, an empirical issue. Are stock prices determined on the basis of dividends?

Although there had been a large body of empirical evidence accumulated by the traditionalists, its validity was now questioned. By including considerations of growth and risk, the strong dividend effect observed in earlier studies was weakened considerably.[39,40]

Then MM did an empirical study of their own.[41] Their theory suggested that stock prices were determined by *expected* future earnings.

---

[36] John Lintner, "Optimal Dividends and Corporate Growth Under Uncertainty," *The Quarterly Journal of Economics*, vol. 78 (February 1964), p. 63.

[37] Ibid., p. 84.

[38] Ibid., pp. 68–91.

[39] Irwin Friend and Marshall Puckett, "Dividends and Stock Prices," *American Economic Review*, vol. 54 (September 1964), pp. 656–82.

[40] James J. Diamond, "Earnings Distribution and Valuation of Shares," *Journal of Finance and Quantitative Analysis* (March 1967), pp. 15–30.

[41] Franco Modigliani and Merton H. Miller, "Some Estimates of the Cost of Capital to the Electric Utility Industry," *American Economic Review*, vol. 56 (June 1966), pp. 333–91.

To do their study, they constructed an "instrumental variable" to serve as a measure of investors' expectations. One of the determinants of this instrumental variable was dividends. When a dividend variable was used in conjunction with the instrumental variable in a regression equation, the dividend variable provided little additional explanation as to variations in stock prices.

There were numerous objections to MM's methodology.[42] Their detractors suggested MM's analysis was biased. By using dividends in constructing their instrumental variable, which was to serve as a measure of expected earnings, MM virtually assured that the introduction of dividends as a separate explanatory variable would have little effect.

In addition to questioning the validity of MM's empiricism, the dividend relevance proponents accumulated additional evidence to support their views. Brigham and Gordon did a regression study[43] to determine if the cost of retained earnings was affected by the firm's retention rate and if the cost of new equity was affected by the firm's debt ratio. They found the cost of retained earnings rose as the retention rate increased and that the cost of new equity increased as leverage increased, *but not by enough to support MM's capital structure irrelevance arguments.*

VanHorne and McDonald tested[44] MM's arguments as to the substitutability of retained earnings and new stock. They examined two industries and the companies within those industries which had sold new stock while still paying cash dividends. The authors found a general preference for dividend payments, even though the firms had to sell that much more new stock, incurring the attendant flotation costs. Such a finding is counter to the MM position, which treats new equity and retained earnings as perfect substitutes.

However, the empirical evidence is not one-sided. The MM arguments have been supported in a number of instances. Their models suggest that the investment policy of a firm should be independent of its dividend policy. Although some would object,[45] there is evidence to support this contention.[46]

---

[42] See, for example, the papers by (1) Jean Crocket and Irwin Friend, (2) Myron J. Gordon, and (3) Alexander A. Robichek, John G. McDonald, and Robert C. Higgins, all entitled "Some Estimates of the Cost of Capital to the Electric Utility Industry, 1954–57: Comment," and appearing in *American Economic Review*, vol. 57 (December 1967), pp. 1258–88.

[43] Eugene F. Brigham and Myron J. Gordon, "Leverage, Dividend Policy and the Cost of Capital," *Journal of Finance*, vol. 23 (March 1968), pp. 85–103.

[44] James C. VanHorne and John McDonald, "Dividend Policy and New Equity Financing," *Journal of Finance*, vol. 26 (May 1971), pp. 507–19.

[45] Phoebus J. Dhymes and Mordeci Kurz, "Investment, Dividend and External Finance Behavior of Firms," in R. Ferber, ed., *Determinants of Investment Behavior*, New York, National Bureau of Economic Research; distributed by Columbia University Press, 1967.

[46] Eugene F. Fama, "The Empirical Relationship Between the Dividend and Investment Decisions of Firms," *American Economic Review*, vol. 64 (June 1974), pp. 304–18.

The results of the 1966 empirical study by MM has been supported with a less elaborate statistical design. This study does not use the instrumental variable approach and is therefore not subject to the same criticisms.[47]

MM's suggestion of a "clientele effect" has been vindicated. Examination of prices of stocks around the dates when the firms pay dividends suggests that different payout policies attract buyers that are in different tax brackets.[48]

The MM contention of an "information effect" has also found support.[49] However, this evidence can be characterized as weak. The market seems to be relatively efficient in anticipating the information in the dividends.[50] Further, such information is of limited usefulness—dividends appear to be poor predictors of future earnings.[51]

However, the lack of predictive content is not unique to dividends. The residual theory, as embodied in the Walter and Gordon models, suggests that high retention rates and high rates of return on company projects should predict high rates of earnings growth. This does not seem to be the case.[52] This can be partially explained. Evidence suggests that retained earnings are sometimes utilized for very low return investments.[53]

There has also been a theoretical counterargument to the risk exposure effects of earnings retention as suggested in Gordon's 1962 paper. By using an arbitrage argument similar to that in MM's 1958 paper, it has been shown that investors can create "homemade dividends" in the same way they manufacture "homemade leverage."[54] If the firm does not pay out as much as the investors want, they can sell some of the stock, increasing current income and reducing future risk exposure.

*The Literature in Retrospect.* It may be difficult to discern a pattern in the literature, and it is quite likely some will find fault with this

---

[47] Robert C. Higgins, "Growth, Dividend Policy, and Capital Costs in the Electric Utility Industry," *Journal of Finance*, vol. 29 (September 1974), pp. 1189–1201.

[48] Edwin J. Elton and Martin J. Gruber, "Marginal Shareholder Tax Rates and the Clientele Effect," *Review of Economics and Statistics*, vol. 52 (February 1970), pp. 68–74.

[49] Ross Watts, "The Information Content of Dividends," *Journal of Business* (April 1973), pp. 191–211.

[50] Richardson R. Pettit, "Dividend Anouncements, Security Performance, and Capital Market Efficiency," *Journal of Finance*, vol. 27 (December 1972), pp. 993–1007.

[51] James S. Ang, "Dividend Effect: Information Content or Partial Adjustment," *Review of Economics and Statistics* (February 1975), pp. 65–70.

[52] Joseph E. Murphy, "Return on Equity Capital, Dividend Payout, and Growth of Earnings Per Share," *Financial Analyst Journal*, vol. 23 (May–June 1967), pp. 91–93.

[53] William J. Baumol, Peggy Heim, Burton G. Malkiel, and Richard E. Quandt, "Earnings Retention, New Capital, and Growth of the Firm," *Review of Economics and Statistics*, vol. 52 (November 1970), pp. 345–55.

[54] Robert C. Higgins, "Dividend Policy and Increasing Discount Rates: A Clarification," *Journal of Financial and Quantitative Analysis*, vol. 7 (June 1972), pp. 1757–62.

characterization. Traditionalists believed that dividends were an important factor in the determination of stock prices. Their statistical studies reflected, and reinforced, these beliefs. The theoretical models of that phase started from the assumption of dividend relevance and used the standard machinery of economics (present value) to define stock values.

Miller and Modigliani did not assume dividend relevance. They started from perfect market assumptions and found that in such a setting dividends were irrelevant to stock valuation. However, they went further—they postulated dividend irrelevance even under more generalized conditions. They suggested why this could be the case and why existing statistical evidence was insufficient to refute their contentions.

The traditionalists have since refined their theories and their empiricism. The new theories suggest why dividends should be relevant to stock valuation—the effects of earnings retention on investment risk and shareholders' aversion to such risks. The empirical tests have been improved, reducing the biases created by omitted factors and questionable variable definitions.

However, the theories and evidence have not resolved the dividend policy issue. If domestic capital markets were perfect, there should be no concern over dividend policy. Further, even if the markets do have some inefficiencies, clientele effects may erase them. But U.S. capital markets have more than minor inefficiencies. One obvious consideration is the tax system. Effective tax rates on dividends are much higher than those on capital gains for individuals. However, the nominal tax rate on dividends is very low for corporate investors. Whether the clientele effect can erase the tax effect and other such market imperfections is not yet known. Whether dividend policy is relevant, for some firms or for all firms, remains an unanswered empirical question.

# part V
# EXPANSION AND GROWTH

The normal expectation of a typical business firm is growth. Over its economic life a business firm may expand internally, externally, or in both directions. Internal expansion may be financed with funds from operations or with funds from external sources—or with a combination of both. External expansion is accomplished by a combination of two or more companies. External growth of business corporations may be achieved through various legal means, such as purchase, lease, holding company, voting trust, consolidation, and merger, as well as through cooperative efforts by means of trade associations, community of interest, voluntary chains, and jointly owned facilities.

The economies resulting from size often create additional incentive for growth and expansion, both internal and external. In the past, the general public has been prone to identify expansion in size with monopoly, and this attitude is reflected in the enactment of antitrust laws and provisions for regulation. Both internal and external expansion and growth are considered in this section.

# 21

# Growth of Business Enterprises

A so-called growth company is usually one having aggressive management, high depreciation charges, large capital expenditures, low dividends relative to earnings, frequent stock dividends, new product development, and rapidly increasing sales over a recent period of years. The topics discussed in this chapter include growth factors, optimum size, types of expansion, major combination movements, alternatives to mergers and consolidations, and public policies relative to business acquisitions.

## Growth Factors

In an expanding economy, growth of business concerns is to be expected; but, after a firm has reached its optimum size, there may be economic justification for creating new firms to care for the expanding needs of the economy rather than increasing the size of existing firms. Although it may be argued that existing firms ought to assume the burden of providing more goods and services, management must recognize that lower profits result from pushing output and sales beyond the optimal point. The danger of overexpansion in a dynamic economy is less than in a static or declining one, but the danger is there nevertheless.

Two main reasons for growth of business firms have been: (1) the increase in population and in the average income of the consumer; and (2) technological improvements in communications, transportation, and production.

*Social Factors.* The optimum size of a business firm is the size that enables it to produce most efficiently at the lowest possible per unit cost, thus permitting its product to be sold at the lowest possible price. In a competitive society, business firms that cannot meet this competition will tend to be forced out of business. If the output of the lowest-cost firm is sufficient to meet the entire demand of the economy, it could obtain a monopoly. This point looms large whenever the proper size of business firms is debated on social, political, and economic grounds. One of the arguments is that elimination of small business firms entails a loss in social values for which the greater efficiency of large business units does not compensate. Another argument is the possibility that monopolists will exploit the general public by overcharging consumers for their products.

The popular attitude toward large business firms is reflected in public policy that has been directed toward preserving small and medium-sized business units in fields where they can succeed if properly managed. The approach has been both positive and negative—protection and aid to small business units, on one hand, and control and regulation of large units, on the other. The activities of the Small Business Administration and the preferential tax treatment of small business units exemplify the positive approach. The negative approach is illustrated by provisions for control and regulation of combinations under the Sherman Antitrust Act of 1890 and the Clayton Act of 1914, as amended.

Unfortunately, the concept of monopoly is usually associated with size and there is often little relationship between the two. As an illustration a small business concern such as a store in an isolated community may hold a much more monopolistic position than a large one in a city where there are many competitors. Perhaps the greater accessibility to different markets that has been made possible by automobiles and good roads has done more to break up monopolies than all the national and state antimonopoly laws that have been enacted. At the same time, consumers have profited from the greater efficiency of modern merchandising that has accompanied an increase in the size of stores and other business units.

In some industries, such as public utilities and transportation, service is provided more economically on a noncompetitive basis. The cost of telephone service would be higher if ten companies operated in a single city than if a single company provided this service. State and local governments have given monopoly status not only to electric, gas, telephone, water, and public-warehouse companies but also to railroads and other transportation companies. The rates and practices of these companies have long been subjected to regulation by federal, state, and local public-service commissions. The geographical area served by such companies is limited by their franchises, and their growth depends in part on finding new customers for their services. Hence, these companies are the chief sponsors of new industries in many areas. Usually, although there are numerous exceptions, regulated companies are not considered growth companies in the sense that their prospects for future expansion are at a rate above the average of other nonregulated companies.

Since 1917, a change has taken place in the public attitude toward large business units, and this is reflected in some of the laws passed by Congress that have encouraged, rather than discouraged, combinations and expansion of business firms. These acts include the Webb-Pomerene Act of 1918, which permits U.S. firms to form combinations for export purposes, and the Transportation Act of 1920, which directed the Interstate Commerce Commission to draw up plans (which were never carried out) for consolidation of the railroads. In fact, some acts of Congress have even seemed to challenge the effectiveness of competition; this is illustrated by the National Recovery Act of 1933, which encouraged formulation of codes of fair competition (declared unconstitutional by the Supreme Court in 1935). At the same time that growing tolerance and acceptance of large corporations developed, provisions for the regulation of these corporations were strengthened to prevent abuses that could accompany expansion and combinations in business units; for example, the Interstate Commerce Commission, Federal Trade Commission, and Securities and Exchange Commission were created.

The use of cutthroat competition to eliminate other companies in the same field is practically a thing of the past, but the Department of Justice has followed a policy of maintaining competition by enforcement of antitrust laws. The average size of business firms in the United States, as would be expected in a growing economy, has increased during the present century; but the tenacity of small, local owned and operated business units is well documented.

## Determination of the Optimum Size

In a free-enterprise system, a particular firm's optimum size is determined largely by the value of the firm's final product and by technological, managerial, marketing, and financial factors.

*Value of Final Product.* Other things being equal, the optimum-sized business unit tends to vary directly with the value of the final product—large, if the value of the final product is large, as in the shipbuilding, aircraft, and automotive industries; and small, if the value of the final product is small, as in the service industries such as barber shops, beauty parlors, and shoe-repair shops. This does not mean there will be no large business units in the service industry, because there are giant public-utility and transportation companies. Nor does it mean that the value of the final product of large companies is always large, because just the opposite is often the case. So the value of the final product is only one of many factors that influence the optimum size of a business firm.

*Technological Factors.* Laborsaving machines and division of labor that may be employed for economic advantage tend to increase the size of business firms. The minimum-sized business unit will be relatively large if its operations entail production that (1) requires large outlays for machinery, (2) may be subdivided, and (3) is suitable for "occupational specialization" (for example, production of automobiles, aircraft, and other durable producers' and consumers' goods).

The trend is toward designing and building more and better machines; but their purchase by a business firm must be justified on the basis of their income productivity. For example, an individual press used in the automobile industry may cost as much as $250,000 and the interest, depreciation, and other fixed charges thereon may be $250 per day. If the daily capacity of the press is 1,000 parts, fixed charges are 25 cents per part; but, if only 100 parts can be used per day, fixed charges are $2.50 per part. If other operations can be stepped up to use 1,000 parts daily, it may be profitable to acquire the press. Therefore, such a business firm is under pressure to increase production to the point where expensive machines can be utilized to capacity. Thus, a firm should be large enough to employ machinery profitably; or, conversely, a firm should limit acquisition of fixed assets to those it can use advantageously (which may result in its being at a competitive disadvantage compared to a larger firm).

The optimum size of a single business unit, considered from a technological point of view, does not prevent the formation of business concerns that operate several plants, stores, and other outlets under one management. Technological factors tend to determine the minimum rather than the maximum size of individual units, as illustrated by chain stores in grocery, drug, and general merchandise lines, and multiple plants and outlets operated by manufacturing firms such as General Electric and General Motors.

*Marketing Factors.* The cost of marketing a product rather than its value is sometimes the only justification for business expansion. Among the most expensive activities of some business firms is sales promotion, and this entails marketing research, study, advertising, and planning. Brand-name goods, regardless of the price of individual items, are sold in a national or international market; the marketing process requires large outlays for advertising, selling, and marketing organizations throughout the trade area. Some products, such as cigarettes, could be produced economically by small firms; however, the marketing costs may be so great as to necessitate their allocation over a large volume of sales, best achieved by a large business firm. Sometimes a business concern can increase and stabilize its sales volume by adding other products that appeal to the same market and can be distributed through existing facilities.

*By-Products.* In order for a business firm to maintain its competitive position, management may be forced to increase the size of the business unit so as to utilize the by-products of production profitably; but these must be available in quantities sufficient to justify expenditures for facilities to process them. This tends to put additional pressure on management to expand operations not only to utilize by-products but also to increase the output of the primary product in order to be assured a sufficient amount of by-products to make its utilization profitable.

***Managerial Skill.*** In achieving the optimum-sized business firm as distinguished from the optimum size of individual plants or units, management may capitalize on the economies resulting from the use of specialized skills in production, distribution, research, and financing that may be denied small firms. By using specialized skills, a business firm may find it advantageous to operate multiple plants, chains of stores, hotels, or service stations under one management. However, if top management is too far removed from the operations of individual units, this type of combination may be unprofitable. In other words, the cost of coordinating and formulating general policies must be weighed against the advantages of unified management and the services of specialists.

Industrial companies manufacturing tens of thousands of individual products for consumers, producers, and the government have been able to meet the challenge of size through decentralization of management. Under decentralized management arrangements, individuals have been made responsible for organizing and managing divisions or units of large business firms on a semi-independent basis. Along with such responsibility goes the authority to plan and budget, formulate production schedules, establish inventory levels, estimate the cash flow and cash needs, and so on. Nevertheless, decentralized management must conform to policies established by corporate management that are binding on all employees, and those responsible for management in the decentralized plan are provided with instruction manuals as to the company's policies on matters of overall interest to the company. Company policies pertain to items such as appropriations for major improvements, compliance with antitrust laws, maintenance of the company's salary structure, and use of the companys' name and symbols. The divisions or units operate under the principle of reserved authority, which permits the corporation's officers at the top level to change policies when appropriate.

***Financing Costs.*** The cost of financing is a problem common to all business firms. However, large, well-known firms have the advantage of being able to borrow in the capital market (where interest rates may be lower than those charged by banks and other lenders) and to increase equity capital through the public sale of stock. Although interest charges are usually a smaller item in the cost of operating a business firm, the ability to obtain funds is of prime importance. As noted in preceding chapters, larger firms have decided advantages over smaller firms not only in costs of borrowing but also in availability of funds. Growth is seldom determined wholly by the ease and cheapness of external financing because a successful business firm also will have internal funds and will be able to use these funds from operations to finance expansion.

***Determination of Size.*** The decision of management as to the appropriate size of any individual business enterprise may differ from the optimum as determined by technological, managerial, marketing, financial, and other factors. However, at any one time, management will be making adjustments because of the influence of one or more of these factors. As already noted, if there is a conflict between the ideal technological unit and the ability of centralized management, the solution may be to appoint divisional managers for plants, stores, or other units and to give them the power to operate these units, in large part, as separate business entities. However, failure to find or conform to the various optima may result in failure of a business firm or, at least, in its functioning at an uneconomical level. The problem is a challenging and continuing one because of fluctuations in the economy caused by changes in the general price level or individual and group prices within the general price structure, in technology, in the tax structure, and in the demands of the general public. The adaptation to these changes by key executives of a business firm may be the most important factor in explaining expansion and the direction it takes.

## Types of Expansion

*Direction of Expansion.* Expansion of business firms customarily takes one of the following directions: horizontal, vertical, and conglomerate or heterogeneous. Horizontal expansion is exemplified by the combination of similar stores, plants, or other business units under one management. Vertical expansion consists of bringing together two or more successive stages in production under one management—in the steel industry this would include iron mining, transporting and refining the ore, converting ore into steel, and distributing steel and steel products. Conglomerate or heterogeneous expansion consists of bringing under one management products or activities that have no apparent similarity either in the nature of the products or their marketing requirements.

*Diversification.* Some diversification is characteristic of big business firms. While most of the acquired units produce items closely related to the firm's markets, original products, and technology, a considerable amount of current combination encompasses nonrelated units. At present, enforcement of antitrust laws by the federal government has made it easier for corporate management to acquire noncompetitive companies in other industries. In addition, the high corporate income tax has made it desirable, in some cases, for profitable companies to acquire those in which there has been a loss. Under the provisions of the Internal Revenue Code, net operating losses of corporations may be carried back three years and carried forward seven years, applying the losses against taxable income. After the acquisition has been completed, amended tax returns will be filed for the years in which the carry-back is applicable. Thus, a firm showing past losses can be merged into a profitable one thereby reducing the taxable income of the surviving firm. The income taxes will be lowered thereby qualifying the surviving firm for a tax refund. Thus, a firm that has sustained recent losses is a more attractive merger candidate than it would be otherwise.

The increase in conglomerate-type activity has prompted consideration of the motives behind such mergers and acquisitions. The merging firm's management apparently has forecast a rate of return on the investment higher than its cost of capital. It is expected that the new entity might create a "synergism," that is, the surviving firm is more profitable than the simple sum of the formerly individual companies. However, in many instances there is no evident operational or economic relationship between the merged companies. Why then do they merge? One motive which has been suggested is the desire for diversification.

The idea that a conglomerate can reduce its risk or, alternatively, stabilize its earnings by branching out into a number of dissimilar business operations can be attributed to the theory of portfolio selection introduced by Markowitz[1] and Tobin.[2] The theory involves the selection of preferred combinations of securities on the basis of two characteristics: expected return, a measure of profitability; and standard deviation of the return, a measure of riskiness. The objective is to select combinations of securities which will simultaneously maximize the return for a given level of risk, and minimize the risk for a given return.

In the two-parameter model of Markowitz, expected portfolio return is simply the weighted average of individual returns.[3] However, the standard deviation of portfolio return is not an average of individual standard deviations but a function of the correlation between the returns of the individual securities making up the portfolio, the proportional amount invested in each security, and the standard deviation of each security.[4] Thus, when the correlation of returns is less than perfect

---

[1] Harry M. Markowitz, *Portfolio Selection: Efficient Diversification of Investments* (New York: John Wiley & Sons, 1959).

[2] James Tobin, "Liquidity Preference as Behavior Towards Risk," *Review of Economic Studies*, vol. 6, no. 1 (February 1958).

[3] Mathematically,
$$E(R_p) = \sum_{j=1}^{m} X_j E(R_j).$$

[4] $\sigma_p = \sqrt{\sum_{i=1}^{m} \sum_{j=1}^{m} X_i X_j \sigma_i \sigma_j C_{ij}}$

where:

- $X$ is proportion invested in each security;
- $E(R_p)$ is expected return on the portfolio;
- $E(R_j)$ is expected return on the security $j$;
- $m$ is number of securities comprising portfolio;
- $\sigma_i$ is the standard deviation of expected returns;
- $C_{ij}$ is the correlation coefficient between security $i$ and security $j$; and
- $\sigma_p$ is the standard deviation of the portfolio.

(1.0), the standard deviation of the portfolio return will be less than the simple weighted average of the individual standard deviations.

These principles of portfolio theory can be applied to conglomerate activity if we think of the conglomerate as being composed of a number of individual activities. In this way it is somewhat analogous to an investor forming a portfolio of individual securities. Similarly, the conglomerate's total expected rate of return is the weighted average of all the rates of return for each individual activity. However, the standard deviation of the conglomerate's return will not be the weighted sum of the standard deviations of the separate activities. Here lies the purported motive for conglomerate merger.

Since it is usually assumed that a systematic relationship exists between the riskiness of a firm, as measured by the variability of its income, and the market value of its stock, the firm must seek to minimize the risk of its total operations if it wishes to increase or maximize its market value. If a business segment is added whose return is just as variable as current operations (i.e., perfectly correlated with), overall risk will not change. However, where segments are added whose returns are less than perfectly correlated with other activities, overall risk is reduced. This is the diversification effect and intuitively assumes that income fluctuations in one business segment are offset by income fluctuations in other business segments.

From the standpoint of maximizing shareholder wealth, conglomerate mergers for diversification alone have been questioned.[5] Some authors have shown that the same result can be achieved by the individual investor simply by buying securities in the various activities in the same proportion as the individual segments would have contributed to the total conglomerate return. The value of the individual firms prior to the merger would reflect this possibility. Therefore, after the merger no increase in market value for the combined entity is possible or should even be expected.

Several authors have provided some justification for the diversification motive in a conglomerate merger. The merger for diversification purposes may be desirable if viewed from management's standpoint. Weston and Mansinghka noted such a rationale where it is "diversification to avoid adverse effects on profitability from developments taking place in the firm's traditional product market areas."[6] Additionally, it has been claimed that "the more stable income stream produced by a merger will induce lenders to increase the limits on lending to the newly created firm above

---

[5] Haim Levy and Marshall Sarnat, "Diversification, Portfolio Analysis, and the Uneasy Case for Conglomerate Mergers," *Journal of Finance*, vol. 25 (September 1970), p. 796.

[6] J. Fred Weston and Surendra K. Mansinghka, "Tests of the Efficiency Performance of Conglomerate Firms," *Journal of Finance*, vol. 26 (September 1971), p. 919.

the sum of the original limits that were obtained for the merger parties individually."[7]

***Internal and External Expansion.*** Expansion of business firms may result from internal or external growth, or from a combination of both. Internal growth may result from the application of retained earnings or funds raised from outside sources.[8] In other words, internal growth, as defined here, includes all growth except that resulting from complete or partial absorption of other business units. External growth may result from acquisition of assets by merger, by consolidation, by lease, by the holding-company device, or by some modification of one or more of these methods.

In a merger, the absorbing firm retains its identity and the firm absorbed loses its identity; in a consolidation, all participants lose their identities and a new firm emerges; in a lease or holding-company arrangement, all participants retain their identities but control passes, to a great extent, from the lessor or subsidiary companies to the lessee or holding company. Although there are technical differences among the devices used to achieve external growth, the terms merger, consolidation, amalgamation, and combination are often used without distinction; perhaps the word "combination" could be used with some degree of accuracy to cover all forms of expansion resulting from transfer of ownership or control of other business units.

Internal expansion has advantages over external expansion in that it avoids valuation problems and alteration costs incurred in remodeling facilities acquired; permits locating new facilities or relocating existing ones to take advantage of low taxes, abundant labor supply, cheap power, low-cost raw materials, and convenient transportation facilities; and it avoids the necessity for obtaining stockholders' consent to combine and deal with dissenting minority stockholders and creditors of the firm or firms to be transferred. New facilities and equipment permit management to take advantage of new technological advances and to strengthen the position of the firm as a low-cost producer. Offsetting this advantage, time and financial resources are required to build, equip, and staff new plants;

---

[7] Wilbur G. Lewellen, "A Pure Financial Rationale for the Conglomerate Merger," *Journal of Finance*, vol. 26 (May 1971), p. 521.

[8] Over a period of years, the growth traced to combination may affect the competitive position of a business firm, which, in turn, will be reflected in its earnings and therefore the amount of expansion financed with retained earnings. For example, when "organized fifty years ago, American Can acquired virtually a monopoly of can-making by merging more than 100 can-making firms. Its size gave it unique bargaining power and for many years it obtained secret rebates in buying tin plate from the U.S. Steel Corporation." (George W. Stockings, "Book Reviews," *Journal of Finance*, vol. 9 [December 1954], pp. 942–43.) As recognized previously, the point is that it is impossible to distinguish between the effects of combination and internal expansion in explaining the size of modern business units.

if new products are included in the expansion, time and money will be required to advertise and to develop a market for them. Finally, additional funds may be needed to finance working-capital assets, such as inventories and receivables. If funds from operations are not sufficient to finance needs, the firm will have to borrow from banks, other lenders, or in the money market.

External expansion has advantages over internal expansion in that little or no time is lost in putting plans and facilities into operation because a going concern usually includes an experienced staff, outlets for products, goodwill, and a ready market. Usually, combinations do not increase an industry's total productive capacity, and, so, external expansion may lessen the danger of cutthroat competition. Expansion of a particular business firm will be influenced by the firm's financial position and the attitude of management toward diversification.

*Timing of Expansion.* Since external expansion represents changes in ownership and internal expansion represents capital formation, there may be no relationship between the timing of the two. Internal expansion tends to coincide with movements of the business cycle, but this is not necessarily true of combinations. If, as one group contends, the chief motive behind combination is the achievement of economies of operation, the combination movement should be greatest during periods of business depression. If, as a second group contends, combinations are due to the activities of promoters, the combination movement would be greatest during stock-market booms, when common stock is easier to sell.[9] Neither of these factors completely explains the various combination movements, but both have been important to some degree in the three major movements in the United States (along with political atmosphere, stage of economic development in the United States, tax factors, and other reasons noted below).

## Three Major Combination Movements

An analysis of the three major merger or combination movements in the United States (1898–1903; 1920–31; and 1951–71) shows that distinct sets of forces explain each of these movements. This section discusses the most distinctive features of each period.

*First Period.* The important factors in the first combination movement include relaxation of business-corporation laws to permit corporations to hold stock in other corporations; achievement of combination without violation of the Sherman Act, which prohibited collusive activi-

---

[9] When W. F. Mueller, Director of the Federal Trade Commission, testified before the Senate Antitrust and Monopoly Subcommittee, he stated that a study of mergers showed "particularly close relationship between merger activity and stock prices." However, it was not "clear just how 'conditions' in the stock market encourage mergers." (*New York Times,* March 17, 1965, p. 65.)

ties but permitted combinations if the issue of monopoly was not raised; development of transportation facilities and national markets, which permitted economical operations of large-scale, multiunit business concerns; improvements in managerial techniques; and development of financial markets.

The first wave of business combination was one wherein many business firms in the same line of activity were brought under one management. Destructive competition was greatly reduced and the stage was set for cost reductions, price increases, and profit expansion. Some combinations were of the vertical type, but most of them were horizontal in nature (such as tinplate, shoe manufacturers and sugar-refining companies). Promoters made use of the holding-company device as well as the old charter (merger) and new charter (consolidation) methods in bringing together different business units under one management. Very little thought was given to diversification, and the apparent aim of management was to reduce costs and obtain better control over markets. The merger movement of this period proved to be beneficial to the promoters, investment bankers, founders of absorbed or consolidated companies that received stock in the absorbing or new company, the general public that invested in the new companies, and consumers who obtained better products (although there were exceptions).

*Second Period.* The predominant factor in the merger movement of the 1920s was the stock-market boom, which facilitated the sale of securities issued by new combinations. The fact that many of the combinations were vertical and horizontal types of expansion seems to suggest that the motives for expansion were to assure the growing firm an adequate supply of raw materials and to make advertising, selling, and distributing organizations more effective. In the second merger movement, economies in business operations were basic—economies in buying and selling, in the use of personnel, and so forth—but promotional opportunities and underwriters' profits were also important factors.

The background for this merger movement is found in developments that occurred during World War I, when pressure was brought to bear on firms to combine in order to increase production by increasing efficiency in the use of labor, and capital, (even the federal government found it expedient to take over and operate the railroads under a unified system and under centralized control). The War Industries Board insisted on standardization of products and elimination of competition among agencies purchasing war supplies—and even resorted to price fixing. These wartime controls demonstrated the advantages of centralized management; the combination movement of 1920s, which reached its peak during 1927–29, was an extension of this movement under private control. Among those affected were public utilities, mining and oil industries, manufacturers, hotels, motion pictures, retail chain stores, and other divisions of the service industry. One of the most significant aspects of expansion during this period was the growth in holding companies in the public-utility field. (see Chapter 23). At the beginning of 1930, the 200 largest nonfinancial corporations controlled about 50 percent of nonbanking corporate wealth.

**Third Period.** In the merger movement beginning in the 1950s, the motivating factors included tax advantage, relatively low prices of common stock, and postwar shortages and a seller's market, which made it expedient to form combinations rather than await plant construction. The desire to secure market control seems to have been relatively unimportant during this merger period. Perhaps the decrease in monopoly-type mergers can be explained by a realization that many of the economies of size had already been achieved; limitations on management, technological changes, etc.; more vigorous enforcement of antitrust laws; and a decline in the influence of investment bankers who, in the past, had not only instigated plans for combinations but also had helped finance them.

The third wave of mergers, consolidations, and acquisitions tapered off about 1971. The principle that seemed to motivate many of these combinations was the need for diversification so as to stabilize income over the business cycle. A second factor was that changes in methods of production and consumer demand were so rapid as to put a one-product company out of business overnight. By acquiring a second firm, management could diversify its business and increase output. The conglomerate or heterogeneous type of combination has brought under the control of one management producers of such unrelated items as cigarette lighters and aircraft parts; anthracite coal and men's and boys' underwear; road-building equipment, fishing rods, steel, and glass; and woolen and worsted fabrics and precision sheet metal goods.[10]

In the third combination movement, which extended into the 1970s, conglomerates seem to be designed to economize on marketing and management resources and expenditures (note the variety of products advertised by one company during a TV program). Some industrial companies are still looking for ailing concerns to absorb so as to obtain the advantage of carrying forward a tax loss that can be applied against future earnings. The small size and inadequate cash flow of many business firms makes it uneconomical for them to continue in operation as independent business units; consequently, many of them are absorbed by larger firms that are capable of operating their facilities on an economical basis. Thus, many business firms are attempting to improve their competitive positions in their own industries or taking on the output of entirely new products in a line not related to their original business activities. However, the Justice Department has been successful in preventing certain rumored or proposed mergers, as exemplified by those of Bethlehem Steel and

---

[10] Stanley H. Brown, "Textron: How to Manage a Conglomerate," *Fortune*, April 1964, pp. 154 ff.

Youngstown Steel and Tube Company, and Texaco, Inc. and Superior Oil Company of California—"when the effects may be substantially to lessen competition or to tend to create a monopoly."

One important aspect of the third merger movement has been the creation of foreign units by U.S. business concerns. In establishing foreign units, there has been an increase in emphasis on joint ventures—the shared ownership approach—with foreign businessmen and investors. These joint ventures may be voluntary (when managers of U.S. companies feel the market can be served better with local cooperation) or required by the government where the plant is located.

Frequently, local suppliers are given preference when equivalent service, price, and quality of goods are offered; therefore, U.S. firms have recognized the need for building plants abroad if they are to avoid losing their foreign markets to competitors. Customers generally feel their needs are supplied better by a local firm because it is easier to replace goods when the supply lines are short. As a result of being supplied locally, the customers' inventories are smaller and better suited to the local markets.[11]

U.S. business corporations engaged in foreign business may find there is no substitute for foreign locations in some areas because of tariff barriers and the need to be near markets. Theoretically, tariffs are levied to equalize competition—to compensate for differences in conditions at home and abroad due to differences in shipping charges, prices of raw materials, domestic taxes, wages, and efficiency. However, the ideal supposedly sought through tariffs is seldom achieved.

## Alternatives to Mergers and Consolidations

The most common type of intercorporate relationship is the ownership of stock or assets of another company. The promoters of a merger or consolidation may expedite acceptance of their plan by purchasing or acquiring voting shares of the corporations they wish to acquire. If these promoters secure representation on the boards of directors of the respective corporations, they may create an atmosphere friendly to the merger or consolidation and may assist in drawing up the plan. Sometimes, after obtaining control of other corporations, a group may find it expedient to operate the corporations as separate entities rather than effect a formal merger or consolidation. The 1950 amendment of the Clayton Act prohibits acquisition by a corporation of stock or assets of another corpo-

---

[11] Although the charge has frequently been made, the building of plants abroad may not adversely affect employment at home. The foreign business of U.S. companies served through local outlets has added to their volume of business, and foreign production may not have replaced U.S. production (foreign plants have supplied foreign markets). While U.S. corporations are building plants in foreign countries, foreign companies also are building manufacturing facilities in the United States.

ration if "the effect of such acquisition may be substantially to lessen competition or tend to create a monopoly," but the presumption is that such acquisitions will not be disapproved unless economic evidence can be shown that competition would thereby be substantially reduced or that monopolistic elements are present.

***Purchase of Assets.*** When a company buys all or part of the assets of another company, the cash thus obtained by the seller may be used to start a different type of business or may be distributed on a pro rata basis to stockholders. As an illustration, in 1949, Penick & Ford, Ltd., a food-processing firm, sold its assets for cash to the R. J. Reynolds Tobacco Company (now R. J. Reynolds Industries, Inc.) and distributed $22 per share of stock held to each of its stockholders. Graham Paige, an automobile producer, sold its property to Kaiser Industries and used the cash to start an investment company. Later, the company (Graham Paige) acquired Madison Square Garden and, in 1962, changed the company name to Madison Square Garden Corporation. From 1962 to 1977, the company's principal business was the operation of Madison Square Garden, the ownership of the New York Rangers hockey team, the New York Knickerbockers basketball team, Roosevelt Raceway, Inc., Arlington Park-Washington Park Race Track, Inc., and office and hotel interests. In 1977, Gulf and Western Industries, Inc., a conglomerate owning 81 percent of Madison Square Garden, purchased the remaining stock for $10 a share. Madison Square Garden Corporation was then merged into Gulf and Western Industries.[12]

If a corporation sells its assets for cash, it generally has no gain or loss when it distributes the cash in exchange for its stock in a liquidation. The transaction is viewed as a sale of the stock by the shareholder to the corporation. However, each stockholder has a gain or a loss depending upon the amount received in relation to the purchase price.

***Lease Method.*** The lease method is perhaps the easiest way to acquire assets of other corporations, and a number of railroad systems have been created by this means. In the industrial field, the lease arrangement is limited largely to rental contracts covering real property; however, some companies rent or lease machines of different types. Lease agreements are not considered business transfers because they do not represent a change in ownership of business assets (see Chapter 14).

The degree of ease in acquiring assets is often the predominant factor in determining the procedure that will be followed in effecting combinations; however, other factors such as the permanency of the combination should be considered. If the problem faced by management is a temporary one, such as catching up with current or anticipated demand, it may be better to subcontract for parts or other units needed rather than resort to external expansion. Because the economies resulting from operating multi-

---

[12] *Wall Street Journal,* August 22, 1977, p. 12.

plant firms are limited and the threat of antitrust legal action may be present, the permanent policy of management may be to contract with independent firms for many of the things needed in operations. The ability to make such contractual arrangements has been a factor in the decline of vertical expansion. However, if the motive of management is to stabilize output, avoid duplication of marketing facilities, prorate advertising or sales costs over a larger sales volume, or obtain the benefits of centralized research, a more permanent type of combination may be sought. Thus, a horizontal combination may be arranged in order to use a single sales force.

Business arrangements whereby control rather than absorption of business units is sought have greater flexibility than permanent combinations. Although lease arrangements offer certain advantages, such contracts are usually long-term and rental charges may become burdensome during business recessions. Burdensome fixed charges may be avoided when control is secured through stock ownership. Control through acquisition of voting shares is the most flexible method of acquiring other business firms because the resulting combination can be dissolved by a parent corporation simply by selling the shares of the subsidiary.

*Holding Company.* The holding company, a corporation that holds shares of other companies in order to vote the stock and thereby achieve a common group policy, is the best illustration of the flexibility of the corporate form of business enterprise. The holding-company device is used to keep control of existing companies, to promote a new venture through creation of a new corporation, or to set the stage for a merger or consolidation at a future time. As compared to the total risks assumed in permanent combinations, a holding company's risks are limited to its investments in its subsidiary companies. The right of business corporations to acquire stock of other corporations is usually conferred by statute; it is at variance with the common law principle that stock ownership by one corporation of a second corporation is not in keeping with the purposes for which the corporation was created. A pure holding company is a corporation organized for control purposes; it is not, at the same time, an operating company. A pure holding company may assume managerial, research, financial, and other activities that would make it similar to the head office of an industrial or merchandising enterprise having multiple plants, stores, or other outlets (see Chapter 23).

*Community of Interest.* Sometimes the advantages accruing from external growth may be obtained in whole or in part by the establishment of a community of interest through interlocking directorates or ownership of common stock in several corporations by one or more persons; voluntary chains or retail units linked by contract to a central organization in order to obtain the benefits of unified management; or trade associations, where business firms join in research projects, studies, and publications on matters of mutual interest. If the result of any of these arrangements is to decrease competition, the courts may declare them illegal.

Pools have been established by owners of patents and copyrights when individual exploitation was not feasible or the rights of others were so similar that licensing seemed preferable. Antitrust suits may follow if the resulting degree of cooperation exceeds that covered by patent monopoly, such as market control, prevention of competition, or price fixing.

The use of trademarks as a basis for the franchise business has brought hundreds of small companies, located in different areas, into nationwide cooperative ventures under the general supervision of the parent companies. However, the practice of creating exclusive territories has been attacked as being illegal. As a general rule, it is legal for business firms to combine in order to own and finance some venture. This is true for railroad and bus terminals and for wholesale markets if competitors are permitted to use them. This policy was extended to pipelines when nine oil companies organized the Colonial Pipeline Company to carry oil to Eastern markets.[13]

Trade associations, whose chief function is to gather and distribute information to members, may be declared to be operating illegally if the statistical information is linked to customer assignment to market territories, price fixing, or limitation of production. However, there are some practices that have been legalized by congressional action, such as cooperative buying at a lower price when there is a cost saving (as authorized by the Robinson-Patman Act), and selling abroad, which is encouraged by the Webb-Pomerene Act that permits exporters to form marketing groups.

## Public Policies Relative to Business Acquisitions

In selecting the form a business acquisition is to take (merger, consolidation, etc.), management is bound by public policy, which has the preservation of competition among industrial companies as one of its aims. By their nature, public-utility, railroad and airline companies are so-called natural monopolies of organization; therefore, public policy has stressed regulation rather than preservation of competition in these fields. In addition to being uneconomical and unprofitable, it would not serve public interest for two or more telephone, electric and gas, and water companies to operate within a city; therefore, no effort has been made to maintain competition in such instances.

In general, the antimonopoly movement has been directed toward preserving competition in industrial fields; but, as evidenced by legisla-

---

[13] The oil companies that organized the Colonial Pipeline Company were the following: American, Continental, Cities Service, Phillips, Pure, Sinclair, Socony, Texaco, and Gulf.

tive action, there has been a lack of consistency in public policy. In fact, the federal government has passed laws that have decreased competition in certain fields, as illustrated by statutes, providing for price support of agricultural products, fluid milk, and labor.[14] The National Recovery Act of 1933 was declared unconstitutional by the Supreme Court in 1935, but it was the most sweeping of the acts passed by Congress to stabilize prices. During the first month after passage of this act, 400 "codes of fair practice" were approved in spite of the fact that many of them included provisions of a monopolistic nature.

Prior to 1890, cases involving the issue of "restraint of trade" came before state courts, which sometimes ruled that contracts having control of prices as their purpose were unenforceable and that there was criminal conspiracy against the public interest. To avoid the legal hazard of being a party to unenforceable agreements or being charged with criminal conspiracy, business combinations were formed by organizing voting trusts—issuing trust certificates by a common-law trust in exchange for the stock of competing companies. The trustees of the corporations made all decisions concerning them. If the rights of trustees were challenged in one state, they could reorganize in a second state and continue operations.

The Sherman Antitrust Act of 1890 was directed at monopoly and restraint of trade in interstate commerce, and the Antitrust Division of the Department of Justice is responsible for the enforcement of federal antitrust laws.[15] With the realization that mere size is not necessarily an indication of unreasonable restraint of trade or unfair trade practices, there has been a change in the attitude of Congress, the courts, and the general public toward combinations. In their effects on competition, some mergers are bad, some good, and some neutral. If all mergers or combinations were bad, making them illegal would be a simple way to handle the problem.

While public policy may be served by increasing or preserving competition through prevention of combinations, a monopolistic situation may result from internal growth. This may be accompanied by building additional capacity for supplying an expanding market in new as well as old areas, developing new products for diversification or replacement

---

[14] Among the acts permitting monopolistic practices are the Bituminous Coal Conservation Act of 1935, declared unconstitutional and replaced by a second act in 1937, which has withstood the test of constitutionality; the Connally Hot Oil Act of 1935, forbidding interstate commerce in excess of state petroleum quotas; the Railway Labor Act of 1926; the Norris–La Guardia Act of 1932; the National Labor Relations Act of 1935; and the Taft–Hartley Act of 1947. Other acts of Congress have placed parity price floors under agricultural prices.

[15] The assistant attorney general for the Antitrust Division of the Department of Justice is charged with the enforcement of the antitrust and 30 kindred acts. The division receives complaints and conducts investigations (in cooperation with the Federal Bureau of Investigation) that may lead to criminal prosecutions or suits in equity to break monopolies or restraints of interstate or foreign trade.

of old ones, and obtaining customers of other companies and employing their key personnel. Although combinations account for the origin of some large firms, their current positions within their industries may have been due as much to internal as to external growth. A second aspect of the combination movement is that some of the ends sought may be attained by means short of formal combination. Price stabilization and limitations on competition may be achieved in industries wherein there is considerable concentration through trade associations; informal contacts through publications, and dinner meetings; interlocking directorates and officers; and price leadership, governmental regulation, or other miscellaneous means.

> The Government is involved in economic activity for many different reasons . . . it must facilitate competition and improve the efficiency of markets; it must impose detailed regulations where the market does not offer sufficient safeguards to consumers' interests because of inevitable monopolistic conditions.[16]

These governmental safeguards, such as the Sherman Antitrust Act and the Clayton Act, are implemented by several permanent commissions created by Congress.

**Federal Trade Commission.** The Federal Trade Commission (FTC) was created in 1914, and its powers have been enlarged by subsequent acts of Congress. At present the functions of the FTC include promoting "free and fair" competition in interstate trade by preventing price-fixing agreements, boycotts, combinations in restraint of trade, and unfair or deceptive acts, including false advertising, price discrimination, and so on; safeguarding the life and health of the public by preventing the dissemination of false advertisements of drugs, cosmetics, and food; and making available factual data concerning economic and business conditions as a basis for legislation and for the protection and guidance of the public. The basic function is to prevent the free-enterprise system from being "stifled by a monopoly or corrupted by unfair or deceptive trade practices." The Clayton Act (1914) was passed "to supplement existing laws against unlawful restraints and monopolies." As amended, the act makes illegal any practices that may decrease competition, including acquisition of stock and interlocking directorates. The FTC issues complaints, holds hearings, gives advisory opinions, issues regulations, and enters "cease-and-desist" orders in case of proved violations. A business firm may appeal such an order to the circuit court of appeals, which may affirm, modify, or set aside orders of the commission.[17]

---

[16] *Economic Report of the President Transmitted to the Congress February, 1970* (Washington, D.C.: U.S. Government Printing Office, 1970), p. 92.

[17] "Any individual or firm against which FTC has issued an order to cease and desist may petition a U.S. Court to review and set aside the order." (Federal Trade Commission, *Annual Report for the Year Ended June 30, 1964* [Washington, D.C.: U.S. Government Printing Office, 1965], p. 31.)

*Interstate Commerce Commission.* The Interstate Commerce Act of 1887 provided for regulation of transportation companies but gave more or less tacit admission that certain monopolistic aspects are present in this type of business. Subsequent legislation by Congress broadened the the scope and strengthened the authority of the Interstate Commerce Commission (ICC). At present, it has jurisdiction over common carriers (railroads, water, motor), express companies, sleeping-car companies, pipelines, and freight forwarders engaged in interstate commerce. The ICC regulates foreign commerce to the extent that it takes place in the United States. At the same time that the commission protects the public interest by preventing overcharging for services and so on, it must assist in developing, coordinating, and preserving a national transportation system.

The ICC has the following powers in dealing with companies coming under its jurisdiction: it may permit pooling or division of traffic, service, or earnings; it supervises the use of rolling stock and special equipment by various companies (exchange, and return); it passes on proposed consolidations, mergers, and acquisitions of control; and it requires annual reports and prescribes the forms of the accounts, records, and memorandums to be kept.

*Securities and Exchange Commission.* Under provisions of the Public Utility Holding Company Act of 1935, the Securities and Exchange Commission (SEC) "regulates interstate public-utility holding company systems engaged in the electric utility business and/or retail distribution of gas."[18] (The Federal Power Commission supervises wholesale distribution of gas between states.) Among the duties of the SEC are the responsibility for physical integration of public-utility companies and related functional properties and the elimination of unnecessary holding companies (see Chapter 23). The result has been that the SEC has been responsible for the merger of many operating companies into 20 holding-company systems registered under the act as of year-end 1975.[19] The SEC has been active not only in promoting mergers and holding-company combinations but also in destroying them.

*Federal Power Commission.* The Federal Power Commission (FPC) was created in 1920, but its present form of organization dates primarily from June 1930. The commission is responsible for licensing hydroelectric projects on government lands (excluding power projects in national parks or national monuments) and on navigable waters of the United States. The commission has jurisdiction over the transmission and sale at wholesale of electric energy in interstate commerce and public utilities

---

[18] Securities and Exchange Commission, *42nd Annual Report, for the Fiscal Year Ended June 30, 1976* (Washington, D.C.: U.S. Government Printing Office, 1977), p. 145.

[19] Ibid., p. 145.

engaged therein (Title II of the Public Utility Act of August 26, 1935) and the transportation and sale of natural gas in interstate commerce for resale and natural gas companies engaged therein (Natural Gas Act of June 21, 1938, as subsequently amended.[20]

The FPC prescribes and enforces a system of accounts to be maintained by companies under its jurisdiction and passes on the issuance of securities and the transfer of assets by these companies. In arriving at rates or charges for electric energy sold at wholesale in interstate commerce and for natural gas sold by companies under its jurisdiction, the commission cooperates closely with state regulatory agencies.

*Federal Communications Commission.* The Federal Communications Commission (FCC) was provided for by the Communications Act of 1934 and the commission now administers that act as amended. Its jurisdiction pertains to wire, radio, and television companies that operate in interstate and foreign communication. Charges and practices are subject to review by the commission, which is authorized to issue licenses, classify radio and television stations, prescribe the nature of their services, assign frequencies, and make regulations to carry out the purposes of the act. The FCC may issue and revoke or modify licenses; the assignment or transfer of control of licenses is prohibited except upon the written consent of the commission.

**Summary**

A business firm's optimum size is influenced by social, technological, managerial, distributional, and financial factors, as well as the profitability of processing by-products. To ignore these factors may result in the failure of the business concern. Because these factors—as well as those of public demand and general prices—are subject to change, the problem is a continuing one. To achieve or maintain its optimum size, a business firm may find it necessary to expand either through external or internal growth.

External growth results from acquisitions of assets by means of merger, consolidation, or combination with other business units by use of the lease, holding company, or some other device. Internal growth results from the application of retained earnings or of funds raised from outside sources. The expansion of a business firm may take any one of the following directions: horizontal, vertical, or conglomerate—or it may involve a combination of these.

---

[20] The Commission's powers have been enlarged by the Flood Control Acts of 1938 and the River and Harbor Acts of 1945 and subsequent years and other acts, including the Tennessee Valley Authority Acts, Bonneville Project Act, and Fort Peck Project Act. See also the latest edition of the *United States Government Organization Manual* (Washington, D.C.: U.S. Government Printing Office).

The forms of business transfers and the methods used to effect them have been influenced by public policy as reflected in statutes such as the Interstate Commerce Act of 1887, the Sherman Antitrust Act of 1890, and the Clayton Act of 1914. In the industrial field, public policy has stressed the preservation of competition; but, as evidenced by legislative action, there has been a lack of consistency in public policy with the result that, in some instances, competition has decreased as the result of legislative action. Public policy as to the public-utility, railroad, and airline industries has been directed toward providing regulation rather than preserving competition, and the Federal Trade Commission and the Interstate Commerce Commission were created to protect the public by preventing abuses that could stem from the monopolistic aspects of the "public necessity" companies under their jurisdictions.

## QUESTIONS

1. "The normal expectation of a typical business firm is growth." Businesses cannot grow indefinitely. What are some of the factors that limit rate of growth and final size?
2. List possible advantages for internal over external expansion. Do the same for external over internal expansion.
3. What criteria should one examine to determine whether optimum size has been obtained?
4. Through diversification a corporation reduces the chance of loss inherent in having only one product line. That is, there is a lower probability of several different products having a sales slump simultaneously. Doesn't diversification also reduce the probability of extraordinarily high rates of return?
5. In a merger between two companies, must both companies be issued new stock certificates? In a consolidation?
6. In 1960 several large electrical-equipment manufacturers were convicted of price fixing. As a result these manufacturers were sued by their customers for amounts up to three times the damages incurred through price fixing. Why should the law allow for penalities greater than the original loss?
7. The Robinson-Patman Act permits manufacturers to charge one customer more than another only if the price differentials can be attributed to higher costs. How might a supplier justify a low price for a consolidated firm consisting of three companies now paying relatively high prices for raw materials?
8. In explaining sales of closely held companies, the tax structure has had an influence because of the impact of estate taxes and the lower tax on capital gains. Could the same results be achieved if all or part of the owners' shares were distributed publicly?
9. "The antimonopoly movement has been directed toward preserving competition in industrial fields; but, as evidenced by legislative action, there has been a lack of consistency in public policy." Justify this statement.

## PROBLEM

1. Use Moody's Industrial Manual for the years 1972 and 1976 to analyze whether General Electric, Dow Chemical, and Gulf and Western Industries grew externally or internally.

# 22

# Business Combinations

External growth of business corporations may be achieved through various legal means, such as purchase, lease, holding company, voting trust, consolidation, and merger, as well as through cooperative efforts by means of trade associations, community of interest, voluntary chains, and jointly owned facilities. The number of major mergers and assets acquired reached a peak in 1968 (1,829 mergers).[1] Since the peak in 1968 the numbers of mergers has declined; in 1975 there were 859 mergers and acquisitions. Practically every major corporation has been involved in one or more mergers since 1950.

In this chapter the subject of business combinations is dealt with under the headings of promotion, forms of combination, influence of payment procedure, and dissenting stockholders and creditors.

**Promotion**

The transfer of ownership of corporations and business combinations discussed in the preceding chapter may be the result of the efforts of either professional promoters or investment bankers. Although such promotions are rarely the primary activity of an investment banking firm, the latter is equipped to perform such functions more efficiently than an independent professional promoter or any other financial institution.

The suggestion for the acquisition of a company may come from an accounting firm such as Peat, Marwick, Mitchell & Company or Arthur

---

[1] A merger is defined as "major" if the consideration paid is at least $700,000 in cash, notes, or securities. ("Mergers on Parades," *Mergers and Acquisitions*, vol. 8, no. 1 [Spring 1973], pp. 80–81.)

Andersen & Company; a commercial bank such as the First National City Bank of New York or the Morgan Guaranty Bank and Trust Company of New York; or a public relations man, a management consultant, a manufacturing or distributing firm that helped organize and finance a particular firm in order to promote its products, or an investment banking firm. For their services, merger brokers collect fees that vary from 1 percent of the purchase price on large deals to 3 percent on small ones.

Investment banking houses, because of their broad experience and close contacts with many different business firms, are in a position to facilitate the acquisitions, mergers, and combinations of business corporations. A large investment house will have 50 or more directors on corporations' boards of directors, will act in an advisory capacity and raise capital for 100 or more large corporations, and will have contacts with hundreds of other business firms. The major investment houses keep one list of corporations that wish to diversify their products by purchasing other business firms or by merging with them and another list of firms that meet the specifications of the first group. This knowledge, together with their facilities, makes it possible for the investment houses to assist in bringing about these combinations and to handle the financial details resulting from such mergers and acquisitions. In other cases, an investment banker may search out business firms and promote a merger by bringing the parties together, helping with the negotiations, giving advice as to the details of financing, and handling the sale of the securities to the public.

The person or firm that negotiates a merger or combination is seldom the one who operates the corporation after it has been formed; hence, the successful promotion of a merger does not ensure the success of the newly created corporation. Unless management gives sufficient attention to the justification of the acquisition of new operating facilities and their incorporation into current activities of the firm, a merger is likely to be doomed to failure. The most successful combinations are those wherein management has set up sound operating objectives for acquired firms and provided the leadership necessary to formulate policies as to budgeting, compensation, financial control, personnel, and other corporate matters. Since 1950 the larger acquisitions typically have been of the conglomerate type. The management of Textron, Inc., has combined a large number of small companies whose operations were unrelated by merchandising or production procedures. Although many other corporations have been involved in conglomerate mergers, few have gone as far as Textron. Gulf and Western Industries (mentioned in the previous chapter) is another prime example of a conglomerate.

When two or more existing corporations are to be combined, a major problem of the promoter is to select the form of combination. In making a choice, consideration must be given to the ease of arrangement and financing, the degree to which managerial control will be jeopardized, flexibility of organization, permanence, and taxation.[2] Compromise will be necessary because no combination is likely to be satisfactory on all counts to all parties.

## Forms of Combination

The types of combinations considered in this section include the lease arrangement, holding company, voting trust, and consolidation or merger.

*Lease Arrangement.* Of the different types of combinations, the least expensive to organize is one where a company leases the assets of a second company in order to use them. The lease arrangement is also the least disturbing to the absorbing company and the least damaging to the existing tax structure. No cash may be needed to acquire additional facilities, and negotiations are reduced to a minimum because only the consent of stockholders of the leased company is required. The intercorporate lease usually includes all the leased corporation's property including real estate and working capital. It is not uncommon for the leasing (lessee) company to operate the leased property through a subsidiary.

The terms of a lease arrangement may permit the leasing company (lessee) to assume the corporate powers of the firm whose assets are leased, leaving the latter company with little more than a corporate shell. However, the firm whose assets are leased will retain its corporate identity; therefore, a stock transfer book will be maintained. The leased firm will receive lease payments and distribute them, after expenses, to its stockholders, who will continue to hold annual meetings and elect a board of directors.

The chief disadvantages of the lease type of combination are that (1) it is not permanent, being limited to a number of years; (2) it may result in high fixed charges that may adversely affect the leasing firm's (lessee's) credit; (3) property acquired through a lease may not be used as security for mortgage notes or bonds; and (4) the tax situation would be unfavorable because two corporate structures are involved.

Little use has been made of the lease as a devise for intercorporate combinations, except for railroads, mining companies, and infrequently department stores. The existence of high corporate income taxes has been an important factor in the termination of many leases and the ultimate merger of the companies.

---

[2] Under the Premerger Notification Program of the Federal Trade Commission, all corporations subject to FTC jurisdiction and having total assets of $250 million or more are required to file a special report whenever an acquisition of a firm with $10 million or more in total assets is made. (*Annual Report of the Federal Trade Commission, 1971*, p. 31.) After mid-1978 firms having total assets of $100 million or more are required to file a special report whenever an acquisition of a firm with at least $10 million in assets is proposed. Companies may not complete the transaction until 30 days after filing the report. (*Wall Street Journal*, February 15, 1978, p. 6.)

484    Part V    Expansion and Growth

*Holding Company.* The holding-company device, discussed more fully in the next chapter, leaves intact the existing corporate forms of organization.³ The holding-company method of building corporate systems has the advantage of being more flexible than the lease method because the stock of subsidiaries may be sold at any time. However, selling may obligate the holding company to pay a large capital gains tax. Stock of a potential subsidiary corporation may be purchased in the open market; therefore, no stockholder approval is needed. It is only when shareholders of acquired companies are asked to exchange their stock for the stock of the holding company that consent is necessary. In some industries, the approval of government regulatory agencies is necessary for an operating company to be absorbed by a holding company.⁴ The holding-company device of creating a corporate system has the same tax disadvantage as the lease method because two corporate structures are involved. Dividends declared by a subsidiary are taxable to the holding company. However, as noted in Chapter 2, corporations are allowed a deduction of 85 percent of all dividend income earned from domestic corporations if a consolidated return is not filed.

*Voting Trust.* Prior to the wide use of the holding-company method of obtaining control of other corporations, promoters used the trust device. Shareholders of small companies were persuaded to leave their shares in trust with a group of trustees in exchange for trust certificates. Thereby the trustees were empowered to exercise the rights of the owners of the corporation, such as electing directors who operated the company as directed by the trustees. The original Standard Oil trust was of this type, until the Ohio courts declared this arrangement to be against the public interest because it was an illegal grant of authority by the Standard Oil Company of Ohio to the Standard Oil trustees. Later, this trust was reorganized using the holding-company device. However, because voting trusts are contractual in nature, many state governments have made no provisions for them.

In general, state and federal courts sanction voting trusts except when

---

³ Subsidiaries of Norton Simon include the following: Canada Dry Corp., Glass Container Corp., Halson Enterprises Corp., Hunt-Wesson Food Corp., Max Factor Co., McCall Corp., McCall Pattern Co., Norton Simon Communications Inc., Somerset Importers, Ltd., Somerset Wine Co., Southern Cotton Oil Co., Inc., Southern Shell Fish Co., Inc., United Can Co., Wakefield Seafoods, Inc., *Moody's Industrial Manual,* 1976, p. 2302.

⁴ For example, Chemical New York Corp., New York, a bank holding company, applied for approval to acquire voting shares of CNA Nuclear Leasing, Inc., Boston, Mass., a company that is engaged in full-payout leasing of personal property and equipment. "The Board has determined that the public interest benefits that the Board is required to consider under . . . (the Bank Holding Company Act) do not outweigh the possible adverse effects. Accordingly, the application is hereby denied." (*Federal Reserve Bulletin,* vol. 59, no. 9 [September 1973], pp. 698–700.)

*Consolidation or Merger.* The current trend in business combinations is for one company to be formed rather than maintaining several legal corporate entities. In this way the single remaining company is the only taxpayer; and, when a sale of a firm can be avoided by an exchange of stock, no capital-gains or transfer tax will be involved. The capital-gains tax will be deferred until each owner of the stock disposes of it. The cost basis of the stock is still the price at which the owner acquired it. Because two sets of stockholders must be satisfied to complete such a consolidation or merger, it is more difficult to organize than some other forms of combination; however, when completed, managerial control is centralized and continuity is assured.

When a plan for a merger or consolidation is acceptable to all stockholders, the amount of funds needed to bring the combination into existence will be limited to "behind the scenes" promotion expenses and legal costs. However, if some shareholders dissent from the merger, as they have a right to do, cash may be needed to meet their claims. If a settlement is not reached out of court, either the dissenting stockholders or the corporation may file a petition in the appropriate court asking for a finding and determination of the fair value of such shares by an appraiser appointed by the court. (The procedure is discussed later in this chapter.)

When a merger is effected through an exchange of stock, the capital-gains tax is avoided and, for tax purposes, the absorbing company may report acquired assets at the current price. When stock of a company to be merged is acquired in the capital market, rumors of the pending merger tend to inflate the market price and make acquisition of the company unduly expensive. The anticipated effect of a merger is improvement in operating efficiency through property consolidation, combined staff, and other savings that will permit larger and more stable earnings, more cash dividends, and a higher market price for the stock. Irrespective of the origin of the idea of combining with a second company and the procedure followed, the most difficult problems are those associated with the valuation of the acquired company's assets. If the combination is to be effected through an exchange of stock, the acquiring company must be appraised as well as the company to be acquired, which magnifies the problems.

## Influence of Payment Procedure

A public notice of a combination usually reveals the price in the case of an acquisition or the exchange ratio of shares in the case of a merger or a consolidation, but very little of what goes on behind the scenes prior to a combination is revealed. Management is generally more informative in placing merger plans before the stockholders for approval, but, usually, management emphasizes expected advantages to the company and details as to changes in the charter and bylaws that accompany the proposed merger.

The price at which a business firm is acquired may be affected by the method of payment. As an illustration, if a buyer's stock that is selling at a high price, such as 30 times earnings, is to be used to purchase the firm, the buyer may be willing to pay a higher price than he would be willing to pay if cash were to be used. This attitude can be explained by the fact that relatively fewer shares will have to be given to complete an acquisition. Thus, the impact on future earnings will be less than if the price-earnings ratio were lower. In the opposite case, if the buyer's stock is selling at a low price-earnings ratio, the buyer would prefer to use cash in acquiring the firm. If the stock of both firms is selling at the same price-earnings ratio, the mode of payment would tend to have no effect on the price.

If a company with a low price-earnings ratio is acquired by one with a high price-earnings ratio, the seller's earnings per share will be diluted. Assume that Company A is combining with Company B to form a new company, C, and that Company A's price-earnings ratio is 15:1 and its stock is selling at $120 per share; and Company B's price-earnings ratio is 8:1 and its stock is selling at $40 per share. The exchange ratio would be one share of Company A stock ($120) for three shares of Company B stock ($40). To facilitate the exchange of stock, Company A's stock is split three for one with the result that Company C will have 25,000 shares ($5000 \times 3 + 10,000$). The relationships and amount of dilution may be illustrated as follows:

|  | Company A | Company B | Company C |
|---|---|---|---|
| Total earnings | $40,000 | $50,000 | $90,000 |
| Number of shares | 5,000* | 10,000 | 25,000 |
| Earnings per share | $8 | $5 | $3.60 |
| Market value per share | $120 | $40 | n.a. |
| Price-earnings ratio | 15:1 | 8:1 | n.a. |

* Before the stock split.

New Company C would have earnings of $90,000, the number of shares would be increased to 25,000, and the new shares would earn $3.60 per share, as compared with $2.67 (one third of $8) for Company A shareholders and $5 for Company B shareholders. Company A shareholders will have an increase in earnings per share of $2.80 ($3.60 × 3 = $10.80) and Company B shareholders will have a decrease of $1.40 per share ($5 − $3.60). The appreciation of Company A stock is $14,000 (5,000 × $2.80) and the dilution of Company B stock is $14,000 (10,000 × $1.40). The earnings per share, at the time of the merger and after Company A stock had been split, would be $2.67 per share ($8 ÷ 3) and that of Company B would be $5 per share.

In the above case, the question may be asked: Why would management of Company B merge, knowing there would be a dilution in per share earnings? The answer to this question is the key to the reasons for merging. The primary reason is that, in the long run, the expected earnings of the new company formed by the merger will be greater than the total earnings of the two companies if they had not merged. Presumably, an increase in earnings is expected to result from the merging of costs of management, sales forces, advertising, and transportation.

If the products of one company supplement those of the other company, an increase in sales may result. In addition, the acquisition may result in assurance of supplies of raw materials for which there is an increased demand and a dwindling supply.

Figure 22-1 assumes that Company B's earnings were $5.00 per share and not expected to grow, thus explaining the market's assigning it an 8-to-1 price-earnings ratio. Company A's earnings are assumed to be growing, thereby justifying a higher price-earnings ratio of 15 to 1. It is expected that the earnings of Company C will increase through the years ahead. Just how much cannot be determined at the time of the merger, but if there are operating economies such an expectation should be war-

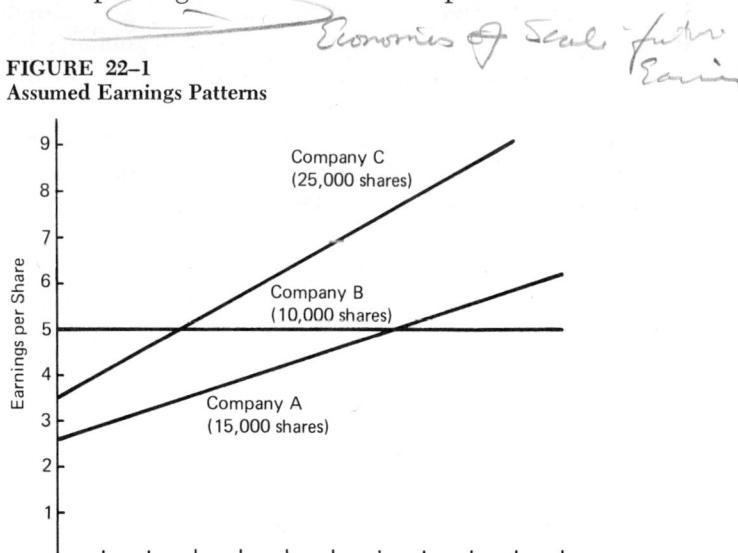

FIGURE 22-1
Assumed Earnings Patterns

ranted. The market will recognize the expected growth in earnings and thereby assign the firm a price-earnings ratio more like former Company A's than Company B's. The expectation of both higher earnings and market prices in the future will more than offset the short-run dilution of earnings of Company B.

If the management of Company B should stop negotiations, the management of Company A may purchase stock of Company B in the open market. Barring any change in the market price of the stock, the result would be the same as if negotiations had not been called off. However, it is unlikely that the price of the stock would remain at $40 per share under these conditions. It may be possible for the managements of the two companies to expedite the sale by offering the seller convertible preferred stock or convertible debentures. The advantages offered the seller would be a higher quality security, stable return, and possible appreciation in value of common stock. Gradual conversion does not noticeably affect earnings or the book value per share of common stock; however, by offering the conversion privilege, the company is merely postponing issuance of common stock and its dilution.

In many instances it is not possible to get market quotations for a small firm that is to be merged. In these cases, the managements must agree on some method of determining its value. The methods employed are varied; valuations may stress book value, expert's appraisals based on the concept of replacement cost new minus depreciation, liquidation value, or capitalization of earnings, to name a few of the more common techniques. Table 22–1 shows a relatively small firm having an uninterrupted, rapidly growing earnings trend. The managements of the firms involved in the merger have agreed to weigh the more recent earnings more heavily than in the earlier years. A five-year earnings period is to be considered with a weight factor of 1 to 5, beginning with the earliest year. The weighted average earnings are then to be capitalized at 10 percent. It should be emphasized that this procedure was agreed upon by both parties, and therefore was a vital part of the entire negotiation process. Other methods could have been used, for example, market value of assets, as long as both parties agreed to the terms.

Table 22–1 was compiled from the firm's income statements for five years beginning with 1974.

The unweighted average earnings for the period 1974–1978 are $100,000. In contrast the weighted earnings are $111,667. If these earnings are capitalized at 10 percent, the firm's value will be estimated to be $1,000,000 and $1,116,670 for the unweighted and weighted earnings, respectively. By using the weighting system shown in Table 22–1, earnings of the most recent years are recognized as being more important than those of the earlier years. If, for example, the earnings pattern is trendless, the results would not differ. Finally, if the firm's earnings are falling, the

**TABLE 22-1**
Valuation of a Firm Based Upon a 10 Percent Capitalization of Weighted Average Earnings

| Year | Net Earnings | Weight Factor | Weighted Average Earnings |
|---|---|---|---|
| 1974 | $65,000 | 1 | $ 65,000 |
| 1975 | 80,000 | 2 | 160,000 |
| 1976 | 105,000 | 3 | 315,000 |
| 1977 | 115,000 | 4 | 460,000 |
| 1978 | 135,000 | 5 | 675,000 |
| Total | $500,000 | 15 | $1,675,000 |
| Average | $100,000 | | $ 111,667 |

Valuation: (1) Unweighted $100,000 ÷ 10% = $1,000,000
(2) Weighted $111,667 ÷ 10% = $1,116,670

present weighting system would give a lesser capitalized value to the firm than if unweighted average earnings are used.

## Dissenting Stockholders and Creditors

*Procedure.* After negotiators have completed their work, a formal agreement is drawn that contains the terms of the merger or consolidation. The next step is the approval of each company's board of directors, which is normally little more than routine because the members are usually informed as to the progress of negotiations. Their approval is indicated in two resolutions: one containing the terms of the merger or consolidation and the second directing that the merger or consolidation plan be submitted to the stockholders for their approval.

The plan submitted to the stockholders contains the names of the corporations in the proposed merger or consolidation; name of the surviving or new corporation; terms and conditions of the proposed merger or consolidation; appropriate change in the articles of incorporation of the surviving corporation or complete charter provisions for the new corporation; method and basis for converting the shares of each corporation into shares, other securities, or obligations of the surviving (merged firm only) or new corporation; and any other provisions with respect to the proposed merger or consolidation that are deemed desirable or necessary.

The stockholders vote for or against the consolidation at a regular or special meeting called by the directors for this purpose. They may vote in person or by proxy and the required legal percentage must approve before management can proceed with the combination plan. If the stockholders of any affected company fail to approve of the plan by the required percentage, the plan may be abandoned temporarily or permanently, or the negotiators may try to meet the objections of the disapproving stockholders.

If the consolidation plan is approved by each corporation's stockholders, the next step is to secure the signature of the presidents and secretaries of the corporations on the agreement, which is filed with the appropriate official of the state wherein the new company is being chartered. When approved, the state official, usually the secretary of state, issues the necessary certificate and thus brings to an end the corporate existence of all participants. If one is a foreign corporation, the required official of the foreign state must be notified in the manner prescribed in the state law (otherwise, it may be required to pay state taxes). When the certificate of organization is approved, it becomes the charter of the new company. The new board of directors is elected immediately and the new corporation takes title to the property of the absorbed corporations and assumes responsibility for their debts and other obligations. According to the terms of the agreement, new stock is distributed among the stockholders in exchange for their old shares, and the next and final step is to care for dissenting stockholders, who are protected by state law.

**Dissenting Stockholders.** In practically every proposed merger or consolidation, some stockholders either vote against the plan or refrain from voting when called upon to approve a combination plan; and, in addition, they may file objection to it in the manner prescribed by state laws.[5] The Texas law specifies that the objection must be filed before or at the regular or special meeting of shareholders. The objection form contains the dissenting shareholders' names and addresses so they may be notified if the combination is approved. If approved, the dissenters make a written demand on the new or remaining firm for payment of a fair value for their shares as of the date the shareholders voted in favor of the combination "excluding any appreciation or depreciation in anticipation" of the change. The demand must state the number and class of shares owned and an estimate of their fair value. If a dissenting shareholder fails to file his demand within the first ten days, he must accept the settlement offered by the corporation.

Within the ten-day period, management of the new corporation will notify the dissenting shareholder that it (1) accepts his "fair value estimate" and will pay him if he will surrender his stock certificates duly endorsed, or (2) tenders management's estimate of a "fair value" and an offer to pay that amount per share within 30 days if he agrees to accept. If this value is accepted and paid, the dissenting stockholder ceases to

---

[5] Texas law, which is similar to the Model Business Corporation Act, permits a shareholder to dissent from (1) any amendment that changes the corporate purpose, (2) any plan of merger or consolidation, and (3) unless "expressly provided" in the charter, any sale, lease, exchange, mortgage, or pledge of all, or substantially all, assets of the corporation without the required votes of approval (two thirds).

have any ownership interest in the company. The rights of the remaining dissenting shareholders, with whom no agreement has been reached, will be determined by the courts.[6]

A petition may be filed by the corporation or dissenting stockholders asking for the determination of fair value of the shares by an appraiser appointed by the court. All of the shareholders notified, as well as the corporation, are bound by the final decision of the court (that is, all who have joined in the petition and have been properly notified).

During the interim between filing the dissent and determination of the value of shares, a stockholder has all the rights and privileges inherent in stock ownership, including cash dividends which are added to the claims of the stockholders. A time limit is placed on the above procedures so that the settlement of claims will not be unduly delayed.

**Rights of Creditors.** Creditors are not permitted to participate in any merger or consolidation, provided the law permitted the combination at the time they became creditors, unless there is fraud or illegal or unfair action. In a case of fraud or illegal or unfair action, creditors may bring legal action against the corporation to stop the combination. However, proposed legal action taken because they do not want to be creditors of a second company is not permissible if they knew their corporation had a right to merge or consolidate when they became creditors.

Secured creditors retain the same liens on assets they had before a merger; thus, they follow the asset of their merged company into the consolidated corporation. The surviving corporation assumes the obligations, penalties, and liabilities of the former corporations and no claims against them are changed, which includes any civil or criminal action in process or pending. However, the after-acquired property clause contained in a mortgage indenture issued by one of the merged companies is not applicable to the new company.

## Summary

The types of combinations discussed in this chapter included the leasing arrangement, holding company, voting trust, and consolidation or merger. In business combinations the problem of valuation is always present. When the firms participating in a merger or consolidation agree upon the respective valuations, the transfer may be effected by negotiating an exchange of securities, or a purchase of assets or stock.

---

[6] Arizona law treats the problem of dissenting shareholders somewhat differently. It provides that:
1. At least two thirds of the stock must vote for the merger.
2. Dissenting stockholders shall be paid in cash the fair value of their stock.
3. Dissenting stockholders must give written notice to the president, secretary, or statutory agent of the corporation not later than two days after the consolidation meeting, and must file an action to fix the value of the shares in the appropriate superior court within 30 days after the meeting.

By using one or more of the generally accepted valuation methods, it may be possible to arrive at a mutually agreeable arrangement for converting the shares of each corporation into shares of the surviving or new corporation. This requires an evaluation of each class of shares to ensure equitable treatment of all shareholders. In some cases, negotiations for mergers or consolidations have lasted for years; in other cases, proposed transfers have never been completed, either because the valuation problem could not be solved to the satisfaction of a sufficient number of stockholders or because of dissension among the chief executives of participating companies (they could not all hold equivalent positions in the new company as there would be only one presidency and one chairmanship of the board of directors to be filled).

The complexity of the problem of relative valuation grows as the number of combined corporations increases. The assets and earning power of a corporation will be the same irrespective of the number of shares distributed, so each shareholder is interested in getting his proportionate share. In order to obtain the necessary affirmative votes, the promoter must convince the required number of shareholders in each group that they are receiving their proportionate shares and that all participants will benefit from the anticipated high earnings that will follow as a result of the merger or consolidation.

If market quotations are not available or are not indicative of the value of each corporation, other means of valuation must be employed. These may include, among others, book value of assets, appraisals by experts, capitalization of net income, or liquidation value. Most state governments provide procedures to protect dissenting stockholders from being forced to take an unfair price for their stock. Maintenance of shareholders' rights during the interim period, and a time limit on events leading to a settlement so that no losses will result from delays, are also generally assured.

## QUESTIONS

1. Among the different legal forms of combinations used by promoters, which ones do not decrease the number of corporations? Which ones do decrease the number of corporations? Explain your answer.

2. What effect does the rate of interest used in capitalization of earnings have on a company's value? Illustrate. How should the earnings to be capitalized be estimated?

3. Arthur Stone Dewing has stated that one of the motives that leads men to expand business enterprises is ambition. That is, the bigger the business, the bigger the person. As president of a small corporation about to be absorbed by a large corporation, how would you view your impending reduction in corporate rank?

4. The rumors of a merger often causes the market price of a company's stock

to rise. Why? Does a merger necessarily increase the value of both companies' stock? Might a merger rumor cause a lower stock price?

5. A corporation is considering the purchase of another corporation's stock for cash. What is the income tax consequence for the selling stockholders?

6. In a prospective merger agreement Corporation A will exchange its shares for Corporation B's stock. What is the income-tax effect on Corporation B's stockholders?

7. A conglomerate firm is considering the acquisition of another corporation with a tax-loss carry-forward. Why is the firm an attractive acquisition?

8. What effect will an increase in the price-earnings ratio have on the buying company's strategy in combinations?

9. What recourse is available to dissenting stockholders if they disapprove of the consolidation plan?

## PROBLEMS

1. The National Corporation is examining the possibility of acquiring the Local Company, whose average yearly income for the past four years has been $50,000. The Local Company has a price-earnings ratio of 10 and earnings have been running about $3 per share. Given the above information, what valuation should the National Corporation place on the Local Company?

2. The Super Machine Company is contemplating the acquisition of either Company X or Company Y. Given the following past earnings trend for the two companies, which would be the best acquisition prospect (earnings in thousands)?

|      | X    | Y    |
|------|------|------|
| 1975 | $50  | $40  |
| 1976 | 40   | 50   |
| 1977 | 80   | 60   |
| 1978 | 70   | 70   |
| 1979 | 60   | 80   |

If the Super Machine Company capitalized weighted average earnings at 14 percent, what would be the valuation of each company?

3. The Sota Corporation is examining the information available on the Diamond Box Corporation in order to determine whether it might be a merger partner.

|                                                  | Sota    | Diamond Box |
|--------------------------------------------------|---------|-------------|
| Total earnings                                   | $20,000 | $8,000      |
| Number of shares outstanding (common stock)      | 10,000  | 8,000       |
| Earnings per share                               | $2      | $1          |
| Market price                                     | $60     | $15         |
| Price-earnings ratio                             | 30:1    | 15:1        |

Assuming that the two companies decide to effect a straight merger, what will be the earnings per share and market price of the new corporation? The Sota shareholders will receive one new share for each of their old shares. The Diamond Box stockholders will receive one new share for each four shares of Diamond Box held. (Assume that the price-earnings ratio for the new company is expected to drop to 25:1.) How do you feel the stockholders of *both* companies might react?

4. The Typewriter Corporation is interested in acquiring the Dictating Corporation. The earnings of the Dictating Corporation for the last five years were (in thousands):

|      |       |
|------|-------|
| 1975 | $500  |
| 1976 | 480   |
| 1977 | 420   |
| 1978 | 450   |
| 1979 | 400   |

The Typewriter Corporation is interested in placing a valuation on the Dictating Corporation. If the Typewriter Corporation agrees to capitalize the weighted average earnings at 15 percent, how much is the Dictating Corporation worth? If you were a stockholder of the Dictating Corporation would you prefer to use the unweighted average earnings capitalized at 15 percent? (Use the methods illustrated in the text.)

# 23

# Control of Corporations by Other Corporations

A corporation may gain control of another corporation by purchasing shares of voting stock and voting such shares through its representatives, as prescribed by the bylaws or the board of directors. The power to acquire and to vote shares in the name of a corporation has permitted control of corporate assets with a relatively small investment. A corporation may acquire the assets of a second company without acquiring the corporate entity, thereby leaving the old company as a going concern. Sometimes the assets of a second corporation are acquired under a lease arrangement without destroying the entity of the lessee. The topics dealt with in this chapter include corporate investments in securities of other corporations, types of holding companies, consolidated financial statements, advantages and disadvantages of holding companies, and regulation of public-utility companies.

### Corporate Investments in Securities

A corporation's cash in excess of its current needs may be invested to secure income; because of their high quality and marketability, short-term government obligations are favored for such investments. However, when investments in short-term securities are adequate to cover all anticipated needs for near-cash, a corporation may choose to invest the remainder in securities of other corporations. Presumably, a corporation making such investments is able to justify the retention of earnings for expansion purposes, otherwise it may be subject to penalties under Section 531–536 (old Section 102) of the Federal Revenue Act dealing with the accumulated earnings tax. This special tax may be imposed if assets are accumulated that do not relate to the raison d'etre of the firm. A second question that may be raised in connection with a corporation's investments in the securities of other corporations pertains to the effect of such stock ownership on the relationship between the two corporations.

**Question of Legality.** At one time the legality of corporate ownership of stock of another corporation was questioned on the ground that it was foreign to the purpose for which the corporation was created. If a corporation held stock of a second corporation, it was under implied powers—the means of accomplishing the purpose for which the corporation was formed. As an illustration, in order for a corporation to protect its interest, it was considered entirely reasonable and necessary to take title to stock that had been pledged as security for a debt, provided it had no intention of keeping the stock as a permanent investment or controlling the other corporation; under different circumstances, it was considered legal for one corporation to accept stock of another corporation in payment for property.

Today, however, the general powers of business corporations, as provided for in statutes, customarily include the right to acquire and otherwise deal in shares or obligations of other domestic and foreign corporations. (There are many corporations, such as investment companies, that have been formed for no other purpose). Holding companies are customarily organized to obtain control of other corporations through ownership of their voting stock. The same results may be obtained by use of voting trusts, as demonstrated by their use toward the end of the last century when voting trusts gained control over competing companies in the petroleum, sugar, and other industries.

Prior to 1888, some corporations were given the power to own stock of other corporations by special acts of state legislatures. In 1868, the Pennsylvania legislature chartered a corporation that was organized for the specific purpose of owning shares of other corporations. Twenty years later, the New Jersey legislature enacted a law permitting corporations to own shares in other corporations. This pioneer statute has been amended and broadened; subsequently, its provisions pertaining to stock ownership have been adopted by other states.

The New Jersey statute appeared at the time "trusts" were under attack in the courts, and many of these so-called trusts were reorganized as New Jersey corporations, with the new corporations acquiring the stock formerly held by the trustees. In exchange for their trust certificates, the former beneficiaries of the voting trusts received shares in the new corporations organized as holding companies. The shift from the use of a voting trust to a holding-company control device met the legal objection that voting trusts were illegal because they deprived stockholders of their voting rights.[1] However, the combination resulting from a holding com-

---

[1] Today, the voting trust is provided for in some business-corporation acts and it is considered legal when not used in restraint of trade. It is most frequently used to

pany may be challenged if the results are not in the public interest (if it reduces competition, restrains trade, or creates a monopoly).

One of the more important aspects of the "merger" movement of 1920–31 was the extensive use of the holding-company device in the public-utility field and a lesser extent in other industries. By 1930, ten groups of holding companies controlled about three-fourths of the nation's electric-light and power industry. Promoters were able, with relatively small investments, to control vast networks of companies by owning small amounts of voting stock and by pyramiding holding companies (layers of three or more above operating companies were not unusual). During the depression, dividends of operating companies were greatly reduced or eliminated and the funds needed to pay the charges on the various securities of holding companies shrank or disappeared. Even before the federal government made provisions for reorganization of the light and power industry, many of the systems were reorganized and some had disappeared.

A holding company is usually organized as a corporation (but it may be a business trust or joint-stock company) that controls one or more corporations through stock ownership. Sometimes a corporation may control a second corporation by owning only a small percentage of its stock; but control can be assured only by ownership of 50 percent plus one share of the voting stock. However, as defined in the Public Utility Holding Company Act, "any company which directly or indirectly owns, controls, or holds with power to vote, 10 percentum or more of the outstanding voting securities of a public-utility company" is a holding company. Investment companies customarily limit their investments in any one company to 5 percent or less of the voting stock in order to prevent being classified as holding companies and to meet the requirement contained in the Investment Company Act to qualify as a diversified company. If an investment company did not meet this provision it would lose the tax benefit granted diversified investment companies which permits them to pay out 90 percent or more of their earnings without paying corporate income taxes on the portions distributed.

***Influence on Management Policies.*** In December 1950, Congress amended the Clayton Act so that the Federal Trade Commission can rule against the acquisition by one industrial corporation of the stock of a second corporation if adverse effects on competition are expected; the Interstate Commerce Commission passes on acquisition of stock by railroad companies; and the Securities and Exchange Commission passes on acquisition of stock by public-utility holding companies.

---

retain contol of a particular company. For example, in 1952, three directors of the Hamilton Watch Company established a voting trust in which about 40 percent of the voting shares were deposited in order to prevent the Benrus Watch Company from obtaining control. The latter owned about 25 percent of the voting stock of the Hamilton Watch Company. The voting trust agreement was for ten years.

The extent to which a corporation that has invested in a second corporation may influence the latter's policies is difficult to appraise. If the investing corporation follows the typical small investor's policy of assigning proxies to management, it may avoid any outward appearance of influencing management. If the investing corporation holds stock in a corporation that is a competitor, a supplier, or a customer, it may be more difficult to prove that competition will not be adversely affected. In 1954, after having been in the court for about five years, the federal court dismissed the case brought by the Justice Department against E. I. du Pont de Nemours & Company, General Motors Corporation, United States Rubber Company, Christiana Securities Company, Delaware Realty & Investment Company, and more than 100 individuals.[2] This decision was appealed by the government to the U.S. Supreme Court for reversal of Judge LaBuy's decision, argued before the Court, and remanded to the Chicago U.S. District Court with instructions to eliminate "the effects" of the stock ownership.[3] The basic issue in the duPont case was whether General Motors stock (63 million shares, or about 23 percent of the total number of shares outstanding) was acquired for investment purposes or to give duPont a dominant position as a supplier of automobile finishes and fabrics to General Motors. The acquisition raised the question of the applicability of the law to vertical stock acquisitions as well as to already accepted horizontal acquisitions, and the majority of the Supreme Court ruled in favor of including vertical acquisitions.

The suspicion of collusion between two or more corporations because of stock ownership may be impossible to prevent even by prohibiting corporations from buying stock of other corporations. Although commercial banks' and financial institutions' investments in corporations are pro-

---

[2] Judge Walter J. LaBuy in the United States District Court in Chicago ruled that the government's complaint in the so-called General Motors suit should be dismissed because, to quote from the "Conclusion" of the opinion: "It may be that a violation of the Clayton Act can be made out in the absence of an actual restraint of trade where it is established that there is a reasonable probability that a condemned restraint will result from an acquisition of stock. The acquisition challenged by the Government—duPont's investment in General Motors—took place over thirty years ago. In those many intervening years the record discloses that no restraint of trade has resulted. . . . The Government has failed to prove conspiracy, monopolization, a restraint of trade, or any reasonable probability of a restraint, and for those reasons the Amended Complaint should be dismissed." (Cited in "Letter to the Stockholders," E. I. du Pont de Nemours & Company, Wilmington, Delaware, December 8, 1954.) This decision was reversed and sent back to the Chicago court for settlement.

[3] In compliance with the final judgment of Judge LaBuy (entered March 1, 1962 in U.S. District Court in Chicago), duPont distributed 62,551,553 shares of General Motors common stock to duPont stockholders—on July 9, 1962, 22,991,492 shares; on January 4, 1964, 16,557,983 shares; and on January 4, 1965, 23,002,678 shares. In addition, duPont management sold 447,847 shares in the market (E. I. du Pont de Nemours & Company *Annual Report 1964* [Wilmington, Delaware, 1965], p. 33). Under Public Law 87–403 (February 2, 1962), the market value of General Motors shares will be treated as a return of capital to individual stockholders on which no tax will be levied unless the value of General Motors shares exceeds the cost of the shareholder's duPont stock. If this occurs, the excess will be treated as a capital gain.

hibited or greatly limited, they influence the policies of corporations because of debtor-creditor relationships. The same suspicion of collusion could exist between business firms due to the debtor-creditor relationship established when goods are sold on credit and when loans are made. The opportunity for antisocial practices is present whenever two or more individuals, business firms, or corporations deal with one another.

Sometimes, one company invests in the common stock of a second company for defensive reasons—to prevent a competitor from assuming control and taking its business. Moves by management of one company to seek control of a second company by investing in its stock are not always approved by the first company's stockholders, and management of the second company may take legal or other action to prevent it.

**Community of Ownership.** When two or more corporations cooperate to finance a new corporation, cooperative ownership results (a situation that is being encouraged by the Small Business Administration). A corporation may be created to carry on a research project, to facilitate a buying program, to collect and disseminate information, to develop a new process or invention, or to develop mutually owned or collectively used real estate, such as terminal facilities of railroads. In some cases, the mutually owned corporation may be created to comply with some provision in a state law (such as gas-collecting and -processing corporations formed to use waste products of the petroleum industry where "flaring" in oil fields has been prohibited).

The concept of mutual ownership of one corporation by several corporations exists in reverse when one holding or operating company owns the controlling interest in several other companies. Between these two extremes, there may be an intermingling of ownership wherein operating companies may own and be owned by all the other companies in a group. If the small amount of stock a director may be required to own to qualify as a director is disregarded, theoretically, a perfect corporate community of ownership could be achieved by prorating ten percent of the common stock of each 11 corporations among the other 10 corporations in the group. Dividends on stock would be paid only to other corporations, and no noncorporate owner would receive an investment income from the common stock of any of the 11 corporations. Although such intermingling of corporate stock to exclude noncorporate owners from ownership is possible, usually a "community of interest" is one formed by a small group of persons who, through stock ownership in different corporations, elect directors and otherwise influence the policies of the corporations.

## Types of Holding Companies

At one time the classification of holding companies as "holding" and "operating-holding" companies was descriptive, but that is no longer the case. More accurately, a holding company is a managerial corporation that performs the same services for its subsidiaries as the head office of a large company performs for its divisions, stores, or other units; and an operating-holding company is an operating company that controls one or more subsidiary companies. Most large U.S. industrial corporations may be classified as operating-holding companies. Even a small bank may own subsidiary corporations, one of which may own the bank building, a second which may own and operate the safe deposit business, and a third which may operate the bank's trust business.

*Superholding Companies.* The corporate structure of a combination may consist of several layers, with a superholding company controlling holding companies that control holding companies—until, eventually, we come to the operating companies that produce the income to support the superstructure of corporations, controlling corporations, *ad extremum.* Congress inserted the "grandfather" clause in the Public Utility Holding Company Act of 1935 and thus limited the number of layers of corporate entities to three—a superholding or holding-operating company, one or more subsidiary holding or holding-operating companies, and operating companies. However, this applies to only those corporations covered by the act, whereas holding companies exist in all fields of business—public utilities, railroads, and other industries and their subdivisions.

*Financing-Holding Companies.* In its simplest form, a holding company has assets that consist of the voting stock of its subsidiaries (in amounts sufficient to ensure control), office equipment, cash, and sundry assets. Some holding companies are at the same time financing companies—financing their subsidiaries by purchasing their bonds or stock. In this case, the financing-holding company may pledge the bonds of its subsidiary for a bond issue of its own. For example, if the smaller subsidiary agrees to pay 7 percent on its bonds, the parent company might pledge them together with those of other subsidiaries for a larger bond issue bearing an interest rate of perhaps 6 or 6.5 percent. If and when a holding company acts as a financing company in this way, the result is an expansion of its assets to include more than the voting stock of its subsidiaries. The greatest change in the assets of a holding company occurs when the assets of subsidiaries are absorbed by merger or consolidation and the company becomes a holding-operating company.

When a wholly-owned subsidiary sells stock, it will be to the parent company. For instance, the New York Telephone Company may announce plans for the sale of additional stock, all of which will be purchased by the American Telephone and Telegraph Company. The funds received for the stock will be given back to the American Telephone and Telegraph Company in payment for advances made by the parent company.

*Operating-Holding Companies.* In addition to being holding companies, operating-holding companies produce goods and services that are sold to the general public. If corporation A owns all the stock of operating company B, it will be simple to obtain the approval of B for a merger of A and B. The accounting procedure would be to delete corporation B stock as an investment of corporation A and replace it with "plant, equipment, and other assets" formerly owned by the acquired corporation. Adjustment for the difference between values may be made by crediting or charging the "capital surplus" of corporation A. If there are minority stockholders, their shares may be purchased for cash or exchanged for new stock, usually at the option of the minority stockholders. If there are dissenting shareholders, their claims may, if necessary, be settled through court proceedings, as previously noted. Subsidiary corporations are being absorbed practically every day by operating-holding companies (with the general public taking little notice of the act). Many corporations, such as General Motors and United States Steel, that were organized as holding companies have become operating-holding companies with the emphasis properly placed on their operating activities.

## Consolidated Financial Statements

A factor in the decline of pure holding companies is the widespread practice of consolidating the returns of the parent and subsidiary corporations which show combined income and assets. If the parent company owns 80 percent of the voting power of all the classes of stock and at least 80 percent of the nonvoting stock of a subsidiary, it may choose to file a consolidated return for federal income tax purposes. Otherwise, the dividend paid by the subsidiary to the parent would be subject to taxation as corporate income to the parent firm. However, when there is no consolidated return for tax purposes, 85 percent of the dividends are not subject to taxation.

Customarily, a consolidated return will cover all subsidiaries, provided the business units are not dissimilar in nature; the parent company's investment is 50 percent or more (if less, the subsidiary is sometimes referred to as an affiliate); the intercompany transactions are large; and the fiscal years are similar. Special situations may justify the exclusion of the subsidiary when the situation is the opposite of those cited above, when it is located in a foreign country, or when it is in the process of being liquidated or sold.

Among the best-known operating-holding companies in the United States is the American Telephone and Telegraph Company system, which provides long-distance telephone service for its customers, controls its telephone and other subsidiary companies through stock ownership, and has investments in other companies affiliated with it (see Table 23–1). Early control of the basic patents permitted the American Telephone and Telegraph Company to attain a position of prominence in the communications industry. Local units were combined with regional ones to in-

## TABLE 23-1

### Bell System Consolidated Balance Sheet Detail
($000)

| Investment in subsidiaries consolidated—December 31, 1976 | Percent Ownership | Equity Application to AT&T Co. | Note* and Advances |
|---|---|---|---|
| New England Tel. & Tel. Co. | 86.0 | $ 1,509,606 | $ — |
| New York Tel. Co. | 100.0 | 4,415,529 | — |
| Empire City Subway Co. (Ltd.) | 100.0 | 13,755 | — |
| New Jersey Bell Tel. Co. | 100.0 | 1,598,410 | 20,000 |
| Bell Tel. Co. of Pennsylvania | 100.0 | 1,629,188 | 18,000 |
| Diamond State Tel. Co. | 100.0 | 131,835 | 1,400 |
| Chesapeake & Potomac Tel Co. | 100.0 | 297,755 | 6,300 |
| Chesapeake & Potomac Tel. Co. of Maryland | 100.0 | 804,500 | 8,800 |
| Chesapeake & Potomac Tel. Co. of Virginia | 100.0 | 836,822 | 6,900 |
| Chesapeake & Potomac Tel. Co. of West Virginia | 100.0 | 248,076 | 6,200 |
| Southern Bell Tel. & Tel. Co. | 100.0 | 3,368,800 | 10,000 |
| South Central Bell Tel. Co. | 100.0 | 2,616,981 | — |
| Ohio Bell Tel. Co. | 100.0 | 1,219,631 | 20,000 |
| Michigan Bell Tel. Co. | 100.0 | 1,465,149 | 31,500 |
| Indiana Bell Tel. Co., Inc. | 100.0 | 609,232 | 56,000* |
| Wisconsin Tel. Co. | 100.0 | 576,673 | 19,400 |
| Illinois Bell Tel. Co. | 100.0 | 1,885,732 | — |
| Northwestern Bell Tel. Co. | 100.0 | 1,512,416 | — |
| Southwestern Bell Tel. Co. | 100.0 | 4,077,164 | 138,000 |
| Mountain States Tel. & Tel. Co. | 88.6 | 1,490,514 | — |
| Malheur Home Tel. Co. | 88.6 | 1,015 | — |
| Pacific Northwest Bell Tel. Co. | 89.3 | 784,735 | 16,100 |
| Pacific Tel. & Tel. Co. & Sub. | 89.8 | 3,254,837 | — |
| Bell Tel. Co. of Nevada (wholy owned by Pacific) | | | |
| 195 Broadway Corporation | 100.0 | 238,099 | 59,335 |
| Eastern Tel. & Tel. Co. | 100.0 | 4,195 | — |
| Transoceanic Communications, Inc. | 100.0 | 6,975 | 550 |
| Transoceanic Cable Ship Co., Inc. | 100.0 | 5,197 | — |
| Transpacific Communications, Inc. | 100.0 | 15,009 | 2,000 |
| Total | | $34,617,821 | $420,485 |

| | Percent Ownership | Cost | | | Proportionate Interest in Net Assets in Excess Of Such Cost | Total |
| --- | --- | --- | --- | --- | --- | --- |
| | | Stock | Advances | Total | | |
| Other investments at equity—December 31, 1976 | | | | | | |
| Western Electric Co., Inc | 100.0 | $1,451,010 | — | $1,451,010 | $1,810,615 | $3,261,615 |
| Bell Tel. Laboratories, Inc | 50.0 | 141,000 | $11,000 | 152,000 | — | 152,000 |
| The So. New England Tel. Co. | 17.6 | 55,545 | 5,700 | 61,245 | 29,659 | 90,904 |
| Cincinnati Bell Inc. | 25.7 | 24,345 | 1,600 | 25,945 | 24,543 | 50,488 |
| The Champaign Tel. Co. | 50.0 | 557 | — | 557 | 1,194 | 1,751 |
| Cuban American Tel. & Tel. Co. | 50.0 | 163 | — | 163 | 1,412 | 1,575 |
| American Bell Inc. | 100.0 | 500 | 500 | 1,000 | 311 | 1,311 |
| American Bell Int'l, Inc. | 100.0 | 4,000 | — | 4,000 | 578 | 4,578 |
| Texas Compensation Ins. Co. | 100.0 | 150 | — | 150 | 266 | 416 |
| Southwestern Bell Tel. Co of Arkansas | 100.0 | 1 | 6 | 7 | 3 | 10 |
| Total | | $1,677,271 | $18,806 | $1,696,077 | $1,868,581 | $3,564,648 |

Source: American Telephone and Telegraph Company.

crease efficiency and permit rate stability. The AT&T system consists of the American Telephone and Telegraph Company, 26 subsidiary telephone companies, certain subsidiaries not consolidated, and an investment interest in other companies. The subsidiaries not consolidated include the Bell Telephone Laboratories, Inc., which is the research and development company (Western Electric owns the other 50-percent interest); the Western Electric Company, Inc., which is the manufacturing company for AT&T; the Southern New England Telephone Co., and Cincinnati Bell Inc., with AT&T owning only a minority interest in both of these subsidiaries. Western Electric manufactures most of the equipment and apparatus used by the consolidated and other telephone companies. Items purchased from Western Electric by telephone companies are entered to their accounts at cost to them, including the return to Western Electric on this business.

In the past, increases in telephone rates have been a relatively minor factor in the growth of earnings of the American Telephone and Telegraph Company but new markets and increases in operating efficiency have been important factors. The Bell system is one of the leaders in electronics and space research and is frequently classified as a moderate growth company. In addition to the Bell system, there are independent telephone companies in the United States served by the AT&T long-distance communications system.

As a result of a series of mergers, the United States Steel Corporation can be classified as an operating-holding company. Today, many of the properties that were operated by subsidary corporations are being operated as divisions. The United States Steel Corporation is the largest steel producer, a major coal and chemical producer, and, through a subsidiary, one of the largest cement producers in the United States.

## Advantages and Disadvantages of Holding Companies

Although there has been a tendency for large holding companies to simplify their organizations by eliminating some of their subsidiary corporations by absorption, there also has been a development in the opposite direction, wherein some operating companies have organized and operate new subsidiary corporations. The holding-company device may also be used to acquire control of an existing company that is an important supplier, customer, competitor, or firm whose products or services will complement or complete those of the acquiring corporation. The holding-company device also offers a means whereby the promoters may embark on a new venture without assuming any risks other than the amount invested in the venture. At the same time, there may be legal, administrative, tax, and other advantages in using the holding-company device to acquire and operate subsidiaries or affiliates as compared to other ways of arranging combinations.

*Advantages.* As a device to promote the growth of business firms, managements choose holding companies over mergers and consolidations for widely varied reasons. Advantages frequently attributed to the holding-company device are included in the following listing.

1. It is not necessary to obtain formal approval of stockholders before or after control of a company has been achieved. If the promoter can arrange with a few large stockholders to sell their shares or exchange them for shares of the holding company, the consent of the other stockholders is not necessary (assuming that over 50 percent of the voting stock has been acquired). Although the stock could be purchased through normal channels, this method would tend to raise the price per share and would take considerable time. A third method of acquiring controlling interest is to offer a price for the stock above the market price if the total pledges to sell are made by a specified time and if the total shares reach a specified amount. In acquiring a company, one or more of these methods may be used.

2. The holding company permits management to conserve cash because there are no legal requirements that dissenting shareholders must be paid, as in consolidations, mergers, and, usually, in leasing and purchasing the assets. In acquiring stock, there is also the possibility that an exchange can be arranged. With a relatively small investment, the holding-company device permits obtaining control over assets valued at many times the investment. (Theoretically, by pyramiding holding companies upon holding companies, one could control all of the corporate wealth of the country with one dollar.) After obtaining ownership of the stock of a subsidiary company, the stock may be used as collateral for notes or bond issues, which would further reduce the amount of cash needed by the holding company.

3. Less risk is assumed in using the holding-company device of achieving external growth than in using a merger or consolidation. The holding company does not guarantee or assume responsibility for the debts of its subsidiaries, which is always advantageous, and especially so when the courts may require that a combination be broken up or there is a large risk element in the venture. If some mistakes are made, it is easier to dispose of an unprofitable company than an unprofitable division of a company, or assets, liabilities, and personnel that have been integrated.[4]

When subsidiary companies are operated as separate legal entities, the holding company may liquidate its investment in an unprofitable subsidiary with a minimum of loss; and, if a subsidiary fails, the parent corporation's loss is usually limited to its investment in the stock of the subsidiary. As an illustration, many merchandising and service companies minimized their losses during the 1930s by incorporating their real estate

---

[4] One of the largest banks in New York was confronted with the problem of de-integrating until the merger was approved by Congress.

properties separately. However, since that time the courts on several occasions have redefined the responsibilities of a parent corporation for the debts of its subsidiaries. No longer may a parent corporation be sure it is not responsible for the debts of a bankrupt subsidiary corporation. Sometimes the debts of a subsidiary have been incurred for the benefit of the parent corporation or other subsidiary companies in the system or combination. If it can be shown that the subsidiary was used as the agent, adjunct, or instrumentality of the parent corporation, the latter may be held responsible for the debts of the subsidiary (the so-called instrumentality rule).

When a parent corporation is guilty of unfair treatment or mismanagement of a subsidiary corporation, it cannot avoid responsibility for the debts of the subsidiary. However, as noted by the Securities and Exchange Commission, each case wherein the issue of mismanagement or unfair treatment of a subsidiary arises calls for careful analysis of a complicated set of facts to determine the degree of responsibility of the parent corporation. In order to prevent creditors of a subsidiary from collecting assets from the parent corporation when those of the subsidiary are inadequate to cover claims, the following steps should be taken by management: (1) The subsidiary should be set up as a separate unit sufficiently strong to bear any financial strain to which it would normally be subjected. (2) Management of the two corporations should function separately and the day-to-day business and financial records should be kept separately. (3) Those with whom the two corporations come in contact should be kept aware of the fact that they are separate entities.

4. A corporation may organize separate subsidiaries incorporated in the states or foreign countries wherein they operate in order to offset restrictions placed on business activities of foreign corporations. For example, if one or several different activities carried on by a corporation are subject to special regulation, all the corporation's affairs might be brought under review and state regulation. For instance, a firm owning more than one racetrack probably would find it more convenient dealing with the regulatory authorities if each track were incorporated separately.

The spread of U.S. business corporations throughout the world has increased the creation of holding companies, because it is easier to maintain goodwill and avoid discriminatory regulation when producing or selling through the facilities of a local or domestic corporation. A considerable amount of criticism of U.S. corporate ventures in foreign countries has been eliminated by permitting local investors to buy the stock of the foreign subsidiaries of U.S. corporations. There are other economic advantages of local ownership interest, such as avoiding discriminatory restrictions on foreign companies (reporting, quotas, tariff walls, etc.) and anti-U.S. and "buy at home" campaigns.

**Disadvantages.** Sometimes, a parent corporation may avoid paying taxes on earnings outside its state of incorporation by operating through a subsidiary, which would limit taxes paid in that state to those on the earnings from operation within the state. The tax advantages derived from separate incorporation must be weighed against the expenses incurred in creating and maintaining separate corporate organizations, paying state organization and franchise taxes, reporting to state regulatory agencies, and paying higher federal income taxes.

1. The greatest penalty associated with operating separate corporate units is probably that due to the federal income tax laws. To file a consolidated tax return, a parent company must own 80 percent of its subsidiary company's voting stock and at least 80 percent of each class of nonvoting stock, except preferred. In a consolidated tax return, the parent corporation is able to adjust its income and expenses by canceling out intercompany transactions. The savings that result may make it desirable for the parent corporation to increase its equity holdings in its subsidiaries.

2. From a social point of view, the holding-company device makes it possible for unscrupulous or unqualified promoters with no business experience and with a relatively small amount of funds to obtain control over a large number of business firms.[5] By replacing qualified directors, the promoter may seriously weaken the subsidiary companies. Strong companies may be exploited by a weak one owned by the promoter, and the only defense available to minority stockholders of the exploited companies is to sue the promoter.

## Regulation of Public-Utility Companies

During the 1920s, the holding company had an extensive growth in the electric-power and light and gas industries. The promoters of these holding companies were not always motivated by the desire to improve or increase the efficiency of operating companies. At the beginning of the industry—its most speculative period—hundreds of companies were developed throughout the country that were locally financed, operated, and controlled. With improvements in methods of production, most of these companies reduced rates and increased profits. The public-utility holding-company system developed when suppliers entered the field to acquire companies in order to protect their markets.

In 1905, the General Electric Company organized the Electric Bond and Share Company to give financial assistance to utility companies that purchased General Electric products. Stone and Webster was formed to keep its engineering and managerial service business; and investment bankers organized systems so they could control operating companies and keep their financing business. Past abuses are considered here in some

---

[5] See, for example, George J. McManus, "Holding Companies are Losing Their Grip," *Iron Age*, vol. 210, no. 5 (August 3, 1972), p. 56.

detail because they could develop in the current holding-company movement in fields other than public utilities.

**Regulated Firms.** Public-utility and railroad companies differ from other corporations in that they (1) render necessary services, (2) are "natural monopolies" because they give their best service when operating under monopolistic conditions, (3) require large capital outlays, (4) have incomes that tend to be fairly steady, and (5) are subject to service and rate regulations. The principle of rate regulation is based on the concept that the general public must be protected from excessive rates that could be charged by a company having a monopoly; at the same time, the company must be permitted to earn a fair return on capital. Rate regulation necessitates evaluation of assets, because net income of $1 million may be "fair" on a valuation of $16 million but inadequate on a $22-million valuation.

Customarily, the jurisdiction of state public-service commissions is limited to operating companies, and certain information they need may be in the files of holding companies over which they have no jurisdiction. In the past, financial practices originating with holding companies and their promoters often led to inflated values of assets and expenses of operating companies. Following intensive investigation of public-utility holding companies from 1928 to 1935 by the Federal Trade Commission and after congressional hearings, Congress passed the Public Utility Holding Company Act of 1935.[6] The law pertains to holding companies and their subsidiaries in the electric-light and gas industries engaged in transmitting and selling electric energy and gas in interstate and foreign commerce. In passing the act, the aim of Congress was to correct the abuses that were characteristic of organizing, financing, and operating holding-company systems. Public-utility operating companies were being regulated by state or local agencies whose authority did not cover the activities of holding companies.

Often, the securities issued by holding companies were based on "fictitious asset values and paper profits from intercompany transactions" issued in anticipation of revenue from subsidiaries, which, if realized, would burden consumers and require the operating companies to support an overcapitalized holding-company superstructure. When dealing with subsidiaries, managements of holding companies made excessive charges for services, construction work, equipment, and materials. In addition, the holding company's control over subsidiaries was used to obtain funds from them in the form of dividend payments and loans; and their assets were used as security for notes and bonds sold to the public by the holding company. As a result, many of the speculative ventures of the pro-

---

[6] See House Committee on Interstate and Foreign Commerce, *Public Utility Holding Companies* (Hearings on H.R. 5423, 74th Cong., 1st sess.; Washington, D.C.: U.S. Government Printing Office, 1935, 3 vols.).

moter and manipulator were financed by the operating companies. Accounting systems were sometimes kept in a form to conceal the true position of the operating companies and their relations to the holding company. Added confusion resulted from the existence of pyramiding holding companies—holding companies that owned holding companies that owned holding companies, and so on, until the operating companies that supported all the other companies were at the bottom of the pyramid. This expansive holding-company structure permitted the promoters to increase the amount of assets they controlled with a small amount invested in voting stock of the "peak" holding company.

**Public Utility Holding Company Act.** Under provisions of the Public Utility Holding Company Act of 1935, the electric and gas holding companies are required to register with the Securities and Exchange Commission, and, after registration, the commission has three main functions pertaining to them. First, the commission must require physical integration of public-utility companies and functionally related properties of holding-company systems. The purpose is to simplify the intercorporate financial structure and the relationship among units of a holding-company system. Second, it is required to supervise the financing of "intercompany" transactions, servicing arrangements, and certain accounting practices of the holding company and corporations in the system. The third major function pertains to the exempt provisions of the act and to the rights and status under the act of persons and companies.[7]

The commission has the power to approve or disapprove the issuance of securities by the holding companies and their subsidiaries (and to place a ban on unsecured bonds, preferred stock, no-par stock, and nonvoting stock without the commission's specific approval); to control intercompany transactions, such as loans, sales of securities, charges for managerial services, and sales and construction contracts; to approve or disapprove the acquisition of subsidiaries; and to require periodic reports and the use of prescribed accounts, records, and statement forms.

In giving the SEC detailed powers over the business activities of public-utility holding companies, Congress sought to correct inefficiencies resulting from the growth of uneconomical systems, creation of top-heavy capital structures, and inflation of operating costs and capital values. When a holding company deals with an operating subsidiary company, bargaining at arm's length is absent. In the past, this situation sometimes led to "upstream" loans (from operating companies to the holding company) and to service, interest, and other intercompany charges that were not related to actual costs (with the operating companies' customers and minority stockholders being exploited). The abuses that were pre-

---

[7] Securities and Exchange Commission, *42nd Annual Report, for the Fiscal Year Ended June 30, 1976* (Washington, D.C.: U.S. Government Printing Office, 1977, p. 145).

valent included keeping the books of the holding company out of the jurisdiction of state regulatory bodies, padding and manipulating expenses, creating secret reserves, releasing inaccurate information about financial positions of subsidiary companies, and manipulating market prices of stocks.

**Rehabilitation of Holding Companies.** One of the most serious problems faced by the SEC was that of rehabilitating holding-company systems. The excessive prices paid for operating units led to overcapitalization of holding-companies, which broke down during the depression of the 1930s and resulted in heavy losses to investors.

The irresponsible financial practices of holding companies were harmful to their operating subsidiary companies, and the latter were left with large fixed charges, dividend arrearages on preferred stock, and excessive issues of preferred and common stock. During the early 1930s, some holding companies depended on their operating companies for loans and dividends; and, in most cases, the loans were made and the dividends were voted even though doing so was not warranted. In other cases, the holding companies used the credit of the operating companies to obtain funds for ventures unrelated to the activities of the operating companies.

Since 1935, considerable progress has been made in "squeezing the water out of inflated valuations," reducing costs of operations, increasing net earnings, and simplifying holding-company systems. Both disinvestment in nonintegrated properties and simplification of corporate structure are still taking place—but at a much slower rate, because integration of public-utility companies is almost complete. When completed, each holding-company system will resemble operating-holding companies such as Commonwealth Edison Company, Consolidated Edison Company of New York, and other large companies of this type. Because of better organization and management, the public-utility industry generally has been able to keep pace with the rapid growth in demand for its services.

At the end of calendar 1975 there were 20 holding companies registered under the Act, including 18 "active" registered holding-company systems, including 3 subholding companies, and 2 small "non-active" systems. In all, 165 companies were in the active holding-company systems.[8]

---

[8] The three subholding companies were the Potomac Edison Company and Monongahela Power Company, public-utility subsidiary companies of Allegheny Power Systems, Inc., and Southwestern Electric Power Company, a public-utility subsidiary company of Central and South West Corporation. (Ibid., pp. 145 and 147.)

**Summary**

The right of corporations to own stock in other corporations has been established by statutes, and the development of both investment companies and holding companies stems from these enabling acts. When the purpose of acquiring stock of other corporations is control, a parent-subsidiary relationship results; when the purpose is investment, the investor corporation usually limits its stock ownership in any one corporation to avoid being classified as a holding company. When expansion is considered, it is agreed it is cheaper to acquire control over a second corporation than to effect a merger, consolidation, or outright purchase. All the holding company needs to do is to acquire, by purchase or exchange, enough of the voting stock of a second corporation to assure control. When the voting stock of an operating company represents only a small part of its capital structure, control can be obtained by a relatively small investment. If management of the holding company can arrange an exchange of its bonds, preferred stock, or nonvoting common stock for the operating company's voting stock, control can be obtained with no cash outlay and no dilution of voting rights of the holding company's stock.

A pure holding company is a nonoperating company that controls the operations of subsidiaries through voting privileges obtained by stock ownership; an operating-holding company, as the name suggests, is both a holding company and an operating company. Most of the major corporations in the United States are of the latter type. In financial reporting, subsidiaries are sometimes treated as units of a system and, sometimes, consolidated financial reports are made. The practice followed depends on factors such as the percentage of ownership of the parent in the subsidiary, the volume of intercompany transactions, and the degree of similarity in operations. The relative advantages and disadvantages of large holding companies depend on managerial, risk, legal, and tax factors.

The Public Utility Holding Company Act of 1935, which pertains to registered electric and gas holding companies and their operating subsidiaries having properties in more than one state, limited the layers of corporate entities to three and gave the Securities and Exchange Commission detailed powers over the financial activities of public-utility holding companies. Since 1935, a great deal of progress has been made in simplifying capital structures, deflating valuations of corporate assets, reducing operating costs, and increasing net earnings. As a consequence, the industry generally has been able to keep pace with the increased demand for service.

## QUESTIONS

1. Identify: (*a*) holding company, (*b*) subsidiary company, (*c*) affiliated company, (*d*) pure holding company, (*e*) operating-holding company, (*f*) grandfather clause.
2. May it be cheaper to acquire control over a second corporation by stock ownership than to effect a merger, consolidation, or outright purchase? Explain.
3. Analyze: "What you have in mind. . . . Where I have . . . an operating

company, and I sell the common stock to Company B; Company B issues ... bonds and preferred to pay for that common stock, and also issues common stock, and then Company C takes that common stock, and Company C issues securities on it. ... And that common stock passes to Company D and it in turn issues and so on." (House Committee on Interstate and Foreign Commerce, *Public Utility Holding Companies* [Hearings on H.R. 5423, 74th Cong., 1st sess.; Washington, D.C.: U.S. Government Printing Office, 1935], p. 1525.)

4. Why is the use of debt in a holding-company's capital structure more risky than the use of debt in an operating company?
5. The Public Utility Holding Company Act of 1935 limits the number of public-utility holding-company layers to three, including the operating companies. How does this constraint reduce the possibility of collapsing utility-company pyramids?
6. Discuss some of the advantages and disadvantages of a holding company.
7. Discuss what is meant by the phrase "community of interest."
8. How can a holding company finance its subsidiaries?
9. What are some of the reasons for the decline in *pure* holding companies?
10. What are some of the tax and legal advantages and disadvantages for a holding company when it operates its subsidiary companies as separate legal entities?
11. How has the Clayton Act affected the growth of holding companies?

## PROBLEMS

1. The Pima Company is a holding company owning the entire common stock of operating companies Alpha and Beta. Balance sheets for the two subsidiaries as of December 31, 1978 are identical and appear as below:

Balance Sheet, December 31, 1978
(in millions)

| | | | |
|---|---|---|---|
| Current assets | $ 6 | Current liabilities | $ 1 |
| Fixed assets | 4 | Bonds (8%) | 2 |
| | | Preferred stock (6%) | 2 |
| | | Common stock | 4 |
| | | Retained earnings | 1 |
| Total assets | $10 | Total liabilities | $10 |

Each operating company earns $1 million annually before taxes and before interest and preferred dividends. A 50-percent tax rate is assumed.
  a. What is the annual rate of return on each subsidiary's net worth (common stock plus retained earnings)?
  b. If the Pima Company has fixed-interest charges of $500,000, how much is available annually for distribution to Pima's stockholders?
  c. If ownership of 30 percent of the holding company's common stock with a total market value of $10 million is sufficient to control all three firms, what percentage would this be of the total assets of the operating companies?

2. Compute the earnings available to Holding Company A, if its operating company pays out *all* earnings in dividends, from the following figures (in thousands):

HOLDING COMPANY A

| | |
|---|---|
| Common stock of operating company | $ 50 |

*Operating Company*

| | |
|---|---|
| Total assets | $250 |
| Debt (5%) | 125 |
| Preferred stock (6%) | 25 |
| Common stock equity | 100 |

Assume a 50-percent tax rate. The 1978 earnings before interest and taxes for the operating company were $50,000.

## ADDITIONAL READINGS

Alberts, W. W., and J. E. Segall (eds.). *The Corporate Merger*. Chicago: University of Chicago Press, 1966.

Ansoff, H. I., and J. F. Weston. "Merger Objectives and Organizational Structure," *Quarterly Review of Economics and Business*, vol. 2 (August 1962), pp. 49–58.

Arndt, R. E. "Return on Investment, Earnings Growth Rates, and P/E Growth Theory, in Merger Planning," *Mergers & Acquisitions*, vol. 8 (Spring 1973), pp. 42–58.

Babcock, G. C. "The Concept of Sustainable Growth," *Financial Analysts Journal*, vol. 26 (May–June 1970), pp. 108–14.

Beman, L. "What We Learned from the Great Merger Frenzy," *Fortune*, vol. 87 (April 1973), pp. 70 ff.

Cheney, R. E. "What's New on the Corporate Takeover Scene," *Financial Executive*, vol. 40 (April 1972), pp. 18–21.

Davis, R. F. "Compatibility in Corporate Marriages," *Harvard Business Review*, vol. 46 (July–August 1968), pp. 86–93.

Foster, E. M. "The Price-Earnings Ratio and Growth," *Financial Analysts Journal*, vol. 26 (January–February 1970), pp. 139–47.

Gort, M. *Diversification and Integration in American Industry*. Princeton, N.J.: Princeton University Press, 1962.

Higgins, R. C., and L. D. Schall. "Corporate Bankruptcy and Conglomerate Merger," *Journal of Finance*, vol. 30 (March 1975), pp. 93–114.

Kelley, E. M. *The Profitability of Growth Through Mergers*. University Park: Pennsylvania State University, 1967.

Levinson, H. "A Psychologist Diagnoses Merger Failure," *Harvard Business Review*, vol. 48 (March–April 1970), pp. 139–47.

McCarthy, G. D. *Acquisitions and Mergers*. New York: Ronald Press Co., 1963.

―――. "Premeditated Mergers," *Harvard Business Review*, vol. 39 (January–February 1961), pp. 74–82.

MacDougal, G. E., and F. V. Malek. "Master Plan for Merger Negotiations," *Harvard Business Review*, vol. 48 (January–February 1970), pp. 71–82.

Mahoney, J. D. "The Corporate Takeover: from Duel to Blitzkrieg," *Management Review*, vol. 61 (November 1972), pp. 2–12.

Reilly, F. K. "What Determines the Ratio of Exchange in Corporate Mergers?", *Financial Analysts Journal*, vol. 18 (November–December 1962), pp. 47–50.

Rockwell, W. F. "How To Acquire a Company," *Harvard Business Review*, vol. 46 (September–October 1968), pp. 121–24.

Shad, J. S. R. "The Financial Realities of Mergers," *Harvard Business Review*, vol. 47 (November–December 1969), pp. 133–46.

Shick, R. A., and F. C. Jen. "Merger Benefits to Shareholders of Acquiring Firms," *Financial Management*, vol. 3 (Winter 1974), pp. 45–53.

Silberman, I. H. "A Note on Merger Valuation," *Journal of Finance*, vol. 23 (June 1968), pp. 528–34.

Wakefield, B. R. "Mergers and Acquisitions," *Harvard Business Review*, vol. 43 (September–October 1965), pp. 6–19.

# part VI
# FINANCIALLY DISTRESSED BUSINESS FIRMS

The problems of financially distressed business firms and their solutions are considered in this section under the headings of recapitalization, reorganization, and liquidation of business firms. Recapitalizing a business firm refers to remodeling its capital structure. This is done for various reasons, including attainment of more economical financing, avoidance of financial strain, and preparation for listing on a stock exchange.

The reorganization of a business firm may refer to managerial changes, but, as used here, it means a revision of the firm's capital structure necessitated by default on interest and principal payments or other obligations. Broadly speaking, the principal difference between recapitalization and reorganization is that the first is voluntary while the second is forced on a business firm by creditors.

Liquidation of a business concern ordinarily means that its assets are converted into cash in order to discharge liabilities, with any remaining cash to be distributed to owners. If a firm is incorporated, additional legal steps are necessary in order to dissolve the corporation.

# 24

# Recapitalizations of a Business Firm

Recapitalization of a corporation is the rearrangement of the amount of its bonds, long-term notes, and stock, not for the purpose of raising additional capital but to change the corporation's capital structure. As an illustration, a corporation is recapitalized when it replaces mortgage bonds with preferred stock or with common stock in order to reduce fixed charges. Changes in a corporation's financial position may make modification in its capital structure desirable or necessary in order to avoid financial hardship. The term "recapitalization" as used here does not refer to recapitalization under reorganization plans. Once a default on interest or principal payment occurs, the right of management to take corrective action passes to a large extent from the corporation to its creditors; and the changes in the capital structure that follow are called reorganizations (see Chapter 25).

Voluntary recapitalization is considered in this chapter under the headings: changes in capital structure, recapitalization of common stock, distribution of capital, reclassification of stock, recapitalization of preferred stock, redemption of stock, and recapitalization of debt.

### Changes in Capital Structure

The concept that a corporation's power to issue securities stems from the general or special statute under which the corporation is organized is deeply embedded in corporation law. By actions of directors and stockholders, modern corporation codes permit additional shares to be authorized by charter amendment.[1]

---

[1] *Uniform Commercial Code, 1972 Official Text with Comments* (Philadelphia: American Law Institute; or Chicago: National Conference of Commissioners on Uniform State Laws, 1972, pp. 517–18.)

***Contractual Rights.*** The capital structure of a business corporation includes its long-term debt and owners' equity. The rights of owners are determined by contracts as interpreted by state and federal courts. The rights of stockholders are specified in the corporate charter or certificate of incorporation and sometimes in the bylaws, and the rights of creditors are found in the trust indentures or loan agreements. Although the financial conditions of a business firm and the environment in which it operates are changing continuously, its contracts with security holders are difficult to modify to conform to changing conditions. In the light of conditions (1979), a noncallable, ten-year, 10-percent bond might seem unrealistic and foolhardy to the financial manager of the mid-1980s. A mortgage-bond indenture may contain the after-acquired property clause, although the plant and other facilities of the corporation may have appreciated a hundredfold in value since the bond issue was negotiated. Although the corporation may issue second-mortgage bonds, the penalty would probably be a higher interest rate due to the prejudice against junior bonds. In such a case, a modification of the basic contract seems to be justified.

***Modification of Terms.*** The financial position of a business concern may be so severely strained because of operating deficits that some adjustment in its capital structure may be necessary. Typically, this financial stress is first recognized by a request for a modification of a short-term bank loan by the firm. By asking for a longer maturity the firm hopes to be able to halt the operating deficits, and enable itself to pay off the loan when it matures.

When a business corporation's earnings after taxes are large enough to permit it to increase retained earnings, it builds a larger equity cushion to protect itself against losses that may result from adverse changes in its financial position. Retention of income has been a major feature of corporations' financial policies since 1945. A secondary consequence of this situation has been the widespread use of stock splits in order to increase the number of shares and to keep their market price within a more popular trading range. When a stock climbs too far over the $100-market-price range, it frequently becomes a candidate for a stock split. For example, Digital Equipment Corporation split its stock 3-for-1 on November 8, 1976, when the stock was selling at $172-7/8 at the time of the announcement.

If the stock of some companies were not split periodically, the market price would be so high as to preclude regular trading. The number of a corporation's shares may be changed by other means; but, like any change in capital structure, the purpose is, or should be, to strengthen the corporation's financial position, to broaden the market for its securities, and to facilitate future financing.

The simplest method of changing the capital structure of a corporation is to increase or decrease retained earnings. Some companies depend on this method of financing more than others. The distribution of capital among debt, preferred stock, and equity of any corporation is influenced not only by managerial policy but also by the economic environment and the industry wherein the firm operates (see Table 24-1). Public-utility companies finance relatively more with debt than do railroads and industrial companies. As a consequence, industrial companies and railroads use retained earnings and common-stock issues more extensively than public-utility companies.

TABLE 24-1
Capital Structures* (amounts in thousands)

| Item | Industrial | | Railroad | | Public Utility | |
|---|---|---|---|---|---|---|
| | Amount | Percent | Amount | Percent | Amount | Percent |
| Noncurrent debts | $ 364,129 | 19.9 | $391,248 | 39.3 | $270,670 | 52.8 |
| Preferred stock | ... | ... | 4,391 | 0.4 | 59,360 | 11.5 |
| Common stock | 441.414 | 24.2 | 209,257 | 21.1 | 103,660 | 20.2 |
| Retained earnings | 1,046,273 | 55.9 | 387,114 | 39.2 | 79,185 | 15.5 |
| Total Liabilities and Equity | $1,851,816 | 100.0 | $992,010 | 100.0 | $512,875 | 100.0 |

* Statistics from balance sheets of three companies, the names of which are withheld.

## Recapitalization of Common Stock

The least complicated method of changing the common stock in the capital structure of a business corporation is to increase the number of shares outstanding as provided for in the articles of incorporation or the charter of the corporation as amended. When a change is to be made in the aggregate amount of capital, the number of shares authorized, or the par value, the approval of the stockholders, as well as of the board of directors, is necessary. Thus, management does not have a free hand in using common stock as a financing device, and it is not unusual for a clash in the interests of management and stockholders to prevent financing with issues of stock. Differences between the economic needs and the legality of financial proposals are often unreconcilable.

**Charter Amendment Procedure.** The corporation laws of most states make statutory provisions for amending the articles of incorporation of companies chartered therein. These procedures must be followed regardless of how trivial or routine the proposed changes seem to be. First, the corporation's board of directors adopts a resolution containing the proposed amendment and directing that it be submitted at an annual or special meeting of the shareholders. Second, a notice containing the proposed amendment, or a summary of the changes contained therein, is mailed to each shareholder of record within 10 and not more than 50 days before the date of the meeting. At this meeting, management takes the vote on the proposed amendment; and, if approved by two-thirds or more of those entitled to vote thereon, it becomes part of the corporation's charter. When class voting is permitted, each class of shareholders must give enough affirmative votes before the amendment can be adopted. For example, although the common stockholders may approve the refinancing of a preferred-stock issue, the amendment will fail if rejected by a much smaller number of preferred stockholders. Furthermore, changes in the charter that permit an increase in the amount of common or preferred stock are time-consuming. However, organizers of corporations may provide for future changes in corporate needs by providing for flexibility in financing in the original charter. For example, the corporation's charter may provide for the issue of 10 million shares of common stock with a par value of $25, although only 1 million shares may be issued originally.

**Right to Amend.** State corporation acts usually specify the items that may be changed by following the proper amendment procedures. New clauses may be added if they contain the types of provisions that could have been included originally and others that may be necessary to effect change, exchange, cancellation, or reclassification of shares or the rights of shareholders. More specifically, the charter permits the board of directors and shareholders to (1) increase or decrease the par value of authorized shares of any class having par value, (2) change the par value shares into the same or a different number of shares without par value, (3) change shares of no-par value stock into the same or a different number of shares having par value, and (4) change shares of any class with or without par value into a different number of shares of the same class or other classes.

**Stock Splits.** Changes in the par or stated value of stock are significant when management wishes to change the number of shares of stock outstanding for various reasons, such as increasing or decreasing the market price of the stock and creating a capital surplus (see below). Management may provide for recapitalization of common stock by splitting the shares outstanding, with no other change in the corporation's capital structure. A stock split of two new shares for one old share would reduce the par value and double the number of shares of common stock. Splitting up the corporation's stock may or may not result in an increase in the number of stockholders. The assumption that the more shares outstanding, the more shareholders, is not always valid; but there is a tendency for the number of shareholders to increase following a lowering of the market price resulting from a stock split. As an illustration, the Atchison, Topeka, and Santa Fe Railway split its common shares 5-for-1 when there were 40,000 common stockholders; by 1967, the number of stockholders had increased to about 109,000. At the close of 1976, Santa Fe Industries, Inc., the successor corporation to the railroad set up in 1967 to permit diversification, had over 94,036 common and 5,079 preferred stockholders.

The specific reasons for attempting to increase the number of shareholders include the following: to meet the qualifications for listing the company's shares on a national stock exchange; to obtain a wider market for shares offered under preemptive rights; to increase the interest of the public in the company's products or services; to disseminate ownership more widely in order to facilitate control of the company by existing management; and to anticipate a public offering of stock.

A stock split may be favored by management of some corporations, such as growth companies, in order to avoid the appearance of excessive per-share earnings. In other instances, management may want to pave the way for a combination with a second company. If the number of shares is increased and their aggregate market value is in excess of their equivalent in old shares, a better exchange ratio or price may be obtained for the company's assets. For instance, if the company's stock had been selling for $300 per share, a 10-for-1 split would reduce the price to approximately $30. However, after the announcement of an impending stock split, the price of the stock usually increases in expectation of higher cash dividends; but, if such a dividend increase does not materialize, the price will tend to decline.

A price decline of a low-priced stock is less apparent than the same percentage decline of a higher-priced stock—a decline of 10 percent or $3 per share on a $30 stock tends to be less disturbing than a $30 decline in a $300 stock. This illusion of stability in market price for low-priced stocks is also applicable to earnings. A stock split increases the number of shares outstanding, decreases the par or stated value of each share, and lowers the book value per share, but has no effect on the total amount of net worth or the total of any of the items in the stockholders' section of the corporation's balance sheet (see Table 24–2). The stock split of 2-for-1 resulted in an increase in the number of shares of common stock from 400,000 to 800,000 and a reduction in the par value of the stock from $20 to $10.

TABLE 24–2
Effect of Stock Split (in millions)

| Capital Structure before Stock Split | | Capital Structure after Stock Split | |
|---|---|---|---|
| Noncurrent debt | $ 5 | Noncurrent debt | $ 5 |
| Preferred stock (10,000 shares, par $100) | 1 | Preferred stock (10,000 shares, par $100) | 1 |
| Common stock (400,000 shares, par $20) | 8 | Common stock (800,000 shares, par $10) | 8 |
| Retained earnings | 3 | Retained earnings | 3 |
| Total | $17 | Total | $17 |

**Reverse Stock Splits.** Recapitalization of a corporation's stock may result from a reverse stock split, which takes place most commonly when general business is depressed and the corporation taking such action has deficits to show on its balance sheet. Corporation laws usually permit a corporation to apply its capital surplus to the reduction or elimination of deficits by resolution of the board of directors after all retained earnings have been used. A capital surplus may be created by reducing the par value of stock without changing the number of shares outstanding or by reducing the number of shares without changing the par value (see Table 24–3).

TABLE 24–3
Effects of Reverse Stock Split (in millions)

| Capital Structure before Reverse Stock Split | | Capital Structure after Reverse Stock Split | |
|---|---|---|---|
| Noncurrent debt | $ 5 | Noncurrent debt | $ 5 |
| Preferred stock (10,000 shares, par $100) | 1 | Preferred stock (10,000 shares, par $100) | 1 |
| Common stock (800,000 shares par $10) | 8 | Common stock (400,000 shares, par $10) | 4 |
| Retained earnings | (1) | Capital surplus | 3 |
| Total | $13 | Total | $13 |

Corporate management may favor a reverse stock split in order to bring the market price of the stock into a more popular trading zone, that is, to reduce the number of shares so as to increase the price. The theory behind the reverse stock split is that the investor type of stockholder shows little interest in stocks selling for $2 to $3 per share, but would be interested if the stock were selling for $20 or $30 per share.[2] There are good reasons for questioning this premise; but trading in a higher-priced zone may be advantageous to speculators because most brokers refuse to accept low-priced stock as collateral for loans. A more fundamental reason for the reverse stock split is the expectation of management that the credit rating of the corporation will thereby be improved and it will be able to secure loans at lower interest rates, with less security, for longer periods of time, and under more favorable terms. But these expectations may not follow unless earnings improve, which requires something more basic than a decrease in the number of shares of stock outstanding. Nevertheless, with the reduction in the number of shares outstanding, the earnings per share will increase even though net earnings of the firm do not improve significantly. The higher earnings per share will support a higher market price for the new shares.

---

[2] One of the most famous reverse stock splits occurred on April 26, 1938, when Cities Service Company's authorized common stock was changed from 50 million no-par shares to 5 million $10 par shares, for a 1-to-10 reverse split, and given one half vote per share. At the same time, 348,000,724 treasury shares were canceled. Subsequently, in 1955, the authorized shares of the company were increased to 20 million, with one vote per share.

*Use of Capital Surplus.* Because of the ease of changing par or stated value of common stock, it is the method of recapitalization most commonly used when an increase in capital surplus is desired. The use of capital surplus is subject to legal requirements, but its existence permits a corporation to eliminate a retained earnings deficit, reduce the book value of tangible fixed assets, and write down goodwill and other intangible assets. A reduction in value of assets would make possible a reduction in depreciation charges; the resulting decline in expenses would cause reported net income to increase and thus make dividend payments possible. However, if the reduction in the valuation of assets is excessive, the resulting understatement of depreciation charges and overstatement of earnings may encourage management to recommend the declaration of excessive dividends.

*New Classes of Shares.* A business corporation's charter may be amended so as to permit it to (1) create classes of stock having rights and preferences either prior and superior or subordinate and inferior to the shares of any class then authorized; (2) cancel or change the rights of holders of any shares of any class to receive dividends that have accrued but have not been declared; (3) divide any special or preferred class of shares into series and determine the difference between it and other series as to dividends, security, and other variations; and (4) change the title to all or any of its shares pertaining to preferences, limitations, and relative rights. Although it does not follow that a corporation may make any of these changes in its charter, this list suggests efforts made by state legislatures in authorizing amendments that would permit domestic corporations to meet their financial needs by changing the capital stock part of their capital structures.

*Reacquired Shares.* The capital structure of a corporation is affected when reacquired shares are canceled and a capital surplus is created, but only to the extent of the difference in the par or stated value and the cost of reacquiring them. When a company's stock having a par value of $25 is reacquired in the market at $20, according to the laws of most states, the capital surplus may not be increased by more than $5 per share. Stock may be reacquired by management by purchase in the open market when selling below par or stated value, from gifts to the corporation by stockholders, or in response to a request for tender of stock at a specific price below par or stated value.

As in other cases, when the amount of capital is changed, the facts are filed with and a record kept by the secretary of state. The board of directors of a corporation may at any time pass a resolution canceling all or any part of its reacquired shares other than redeemable shares (see below). The statement of cancellation that is made out and filed with the secretary of state must contain certain specified information. When the secretary of state verifies that the corporation has met the requirements of the law, including the payment of fees and franchise taxes, the secretary dates and endorses the original duplicate with the word "filed," keeps one copy on file in the office, and returns the other to the corporation. The effect of the filing is to reduce the amount of stated capital of the corporation.

## Distribution of Capital

A reduction in the capital account of a corporation can be accomplished by the distribution of a "liquidating dividend." If management finds it advisable to liquidate some of its business, it must have the approval of both the board of directors and two-thirds of the stockholders (there may be exceptions, such as with mining companies). Then, management may distribute property to the shareholders, which is charged to the stated capital or capital surplus. Legally, such distributions may not be made if the company is insolvent or if the distribution would cause it to become insolvent. Nor is the amount of the distribution to any one class of shareholders legal if it reduces the net assets of the corporation below the aggregate amount payable to preferential shareholders in case of voluntary liquidation.

Instead of a partial liquidation, there may be complete liquidation of a corporation's assets. In this case, after satisfying the demands of creditors and preferred stockholders, the remaining cash obtained from the sale of assets is distributed to common stockholders on a pro rata basis. Liquidations may take years to complete. For example, in April 1965, the managers of Overland Corporation, formerly Willys-Overland, stated that a financial distribution of the assets in a special fund, created in 1953 from the assets of the old company, would be distributed to 1,500 shareholders. They received 92.89 cents for each certificate surrendered. Willys-Overland Motors, which produced Jeeps, had sold its principal assets to Kaiser Industries Corporation and started operating in 1953 as an investment company. In November 1962, it had merged with Empire Securities, whose shareholders received the same amount per share as the certificate holders of the Overland Corporation.[3]

Some corporation laws permit a corporation's board of directors to distribute cash dividends paid out of capital surplus to the holders of cumulative preferred shares if the corporation has no retained earnings and is not insolvent or would not be made insolvent by the payment.

## Reclassification of Stock

Reclassification of one type of stock into another type of stock is a common procedure for changing the capital structure of a business corporation. When preferred stock is reclassified as common stock, the effect

---

[3] *Wall Street Journal*, April 6, 1965, p. 12.

is to increase the book value of the aggregate amount of common stock and to reduce the amount of preferred stock. Since the exchange is usually "sweetened" with a cash payment, the retained earnings of the corporation may be reduced. In some cases, the reclassification may involve different series or issues of preferred stock that bear different dividend rates. For example, a single type of preferred shares may be exchanged for two new preferred issues, one of which will have a priority senior to the other.

The reasons for reclassifying stock vary widely among business firms. In many cases since 1945, the reason for reclassification has been to eliminate a noncallable high-dividend preferred-stock issue. Another reason is to eliminate large arrearages that have accumulated on cumulative preferred stock. After the arrearages have been discharged, the financial structure of the firm should be in line with earnings, so any future embarrassment that tends to accompany large overdue obligations may be avoided. Arrearages infrequently may be paid in full with cash. More frequently, however, they are financed by a combination of cash, preferred stock having a priority senior to the existing issue in arrears, and additional common stock.

Simplification of a corporation's capital stock would result if common stock were given in exchange for preferred stock. In addition, management may find it advantageous to reclassify preferred stock into common stock in order to increase the firm's bargaining position in case of future combination with other corporations. The earnings per share accruing to holders of common stock may be increased if the dividends on preferred stock are eliminated. The acquisition of a second company by an exchange of stock may be facilitated by having but one class of stock. It should be pointed out at this point that management must negotiate with the preferred stockholders before any reclassification into common stock can take place.

Sometimes the reason for reclassification is to enable large stockholders to liquidate part of their investment by reclassifying some of the common stock into nonvoting preferred stock. The latter could be sold without reducing management's ability to control the company by keeping majority control over common stock. The owners of a closely held corporation may want to liquidate part of their investment through a public sale. In order to prepare for the change, management may revamp the corporation's capital structure by reducing the par value of the stock, increasing the number of shares, and bringing the capital structure in line with prevailing market sentiments and economic conditions.

As will be discussed more fully in the next section, one result of reclassification of different classes of stock may be to increase the number of shares of common stock and to dilute the rights and privileges of common stockholders. In the case where the par or stated value of one class of stock is greater than the par or stated value of the stock for which it is exchanged, the capital surplus must be adjusted to account for the difference. Finally, legal action may be responsible for reclassification of stock, as in the public-utility industry.

## Recapitalization of Preferred Stock

***Contractual Rights.*** Many of the principles applicable to the adjustment of the common-stock section of the capital structure are equally applicable to the preferred-stock section. Both classes of stockholders are owners, and their contractual relations to their firm are legally different from those of creditors. As in the case of common stock, changes in the rights and privileges of preferred stockholders necessitate changes in the articles of incorporation or the charter of the corporation. A number of the problems entailed in common-stock recapitalization are also applicable to preferred-stock recapitalization, but preferred stockholders have preference over common stockholders and these preferences may conflict seriously with the financial well-being of the corporation.

***Right to Amend.*** When there is a conflict of interest between preferred stockholders and the welfare of the company, management should initiate the procedure for its solution, which requires a change in the corporation's charter. Most state corporation laws permit the board of directors and shareholders to authorize and establish series of preferred stock or classes of shares and to fix the relative rights and preferences of each series or class. A corporation's charter may be amended to revoke, diminish, or enlarge the authority of the board of directors to eliminate such stock and the preferences. If the existing preferred stockholders would be affected adversely by such amendments, it would be necessary to obtain their approval before such changes would be effective.

***Reasons for Recapitalization.*** Recapitalization of preferred stock may be motivated by a desire or necessity to simplify the corporation's capital structure, reduce voting stock outstanding, create a better capital structure for future financing, and bring the capital structure in line with earnings. Preferred stock is relatively unimportant in the capital structures of most business corporations; but, for some companies, its presence has created serious problems.

The features and restrictions under which preferred stock is issued may be burdensome to management. A common criticism is that dividend rates on noncallable preferred stock may be too high, being out of line with current economic conditions, and should be eliminated or reduced. A second reason for recapitalization of preferred stock is the limitation placed on management by the terms under which the stock was issued. The protective features may specify that no additional long-term debt or preferred stock is to be issued as long as this issue of preferred stock is outstanding. In other instances preferred stockholders may be given the right to approve or disapprove all additional debt or other preferred stock issues having claims superior to the outstanding preferred stock. In some cases, preferred stock may be issued under conditions that require management to provide for retirement of the issue by establishing a sinking fund, which may be burdensome. However, the most serious problems that necessitate recapitalization of preferred stock are arrearages on cumulative preferred stock.

**Arrearages on Preferred Stock.** When business corporations finance with preferred-stock issues, the cumulative feature is usually included to make the securities attractive to investors. Then, if dividends are not paid one year, they accumulate as claims against the corporation that must be paid before dividends can be paid on common stock. This situation may exist in partnerships if claims of limited partners are permitted to accumulate. Although preferred-stock dividends are contingent rather than fixed charges, allowing them to accumulate tends to affect the position of the business enterprise adversely.

Arrearages of preferred-stock dividends and unpaid claims of limited partners may not cause actual insolvency, but they may affect a firm's credit position so adversely as to lead indirectly to financial strain or failure. The existence of arrearages may make it difficult to sell stock or to borrow; as a result, the business firm may be thrown on its own resources, which may not be adequate to meet some emergency need for funds.

**Recapitalization Plan.** Any plan for recapitalization of preferred stock should have sufficient merit to make it possible for management to sell it to stockholders on the basis that the proposed changes will strengthen the corporation and further the interests of all concerned. If prospects point to a continued weakening in the competitive position of the corporation, the alternative to acceptance of some compromise plan might be reorganization, liquidation, or consolidation with another company. One of the objectives of a plan for eliminating dividend arrearages is to avoid or lessen the cash drain required in paying accumulated dividends; but some cash payments may be necessary to satisfy dissenting preferred stockholders. Stockholders are usually offered one or more of the following in exchange for their preferred stock and the dividend arrearages: additional noncumulative preferred stock; new preferred stock with a lower dividend rate, conversion privilege, participation feature, or seniority over outstanding preferred stock; common stock; or cash. On some occasions, preferred stockholders may be offered bonds or other credit instruments.

After a plan has been effected, unless earnings are sufficient to pay charges on the obligations that have replaced the old preferred stock, new dividend arrearages will accumulate unless the new preferred stock is made noncumulative. If bonds or other types of debt instruments are used, a more serious problem than the former one may result because fixed charges (interest) have replaced contingent charges (dividends).

If a recapitalization plan is to provide permanent financial relief, the corporation may recapitalize with common stock or noncumulative preferred stock with a lower dividend rate.

One of the more popular recapitalization plans consists of the offering of a small amount of cash, noncumulative preferred stock, and common stock. The cash is given as a sort of bonus to sweeten the transaction in order to encourage acceptance. The new preferred stock may be given preference over the old and, if and when it is exchanged, the new stockholders may be given the right to convert the new preferred stock into common stock. The new dividend rate will be below the old rate and the call feature will usually be added if it was lacking in the old issue. If the old stock had the call feature, the new call price will be more favorable (lower) to the company. Either preferred or common stock may be used to capitalize the dividend arrearages. Because the dividend arrearage is the "consideration," the amount of stock offered will be limited so that the shares are "fully paid and nonassessable." As an illustration, if the dividend arrearage on each share is $50 and the par value of the stock is $10, no more than five shares would be offered in exchange for the dividend arrearage on each preferred share.

Any plan adopted should (1) avoid impairment of the firm's working-capital position by paying off preferred stockholders with too much of its cash, (2) improve the market price and stability of the company's securities, (3) resume payment of dividends on both preferred and common stock if earnings justify doing so, (4) eliminate all arrearages, and (5) provide a capital structure that will strengthen the corporation financially and economically.

**Conflicting Interests.** The bargaining position of common stockholders is usually inferior to that of preferred stockholders in recapitalization of preferred-stock dividend arrearages, because dividends cannot be paid on common stock until dividend arrearages have been eliminated. Nevertheless, common stockholders may be reluctant to accept a settlement plan for dividend arrearages that would give preferred stockholders a share in future earnings above the amount of the old preferred-stock dividend rate.

If current earnings are large and the earning trend is expected to continue, common stockholders may take the position that retained and current earnings warrant settling arrearages in cash, thus protecting their interests in future income, retained earnings, and voting power from the dilution that would occur if old preferred stockholders were given common stock in settlement of their claims. Although common stockholders may object to a proposed plan that calls on them to share their ownership privileges, they realize that elimination of dividend arrearages may permit the corporation to pay cash dividends on common stock at an earlier date.

In voting on a plan to settle their claims to accumulated dividends, preferred stockholders are concerned with their prospects for future dividends on preferred or common stock and the proportionate amount of earnings that will be available for this purpose. Their decision to accept or reject a recapitalization plan may rest on their appraisal of future earnings and how they are to share in them under the proposed recapitalization plan as compared to their current rights to dividends including arrearages. However, a recapitalization of preferred stock with dividends in arrears is usually followed by an improvement in the market value of the corporation's outstanding common stock, because it places the common stockholders closer to dividend payments.

Corporations rarely settle large dividend arrearages in cash, as provided in preferred-stock contracts; if management fails to work out a recapitalization plan that is acceptable to stockholders, it may use indirect methods to achieve its ends. Management may succeed in gaining shareholders' support for a merger or consolidation in which the dividend arrearages will be absorbed in the exchange of stock. If a majority of stockholders accept such an arrangement, the dissenting minority stockholders can be paid off in cash, as is usually done in other mergers or consolidations.

## Redemption of Stock

A firm may wish to redeem stock under certain circumstances. For example, a wasting-asset corporation (such as a coal or a copper mine) may redeem stock to permit the corporate structure to reflect the declining natural resource reserves. Or, a firm may sell off or close part of its product line, thereby enabling the capital structure to shrink. Future operations will be on a reduced scale; as a consequence, financial requirements presumably will be less.

*Restrictions on Redemption.* In order to protect creditors as well as stockholders, corporation laws customarily contain restrictions applicable to the redemption of stock. The restrictions found in corporation laws pertain to both redeemable and nonredeemable shares. When redeemable shares are purchased, they may be treated as authorized but unissued shares, unless the articles of incorporation specify that they may not be reissued. In the latter case, this would amount to an amendment to the corporation's charter and would result in a reduction in the amount of authorized capital. Otherwise, reacquired shares are restored to the status of authorized but unissued shares.

Action may be taken to amend a corporation's charter so as to reduce the amount of stated capital represented by shares with or without par value without any cancellation in the number of shares outstanding. The surplus that results from this reduction in par or stated value or capital stock must be treated as capital surplus. After eliminating the retained earnings, part of the capital surplus may be used to eliminate deficits arising from losses.

**Procedure for Redemption.** With a change in financial conditions, corporate management may want to redeem or retire some or all of a particular class of stock, subject to the provision that the total amount of capital may not be reduced below a given amount, such as $1,000. In order to protect shareholders, the charters of corporations customarily specify the procedures to be followed in redeeming shares. If only part of a certain class of shares is to be redeemed, those to be redeemed must be selected by lot. The redemption is effected by call and written or printed notice, which must contain (1) name of class or series of shares, or parts thereof, to be redeemed; (2) date fixed for redemption; (3) redemption price; and (4) place of payment on the surrender of share certificates. The notice of redemption must be given to each shareholder not less than 20 nor more than 50 days before the date set for redemption. After a share of preferred stock has been called, "the security represents only a right to the funds set aside for redemption."[4]

Payment for stock called for redemption may be at a bank or trust company in which the company has made a deposit for this purpose. If the sum is sufficient to pay the redemption price, the state corporation law may absolve the corporation of any further liability to pay. The dividends cease to accrue after the date set for redemption, the shares are no longer classified as outstanding, and the shareholders have no more rights except to receive their payments from the bank or trust company when they surrender their stock certificates. If the holder does not surrender his certificates within six years, the bank or trust company returns the balance of the deposit to the corporation, which has been relieved of all its responsibility for the shares.

**Cancellation of Shares.** After a statement of cancellation has been filed, redeemable shares that have been purchased or redeemed are restored to the status of authorized but unissued shares unless the corporate charter provides that the reacquired shares shall not be reissued. In the latter case, the filing of the statement of cancellation operates as an amendment that eliminates the right of reissue and decreases the authorized capital of the corporation.

The statement of cancellation of shares, which must be in duplicate, is signed by the president or vice president and the secretary or assistant secretary of the corporation and verified by one of the officers signing the statement. It must contain (1) the name of the corporation, (2) a copy of the resolution approving the reduction with the date of its adoption, (3) the number of shares outstanding and the number entitled to vote on the resolution, (4) the number of shares voted for and against the

---

[4] *Uniform Commercial Code, 1972,* p. 528.

reduction, and (5) how the reduction was effected and the dollar amount of stated capital after the change.

Corporation laws place limits on the amount that the capital of a corporation may be reduced in order to protect creditors and shareholders. For example, the aggregate stated capital of a corporation may not be decreased to an amount equal to or less than the amounts payable in case of voluntary liquidation to shareholders having preferential shares or other nonpreferential par value shares. In no case may the stated value of the corporation's capital be reduced to less than $1,000 (or some other minimum sum as stated in the state's corporation law).

## Recapitalization of Debt

With the passage of time, the provisions in debt contracts tend to be more out-of-date than those in preferred-stock issues. Changes in economic conditions and in the financial positions of corporations increase the seriousness of unfavorable provisions in debt contracts, which is compounded by the increase in debt relative to equity in many financial structures. An example of this may be a corporation with a capitalization ratio of 60-percent debt and 40-percent equity. Problems with debt issues are bound to be more difficult for such a firm than one having 40-percent debt and 60-percent equity in its financial structure.

**Legal Background.** Customarily, corporations' charters permit them to make contracts and incur liabilities, such as borrowing money at interest rates negotiated by management; issuing notes, bonds, and other evidences of indebtedness; and securing these liabilities with pledges of corporate income and corporate property. In addition, business corporation laws usually permit corporations to lend their funds for any corporate purpose and to hold real or personal property as security for them.

The relationship between creditors and business firms in need of adjustment are in the form of contracts that may be more difficult to change than provisions in corporations' charters covering the rights and privileges of stockholders. Interest payments, unlike dividends, are fixed charges that cannot be "passed." While stocks usually have no maturity date and therefore present no problem of retirement, debt obligations customarily have maturity dates and their eventual retirement must be anticipated.[5]

***Adjustment Problems.*** Adjustments commonly made to solve debt problems that affect a corporation's capital structure are: (1) a reduc-

---

[5] Article 8 of the *Uniform Commercial Code* deals with bearer bonds, formerly covered by the Uniform Negotiable Instruments Law, and with registered bonds not previously covered by any uniform law. It also covers certificates of stock, formerly provided for by the Uniform Stock Transfer Act, and additional types of investment paper not covered by any uniform act. (*Uniform Commercial Code, 1972*, p. 514.)

tion in the interest rate, (2) extension of the maturity date, (3) reduction in the amount of principal, (4) modification of debt-retirement requirements, (5) relaxation of requirements to maintain certain ratios specified in the trust indenture, and (6) release of pledged assets so they may be used to secure new loans.

1. If interest payments, which are fixed charges, become burdensome, management may open negotiations with lenders for their downward adjustment. Since corporate debts are held primarily by institutional investors, such as commercial banks, insurance companies, and pension funds, it is easier to arrange interest adjustments than if there were thousands of individual creditors. Institutional investors are well informed as to the financial status of the corporations whose debt obligations they hold; hence, the interest-rate reductions they agree to are usually justified by the facts of the case.

2. A common method used by management to make adjustments in corporate debts is negotiating with creditors for the extension of maturities of debts. Although a corporation may be able to finance all fixed charges and other current needs for cash and have an adequate fund for working-capital purposes, it may be unable to meet a maturing long-term loan or bond issue. When these debt obligations are held by one or a few lenders, such as insurance companies, savings institutions, or pension funds, it may be relatively easy to negotiate for an extension of the maturity date; but, if the individual bonds are widely held, it may be next to impossible to arrange for an extension. In the latter case, the best that management may be able to do is to arrange for an extension with the larger creditors and retire the bonds held by others.

3. Another common method used by management is to negotiate with creditors for the reduction of the principal amount of debts. This type of adjustment is made in hardship cases, when corporations are unable to pay off maturing obligations or refund them in full.

4. Provisions in trust indentures requiring funds to be set aside for sinking-fund or installment payments may become financially disturbing to the debtor corporation if they would leave the corporation stripped of cash and short-term investments used to replenish cash. Under favorable circumstances, modificatioins may be made in corporate debt-retirement requirements.

5. When it becomes a hardship for corporate management to maintain ratios specified in trust indentures or loan agreements, concessions by creditors may be the only alternative to reorganization of the debtor corporation. Under some circumstances, it may be possible for corporate management to negotiate a relaxation of some of the indenture requirements inserted to protect creditors from nonliquidity or insolvency of the corporation.

6. In some cases, corporate management may be able to convince

secured creditors that the earnings of the company and their chances of obtaining repayment of their loan would be enhanced if management could borrow at a lower interest rate or under more favorable terms with a secured loan rather than an unsecured loan. Hence, both the company and the creditors would find it advantageous if the security behind the first loan were released for use as security for the second loan. In the final analysis, the security for loans is the amount of earnings after taxes that may be applied to interest and principal repayment; so the lenders may not be sacrificing materially by releasing pledged assets.

**Summary**

Recapitalization of a business corporation occurs whenever there is any change in its capital structure. Such changes may take place in the relative amount or proportion of debt or equity. In any case of voluntary recapitalization, the contractual rights of stockholders and creditors must be taken into consideration. These contractual rights as specified by law or as provided for in contracts may hamper the corporation to such a degree that modification may be required if the business is to continue to operate.

Modifications of capital structure may entail the exchange of debt obligations for equities or preferred stock for common stock. Changes may be made in the par value or the number of shares outstanding, in the case of common stock, by means of a stock split or by a reverse split, or by reacquisition of outstanding shares. In any case, charter amendments are required for basic changes in a corporation's capitalization and such amendments require following statutory procedures to assure validity.

When reclassification of stock is the procedure used to change a corporation's capital structure, it usually involves the elimination or reclassification of noncallable high-dividend preferred-stock issues, either to simplify the firm's capital structure or to eliminate dividend arrearages on preferred stock. Other reasons for eliminating preferred stock are to improve the corporation's bargaining power in case of future combination with other corporations and to increase earnings per share on common stock.

Recapitalization of corporate debt is usually necessitated by changes in economic conditions and in the financial positions of business corporations. With the increase in the relative amount of debt in corporate capital structures, the unfavorable provisions in debt contracts cause increasingly serious difficulties for financial managers of corporations. The holding of debt obligations by institutional investors facilitates adjustments in debt contracts that affect capital structure. These adjustments commonly include reductions in interest rates and amount of principal; extensions in maturity dates; modifications of debt-retirement provisions and in other trust-indenture and loan-agreement requirements; and the release of pledged assets for use in securing new loans.

## QUESTIONS

1. Distinguish among (a) recapitalization, (b) reorganization, and (c) liquidation of a business firm.
2. What factors may cause the cash position of a business firm to deteriorate?
3. What should be the objectives of management in working out an arrangement for eliminating preferred-stock dividend arrearages?
4. (a) What adjustments may be made in common stock to improve the capital structure of a corporation? (b) What is meant by a reverse stock split? When may it be used by management?
5. What are some of the reasons why a firm might change its common stock from a high-par value to a low- or no-par value stock?
6. Why might a corporation exchange its old common stock outstanding for new types of classes of common stock?
7. What is a "liquidating dividend" and how might it be used?
8. Why do corporations exchange their outstanding preferred issues for common stock?
9. Discuss: "Companies can share their profits with shareholders in a number of ways."
10. Explain: "Sinking-fund provisions in a trust indenture may be so exacting as to impair the operations of a company, with the result that the security or earning power behind the issue is weakened." How may management solve this problem?
11. Why might a corporation propose a 1-for-5 reverse split and subsequent rights offerings to shareholders?

## PROBLEMS

1. What effect will the exchange of common stock for preferred stock have on the Diamond Construction Company's balance sheet? How will this change affect the earnings per share of the common stockholders if the earnings before interest and taxes are $1 million? (Assume a 50-percent tax rate.)

    Long-Term Capital Structure
    (in millions)

    | | |
    |---|---|
    | Bonds, 8% | $ 5 |
    | Preferred stock, 5% | 2 |
    | Common stock (no-par, 1 million shares) | 10 |
    | Retained earnings | 3 |
    | Total | $20 |

2. Given the following capital structure of the Seashore Corporation (figures in thousands):

|  |  |
|---|---|
| Long-term debt, 8% | $1,000 |
| Preferred stock (20,000 shares, par $10) | 200 |
| Common stock (50,000 shares, par $20) | 1,000 |
| Retained earnings | 500 |
| Total | $2,700 |

If the Seashore Corporation decides to initiate a 4-for-1 stock split, how will its capital structure be affected? Discuss some of the reasons why management may favor such a move.

3. What would happen to the Seashore Corporation's capital structure if management favored a 4-for-1 reverse split? The par value of the new shares was changed to $10. Discuss some of the reasons why management might favor a reverse split.
4. The Sunshine Manufacturing Company is considering several alternative methods of recapitalization. Its capital structure in 1979 was as follows (assume a 50-percent tax rate):

Liabilities and Equities<br>(in thousands)

|  |  |
|---|---|
| Bonds, 6% | $ 4,000 |
| Preferred stock, 5% (100,000 shares, $20 par) | 2,000 |
| Common stock (500,000 shares, $5 par) | 2,500 |
| Retained earnings | 1,500 |
| Total | $10,000 |

What effect would the following methods of recapitalization have on its capital structure, given that the company anticipates earnings before interest and taxes in 1980 of $800,000? What reaction might be expected by the common shareholders in each case?

a. The outstanding debt is refunded by issuing common stock at $5.00 a share.

b. The outstanding preferred stock is replaced by a 6-percent bond issue.

# 25

# Reorganization of Business Firms

Financial reorganization is the revision of the financial structure of a business firm necessitated by its failure to meet interest, debt repayment, or other obligations. Thus, a business enterprise that cannot meet its maturing obligations is insolvent in a "temporary," "technical," or "equity" sense. At the same time, if the business firm has liabilities in excess of its assets, it is insolvent in the "true" or "bankruptcy" sense. A business firm could be insolvent in the equity sense without being insolvent in the bankruptcy sense; conversely, it could be solvent in the equity sense and insolvent in the bankruptcy sense. An insolvent firm may operate indefinitely as long as it meets its obligations as they come due.

When a business concern is in default on its obligations, its creditors may take action either out of court or in court to liquidate the business firm (see Chapter 26) or they may adjust the business debts either out of court or in court so that the business firm can continue to function. The most important of the adjustment procedures that may be followed are considered in this chapter.

## Financial Structure

The financial plan of a corporation is the projection of issues of stocks and bonds and other debts at the time the corporation is organized or reorganized; but, due to numerous factors, at a later date the financial structure of a business firm may bear little resemblance to the original plan. A study of the financial position of a firm will include a review not only of its capital structure but also of its short-term obligations. There is no longer a sharp division between the credit and capital needs of businesses; hence, the presentation in Table 25–1 of financial structures of

**TABLE 25-1**
Financial Structures * (dollars in thousands)

| Item | Industrial | | Railroad | | Public Utility | |
|---|---|---|---|---|---|---|
| | Amount | Percent | Amount | Percent | Amount | Percent |
| Current liabilities | $ 739,277 | 28.9 | $ 69,958 | 6.6 | $ 39,361 | 7.1 |
| Noncurrent debts | 364,129 | 14.2 | 391,248 | 36.8 | 270,670 | 49.0 |
| Total Liabilities | $1,103,406 | 43.1 | $ 461,206 | 43.4 | $310,031 | 56.1 |
| Preferred stock | ... | ... | $ 4,391 | 0.4 | $ 59,360 | 10.8 |
| Common stock | $ 441,414 | 17.2 | 209,257 | 19.8 | 103,660 | 18.8 |
| Retained earnings | 1,016,273 | 39.7 | 387,114 | 36.4 | 79,185 | 14.3 |
| Total Owners' Equity | $1,457,687 | 56.9 | $ 600,762 | 56.6 | $242,205 | 43.9 |
| Total Liabilities and Equity | $2,561,093 | 100.0 | $1,061,968 | 100.0 | $552,236 | 100.0 |

* Statistics from balance sheets of three companies, the names of which are withheld.

business firms seems more appropriate than a presentation of capital structures would be.

As is to be expected, the short-term indebtedness of industrial companies is proportionately larger than the current liabilities of railroads and public-utility companies. Compared with industrial firms and railroads, public-utility companies are more prone to go into debt, and their financial structures are dominated by long-term debt. While railroads and industrial companies may issue preferred stock, this means of financing is used to a much greater extent by public-utility companies.

The amount of financing with common stock equity is relatively more important for industrial and railroad companies than for public-utility firms. Public utilities are subject to rate regulation, and generally may not retain earnings in anticipation of future expansion requirements. Since improvements or expansion of their facilities are normally large, external financing with bonds and preferred and common stock are characteristics of the industry. A larger proportion of debt is possible because of the existence of the physical plant and more stable earnings due to the nature of the services provided.

In the history of the United States, the most significant peacetime industry reorganization occurred in the public-utility industry following the passage of the Public Utility Holding Company Act of 1935. Congress made mandatory the reorganization of public-utility systems and the elimination of unnecessary holding and operating companies—a movement management had started in 1930.[1] Most operating companies had been kept in good condition throughout the depression; hence, most

---

[1] In 1930, the North American Company sold to the Pacific Gas and Electric Company its controlling interest in the San Joaquin Light and Power Corporation, the Great Western Power Company, and the Midland Counties Public Service Corporation—a logical development because these companies were physically interconnected with the properties of the Pacific Gas and Electric Company.

attention was directed toward correcting financial abuses that developed during the rapid expansion of the industry during the 1920s.[2] Most of the unnecessary holding and operating companies have been eliminated; at the present time, the companies in the industry are among the most efficiently organized and operated in the country.

### Inadequacy of Working Capital

The capital structure of a business firm excludes its short-term liabilities, but financial difficulties that lead to involuntary recapitalization often originate among current liabilities. Usually, a weakening of a firm's current financial position is one of the first indications that it is encountering financial difficulties. The cash position is particularly important because the continuing operation of a business depends not only on paying debts when due but also on acquiring labor and goods and materials with which to operate.

*Importance of a Cash Budget.* If a business firm prepares a cash budget, management can compare estimated disbursements with estimated receipts plus bank balances to ascertain whether loans will be required during the budget period. A sharp increase in required disbursements or a sharp decline in receipts will have an adverse effect on the cash position of a business firm. An increase in disbursements may be caused by losses resulting from hurricanes, tornadoes, fires, fraud, and other causes that may be covered by insurance; but the firm may be faced with a costly interruption in operations as well as a sharp increase in expenditures for replacement of property for which adequate funds may not be available.

*Importance of Sales.* Financial difficulties are frequently caused by a decrease in receipts rather than by an increase in expenditures. As an illustration, when sales decline and outstanding receivables are not collected promptly, the situation is one wherein working-capital assets are frozen, or at least congealed. If current obligations are small, the firm may be able to "weather the storm"; if they are large, the hackneyed term "excessive short-term indebtedness" may be used to explain the firm's difficulties. In either event, the firm's difficulties are the result of a decline in sales or collections or both. Sometimes an increase in sales will lead to plant expansion; later, if sales decline, fixed charges may be too large.

A decline in sales is usually followed or accompanied by a situation wherein inventories are excessive. Such a situation may result if the business firm has been guilty of "speculation in inventories," that is, overbuying in anticipation of higher prices. In addition to having mis-

---

[2] The rapid growth of the public-utility industry was financed in part by equipment-manufacturing and construction companies and holding companies. The public-utility companies were among the first to use open-end mortgages freely.

judged the market, management may have made poor selections of goods or products to be manufactured and sold. In other cases, excessive returns may be caused by too liberal a policy as to returning of goods or canceling orders. When customers want to return goods or cancel orders for no other reason than a downward trend in prices, management may counteract this movement by lowering prices or offering larger cash discounts.

**Importance of Management.** While sales are important to a business firm, collections are equally important. A deficiency in either is, in the final analysis, the fault of management. When so-called reasons for business failures are analyzed, most of them point directly or indirectly to poor management. The validity of the conclusion that most failures are due to poor management is substantiated by the fact that usually there are other business concerns in the same field that are operating profitably.

Because inadequacy of working capital is a common weakness among business firms, sound managerial procedure calls for giving this problem primary attention. Management may keep its fingers on the pulse of the firm's affairs by computing its current, inventory, and collection ratios and comparing them to those of other firms in the same line of trade or industry. Otherwise, management may be satisfied with a business concern's rate of growth without being aware of the fact that the firm's position has deteriorated because current liabilities have increased more than current assets.

In addition to giving attention to a firm's current and other ratios, management should examine the quality of current assets and the nature of current liabilities. A current ratio of 1.5:1 may be considered unsatisfactory; but, if current assets are in the form of bank balances, the ratio may be adequate. On the other hand, a ratio of 3:1 may seem satisfactory; but if current assets are predominately in the form of inventories of questionable market value, the ratio may be unsatisfactory. Hence, the quality of current assets is as important a factor in appraising the current position of a business as the amount of current liabilities. Among the ratios that may be used to test the quality of current assets are cash and short-term investments to current assets, and inventory to current assets.

The tools of financial analysis may include pro forma statements, which necessitate not only the construction of income and balance-sheet statements at the end of an accounting period but also the construction of other statements that project the business firm's operations through the next fiscal year. Management must assume certain results from operations, including the effects of the use of new funds obtained from bank loans, open-market financing, and other sources. After the anticipated effects of new funds are projected on the balance sheet, a ratio analysis of the hypothetical balance sheet should indicate if borrowed funds and the use thereof will strengthen or weaken the business firm.

When the financial position of a business firm becomes strained because of a slowing down in the circuit flow of its working-capital assets, it may be able to obtain cash by selling, assigning, or pledging accounts receivable; selling nonessential fixed and other assets; liquidating inventories by using devices such as "clearance" and "end-of-the-month" sales; and applying pressure to collect past-due accounts. The firm may also conserve its cash or reduce cash drain by using trade credit more fully and refraining from taking cash discounts; reducing salaries (in rare instances, employees have accepted temporary delays in receipt of salaries); and reducing operating expenses for items such as maintenance, advertising, etc. A firm that reduces operating expenses may find the reduction helpful not only in easing its financial strain but also in negotiating with creditors for extensions of maturities of debts and for new loans.

## Excessive Indebtedness

A loss of cash results when interest and principal payments on debts are met (which tend to come at the wrong time, unless planned for in advance); hence, "excessive indebtedness" usually appears among the stated reasons for business firms' financial difficulties not only because the payments reduce a business concern's resources but also because these obligations place the borrower in a position where creditors can demand payment irrespective of the inconvenience caused the borrower.

Customarily, there are provisions in long-term-debt contracts that require assets to be set aside periodically for debt retirement: in sinking-fund bond issues, to retire bonds at maturity; in serial-bond issues, to retire bonds as they mature each year; and in term loans, to meet installment payments on the principal. In most cases, the debt contract requires the debtor to meet certain financial standards, including maintenance of a specified current ratio. Because a financially strained firm normally exhausts its sources of short-term credit first, a decrease in its current ratio below the standard specified may indicate that a default is imminent.

A default on a debt may indicate more than nonpayment of interest and principal, as illustrated by the following:

> The following will be Events of Default: (a) default in the payment of any interest when due, continued for 30 days; (b) default in the payment of principal (or premium, if any) when due; (c) default in the deposit of any Sinking Fund payment when due; (d) default in the performance of any other covenant of the Company, continued for 60 days after written notice; (e) acceleration of any indebtedness for money borrowed by the Company or any consolidated Subsidiary under the terms of the instrument under which such indebtedness is or may be outstanding, if such acceleration is not annulled, or such indebtedness is not paid, within 10 days after written notice; and (f) certain events in bankruptcy, insol-

vency or reorganization. If an Event of Default shall occur and be continuing, the Trustee or the Holders of 25% in principal amount of the Outstanding Debentures may declare the Debentures due and payable immediately.

The Holders of a majority in principal amount of the Outstanding Debentures may direct the time, method and place of conducting any proceeding for any remedy available to the Trustee or exercising any trust or power conferred on the Trustee, provided that such direction shall not be in conflict with any rule of law or the Indenture. Before proceeding to exercise any right or power under the Indenture at the direction of such Holders, the Trustee shall be entitled to receive from such Holders reasonable security or indemnity against the costs, expenses and liabilities which might be incurred by it in compliance with any such direction.

The Company will be required to furnish to the Trustee annually a statement as to the fulfillment by the Company of all of its obligations under the Indenture.[3]

Finally, a bond indenture or a term-loan agreement usually contains an acceleration clause that makes outstanding obligations covered by the contract due and payable at the option of creditors if any term of the contract is violated. If creditors use the acceleration clause to call unpaid balances on outstanding debts, business management may be confronted with a cash demand that may necessitate an adjustment of the debt or liquidation of the firm.

When a business firm has incurred heavy losses, it may be able to prevent default on current obligations by using funds from operations accounted for as depreciation and other allowances; but, in so doing, the firm is liquidating assets and this could lead to insolvency in the bankruptcy sense. This type of gradual liquidation is most serious to intermediate- and long-term creditors who, in case of forced liquidation, look to receipts from sales of fixed assets to cover their claims. Term-loan agreements and bond indentures usually place restrictions on additional borrowing; therefore, a business firm bound by such contracts, while being required to use cash to pay interest and to repay principal, may not be able to borrow when the need for additional funds is greatest.

If earnings decline sharply, the resulting situation may be described as one where fixed assets are excessive, but it would be more accurate to describe it as a situation resulting from unprofitable expansion. Overexpansion may result from enlarging or improving the appearance of retail establishments or manufacturing plants, constructing new buildings, and so on. If improvements financed with borrowed funds are less productive than anticipated, the combination of lower earnings plus the additional debt charges may cause financial strain. Even when fixed-capital expansion is not financed with long-term debt, it may still cause a serious

---

[3] Dayton-Hudson Corporation, *Prospectus, 9¾% Sinking Fund Debentures Due June 1, 1995* (Minneapolis), p. 22.

shortage of working-capital assets, and this may necessitate borrowing under unfavorable conditions.

Poor administration of earnings is a second cause of fixed assets becoming top-heavy. If inadequate allowances are made for depreciation, profits will be overstated, and, on the basis of high profits, sole proprietors or partners may make heavy withdrawals from their business firms and boards of directors of corporations may declare excessive cash dividends. This loss of cash causes a business firm's working-capital position to be weakened and its net worth to be reduced

Once a business firm is faced with insolvency because of inability to meet long-term obligations, it may use the same remedial devices to obtain cash as used by firms having inadequate working capital (see above). In some cases, the problem may be solved temporarily by obtaining an emergency loan; but it may be solved permanently by increasing net worth—if the business is incorporated, by selling stock, and, if unincorporated, by taking in partners. The future prospects of the firm and the ability of management to attract additional investors will determine whether or not either method is practical. If a firm's working capital is adequate, bondholders and other long-term creditors may consent to an extension of maturities of debts.

The decline in wholesale commodity prices looms large among the reasons given for the concentration of business failures in certain years. If, for example, 20 percent of the business enterprises in the United States are marginal, it is not illogical to assume that losses taken on inventories during periods of falling prices are sufficient to eliminate the margin of profit that has kept them in business during good or normal times. Only those firms with adequate working capital that keep liabilities, inventories, receivables, and fixed assets within bounds will be able to take in stride lower profits or losses on inventories during recession periods.

During a business recession, a decline in sales volume may be more significant than a decline in prices as a factor in business failures. Even though prices may be fairly stable, as in the durable-goods-producing industries (machines, tools, equipment, automobiles, etc.) the demand may be so depressed as to cause serious financial strain. As an illustration, if an annual sales volume of 10,000 units (or some other figure) is needed to cover a firm's fixed charges any substantial decline in sales below this figure may cause financial strain. On the other hand, if demand is stable (as for necessities among consumers' goods), part of the strain due to lower prices would tend to be neutralized.

In some industries, labor costs are a relatively high proportion of total costs; in others, they are relatively small. Wage rates are hard to adjust downward; therefore, the degree of flexibility in adjusting operating expenses to meet declining prices varies among industries. A firm in an industry where labor costs are proportionately high is subject to a double squeeze on profits—lower sales receipts and relatively high labor costs.

Management must be aware of the business cycle, the characteristics of its industry, and other factors pertinent to the business enterprise; it adjusts production, market, and financial policies to these risks. Although price history is an important factor in explaining periodic fluctuations in the number of business failures, weakness in capital structure probably accounts for much of the correlation between declines in commodity prices and increases in business failures. A business firm in an industry sensitive to cyclical changes will be subjected to extreme fluctuations in financial needs.

## Out-of-Court Adjustments

There are several remedies available to creditors before resort is made to the courts. In general, the creditors must feel that they will receive a higher percentage of their claims by these adjustments than they would receive by using the courts, or else the latter procedure would be followed immediately.

*Extensions.* An extension is an arrangement where creditors agree not to press for payment of overdue debts until the lapse of a specified period of time. Usually, the obligations in default are short-term, but they may be long-term debts or even sinking-fund commitments as required by trust indentures. Because trade creditors ordinarily advance credit that is unsecured, they tend to be at a disadvantage in both reorganizations and liquidations of debtor firms. Although more numerous, individual trade suppliers usually have less at stake than financial institutions and other large creditors. This situation gives these small creditors a "nuisance" advantage in dealing with the debtor firm and the other creditors (see below).

**Simple Extensions or "Workouts."** Customarily, a simple extension or "workout" is one where a single financial institution, such as a bank or finance company, assumes the leading role in the rehabilitation proceedings. The assumption is that the chief creditor (usually a bank) has decided to "stay with" the debtor rather than force liquidation of the business firm. When negotiating the extension of credit, the bank is confronted with the choice of extending the maturity of all or part of the firm's debt. Sometimes the debtor will be able to pay part of the bank loan, and, often, the bank will accept a partial payment and extend the maturity of the balance.

When many small creditors (such as trade creditors) are pressing for payment, the bank may agree not only to extend the maturity of its outstanding loan but also to make an additional loan so these creditors may be paid in full. As a result, the business firm's total debt will not be reduced but will be consolidated and owed to a bank willing to work with the debtor.

As a condition for advancing additional funds, the bank usually demands added protection; if the firm is incorporated, the officers, directors, or large stockholders may be required to endorse the promissory notes of the corporation. This endorsement means that the personal debt-paying ability of large equity holders or those responsible for the operations of the business firm has been added to that of the corporation. If the officers, directors, and others closely linked to the firm have claims against the corporation, they may be required to subordinate their claims to those of the bank.[4]

In administering a workout, a bank usually insists that the debtor curtail business activities. The workout budget usually specifies that all capital outlays cease, that administrative expenses be sharply reduced, and that purchases be adjusted downward to a basis of much lower production or sales expectations. When arranging a workout, the bank is hopeful of keeping alive one of its business customers; the average bank is frequently confronted with this problem of saving financially embarrassed business customers.

If a workout does not result in an improvement in the business firm's position during the initial or supplementary extension period, other plans may be made. Often, a bank will change its position toward the debtor firm because of some act of other creditors, the debtor's failure to follow the workout budget, or the firm's disappointing performance as checked against expectations.

*Creditors' Committee.* A bank that is one of a number of large creditors cannot afford to stand aside while other creditors receive the major part of the business assets, leaving it little or nothing in case of ultimate liquidation. After working with a business firm, a bank may want extensions of maturities of debts broadened to include the claims of all creditors; or, at the beginning of negotiations for an extension, a bank and two or more creditors may participate in the proceedings. Later, a meeting of all creditors may be called.

The one who calls the creditors' meeing may be a representative of a trade, credit, or manufacturers' association, or of an adjustment bureau (operated by a local association affiliated with the National Association of Credit Management). Adjustment bureaus work in arranging for extensions as well as serving as participants in all types of adjustment and liquidation proceedings.

Either the debtor firm or its creditors may initiate the negotiations for an extension through an adjustment bureau. At the initial meeting of

---

[4] A bank may have a provision in the subordination agreement permitting it to file upon and receive dividends of the subordinated creditors. If a firm has liabilities of $75,000 and assets of $30,000 upon liquidation and the indebtedness is divided equally among the bank, subordinated creditors, and unsecured creditors, each group's "dividend" would be $10,000. Then, if the bank is assigned the $10,000 received by the subordinated creditors, its loss would be reduced to $5,000 ($25,000 — $20,000 rather than $25,000 — $10,000).

the principal creditors called by the adjustment bureau, the debtor is asked to attend and provide any requested records or other information. The bureau may be asked to study the debtor's financial situation and make a report thereon at a formal meeting of the creditors. At this formal meeting, the firm's financial position is discussed and a creditors' committee is usually elected. This committee works out the extension agreement, which becomes a valid contract as soon as all creditors agree in writing; but, if some do not sign, the whole agreement may be called off or some arrangement may be made whereby the minority creditors will be paid off in cash.

While there is no specified form for the extension agreement, it must cover the extension period and provide for control of the business by a creditors' committee for as long as the agreement is in effect. The debtor must sign papers permitting the committee to retain control and operate the business.[5]

In some cases, there may be several contracts; in others, a single contract may be worked out to provide for the extension of old claims, advances of new funds (which may be given priority in repayment), the transfer of management to the creditors' committee, and the return of management to owners when the debts are paid in full. The same contract provisions may be worked out from year to year, provided the firm's financial position is improving, or they may be terminated at the end of one year.

The size of a creditors' committee depends on the number of creditors, the variety of interests involved, and the size of the business firm. Although existing personnel of the business firm may be retained, the committee assumes responsibility for making policy decisions. The creditors' committee has a chairman, usually a banker, who is responsible for seeing that decisions are carried out. Sometimes, the committee will appoint a trained executive to act as treasurer or controller of the business. In a relatively short time, this official should be in a position to tell the committee whether the business ought to be continued or liquidated.

The function of the new or reorganized management is to correct those conditions that precipitated the business concern's difficulties. The financial difficulties of such firms may be solved by changing credit and collection policies; reducing inventories; introducing new products; liquidating advances to directors, officers, or others; and reducing wages, salaries, and other expenses. If the plans of the creditors' committee are carried

---

[5] The papers used to give the creditors' committee control will depend on the form of business organization. If it is a corporation, a voting trust may be set up giving the trustees power to elect directors and appoint officers and to liquidate the business if it seems desirable to do so. Another arrangement is to deposit 51 percent of the voting stock in escrow. A partnership or single proprietorship may file a chattel mortgage on assets with the committee and sign documents authorizing the committee to approve purchases, sales, payments, and salaries and to countersign checks of the firm.

out successfully, profits will increase, net working capital will be built up, debts will be liquidated, and the firm will be in a position to obtain new credit when needed. Then the creditors' committee will be discharged and the control of the business firm will be returned to its owners.

The advantages claimed for the creditors'-committee method of reorganizing business enterprises include the following: (1) The expenses and costs are usually less than when other methods are used. (For example, members of the creditors' committee often serve without compensation and any payment made to them usually follows successful reorganization of the business firm.) (2) Reorganization usually takes place without the unfavorable publicity that would handicap the firm's normal business operations. (3) Although some changes in the firm's personnel may be necessary, a creditors' committee reorganization has the advantage of keeping intact most of the staff to resume management as soon as the committee's control is released to the owners. (4) A creditors' committee may act promptly in settling claims of creditors and thus expedite return of the business firm to its owners. (5) Usually, the committee's representative will take prompt action in case the plans do not work out as anticipated. Under certain circumstances, the firm may be provided with additional funds to finance new activities; under other circumstances, it may move in the opposite direction, to turn existing assets of the firm into cash as soon as possible in order to minimize creditors' losses.

Among the reasons for the lack of popularity of the creditors'-committee form of business reorganization is the inability of such a committee to stop actions of noncooperative creditors who are trying to collect their claims. When two or more creditors sign an agreement with the debtor for an extension of their claims, a binding contract is created. But, since no creditor is forced to sign such an agreement, those who do not are free to demand payment when their claims come due. Many small and some large nonsigners take advantage of this situation to demand payment; as a result, participants in the creditors' committee sometimes find it necessary to make advances to the business concern to prevent further deterioration in its affairs. Sometimes, creditors are in no position to make extensions, as happened so often during the early 1930s. Under such circumstances, the creditors'-committee plan for reorganization may not be feasible.

The creditors' committee also lacks the power, possessed by the courts, to exclude questionable claims and to set aside unprofitable contracts, such as leases. The success of a creditors'-committee reorganization plan depends largely on two factors: the ability of the chief creditors to negotiate a binding agreement among creditors for extension of most of the debtor's obligations and the full cooperation of the owners of the firm with the creditors' committee.

While most extension agreements pertain to the debts of small business firms, sometimes holders of long-term obligations of large business units are asked to agree to the extension of the maturities of their bonds and notes. If the outlook for the company seems favorable, an agreement can usually be arranged with the large creditors; but, often, the small dissenting bond or note holders (hold-outs) must be paid in full.

*Composition Settlements.* Another type of voluntary adjustment that requires the same type of cooperation among creditors and between them and the financially distressed business firm is the composition settlement. A composition settlement is an arrangement wherein the debtor agrees to pay and the creditors assent to receive a percentage of the obligations as full payment, thus to liquidate the debts of the business enterprise. If a debtor realizes that his business firm's position is in danger of becoming hopeless, he may negotiate with creditors to pay them a part of their claims (such as 25, 50, or 75 cents on the dollar). In other cases, the initiative may be taken by a banker, a group of creditors, or a representative of an adjustment bureau who is fully aware of the debtor's position. (As an illustration, a settlement may follow termination of an extension agreement.) Often, a composition settlement is negotiated with the assistance of an adjustment bureau, as in the case of the extension discussed above. Usually, provisions are made for the supervision of the business firm by a creditors' committee until the settlement is completed.

While the details of a composition settlement usually provide for a reduction in creditors' claims by a uniform percentage, there may be exceptions in favor of small creditors who often take advantage of their "nuisance value" to gain better treatment. Before resorting to the more expensive bankruptcy proceedings, the larger creditors may agree that small creditors be paid in full if their claims do not exceed a certain amount, such as $100.

In some composition settlements, provisions are made for the payment of adjusted claims on a stated date or dates, with no provision for further extensions and for dissolution of the creditors' committee when all obligations have been met. In other cases, provisions may be made for settlement of part of the adjusted claims in cash and the remainder in notes payable to the individual creditors, and for dissolution of the creditors' committee either upon delivery of the cash and notes or when all obligations have been met. In all cases, when the creditors' committee is dissolved, all control documents are returned to the business firm.

Every creditor, when offered a composition settlement, has a difficult decision to make. He will want assurance that the offer represents the maximum the debtor can pay, that the debtor has done all he can to meet his obligations, and that an accurate picture of the debtor's financial condition has been presented.

Composition settlements may have an advantage over extensions in that creditors receive some cash at once; but, if the settlements include notes that mature in one, two, or more years, creditors are still faced with collection problems just as they would be in extensions. If the business firm is unable to meet these notes at maturity, it may be involved in new financial difficulties before it has extricated itself from the old. If liquidation of the debtor firms is to take place, creditors might be wise to refuse a composition settlement when the offer is made.

The success of any out-of-court adjustment depends on the willingness of all large creditors to make concessions and of some of them to serve as members of a supervisory committee (usually a thankless position). In addition, banks and other financial institutions may be expected to advance additional funds to the firm, and the major trade creditors may be expected to continue to sell merchandise on regular terms to the business firm. If major creditors refuse to make commitments in extensions or composition agreements, the debtor's financial position will tend to deteriorate.

## Reorganization under the Federal Bankruptcy Act

Article I, Section 8, of the United States Constitution states that "Congress shall have power . . . to establish . . . uniform laws on the subject of bankruptcy throughout the United States." This power was used by Congress in 1800, 1841, 1876, and 1898; although frequently amended, the Bankruptcy Act of 1898 is still in force. The Chandler Act, or Bankruptcy Act of 1938, was the last important revision until 1978.

The federal bankruptcy law contains chapters and sections that cover not only liquidation of insolvent business enterprises but also their reorganizations. The first seven chapters of the Bankruptcy Act contain statutory procedures for liquidation of insolvent business concerns; the chapters added during the 1930s provide for reorganizations.

Prior to the passage of the Bankruptcy Act of 1938, there were many instances where a public need existed for the continuance of services provided by business firms that were unable to pay their obligations or were insolvent in the bankruptcy sense. Examples of such business firms include companies that provide water, gas, electricity, and transportation services. The procedures followed in such cases, where the public interest outweighed the interests of creditors, were developed into a body of rules supplementary to common and statutory law; but, as Congress added new chapters to the Bankruptcy Act, what was formerly called "equity" law became statutory law.

In equity proceedings, a receiver was appointed by the appropriate court (usually a federal court) to operate the business. The receiver was made responsible for operating the firm efficiently and keeping the property intact (preventing seizure by creditors); however, the receiver was not given the responsibility for working out a plan of reorganization. This was usually done by large investors, officers and directors of the corporation, and investment bankers who had underwritten the issues in default. These interested parties took the leadership in the organization of protective committees, but they had to contend with "outsiders" who appointed themselves as members of self-created "protective committees" for the purpose of claiming expenses and fees that were to be paid out of the proceeds from the corporation's assets.

Under the old equity proceedings, there were usually too many protective committees to work efficiently; and, as a result, a reorganization committee was usually selected from among those who made up the stronger protective committees. After the reorganization plan was completed, the next step was to gain approval of its fairness from the court. The final step was the formality of a foreclosure sale from the old to the new company, with the settlement of the claims being made in new securities and with dissenting interests being paid off in cash.

The weaknesses of equity receivership included excessive costs of reorganization, which reduced the share remaining for creditors and other security holders; domination by bankers and "insiders" of the reorganization proceedings, which worked to the disadvantage of general creditors; and creation of reorganization plans that failed to meet the test of feasibility. Under Chapter X of the Bankruptcy Act, "Reorganizations," the Securities and Exchange Commission has been able to limit exploitation by both outsiders and officers of the business firms involved.

The provisions made by Congress since 1932 for reorganizations do not cover all the possible situations that could confront business firms (such as who may vote a block of stock formerly held in trust and whether a favorable vote on a proposed merger is legal). However, equity proceedings are now almost a thing of the past in reorganizations of business firms, because arrangements for less complicated cases are provided for under Chapter XI, for more complicated cases and large corporations other than railroads under Chapter X, and for railroads under Chapter VIII.

*Arrangements under Chapter XI.* An arrangement is defined in the statute as a "plan of a debtor for the settlement, satisfaction or extension of the time of payment of his unsecured debts." The petition to effect an arrangement must be filed by a debtor, not a creditor. It is usually filed in the district court in which the business is located, but it may be transferred to any district court for the convenience of the creditors. The petition will identify the petitioner (name, address, and occupation or place of business); state that bankruptcy proceedings are not pending under other sections of the law; state that the petitioner is either insolvent because liabilities exceed assets or because he is unable to meet his obligations as they mature; contain the proposed plan or arrangement; include annexed schedules containing a full statement of debts and an inventory of assets; and contain exhibits showing executory contracts and a statement of the full and true nature of the petitioner's affairs.

The arrangement may include provisions for treatment of all secured creditors in the same way or division of debts into classes to be treated differently; rejection of contracts; specific undertakings of the debtor during any period of extension, including the payment of accounts receivable; termination of any period of extension provided by the arrangement; continuation of the business with or without supervision or control by a receiver, creditors' commitee, or otherwise; payment of debts incurred after filing of the petition; supervision by the court until provisions of the arrangement are performed; and other appropriate measures.

Following the filing of the petition, the court may (on application of creditors) appoint a trustee or receiver for the petitioner's property and one or more appraisers to prepare an inventory of his assets. The debtor may remain in possession of his property, and he may be ordered to file an approved surety bond to indemnify the "estate" against subsequent loss, pending confirmation of an arrangement.

The bankruptcy law requires that an official meeting of the creditors be called; but, before proceedings reach this stage, much work will have been done by creditors and an adjustment bureau that may have entered the case. Informal meetings may have taken place and a creditors' committee may have been selected; in this case, the committee may have met with the debtor to review the plan of arrangement and possibly revise it. The creditors' committee or the adjustment bureau may have arranged with the court for an investigation of the debtor's affairs (books, inventories, and records), keeping the court informed as to the creditors' wishes and making reports to the creditors.

The referee or judge presides at the first official meeting, allows or disallows claims filed by creditors, and examines the debtor and other witnesses that may be called or that may appear. The plan proposed by the debtor may be accepted or altered; if altered, the debtor must accept the modifications. Creditors present or represented at the meeting have the right to examine the debtor and other witnesses and to suggest changes in the arrangement. The proposed arrangement may not be presented for confirmation until it has been accepted in writing by a majority in number and in amount of proven and allowed claims of each class of creditors. If the plan is not accepted, the first official meeting may be adjourned for a stated period of time. If no agreement is reached at later meetings, the debtor business will be liquidated through bankruptcy proceedings (see Chapter 26).

Assuming that an arrangement is accepted in writing by a majority of each class of creditors, it will go into effect when it is confirmed by the court. Before the court confirms the arrangement, it must apply five tests: Have provisions of Chapter XI of the Bankruptcy Act been observed? Is the arrangement to the best interests of the creditors? Is the plan fair, equitable, and feasible? Has the debtor been guilty of any acts or failed to perform any duties that would be a bar to the discharge of a bankrupt? Has the proposal and its acceptance been made in good faith and not made or procured by means, promises, or acts forbidden in the act? When action is brought under Chapter XI and the facts indicate that proceedings should be under Chapter X, under Rule 11–15 of the Bankruptcy Procedure which became effective as of July 1, 1974, the Commission as well as other parties in interest, except the debtor, have 120 days from the first date set for the first meeting of creditors to file a motion. The time may be extended for good cause. A motion made by the debtor for transfer, however, may be made at any time. The rule requires a showing that a Chapter X reorganization is feasible. This in effect means that a motion can be granted only if the court finds both that Chapter XI is inadequate and reorganization under Chapter X is possible.[6]

After an arangement has been confirmed by the court, it becomes binding not only on those creditors who have approved it but also on all others. The referee or judge determines the time when the debtor is to make his payments and directs the receiver, trustee, or some other person to receive and disburse them. The debtor is discharged by the court as to all debts covered by the arrangement, but the confirmation and discharge may be set aside by the court within six months upon petition of a creditor if fraud was employed in obtaining the arrangement. Such a petition would be followed by new hearings and perhaps a new arrangement or the liquidation of the debtor as a bankrupt.

One advantage of an arrangement is that it compels the minority group of creditors to accept a plan approved by the majority. Since the court must approve claims, an additional advantage of an arrangement is that it offers protection against questionable, fraudulent, and unreasonable claims. The disadvantages of arrangements, as compared to extensions or composition settlements outside the courts, are that costs and expenses are greater and proceedings less flexible, more time-consuming, and usually unfavorable in that they may involve adverse, widespread publicity. However, when there are a large number of creditors or a few noncooperative large creditors, the best solution to the problem may be to work out a reorganization (arrangement) under supervision of a federal court as provided for in Chapter XI of the federal bankruptcy law.[7]

*Reorganization under Chapter X.* Chapter X of the Bankruptcy Act provides for the reorganization of corporations, other than railroads, under the supervision of the federal courts. This chapter is designed to cover the reorganization of large corporations in which there is public interest because of investments in the securities issued by such corpora-

---

[6] Securities and Exchange Commission, *42nd Annual Report, for the Fiscal Year Ended June 30, 1976* (Washington, D.C.: U.S. Government Printing Office, 1977, p. 159.) The W. T. Grant filing of a Chapter XI petition on October 2, 1975, triggered the single largest attempted business rehabilitation instituted under the Bankruptcy Act. There were $1.02 billion and $1.03 billion in assets and liabilities, respectively. However, on April 13, 1976, Grant was adjudicated a bankrupt and a straight liquidating bankruptcy trustee was appointed thereafter. Ibid., p. 160.

[7] See "Emersons Ltd. Petitioned for Chapter 11 Status after its Credit Talks Failed," *Wall Street Journal,* February 11, 1977, p. 31.

tions. The petition to reorganize under Chapter X may be filed by the debtor corporation, three or more creditors having claims of $5,000 or more, or an indenture trustee. The first is called a voluntary petition and the last two are called involuntary petitions; in practice, the first type is the most common.

A voluntary petition, which is usually filed in the district court where the head office is located, must state that the corporation is insolvent or unable to pay its debts as they mature; present facts showing why relief is sought under Chapter X and give details as to the nature of the business; disclose the corporation's assets, liabilities, capital stock, and financial condition; reveal the nature of all pending legal proceedings, including the status of any plan of reorganization, readjustment, or liquidation in connection with or independent of any judicial proceedings; and give the reasons why the petitioner, or petitioners, asks that a reorganization plan be effected. If the judge is convinced that the petition of a debtor has been filed in good faith and meets the requirements of Chapter X, he may enter an order approving the petition; otherwise, he is required to dismiss it. If the petition has been filed by creditors or an indenture trustee (an involuntary petition), the debtor may file an answer within ten days, or within a longer period if the court permits. Answers may also be filed by other creditors, an indenture trustee, or any stockholder if the company is solvent in the bankruptcy sense (assets still exceed liabilities). Customarily, the judge will reject the petition if the creditors acquired their claims for the purpose of filing the petition, if adequate relief could be obtained under Chapter XI, if a reasonable plan of reorganization cannot be effected, or if interests of creditors and shareholders can be served best by a prior proceeding that is pending in the courts.

If the debtors' liabilities are more than $250,000, the judge must appoint one or more trustees to conduct the business pending reorganization or liquidation. For smaller corporations, the judge may leave the debtor in possession and appoint an examiner to perform the functions of the trustees. Trustees and their attorneys must be disinterested (this term is defined in the law so as to bar not only creditors, officers, and stockholders of the debtor but also investment bankers, lawyers, and others who have assisted in the issuance of securities of the debtor corporation). In order to assist in management of the business pending reorganization, the judge may appoint an employee, officer, or director as an additional trustee.

After the decision as to management is made, a date is set for the trustees to present schedules of assets and liabilities (including liens, contracts, and similar obligations) and names and addresses of creditors and stockholders of each class. The judge may also direct the trustees to investigate past management of the firm and to report any facts pertaining to fraud, misconduct, mismanagement, and irregularities on the part of directors, officers, and others. Out of this investigation, factual information may be brought forth to form the basis for prosecution of individuals for past acts. A hearing of interested parties must be called not less than 30 nor more than 60 days after the petition has been signed. At this hearing, objections to continuance of existing management or to the appointment of any trustee may be heard.

Unlike proceedings under Chapter XI and the older equity proceedings, the basic responsibility for presenting a plan of reorganization falls on the trustee rather than on management or security holders. In rare cases wherein the debtor is left in possession (as may be true if liabilities are less than $250,000), an examiner may be given responsibility for filing a plan of reorganization. Nevertheless, creditors and stockholders are permitted to submit proposals for reorganization. Thus, not just one plan but several may be presented at a second meeting of interested parties.

The plan for reorganization must conform to certain statutory requirements so as to meet the tests of being "fair, equitable and feasible." The plan must specify what claims, if any, are to be paid in full in cash; provisions altering or modifying rights of creditors and stockholders; provisions for rejecting any executory private contracts; exclusion of creditors or stockholders or any class thereof that are not to be affected by the plan; treatment of all or any part of the property of the debtor; and payment of all costs and administrative expenses and other allowances (such as those of committees of stockholders and creditors) that may be approved by the judge.

The judge is required to hold a hearing on the reorganization plan following the expiration of the time given to the trustee to file a plan. At this hearing, objections to the plan may be submitted, amendments may be proposed, and substitute plans of creditors or stockholders may be considered. The committee representing unsecured creditors (often working with adjustment bureaus, as in other types of adjustments), secured creditors, stockholders, leaseholders, and others may work together and arrive at a plan that will be acceptable to all; but, more often, they will submit several plans. Following this hearing, the judge must submit the plan or plans to the Securities and Exchange Commission if the indebtedness exceeds $3 million, but such submission is discretionary if the sum is less than $3 million.[8]

The role of the SEC under Chapter X of the Bankruptcy Act is advisory, with the commission having no power to veto or to require the

---

[8] The SEC was a party in a total of 124 reorganization proceedings in fiscal 1976. During the year, 9 proceedings were closed, leaving 115 in which the commission was a party at fiscal year-end. (See *Securities and Exchange Commission, 42nd Annual Report, for the Fiscal Year Ended June 30, 1976* [Washington, D.C.: U.S. Government Printing Office, 1977], p. 152.)

adoption of a reorganization plan. In effect, the commission's technical staff is placed at the disposal of the judge, who may or may not accept its recommendations. The SEC is well prepared for its advisory role, having regional offices staffed with accountants, analysts, and lawyers who keep in close touch with all the hearings, parties, and issues involved in reorganizations. While the reorganization is in process, the commission may be called upon by creditors, stockholders, and others for advice and suggestions as to the proper procedures to be followed. Usually, the SEC participates in proceedings in which there is a "substantial public investor interest" or where "an unfair plan has been or is about to be proposed, public security holders are not represented adequately, the reorganization proceedings are being conducted in violation . . . of the Act, the facts indicate that the Commission can perform a useful service, or the Judge requests the Commission's participation."[9]

Since the federal law states that a trustee must be disinterested, the SEC may present evidence before the judge that will lead to either the resignation or removal of trustees not qualified under the act. The commission may object to the appointment of a second trustee (who may be an officer, director, or employee) on the grounds that the appointment is unnecessary; but, if an officer, director, or employee is appointed, the commission may work to prevent encroachment upon the function of the disinterested trustee.

The SEC also insists that trustees comply with that section of the law that requires trustees to give security holders reports on their investigations of property, liabilities, and financial conditions of the debtor and the operation of the business (often the commission assists in the preparation of such reports). The commission may undertake investigation as to possible courses of action to be followed in case of mismanagement, fraud, or other types of misconduct by officers, directors, and other insiders. It is also active in investigations of conditions under which creditors' and other committees are selected and function.

In appraising a proposed reorganization plan, the SEC must pass on its fairness, equitableness, and feasibility. In judging the fairness and equitableness of a plan, emphasis is on legal and contractual priority provisions for settling claims in cash or securities. Junior claimants may participate only to the extent that the debtor's property has value after satisfaction of all prior claims or that they make additional contributions necessary to the reorganization of the debtor firm. In arriving at valuation of the property, the commission stresses the "appropriate capitalization of reasonable prospective earnings."

In arriving at the value of assets, the greatest amount of disagreement arises in estimating future earnings and in arriving at the interest rate at

---

[9] Ibid., p. 151.

which these prospective earnings are to be capitalized.[10] If anticipated earnings are high and the rate of their capitalization is low, the total value of the property may justify the inclusion of common stockholders in the plan. On the other hand, if anticipated earnings are low and the rate of their capitalization is high, common stockholders may be either excluded or permitted to reacquire an interest in the company by contributing a specific amount of cash for each share of stock held. The SEC is concerned with the adequacy of working capital, the relationship of capital structure and bonded debt to property values, the effect of a new capitalization on the company's prospective credit, the adequacy of prospective earnings relative to interest requirements and dividends on preferred and other stock, and the prevention of the need for future reorganization.

After the advisory report of the SEC is made, copies of the report are made available to the parties appearing at the proceeding. Summaries or copies of the report are sent to all creditors and security holders when they are requested to vote on the reorganization plan. The report may or may not be the basis for approval, disapproval, or modification of the reorganization plan. Before the judge approves a reorganization plan, it must comply with the provisions of the law covering fairness, equitableness, and feasibility; after the plan is approved, the judge then sets a time limit for its acceptance by the security holders.

In the Westec Corporation Case, the SEC filed an advisory report on the trustee's plan of reorganization.[11] The plan provided for the participation of common stockholders, since the company was solvent, and for the participation, as a separate class, of those stockholders who had purchased their stock in the open market in a specified period during which, as the trustee's report disclosed, major manipulations in the Westec stock had occurred.

Acceptance of a reorganization plan under Chapter X requires approval of two thirds of each class of claims (amount of claims, not number of claimants) affected. Not included among those affected are secu-

---

[10] In commenting on its wide experiences with the fairness and feasibility of reorganization plans under Chapter X of the National Bankruptcy Act, the Securities and Exchange Commission wrote as follows: "The Commission has consistently stated that the proper method of valuation for reorganization purposes is primarily an appropriate capitalization of reasonable prospective earnings." The commission commented further, "In recent years the Commission has encountered difficulties because the parties are disposed to base values and capital structures upon inflated war earnings, either because they overlook the extent to which earnings are inflated or hope such earnings will continue long enough to permit debt to be scaled down to manageable proportions." (Securities and Exchange Commission, *10th Annual Report, for the Fiscal Year Ended June 30, 1944* [Washington, D.C.: U.S. Government Printing Office, 1945], pp. 150 ff.)

[11] See "Westec Reorganization Gets Approval by SEC," *Wall Street Journal*, February 11, 1969, p. 17.

rity holders whose claims have not been disturbed, as might be the case with first-mortgage bondholders, and others, such as common stockholders, whose claims have been wiped out entirely. A plan is considered to be accepted by a class of security holders if two thirds of the amount of claims filed and allowed are accepted in writing. Although a class of creditors or stockholders votes to reject a plan that is acceptable to other classes, the plan may be put in effect if provisions are made to protect the interest of dissenters.

Customarily, each class of security holders more or less has its own self-appointed protective committee; for such a committee to be truly representative, it must have either proxies to act for security holders or physical possession of the securities. The latter may be arranged, first, by contracting with a bank or trust company to accept the securities in exchange for certificates of deposit, if and when deposited, and, then, by soliciting the deposit of securities.

After accepting a reorganization plan, the judge calls a final hearing. At this point the plan may still be altered on the proposal of interested parties if, in the opinion of the judge, the change does not have an adverse effect on the interests of other security holders. The judge will confirm the final plan if convinced it is fair, equitable, and feasible and otherwise meets the requirements of the law.[12]

Confirmation means that the reorganization plan is binding on the corporation, its creditors, and its stockholders. As in cases under Chapter XI, confirmation and discharge can be set aside within six months if fraud is involved. The judge may specify that claims that have not been filed or presented within five years will be set aside and any securities or cash remaining with the corporation will become its property or the property of any corporation organized to succeed it.

The judge must pass on the claims of creditors, trustees, attorneys, and others for costs and expenses incurred during the reorganization proceedings. Prior to the 1938 amendment, under equity proceedings, insiders or others in no way connected with the corporation prior to reorganization proceedings often purchased securities of the debtor corporation and organized and controlled "protective committees" to further their own interests. The present law provides for regulation of indenture trustees and persons or committees representing stockholders in reorganization proceedings. Under oath, every representative is required to file a statement

---

[12] Other requirements of the law are: (1) claims of the U.S. Treasury Department must be satisfied; (2) the proposal and plan must have been made and procured in good faith and not by means or promises forbidden by the act; (3) costs and expenses incident to reorganization must have been fully disclosed and must be reasonable, or, if they are to be fixed after confirmation, they are to be subject to the approval of the judge; and (4) the interests of directors, officers, and others who are to manage the corporation must be compatible with those of creditors and stockholders and consistent with public policy.

showing the authority under which he is empowered to act for the creditors or stockholders, giving pertinent facts and circumstances under which this power was granted and indicating circumstances under which securities held by persons represented were acquired. The judge may disregard any proxy, power of attorney, indenture, or depository agreement determined to be unfair or not consistent with public policy. The court seeks to protect the "estate" from exorbitant charges and at the same time provide equitable allowances to creditors' committees and others, when merited.

The SEC has been helpful in reorganizations by presenting facts that have resulted in keeping down the costs of reorganizations. These have included exposure of the lack of qualifications of members of committees and the unreasonableness of claims for services rendered.

**Amendments to the Bankruptcy Act.** The first major revision of the bankruptcy laws in 40 years was enacted in 1978. Perhaps the main reason for the amendments was the explosive growth of consumer credit in the 1970s. As a consequence, an enormous increase in the number of personal bankruptcies strained the existing system. The bankruptcy courts handled over 200,000 cases in the year ending June 30, 1978, 85 percent of them involving consumers, as compared to only 10,000 cases in 1946. Two major changes were enacted: (1) a new network of federal courts having exclusive jurisdiction over bankruptcy cases are to be established; and (2) more rights have been conferred upon debtors than formerly existed. Among other things, the new rules will make it easier for individuals and small business owners with fairly steady incomes to reschedule debts for full or partial payment within three years instead of liquidating property in full bankruptcy.

Before enactment of the new amendments, as noted above, corporate reorganizations used either Chapter X or XI. The 1978 legislation merged these chapters into a new Chapter XI thereby giving creditors and stockholders more leeway in negotiating a settlement plan. The new amendments will ease somewhat the absolute priority rule. Corporate debtors will be permitted to negotiate a restructuring of debt with all creditors and stockholders. If it is the finding of the court that the position of the various claimants will be no worse than it would be under a straight liquidation, then a reorganization plan can be cleared by a favorable vote of those affected. The new law goes into effect October 1, 1979. Of course, as is the case with much new legislation, it will take considerable time before an identifiable pattern will emerge under the new changes thereby permitting comparisons to be drawn with former Chapters X and XI reorganizations. Therefore, it is still too early to say how the 1978 amendments will change bankruptcy proceeding in the years ahead.

**Reorganization under Chapter VIII.** The provisions for reorganization of railroads are contained in Chapter VIII of the Bankruptcy Act, which was added in 1933 as Section 77.[13] Although the general procedures for reorganization of railroads are the same as for reorganizations of public-utility and industrial companies under Chapter X, the Interstate Commerce Commission has the key role in railroad reorganizations. In some cases, the federal district court cannot proceed with reorganization proceedings until the ICC has acted.

Reorganization proceedings may be initiated by filing a petition in the appropriate federal district court by the railroad with the approval of the ICC or by creditors whose claims are equal to 5 percent or more of the company's total indebtedness, 10 percent of all creditors, or 25 percent of any class of creditors. After proper notice and a hearing, the court appoints a trustee, who must be approved by the ICC. The trustee, whose primary function is to operate the railroad, may be a former employee of the company; but, in the case of larger railroads, one or more additional independent trustees must be appointed.

The ICC is responsible for holding hearings on plans submitted by the trustee or on behalf of 10 percent or more of any class of creditors or stockholders, and it must submit a reorganization plan to the court. By rulings of the U.S. Supreme Court, the ICC's findings as to valuation of assets and other facts are final and are not subject to review by the federal district court. Consequently, the jurisdiction of the court is limited to determining the procedures followed conform to the law. However, the court may object to the commission's plan and insist that it be reconsidered.

Creditors, stockholders, and other interested parties are permitted to file objections to the ICC plan; arrangements will then be made for a hearing at which opposition to the plan will be heard. When the court approves a plan, it will direct the ICC to conduct the voting. Then, a certified copy of the plan, which must be accepted or rejected in writing by the different classes of claimants, will be sent to all interested parties. The results will be reported to the court, which will confirm the plan if approval of the necessary two-thirds of each class of affected security holders has been obtained. However, the judge may confirm a plan of reorganization that has not been accepted by two thirds of each class of security holders affected if he finds that it makes adequate provisions for fair and equitable treatment of the claims or interests of those rejecting it, if the rejections are not reasonably justified, or if the plan otherwise conforms to all the requirements of the law.

**The Mahaffie Act.** In April 1948, Congress enacted the Mahaffie Act, which provides for a simple procedure for a mild reorganization of railroads. By adding Section 20b to the Interstate Commerce Act, Congress

---

[13] On June 21, 1970, the Penn Central Company filed under Section 77 of the federal Bankruptcy Act a petition covering its subsidiary, the Penn Central Railroad. (*Wall Street Journal*, June 22, 1970, p. 3.)

permitted a railroad, with the approval of the Interstate Commerce Commission, to propose a recapitalization or readjustment of the company's funded debt to the creditors. When the proposed modification is approved by holders of 75 percent of the aggregate principal (more than 75 percent if the principal amount is held by fewer than 25 holders), the ICC may enter an order approving the change. Minority creditors have the right of judicial review, as under any other order issued by the ICC.

Before the ICC permits the readjustment plan to be submitted to secured creditors, it will have had public hearings on the proposals and will have determined if the proposals are within the scope of the law and in the best interest of the public, the carrier, and the different classes of security holders (those directly as well as indirectly affected). If readjustments can be made under the provisions of the Mahaffie Act, the result could be the avoidance of the expensive, long-drawn-out proceedings that characterize reorganizations under Chapter VIII.

**Reorganization Plans.** In financial reorganizations of corporations under supervision of the courts, the statutes require that plans be "fair and equitable." The U.S. Supreme Court has interpreted this to mean that the doctrine of "absolute priority" must be followed in treatment of security holders. Thus, senior security-holders' claims must be satisfied in full before junior security holders are permitted to participate. After the valuation of the firm, common stockholders may have no equity in the corporation; therefore, they may not be permitted to participate in the reorganization plan. In this case, they may appeal to the Supreme Court for modification of the reorganization plan; if they are successful, a new plan may be formulated. (Other security holders have the same privilege of appeal.)

In order to make a new plan feasible, one class of security holders may have to accept two or more classes of junior securities in exchange for those they hold. As an illustration, each holder of a $1,000 first-mortgage bond may be requested to accept a $500 first-mortgage bond and preferred stock or common stock for the remainder of the principal and accrued interest claims against the corporation; second-mortgage bondholders may receive only preferred and common stock; old preferred stockholders may receive only common stock; and old common stockholders may receive only the privilege of buying new common stock or they may hold no rights at all in the reorganized corporation.[14] The objectives

---

[14] Drew National Corp. concluded its Chapter XI proceedings which were begun in August, 1975. Under the approved plan, creditors with allowable claims up to $500 are to receive a 20 percent payment within 30 days. Creditors with claims over $500 are to receive prorated shares of a sum equal to 40 percent of the total allowable claims over $500, or $4 million, whichever is greater. An initial $150,000 is to be paid within 30 days, and the balance is payable in quarterly installments over 15 years. In addition, the creditors will receive 1.5 million shares of common stock which will represent 31 percent of the total shares outstanding after the new shares are issued. (*Wall Street Journal*, October 18, 1977, p. 3.)

of a reorganization plan should be to reduce fixed charges, eliminate burdensome leases and debt obligations, assure adequate working capital, permit the raising of new capital in the future, and pave the way for a sound financial policy.

## Summary

When a business enterprise cannot meet its maturing debt obligations, the situation may be handled by an adjustment outside of the courts or by an arrangement or reorganization under supervision of the courts. A firm may be able to meet its obligations if given time; and, if creditors choose to stay with the firm, a credit extension may be worked out. The chief creditor, usually a commercial bank, will be influenced by the size, number, and nature of the debts and by the action taken by other creditors. When there are a number of large creditors, the extension plan may be formulated and administered by a creditors' committee. Either the debtor or the creditors may negotiate an extension through an adjustment bureau. The extension plan worked out by the creditors' committee becomes binding on the debtor and those creditors who sign the contract, but nonsigners are free to demand payment when their claims come due.

In other cases, a composition settlement may be effected wherein creditors agree to accept a percentage of the obligations as full payment. Usually, composition settlements are negotiated and administered in the same way as extensions, with a creditors' committee supervising the business firm until the settlement is completed.

During the 1930s, Congress added several sections to the federal Bankruptcy Act to provide for reorganization of business concerns. Under the provisions of Chapter XI of the Bankruptcy Act, an "arrangement," defined as a "plan of a debtor for the settlement, satisfaction, or extension of the time of payment of his unsecured debts," may be effected through a petition filed by the debtor. A petition to reorganize under Chapter X of the act may be filed by the debtor, by creditors, or by an indenture trustee.

In railroad reorganizations, under Chapter VIII of the Bankruptcy Act, plans are filed with the Interstate Commerce Commission. Since the U.S. Supreme Court has ruled that the ICC's findings as to valuation and other facts are final, they are not subject to review by the courts, although questions of law are. When Congress amended the Interstate Commerce Act in 1948, it provided for ways whereby funded debts could be adjusted outside the bankruptcy courts by order of the Commission; however, like other orders of the ICC, such arrangements are subject to judicial review.

In 1978 the first major revision of the bankruptcy act since 1938 was enacted. The amendments in the existing act are concerned with establish-

## 25 Reorganization of Business Firms

ing a new system of bankruptcy courts and with changes strengthening the rights of debtors. The new law goes into effect October 1, 1979.

## QUESTIONS

1. Identify: (a) an extension or "workout," (b) creditors' committee, (c) adjustment bureau, and (d) composition settlement.
2. What are the objectives of any sound reorganization plan?
3. What is the difference between "technical insolvency" and "bankruptcy"? Give an example of each situation.
4. Why is a voluntary composition settlement less likely if the major portion of an insolvent firm's debt is owed to many small creditors as opposed to one large creditor?
5. Legal settlements are, for the most part, effected under Chapters VIII, X, and XI of the Bankruptcy Act. What are the main differences of these provisions?
6. How many creditors are necessary to force a corporation into bankruptcy? What is the minimum total claim of the creditors required by the court for a bankruptcy petition?
7. Why is reorganization usually preferable to liquidation?
8. What is the "absolute priority" doctrine? Why would well-secured bondholders be more likely to favor this doctrine than common stockholders?
9. Analyze: Under the SEC's plan for reorganization of Yuba Consolidated Industries, Inc.: (1) creditors whose claims dated from March 1960 would receive 100 percent of their $6,234,218 claims in cash ($884,415), preferred stock ($4,632,650), and common stock ($717,153), representing 10.47 percent of the equity in the new company; (2) creditors whose claims predated March 1960 would receive 90.9 percent of their claims of $2,323,364 in cash ($165,585), preferred stock ($867,310), and common stock ($1,079,929), representing 15.77 percent of the equity of the company; (3) the holders of $6,170,500 of subordinated debentures would receive $5,050,918 in common stock, representing 73.6 percent of the company's common stock; and (4) current stockholders would receive nothing. (*Wall Street Journal*, May 5, 1965, p. 6.)
10. If a company fails to pay interest on its bonds before reorganization, should the new securities offered in exchange for the bonds be based on the current depressed market value or on the principal amount of the bonds?

## PROBLEMS

1. The capital structure of the XYZ Company is as shown (in millions of dollars):

Short-term debt:
  Accounts payable .................... $ 1
  Notes payable ....................... 2
Long-term debt:
  First mortgage, 7% .................. 2
  Second mortgage, 8% ................. 4
Preferred stock, par value $100 ........ 1
Common stock, par value $10 ............ 2
Paid-in surplus ........................ 1
Retained earnings ..................... (3)

The aggregate market value of the firm's assets is $10 million. The value of the fixed assets on which both the mortgages have a lien is $4 million.

Develop a plan of reorganization that meets the statutory requirements of being "fair, equitable, and feasible."

2. On December 31, 1978, the ABC Company filed a voluntary petition in bankruptcy under Chapter X. At that time, it had the following balance sheet:

ABC COMPANY
Balance Sheet, December 31, 1978
(in thousands)

| | | | |
|---|---:|---|---:|
| Cash .................... | $ 100 | Accounts payable ......... | $ 1,000 |
| Accounts receivable ...... | 500 | Notes payable, 7% ........ | 1,000 |
| Inventory ................ | 1,400 | First mortgage, 6% ....... | 2,000 |
| Fixed Assets ............. | 10,000 | Debentures, 7% ........... | 3,000 |
| | | Preferred stock .......... | 1,000 |
| | | Common stock ............. | 2,000 |
| | | Retained earnings ........ | 2,000 |
| Total Assets ....... | $12,000 | Total Liabilities .... | $12,000 |

The ABC Company can probably earn $600,000. It is determined that 10 percent is an appropriate rate of capitalization.

How would you reorganize the firm?

3. In *Arlington Discount Company,*[*] the debtor was engaged in the business of purchasing, at a discount, second mortgages and installment land-contract receivables. It proposed an arrangement under Chapter XI whereby the 400 holders of $1,194,000 of subordinated certificates of indebtedness would receive 5 percent of their claims in cash at confirmation, 60 percent in noninterest-bearing notes, and the balance in preferred stock. The SEC's motion under Section 328 was based on the need for an impartial investigation of management activities and for a comprehensive reorganization under Chapter X, including an adjustment of secured debt, rather than a simple arrangement of unsecured debts. The court granted the SEC's motion and the debtor filed an amended Chapter X petition, which the court approved.

Why did the SEC request that the arrangement under Chapter XI be shifted to Chapter X?

---

[*] Securities and Exchange Commission, *33rd Annual Report, for the Year Ended June 30, 1967* (Washington, D.C.: U.S. Government Printing Office, 1968), p. 140.

# 26

# Liquidation of Business Firms

In the area of business finance, attention is customarily directed toward the problems associated with the organization, operation, and expansion of going concerns; however, many firms must be liquidated and the likelihood of financial loss to owners or investors and creditors is highly probable. Essentially, liquidation is the process of converting a firm's assets into cash and distributing it in the order of priority of claims of the various classes of creditors and owners. The liquidation of a business firm may be presided over by management, creditors, or an appropriate judicial officer. If the economy is to be strengthened, the buyers of the assets of a liquidated firm must be able to use them more efficiently than the original owners—an economic aspect of business failure that should not be ignored.

This chapter deals with the liquidation of business concerns under the following headings: liquidation of solvent business enterprises, liquidation of insolvent business firms outside federal courts, dissolution of corporations, liquidation under the federal bankruptcy law, and greater protection for creditors (including creditor business firms, as provided by current laws).

## Liquidation of Solvent Business Enterprises

Statistics of the number of business enterprises that have been discontinued for any reason appear periodically in the *Survey of Current Business*. Studies based on the statistics of business discontinuations for certain years have shown that less than one half are due to failure. Although business transfers are not classified as business discontinuations, the purpose in some of these transfers is to prevent or minimize losses. Dissolution of old business firms and formation of new firms is a normal aspect of U.S. business.

The rate of business discontinuations may be much more rapid than the rate at which new business firms are established, as exemplified during the early years of World War II; but the more normal condition is for the number of terminations to be less than the number of new business organizations. While some business discontinuations are due to failure, many are terminated voluntarily for various reasons. Sometimes a business firm disappears not because of inefficiency but rather because of an unusually high degree of efficiency that leads to the firm's acquisition by a second company in order to obtain its trademarks, patents, products, personnel, or trade customers. In other instances, owners of profitable businesses sell them because there is no suitable succession to present management or because a buyer's offer is too attractive to refuse.

During periods of external growth, corporations are acquired and holding-company structures are simplified by reducing the number of corporations. Management seeks simplification of corporate structures in order to obtain more economical financing, reductions in taxes and overhead costs, greater efficiency in production and marketing, and for legal reasons. In replacing the holding company, corporate adjustments usually take the form of dissolving subsidiary corporations and operating them as divisions. Other intracorporate adjustments may take the form of merging some of the subsidiaries with each other or with the parent company. In order to perform some specialized function for the corporate group, a separate corporation may be created.

Some business firms are purchased not because of their profitability but rather because they have been operating at a loss. Such acquisitions enable buyers to reap substantial tax benefits under the provisions of the Internal Revenue Code, which permit a loss to be carried forward seven years or back three years.[1] Although the Internal Revenue Service has made its regulations concerning the acquisition of companies to obtain tax losses more restrictive, the possible tax write-off is often the most valuable advantage obtained in the acquisition of a money-losing company.

Voluntary liquidations are normal in wasting-assets industries. After a natural resource has been fully exploited or depleted, the company's alternative to liquidation is either to shift to some other industry or to acquire new assets in the same field in another location, which most ma-

---

[1] An illustration of the application of the federal tax write-off provision is this: Assuming that the X Company had a loss of $1 million in 1978, it may claim a refund on taxes paid in 1975, 1976, and 1977; but, if it had no profits and paid no taxes during those three years, it may obtain a tax advantage by carrying the loss forward up to the next seven years. In effect, the first $1 million of net profit earned before the expiration of seven years will be tax free. A second corporation may offer to buy the X Company to acquire not only its assets but also its "no-tax on the next $1 million."

jor companies are able to do. A lumber company that follows a policy of replanting rather than one of depleting the supply of timber may be an exception. As noted in a preceding chapter, wasting-assets companies recover capital invested out of earnings, which are accounted for as allowances for depletion. The distribution of depletion allowances to owners as dividends amounts to a gradual liquidation of the business concern.

For a small firm, a policy of using depletion allowances to acquire new assets in the same field may not be feasible; and, if management is highly specialized, to enter a new field of production may be unwise. The return of capital in the form of depletion-allowance distributions may not be taxed as ordinary dividend distributions; stockholders are usually informed as to what portion of their dividends is being paid out of current profits (taxable) and what portion is capital distribution.

A business enterprise may, for one of a number of reasons, liquidate its business in part by converting some of its assets into cash and reducing its capitalization by retirement of long-term debt, preferred stock, or part of its outstanding common stock. A decrease in capital structure and a corresponding decrease in operations may permit a business firm to concentrate on that part of its business that is most profitable and avoid financial difficulties that could lead to insolvency. In some cases, a company may have no choice as to the disposal of part of its business owing to unfavorable court or legislative action. This is illustrated by the liquidation of many holding companies as a result of the passage of the Public Utility Holding Company Act of 1935.

Sometimes, combinations of business units created through the holding-company device or other means will not be successful for various reasons. When an acquired unit is operated as a separate division, financial trouble may be caused by lack of adequate budgeting and control. The most successful acquisitions result when a system of control is established immediately and when the system calls for regular reports as well as current information on management of cash, inventory, accounts receivable, and plans for future financing of current and fixed assets.[2]

In some cases, corporate management, realizing that the prospects of the business concern are uncertain, will liquidate immediately in preference to waiting until the company becomes hopelessly insolvent. In other cases, when firms encounter difficulties in raising needed capital and meeting current obligations, they will choose to liquidate. Among the common causes for changes in business prospects are new inventions, changes in methods of operation, shifts in public demands for products, and local changes in streets or highways that can completely disrupt the operations of retailers and service companies. Even though business prospects are excellent, and enterprise may be liquidated because of the

---

[2] M. VanMesdag, "Why Too Many Mergers Come Unstuck," *The Director*, vol. 24 (April 1972), p. 54.

death or retirement of a proprietor, a partner, a key official, or someone else on whom the success of the business depends. Other reasons for voluntary liquidations include disagreements among owners as to business policy, and decisions of owners to start new business ventures, accept more profitable employment elsewhere, convert personal assets into liquid form in anticipation of inheritance taxes, or diversify holdings. The combinations and variations of reasons why business firms are voluntarily liquidated are almost without limit.

Provisions for voluntary liquidation of firms are made by states' corporation laws. If a corporation has not commenced business or sold shares, dissolution may be achieved by incorporators within two years by filling out the "Articles of Dissolution" and filing it with the secretary of state. When the forms are signed and returned to the incorporators, the existence of the corporation ceases. Voluntary liquidation of small corporations with a limited number of shareholders may take place after written consent of all shareholders, including those without voting privileges. After written consent is obtained, the document with the signatures is presented to the corporation's president, vice president, secretary, or assistant secretary, who executes a statement of intent to dissolve in duplicate. The documents may or may not be filed with the secretary of state, but they should be preserved.

For dissolution of most corporations, the following procedure is used: The resolution to dissolve is approved by the board of directors and then submitted to the shareholders at a regular or special meeting. When the resolution is approved by at least a two-thirds vote of all shareholders, a "statement of intent to dissolve" is filed with the secretary of state. After filing, the corporation must notify all creditors in writing. Then, it proceeds with the liquidation of the corporate assets, uses the cash to discharge its obligations to its creditors, and distributes the remaining cash and other property among the stockholders in exchange for their stock certificates. If the liquidation is to take considerable time, property may be surrendered to a trustee in order to avoid annual fees and other expenses that are normally paid by a corporation.

## Liquidation of Insolvent Business Firms outside Federal Courts

As in the case of reorganization proceedings, insolvent business enterprises may be liquidated either out of court or under the supervision of state or federal courts. Business firms liquidated because of legal action are usually small ones, whereas large firms are usually permitted to reorganize. When the problems are uncomplicated and mutual trust exists between the debtor and his creditors, arrangements may be made for liquidation under supervision of a creditors' committee. If the problems are complicated, the procedure may entail a common-law or statutory assignment or a state court receivership. Since federal law has precedence over state law in bankruptcy cases, either the debtor or creditors may have a case transferred by petition to a federal court.

***Creditors' Committee.*** The problems associated with organizing a creditors' committee and negotiating a liquidation agreement (among creditors and with the debtor) are, in general, the same as those present in formulating an adjustment agreement, extension, or composition settlement. In fact, an adjustment attempt is sometimes followed by a decision of the creditors and debtor to liquidate the business. The distinguishing characteristic of a liquidation by a creditors' committee is the assumption of all managerial powers by the creditors.

If a firm is incorporated, liquidation of assets is followed by dissolution of the corporation; but proprietors and partners continue to live, and, to them, obtaining a discharge or release of all liabilities at the time of liquidation is of utmost importance. On the other hand, creditors prefer that liabilities be kept alive, because the debtor may acquire assets in the future that could be seized to settle unpaid claims. Unless a release or discharge from the unpaid balances of the debts can be obtained from all creditors, the debtor may prefer to file a petition in bankruptcy and have the proceedings transferred to a federal court. A threat to do so may result in concessions from creditors who are reluctant to sign a release; in addition, uncooperative or recalcitrant creditors may be subjected to pressure from other creditors who favor an out-of-court settlement, which is generally to the advantage of the creditors. As in the case of composition settlements or extension agreements, uncooperative small creditors may be paid in full; but, in other cases, the only feasible solution may be to resort to the federal courts.

When there are a small number of creditors and they trust the debtor, they may permit him to liquidate his business and prorate the cash among them with or without supervision of a creditors' committee. Sometimes, a representative of the local adjustment bureau of the National Association of Credit Management will work closely with the debtor and creditors in liquidation proceedings. The representative will act not only as an adviser but also a depository and distribution agent for funds to be given to creditors. If evidence of fraud or unfair treatment appears, all proceedings may be stopped by either the creditors or the debtor and federal bankruptcy proceedings may be initiated.

***Common-Law Assignments.*** A debtor who feels the business is hopelessly insolvent may make an assignment of all the assets to a trustee (also called an assignee) who is to manage and hold them in trust for the benefit of the creditors pending settlement of creditors' and other claims against these assets. It is a transfer of the title with the intent, at the time of the assignment, to part with all interest in the assets being transferred. Such assignments may be effected under state statutes or under common law. A common-law assignment is usually conducted under a committee of creditors, which means that the publicity associated with a statutory assignment may be avoided (the latter being a matter of public record). The common-law assignment or one made under the state law is an act of bankruptcy; as such, it permits the creditors to petition the debtor into bankruptcy within four months. Thus, both common-law and statutory assignments require the consent of creditors.

While the initiative in making an assignment of assets is taken by the debtor, it is usually with the consent of the chief creditors; and, while the debtor selects the trustee, this advantage is theoretical because so-called voluntary assignments are commonly made under pressure of creditors, who are instrumental in the selection of the trustee or assignee. The assignee is the trustee for the creditors; and, as in any trust, the beneficiaries have remedies against the trustee for improper or illegal actions in administering trust affairs. While assignment may be approved by either state or federal courts, some are set aside because of fraud.

Sometimes a banker who has been closely connected with the business firm (as one who has been active in a previously attempted workout) is selected as the trustee; but, in other cases, assignments may be made to friends, lawyers, adjustment bureaus, credit management associations, or trade associations. Since the plan to liquidate a business may follow an unsuccessful attempt to rehabilitate the firm under supervision of a creditors' committee, the best results may be obtained by using the same individuals to work out the liquidation proceedings.

To be effective, all creditors must accept the assignment arrangement; and once creditors have consented to an assignment, they may not file petitions in bankruptcy. Often, a representative of an adjustment bureau is selected to be the original or replacement assignee because he is well qualified to obtain the signatures of all creditors. Willingness of creditors to accept an assignment agreement depends on their confidence in the ability of the trustee as well as their satisfaction as to the good faith of the debtor.

The legal procedure for the transfer of assets from the debtor to the trustee varies, but it may be done by executing a chattel mortgage, power of attorney, or deed of trust. The function of the trustee is to preserve, collect, and distribute assets for the benefit of creditors without preference, except as may be prescribed in the instrument of assignment. The advantages of using an assignment as the method of transferring title to property for the benefit of creditors are: (1) it is less expensive than bankruptcy proceedings; (2) the trustee has sufficient time to liquidate assets because there is no time limit set for termination of the trust; and (3) the administration of the estate is private, rather than a public matter as in bankruptcy cases.

The disadvantages of using an assignment in liquidating an insolvent firm are: (1) the trustee is personally liable to all creditors for any actions, therefore, the trustee may be ultraconservative in carrying out the duties despite the fact that the trustee has a great deal of freedom in selling assets and in administering the affairs of the estate; (2) an assignment may be upset and the proceedings transferred to a federal or state court, which would mean a delay in settling the affairs of the debtor; (3) the trustee lacks powers possessed by the court, such as the right to examine the debtor under oath and to recover preferential payments made to certain creditors; and (4) a creditors' committee may work closely with the assignee, but its supervision may not be so effective as that of a court over a receiver. The legal basis for a common-law adjustment is the consent of the creditors, which must be made in compliance with the terms of the instrument of assignment. While common law permits preference to be given in the assignment instrument to some creditors, statutory law generally forbids this practice of discrimination.

Even though assignments may be administered under supervision of state courts, there are territorial limitations on the power of the assignees and there is a lack of uniformity in the laws and requirements of various states. Considered from the viewpoint of the debtor, the most serious objection to a common-law or statutory assignment may be the inability to secure a release from creditors, particularly those from outside of the state, from the unpaid portion of the debts. (A debtor may bring about a petition in bankruptcy by making an assignment that would cause creditors to take action to have the proceedings transferred to a federal court.)

Although states have provisions for receivership and liquidation of insolvent business enterprises, the federal bankruptcy law; with its provisions for reorganizations and for the discharge of debtors, has largely superceded these state statutes. There may be no advantage in proceeding under state courts since dissenting creditors may have almost any settlement reached therein transferred to a federal court. In addition, state courts have limited territorial jurisdiction. However, while creditors have the right to transfer a liquidation proceeding from a state court to a federal bankruptcy court, they may choose not to do so because the costs involved are generally greater.

The chief differences between a statutory and common-law assignment are that the former is recorded and the latter is not, and the administration of a statutory assignment is supervised by a court, while a common-law assignment is supervised by a creditors' committee. Under federal law, an assignment is one of the acts of bankruptcy, but a creditor who has signed an assignment agreement may not file a petition of bankruptcy. Therefore, a creditor should not agree to an assignment unless there is faith in the trustee (who is selected by the debtor). The trustee may be a personal friend of the debtor, a banker, or a lawyer, qualified to perform the required duties. These duties include: (1) giving public notice of the appointment and the assignment; (2) executing bonds as required for trustees; (3) taking possession of the debtor's property as listed along with the other assignment papers; (4) collecting assignor's debts; (5)

selling property assigned to the trustee; (6) paying expenses and distributing liquidating dividends to creditors from time to time out of the proceeds; (7) releasing surplus funds to the assignor; and (8) closing the estate by filing an accounting with the proper local official.

*Statutory Assignments.* Although all states have provisions for statutory assignments, they are used less frequently than common-law assignments. Although there are some differences between the two, in general, they are similar. In common-law assignments, preferences may be given to certain classes of creditors that may or may not be permitted under state statutes. After assignments have been initiated, the creditors may request the appropriate state court to replace the original assignee. The instrument used in making an assignment is prescribed by law and it must be filed in the appropriate public office (thereby giving publicity to the proceedings). Final accounting must be made by the trustee to the appropriate state court.

*State-Court Receivership.* State laws also may have provisions for liquidation and rehabilitation of business firms or for seizure of specific assets that are involved in litigation. To carry out these objectives, receivers may be appointed by an appropriate state court. The purpose of receivership is to protect the interests of majority parties, which may necessitate operating a business even though it means that the legal or contractual rights of minority parties are temporarily set aside (as in seizure of assets, the loss of which would cripple a firm). In other cases, the situation may be such that the interests of all except certain minority parties are best served if the assets are liquidated. State receiverships may be available only in specified instances and then only when other remedies are not available. In some states, a state-court receiver operates in liquidations like a statutory assignee; but, being an officer of the court, the receiver is selected by the court and not by the creditors or the debtor.

## Dissolution of Corporations

Business-corporation acts provide for both voluntary and involuntary dissolution of corporations, the former being outside of the court and the latter being under court supervision. Sometimes a dissolution proceeding that starts on a voluntary basis is shifted to the courts at the request of either the corporation or the dissenting creditors. Irrespective of how a corporation is dissolved, creditors of the debtor corporation face different problems than those faced by creditors of an unincorporated business firm in process of dissolution.

The fact that a corporation ceases to exist upon dissolution means that its creditors must file and collect claims against the corporation before dissolution. As noted previously, single proprietors and partners live on after the liquidation of their business firms and they may be held responsible for unpaid balances unless a release or discharge is obtained from the creditors. However, a corporation may retain assets and place them in trust as a reserve to satisfy liabilities and other claims against a company.

The simplest procedure for dissolution of a corporation is by written consent of all stockholders. Since this method of initiating a dissolution procedure requires the signatures of all stockholders, it is used only when there are but a few stockholders. In most cases, the initiative for voluntary dissolution is taken by the corporation. This involves the adoption of a resolution by the board of directors that the corporation be dissolved and, subsequently, the affirmative vote of at least the required percentage of shares outstanding (usually two thirds). Irrespective of the method used, a "statement of intent to dissolve" must be filed with the secretary of state or the appropriate state official.

Filing the statement of intent to dissolve gives creditors of the corporation an opportunity to present their claims against the corporation. In addition, the corporation must give written notice to each known creditor or other claimant and must cease doing business, except that which is incidental to the winding up of its affairs. Normally, the corporation continues to exist until a certificate of dissolution is issued by the secretary of state. Some state laws provide that voluntary dissolution proceedings may be revoked at any time prior to issuance of a certificate of dissolution by the secretary of state. If voluntary dissolution proceedings have not been revoked and if all provisions of the law have been met, the secretary of state will issue a certificate of dissolution.

Sometimes a corporation is dissolved but the business is not discontinued; in this case, the corporation's legal existence ceases, but the business may be operated as an unincorporated business firm or the assets may be absorbed by a second corporation or a new corporation, as in a merger or consolidation. Section 11 (b) of the Public Utility Holding Company Act of 1935, which requires the public-utility systems to dissolve or reorganize companies that do not fit into "a single integrated public-utility system" or that "unduly or unnecessarily complicate the structure," has probably been responsible for the dissolution of more corporations than any act in modern history.

In addition to voluntary surrender of charters, corporations may be dissolved through state judicial proceedings. The attorney general may take dissolution action in the appropriate state court for such causes as failure to file an annual report as required by law; failure to pay fees, franchise taxes, or penalties prescribed by law; and failure to maintain a registered agent in the state. In addition, legal action to dissolve a corporation may result if the corporation exceeds or abuses the authority conferred on it by law or if misrepresentation has been made of any material matters in reports and other documents submitted by such corporation as required by the statutes. However, if a corporation eliminates the cause of action before dissolution, legal proceedings to dissolve the corporation usually cease.

Other reasons for involuntary dissolution of corporations may include (1) the occurrence of some contingency provided for in the charter, such as consolidation or merger; (2) failure to commence business within a certain period of time; (3) expiration of the period for which the corporation was chartered; (4) an act of the state legislature; or (5) failure or losses. However, liquidation and dissolution result most frequently because a corporation is technically insolvent.

A state court may appoint a receiver to liquidate a corporation when other remedies available either at law or equity are deemed inadequate. The receiver has all the duties and powers customarily bestowed on receivers. The court will enter a decree dissolving the corporation after the costs and expenses of such proceedings have been paid, all debts and other liabilities have been discharged, and the remaining property—if any—has been distributed to the shareholders. If the assets are insufficient to satisfy all costs, expenses, debts, and other liabilities, the court will enter a decree dissolving the corporation after assets are distributed equitably as far as they will go in payment. For reasons already considered, most corporations that are insolvent are liquidated under supervision of the federal courts (see below).

### Liquidation under the Federal Bankruptcy Act

The current bankruptcy law of the federal government dates from 1898, but it has been amended frequently by Congress and interpreted and supplemented by general orders and rules adopted or prescribed by the Supreme Court of the United States. In order to bring about uniformity in procedures, the Supreme Court has adopted official forms to be employed by officers of the bankruptcy courts, debtors, creditors, and other parties. In addition, other supplementary but unofficial forms are available to cover contingencies in bankruptcy proceedings.

*Purpose of the Bankruptcy Act.* With regard to liquidating insolvent business concerns, the federal Bankruptcy Act has two main purposes: (1) to convert the assets of insolvent debtors into cash so as to pay the claims of secured creditors according to the priority of their claims and to distribute the remainder to other creditors in proportion to their claims as filed and allowed by the court; and (2) to relieve honest but unfortunate debtors of the obligation for unpaid portions of their debts in order to give them the opportunity to renew their business activities without being subjected to past claims that might make continuance in business impossible. This discharge of the bankrupt is now considered to be only a secondary objective of bankruptcy proceedings, because now emphasis is on the protection of creditors against fraud prior to or during liquidation proceedings and the equitable distribution among them of the debtors' available assets.

**Voluntary and Involuntary Bankruptcy Petitions.** Bankruptcy proceedings for liquidation purposes under federal law are initiated by a petition filed either by the debtor or by the creditors on an official form in which the petitioners request that the debtor be adjudged a bankrupt.[3] If the petition is filed by the debtor, voluntary bankruptcy is involved; if filed by creditors, involuntary bankruptcy is involved. Petitions may be filed by or against persons, partnerships, and corporations (except municipal corporations, railroads, insurance companies, incorporated banks, or savings and loan associations).[4]

**Acts of Bankruptcy.** An involuntary petition of bankruptcy must allege that the debtor has committed, within the four months preceding the filing of the petition, one or more of the following six acts of bankruptcy: (1) committing fraud while insolvent, such as transferring, concealing, or removing assets with the intent to hinder, delay, or defraud creditors; (2) giving one or more creditors a preference or an advantage over others while insolvent, such as transferring or permitting legal seizure of assets; (3) permitting any creditor to obtain a lien on property while insolvent (a passive way to give preference); (4) making a general assignment for the benefit of creditors, whether or not the debtor is insolvent at the time; (5) permitting appointment of a receiver or trustee to take charge of the property while insolvent in either the bankruptcy or equity sense; and (6) admitting in writing inability to pay debts and willingness to be adjudged a bankrupt whether solvent or insolvent at the time.

**Adjudication.** If forms are filled out properly, the judicial decision on a voluntary bankruptcy petition is made immediately; but, in involuntary proceedings, the debtor (defendant) is given an opportunity to make and answer charges. He may deny having been insolvent at the time the alleged bankruptcy act was committed, or he may question the court's jurisdiction, and so on. A hearing will be held at which evidence may be submitted by creditors in favor of and opposed to the debtor. Then the case will either be dismissed for lack of evidence or the debtor will be adjudged a bankrupt. If no answer is filed by the defendant, which is the ordinary procedure, he will be adjudged a bankrupt by default. So, bankrupt companies are those that have been declared bankrupt by a federal court.

---

[3] When there are 12 or more creditors, the petition must be filed by 3 or more creditors having provable claims totaling $500 or more in excess of any specific security they may have; but, if the number of creditors is less than 12, a single creditor may file if he has unsecured claims of $500 or more.

[4] The term corporation, as used in the Bankruptcy Act, includes partnership associations, joint-stock companies, business trusts, and unincorporated companies. Creditors may not file a petition in bankruptcy against persons owing less than $1,000, against wage earners whose compensation does not exceed $1,500 a year, or against farmers engaged chiefly in tilling the soil.

***Referee in Bankruptcy.*** After adjudication, the case is transferred to a referee in bankruptcy. This judicial officer is appointed for a term of six years; but, because appointments may be renewed, his tenure of office may be prolonged indefinitely. Referees may perform all the duties conferred on the courts by the federal Bankruptcy Act, subject to review by the judge. Among the more important duties of a referee in bankruptcy are: (1) to see that the bankrupt files a schedule of assets and a list of creditors properly; (2) to notify creditors and other interested parties of meetings and actions in the proceedings; (3) to keep and furnish requested information to the court and interested parties; (4) to declare liquidating dividends to be distributed to creditors and to prepare dividend sheets showing dividends declared and to whom payable; and (5) to keep all records of the case until its conclusion and then to transmit them to the clerk of the court, where these records will remain open for inspection. (Since real estate is commonly involved, such records are valuable to abstractors in tracing changes in title to real property.)

***Receiver in Bankruptcy.*** Before the selection of a trustee to take charge of the bankrupt's estate in liquidation proceedings, a receiver may be appointed by the judge to take possession of all or part of the debtor's property and to prevent further deterioration of the estate. Action is usually taken upon petition by creditors either before or after the hearings on the bankruptcy petition. The tour of duty of an appointed receiver may be a short one, but this is unlikely, since bankruptcy proceedings are apt to be drawn out over a long period of time. A receiver's primary function is to preserve, not to administer, the debtor's estate; perishable assets may be sold, and such other duties performed as are defined in the order of the judge or referee who made the appointment. If no receiver is appointed, it is the duty of the bankrupt to preserve the value of the property pending appointment of a trustee. The appointment of a receiver in bankruptcy can be justified only when such action is absolutely necessary to preserve the estate. Title to the property remains with a bankrupt until a trustee has been selected.

***Action by Creditors.*** The trustee in liquidation proceedings under the federal Bankruptcy Act is the officer of the court who takes charge of the administration and settlement of the bankrupt estate. He is selected at the first meeting of the creditors, but his election is subject to the approval of the judge or referee. If creditors cannot elect one or more trustees (there may be three) by a majority vote, the trustee or trustees may be appointed by the court. The referee calls and presides over the meeting of the creditors soon after the debtor is adjudged a bankrupt. Usually, the creditors select a committee to represent them in later proceedings (such as consulting with and advising the trustee in the performance of his duties). Since bankruptcy proceedings are conducted in the interest of general creditors, secured creditors are not permitted to vote except when their claims exceed the probable value of pledged assets.

Creditors may be represented at creditors' meetings by proxy or attorney; no given quorum is required at such meetings.

The creditors must file a "proof of claim," which means they must present a sworn statement setting forth their claims upon forms and in a manner prescribed by the Supreme Court of the United States. It is a crime punishable by imprisonment for a period not exceeding five years to present a false proof of claim against the bankrupt's estate. After claims are filed (proved), they are either allowed or rejected. Before the election of a trustee, either a creditor or the bankrupt may object to a claim, thereby making it subject to reexamination. After election and confirmation, the trustee handles such matters.

**Trustee in Bankruptcy.** The trustee acquires all the bankrupt's property as of the date of the filing of the bankruptcy petition. The trustee has the power or right to acquire or reacquire property fraudulently transferred; property held by an assignee; and property committed to or invested in the bankrupt by inheritance, bequest, or otherwise within six months after such bankruptcy is filed.

After taking title to the bankrupt's property, the trustee's duty is to liquidate it as soon as possible under supervision of the court; therefore, persons having selling ability and experience in the same line of business as the bankrupt are often elected as trustees. Receipts are deposited in one of the depositories (banks) designated for the receipt of bankruptcy-court funds. Obligations are met in the order of their priority as follows: (1) actual and necessary expenses of preserving the bankrupt estate; (2) wages due workmen and other employees earned within three months before commencement of bankruptcy proceedings but not to exceed $600; (3) creditors' costs incurred in preventing discharge of the bankrupt under an arrangement or other proceedings and in convicting any person for an offense under the act; (4) taxes due the federal, state, and local governments; (5) debts given priority by federal and state law; and (6) general creditors.

Following liquidation and distribution of assets, a final hearing is called at which the trustee gives an accounting to the creditors and the referee. If no objections are raised, the trustee's accounts will be approved by the referee and the court will discharge the bankrupt.

**Discharge of the Bankrupt.** The discharge of the bankrupt is a release granted by the court from all debts that remain unsatisfied, except (1) taxes due to the federal, state, and local governments; (2) liabilities for obtaining property by false pretenses, malicious injuries, alimony, support of husband or wife and child, and similar personal liabilities; (3) unscheduled claims; (4) claims against the bankrupt arising because of fraud, embezzlement, and so on while acting in a fiduciary capacity; (5) wages earned within three months prior to bankruptcy proceedings; and (6) money deposited by employees as security for faithful performance of duties during their term of employment.

A discharge may not be allowed if the bankrupt has (1) committed certain offenses punishable by imprisonment under the bankruptcy act, (2) destroyed records, (3) made fraudulent transfers of assets, (4) been granted a discharge in bankruptcy within six previous years, (5) refused to obey orders of the court, or (6) failed to explain satisfactorily deficiencies or losses in assets.

The judge of the bankruptcy court may reopen the case before the lapse of a reasonable amount of time on the application of the creditors (the common reason for doing so is the discovery of new assets). In this case, a new trustee will be elected and the foregoing procedures will be repeated.

## Greater Protection for Creditors

Since the passage of the Chandler Act of 1938, most of the major abuses that formerly marred bankruptcy proceedings have been eliminated. No longer are persons relatively safe from prosecution if they participate in fraudulent bankruptcies. In the past, bankruptcy assets remaining for creditors were greatly reduced because, too often, referees, trustees, receivers, and creditors' attorneys combined to "milk" the bankrupt's assets for personal gain. In bankruptcy and reorganization cases, the court must settle the problem of determining the amount of funds to be paid (out of what is left of the debtor's estate) to various committees and others for services and expenses incurred in the proceedings.

Although the Securities and Exchange Commission receives no compensation, it has been helpful to the courts in examining applications for compensation. In the R. Hoe & Co., Inc., case, three applicants sought compensation totaling $1,087,000. the SEC recommended compensation of $367,000, and the court awarded allowances totaling $550,000.[5] The trustee of the Canadaigua Enterprises Corporation requested a final allowance of $750,000. The Commission contended that the request was excessive, and recommended a final allowance of $240,000, but the court granted an award of $310,000.[6] In the Farmington Manufacturing Company case, the Court of Appeals for the Fourth Circuit held that the lower court's award of $350,000 for a Chapter X trustee was insufficient and adopted the Commission's recommendation of $575,000 for services rendered through June 30, 1973.[7]

The remuneration of officials and other participants in bankruptcy

---

[5] Securities and Exchange Commission, *37th Annual Report, for the Fiscal Year Ended June 30, 1971* (Washington, D.C.: U.S. Government Printing Office, 1972), pp. 194–95.

[6] Ibid., p. 195.

[7] Securities and Exchange Commission, *42nd Annual Report, for the Fiscal Year Ended June 30, 1976* (Washington, D.C.: U.S. Government Printing Office, 1977), p. 158.

proceedings is controlled by law and regulations, and the qualities of ability and integrity are emphasized in selecting appointees. However, if creditors would participate more actively in bankruptcy proceedings, even better administration and more vigorous criminal prosecution of fraudulent debtors might result.

The Chandler Act provides opportunities for closer and more intelligent control by creditors by requiring (1) the selection of a creditors' committee of three or more at the first creditors' meeting and giving the committee official standing to advise and to consult with the trustee; (2) notice be given of all applications for compensation (attorneys for the bankrupt, the referee, the receiver, the trustee, the creditors, and any others); (3) information be provided as to sale of assets, compromises of claims if more than $1,000, and other similar matters; and (4) exclusion of creditors with claims of less than $50 in computing the number eligible to vote at creditors' committee meetings when trustees are selected.

The act also makes provisions for (1) mandatory examination of bankrupts (instead of merely permissive examination); (2) criminal action applicable to debtors in reorganization as well as in bankruptcy; (3) classification of sections pertaining to liens, preferences, and fraudulent transfers; and (4) appointment of an equity receiver being construed as an act of bankruptcy. As noted in the preceding chapter, greater protection was given to security holders in Chapter X of the Bankruptcy Act by (1) providing for the appointment of a disinterested trustee by the judge (if indebtedness is over $250,000) who is to assume the leading role in evolving a plan of reorganization; (2) requiring the submission of the plan to the Securities and Exchange Commission (if indebtedness exceeds $3 million); and (3) requiring the trustee to ascertain whether any basis exists for charges of fraud, misconduct, or mismanagement, when so directed by the court.

Under the most favorable conditions, bankruptcy proceedings are expensive; therefore, trade associations try to hold down the costs of rehabilitation of financially embarrassed business firms and liquidation of others by out-of-court settlements (these settlements exceed in number those made under supervision of the courts). When nonbankruptcy proceedings are used for liquidation purposes, adjustment bureaus may perform the functions of creditors' committees or, at least, cooperate closely with them. Usually, adjustment bureaus have both an intimate knowledge of the debtors' affairs and contacts with their chief suppliers, who are usually most numerous among unsecured creditors. It is due, in part, to the activities of credit adjustment bureaus that more cases are being adjusted out of court and costs of court cases have been reduced. Nevertheless, sight must not be lost of the fact that, to the extent creditors are not permitted to seize assets at random by court proceedings, a firm is not faced with a situation wherein the seizure of certain assets would prevent the efficient use of all the company's property.

## Summary

A business enterprise may be liquidated by procedures involving common consent of the debtor and creditors, common-law or statutory assignments, corporate dissolution, state-court receivership, or federal bankruptcy proceedings. During any year, many business discontinuations are voluntary liquidations of solvent business enterprises. Many are proprietorships and partnerships where death or retirement of owners often leads to dissolution of the business firm. In some cases—such as firms in wasting-assets industries—voluntary liquidations are common; sometimes the threat of insolvency may lead to voluntary liquidation to minimize or prevent losses.

Insolvent business enterprises may be liquidated voluntarily or involuntarily, either outside of courts or under the supervision of state or federal courts. When liquidated outside of courts, the procedure may be a common-law assignment under supervision of a creditors' committee. Although similar in most respects to common-law assignment, statutory assignment is a matter of public record since it necessitates filing with the appropriate public official.

When insolvent business concerns are liquidated under the federal Bankruptcy Act, the bankruptcy proceedings may be initiated by a petition filed by the debtor or creditors. An involuntary petition, one initiated by creditors, must allege that the debtor has committed one or more of the six acts of bankruptcy within four months preceding the filing of the petition. If the debtor is adjudged a bankrupt, a referee in bankruptcy is appointed. Before the appointment of a trustee, a receiver in bankruptcy may be appointed to preserve the debtor's estate.

The trustee, selected by creditors, subject to approval of the judge or referee, is the officer of the court who administers and settles the bankrupt's estate. After liquidation and distribution of assets, barring objections, the trustee's accounts are approved by the referee and the court discharges the bankrupt from all debts remaining unsatisfied (with minor exceptions, as provided in the statutes).

The Chandler Act of 1938 provides for greater protection of creditors by introducing safeguards against fraudulent bankruptcies and control over remuneration of officials in bankruptcy proceedings. Now, the discharge of the bankrupt is a secondary objective of bankruptcy proceedings; the primary purposes are to protect creditors against fraud prior to and during liquidation proceedings and to ensure the equitable distribution of the debtor's available assets among the creditors.

## QUESTIONS

1. Distinguish between (*a*) business failure and business discontinuation, (*b*) liquidation and dissolution of a business concern, and (*c*) voluntary and involuntary liquidation of a business firm.

26 Liquidation of Business Firms

2. Why is it important for an owner of an unincorporated business firm to obtain a release or discharge for unpaid balances of debts in liquidation proceedings? How does his position differ from that of stockholders of a corporation?
3. Distinguish between common-law and statutory assignments. What are the advantages and disadvantages of each?
4. Why are large corporations most commonly liquidated or reorganized under supervision of the federal courts?
5. When bankruptcies occur, what is the order of priority in which obligations are settled? Is this rule applicable to reorganizations under supervision of the courts?
6. At one time, the emphasis in bankruptcy proceedings was on the protection of the bankrupt. What is the current approach? Explain.
7. Why are liquidations more likely for industrial firms than for public-utility or railroad corporations?

## PROBLEMS

1. The Air-Space Corporation has been liquidated and its assets were sold for $200,000 cash. Given the corporation's liabilities and stockholders' equity shown, how would you distribute its cash among its investors and creditors? (Assume all debt is unsecured.)

    | | |
    |---|---|
    | Debentures | $ 300,000 |
    | Accounts payable | 100,000 |
    | Preferred stock | 200,000 |
    | Common stock | 3,000,000 |

2. The Hardy Corporation was forced to liquidate its assets, which were sold for $40,000 cash. How much of the cash is distributed to each class of investors and creditors? Assume the corporation balance sheet before liquidation contained the following:

    | | |
    |---|---|
    | Bank loan | $15,000 |
    | Accounts payable | 15,000 |
    | Debentures | 20,000 |
    | Preferred stock | 30,000 |
    | Common stock | 50,000 |
    | Property taxes | 5,000 |

    (Assume the bank loan is unsecured.)

3. A corporation is forced to liquidate. The liquidation brings in $40,000 from fixed assets, $25,000 from accounts receivable, and $22,000 from inventories.

    Balance Sheet (before Liquidation)

    | | | | |
    |---|---|---|---|
    | Cash in bank | $ 10,000 | Accounts payable | $ 30,000 |
    | Accounts receivable | 80,000 | First-mortgage bond | 25,000 |
    | Inventories | 40,000 | Second-mortgage bond | 15,000 |
    | Plant and equipment | 70,000 | Debentures | 20,000 |
    | | | Common stock | 100,000 |
    | | | Retained earnings | 10,000 |
    | Total Assets | $200,000 | Total Liabilities | $200,000 |

The first- and second-mortgage bonds are secured by the plant and equipment. How will the cash be distributed among the firm's creditors?

4. A Tucson, Arizona business is being liquidated. The balance sheet prior to liquidation is as follows:

| | | | | |
|---|---|---|---|---|
| Cash on hand | $ 2,000 | Bank loan (1st Nat'l.) | | $ 6,000 |
| Bank deposit (1st Nat'l.) | 1,000 | Accounts payable | | 12,000 |
| Accounts receivable | 3,000 | Common stock | | 1,000 |
| Inventory | 5,000 | Retained earnings | | 4,000 |
| Equipment | 12,000 | | | |
| Total Assets | $23,000 | Total Liabilities | | $23,000 |

In liquidation the following amounts were realized:

| | |
|---|---|
| Cash | $ 2,000 |
| Accounts receivable | 2,000 |
| Bank deposit | 1,000 |
| Inventory | 3,000 |
| Equipment | 4,000 |
| Total | $12,000 |

The accounts receivable were pledged to the bank to secure its loan. (Assume the right of offset in both cases below.)

*a.* How much does the bank receive in final payment on the loan?

*b.* What would the bank have received if it had *not* had a lien on the accounts receivable?

*c.* What do the trade creditors and common stockholders receive in each case?

# ADDITIONAL READINGS

Altman, E. I. "Financial Ratios, Discriminant Analysis, and the Prediction of Corporate Bankruptcy," *Journal of Finance,* vol. 23 (September 1968), pp. 589–610.

———. "Corporate Bankruptcy Potential, Stockholder Returns and Share Valuation," *Journal of Finance,* vol. 24 (December 1969), pp. 887–900.

Bonham, H. B. "Creditor's Right to Inside Information," *Financial Analysts Journal,* vol. 26 (January–February 1970), pp. 115–18.

Edmister, R. O. "An Empirical Test of Financial Ratio Analysis for Small Business Failure Prediction," *Journal of Financial and Quantitative Analysis,* vol. 7 (March 1972), pp. 1477–93.

Fergusson, D. A. "Preferred Stock Valuation in Recapitalizations," *Journal of Finance,* vol. 13 (March 1958), pp. 48–69.

Murray, R. F. "The Penn Central Debacle: Lessons for Financial Analysis," *Journal of Finance,* vol. 26 (May 1971), pp. 327–32.

Weintraub, B., and L. Harris. *Practical Guide to Bankruptcy and Debtor Relief.* Englewood Cliffs, N.J.: Prentice-Hall, Inc., 1964.

## Appendix A: Present Value of $1

| Year | .0075 | .0100 | .0150 | .0200 | Rate .0400 | .0500 | .0600 | .0700 |
|---|---|---|---|---|---|---|---|---|
| 1 | 0.993 | 0.990 | 0.985 | 0.980 | 0.962 | 0.952 | 0.943 | 0.935 |
| 2 | 0.985 | 0.980 | 0.971 | 0.961 | 0.925 | 0.907 | 0.890 | 0.873 |
| 3 | 0.978 | 0.971 | 0.956 | 0.942 | 0.889 | 0.864 | 0.840 | 0.816 |
| 4 | 0.971 | 0.961 | 0.942 | 0.924 | 0.855 | 0.823 | 0.792 | 0.763 |
| 5 | 0.963 | 0.951 | 0.928 | 0.906 | 0.822 | 0.784 | 0.747 | 0.713 |
| 6 | 0.956 | 0.942 | 0.915 | 0.888 | 0.790 | 0.746 | 0.705 | 0.666 |
| 7 | 0.949 | 0.933 | 0.901 | 0.871 | 0.760 | 0.711 | 0.665 | 0.623 |
| 8 | 0.942 | 0.923 | 0.888 | 0.853 | 0.731 | 0.677 | 0.627 | 0.582 |
| 9 | 0.935 | 0.914 | 0.875 | 0.837 | 0.703 | 0.645 | 0.592 | 0.544 |
| 10 | 0.928 | 0.905 | 0.862 | 0.820 | 0.676 | 0.614 | 0.558 | 0.508 |
| 11 | 0.921 | 0.896 | 0.849 | 0.804 | 0.650 | 0.585 | 0.527 | 0.475 |
| 12 | 0.914 | 0.887 | 0.836 | 0.788 | 0.625 | 0.557 | 0.497 | 0.444 |
| 13 | 0.907 | 0.879 | 0.824 | 0.773 | 0.601 | 0.530 | 0.469 | 0.415 |
| 14 | 0.901 | 0.870 | 0.812 | 0.758 | 0.577 | 0.505 | 0.442 | 0.388 |
| 15 | 0.894 | 0.861 | 0.800 | 0.743 | 0.555 | 0.481 | 0.417 | 0.362 |
| 16 | 0.887 | 0.853 | 0.788 | 0.728 | 0.534 | 0.458 | 0.394 | 0.339 |
| 17 | 0.881 | 0.844 | 0.776 | 0.714 | 0.513 | 0.436 | 0.371 | 0.317 |
| 18 | 0.874 | 0.836 | 0.765 | 0.700 | 0.494 | 0.416 | 0.350 | 0.296 |
| 19 | 0.868 | 0.828 | 0.754 | 0.686 | 0.475 | 0.396 | 0.331 | 0.277 |
| 20 | 0.861 | 0.820 | 0.742 | 0.673 | 0.456 | 0.377 | 0.312 | 0.258 |
| 21 | 0.855 | 0.811 | 0.731 | 0.660 | 0.439 | 0.359 | 0.294 | 0.242 |
| 22 | 0.848 | 0.803 | 0.721 | 0.647 | 0.422 | 0.342 | 0.278 | 0.226 |
| 23 | 0.842 | 0.795 | 0.710 | 0.634 | 0.406 | 0.326 | 0.262 | 0.211 |
| 24 | 0.836 | 0.788 | 0.700 | 0.622 | 0.390 | 0.310 | 0.247 | 0.197 |
| 25 | 0.830 | 0.780 | 0.689 | 0.610 | 0.375 | 0.295 | 0.233 | 0.184 |

| | | | | | | |
|---|---|---|---|---|---|---|
| 26 | 0.823 | 0.772 | 0.679 | 0.598 | 0.361 | 0.281 | 0.220 | 0.172 |
| 27 | 0.817 | 0.764 | 0.669 | 0.586 | 0.347 | 0.268 | 0.207 | 0.161 |
| 28 | 0.811 | 0.757 | 0.659 | 0.574 | 0.333 | 0.255 | 0.196 | 0.150 |
| 29 | 0.805 | 0.749 | 0.649 | 0.563 | 0.321 | 0.243 | 0.185 | 0.141 |
| 30 | 0.799 | 0.742 | 0.640 | 0.552 | 0.308 | 0.231 | 0.174 | 0.131 |
| 31 | 0.793 | 0.735 | 0.630 | 0.541 | 0.296 | 0.220 | 0.164 | 0.123 |
| 32 | 0.787 | 0.727 | 0.621 | 0.531 | 0.285 | 0.210 | 0.155 | 0.115 |
| 33 | 0.781 | 0.720 | 0.612 | 0.050 | 0.274 | 0.200 | 0.146 | 0.107 |
| 34 | 0.776 | 0.713 | 0.603 | 0.510 | 0.264 | 0.190 | 0.138 | 0.100 |
| 35 | 0.770 | 0.706 | 0.594 | 0.500 | 0.253 | 0.181 | 0.130 | 0.094 |
| 36 | 0.764 | 0.699 | 0.585 | 0.490 | 0.244 | 0.173 | 0.123 | 0.088 |
| 37 | 0.758 | 0.692 | 0.576 | 0.481 | 0.234 | 0.164 | 0.116 | 0.082 |
| 38 | 0.753 | 0.685 | 0.568 | 0.471 | 0.225 | 0.157 | 0.109 | 0.076 |
| 39 | 0.747 | 0.678 | 0.560 | 0.462 | 0.217 | 0.149 | 0.103 | 0.071 |
| 40 | 0.742 | 0.672 | 0.551 | 0.453 | 0.208 | 0.142 | 0.097 | 0.067 |
| 41 | 0.736 | 0.665 | 0.543 | 0.444 | 0.200 | 0.135 | 0.092 | 0.062 |
| 42 | 0.731 | 0.658 | 0.535 | 0.435 | 0.193 | 0.129 | 0.087 | 0.058 |
| 43 | 0.725 | 0.652 | 0.527 | 0.427 | 0.185 | 0.123 | 0.082 | 0.055 |
| 44 | 0.720 | 0.645 | 0.519 | 0.418 | 0.178 | 0.117 | 0.077 | 0.051 |
| 45 | 0.714 | 0.639 | 0.512 | 0.410 | 0.171 | 0.111 | 0.073 | 0.048 |
| 46 | 0.709 | 0.633 | 0.504 | 0.402 | 0.165 | 0.106 | 0.069 | 0.044 |
| 47 | 0.704 | 0.626 | 0.497 | 0.394 | 0.158 | 0.101 | 0.065 | 0.042 |
| 48 | 0.699 | 0.620 | 0.489 | 0.387 | 0.152 | 0.096 | 0.061 | 0.039 |
| 49 | 0.693 | 0.614 | 0.482 | 0.379 | 0.146 | 0.092 | 0.058 | 0.036 |
| 50 | 0.688 | 0.608 | 0.475 | 0.372 | 0.141 | 0.087 | 0.054 | 0.034 |

## Appendix A: Present Value of $1 (continued)

Rate

| Year | .0800 | .0900 | .1000 | .1100 | .1200 | .1300 | .1400 | .1500 |
|---|---|---|---|---|---|---|---|---|
| 1 | 0.926 | 0.917 | 0.909 | 0.901 | 0.893 | 0.885 | 0.877 | 0.870 |
| 2 | 0.857 | 0.842 | 0.826 | 0.812 | 0.797 | 0.783 | 0.769 | 0.756 |
| 3 | 0.794 | 0.772 | 0.751 | 0.731 | 0.712 | 0.693 | 0.675 | 0.658 |
| 4 | 0.735 | 0.708 | 0.683 | 0.659 | 0.636 | 0.613 | 0.592 | 0.572 |
| 5 | 0.681 | 0.650 | 0.621 | 0.593 | 0.567 | 0.543 | 0.519 | 0.497 |
| 6 | 0.630 | 0.596 | 0.564 | 0.535 | 0.507 | 0.480 | 0.456 | 0.432 |
| 7 | 0.583 | 0.547 | 0.513 | 0.482 | 0.452 | 0.425 | 0.400 | 0.376 |
| 8 | 0.540 | 0.502 | 0.467 | 0.434 | 0.404 | 0.376 | 0.351 | 0.327 |
| 9 | 0.500 | 0.460 | 0.424 | 0.391 | 0.361 | 0.333 | 0.308 | 0.284 |
| 10 | 0.463 | 0.422 | 0.386 | 0.352 | 0.322 | 0.295 | 0.270 | 0.247 |
| 11 | 0.429 | 0.388 | 0.350 | 0.317 | 0.287 | 0.261 | 0.237 | 0.215 |
| 12 | 0.397 | 0.356 | 0.319 | 0.286 | 0.257 | 0.231 | 0.208 | 0.187 |
| 13 | 0.368 | 0.326 | 0.290 | 0.258 | 0.229 | 0.204 | 0.182 | 0.163 |
| 14 | 0.340 | 0.299 | 0.263 | 0.232 | 0.205 | 0.181 | 0.160 | 0.141 |
| 15 | 0.315 | 0.275 | 0.239 | 0.209 | 0.183 | 0.160 | 0.140 | 0.123 |
| 16 | 0.292 | 0.252 | 0.218 | 0.188 | 0.163 | 0.141 | 0.123 | 0.107 |
| 17 | 0.270 | 0.231 | 0.198 | 0.170 | 0.146 | 0.125 | 0.108 | 0.093 |
| 18 | 0.250 | 0.212 | 0.180 | 0.153 | 0.130 | 0.111 | 0.095 | 0.081 |
| 19 | 0.232 | 0.194 | 0.164 | 0.138 | 0.116 | 0.098 | 0.083 | 0.070 |
| 20 | 0.215 | 0.178 | 0.149 | 0.124 | 0.104 | 0.087 | 0.073 | 0.061 |
| 21 | 0.199 | 0.164 | 0.135 | 0.112 | 0.093 | 0.077 | 0.064 | 0.053 |
| 22 | 0.184 | 0.150 | 0.123 | 0.101 | 0.083 | 0.068 | 0.056 | 0.046 |
| 23 | 0.170 | 0.138 | 0.112 | 0.091 | 0.074 | 0.060 | 0.049 | 0.040 |
| 24 | 0.158 | 0.126 | 0.102 | 0.082 | 0.066 | 0.053 | 0.043 | 0.035 |
| 25 | 0.146 | 0.116 | 0.092 | 0.074 | 0.059 | 0.047 | 0.038 | 0.030 |

| | | | | | | | | |
|---|---|---|---|---|---|---|---|---|
| 26. | 0.135 | 0.106 | 0.084 | 0.066 | 0.053 | 0.042 | 0.033 | 0.026 |
| 27. | 0.125 | 0.098 | 0.076 | 0.060 | 0.047 | 0.037 | 0.029 | 0.023 |
| 28. | 0.116 | 0.090 | 0.069 | 0.054 | 0.042 | 0.033 | 0.026 | 0.020 |
| 29. | 0.107 | 0.082 | 0.063 | 0.048 | 0.037 | 0.029 | 0.022 | 0.017 |
| 30. | 0.099 | 0.075 | 0.057 | 0.044 | 0.033 | 0.026 | 0.020 | 0.015 |
| 31. | 0.092 | 0.069 | 0.052 | 0.039 | 0.030 | 0.023 | 0.017 | 0.013 |
| 32. | 0.085 | 0.063 | 0.047 | 0.035 | 0.027 | 0.020 | 0.015 | 0.011 |
| 33. | 0.079 | 0.058 | 0.043 | 0.032 | 0.024 | 0.018 | 0.013 | 0.010 |
| 34. | 0.073 | 0.053 | 0.039 | 0.029 | 0.021 | 0.016 | 0.012 | 0.009 |
| 35. | 0.068 | 0.049 | 0.036 | 0.026 | 0.019 | 0.014 | 0.010 | 0.008 |
| 36. | 0.063 | 0.045 | 0.032 | 0.023 | 0.017 | 0.012 | 0.009 | 0.007 |
| 37. | 0.058 | 0.041 | 0.029 | 0.021 | 0.015 | 0.011 | 0.008 | 0.006 |
| 38. | 0.054 | 0.038 | 0.027 | 0.019 | 0.013 | 0.010 | 0.007 | 0.005 |
| 39. | 0.050 | 0.035 | 0.024 | 0.017 | 0.012 | 0.009 | 0.006 | 0.004 |
| 40. | 0.046 | 0.032 | 0.022 | 0.015 | 0.011 | 0.008 | 0.005 | 0.004 |
| 41. | 0.043 | 0.029 | 0.020 | 0.014 | 0.010 | 0.007 | 0.005 | 0.003 |
| 42. | 0.039 | 0.027 | 0.018 | 0.012 | 0.009 | 0.006 | 0.004 | 0.003 |
| 43. | 0.037 | 0.025 | 0.017 | 0.011 | 0.008 | 0.005 | 0.004 | 0.002 |
| 44. | 0.034 | 0.023 | 0.015 | 0.010 | 0.007 | 0.005 | 0.003 | 0.002 |
| 45. | 0.031 | 0.021 | 0.014 | 0.009 | 0.006 | 0.004 | 0.003 | 0.002 |
| 46. | 0.029 | 0.019 | 0.012 | 0.008 | 0.005 | 0.004 | 0.002 | 0.002 |
| 47. | 0.027 | 0.017 | 0.011 | 0.007 | 0.005 | 0.003 | 0.002 | 0.001 |
| 48. | 0.025 | 0.016 | 0.010 | 0.007 | 0.004 | 0.003 | 0.002 | 0.001 |
| 49. | 0.023 | 0.015 | 0.009 | 0.006 | 0.004 | 0.003 | 0.002 | 0.001 |
| 50. | 0.021 | 0.013 | 0.009 | 0.005 | 0.003 | 0.002 | 0.001 | 0.001 |

Appendix A: Present Value of $1 (concluded)

Rate

| Year | .1600 | .1800 | .2000 | .2200 | .2400 | .2500 | .3000 | .4000 |
|---|---|---|---|---|---|---|---|---|
| 1 | 0.862 | 0.847 | 0.833 | 0.820 | 0.806 | 0.800 | 0.769 | 0.714 |
| 2 | 0.743 | 0.718 | 0.694 | 0.672 | 0.650 | 0.640 | 0.592 | 0.510 |
| 3 | 0.641 | 0.609 | 0.579 | 0.551 | 0.524 | 0.512 | 0.455 | 0.364 |
| 4 | 0.552 | 0.516 | 0.482 | 0.451 | 0.423 | 0.410 | 0.350 | 0.260 |
| 5 | 0.476 | 0.437 | 0.402 | 0.370 | 0.341 | 0.328 | 0.269 | 0.186 |
| 6 | 0.410 | 0.370 | 0.335 | 0.303 | 0.275 | 0.262 | 0.207 | 0.133 |
| 7 | 0.354 | 0.314 | 0.279 | 0.249 | 0.222 | 0.210 | 0.159 | 0.095 |
| 8 | 0.305 | 0.266 | 0.233 | 0.204 | 0.179 | 0.168 | 0.123 | 0.068 |
| 9 | 0.263 | 0.225 | 0.194 | 0.167 | 0.144 | 0.134 | 0.094 | 0.048 |
| 10 | 0.227 | 0.191 | 0.162 | 0.137 | 0.116 | 0.107 | 0.073 | 0.035 |
| 11 | 0.195 | 0.162 | 0.135 | 0.112 | 0.094 | 0.086 | 0.056 | 0.025 |
| 12 | 0.168 | 0.137 | 0.112 | 0.092 | 0.076 | 0.069 | 0.043 | 0.018 |
| 13 | 0.145 | 0.116 | 0.093 | 0.075 | 0.061 | 0.055 | 0.033 | 0.013 |
| 14 | 0.125 | 0.099 | 0.078 | 0.062 | 0.049 | 0.044 | 0.025 | 0.009 |
| 15 | 0.108 | 0.084 | 0.065 | 0.051 | 0.040 | 0.035 | 0.020 | 0.006 |
| 16 | 0.093 | 0.071 | 0.054 | 0.042 | 0.032 | 0.028 | 0.015 | 0.005 |
| 17 | 0.080 | 0.060 | 0.045 | 0.034 | 0.026 | 0.023 | 0.012 | 0.003 |
| 18 | 0.069 | 0.051 | 0.038 | 0.028 | 0.021 | 0.018 | 0.009 | 0.002 |
| 19 | 0.060 | 0.043 | 0.031 | 0.023 | 0.017 | 0.014 | 0.007 | 0.002 |
| 20 | 0.051 | 0.037 | 0.026 | 0.019 | 0.014 | 0.012 | 0.005 | 0.001 |
| 21 | 0.044 | 0.031 | 0.022 | 0.015 | 0.011 | 0.009 | 0.004 | 0.001 |
| 22 | 0.038 | 0.026 | 0.018 | 0.013 | 0.009 | 0.007 | 0.003 | 0.001 |
| 23 | 0.033 | 0.022 | 0.015 | 0.010 | 0.007 | 0.006 | 0.002 | 0.000 |
| 24 | 0.028 | 0.019 | 0.013 | 0.008 | 0.006 | 0.005 | 0.002 | 0.000 |
| 25 | 0.024 | 0.016 | 0.010 | 0.007 | 0.005 | 0.004 | 0.001 | 0.000 |

| | | | | | | | |
|---|---|---|---|---|---|---|---|
| 26....0.021 | 0.014 | 0.009 | 0.006 | 0.004 | 0.003 | 0.001 | 0.000 |
| 27....0.018 | 0.011 | 0.007 | 0.005 | 0.003 | 0.002 | 0.001 | 0.000 |
| 28....0.016 | 0.010 | 0.006 | 0.004 | 0.002 | 0.002 | 0.001 | 0.000 |
| 29....0.014 | 0.008 | 0.005 | 0.003 | 0.002 | 0.002 | 0.000 | 0.000 |
| 30....0.012 | 0.007 | 0.004 | 0.003 | 0.002 | 0.001 | 0.000 | 0.000 |
| 31....0.010 | 0.006 | 0.004 | 0.002 | 0.001 | 0.001 | 0.000 | 0.000 |
| 32....0.009 | 0.005 | 0.003 | 0.002 | 0.001 | 0.001 | 0.000 | 0.000 |
| 33....0.007 | 0.004 | 0.002 | 0.001 | 0.001 | 0.001 | 0.000 | 0.000 |
| 34....0.006 | 0.004 | 0.002 | 0.001 | 0.001 | 0.001 | 0.000 | 0.000 |
| 35....0.006 | 0.003 | 0.002 | 0.001 | 0.001 | 0.000 | 0.000 | 0.000 |
| 36....0.005 | 0.003 | 0.001 | 0.001 | 0.000 | 0.000 | 0.000 | 0.000 |
| 37....0.004 | 0.002 | 0.001 | 0.001 | 0.000 | 0.000 | 0.000 | 0.000 |
| 38....0.004 | 0.002 | 0.001 | 0.001 | 0.000 | 0.000 | 0.000 | 0.000 |
| 39....0.003 | 0.002 | 0.001 | 0.000 | 0.000 | 0.000 | 0.000 | 0.000 |
| 40....0.003 | 0.001 | 0.001 | 0.000 | 0.000 | 0.000 | 0.000 | 0.000 |
| 41....0.002 | 0.001 | 0.001 | 0.000 | 0.000 | 0.000 | 0.000 | 0.000 |
| 42....0.002 | 0.001 | 0.000 | 0.000 | 0.000 | 0.000 | 0.000 | 0.000 |
| 43....0.002 | 0.001 | 0.000 | 0.000 | 0.000 | 0.000 | 0.000 | 0.000 |
| 44....0.001 | 0.001 | 0.000 | 0.000 | 0.000 | 0.000 | 0.000 | 0.000 |
| 45....0.001 | 0.001 | 0.000 | 0.000 | 0.000 | 0.000 | 0.000 | 0.000 |
| 46....0.001 | 0.000 | 0.000 | 0.000 | 0.000 | 0.000 | 0.000 | 0.000 |
| 47....0.001 | 0.000 | 0.000 | 0.000 | 0.000 | 0.000 | 0.000 | 0.000 |
| 48....0.001 | 0.000 | 0.000 | 0.000 | 0.000 | 0.000 | 0.000 | 0.000 |
| 49....0.001 | 0.000 | 0.000 | 0.000 | 0.000 | 0.000 | 0.000 | 0.000 |
| 50....0.001 | 0.000 | 0.000 | 0.000 | 0.000 | 0.000 | 0.000 | 0.000 |

## Appendix B: Present Value of an Annuity of $1

Rate

| Year | .0075 | .0100 | .0150 | .0200 | .0400 | .0500 | .0600 | .0700 |
|---|---|---|---|---|---|---|---|---|
| 1 | 0.993 | 0.990 | 0.985 | 0.980 | 0.962 | 0.952 | 0.943 | 0.935 |
| 2 | 1.978 | 1.970 | 1.956 | 1.942 | 1.886 | 1.859 | 1.833 | 1.808 |
| 3 | 2.956 | 2.941 | 2.912 | 2.884 | 2.775 | 2.723 | 2.673 | 2.624 |
| 4 | 3.926 | 3.902 | 3.854 | 3.808 | 3.630 | 3.546 | 3.465 | 3.387 |
| 5 | 4.889 | 4.853 | 4.783 | 4.713 | 4.452 | 4.329 | 4.212 | 4.100 |
| 6 | 5.846 | 5.795 | 5.697 | 5.601 | 5.242 | 5.076 | 4.917 | 4.767 |
| 7 | 6.795 | 6.728 | 6.598 | 6.472 | 6.002 | 5.786 | 5.582 | 5.389 |
| 8 | 7.737 | 7.652 | 7.486 | 7.325 | 6.733 | 6.463 | 6.210 | 5.971 |
| 9 | 8.672 | 8.566 | 8.361 | 8.162 | 7.435 | 7.108 | 6.802 | 6.515 |
| 10 | 9.600 | 9.471 | 9.222 | 8.983 | 8.111 | 7.722 | 7.360 | 7.024 |
| 11 | 10.521 | 10.368 | 10.071 | 9.787 | 8.760 | 8.306 | 7.887 | 7.499 |
| 12 | 11.435 | 11.255 | 10.908 | 10.575 | 9.385 | 8.863 | 8.384 | 7.943 |
| 13 | 12.342 | 12.134 | 11.732 | 11.348 | 9.986 | 9.394 | 8.853 | 8.358 |
| 14 | 13.243 | 13.004 | 12.543 | 12.106 | 10.563 | 9.899 | 9.295 | 8.745 |
| 15 | 14.137 | 13.865 | 13.343 | 12.849 | 11.118 | 10.380 | 9.712 | 9.108 |
| 16 | 15.024 | 14.718 | 14.131 | 13.578 | 11.652 | 10.838 | 10.106 | 9.447 |
| 17 | 15.905 | 15.562 | 14.908 | 14.292 | 12.166 | 11.274 | 10.477 | 9.763 |
| 18 | 16.779 | 16.398 | 15.673 | 14.992 | 12.659 | 11.690 | 10.828 | 10.059 |
| 19 | 17.647 | 17.226 | 16.426 | 15.678 | 13.134 | 12.085 | 11.158 | 10.336 |
| 20 | 18.508 | 18.046 | 17.169 | 16.351 | 13.590 | 12.462 | 11.470 | 10.594 |
| 21 | 19.363 | 18.857 | 17.900 | 17.011 | 14.029 | 12,821 | 11.764 | 10.836 |
| 22 | 20.211 | 19.660 | 18.621 | 17.658 | 14.451 | 13.163 | 12.042 | 11.061 |
| 23 | 21.053 | 20.456 | 19.331 | 18.292 | 14.857 | 13.489 | 12.303 | 11.272 |
| 24 | 21.889 | 21.243 | 20.030 | 18.914 | 15.247 | 13.799 | 12.550 | 11.469 |
| 25 | 22.719 | 22.023 | 20.720 | 19.523 | 15.622 | 14.094 | 12.783 | 11.654 |

| | | | | | | | |
|---|---|---|---|---|---|---|---|
| 26 | 23.542 | 22.795 | 21.399 | 20.121 | 15.983 | 14.375 | 13.003 | 11.826 |
| 27 | 24.359 | 23.560 | 22.068 | 20.707 | 16.330 | 14.643 | 13.211 | 11.987 |
| 28 | 25.171 | 24.316 | 22.727 | 21.281 | 16.663 | 14.898 | 13.406 | 12.137 |
| 29 | 25.976 | 25.066 | 23.376 | 21.844 | 16.984 | 15.141 | 13.591 | 12.278 |
| 30 | 26.775 | 25.808 | 24.016 | 22.396 | 17.292 | 15.372 | 13.765 | 12.409 |
| 31 | 27.568 | 26.542 | 24.646 | 22.938 | 17.588 | 15.593 | 13.929 | 12.532 |
| 32 | 28.356 | 27.270 | 25.267 | 23.468 | 17.874 | 15.803 | 14.084 | 12.647 |
| 33 | 29.137 | 27.990 | 25.879 | 23.989 | 18.148 | 16.003 | 14.230 | 12.754 |
| 34 | 29.913 | 28.703 | 26.482 | 24.499 | 18.411 | 16.193 | 14.368 | 12.854 |
| 35 | 30.683 | 29.409 | 27.076 | 24.999 | 18.665 | 16.374 | 14.498 | 12.948 |
| 36 | 31.447 | 30.108 | 27.661 | 25.489 | 18.908 | 16.547 | 14.621 | 13.035 |
| 37 | 32.205 | 30.800 | 28.237 | 25.969 | 19.143 | 16.711 | 14.737 | 13.117 |
| 38 | 32.958 | 31.485 | 28.805 | 26.441 | 19.368 | 16.868 | 14.846 | 13.193 |
| 39 | 33.705 | 32.163 | 29.365 | 26.903 | 19.584 | 17.017 | 14.949 | 13.265 |
| 40 | 34.447 | 32.835 | 29.916 | 27.355 | 19.793 | 17.159 | 15.046 | 13.332 |
| 41 | 35.183 | 33.500 | 30.459 | 27.799 | 19.993 | 17.294 | 15.138 | 13.394 |
| 42 | 35.914 | 34.158 | 30.994 | 28.235 | 20.186 | 17.423 | 15.225 | 13.452 |
| 43 | 36.639 | 34.810 | 31.521 | 28.662 | 20.371 | 17.546 | 15.306 | 13.507 |
| 44 | 37.359 | 35.455 | 32.041 | 29.080 | 20.549 | 17.663 | 15.383 | 13.558 |
| 45 | 38.073 | 36.095 | 32.552 | 29.490 | 20.720 | 17.774 | 15.456 | 13.606 |
| 46 | 38.782 | 36.727 | 33.056 | 29.892 | 20.885 | 17.880 | 15.524 | 13.650 |
| 47 | 39.486 | 37.354 | 33.553 | 30.287 | 21.043 | 17.981 | 15.589 | 13.692 |
| 48 | 40.185 | 37.974 | 34.043 | 30.673 | 21.195 | 18.077 | 15.650 | 13.730 |
| 49 | 40.878 | 38.588 | 34.525 | 31.052 | 21.341 | 18.169 | 15.708 | 13.767 |
| 50 | 41.566 | 39.196 | 35.000 | 31.424 | 21.482 | 18.256 | 15.762 | 13.801 |

**Appendix B: Present Value of an Annuity of $1 (continued)**

| Year | .0800 | .0900 | .1000 | .1100 | .1200 | .1300 | .1400 | .1500 |
|---|---|---|---|---|---|---|---|---|
| 1 | 0.926 | 0.917 | 0.909 | 0.901 | 0.893 | 0.885 | 0.877 | 0.870 |
| 2 | 1.783 | 1.759 | 1.736 | 1.713 | 1.690 | 1.668 | 1.647 | 1.626 |
| 3 | 2.577 | 2.531 | 2.487 | 2.444 | 2.402 | 2.361 | 2.322 | 2.283 |
| 4 | 3.312 | 3.240 | 3.170 | 3.102 | 3.037 | 2.974 | 2.914 | 2.855 |
| 5 | 3.993 | 3.890 | 3.791 | 3.696 | 3.605 | 3.517 | 3.433 | 3.352 |
| 6 | 4.623 | 4.486 | 4.355 | 4.231 | 4.111 | 3.998 | 3.889 | 3.784 |
| 7 | 5.206 | 5.033 | 4.868 | 4.712 | 4.564 | 4.423 | 4.288 | 4.160 |
| 8 | 5.747 | 5.535 | 5.335 | 5.146 | 4.968 | 4.799 | 4.639 | 4.487 |
| 9 | 6.247 | 5.995 | 5.759 | 5.537 | 5.328 | 5.132 | 4.946 | 4.772 |
| 10 | 6.710 | 6.418 | 6.145 | 5.889 | 5.650 | 5.426 | 5.216 | 5.019 |
| 11 | 7.139 | 6.805 | 6.495 | 6.207 | 5.938 | 5.687 | 5.453 | 5.234 |
| 12 | 7.536 | 7.161 | 6.814 | 6.492 | 6.194 | 5.918 | 5.660 | 5.421 |
| 13 | 7.904 | 7.487 | 7.103 | 6.750 | 6.424 | 6.122 | 5.842 | 5.583 |
| 14 | 8.244 | 7.786 | 7.367 | 6.982 | 6.628 | 6.302 | 6.002 | 5.724 |
| 15 | 8.559 | 8.061 | 7.606 | 7.191 | 6.811 | 6.462 | 6.142 | 5.847 |
| 16 | 8.851 | 8.313 | 7.824 | 7.379 | 6.974 | 6.604 | 6.265 | 5.954 |
| 17 | 9.122 | 8.544 | 8.022 | 7.549 | 7.120 | 6.729 | 6.373 | 6.047 |
| 18 | 9.372 | 8.756 | 8.201 | 7.702 | 7.250 | 6.840 | 6.467 | 6.128 |
| 19 | 9.604 | 8.950 | 8.365 | 7.839 | 7.366 | 6.938 | 6.550 | 6.198 |
| 20 | 9.818 | 9.129 | 8.514 | 7.963 | 7.469 | 7.025 | 6.623 | 6.259 |
| 21 | 10.017 | 9.292 | 8.649 | 8.075 | 7.562 | 7.102 | 6.687 | 6.312 |
| 22 | 10.201 | 9.442 | 8.772 | 8.176 | 7.645 | 7.170 | 6.743 | 6.359 |
| 23 | 10.371 | 9.580 | 8.883 | 8.266 | 7.718 | 7.230 | 6.792 | 6.399 |
| 24 | 10.529 | 9.707 | 8.985 | 8.348 | 7.784 | 7.283 | 6.835 | 6.434 |
| 25 | 10.675 | 9.823 | 9.077 | 8.422 | 7.843 | 7.330 | 6.873 | 6.464 |

| | | | | | | |
|---|---|---|---|---|---|---|
| 26 | 10.810 | 9.929 | 9.161 | 8.488 | 7.896 | 7.372 | 6.906 | 6.491 |
| 27 | 10.935 | 10.027 | 9.237 | 8.548 | 7.943 | 7.409 | 6.935 | 6.514 |
| 28 | 11.051 | 10.116 | 9.307 | 8.602 | 7.984 | 7.441 | 6.961 | 6.534 |
| 29 | 11.158 | 10.198 | 9.370 | 8.650 | 8.022 | 7.470 | 6.983 | 6.551 |
| 30 | 11.258 | 10.274 | 9.427 | 8.694 | 8.055 | 7.496 | 7.003 | 6.566 |
| 31 | 11.350 | 10.343 | 9.479 | 8.733 | 8.085 | 7.518 | 7.020 | 6.579 |
| 32 | 11.435 | 10.406 | 9.526 | 8.769 | 8.112 | 7.538 | 7.035 | 6.591 |
| 33 | 11.514 | 10.464 | 9.569 | 8.801 | 8.135 | 7.556 | 7.048 | 6.600 |
| 34 | 11.587 | 10.518 | 9.609 | 8.829 | 8.157 | 7.572 | 7.060 | 6.609 |
| 35 | 11.655 | 10.567 | 9.644 | 8.855 | 8.176 | 7.586 | 7.070 | 6.617 |
| 36 | 11.717 | 10.612 | 9.677 | 8.879 | 8.192 | 7.598 | 7.079 | 6.623 |
| 37 | 11.775 | 10.653 | 9.706 | 8.900 | 8.208 | 7.609 | 7.087 | 6.629 |
| 38 | 11.829 | 10.691 | 9.733 | 8.919 | 8.221 | 7.618 | 7.094 | 6.634 |
| 39 | 11.879 | 10.726 | 9.757 | 8.936 | 8.233 | 7.627 | 7.100 | 6.638 |
| 40 | 11.925 | 10.757 | 9.779 | 8.951 | 8.244 | 7.634 | 7.105 | 6.642 |
| 41 | 11.967 | 10.787 | 9.799 | 8.965 | 8.253 | 7.641 | 7.110 | 6.645 |
| 42 | 12.007 | 10.813 | 9.817 | 8.977 | 8.262 | 7.647 | 7.114 | 6.648 |
| 43 | 12.043 | 10.838 | 9.834 | 8.989 | 8.270 | 7.652 | 7.117 | 6.650 |
| 44 | 12.077 | 10.861 | 9.849 | 8.999 | 8.276 | 7.657 | 7.120 | 6.652 |
| 45 | 12.108 | 10.881 | 9.863 | 9.008 | 8.283 | 7.661 | 7.123 | 6.654 |
| 46 | 12.137 | 10.900 | 9.875 | 9.016 | 8.288 | 7.664 | 7.126 | 6.656 |
| 47 | 12.164 | 10.918 | 9.887 | 9.024 | 8.293 | 7.668 | 7.128 | 6.657 |
| 48 | 12.189 | 10.934 | 9.897 | 9.030 | 8.297 | 7.671 | 7.130 | 6.659 |
| 49 | 12.212 | 10.948 | 9.906 | 9.036 | 8.301 | 7.673 | 7.131 | 6.660 |
| 50 | 12.233 | 10.962 | 9.915 | 9.042 | 8.304 | 7.675 | 7.133 | 6.661 |

**Appendix B: Present Value of an Annuity of $1 (concluded)**

Rate

| Year | .1600 | .1800 | .2000 | .2200 | .2400 | .2500 | .3000 | .4000 |
|---|---|---|---|---|---|---|---|---|
| 1 | 0.862 | 0.847 | 0.833 | 0.820 | 0.806 | 0.800 | 0.769 | 0.714 |
| 2 | 1.605 | 1.566 | 1.528 | 1.492 | 1.457 | 1.440 | 1.361 | 1.224 |
| 3 | 2.246 | 2.174 | 2.106 | 2.042 | 1.981 | 1.952 | 1.816 | 1.589 |
| 4 | 2.798 | 2.690 | 2.589 | 2.494 | 2.404 | 2.362 | 2.166 | 1.849 |
| 5 | 3.274 | 3.127 | 2.991 | 2.864 | 2.745 | 2.689 | 2.436 | 2.035 |
| 6 | 3.685 | 3.498 | 3.326 | 3.167 | 3.020 | 2.951 | 2.643 | 2.168 |
| 7 | 4.039 | 3.812 | 3.605 | 3.416 | 3.242 | 3.161 | 2.802 | 2.263 |
| 8 | 4.344 | 4.078 | 3.837 | 3.619 | 3.421 | 3.329 | 2.925 | 2.331 |
| 9 | 4.607 | 4.303 | 4.031 | 3.786 | 3.566 | 3.463 | 3.019 | 2.379 |
| 10 | 4.833 | 4.494 | 4.192 | 3.923 | 3.682 | 3.571 | 3.092 | 2.414 |
| 11 | 5.029 | 4.656 | 4.327 | 4.035 | 3.776 | 3.656 | 3.147 | 2.438 |
| 12 | 5.197 | 4.793 | 4.439 | 4.127 | 3.851 | 3.725 | 3.190 | 2.456 |
| 13 | 5.342 | 4.910 | 4.533 | 4.203 | 3.912 | 3.780 | 3.223 | 2.469 |
| 14 | 5.468 | 5.008 | 4.611 | 4.265 | 3.962 | 3.824 | 3.249 | 2.478 |
| 15 | 5.575 | 5.092 | 4.675 | 4.315 | 4.001 | 3.859 | 3.268 | 2.484 |
| 16 | 5.668 | 5.162 | 4.730 | 4.357 | 4.033 | 3.887 | 3.283 | 2.489 |
| 17 | 5.749 | 5.222 | 4.775 | 4.391 | 4.059 | 3.910 | 3.295 | 2.492 |
| 18 | 5.818 | 5.273 | 4.812 | 4.419 | 4.080 | 3.928 | 3.304 | 2.494 |
| 19 | 5.877 | 5.316 | 4.843 | 4.442 | 4.097 | 3.942 | 3.311 | 2.496 |
| 20 | 5.929 | 5.353 | 4.870 | 4.460 | 4.110 | 3.954 | 3.316 | 2.497 |
| 21 | 5.973 | 5.384 | 4.891 | 4.476 | 4.121 | 3.963 | 3.320 | 2.498 |
| 22 | 6.011 | 5.410 | 4.909 | 4.488 | 4.130 | 3.970 | 3.323 | 2.498 |
| 23 | 6.044 | 5.432 | 4.925 | 4.499 | 4.137 | 3.976 | 3.325 | 2.499 |
| 24 | 6.073 | 5.451 | 4.937 | 4.507 | 4.143 | 3.981 | 3.327 | 2.499 |
| 25 | 6.097 | 5.467 | 4.948 | 4.514 | 4.147 | 3.985 | 3.329 | 2.499 |

| | | | | | | |
|---|---|---|---|---|---|---|
| 26 | 6.118 | 5.480 | 4.956 | 4.520 | 4.151 | 3.988 | 3.330 | 2.500 |
| 27 | 6.136 | 5.492 | 4.964 | 4.524 | 4.154 | 3.990 | 3.331 | 2.500 |
| 28 | 6.152 | 5.502 | 4.970 | 4.528 | 4.157 | 3.992 | 3.331 | 2.500 |
| 29 | 6.166 | 5.510 | 4.975 | 4.531 | 4.159 | 3.994 | 3.332 | 2.500 |
| 30 | 6.177 | 5.517 | 4.979 | 4.534 | 4.160 | 3.995 | 3.332 | 2.500 |
| 31 | 6.187 | 5.523 | 4.982 | 4.536 | 4.161 | 3.996 | 3.332 | 2.500 |
| 32 | 6.196 | 5.528 | 4.985 | 4.538 | 4.162 | 3.997 | 3.333 | 2.500 |
| 33 | 6.203 | 5.532 | 4.988 | 4.539 | 4.163 | 3.997 | 3.333 | 2.500 |
| 34 | 6.210 | 5.536 | 4.990 | 4.540 | 4.164 | 3.998 | 3.333 | 2.500 |
| 35 | 6.215 | 5.539 | 4.992 | 4.541 | 4.164 | 3.998 | 3.333 | 2.500 |
| 36 | 6.220 | 5.541 | 4.993 | 4.542 | 4.165 | 3.999 | 3.333 | 2.500 |
| 37 | 6.224 | 5.543 | 4.994 | 4.543 | 4.165 | 3.999 | 3.333 | 2.500 |
| 38 | 6.228 | 5.545 | 4.995 | 4.543 | 4.165 | 3.999 | 3.333 | 2.500 |
| 39 | 6.231 | 5.547 | 4.996 | 4.544 | 4.166 | 3.999 | 3.333 | 2.500 |
| 40 | 6.233 | 5.548 | 4.997 | 4.544 | 4.166 | 3.999 | 3.333 | 2.500 |
| 41 | 6.236 | 5.549 | 4.997 | 4.544 | 4.166 | 4.000 | 3.333 | 2.500 |
| 42 | 6.238 | 5.550 | 4.998 | 4.544 | 4.166 | 4.000 | 3.333 | 2.500 |
| 43 | 6.239 | 5.551 | 4.998 | 4.545 | 4.166 | 4.000 | 3.333 | 2.500 |
| 44 | 6.241 | 5.552 | 4.998 | 4.545 | 4.166 | 4.000 | 3.333 | 2.500 |
| 45 | 6.242 | 5.552 | 4.999 | 4.545 | 4.166 | 4.000 | 3.333 | 2.500 |
| 46 | 6.243 | 5.553 | 4.999 | 4.545 | 4.166 | 4.000 | 3.333 | 2.500 |
| 47 | 6.244 | 5.553 | 4.999 | 4.545 | 4.166 | 4.000 | 3.333 | 2.500 |
| 48 | 6.245 | 5.554 | 4.999 | 4.545 | 4.167 | 4.000 | 3.333 | 2.500 |
| 49 | 6.246 | 5.554 | 4.999 | 4.545 | 4.167 | 4.000 | 3.333 | 2.500 |
| 50 | 6.246 | 5.554 | 4.999 | 4.545 | 4.167 | 4.000 | 3.333 | 2.500 |

## Appendix C: Compound Value of $1

| Year | .0075 | .0100 | .0150 | .0200 | .0400 | .0500 | .0600 | .0700 |
|---|---|---|---|---|---|---|---|---|
| 1 | 1.008 | 1.010 | 1.015 | 1.020 | 1.040 | 1.050 | 1.060 | 1.070 |
| 2 | 1.015 | 1.020 | 1.030 | 1.040 | 1.082 | 1.103 | 1.124 | 1.145 |
| 3 | 1.023 | 1.030 | 1.046 | 1.061 | 1.125 | 1.158 | 1.191 | 1.225 |
| 4 | 1.030 | 1.041 | 1.061 | 1.082 | 1.170 | 1.216 | 1.262 | 1.311 |
| 5 | 1.038 | 1.051 | 1.077 | 1.104 | 1.217 | 1.276 | 1.338 | 1.403 |
| 6 | 1.046 | 1.062 | 1.093 | 1.126 | 1.265 | 1.340 | 1.419 | 1.501 |
| 7 | 1.054 | 1.072 | 1.110 | 1.149 | 1.316 | 1.407 | 1.504 | 1.606 |
| 8 | 1.062 | 1.083 | 1.126 | 1.172 | 1.369 | 1.477 | 1.594 | 1.718 |
| 9 | 1.070 | 1.094 | 1.143 | 1.195 | 1.423 | 1.551 | 1.689 | 1.838 |
| 10 | 1.078 | 1.105 | 1.161 | 1.219 | 1.480 | 1.629 | 1.791 | 1.967 |
| 11 | 1.086 | 1.116 | 1.178 | 1.243 | 1.539 | 1.710 | 1.898 | 2.105 |
| 12 | 1.094 | 1.127 | 1.196 | 1.268 | 1.601 | 1.796 | 2.012 | 2.252 |
| 13 | 1.102 | 1.138 | 1.214 | 1.294 | 1.665 | 1.886 | 2.133 | 2.410 |
| 14 | 1.110 | 1.149 | 1.232 | 1.319 | 1.732 | 1.980 | 2.261 | 2.579 |
| 15 | 1.119 | 1.161 | 1.250 | 1.346 | 1.801 | 2.079 | 2.397 | 2.759 |
| 16 | 1.127 | 1.173 | 1.269 | 1.373 | 1.873 | 2.183 | 2.540 | 2.952 |
| 17 | 1.135 | 1.184 | 1.288 | 1.400 | 1.948 | 2.292 | 2.693 | 3.159 |
| 18 | 1.144 | 1.196 | 1.307 | 1.428 | 2.026 | 2.407 | 2.854 | 3.380 |
| 19 | 1.153 | 1.208 | 1.327 | 1.457 | 2.107 | 2.527 | 3.026 | 3.617 |
| 20 | 1.161 | 1.220 | 1.347 | 1.486 | 2.191 | 2.653 | 3.207 | 3.870 |
| 21 | 1.170 | 1.232 | 1.367 | 1.516 | 2.279 | 2.786 | 3.400 | 4.141 |
| 22 | 1.179 | 1.245 | 1.388 | 1.546 | 2.370 | 2.925 | 3.604 | 4.430 |
| 23 | 1.188 | 1.257 | 1.408 | 1.577 | 2.465 | 3.072 | 3.820 | 4.741 |
| 24 | 1.196 | 1.270 | 1.430 | 1.608 | 2.563 | 3.225 | 4.049 | 5.072 |
| 25 | 1.205 | 1.282 | 1.451 | 1.641 | 2.666 | 3.386 | 4.292 | 5.427 |

| | | | | | | | |
|---|---|---|---|---|---|---|---|
| 26 | 1.214 | 1.295 | 1.473 | 1.673 | 2.772 | 3.556 | 4.549 | 5.807 |
| 27 | 1.224 | 1.308 | 1.495 | 1.707 | 2.883 | 3.733 | 4.822 | 6.214 |
| 28 | 1.233 | 1.321 | 1.517 | 1.741 | 2.999 | 3.920 | 5.112 | 6.649 |
| 29 | 1.242 | 1.335 | 1.540 | 1.776 | 3.119 | 4.116 | 5.418 | 7.114 |
| 30 | 1.251 | 1.348 | 1.563 | 1.811 | 3.243 | 4.322 | 5.743 | 7.612 |
| 31 | 1.261 | 1.361 | 1.587 | 1.848 | 3.373 | 4.538 | 6.088 | 8.145 |
| 32 | 1.270 | 1.375 | 1.610 | 1.885 | 3.508 | 4.765 | 6.453 | 8.715 |
| 33 | 1.280 | 1.389 | 1.634 | 1.922 | 3.648 | 5.003 | 6.841 | 9.325 |
| 34 | 1.289 | 1.403 | 1.659 | 1.961 | 3.794 | 5.253 | 7.251 | 9.978 |
| 35 | 1.299 | 1.417 | 1.684 | 2.000 | 3.946 | 5.516 | 7.686 | 10.677 |
| 36 | 1.309 | 1.431 | 1.709 | 2.040 | 4.104 | 5.792 | 8.147 | 11.424 |
| 37 | 1.318 | 1.445 | 1.735 | 2.081 | 4.268 | 6.081 | 8.636 | 12.224 |
| 38 | 1.328 | 1.460 | 1.761 | 2.122 | 4.439 | 6.385 | 9.154 | 13.079 |
| 39 | 1.338 | 1.474 | 1.787 | 2.165 | 4.616 | 6.705 | 9.704 | 13.995 |
| 40 | 1.348 | 1.489 | 1.814 | 2.208 | 4.801 | 7.040 | 10.286 | 14.974 |
| 41 | 1.358 | 1.504 | 1.841 | 2.252 | 4.993 | 7.392 | 10.903 | 16.023 |
| 42 | 1.369 | 1.519 | 1.869 | 2.297 | 5.193 | 7.762 | 11.557 | 17.144 |
| 43 | 1.379 | 1.534 | 1.897 | 2.343 | 5.400 | 8.150 | 12.520 | 18.344 |
| 44 | 1.389 | 1.549 | 1.925 | 2.390 | 5.617 | 8.557 | 12.985 | 19.628 |
| 45 | 1.400 | 1.565 | 1.954 | 2.438 | 5.841 | 8.985 | 13.765 | 21.002 |
| 46 | 1.410 | 1.580 | 1.984 | 2.487 | 6.075 | 9.434 | 14.590 | 22.473 |
| 47 | 1.421 | 1.596 | 2.013 | 2.536 | 6.318 | 9.906 | 15.466 | 24.046 |
| 48 | 1.431 | 1.612 | 2.043 | 2.587 | 6.571 | 10.401 | 16.394 | 25.729 |
| 49 | 1.442 | 1.628 | 2.074 | 2.639 | 6.833 | 10.921 | 17.378 | 27.530 |
| 50 | 1.453 | 1.645 | 2.105 | 2.692 | 7.107 | 11.467 | 18.420 | 29.457 |

**Appendix C: Compound Value of $1 (continued)**

Rate

| Year | .0800 | .0900 | .1000 | .1100 | .1200 | .1300 | .1400 | .1500 |
|---|---|---|---|---|---|---|---|---|
| 1 | 1.080 | 1.090 | 1.100 | 1.110 | 1.120 | 1.130 | 1.140 | 1.150 |
| 2 | 1.166 | 1.188 | 1.210 | 1.232 | 1.254 | 1.277 | 1.300 | 1.323 |
| 3 | 1.260 | 1.295 | 1.331 | 1.368 | 1.405 | 1.443 | 1.482 | 1.521 |
| 4 | 1.360 | 1.412 | 1.464 | 1.518 | 1.574 | 1.630 | 1.689 | 1.749 |
| 5 | 1.469 | 1.539 | 1.611 | 1.685 | 1.762 | 1.842 | 1.925 | 2.011 |
| 6 | 1.587 | 1.677 | 1.772 | 1.870 | 1.974 | 2.082 | 2.195 | 2.313 |
| 7 | 1.714 | 1.828 | 1.949 | 2.076 | 2.211 | 2.353 | 2.502 | 2.660 |
| 8 | 1.851 | 1.993 | 2.144 | 2.305 | 2.476 | 2.658 | 2.853 | 3.059 |
| 9 | 1.999 | 2.172 | 2.358 | 2.558 | 2.773 | 3.004 | 3.252 | 3.518 |
| 10 | 2.159 | 2.367 | 2.594 | 2.839 | 3.106 | 3.395 | 3.707 | 4.046 |
| 11 | 2.332 | 2.580 | 2.853 | 3.152 | 3.479 | 3.836 | 4.226 | 4.652 |
| 12 | 2.518 | 2.813 | 3.138 | 3.498 | 3.896 | 4.335 | 4.818 | 5.350 |
| 13 | 2.720 | 3.066 | 3.452 | 3.883 | 4.363 | 4.898 | 5.492 | 6.153 |
| 14 | 2.937 | 3.342 | 3.797 | 4.310 | 4.887 | 5.535 | 6.261 | 7.076 |
| 15 | 3.172 | 3.642 | 4.177 | 4.785 | 5.474 | 6.254 | 7.138 | 8.137 |
| 16 | 3.426 | 3.970 | 4.595 | 5.311 | 6.130 | 7.067 | 8.137 | 9.358 |
| 17 | 3.700 | 4.328 | 5.054 | 5.895 | 6.866 | 7.986 | 9.276 | 10.761 |
| 18 | 3.996 | 4.717 | 5.560 | 6.544 | 7.690 | 9.024 | 10.575 | 12.375 |
| 19 | 4.316 | 5.142 | 6.116 | 7.263 | 8.613 | 10.197 | 12.056 | 14.232 |
| 20 | 4.661 | 5.604 | 6.727 | 8.062 | 9.646 | 11.523 | 13.743 | 16.367 |
| 21 | 5.034 | 6.109 | 7.400 | 8.949 | 10.804 | 13.021 | 15.668 | 18.822 |
| 22 | 5.437 | 6.659 | 8.140 | 9.934 | 12.100 | 14.714 | 17.861 | 21.645 |
| 23 | 5.871 | 7.258 | 8.954 | 11.026 | 13.552 | 16.627 | 20.362 | 24.891 |
| 24 | 6.341 | 7.911 | 9.850 | 12.239 | 15.179 | 18.788 | 23.212 | 28.625 |
| 25 | 6.848 | 8.623 | 10.835 | 13.585 | 17.000 | 21.231 | 26.462 | 32.919 |

| | | | | | | | | |
|---|---|---|---|---|---|---|---|---|
| 26 | 7.396 | 9.399 | 11.918 | 15.080 | 19.040 | 23.991 | 30.167 | 37.857 |
| 27 | 7.988 | 10.245 | 13.110 | 16.739 | 21.325 | 27.109 | 34.390 | 43.535 |
| 28 | 8.627 | 11.167 | 14.421 | 18.580 | 23.884 | 30.633 | 39.204 | 50.066 |
| 29 | 9.317 | 12.172 | 15.863 | 20.624 | 26.750 | 34.616 | 44.693 | 57.575 |
| 30 | 10.063 | 13.268 | 17.449 | 22.892 | 29.960 | 39.116 | 50.950 | 66.212 |
| 31 | 10.868 | 14.462 | 19.194 | 25.410 | 33.555 | 44.201 | 58.083 | 76.144 |
| 32 | 11.737 | 15.763 | 21.114 | 28.206 | 37.582 | 49.947 | 66.215 | 87.565 |
| 33 | 12.676 | 17.182 | 23.225 | 31.308 | 42.092 | 56.440 | 75.485 | 100.700 |
| 34 | 13.690 | 18.728 | 25.548 | 34.752 | 47.143 | 63.777 | 86.053 | 115.805 |
| 35 | 14.785 | 20.414 | 28.102 | 38.575 | 52.800 | 72.069 | 98.100 | 133.176 |
| 36 | 15.968 | 22.251 | 30.913 | 42.818 | 59.136 | 81.437 | 111.834 | 153.152 |
| 37 | 17.246 | 24.254 | 34.004 | 47.528 | 66.232 | 92.024 | 127.491 | 176.125 |
| 38 | 18.625 | 26.437 | 37.404 | 52.756 | 74.180 | 103.987 | 145.340 | 202.543 |
| 39 | 20.115 | 28.816 | 41.145 | 58.559 | 83.081 | 117.506 | 165.687 | 232.925 |
| 40 | 21.725 | 31.409 | 45.259 | 65.001 | 93.051 | 132.782 | 188.884 | 267.864 |
| 41 | 23.462 | 34.236 | 49.785 | 72.151 | 104.217 | 150.043 | 215.327 | 308.043 |
| 42 | 25.339 | 37.318 | 54.764 | 80.088 | 116.723 | 169.549 | 245.473 | 354.250 |
| 43 | 27.367 | 40.676 | 60.240 | 88.897 | 130.730 | 191.590 | 279.839 | 407.387 |
| 44 | 29.556 | 44.337 | 66.264 | 98.676 | 146.418 | 216.497 | 319.017 | 468.495 |
| 45 | 31.920 | 48.327 | 72.890 | 109.530 | 163.988 | 244.641 | 363.679 | 538.769 |
| 46 | 34.474 | 52.677 | 80.180 | 121.579 | 183.666 | 276.445 | 414.594 | 619.585 |
| 47 | 37.232 | 57.418 | 88.197 | 134.952 | 205.706 | 312.383 | 472.637 | 712.522 |
| 48 | 40.211 | 62.585 | 97.017 | 149.797 | 230.391 | 352.992 | 538.807 | 819.401 |
| 49 | 43.427 | 68.218 | 106.719 | 166.275 | 258.038 | 398.881 | 614.239 | 942.311 |
| 50 | 46.902 | 74.358 | 117.391 | 184.565 | 289.002 | 450.736 | 700.233 | 1083.657 |

Appendix C: Compound Value of $1 (concluded)

| Year | .1600 | .1800 | .2000 | .2200 | .2400 | .2500 | .3000 | .4000 |
|---|---|---|---|---|---|---|---|---|
| 1 | 1.160 | 1.180 | 1.200 | 1.220 | 1.240 | 1.250 | 1.300 | 1.400 |
| 2 | 1.346 | 1.392 | 1.440 | 1.488 | 1.538 | 1.563 | 1.690 | 1.960 |
| 3 | 1.561 | 1.643 | 1.728 | 1.816 | 1.907 | 1.953 | 2.197 | 2.744 |
| 4 | 1.811 | 1.939 | 2.074 | 2.215 | 2.364 | 2.441 | 2.856 | 3.842 |
| 5 | 2.100 | 2.288 | 2.488 | 2.703 | 2.932 | 3.052 | 3.713 | 5.378 |
| 6 | 2.436 | 2.700 | 2.986 | 3.297 | 3.635 | 3.815 | 4.827 | 7.530 |
| 7 | 2.826 | 3.185 | 3.583 | 4.023 | 4.508 | 4.768 | 6.275 | 10.541 |
| 8 | 3.278 | 3.759 | 4.300 | 4.908 | 5.590 | 5.960 | 8.157 | 14.758 |
| 9 | 3.803 | 4.435 | 5.160 | 5.987 | 6.931 | 7.451 | 10.604 | 20.661 |
| 10 | 4.411 | 5.234 | 6.192 | 7.305 | 8.594 | 9.313 | 13.786 | 28.925 |
| 11 | 5.117 | 6.176 | 7.430 | 8.912 | 10.657 | 11.642 | 17.922 | 40.496 |
| 12 | 5.936 | 7.288 | 8.916 | 10.872 | 13.215 | 14.552 | 23.298 | 56.694 |
| 13 | 6.886 | 8.599 | 10.699 | 13.264 | 16.386 | 18.190 | 30.288 | 79.371 |
| 14 | 7.988 | 10.147 | 12.839 | 16.182 | 20.319 | 22.737 | 39.374 | 111.120 |
| 15 | 9.266 | 11.974 | 15.407 | 19.742 | 25.196 | 28.422 | 51.186 | 155.568 |
| 16 | 10.748 | 14.129 | 18.488 | 24.086 | 31.243 | 35.527 | 66.542 | 217.795 |
| 17 | 12.468 | 16.672 | 22.186 | 29.384 | 38.741 | 44.409 | 86.504 | 304.913 |
| 18 | 14.463 | 19.673 | 26.623 | 35.849 | 48.039 | 55.511 | 112.455 | 426.879 |
| 19 | 16.777 | 23.214 | 31.948 | 43.736 | 59.568 | 69.389 | 146.192 | 597.630 |
| 20 | 19.461 | 27.393 | 38.338 | 53.358 | 73.864 | 86.736 | 190.050 | 836.683 |
| 21 | 22.574 | 32.324 | 46.005 | 65.096 | 91.592 | 108.420 | 247.065 | 1171.356 |
| 22 | 26.186 | 38.142 | 55.206 | 79.418 | 113.574 | 135.525 | 321.184 | 1639.898 |
| 23 | 30.376 | 45.008 | 66.247 | 96.889 | 140.831 | 169.407 | 417.539 | 2295.857 |
| 24 | 35.236 | 53.109 | 79.497 | 118.205 | 174.631 | 211.758 | 542.801 | 3214.200 |
| 25 | 40.874 | 62.669 | 95.396 | 144.210 | 216.542 | 264.689 | 705.641 | 4499.880 |

| | | | | | | | |
|---|---|---|---|---|---|---|---|
| 26 | 47.414 | 73.949 | 114.475 | 175.936 | 268.512 | 330.872 | 917.333 | 6299.831 |
| 27 | 55.000 | 87.260 | 137.371 | 214.642 | 332.955 | 413.590 | 1192.533 | 8819.764 |
| 28 | 63.800 | 102.967 | 164.845 | 261.864 | 412.864 | 516.988 | 1550.293 | 12347.670 |
| 29 | 74.009 | 121.501 | 197.814 | 319.474 | 511.952 | 646.235 | 2015.381 | 17286.737 |
| 30 | 85.850 | 143.371 | 237.376 | 389.758 | 634.820 | 807.794 | 2619.996 | 24201.432 |
| 31 | 99.586 | 169.177 | 284.852 | 475.505 | 787.177 | 1009.742 | 3405.994 | 33882.005 |
| 32 | 115.520 | 199.629 | 341.822 | 580.116 | 976.099 | 1262.177 | 4427.793 | 47434.807 |
| 33 | 134.003 | 235.563 | 410.186 | 707.741 | 1210.363 | 1577.722 | 5756.130 | 66408.730 |
| 34 | 155.443 | 277.964 | 492.224 | 863.444 | 1500.850 | 1972.152 | 7482.970 | 92972.223 |
| 35 | 180.314 | 327.997 | 590.668 | 1053.402 | 1861.054 | 2465.190 | 9727.860 | 130161.112 |
| 36 | 209.164 | 387.037 | 708.802 | 1285.150 | 2307.707 | 3081.488 | 12646.219 | 182225.556 |
| 37 | 242.631 | 456.703 | 850.562 | 1567.883 | 2861.557 | 3851.860 | 16440.084 | 255115.779 |
| 38 | 281.452 | 538.910 | 1020.675 | 1912.818 | 3548.330 | 4814.825 | 21372.109 | 357162.090 |
| 39 | 326.484 | 635.914 | 1224.810 | 2333.638 | 4399.930 | 6018.531 | 27783.742 | 500026.926 |
| 40 | 378.721 | 750.378 | 1469.772 | 2847.038 | 5455.913 | 7523.164 | 36118.865 | 700037.697 |
| 41 | 439.317 | 885.446 | 1763.726 | 3473.386 | 6765.332 | 9403.955 | 46954.524 | 980052.775 |
| 42 | 509.607 | 1044.827 | 2116.471 | 4237.531 | 8389.011 | 11754.944 | 61040.882 | 1372073.885 |
| 43 | 591.144 | 1232.896 | 2539.765 | 5169.788 | 10402.374 | 14693.679 | 79353.146 | 1920903.439 |
| 44 | 685.727 | 1454.817 | 3047.718 | 6307.141 | 12898.944 | 18367.099 | 103159.090 | 2689264.815 |
| 45 | 795.444 | 1716.684 | 3657.262 | 7694.712 | 15994.690 | 22958.874 | 134106.817 | 3764970.741 |
| 46 | 922.715 | 2025.687 | 4388.714 | 9387.549 | 19833.416 | 28698.593 | 174338.862 | 5270959.038 |
| 47 | 1070.349 | 2390.311 | 5266.457 | 11452.810 | 24593.436 | 35873.241 | 226640.520 | 7379342.653 |
| 48 | 1241.605 | 2820.567 | 6319.749 | 13972.428 | 30495.860 | 44841.551 | 294632.676 | 10331079.714 |
| 49 | 1440.262 | 3328.269 | 7583.698 | 17046.362 | 37814.867 | 56051.939 | 383022.479 | 14463511.600 |
| 50 | 1670.704 | 3927.357 | 9100.438 | 20796.561 | 46890.435 | 70064.923 | 497929.223 | 20248916.240 |

## Appendix D: Compound Value of an Annuity of $1

| Year | .0075 | .0100 | .0150 | .0200 | .0400 | .0500 | .0600 | .0700 |
|---|---|---|---|---|---|---|---|---|
| 1 | 1.000 | 1.000 | 1.000 | 1.000 | 1.000 | 1.000 | 1.000 | 1.000 |
| 2 | 2.007 | 2.010 | 2.015 | 2.020 | 2.040 | 2.050 | 2.060 | 2.070 |
| 3 | 3.023 | 3.030 | 3.045 | 3.060 | 3.122 | 3.152 | 3.184 | 3.215 |
| 4 | 4.045 | 4.060 | 4.091 | 4.122 | 4.246 | 4.310 | 4.375 | 4.440 |
| 5 | 5.076 | 5.101 | 5.152 | 5.204 | 5.416 | 5.526 | 5.637 | 5.751 |
| 6 | 6.114 | 6.152 | 6.230 | 6.308 | 6.633 | 6.802 | 6.975 | 7.153 |
| 7 | 7.159 | 7.214 | 7.323 | 7.434 | 7.898 | 8.142 | 8.394 | 8.654 |
| 8 | 8.213 | 8.286 | 8.433 | 8.583 | 9.214 | 9.549 | 9.897 | 10.260 |
| 9 | 9.275 | 9.369 | 9.559 | 9.755 | 10.583 | 11.027 | 11.491 | 11.978 |
| 10 | 10.344 | 10.462 | 10.703 | 10.950 | 12.006 | 12.578 | 13.181 | 13.816 |
| 11 | 11.422 | 11.567 | 11.863 | 12.169 | 13.486 | 14.207 | 14.972 | 15.784 |
| 12 | 12.508 | 12.683 | 13.041 | 13.412 | 15.026 | 15.917 | 16.870 | 17.888 |
| 13 | 13.601 | 13.809 | 14.237 | 14.680 | 16.627 | 17.713 | 18.882 | 20.141 |
| 14 | 14.703 | 14.947 | 15.450 | 15.974 | 18.292 | 19.599 | 21.015 | 22.550 |
| 15 | 15.814 | 16.097 | 16.682 | 17.293 | 20.024 | 21.579 | 23.276 | 25.129 |
| 16 | 16.932 | 17.258 | 17.932 | 18.639 | 21.825 | 23.657 | 25.673 | 27.888 |
| 17 | 18.059 | 18.430 | 19.201 | 20.012 | 23.698 | 25.840 | 28.213 | 30.840 |
| 18 | 19.195 | 19.615 | 20.489 | 21.412 | 25.645 | 28.132 | 30.906 | 33.999 |
| 19 | 20.339 | 20.811 | 21.797 | 22.841 | 27.671 | 30.539 | 33.760 | 37.379 |
| 20 | 21.491 | 22.019 | 23.124 | 24.297 | 29.778 | 33.066 | 36.786 | 40.995 |
| 21 | 22.652 | 23.239 | 24.471 | 25.783 | 31.969 | 35.719 | 39.993 | 44.865 |
| 22 | 23.822 | 24.472 | 25.838 | 27.299 | 34.248 | 38.505 | 43.392 | 49.006 |
| 23 | 25.001 | 25.716 | 27.225 | 28.845 | 36.618 | 41.430 | 46.996 | 53.436 |
| 24 | 26.188 | 26.973 | 28.634 | 30.422 | 39.083 | 44.502 | 50.816 | 58.177 |
| 25 | 27.385 | 28.243 | 30.063 | 32.030 | 41.646 | 47.727 | 54.865 | 63.249 |

| | | | | | | | | |
|---|---|---|---|---|---|---|---|---|
| 26 | 28.590 | 29.526 | 31.514 | 33.671 | 44.312 | 51.113 | 59.156 | 68.676 |
| 27 | 29.805 | 30.821 | 32.987 | 35.344 | 47.084 | 54.669 | 63.706 | 74.484 |
| 28 | 31.028 | 32.129 | 34.481 | 37.051 | 49.968 | 58.403 | 68.528 | 80.698 |
| 29 | 32.261 | 33.450 | 35.999 | 38.792 | 52.966 | 62.323 | 73.640 | 87.347 |
| 30 | 33.503 | 34.785 | 37.539 | 40.568 | 56.085 | 66.439 | 79.058 | 94.461 |
| 31 | 34.754 | 36.133 | 39.102 | 42.379 | 59.328 | 70.761 | 84.802 | 102.073 |
| 32 | 36.015 | 37.494 | 40.688 | 44.227 | 62.701 | 75.299 | 90.890 | 110.218 |
| 33 | 37.285 | 38.869 | 42.299 | 46.112 | 66.210 | 80.064 | 97.343 | 118.933 |
| 34 | 38.565 | 40.258 | 43.933 | 48.034 | 69.858 | 85.067 | 104.184 | 128.259 |
| 35 | 39.854 | 41.660 | 45.592 | 49.994 | 73.652 | 90.320 | 111.435 | 138.237 |
| 36 | 41.153 | 43.077 | 47.276 | 51.994 | 77.598 | 95.836 | 119.121 | 148.913 |
| 37 | 42.461 | 44.508 | 48.985 | 54.034 | 81.702 | 101.628 | 127.268 | 160.337 |
| 38 | 43.780 | 45.953 | 50.720 | 56.115 | 85.970 | 107.710 | 135.904 | 172.561 |
| 39 | 45.108 | 47.412 | 52.481 | 58.237 | 90.409 | 114.095 | 145.058 | 185.640 |
| 40 | 46.446 | 48.886 | 54.268 | 60.402 | 95.026 | 120.800 | 154.762 | 199.635 |
| 41 | 47.795 | 50.375 | 56.082 | 62.610 | 99.827 | 127.840 | 165.048 | 214.610 |
| 42 | 49.153 | 51.879 | 57.923 | 64.862 | 104.820 | 135.232 | 175.951 | 230.632 |
| 43 | 50.522 | 53.398 | 59.792 | 67.159 | 110.012 | 142.993 | 187.508 | 247.776 |
| 44 | 51.901 | 54.932 | 61.689 | 69.503 | 115.413 | 151.143 | 199.758 | 266.121 |
| 45 | 53.290 | 56.481 | 63.614 | 71.893 | 121.029 | 159.700 | 212.744 | 285.749 |
| 46 | 54.690 | 58.046 | 65.568 | 74.331 | 126.871 | 168.685 | 226.508 | 306.752 |
| 47 | 56.100 | 59.626 | 67.552 | 76.817 | 132.945 | 178.119 | 241.099 | 329.224 |
| 48 | 57.521 | 61.223 | 69.565 | 79.354 | 139.263 | 188.025 | 256.565 | 353.270 |
| 49 | 58.952 | 62.835 | 71.609 | 81.941 | 145.834 | 198.427 | 272.958 | 378.999 |
| 50 | 60.394 | 64.463 | 73.683 | 84.579 | 152.667 | 209.348 | 290.336 | 406.529 |

**Appendix D: Compound Value of an Annuity of $1 (continued)**

Rate

| Year | .0800 | .0900 | .1000 | .1100 | .1200 | .1300 | .1400 | .1500 |
|---|---|---|---|---|---|---|---|---|
| 1 | 1.000 | 1.000 | 1.000 | 1.000 | 1.000 | 1.000 | 1.000 | 1.000 |
| 2 | 2.080 | 2.090 | 2.100 | 2.110 | 2.120 | 2.130 | 2.140 | 2.150 |
| 3 | 3.246 | 3.278 | 3.310 | 3.342 | 3.374 | 3.407 | 3.440 | 3.472 |
| 4 | 4.506 | 4.573 | 4.641 | 4.710 | 4.779 | 4.850 | 4.921 | 4.993 |
| 5 | 5.867 | 5.985 | 6.105 | 6.228 | 6.353 | 6.480 | 6.610 | 6.742 |
| 6 | 7.336 | 7.523 | 7.716 | 7.913 | 8.115 | 8.323 | 8.536 | 8.754 |
| 7 | 8.923 | 9.200 | 9.487 | 9.783 | 10.089 | 10.405 | 10.730 | 11.067 |
| 8 | 10.637 | 11.028 | 11.436 | 11.859 | 12.300 | 12.757 | 13.233 | 13.727 |
| 9 | 12.488 | 13.021 | 13.579 | 14.164 | 14.776 | 15.416 | 16.085 | 16.786 |
| 10 | 14.487 | 15.193 | 15.937 | 16.722 | 17.549 | 18.420 | 19.337 | 20.304 |
| 11 | 16.645 | 17.560 | 18.531 | 19.561 | 20.655 | 21.814 | 23.045 | 24.349 |
| 12 | 18.977 | 20.141 | 21.384 | 22.713 | 24.133 | 25.650 | 27.271 | 29.002 |
| 13 | 21.495 | 22.953 | 24.523 | 26.212 | 28.029 | 29.985 | 32.089 | 34.352 |
| 14 | 24.215 | 26.019 | 27.975 | 30.095 | 32.393 | 34.883 | 37.581 | 40.505 |
| 15 | 27.152 | 29.361 | 31.772 | 34.405 | 37.280 | 40.417 | 43.842 | 47.580 |
| 16 | 30.324 | 33.003 | 35.950 | 39.190 | 42.753 | 46.672 | 50.980 | 55.717 |
| 17 | 33.750 | 36.974 | 40.545 | 44.501 | 48.884 | 53.739 | 59.118 | 65.075 |
| 18 | 37.450 | 41.301 | 45.599 | 50.396 | 55.750 | 61.725 | 68.394 | 75.836 |
| 19 | 41.446 | 46.018 | 51.159 | 56.939 | 63.440 | 70.749 | 78.969 | 88.212 |
| 20 | 45.762 | 51.160 | 57.275 | 64.203 | 72.052 | 80.947 | 91.025 | 102.444 |
| 21 | 50.423 | 56.765 | 64.002 | 72.265 | 81.699 | 92.470 | 104.768 | 118.810 |
| 22 | 55.457 | 62.873 | 71.403 | 81.214 | 92.503 | 105.491 | 120.436 | 137.632 |
| 23 | 60.893 | 69.532 | 79.543 | 91.148 | 104.603 | 120.205 | 138.297 | 159.276 |
| 24 | 66.765 | 76.790 | 88.497 | 102.174 | 118.155 | 136.831 | 158.659 | 184.168 |
| 25 | 73.106 | 84.701 | 98.347 | 114.413 | 133.334 | 155.620 | 181.871 | 212.793 |

| | | | | | | | | |
|---|---|---|---|---|---|---|---|---|
| 26 | 79.954 | 93.324 | 109.182 | 127.999 | 150.334 | 176.850 | 208.333 | 245.712 |
| 27 | 87.351 | 102.723 | 121.100 | 143.079 | 169.374 | 200.841 | 238.499 | 283.569 |
| 28 | 95.339 | 112.968 | 134.210 | 159.817 | 190.699 | 227.950 | 272.889 | 327.104 |
| 29 | 103.966 | 124.135 | 148.631 | 178.397 | 214.583 | 258.583 | 312.094 | 377.170 |
| 30 | 113.283 | 136.308 | 164.494 | 199.021 | 241.333 | 293.199 | 356.787 | 434.745 |
| 31 | 123.346 | 149.575 | 181.943 | 221.913 | 271.293 | 332.315 | 407.737 | 500.957 |
| 32 | 134.214 | 164.037 | 201.138 | 247.324 | 304.848 | 376.516 | 465.820 | 577.100 |
| 33 | 145.951 | 179.800 | 222.252 | 275.529 | 342.429 | 426.463 | 532.035 | 664.666 |
| 34 | 158.627 | 196.982 | 245.477 | 306.837 | 384.521 | 482.903 | 607.520 | 765.365 |
| 35 | 172.317 | 215.711 | 271.024 | 341.590 | 431.663 | 546.681 | 693.573 | 881.170 |
| 36 | 187.102 | 236.125 | 299.127 | 380.164 | 484.463 | 618.749 | 791.673 | 1014.346 |
| 37 | 203.070 | 258.376 | 330.039 | 422.982 | 543.599 | 700.187 | 903.507 | 1167.498 |
| 38 | 220.316 | 282.630 | 364.043 | 470.511 | 609.831 | 792.211 | 1030.998 | 1343.622 |
| 39 | 238.941 | 309.066 | 401.448 | 523.267 | 684.010 | 896.198 | 1176.338 | 1546.165 |
| 40 | 259.057 | 337.382 | 442.593 | 581.826 | 767.091 | 1013.704 | 1342.025 | 1779.090 |
| 41 | 280.781 | 369.292 | 487.852 | 646.827 | 860.142 | 1146.486 | 1530.909 | 2046.954 |
| 42 | 304.244 | 403.528 | 537.637 | 718.978 | 964.359 | 1296.529 | 1746.236 | 2354.997 |
| 43 | 329.583 | 440.346 | 592.401 | 799.065 | 1081.083 | 1466.078 | 1991.709 | 2709.246 |
| 44 | 356.950 | 481.522 | 652.641 | 887.963 | 1211.813 | 1657.668 | 2271.548 | 3116.633 |
| 45 | 386.506 | 525.359 | 718.905 | 986.639 | 1358.230 | 1874.165 | 2590.656 | 3585.128 |
| 46 | 418.426 | 574.186 | 791.795 | 1096.169 | 1522.218 | 2118.806 | 2954.244 | 4123.898 |
| 47 | 452.900 | 626.363 | 871.975 | 1217.747 | 1705.884 | 2395.251 | 3368.838 | 4743.482 |
| 48 | 490.132 | 684.280 | 960.172 | 1352.700 | 1911.590 | 2707.633 | 3841.475 | 5456.005 |
| 49 | 530.343 | 746.866 | 1057.190 | 1502.497 | 2141.981 | 3060.626 | 4380.282 | 6275.405 |
| 50 | 573.770 | 815.084 | 1163.909 | 1668.771 | 2400.018 | 3459.507 | 4994.521 | 7217.716 |

**Appendix D: Compound Value of an Annuity of $1 (concluded)**

Rate

| Year | .1600 | .1800 | .2000 | .2200 | .2400 | .2500 | .3000 | .4000 |
|---|---|---|---|---|---|---|---|---|
| 1  | 1.000   | 1.000   | 1.000   | 1.000   | 1.000   | 1.000   | 1.000   | 1.000 |
| 2  | 2.160   | 2.180   | 2.200   | 2.220   | 2.240   | 2.250   | 2.300   | 2.400 |
| 3  | 3.506   | 3.572   | 3.640   | 3.708   | 3.778   | 3.812   | 3.990   | 4.360 |
| 4  | 5.066   | 5.215   | 5.368   | 5.524   | 5.684   | 5.766   | 6.187   | 7.104 |
| 5  | 6.877   | 7.154   | 7.442   | 7.740   | 8.048   | 8.207   | 9.043   | 10.946 |
| 6  | 8.977   | 9.442   | 9.930   | 10.442  | 10.980  | 11.259  | 12.756  | 16.324 |
| 7  | 11.414  | 12.142  | 12.916  | 13.740  | 14.615  | 15.073  | 17.583  | 23.853 |
| 8  | 14.240  | 15.327  | 16.499  | 17.762  | 19.123  | 19.842  | 23.858  | 34.395 |
| 9  | 17.519  | 19.086  | 20.799  | 22.670  | 24.712  | 25.802  | 32.015  | 49.153 |
| 10 | 21.321  | 23.521  | 25.959  | 28.657  | 31.643  | 33.253  | 42.619  | 69.814 |
| 11 | 25.733  | 28.755  | 32.150  | 35.962  | 40.238  | 42.566  | 56.405  | 98.739 |
| 12 | 30.850  | 34.931  | 39.581  | 44.874  | 50.895  | 54.208  | 74.327  | 139.235 |
| 13 | 36.786  | 42.219  | 48.497  | 55.746  | 64.110  | 68.760  | 97.625  | 195.929 |
| 14 | 43.672  | 50.818  | 59.196  | 69.010  | 80.496  | 86.949  | 127.913 | 275.300 |
| 15 | 51.660  | 60.965  | 72.035  | 85.192  | 100.815 | 109.687 | 167.286 | 386.420 |
| 16 | 60.925  | 72.939  | 87.442  | 104.935 | 126.011 | 138.109 | 218.472 | 541.988 |
| 17 | 71.673  | 87.068  | 105.931 | 129.020 | 157.253 | 173.636 | 285.014 | 759.784 |
| 18 | 84.141  | 103.740 | 128.117 | 158.405 | 195.994 | 218.045 | 371.518 | 1064.697 |
| 19 | 98.603  | 123.414 | 154.740 | 194.254 | 244.033 | 273.556 | 483.973 | 1491.576 |
| 20 | 115.380 | 146.628 | 186.688 | 237.989 | 303.601 | 342.945 | 630.165 | 2089.206 |
| 21 | 134.841 | 174.021 | 225.026 | 291.347 | 377.465 | 429.681 | 820.215 | 2925.889 |
| 22 | 157.415 | 206.345 | 271.031 | 356.443 | 469.056 | 538.101 | 1067.280 | 4097.245 |
| 23 | 183.601 | 244.487 | 326.237 | 435.861 | 582.630 | 673.626 | 1388.464 | 5737.142 |
| 24 | 213.978 | 289.494 | 392.484 | 532.750 | 723.461 | 843.033 | 1806.003 | 8032.999 |
| 25 | 249.214 | 342.603 | 471.981 | 650.955 | 898.092 | 1054.791 | 2348.803 | 11247.199 |

| | | | | | | | |
|---|---|---|---|---|---|---|---|
| 26 | 290.088 | 405.272 | 567.377 | 795.165 | 1114.634 | 1319.489 | 3054.444 | 15747.079 |
| 27 | 337.502 | 479.221 | 681.853 | 971.102 | 1383.146 | 1650.361 | 3971.778 | 22046.910 |
| 28 | 392.503 | 566.481 | 819.223 | 1185.744 | 1716.101 | 2063.952 | 5164.311 | 30866.674 |
| 29 | 456.303 | 669.447 | 984.068 | 1447.608 | 2128.965 | 2580.939 | 6714.604 | 43214.343 |
| 30 | 530.312 | 790.948 | 1181.882 | 1767.081 | 2640.916 | 3227.174 | 8729.985 | 60501.081 |
| 31 | 616.162 | 934.319 | 1419.258 | 2156.839 | 3275.736 | 4034.968 | 11349.981 | 84702.513 |
| 32 | 715.747 | 1103.496 | 1704.109 | 2632.344 | 4062.913 | 5044.710 | 14755.975 | 118584.519 |
| 33 | 831.267 | 1303.125 | 2045.931 | 3212.460 | 5039.012 | 6306.887 | 19183.768 | 166019.326 |
| 34 | 965.270 | 1538.688 | 2456.118 | 3920.201 | 6249.375 | 7884.609 | 24939.899 | 232428.056 |
| 35 | 1120.713 | 1816.652 | 2948.341 | 4783.645 | 7750.225 | 9856.761 | 32422.868 | 325400.279 |
| 36 | 1301.027 | 2144.649 | 3539.009 | 5837.047 | 9611.279 | 12321.952 | 42150.729 | 455561.390 |
| 37 | 1510.191 | 2531.686 | 4247.811 | 7122.197 | 11918.986 | 15403.440 | 54796.947 | 637786.947 |
| 38 | 1752.822 | 2988.389 | 5098.373 | 8690.080 | 14780.543 | 19255.299 | 71237.031 | 892902.725 |
| 39 | 2034.273 | 3527.299 | 3119.048 | 10602.898 | 18328.873 | 24070.124 | 92609.141 | 1250064.815 |
| 40 | 2360.757 | 4163.213 | 7343.858 | 12936.535 | 22728.803 | 30088.655 | 120392.883 | 1750091.741 |
| 41 | 2739.478 | 4913.591 | 8813.629 | 15783.573 | 28184.715 | 37611.819 | 156511.748 | 2450129.438 |
| 42 | 3178.795 | 5799.038 | 10577.355 | 19256.959 | 34950.047 | 47015.774 | 203466.272 | 3430182.213 |
| 43 | 3688.402 | 6843.865 | 12693.826 | 23494.490 | 43339.058 | 58870.718 | 264507.153 | 4802256.099 |
| 44 | 4279.546 | 8076.760 | 15233.592 | 28664.278 | 53741.432 | 73464.397 | 343860.299 | 6723159.538 |
| 45 | 4965.274 | 9531.577 | 18281.310 | 34971.419 | 66640.376 | 91831.496 | 447019.389 | 9412424.353 |
| 46 | 5760.718 | 11248.261 | 21938.572 | 42666.131 | 82635.066 | 114790.370 | 581126.206 | 13177395.095 |
| 47 | 6683.433 | 13273.948 | 26327.286 | 52053.680 | 102468.482 | 143488.963 | 755465.067 | 18448354.132 |
| 48 | 7753.782 | 15664.259 | 31593.744 | 63506.490 | 127061.917 | 179362.203 | 982105.588 | 25827696.785 |
| 49 | 8995.387 | 18484.825 | 37913.492 | 77478.917 | 157557.778 | 224203.754 | 1276738.264 | 36158776.500 |
| 50 | 10435.649 | 21813.094 | 45497.191 | 94525.279 | 195372.644 | 280255.693 | 1659760.743 | 50622288.099 |

# Author Index

**A**

Abdelsamad, M. H., 177
Abraham, A. B., 274
Adler, M., 274
Alberts, W. W., 513
Albin, P. S., 348
Altman, E. I. 67, 580
Ang, J. S., 211, 455
Ansoff, H. I., 513
Arditti, F. D., 211
Arndt, R. E., 513
Aronson, J. R., 231
Austin, D. V., 334
Ayers, H. F., 422

**B**

Babcock, G. C., 513
Babiak, H., 430
Bacon, P. W., 348, 422
Baker, J. C., 422
Baker, S. H., 89
Barges, A., 230
Barker, C. A., 441
Barnett, A. H., 193
Battista, G. L., 89
Baumol, W. J., 130, 137, 455
Baxter, N. D., 230, 274
Bean, V. L., 110
Beaver, W. H., 67
Beckhart, B. H., 274
Beman, L., 513
Benishay, H., 67, 110
Ben-Shahar, H., 231
Benston, G., 67
Beranek, W., 110, 231
Bernhard, R. H., 177

Bernstein, P. L., 403
Bierman, Harold, Jr., 67, 178, 193, 338
Bildersee, J. S., 368
Block, E., 322
Boness, A. J., 231
Bonham, H. B., 580
Bower, R. S., 285, 294
Bowlin, O. D., 403
Brennan, M. J., 211
Brigham, E. F., 211, 277, 409, 422, 444, 454
Brittain, J. A., 430
Broman, K. L., 422
Brosky, J. J., 274
Brown, R. G., 110
Brown, Stanley H., 470
Butters, J. K., 31
Bryne, R. A., 193

**C**

Campbell, E. D., 422
Carlson, C. R., 212
Cary, W. L., 31
Cates, D. C., 322
Chambers, J. C., 126
Charnes, A., 193
Cheney, R. E., 513
Cohan, A. B., 281
Cooper, A., 193
Crary, D. T., 89, 231
Crocket, J., 454
Crowningshield, G. R., 89

**D**

Daniels, F. L., 274
Davies, R. M., 31
Davis, P. M., 110

Davis, R. F., 513
Dean, J., 178
Denonn, L. E., 274
Dhymes, P. J., 454
Diamond, J. J., 453
Dobrovsky, S. P., 444
Donaldson, G., 67, 89, 368
Durand, D., 211, 446, 451
Duvall R. M., 334

### E

Ederington, L. H., 322
Edmister, R. O., 580
Ellis, C. D., 348, 403
Elton, E. J., 444, 455

### F

Fama, E. F., 430, 441, 444, 454
Farrar D. E., 193
Fergusson, D. A., 368, 580
Fischer, D. E., 368
Fisher, D. J., 274
Fisher, L., 441, 444
Folger, H. R., 178
Foster, E. M., 513
Fraine, H. G., 403
Fredman, A. J., 303
Friend, I., 444, 453, 454

### G

Ghandhi, J. K. S., 89
Glassmire, W. F., Jr., 349
Gordon, M. J., 196, 212, 294, 396, 444, 447–48, 451–52, 454
Gort, M., 513
Green, D. Jr., 422
Greer, W. R., Jr., 193
Grier, P. C., 348
Griffith, R., 110
Gruber, M. J., 444, 455
Guthart, L. A., 348

### H

Haley, C. W., 231
Halford, F. A., 403
Hamada, R. S., 231
Harkavy, O., 444–45
Harris, L., 580
Haslem, J. A., 89
Hass, J. E., 193
Hawkins, C. A., 141
Hayes, D. A., 274
Hayes, S. L., 422
Haynes, W. W., 178
Heebink, D. V., 194
Heim, P., 455
Helfert, E. A., 67
Henderson, G. V., Jr., 193, 212, 285, 295, 444

Hertz, D. B., 193
Hess, A., Jr., 404
Higgins, R. C., 429, 444, 454–55, 513
Hillier, F. S., 193–94
Holzman, R. S., 31
Hopewell, M. H., 403
Horrigan, J. O., 67
Howard, R. H., 89, 231
Hubbard, C. L., 141
Hubbard, P. M., Jr., 349
Hungate, R. P., 274
Hunt, E. H., 177
Hunt, P., 89

### J

Jaedicke, R. K., 67
Jen, F. C., 381, 394, 403, 514
Jenkins, D. O., 284, 295
Jensen, M. C., 441, 444
Johnson, L. R., 445
Johnson, R. E., 403
Johnson, R. W., 110, 178, 287

### K

Kassouf, S. T., 422
Kaufman, G. G., 403
Kelley, E. M., 513
Kortanek, K., 193
Kurz, M., 454

### L

Lawrence, M. H., 31
Lee, S. J., 278
Legg, S. C., 274
Lerner, E. M., 194
Lev, B., 67
Levinson, H., 513
Levy, H., 466
Lewellen, W. G., 110, 212, 283, 287, 422, 467
Lintner, J., 427, 444, 452–53
Long, M. S., 283
Loomis, C. J., 428
Lorie, J. H., 178
Lusztig, P., 178

### M

McCarthy, G. D., 513
McCoin, K. G., 404
McConnell, J. J., 212
McDonald, J. G., 445, 454
MacDougal, G. E., 513
McManus, G. J., 507
Magee, J. F., 110, 194
Mahoney, J. D., 514
Malek, F. V., 513
Malkiel, B. G., 455
Mansinghka, S. K., 466
Mao, J. C. T., 178, 190

# Author Index

Markowitz, H. M., 465
Mayer, T., 250
Mayor, T. H., 404
Mehta, D., 110
Melnyk, Z. L., 231
Meltzer, A. H., 274
Meyers, S. L., 349
Miller, G. R., 322
Miller, M. H., 132, 137, 231, 233–34, 283, 444, 448, 450–51, 453
Mills R. H., 403
Modigliani, F., 231, 233–34, 444, 448, 450–51, 453
Mueller, W. F., 468
Mullick, S. K., 126
Murphy, J. E., 455
Murray, R. F., 67, 580
Myers, S. C., 194, 212

## N

Nair, R. S., 322
Nantell, T. J., 212
Nasland, B., 194
Nelson, J. R., 349, 422

## O

Ofer, A. R., 396
Oh, J. S., 110
O'Meara, J. J., 445
O'Neal, F. H., 349
Orgler, Y. E., 137
Orr, D., 132, 137

## P

Parker, G. C., 126
Parkinson, M., 422
Pease, F., 422
Pettit, R. R., 455
Percival, J. R., 89
Pfahl, J. K., 89, 231
Pinches, G. E., 363, 369
Popma, J., 274
Porterfield, J. T. S., 445
Puckett, M., 444, 453
Pye, G., 404

## Q

Quandt, R. E., 455
Quartes, J. C., 274
Que, A. V., 422
Quirin, G. D., 178

## R

Rappaport, A., 194
Raun, D. L., 89, 126
Reiling, H. B., 422
Reilly, F. K., 514

Robichek, A. A., 178, 194, 212, 454
Rockwell, W. F., 514
Roll, R., 441, 444

## S

Sametz, A. W., 349
Samuelson, P. A., 422
Sandberg, C. M., 212
Santow, L. J., 212, 369
Sarnat, Marshall, 466
Savage, L. J., 178
Schall, L. D., 231, 513
Schwab, B., 178
Schwartz, E., 231
Scott, I. O., Jr., 250
Segall, J. E., 422, 513
Segura, E. L., 126
Selden, R. T., 274
Shad, J. S. R., 514
Shalit, S. S., 89
Shapiro, E., 445, 447
Shelton, J. P., 422
Shick, R. A., 514
Silberman, I. H., 514
Sisson, R. L., 110
Smidt, S., 178
Smith, D. D., 126
Smith, D. T., 32
Smith, K. V., 110
Snyder, A., 110
Solomon, E., 212, 231
Solomon, M. B., Jr., 178
Sommerfeld, R. M., 32
Sorter, G. H., 67
Sprecher, C. R., 369
Sprouse, R. T., 67
Stancill, J. McN., 110
Statland, N. L., 110
Stevenson, R. A., 369
Stiglitz, J. E., 231
Stockings, G. W., 467
Stone, B. K., 274
Stonich, P. J., 178

## T

Taggert, R. A., 396
Thorp, E. O., 422
Tilles, S., 178
Tobin, J., 137, 465
Tysseland, M. S., 211

## U–V

Upton, C. W., 283
Vancil, R. F., 295
Vandell, R. F., 178
Van Horne, J. C., 194, 349, 445, 454
VanMesdag, M., 565
Vinson, C. E., 422

## W–Y

Wakefield, B. R., 514
Walter, J. E., 422, 445, 447, 452
Watts, R., 445, 455
Weil, R. L., 422
Weintraub, B., 580
Wellman, M. T., 274
Wert, J. E., 303, 381, 394, 403
West, R., 338
Weston, J. F., 126, 212, 466, 513
Wilbur, W. L., 404
Wilt, G. A., Jr., 368
Winn, E. L., Jr., 422
Winn, W. J., 404
Wippern, R. F., 231
Wyndham, R., 322
Yuille, E. C., 274

# Subject Index

## A

Absolute priority rule, 557, 559–60
Accelerated depreciation, 24–26
Acceleration clause, 375
Acceptances
 bankers, 241–43
 trade, 241–43
Accounting, for leases, 291, 295–98
Accounting equation, 36
Accounts receivable
 assignment of, 260–62
 collection policies and, 98–99
 credit standards and, 96–97, 101–2
 factoring and factors, 254–60
 financing, 260–62
 management, 93–102
 terms of sale, 97–98
Accumulated earnings tax, 27–28
Activity ratios
 average collection period, 56–57
 inventory turnover, 54–56
Acts
 Bankruptcy, 573
 Chandler, 546–57, 576–77
 Clayton, 471, 476, 498
 Communications, of 1934, 478
 Communications Satellite, 337
 Internal Revenue; see Internal Revenue Code
 Interstate Commerce, 477
 Investment Company, 497
 Mahaffie, 558–59
 Model Business Corporation, 490
 National Recovery, 461
 Natural Gas, 478
 Public Utility, of 1935, 477–78

Acts—*Cont.*
 Public Utility Holding Company, 447, 509
 Securities, of 1933, 305–6
 Securities Exchange, 477
 Sherman Antitrust, 475–76
 Transportation, of 1920, 461
 Trust Indenture, 376
 Uniform Commercial Code, 261, 325
 Uniform Negotiable Instruments, 325
 Uniform Stock Transfer, 325
 Uniform Warehouse Receipt, 262–64
 United States Warehouse, 263
 Webb-Pomerene, of 1918, 461
Additional first-year depreciation, 24–26
Adjudication of bankruptcy, 573
Adjustment bonds, 388–89
Adjustment bureau, 544, 547, 577
Adjustments and reorganizations, 536–61
 out-of-court, 543–48
After-acquired property clause, 375
Amortization; *see* Depreciation allowances
Antidilution clause, 407
Arrangements under Chapter XI, 549–51, 557
Arrearages on preferred stock, 357, 527
Articles of dissolution, 566
Assets
 balance sheet, 36
 current, 38
 defined, 37–38
 excessive, 541
 fixed, 40–41
 noncurrent, 41
 purchase of, 472
Assignment
 accounts receivable, 260–62

611

Assignment—*Cont.*
  common law and statutory, 567–70
Assumed bonds, 392
Average collection period, 56–57
Average cost of capital, 196–98, 204–9
Average rate of return, 159–60

# B

Bailment risk, 264
Balance sheet, 36
  the accounting equation, 36
  assets, 36–38
  effect of leasing on, 291, 296–97
  liabilities, 41–44
  owner's equity, 44–46
  pro forma, 122–23
  retained earnings, 44–46
Balloon note, 266
Bankrupt, discharge of, 575–76
Bankruptcy
  acts of, 573
  dividend payment and, 432, 434
  liquidation under, 572–76
  purpose of federal act, 572–73
  reorganization under federal act, 548–60
  voluntary and involuntary petions, 573
Banks
  accounts receivable financing by, 262
  business loans of, 248–52
  compensatory balance requirement of, 249–51
  financing through commercial, 248–49
Bearer bonds, 371
"Best effort" basis, 302–3
Bill of lading, 262–63
"Blue-sky" laws, 319
Bond indenture; *see* Trust indenture
Bonds
  annuity method of retirement, 378
  assumed, 392
  bearer, 371
  callable, 393–95, 398–99
  collateral, 383–85
  convertible, 405–11
  corporate, 370–71
  debenture, 385–86
  defined, 370–71
  guaranteed, 391–92
  income, 388–89
  interest payments, 371
  joint, 392–93
  maturity, 371, 377
  mortgage, 374–75
  negotiable, 371
  participating, 389–90
  provision for extinction, 393–95
  recapitalization of, 531–33
  refunding, 395–400

Bonds—*Cont.*
  registered, 371–72
  retirement of, 376–81
  serial, 379–81
  sinking-fund, 377, 379
  stabilized, 390
  subordinate debenture, 386–87
  trading provisions, 391
  trust indenture, 374–75
  trustee for, 375–76
  variable payment, 378–79
Borrowers; *see also* Borrowing; Debt; *and* Loans
  legal restrictions on, 373
Borrowing
  reasons for, 265–66
  use of pro forma statement in, 123
Break-even analysis, 71–78
  effects of changing variables, 74
  financial, 80–83
  limitations of, 74–75
  nonlinear, 75–78
  operating, 71–78
Break-even point, 73–74
Budgets, cash, 116–18
Business
  classifications of, 6
  corporations; *see* Corporations
  debts, 373–76
Business acquisitions and public policy, 474–78
Business combinations
  forms of, 483–85
  promotion of, 481–83
Business concerns; *see* Business firms *and* Corporations
Business corporations; *see* Business firms *and* Corporations
Business failures; *see* Bankruptcy *and* Reorganization
Business firms
  classification of, 6
  commercial banking relations of, 250
  financial statements of, 44–47
  growth of, 424–26
  legal forms of organization, 10–11
  liquidation of, 563–77
  reorganization of, 536–56
  retained earnings and, 424–26
  tax problems of, 9–29
  terms indicating equity of, 44–46
  working capital needs of, 90–93
Business transfers; *see also* Mergers and consolidations
  valuation problems in, 486–89
Buying versus leasing, 288–90

# C

Call loans, 252–53

# Subject Index

Call price, 394–95
Call privilege
  bonds, 393–94
  preferred stock, 352–55
Callable bonds, 393–95
Capital
  allocation, 4, 149–52
  budgeting under certainty, 149–70
  budgeting under uncertainty, 179–91
  circulating, 91
  distribution, 355–56, 524
  expenditures, 150–52
  procurement, 4–5
  rationing, 170–73
  working; *see* Working capital
Capital assets, budgeting of, 152–70
  financial planning and, 150–52
Capital budgeting, MM's Proposition III, 233–34
Capital budgeting analysis, 152–70
  benefit estimation, 154–57
  cost estimation, 152–54
  methods, 157–67
Capital budgeting methods
  average rate of return, 159–60
  internal rate of return, 163–67
  IRR versus NPV and PI, 167–70
  net present value, 160–63
  payback, 157–59
  profitability index, 163
  ranking projects, 167–70
Capital gains and losses, 14–15, 19–22
Capital projects, selection of, 152–70
Capital rationing, 170–73
Capital structure, 214–20, 536–38
  changes in, 517–19
  factors influencing, 222–26
  traditional approach, 48, 214–15
Capital structure problem, the
  the debate, 217–19
  the Modigliani-Miller Model, 215–20
  the MM view on capital structure, 219–20
  taxes and optimal capital structure, 217–19
  the traditional view, 214–15
Capital surplus; *see* Surplus
Cash dividends; *see* Dividends
Cash flow, 154–57
  discounted, 160–67
  present value of, 160–63
  probability of, 186–90
  term loans and, 266–67
  under uncertainty, 186–91
Cash flow expectations, use of decision tree, 190–91
Cash recovery period, 157–59
Certainty, risk, and uncertainty, 180–83
Certainty-equivalent approach, 185–86
Certificate of dissolution, 571

Chapter VIII reorganizations, 557–58
Chapter X reorganizations, 551–57
Chapter XI reorganizations, 549–51, 557
Charter, corporate, amendments to, 519–20
Circulating capital, 90–93
Classified common stock, 336–37, 523
Closed- and open-end mortgages, 382–83
Collateral trust obligations, 383–85
  securities pledged for, 384–85
Collection ratio, 56
Collection services, 255
Combination movements, 468–71
Combination plans, 483–86
Commercial banks, 248–52
  application for loan, 251–52
  characteristics of, 248–49
  compensatory balances, 249–51
  lines of credit, 249
  position of, 248
  short-term loans, 252–53
Commercial paper, 134–35, 245–48
  advantages of, 247–48
  borrowers using, 246–47
  characteristics of, 245–46
  dealers, 246
  sources of funds, 247
  yield on, 246
Common-law assignments, 567–70
Common-size statements, 61
Common stock, 323–46
  changes in par or stated value, 520–21
  cost of, 203, 206
  re-acquired, 523–24
  recapitalization, 519–24
  redemption, 529–31
  rights of ownership, 330–32
Community of interest, 473–74
Community of ownership, 499
Compensatory balance, 249–51
Competitive bidding, 306–8
Composition settlements, 547–48
Compound interest, 139–40
Compound value, 139–40
  of an annuity, 141–42
Conglomerate mergers, 282–83
Consent dividends, 437
Consent voting rights, 359
Consolidated financial statements, 501–4
Consolidations; *see also* Mergers and consolidations
  dissenters in, 489–91
Consuming-assets corporations; *see* Wasting-assets corporations
Contingent liabilities, 43
Control of corporations
  by other corporations, 495–510
  by owners, 223
  preservation of, 222

614  Subject Index

Conversion by bond holders
  forced, 410
  voluntary, 410–11
Conversion clause, 406
Conversion privilege
  bonds, 387, 405–11
  preferred stock, 361–63
Convertible bonds
  use of, 406
  valuation of, 407–10
Convertible preferred stock, use in mergers, 363–64
Corporate bonds; see Bonds
Corporate funds, special, 39
Corporate income; see also Dividends and Profit
  taxed as personal, 17
Corporate trustee, 375–76
Corporations; see also Business firms
  control of, by other corporations, 495–511
  debts of, see Bonds; Debt; and Loans
  directors of, 332–34
  dissolution of, 570–72
  investment of, 39
  reorganization of, 536–56
  tax problems of; see Internal Revenue Code
Cost of capital, 196–209
  average, 204–9
  component costs, 198–203, 206
  component weights, 203–8
  defined, 196
  weighted average, 204–9
Cost of common equity, 201–3, 206
Cost of long-term debt, 198–200, 206
Cost of preferred stock, 200–201, 206
Coupon rate, serial bonds and, 379–81
Coverage ratios, 58
Credit; see also Bonds; Debt; and Loans
  agencies, 101
  analysis, 99–102
  collection policies, 98–99
  investigation, 101–2
  revolving, 248
  standards, 96–97
  terms of sale, 97–98
  trade, 240–45
Credit analysis
  by factors, 256
  inventory loans and, 262–64
Creditors
  action by, 574–75
  dissenting, 489–91
  laws to protect, 374
Creditors' committee, 544–47, 567
Cumulative preferred stock, 356–57
Cumulative voting, 335–36
Current assets, 38–41
Current liabilities, 42–43

Current ratio, 51–52
Customers as source of funds, 414–15
Cyclical flexibility in financing, 222–26

D

Debentures, 385–86
Debt; see also Bonds; Loans; and Mortgages
  excessive, 540–43
  extinction, 393–95
  legal characteristics, 221–22
  long-term, 198–200, 206
  preferential tax treatment for, 389
  recapitalization of, 531–33
  retirement of, 376–81
Debt financing
  effects of leverage of, 224
  legal aspects of, 220–22
  tax advantage of, 217
Debt-to-total-assets ratio, 57–58
Decision criteria for long-term financing decisions, 222–26
  control, 223
  earnings per share, 223–24
  flexibility, 224–25
  riskiness, 224
  suitability, 223
  timing, 225–26
Declining-balance method, 24–25
Degree of operating leverage, 83–84
Degree of total leverage, 85–86
Delinquent accounts, 98–99
Demand loans, 352–53
Depreciation, as a cost, 24
Depreciation allowances
  accelerated, 24–25
  income taxes and, 24–25
  recovery of fixed assets and, 24–25
Discharge of bankrupt, 575–76
Disclosure principle, 313
Discounted cash flows, 160–73
  expected present value, 186–91
  internal rate, 163–67
  net present value, 160–63
  profitability index, 163
Dissenting parties to combinations
  creditors, 491
  procedure, 489–90
  stockholders, 490–91
Dissolution of corporations, 570–72
Distribution of capital, 524
Dividend income deduction, 23–24
Dividend payouts, 430–32
Dividend policy, 426–36
  access to capital markets, 435
  bases for, 432–36
  contract restrictions, 434
  debt repayment, 434–35
  dividend payouts, 430–32
  the human element, 436

Dividend policy—*Cont.*
  legal restrictions, 432–34
  the Lintner study, 427–30
  nature of net earnings, 435
  tax aspects, 435–36
  of U.S. corporations, 427–32
  working capital positions, 434
Dividend policy in academic literature, 426–27, 445–56
  the debate concerning dividends, 451–55
  Miller and Modigliani on dividends, 448–51
  in retrospect, 455–56
  the traditional view, 445–48
Dividends
  arrearages on preferred, 357, 527
  cash, 426
  consent, 437
  human element in payment of, 448–51
  legal aspect of, 432–34
  liquidating, 355–56
  mechanics of payments, 436–38
  policies, 426–36
  preferred stock, 356–58
  stock, 439–41
  tax aspect of, 435–36

## E

Earned surplus, *see also* Retained earnings *and* Surplus
Earnings
  debt costs and, 57–58
  dividend policies and, 424–56
  pattern of, 487
  retained; *see* Retained earnings
Economic order quantity
  cash, 130–33
  inventories, 104–6
Employee stock-ownership plans, 415–16
Equipment, financing of, 265
Equity
  legal characteristics, 221–22
  owners, 44–46
  receivership, 549, 553
  terms indicating, 44–46
  trading on the, *see* Financial leverage, effects of
Equity capital
  nature of, 220–22
  retained earnings and, 424–26
  special sources of, 414–18
Escalator clause, 267
Expansion
  direction, 464
  diversification, 464–67
  internal and external, 467–68
  major combination movements, 468–71
  timing of, 468

Extensions, 543–44

## F

Factoring, 254–60
  advances, 258
  agreements, 258
  clients, 259
  collection services, 255–56
  cost of, 256–57
  credit analysis, 256
  effects on sales, 257–58
  financial services, 255
  objections to, 259–60
FASB *Statement No. 13*, 291, 295–98
  background, impact and implementation, 297–98
  classification of leases, 295–96
  reporting of leases, 296–97
Federal Communications Commission, 478
Federal Criminal Code, 374
Federal Power Commission, 477–78
Federal Trade Commission, 476
Field warehousing, 263–64
"FIFO," 55
Financial analysis, 49–62
  acid-test ratio, 52
  activity ratios, 53–57
  average collection period, 56–57
  balance sheet leverage ratios, 57–58
  common-size statements, 61–62
  current ratio, 51–52
  income statement leverage ratios, 58
  inventory turnover ratio, 54–56
  leverage ratios, 57–58
  liquidity ratios, 51–57
  operating ratio, 61–62
  profitability interrelationships, 59–60
  profitability ratios, 58–60
  return on net worth, 59
  return on sales, 59
  return on total assets, 59
  sources of comparative data, 60–61
  total asset turnover, 53–54
Financial breakeven analysis, 80–83
Financial leasing, 282–84
  sale and leaseback financing, 281–82
  straight financial leases, 282–84
Financial leverage, effects of, 78–80
Financial services, 255
Financial statements and analysis, 35–62
  balance sheet, 36–46
  income, 46–47, 58–60, 62
Financial structure; *see* Capital structure
Financing; *see also* Bonds; Debt; Equity capital; *and* Loans
  accounts receivable, 260–62
  through commercial banks, 248–52
  inventory, 262–64
  through investment bankers, 301–19

Financing—*Cont.*
    open-market, 245–48
    secured, 253–54
Financing-holding companies, 500
Fixed capital assets
    definition, 40–41, 149–52
    depreciation allowances and, 24–25
    excessive, 541
    planning for, 150–52
    recovery of investments in, 154–55
    relative importance of, 150
    selection of, 152–70
Fixed costs, 71–72
Flexibility, 224–26
Flow-of-funds statements, 112–14
Forecasting statements, 118–23
    pro forma balance sheet, 122–23
    pro forma income statement, 120–22
Funds
    from operations; *see* Depreciation allowances *and* Retained earnings
    special, 39

## G–H

Growth of business firms, 459–92
Guaranteed bonds, 391–92
Holding companies
    advantages and disadvantages of, 504–7
    device, 473
    regulation of, 507–10
    rehabilitation of, 510
    tax and legal aspects of, 506–7
    types of, 499–501

## I

Income; *see also* Earnings
    taxes and, 9–29
Income bonds, 388–89
Income position indicated by ratios, 58–60, 62
Income statements, 46–47
Income tax structure, 11–17
Industries, national income by, 6
Influence of payment procedure, 486–89
Insolvency; *see* Bankruptcy
Interest rates on loans, term, 267
Internal and external growth and expansion, 459–78
Internal rate of return, 163–67
    versus NPV, 167–70
Internal Revenue Code, 9, 15, 29
    depreciation allowances and, 24–26
    retained earnings and, 27–28
    Section 531, 27–28
    Section 1231, 22
    Subchapter S corporations, 17–19
Internally generated funds, importance of, 424–26

Interstate Commerce Commission
    consolidations and, 477
    powers of, 477
    regulation of security issues, 313–19
    role in Chapter VIII reorganizations, 557–58
    role in Mahaffie Act reorganizations, 558–59
Inventories, 102–7
    control and evaluation of, 102–4
    economic order quantity, 104–7
    financing of, 262–64
    loans on, 262–64
    safety stocks, 106–7
    turnover ratio, 54–55
Inventory financing
    bills of lading, 262–63
    trust receipts, 264
    warehouse receipts, 263–64
Inventory management, 102–7
    order point, 106–7
    order size, 104–6
Investment of surplus funds, 133–35
Investment bankers
    advisory capacity of, 303–4
    corporate financing through, 301–19
    as promoters, 482–83
Investment banking
    distinctive features of, 302–4
    interrelationships among houses, 309–11
Investment tax credit, 22–23
Investments
    of corporations in securities, 39
    planning for capital, 150–52
    special, 39
    temporary, 39

## J–L

Joint bonds, 392–93
Laws; *see* Acts
Lease arrangement, 483
Lease contract, 275–76
Lease method, 472–73
Lease-or-borrow analysis, 285–88
Lease-or-buy analysis, 288–91
Leaseback financing, sale and, 281–82
Leases
    court treatment, 292
    IRS requirements, 291–92
    legal considerations, 291–92
Leasing, 275–98
    accounting for, 291–93
    attitude of lessees, 276
    balance sheet effects of, 291, 295–98
    costs of, 284–90
    definition of, 275–76
    development of, 276
    general aspects of, 275–78
    similarity to debt financing, 280–84

Leasing—*Cont.*
  sources of, 277–78
Legal form of organization, 10
Lenders; *see* Borrowers
Leverage, 68–85
  effects of financial, 78–80
Leverage measurement, 83–86
  degree of financial leverage, 84–85
  degree of operating leverage, 83–84
  degree of total leverage, 85–86
Leverage ratios
  debt-to-total assets, 57–58
  fixed-assets-to-net-worth, 57
  times-interest-earned, 58
Liabilities
  balance sheet, 41–42
  contingent, 43
  current, 42–43
  long-term, 43
  reserves, 43–44
"LIFO," 55
Lines of credit, 249
Liquidating dividend, 355–56, 524
Liquidation of business firms
  under the Federal Bankruptcy Act, 572–76
  insolvent firms, 566–70
  solvent firms, 563–66
Liquidity ratios, 51–52
  acid-test, 52
  average-collection-period, 56–57
  current, 51–52
  inventory-turnover, 54–55
Listing of securities, 318–19
Loans
  application for, 251–52
  bank, 248–49, 252–53
  inventory, 262–64
  secured, 253–54, 260–68
  short-term business, 252–53, 260–68
Long-term debts, cost of, 198–200, 206
Long-term financing, legal characteristics of debt and equity, 220–22

## M

Management of cash, 127–33
Management of working capital, 90–93, 539–40
Manufacturing companies, 6
"Market-out" clause, 305–6
Mercantile credit; *see* Trade credit
Mergers and consolidations, 485
  alternatives to, 471–74
  major movement in, 468–71
  promotion of, 481–83
Modigliani and Miller
  comparative cost of capital calculation, 236
  model, 215

Modigliani and Miller—*Cont.*
  on taxes, capital budgeting and the cost of capital, 231–36
Mortgage bond, 374–75
Mortgage liens, value of, 383
Mortgages, closed-end and open-end, 382–83

## N

National income by industrial origin, 6
Near-cash securities, 133–34
Negotiable certificates of deposit, 135
Negotiable promissory notes, 241
Negotiation of new issues, 305–6
Net operating loss carry-backs and carry-forwards, 26–27
Net present value method, 160–63
  versus IRR, 167–70
  profitability index, 163
New York Stock Exchange, 318–19
  registered bonds and the, 372
Nonannual compounding, 144–45
Nonfinancial leasing; *see* Operational leasing
No-par stock, 324
  changes in, 520–21

## O

Obligations, collateral trust, 383–85
Obsolescence factor; *see also* Depreciation *and* Depreciation allowances
  in leasing, 280
Officers of corporations, privileged subscriptions for, 416–18
Open-book accounts, 243–45
Open-end mortgages, 382–83
Open-market commercial paper, 245–48
Operating and income ratios, 61–62
  net-profit-to-sales, 59
  operating, 61–62
  return-on-assets, 59–60
  return-on-net-worth, 59
Operating breakeven analysis, 71–74
  breakeven point, 72–74
  effects of changing variables, 74
  fixed costs, 71–72
  limitations of, 74–75
  nonlinear, 75–78
  semifixed costs, 72
  variable costs, 72
Operating-holding companies, 500–501
Operating income statement, 61–62
Operating leverage, 69–71
Operational leasing, 278–80
Optimum size of business firms, factors in, 461–64
Ordinary gains and losses, 20
Organization for financial management, tax factors, 10–11, 28–29
Out-of-court adjustments, 543–48

Owners' equity, 44–46
  balance sheet, 44–46
Ownership
  community of, 499
  evidence of, 324–25
  of record, 324–25
  risks of stock, 330–31

## P

Participating bonds, 389–90
  in voting, 390
Partnership association, 10
Partnerships
  general, 10
  limited, 10
Par value stock, 324
  changes in, 520–21
Payback method, 157–59
Payment method in business transfers, 486–89
Perpetual bonds, 371
Pools, 474
Preemptive rights, 339–40
  issues, 341
  justification for, 339–40
  pricing problem, 341–42
Preference bonds, 388–89
Preferred stock
  arrearages on dividends on, 357
  convertible, 361–63
  cost of, 200–201, 206
  dividends, 356–58
  future role of, 365
  recapitalization of, 526–29
  retirement of, 352–55
  use in mergers, 363–64
  voting right, 358–61
  with warrants, 364
Preferred stockholders
  liquidation and dissolution status of, 355–56
  voting rights of, 358–61
Present value, 140–41
  of an annuity, 142–43
Private placement of securities, 311–13
Privileged subscriptions, 340–41
  for key personnel, 416–18
  legal procedures, 342–43
  market for, 341–42
  value of rights, 343–45
Profit; see also Income
  dividends and, 424–36
  planning, 3
Profitability index method, 163
Profitability ratios, 58–60
  net-profit-to-sales, 59
  operating, 58–60
  return-on-assets, 59
  return-on-net-worth, 59
Pro forma statements, 118–23

Project budgets, 151
Promissory notes, 241; see also Commercial paper
  short-term negotiable, 241
Prospectus, 307, 316, 343
Protective committees, 556
Proxies, 333–35
  regulation by SEC, 333–34
Public utilities, regulation of, 507–9
Purchase of assets, 472

## Q–R

Quick assets ratio, 52–53
Ratio analysis, 49–62
Ratios
  credit and, 50
  current, 51–52
  earnings, 58–62
  liquidity, 51–52
  operating, 61–62
  profitability, 58–60
  quick assets, 52
  use of, 49–62
Reacquired shares, 523–24
Real estate mortgage bonds and notes; see Mortgages
Recapitalization of firms, 517–33
  changes in capital structure, 517–19
  common stock, 519–24
  preferred stock, 526–29
Receivables, 39–40; see also Accounts receivable and Factoring
  financing, 260–62
  ratios, 56–57
Receiver in bankruptcy, 574
Receiverships, state court, 570
Reclassification of stock, 524–26
Redemption; see also Bonds
  common stock, 529–31
  preferred stock, 352–55
Referee in bankruptcy, 574
Refunding bond issues
  at maturity, 399–400
  before maturity, 395–99
Registered bonds, 371–72
Registrar, 325, 330
Regulation
  of public utility holding companies, 477, 508–9
  of security issues, 317–19, 374
Reorganization
  composition settlements, 547–48
  creditors' committees, 544–47
  extensions, 543
  financial structure and, 536–38
  inadequacy of working capital and plans, 538–40
  plans, 559–60
  under Chapter VIII, 557–59
  under Chapter X, 551–57

# Subject Index 619

Reorganization—*Cont.*
  under Chapter XI, 549–51
  under federal bankruptcy act, 548–60
  "workouts," 543–44
Repurchase agreements, 134
Reserve accounts, 43–44
Retaining earnings, 44–46
  cost of, 202, 206
  dividend policies and, 426–38, 445–56
  growth of business firms and, 424–26
  importance of, 424–26
  tax on excessive, 27–28
Retirement
  of bonds, 376–81
  of preferred stock, 352–55
Return
  on net worth, 59
  on sales, 59
  on total assets, 59
Return of capital, 154–57
Reverse stock split, 521–22
Right of offset, 250
Rights
  ex-rights, 343–45
  rights on, 343–44
  standby underwriting of, 345
Risk, 180–83
Risk-adjusted discount rate, 184–85
Riskiness, 224
Risks
  collateral and bailment, 264
  creditors, 374

## S

Safety stocks, 106–7
Sale and leaseback, 281–82
Sales, importance of, 538–39
Sales terms, 97–98
  accounts receivable and, 97–98
Secondary distributions, 303
Secondary markets, 317–19
Secondary offerings, 303
Section 531, Internal Revenue Code, 27–28
Section 1231, Internal Revenue Code, 22
Secured financing, 253–54, 260–68
Securities and Exchange Commission
  bankruptcy and, 553–57
  Chapter XI and, 549–51, 557
  consolidations and, 477
  holding companies and, 507–10
  mortgage bonds and, 376
  preferred stockholders and, 360
  proxy solicitation and, 333–34
  public utility companies and, 477–78, 509–10
  rights offerings and, 342
Security interest, 261

Security issues
  listing of, 318–19
  regulation of, 313–19
  secondary market for, 317–19
Semifixed costs, 72
Serial bonds, 379–81
Serial notes, 379
Services
  emphasis on, 6–7
  of factors, 254–56
Short-term loans, 252–53, 260–68
Short-term securities, 133–35
  commercial paper, 245–48
  negotiable certificates, 135
  repurchase agreements, 134
  U.S. Treasury bills, 134
  U.S. Treasury notes, 134
Sinking funds
  for bonds, 377, 379
  for preferred stock, 355
  reserve accounts, 377–78
Small business firms, preferential tax treatment for, 17–19
Special funds, 39
Stabilized bonds, 390
Standby underwriting, 345
State court receivership, 570
Stated capital, 44
  changes in, 520–22
Statements; *see* Financial statements and analysis
Statistical probability, 186–91
  decision-tree analysis, 190–91
Statutory assignment, 570
Stock; *see also* Common stock *and* Preferred stock
  certificates, 324
  dividends, 439
  no-par, 324
  preemptive right, 339–40
  reacquired, 337–38
  reclassification, 524–26
  redemption of, 529–31
  reverse splits, 521–22
  splits, 440, 520–21
  transfer procedure, 325, 330
Stock dividends and stock splits
  effect on owners' equity, 439
  market effect, 440–41
  periodic stock dividends, 439–40
Stock-options for key personnel, 416–18
Stock transfer agent, 325, 330
Stockholders
  common; *see* Common stock
  dissenting, 489–91
  meetings, 332–33
  provisions for voting, 334–36
Subchapter S corporations, 17–19
Subordinated debentures, 386–87
Subscription rights, 414–18

## Subject Index

Subsidiaries; *see* Holding companies
Sum-of-the-years'-digits, 24–25
Superholding companies, 500
Surplus
  capital, 523
  funds, investment of, 133–35
  tax, 27–28
Syndicates, managers, 309–11
Syndication of loans, 268

### T

Tax on retained earnings, 27–28
Tax aspects of holding companies, 506–7
Tax considerations
  accelerated depreciation, 24–26
  accumulated earnings tax, 27–28
  capital gains and losses, 14–15, 19–22
  corporate dividend income, 23–24
  dividend income deduction, 23–24
  Investment tax credit, 22–23
  net operating carry-back and carry-forward, 26–27
  ordinary gains and losses, 20
  ordinary income, 11
  retained earnings, 27–28
  1231 gains and losses, 22
Tax factors and business decisions, 19–28
Tax factors in choosing a form of organization, 10–11
Taxes, MM tax model, 231–33
Temporary investments, 39
Term loans, 265–68
  cash flow and, 266–67
  characteristics of, 265–68
  documents, 268
  flexibility, 268
  interest rates on, 267
  leasing versus, 285–88
  maturities, 267
  purposes of, 265–66
  repayment, 267
  security, 267–68
  syndication, 268
Time value of money, 138–45
  compound value, 139–40
  nonannual compounding, 144–45
  present value, 140
  uneven series of receipts, 144
Total asset turnover, 53–54
Trade acceptances, 241–43
Trade bills, 241–43
Trade credit, 240–45
  acceptances, 241–43
  basic types, 241
  growth of, 240–41
  open-book accounts, 243–45
  promissory notes, 241
Trading on the equity; *see* Financial leverage
Trading provisions as to bonds, 391

Transfers; *see also* Consolidations *and* Mergers and consolidations
  valuation problems in, 486–89
Treasury stock, 337–38, 523–24
Trust indenture
  collateral, 374–75
Trust receipts, 264
Trustee
  in bankruptcy, 575
  corporate, 375–76
Trusts, 496–97
  voting, 484

### U

Uncertainty, 180–83
  certainty-equivalent approach, 185–86
  risk-adjusted discount rate, 184–85
Underwriters; *see* Investment bankers
Undistributed profits; *see* Retained earnings
Uniform Commercial Code, 261, 325
U.S. Treasury bills, 134
U.S. Treasury notes, 134
Unlisted securities, 319
Unsecured bonds; *see* Debentures
Unsecured loans; *see* Loans
"Upstream" loans, 509

### V

Valuation problems in business transfers, 486–89
Value of a right
  rights-off, 344–45
  rights-on, 344
Value maximization, 5–6
Variable costs, 72
Voluntary and involuntary bankruptcy petitions, 573
Voluntary liquidation, 564–66
Voting
  preferred stockholders, 358–61
  provisions for, 334–36
Voting trust, 484–85

### W–Y

Warehouse receipt, 263–64
Warehousing, 263–64
Warrants, to purchase stock, 411–14
  provisions of, 411–12
  use of, 414
  value of, 412–14
Warrants, subscription, 342–43
Wasting-assets corporations
  dividend payments and, 432
  voluntary liquidation of, 564–65
Weighted average cost of capital, 204–9
  determination of the weights, 203–4, 206
  interpretation of the results, 205–8
  qualifications and extensions, 208–9

**Subject Index**

Working capital, 90–93; *see also* Assets *and* Current assets
    accounts receivable and, 93–102
    dividends and, 434
    flow statement, 114

Working capital–*Cont.*
    inadequacy of, 538–40
    kinds of, 91–92
    "Workouts," 543–44
Yield curve, 379–81

*This book has been set linotype, 10 point and 9 point Caledonia, leaded 2 points. Part numbers are 24 and 48 point Craw Modern and chapter numbers are 48 point Craw Modern. Part and chapter titles are 18 point Craw Modern. The size of the type area is 27 by 46½ picas.*